Growing Shrubs and Small Trees in Cold Climates

Also Published by the University of Minnesota Press

Growing Perennials in Cold Climates (revised and updated edition)
Mike Heger, Debbie Lonnee, and John Whitman

Gardening with Prairie Plants: How to Create Beautiful Native Landscapes
Sally Wasowski, photography by Andy Wasowski

Trees and Shrubs of Minnesota
Welby R. Smith

Growing Fruit in the Upper Midwest
Don Gordon

Flowers for Northern Gardens
Leon Snyder Jr.

Gardening in the Upper Midwest
Leon Snyder Jr.

Trees and Shrubs for Northern Gardens
Leon Snyder Jr.
Photography by John Gregor

Wildflowers of the Northern Great Plains
F. R. Vance, J. R. Jowsey, J. S. McLean, and F. A. Switzer

Northland Wildflowers: The Comprehensive Guide to the Minnesota Region
John B. Moyle and Evelyn W. Moyle
Photography by John Gregor

Growing Shrubs and Small Trees in Cold Climates

Debbie Lonnee
Nancy Rose
Don Selinger
John Whitman

Foreword by Edward R. Hasselkus

Revised and Updated Edition

University of Minnesota Press
Minneapolis
London

All photographs by John Whitman, with the exception of the following.

Photographs by Nancy Rose: *Acer ginnala* samaras (page 18), *Amelanchier laevis* Lustre™ (page 20), *Aronia melanocarpa* (page 30), *Berberis thunbergii* var. *atropurpurea* (page 36), *Buxus microphylla* var. *koreana* 'Wintergreen' hedge (page 41), *Cercis canadensis* Minnesota Strain (page 51), *Clethra alnifolia* 'Hokie Pink' (page 60), *Clethra alnifolia* 'Ruby Spice' (page 60), *Cornus alternifolia* (page 67), *Cornus sericea* berries (page 67), *Corylus* hybrid (pages 70 and 74), *Corylus avellana* 'Contorta' (page 74), *Cotinus coggyria* 'Daydream' (page 80), *Cotoneaster apiculatus* (page 81), *Cotoneaster integerrimus* 'Centennial' (page 85), *Cotoneaster adpressus* var. *praecox* (page 85), *Daphne* x *burkwoodii* 'Somerset' (page 87), *Daphne* x *burkwoodii* 'Carol Mackie' foliage (page 90), *Diervilla sessilifolia* 'Butterfly' (page 95), *Diervilla* x *splendens* (page 95), *Exochorda serratifolia* 'Northern Pearls' (page 103), *Exochorda serratifolia* 'Northern Pearls' seed capsules (page 106), *Hamamelis virginiana* (pages 114 and 118), *Hydrangea anomala* ssp. *petiolaris* (page 127), *Ilex verticillata* 'Red Sprite' (page 129), *Ilex verticillata* 'Shaver' (page 133), *Lonicera xylosteum* 'Emerald Mound' (page 149), *Lonicera tataricum* 'Arnold Red' (page 149), *Lonicera hirsuta* (page 148), *Malus* 'David' (page 164), *Malus* 'Donald Wyman' winter fruit (page 165), *Perovskia atriplicifolia* flowers (page 188), *Physocarpus opulifolius* fruits (page 197), *Picea abies* 'Mucronata' (page 203), *Pyrus calleryana* 'Cleveland Select' (page 232), *Rhododendron* 'Mandarin Lights' (page 243), *Rhododendron* x *marjatta* 'Haaga' (pages 242 and 350), *Rhus aromatica* 'Gro-Low' (page 250), *Rhus aromatica* (page 250), *Salix* 'Scarlet Curls' (page 265), *Symphoricarpos albus* flowers (page 287), *Symphoricarpos orbiculatus* 'Variegatus' (page 287), *Syringa reticulata* (page 296), *Syringa vulgaris* 'Beauty of Moscow' (page 296), *Taxus* x *media* 'Taunton' (page 301), *Thuja occidentalis* 'Gold Cargo' (page 351), *Thuja occidentalis* 'Sunkist' (page 306), *Thuja occidentalis* 'Techny' and 'Wintergreen' (page 310), *Vaccinium* 'Northblue' foliage and berries (pages 312 and 316), *Viburnum dentatum* Autumn Jazz® (page 328), *Viburnum trilobum* fruit (page 351), *Weigela florida* 'Variegata' (pages 337 and 350), *Weigela florida* Carnaval® (page 336), *Weigela florida* 'Java Red' (page 336).

Photographs by Don Selinger of Bailey Nurseries, Inc.: *Acer ginnala* (page 13), *Amelanchier* x *grandiflora* 'Autumn Brilliance' (page 25), *Aronia melanocarpa* var. *elata* (page 30), *Euonymus europaeus* 'Aldenhamensis' (page 101), *Forsythia* 'Meadowlark' foliage (page 113), *Hamamelis vernalis* (page 118), *Ilex verticillata* 'Winter Red' (page 133), *Lonicera* 'Mandarin' (page 143), *Magnolia* x *soulangiana* (page 154), *Malus* Camelot® (page 164), *Malus* 'Donald Wyman' fall fruit (page 165), *Physocarpus opulifolius* 'Snowfall' (page 194), *Potentilla* 'Pink Beauty' (page 211), *Prunus* 'Alderman' (page 222), *Pyrus ussuriensis* Mountain Frost® (page 232), *Sorbus alnifolia* (page 271), *Spiraea japonica* 'Magic Carpet' (page 278), *Symphoricarpos* x *doorenbosii* 'Mother of Pearl' (page 287), *Syringa vulgaris* 'Sensation' (page 296), *Viburnum sargentii* 'Onondaga' (page 329), *Viburnum lentago* (page 328), *Viburnum trilobum* 'Wentworth' (page 329).

Photographs by Roger Anderson: *Paeonia* 'Bartzella' and 'First Arrival' (page 181). Photographs by Kasha Furman of Cricket Hill Garden: *Paeonia* 'Luoyang Hong' (page 173); *Paeonia* 'Shan Hu Tai' (page 181). Photograph by Ed Hasselkus: *Amelanchier laevis* (page 25). Photographs by Donna Whitman: *Paeonia* 'Age of Gold' and 'Anna Marie' (page 180).

Some of the plants listed in this book have patents or patents pending. It is illegal to propagate them without the permission of the patent holder.

Page 1: *Daphne* x *burkwoodii* 'Carol Mackie.' Page 343: *Weigela florida* 'Minuet.'

Originally published in 2001 by Contemporary Books, a division of NTC/Contemporary Publishing Group, Inc.

First University of Minnesota Press edition, 2011

Copyright 2001 by John Whitman

Published by the University of Minnesota Press
111 Third Avenue South, Suite 290
Minneapolis, MN 55401-2520
http://www.upress.umn.edu

A Cataloging-in-Publication record is available from the Library of Congress.
ISBN 978-0-8166-7594-4

Printed in China on acid-free paper

The University of Minnesota is an equal-opportunity educator and employer.

CONTENTS

Berberis thunbergii var.
atropurpurea

Chionanthus virginicus

Shrubs and Small Trees by Common Name

Apple (see *Malus*) 157
Arborvitae (see *Thuja*) 306
Arrowwood (see *Viburnum*) 321
Azalea (see *Rhododendron*) 234
Barberry (see *Berberis*) 32
Blueberry (see *Vaccinium*) 312
Boxwood (see *Buxus*) 38
Bridal Wreath (see *Spiraea*) 273
Burning Bush (see *Euonymus*) 96
Bush Cinquefoil (see *Potentilla*) 211
Bush Honeysuckle (see *Diervilla*) 92
Cardinal Bush (see *Weigela*) 331
Cherry (see *Prunus*) 217
Chokeberry (see *Aronia*) 27
Chokecherry (see *Prunus*) 217
Coralberry (see *Symphoricarpos*) 283
Crabapple (see *Malus*) 157
Currant (see *Ribes*) 253
Dogwood (see *Cornus*) 61
Filbert (see *Corylus*) 70
Fir (see *Abies*) 8
Flowering Almond (see *Prunus*) 217
Fringe Tree (see *Chionanthus*) 52
Hazelnut (see *Corylus*) 70
Highbush Cranberry (see *Viburnum*) 321
Holly (see *Ilex*) 129
Honeysuckle (see *Lonicera*) 143
Hortensia (see *Hydrangea*) 120
Inkberry (see *Ilex*) 129
Juneberry (see *Amelanchier*) 20
Juniper (see *Juniperus*) 135
Lilac (see *Syringa*) 289
Maple (see *Acer*) 13
Mockorange (see *Philadelphus*) 189
Mountain Ash (see *Sorbus*) 267
Nannyberry (see *Viburnum*) 321
Ninebark (see *Physocarpus*) 194
Old Man's Beard (see *Chionanthus*) 52
Pear (see *Pyrus*) 226
Pearlbush (see *Exochorda*) 103

Peashrub (see *Caragana*) 43
Petites Poires (see *Amelanchier*) 20
Pine (see *Pinus*) 205
Plum (see *Prunus*) 217
Possum Haw (see *Ilex*) 129
Purple Leaf Sand Cherry (see *Prunus*) 217
Redbud (see *Cercis*) 47
Russian Arborvitae (see *Microbiota*) 169
Russian Cypress (see *Microbiota*) 169
Russian Sage (see *Perovskia*) 184
Sarvisberry (see *Amelanchier*) 20
Sarvis Tree (see *Amelanchier*) 20
Saskatoon Berry (see *Amelanchier*) 20
Serviceberry (see *Amelanchier*) 20
Shadblow (see *Amelanchier*) 20
Shadbush (see *Amelanchier*) 20
Shrub Cinquefoil (see *Potentilla*) 211
Siberian Carpet Cypress (see *Microbiota*) 169
Smokebush (see *Cotinus*) 76
Smoketree (see *Cotinus*) 76
Snowberry (see *Symphoricarpos*) 283
Spiked Alder (see *Clethra*) 56
Spindle Tree (see *Euonymus*) 96
Spirea (see *Spiraea*) 273
Spruce (see *Picea*) 199
Sumac (see *Rhus*) 245
Summersweet (see *Clethra*) 56
Sweet Pepperbush (see *Clethra*) 56
Tree Peony (see *Paeonia*) 173
Wahoo (see *Euonymus*) 96
Wayfaringtree (see *Viburnum*) 321
White Cedar (see *Thuja*) 306
White Forsythia (see *Forsythia*) 107
White Fringe Tree (see *Chionanthus*) 52
Willow (see *Salix*) 259
Winterberry (see *Ilex*) 129
Wintercreeper (see *Euonymus*) 96
Witch Hazel (see *Hamamelis*) 114
Yew (see *Taxus*) 301

Aronia melanocarpa 'Autumn Magic'

Cotoneaster lucidus

Salix matsudana 'Tortuosa'

Magnolia stellata 'Centennial'

FOREWORD

Shrubs and small trees are basic elements of the residential landscape. As the "bones" of the garden, they provide year-round interest through foliage, flowers, fruits, branching patterns, and bark. Evergreens, both coniferous and broadleaf, bring color and interest to the long winters in cold climates.

Depending on their placement and the scale of the landscape, many tall shrubs may serve as small trees. Serviceberries, fringe tree, some dogwoods, common witch hazel, panicle hydrangea, star magnolia, tree lilacs, and some of the viburnums double as shrubs or trees. Among conifers, there is a wide range of sizes of firs, junipers, spruces, pines, and arborvitae.

The authors live and work in Minnesota (USDA Hardiness Zone 4) and have many years of practical experience selecting, growing, propagating, and maintaining a wide range of winter hardy woody plants. More than 950 taxa (species and cultivars) are presented in alphabetical order. For easy reference, tabular information on color (leaf, flower, and fruit), size, and hardiness is presented for each of them.

The five-star rating system, a unique feature of this book, provides the reader with an expert evaluation of each plant for its aesthetic merit and adaptability to cold climates.

Plant selection should always involve matching the particular plant with the conditions of the site. After evaluating your site, the "Where to Plant" designations of site and light and soil and moisture should help guide you to the right plants. Companion plantings are also suggested.

Attractive landscapes *do* require maintenance. Watering, mulching, fertilizing, and weeding apply to plants generally, but proper pruning of shrubs and small trees seems least understood by many gardeners. The following pages solve the mysteries of pruning and help to diagnose insect, disease, and critter problems.

Having selected the best plants to match your site, perhaps you can't find them at local nurseries or garden centers. Nursery sources are listed for each of the 50 genera of shrubs and small trees in this book.

We of colder climates are indebted to Debbie, Nancy, Don, and John for sharing their collective evaluations and experience of growing shrubs and small trees with us. Our landscapes will be the richer for it.

Edward R. Hasselkus
Professor Emeritus of Horticulture
University of Wisconsin–Madison

ACKNOWLEDGMENTS

Many thanks for the help and support of family, friends, and colleagues. Special thanks to Betty Ann Addison, Penny Aguirre, Erik Anderson, Julia Anderson, Roger Anderson, Bob Arntzen, Lloyd Bachman, Gordon Bailey Jr., Gordon Bailey Sr., Rod Bailey, Kim Bartko, David Bedford, Dave Betker, Marty Carlson, Rachelle Cordova, John Doepke, Mervin Eisel, Karol Emmerich, Dave Ferris, Tim Flood, Kasha and David Furman, Kathleen Gagan, Jeff Gilman, Mark Gormel, Ben and Hidekko Gowen, Anne Haines, Ed Hasselkus, Jean Heger, Mike Heger, John Hoage, Stan Hokanson, Don House, Renee Jaegar, Susan Jellinek, Gary Johnson, Tomni Jones, Greta Kessenich, Evelyn King, Roy Klehm, Anne Knudsen, Rebecca Kolls, Mark Kroggel, Margaret Kromer, Jeannie Larson, Helen Lindsay, Jack and Elise Lonnee, Dick McGinnis, Steve McNamara, Elsie Miller, Sue Milliken, John Nolan, Eric Nordlie, Daniel Ochsner, Jerry Olson, Deborah Orenstein, Todd Orjala, Duane Otto, Penny Pease, Jonathan Pedersen, Barb Pederson, Harold Pellett, John and Sally Perkins, Scott Reath, Jayne Roberts, Laurie Robinson, Rick Rogers, David A. Rose, David G. Rose, Carl Rosen, Maggie Sattler, David Schulte, Terry Schwartz, Barbara Selinger, Lee and Jerry Shannon, Susan Simonton, Heather Skinner, Lynn Steiner, David Stevenson, Jim Stolzenburg, Joe Tashjian, Doris Taylor, Rob Taylor, Kristian Tvedten, Patrick Vettling, Donna Whitman, and Kathy Zuzek.

INTRODUCTION

Gardeners who live in cold climates have special considerations when selecting shrubs and small trees. If you live in an area where minimum winter temperatures drop to −20°F (−29°C) or colder, then you know the importance of selecting landscape plants that are well adapted to cold climates. This area extends over most of Canada and across the northern tier of the United States in what are commonly referred to as zones 1 through 5. These zones are highlighted on the zone map on page xiv.

Shrubs and small trees are essential elements in attractive, well-designed landscapes. Often overlooked and underappreciated, these plants provide an incredible diversity of form, size, and seasonal features such as flowers, fruit, and foliage color.

Fortunately, there are many outstanding shrubs and small trees that will thrive in cold climates. In *Growing Shrubs and Small Trees in Cold Climates,* we list more than 950 species and named varieties of these landscape plants. Within this large group of plants you are sure to find one that will perform well in any particular site in your yard, even those difficult spots where few plants thrive. Among the many named varieties listed, you will find both old varieties, which have proven their value over many years, and many exciting newer ones. Included are some of the most recent introductions that look promising,

but if we have not observed these plants through severe winters, we have given them a fairly conservative hardiness rating and noted this in the description.

For each group of plants we have compiled overall information about appearance, growing patterns, planting and maintenance needs, and special uses. This information is presented in simple, everyday language so that anyone can understand even the more sophisticated aspects of growing shrubs and small trees. Some technical terms are included, generally in parentheses, but our main purpose is to help you grow great shrubs, no matter what your level of knowledge or expertise. This growing information is followed with even more detailed information about individual species and named varieties listed in clear, concise, and easy-to-use charts. Particular note is made of the plant features that will provide multiseason interest in the landscape: flowers; the color, texture, shape, and autumn coloration of foliage; stem coloration and texture; fruit color, size, and shape; and even winter interest, including bark coloration and distinctive architectural form.

With all of these factors considered, we then rated each plant on a scale of one to five stars. The highest-rated, five-star plants are those that have the very best combinations of adaptability and ornamental features. There are many excellent plants listed that did not rate a full five stars but will still prove to be

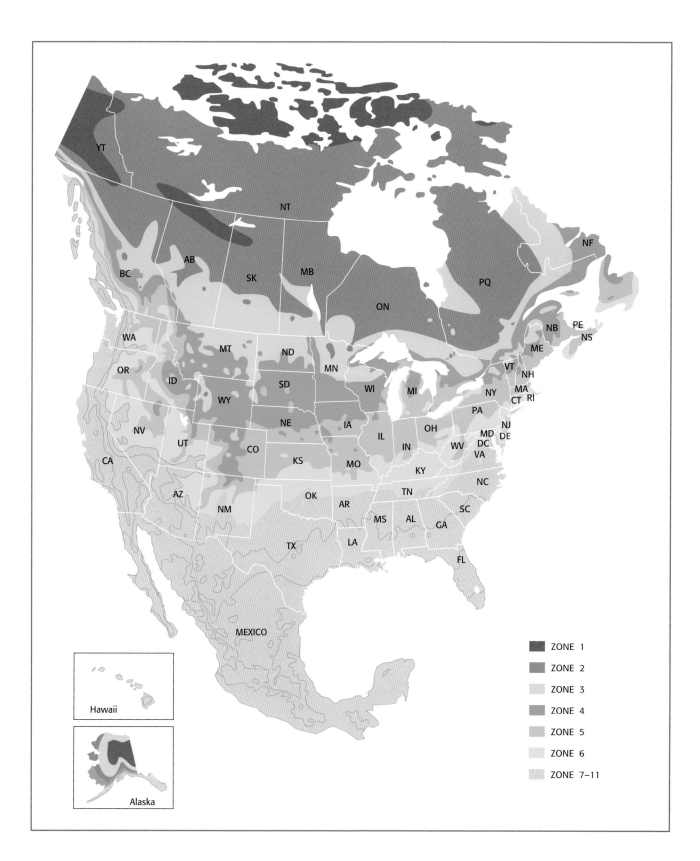

YT

NT

NF

BC

AB

SK

MB

PQ

ON

NB

PE

WA

MT

ND

NS

ME

OR

ID

MN

VT

NH

SD

WI

MI

NY

MA

RI

WY

CT

NV

IA

PA

NJ

UT

NE

IL

OH

MD

DE

CO

IN

WV

DC

CA

KS

MO

KY

VA

AZ

NM

OK

AR

TN

NC

SC

MS

AL

GA

TX

LA

NC

FL

MEXICO

	ZONE 1
	ZONE 2
	ZONE 3
	ZONE 4
	ZONE 5
	ZONE 6
	ZONE 7–11

Hawaii

Alaska

Growing Shrubs and Small Trees in Cold Climates is aimed primarily at gardeners living in zones 1–5. It will also be helpful to gardeners in portions of zone 6. A cold climate is characterized by temperatures that can dip below –20°F (–29°C), as well as by snow during the winter.

useful and beautiful in the landscape. Since individual tastes vary in plants as much as they do in clothes or music, use the ratings and descriptions as a starting point and then discover your own favorites.

In the chart on pages xvi–xvii are some general landscape traits for the major groups (genera) covered in great detail in the individual sections of Part I. It gives a quick overview of each group.

Landscape Use is defined as the range of ways a particular group can be used in your yard. Plant groups lists as "very versatile" or "versatile" can be used in a number of ways. For instance, various types of *Thuja* (Arborvitae) make excellent specimen plants, formal or informal hedges, screens, foundation plantings, mass plantings, and additions to perennial and shrub borders. Plant groups listed as "limited" have fewer ways of being used in the landscape; for instance, their use may be primarily for a low ground cover or as a small specimen. Having more limited use should not be seen as a negative, since these plants often fill a very specific need in the landscape.

Seasonal Interest refers to a group's ornamental features such as flowers, brightly colored autumn foliage, or interesting fruit. Those with "very high" or "high" seasonal interest display ornamental features through most or all of the seasons. *Amelanchier* (Serviceberry), for example, offers lovely spring bloom, colorful summer fruit, stunning autumn foliage color, and attractive bark for year-long seasonal interest. Plant groups with "limited" seasonal interest might have a spectacular show of flowers in spring but lack really interesting features through the rest of the year. *Forsythia* (Forsythia) and *Philadelphus* (Mockorange) fall into this category.

Useful Life Expectancy provides an estimate of how many years you can expect a plant to look good and grow well in your yard. This is a difficult number to predict, since many factors can affect the useful lifespan of a plant. The numbers listed here are based on the assumption of proper planting and reasonable care of the plants. Lifespans will also vary among the species and named varieties within each group.

Maintenance. All landscape plants will benefit from a certain amount of maintenance, even if that just involves light pruning every 3 or 4 years. However, different plant groups require more or less maintenance than others, so the amount of care required for a specific group is listed as "low," "medium," or "high." Examples of factors affecting the rating include need for specialized soils, susceptibility to disease or insect problems that might require regular treatment, and need for frequent or extensive pruning at various times of year.

Preferred Light indicates the level of sunlight that will produce the best growth for a specific group of plants. Many plants are adaptable and will still grow well in somewhat different exposures. But certain features such as how vigorously the plants grow, the amount of flowering and fruit production, and even increased chances for problems with disease or insect infestations may be affected by less than ideal light conditions for that specific group of plants. "Full sun" indicates exposure to direct sunlight throughout the day, certainly no less than 8 hours. "Partial shade" means the plant receives a filtered or broken flow of sunlight, as through the branches of trees or direct light for no more than 4 to 5 hours per day. "Full shade" means the plant receives no direct sunlight throughout the entire day, as under a canopy of tree branches in a wooded area. "Variable" indicates that there is a range of preferred light among the species and named varieties within any given group. Specific light needs within groups with this description are given in individual sections of Part I. In these same sections there may be suggestions for planting shrubs or small trees on specific sides of a home (east, west, north, or south).

The information in *Growing Shrubs and Small Trees in Cold Climates* comes from many years of practical experience in growing, evaluating, selecting, and designing with these trees and shrubs. We have researched many sources of information and gained much insight from the opinions of other landscape plant professionals. We have combined our years of experience in horticultural research, commercial nursery production and management, and garden writing, as well as our avid enthusiasm for growing plants in our own home landscapes, to compile this book. Problems are not glossed over, nor are they exaggerated. We hope to provide some inspiration as well as lots of valuable information to all gardeners who share the challenge of growing plants in cold climates.

We recognize there is always something to be learned. If you have any tips or gardening advice to share, or if you would like to criticize, correct, or add information, please write to us at PO Box 212, Long Lake, MN 55356. Please enclose a self-addressed, stamped envelope if you would like a reply.

MAJOR SHRUB AND SMALL TREE GROUPS

NAME	LANDSCAPE USE	SEASONAL INTEREST	USEFUL LIFE EXPECTANCY	MAINTENANCE	PREFERRED LIGHT
Abies (Fir)	Limited	High	25–50	Low	Full sun
Acer (Maple)	Versatile	High	25–50	Low	Full sun to partial shade
Amelanchier (Serviceberry)	Versatile	Very high	20–50	Low	Variable
Aronia (Chokeberry)	Limited	High	10–15	Low	Full sun
Berberis (Barberry)	Very versatile	Very high	5–15	Medium	Full sun
Buxus (Boxwood)	Limited	High	15–25	Medium	Full sun to partial shade
Caragana (Peashrub)	Limited	Limited	10–20	Low	Full sun
Cercis (Redbud)	Limited	High	15–35	Low	Partial shade
Chionanthus (Fringe Tree)	Limited	High	15–30	Low	Full sun to partial shade
Clethra (Summersweet)	Versatile	High	10–15	Medium	Partial shade to full sun
Cornus (Dogwood)	Very versatile	Very high	10–25	Medium	Variable
Corylus (Hazelnut)	Limited	Limited	10–30	Low	Full sun to partial shade
Cotinus (Smokebush)	Limited	High	10–30	Medium	Full sun
Cotoneaster (Cotoneaster)	Versatile	High	10–20	Medium	Full sun
Daphne (Daphne)	Limited	High	5–10	Low	Full sun
Diervilla (Bush Honeysuckle)	Limited	High	10–25	Low	Partial shade to full sun
Euonymus (Euonymus)	Versatile	High	15–25	Low	Full sun
Exochorda (Pearlbush)	Limited	Limited	15–25	Low	Full sun
Forsythia (Forsythia)	Versatile	Limited	10–15	Medium	Full sun
Hamamelis (Witch Hazel)	Limited	High	15–35	Low	Partial shade to full sun
Hydrangea (Hydrangea)	Versatile	High	10–25	Medium	Variable
Ilex (Winterberry)	Limited	High	10–20	Medium	Full sun
Juniperus (Juniper)	Very versatile	High	15–30	Medium	Full sun
Lonicera (Honeysuckle)	Versatile	Limited	10–15	Medium	Full sun
Magnolia (Magnolia)	Limited	High	25–45	Low	Full sun
Malus (Crabapple)	Versatile	Very high	25–50	Medium	Full sun

Name	Landscape use	Seasonal interest	Useful life expectancy	Maintenance	Preferred Light
Microbiota (Russian Cypress)	Limited	Limited	15–25	Low	Partial shade to full sun
Paeonia (Tree Peony)	Limited	Limited	25–35	Medium	Full sun
Perovskia (Russian Sage)	Limited	Limited	10–15	Medium	Full sun
Philadelphus (Mockorange)	Limited	Limited	10–15	Medium	Full sun
Physocarpus (Ninebark)	Limited	Limited	10–15	Medium	Full sun
Picea (Spruce)	Versatile	High	25–50	Low	Full sun
Pinus (Pine)	Versatile	High	25–50	Low	Full sun
Potentilla (Shrub Cinquefoil)	Versatile	Limited	10–15	Medium	Full sun
Prunus (Almond, Cherry, Plum)	Versatile	High	5–15	Medium	Full sun
Pyrus (Pear)	Versatile	High	15–50	Medium	Full sun
Rhododendron (Azalea)	Limited	High	10–30	High	Variable
Rhus (Sumac)	Limited	High	5–20	Low	Full sun
Ribes (Currant)	Limited	Limited	10–20	Medium	Full sun to partial shade
Salix (Willow)	Versatile	Limited	5–30	Medium	Full sun
Sorbus (Mountain Ash)	Limited	High	15–40	Medium	Full sun
Spiraea (Spirea)	Very versatile	High	10–20	Medium	Full sun
Symphoricarpos (Snowberry)	Limited	Limited	10–15	Low	Variable
Syringa (Lilac)	Versatile	High	15–40	Medium	Full sun
Taxus (Yew)	Versatile	High	20–50	Medium	Full sun to full shade
Thuja (Arborvitae)	Very versatile	High	15–40	Medium	Full sun to partial shade
Vaccinium (Blueberry)	Limited	High	10–20	High	Full sun
Viburnum (Viburnum)	Very versatile	High	15–25	Medium	Variable
Weigela (Cardinal Bush)	Versatile	Limited	5–15	Medium	Full sun
Wisteria (Wisteria)	Limited	Limited	15–30	Medium	Full sun

PART I

The Most Popular Shrubs and Small Trees

The following sections describe more than 950 species (wild) and named varieties (cultivars) of shrubs and small trees. These plants belong to 50 major groups called *genera* (the plural of *genus*). The groups are listed alphabetically by Latin name. The common names are given in the Contents (see page vi). Each section covers one plant group and describes in detail the most simple to the most technical aspects of growing that particular group of shrubs or small trees. Every section follows the same format, so you can easily find the information important to you.

CHAPTER I
INDIVIDUAL LISTINGS

Many terrific shrubs and small trees grow well in cold climates. It is frustrating to read about a specific plant only to find out it will not grow in your area. The plants in this book can stand up to tough conditions. These plants all have distinctive characteristics and each can add a special dimension to your yard. Use this information to combine shrubs and small trees in your own way to make your yard unique and beautiful.

Varieties

More than 950 varieties of shrubs and small trees are listed in Part I. These have all been rated using a five-star system (see page 7). The stars reflect our overall opinion of the plants. The ones with the most stars stand out from the rest. Nevertheless, you should visit local gardens to see these plants for yourself. Seeing actual plants gives you the most accurate picture of what a plant will look like under ideal growing conditions, particularly plants in your area. Since many shrubs and small trees have a completely different look in different seasons, try revisiting gardens throughout the entire year to truly appreciate all they have to offer. No one can describe the exquisite scents of some of these shrubs, nor the richness of their fall coloration, or the delightful taste or beauty of their berries.

Hardiness

The cold hardiness of shrubs and small trees is a complex subject. All of the plants listed in this guide should survive temperatures of –20°F (–29°C) or colder *during their dormant period* in mid winter. However, minimum temperature for survival in mid winter is only one concern for cold-climate gardeners. In fall, shrubs and trees begin to prepare for winter cold through the process of acclimation, or "hardening off." Lack of light and increasingly chilly temperatures trigger this process. Leaves on deciduous shrubs fall off. Growth of all shrubs slows down. Cells begin to change structure so that they will be less likely to be damaged during the dormant season when temperatures dip well below 0°F (–18°C). The cells in flower buds may go through a process known as supercooling. Leaf buds, bark, and other tissues slowly dehydrate. Both supercooling and dehydration prevent the formation of ice crystals within cells. If ice crystals form, they expand, rupture the cell wall (membrane), and kill the cell. In the spring the process is reversed and known as deacclimation. Cells begin to revert to their previous structure as days get longer and temperatures warm up. With each passing day, they are less able to resist freezing.

Clearly then, certain weather patterns can wreak havoc on plants. In the fall, temperatures may drop dramatically before a plant has a chance to harden off fully. In mid winter temperatures may get unseasonably warm only to be followed by sudden temperature drops. This too can damage shrubs. And, finally, during the spring, if warm weather is followed by a late freeze, plants or their often less hardy flower buds can be severely damaged. For this reason, hardiness is not as simple as defining the minimum possible temperature in mid winter as is done in zone maps and in the varietal tables throughout this guide. Shrubs or small trees do not always die immediately from trauma. Their actual death may take several years, which is often puzzling to the home gardener who is not aware of this fact.

Even though you may live in a specific zone as defined on the zone map, your yard may have many microclimates. Large yards with sites ranging from highly protected to highly exposed may represent more than one zone. This often explains why in one yard a shrub may survive and thrive while in another nearby yard it dies back or dies out completely. Or, why in one yard a shrub may survive in a protected area but die back or die out completely in a more exposed site. Zone maps are also misleading in that they don't take into consideration such things as relative humidity, overall daylight versus cloud cover, and similar climatic conditions. The fact that a specific plant may survive to –30°F (–34°C) doesn't tell the whole story. Perhaps, it will only do well in an area with cool summers or high humidity. When specific climatic conditions are required for good growth of a specific plant, this is pointed out.

Finally, knowing the geographical origin of a plant may be critical to your success as well. Specific plants may be native in both cold and warm climates throughout the United States. Unfortunately, those grown from seeds produced by shrubs in the south are rarely hardy in colder climates. Breeders using plants native to colder regions are often able to breed greater cold hardiness into a specific species.

Whenever possible, buy nursery stock grown locally. Shrubs grown in your area have a better chance of surviving in your yard. This is not always possible and you may be willing to take chances on certain shrubs or trees only available from mail-order sources in warmer areas.

The Varieties Charts

The shrubs and small trees listed in the Varieties charts at the end of each section in Part I are presented in a uniform manner. These lists are extremely valuable, representing decades of field testing and observation by experienced growers in cold climates. Many of these plants do quite well in more southerly areas as well, but some thrive only in colder areas.

The Plant Group Genus

The name of each section in Part I represents a group of plants (genus), such as *Prunus*. This group of shrubs and small trees will be used as an example of how the charts at the end of each section are laid out. The plants placed under the heading *Prunus* are there because they have common characteristics.

The Species

In the plant listing, some plant names are in italic typeface. These plants are found naturally in the wild and are referred to as a species. The word species is both singular and plural. *Prunus americana* is a tree that grows wild in many areas of the country.

Variety (var.)

When a wild plant varies somewhat from the species but is quite similar to it, it's referred to as a variety. *Prunus maritima* var. *flava* is an example. *Prunus maritima* is the species, while *flava* is the variety (var.). The only real difference between the two is that the variety produces fruit of a different color. Otherwise, they are almost identical.

Cultivated variety (cultivar)

When a new plant is developed or selected, it is known as a cultivated variety (cultivar) and given a name of the originator's choice. A cultivar will appear with single quotation marks, such as 'Atropurpurea.' Cultivars are genetically identical and often referred to as "named varieties." In some of the plant groups there will be two names given for the same plant. The name most commonly used in selling the plant to the public is listed first. Many names bear either a trademark ™ or registered ® symbol. When bearing these symbols, the single quotes are dropped. For example, Weigela 'Wine & Roses' may be listed as Wine & Roses™. If the plant name is registered, it appears as Wine & Roses®.

A Cross

Sometimes species and cultivars are interbred to create a new plant. *Prunus* × *cistena* is a cross between *Prunus pumila* (a species) and *Prunus cerasifera* 'Atropurpurea' (the previously mentioned cultivar). Crosses can also be made in other ways, but this is a good example.

This system of naming plants can seem somewhat intimidating, but the advantage of knowing the correct name is obvious. By knowing the Latin and cultivar names, you should get the exact plant you want from local nurseries or mail-order sources. If you order by common name, this may not happen because common names vary widely throughout the country and the same common name may be given to completely different plants. Finally, no matter where you are in the world people know plants by their Latin name.

Sources

Each section includes an alphabetized list of mail-order sources for that group of plants. These lists are important because local nurseries may stock a rather limited supply of plants. There are more than 130 mail-order sources listed throughout this guide. The variety of plants offered by individual sources varies considerably. Some companies may specialize in the group of shrubs or small trees highlighted in a particular section or may only sell one or two unusual types within that group. Offerings change frequently. The sources listed in this guide are primarily retail. A few may become wholesale in the future but will generally sell to retail customers willing to spend a minimum amount of money. If you cannot find a specific plant, you can ask these mail-order sources for help. You can also go to *www.plantinfo.umn.edu*. Enter the name of the plant you are looking for. The site will list mail-order sources with their physical or mailing address, telephone number, and web address. There may not always be a match. Also, the site sometimes lists addresses of companies that have gone out of business, no longer sell through the mail, or will only sell to wholesale customers. Even when a source is listed, that source may not have the plant. Some plants listed in this guide or on line will be available one year, not the next, then possibly available a year or two later. However, the majority of the plants listed will be available from local nurseries or a specific mail-order company every year. It is impossible for any site or book to match thousands of plants to suppliers without problems. However, this online site and the source lists in this guide will help you find a specific plant as quickly as possible.

Keep the following tips in mind regarding mail-order sources:

• Most companies now have sites on line that list the shrubs and small trees they sell. Just enter the company's name to get to the site. Many companies sell plants directly to you from these sites.

• If you do not have access to the internet or prefer to deal directly with a person, each source listed has a mailing address and telephone number.

• If contacting a company through the mail, always include a stamped, self-addressed envelope for a reply. If you are requesting a catalog, the company will let you know if there is a charge or will send you one for free.

• You may prefer to call a company to speak to someone directly. They will give you information on catalogs and can answer specific questions regarding their plants.

• Catalogs are less common as costs of printing have risen dramatically. If catalogs are available, there may be a charge. The cost is often applied toward your first purchase.

• Good catalogs include the Latin name of each plant. Use that name when placing an order. When in

Seed Companies

You can grow many shrubs and small trees from either collected or purchased seed. The number of companies offering seed for shrubs and small trees is dwindling. The following are a few that remain:

Angelgrove Tree Seed Co.
P.O. Box 74, Riverhead, Harbour Grace, NL A0A 3P0 Canada
(888) 596-4053

Brandywine Conservancy (seed bank)
P.O. Box 141, Chadds Ford, PA 19317
(610) 388-8327

F.W. Schumacher Co.
P.O. Box 1023, Sandwich, MA 02563
(508) 888-0659

J. L. Hudson, Seedsman (seed bank)
Star Rte. 2, P.O. Box 337, La Honda, CA 94020
(no phone by request)

Sheffield's Seed Co., Inc.
269 Auburn Rd., Rt. 34, Locke, NY 13092
(315) 497-1058

The Fragrant Path
P.O. Box 328, Fort Calhoun, NE 68023
(no phone by request)

doubt, use the Latin in this guide along with the varietal name so that there is no misunderstanding about the plant being ordered. Catalogs that list plants by common name or by color only are not doing their job. Move on to a different company.

- Compare offerings in several catalogs. Make sure to understand the age of the plant being ordered. The more mature a plant, the more expensive it is likely to be.
- Ask whether a plant is growing on its own roots or is grafted. If a plant is grafted, ask what rootstock has been used.
- Buy plants as early in the year as possible since stock may be limited.
- If ordering by phone, get the name of the person you talk to and keep it on file.

- If ordering in writing, note the date you mail the letter. If plants do not arrive as requested, you may have to follow up with a call.
- Many catalogs suggest accepting "substitutions" for plants which are sold out. Whether you are willing to do this is a matter of personal choice. You can avoid this problem by ordering very early.
- Since you are growing plants in a cold climate, specify the date you would like to receive your shipment. Stress this. Plants mailed in extreme cold often die; they also require extra care to keep alive until planting time. However, companies selling bare root plants have to dig them while dormant. Southern suppliers may have to send you plants earlier than you want. See page 364 on how to deal with this situation, a process known as *heeling in.*
- Ask what kind of guarantee the company has for its plants. Plants are most likely to die out, if they are going to, in the winter following the first growing season. You need a guaranty for no less than a year, two if possible.
- When you receive plants in the mail, check to see that you got what you ordered.
- Check the plants on arrival to make sure that they are not dried out, damaged, or dead. Dead cane has a gray look and will crack if bent; also, if you cut into it, it will be brown rather than light white or green. If you sense a problem, contact the company immediately.
- Plant all shrubs as soon as possible after receiving them. Follow the planting instructions provided. The planting instructions in this guide may give you a few extra tips.
- Keep records of orders, and label all plants. If a plant turns out to be an "imposter," let the company know and get a refund. Few companies deliberately mail the wrong plants, but it does happen that plants get mixed up by mistake. Shrubs and small trees grow slowly, and records may have to be kept for years.
- Mail-order sources may choose to restrict sales to specific geographical areas. Generally, this information is made clear in their catalogs and online sites.

- In a few instances, there are legal restrictions that prohibit the sale of plants between certain states or foreign countries. This is to stop the spread of diseases and insect infestations. Mail-order sources generally outline these restrictions in detail.
- The availability of some shrubs varies by year. Occasionally, a specific variety may be in such short supply that the commercial grower must rebuild stock before selling it again. If there is enough demand, the specific variety of shrub will be on the market again in the near future. So let sources know that you want a specific plant.

Using This Growing Guide

Read the chapters in Part II *before* delving into the 50 individual shrub sections in Part I. The chapters in Part II contain specific tips and procedures that may not be found in the rest of the book. Or, they may contain more detailed information on a specific procedure to avoid unnecessary repetition.

While the language is as simple and easy to understand as possible, you may run into unfamiliar words. Read the glossary in advance to understand their meaning. The glossary also contains information related to these terms that will help you be successful in growing shrubs and small trees in cold climates.

The material in individual sections of Part I may appear to be repetitive. However, there are subtle differences in the text. It is these seemingly small

The Five-Star System

STARS HAVE BEEN AWARDED to each shrub or small tree. The highest possible rating is five stars (*****). The process of awarding these stars involved many factors, including rate of growth, vigor, potential landscape use, and multiseasonal interest. Hardiness was also a consideration in awarding stars. While the ratings are subjective, they are based on decades of growing and field testing thousands of varieties of shrubs and small trees. A plant with a low rating can still be lovely and well worth buying if grown properly. With the thousands of shrubs and small trees available in the market and presently being tested, inevitably some fine plants have been left out. New varieties are constantly being evaluated, and the best of these will be added in future editions. If we have missed a superstar you have tested for three or more years in your garden, we would appreciate hearing from you.

points that lead to success with each shrub. There is an advantage to having all of the growing information in each section. You will not be frustrated by having to flip back and forth to get specific facts that vary by plant.

The lists of plants at the end of each section in Part I contain many terrific shrubs and small trees. Note that mail-order catalogs may differ slightly in how these plants are categorized. If you order the plants as listed, the mail-order companies will understand what you're after. And that's what really counts.

Abies balsamea 'Nana'

ABIES

(AY-bees)

FIR

The Firs listed here are unique plants, most commonly used in rock gardens but increasingly in perennial borders. The plants are prized by collectors for the lovely color and texture of their evergreen foliage. They are rarely bothered by diseases or insects. However, they react badly to high heat or drought. They are also extremely slow growing.

new growth or candling has a softer green color than older needles. Needles tend to be flat and often have a different coloration underneath than on the surface. They generally last several years, then drop off. Some Firs will form upright stems (leaders) which initiate vertical growth. While most of the Firs listed in the chart will not produce cones, **Abies koreana** 'Silberlocke' will as it matures.

How Firs Grow

Firs have a relatively shallow, fibrous root system. Plants produce numerous branches covered with needles (leaves) that vary in length by variety. The

Where to Plant

Site and Light Firs prefer full sun but tolerate partial shade. Plant them where they will have good air circulation.

Soil and Moisture Firs prefer well-drained, slightly acidic soils that remain cool and moist throughout the growing season. If soil is compacted, replace it or build a raised bed. Firs grow well in rocky soils as long as the soils are loose. Keep the root system moist and cool by using lots of acidic mulch and watering regularly. As the plants mature, they shade their own root systems, but in early growth they demand more attention.

Spacing Space Firs with their mature size in mind. They can be quite slow growing, but eventually they will take up the space outlined in the chart at the end of this section.

Landscape Use

The dwarf Firs selected make excellent specimen plants in rock gardens and also fit nicely into foundation plantings. Their relatively small size and slow growth rate make them especially valuable in tight spaces. Dwarf Firs added to shrub and perennial borders also make good accent plants because of their interesting coloration and texture.

Planting

Bare Root Rarely sold this way.

Containerized Plants If the soil in the container is dry, soak it thoroughly and let it drain overnight before planting. Carefully remove the plant from the container to avoid shattering the root ball. Plant at the same depth as in the container. Fill in with well-prepared soil, press firmly to get rid of all air pockets, and water immediately. Dissolve acidic water-soluble fertilizer in a gallon (about 4 liters) of water following the directions on the label. Pour ½ cup (about 120 ml) of this starter solution around the base of each plant. If you prefer organic fertilizer, use fish emulsion instead.

Balled and Burlapped Rarely sold this way.

Transplanting

Dig up the plant in early spring before new growth emerges. Keep as much soil around the roots as possible. Plant immediately as you would a containerized plant. With the larger varieties, hire professionals to do this if the plants have already matured over a period of years.

How to Care for Firs

Water Keep the soil evenly moist from spring until the soil freezes in fall. Consistent watering is especially important during the first 2 years. Always saturate the soil deeply with each watering. When the top 2 inches (5 cm) of soil dry out, water. Never let these plants suffer water stress during prolonged dry spells.

Mulch Apply a 1- to 2-inch (2.5- to 5-cm) layer of mulch around each plant as soon as the ground warms up in spring. Good mulches include shredded bark, pine needles, and wood chips. Mulch retains moisture in the soil and helps prevent the growth of weeds. Replenish the mulch as necessary throughout the growing season.

Fertilizing Fertilize every spring with an acidic fertilizer, such as Miracid. Any acidic fertilizers designed for use with evergreens and Rhododendrons are also recommended. Follow the directions on the labels for correct dosage. If using granular fertilizer, saturate the soil to dissolve the particles and carry nutrients into the root zone.

If you prefer organic fertilizers, use alfalfa meal (rabbit pellets), blood meal, bone meal, compost, fish emulsion, Milorganite, or rotted manures. Bone meal must be added to the soil at planting time to be effective. If available locally, use cottonseed meal since it's mildly acidic.

Weeding Prevent the growth of most annual weeds by using mulch. Pull by hand any weeds that do appear. Weeds compete with Firs for available moisture and nutrients and should be removed immediately.

Deadheading Not a consideration.

Pruning If any portion of the plant dies back after a hard winter, snip it off to live stem tissue below. Plants require little to no pruning for good health. Shape or control the plant's size through pruning. Do this in spring after new growth emerges. Cut new growth back by no more than one-half. If a plant forms an upright stem (leader), it is your choice as to whether to cut it off or not. Leave it on for upright form; cut it off to keep the plant in a more controlled shape.

Winter Protection Firs may experience some winter damage in the first year or two. Proper watering until the first freeze is very important. So is placing them in a protected location.

Problems

Insects None serious.

Disease None serious.

Marauders Some people have problems with rabbits and deer nibbling foliage in the winter. Surround plantings with fencing or spray them with repellents if this becomes a problem.

Propagation

Abies balsamea 'Nana' (Dwarf Balsam Fir) and *Abies koreana* 'Silberlocke' (Silberlocke Korean Fir) are propagated from hardwood cuttings. In winter, snip off new growth. Keep cuttings moist and cool but provide bottom heat to stimulate growth. For additional information, see pages 406–8. The other varieties listed at the end of the chapter are usually grafted to the rootstock of varying Firs, but this should be left in the hands of professionals.

Special Uses

None.

Sources

Bloom River Gardens, 39744 Deerhorn Rd., Springfield, OR 97478, (541) 726-8997

Evermay Nursery, 84 Beechwood Ave., Old Town, ME 04468, (207) 827-0522

ForestFarm, 990 Tetherow Rd., Williams, OR 97544, (541) 846-7269

Fraser's Thimble Farms, 175 Arbutus Rd., Salt Spring Island, BC V8K 1A3 Canada, (250) 537-5788

Girard Nurseries, P.O. Box 428, Geneva, OH 44041, (440) 466-2881

Greer Gardens, 1280 Goodpasture Island Rd., Eugene, OR 97401, (541) 686-8266

Heronswood Nursery, 300 Park Ave., Warminster, PA 18974, (877) 674-4714

Hortico, Inc., 723 Robson Rd., RR# 1, Waterdown, ON L0R 2H1 Canada, (905) 689-6984

Klehm's Song Sparrow Perennial Farm, 13101 E Rye Rd., Avalon, WI 53505, (800) 553-3715

Porterhowse Farms, 41370 SE Thomas Rd., Sandy, OR 97055, (503) 668-5834

River Rock Nursery, 19251 SE Hwy 224, Damascus, OR 97089, (503) 658-4047

Siskiyou Rare Plant Nursery, 2115 Talent Ave., Talent, OR 97540, (541) 535-7103

Wavecrest Nursery, 2509 Lakeshore Dr., Fennville, MI 49408, (888) 869-4159

Whitney Gardens & Nursery, P.O. Box 170, Brinnon, WA 98320, (360) 796-4411

Abies balsamea 'Nana'

Abies concolor 'Compacta'

Abies lasiocarpa var. *arizonica* 'Compacta'

Abies lasiocarpa 'Green Globe'

VARIETIES

Dwarf conifers grow very slowly. Take this into consideration when noting height and width of individual plants listed. It may take *decades* for some plants listed to reach these dimensions.

VARIETY	FOLIAGE COLOR	HEIGHT/WIDTH	HARDINESS
Abies balsamea			
(Dwarf Balsam Fir)			
'Nana'***	Dark green	2'/3'	−40°F
'Piccolo'***	Dark green	2'/3'	−40°F

These shrubs have an attractive, mounded form that is both neat and controlled. 'Nana' has very short needles, deep green on top, silvery underneath. New growth in spring is light green but turns deep blue to dark green as it matures. 'Piccolo' has rounded elongated needles angled downward and is ideal for rock gardens. Brush against them for that wonderful scent that makes Balsam Firs so much in demand as Christmas trees. They are extremely slow growing. Buy these plants growing on their own roots to ensure the tight, uniform appearance desired.

VARIETY	FOLIAGE COLOR	HEIGHT/WIDTH	HARDINESS
Abies concolor			
(White Fir)			
'Archer' ('Archer's Dwarf')***	Blue	6'/3'	−40°F
'Compacta'****	Blue gray	9'/6'	−40°F
'Scooter'***	Yellow green	3'/3'	−40°F

'Archer' starts off as a mound. It takes more than 10 years for it to form a small, lovely cone-shaped plant with radiating tiered branches. 'Compacta,' also grows very slowly and its needles are shorter than the species but have a wonderful rich coloration. The plant can have a somewhat dense irregular form, but it is still very appealing. 'Scooter' forms a flattened bun with horizontal branches and shorter needles than the species.

VARIETY	FOLIAGE COLOR	HEIGHT/WIDTH	HARDINESS
Abies koreana			
(Korean Fir)			
'Silberlocke' ('Hortsmann's Silberlocke')***Silver		12'/3'	−20°F

The species is a lovely tree with interesting purple cones. 'Silberlocke' has become one of the most popular selections. The silver white undersides of its green needles, their unusual way of curling up at the tips, and the overall twisting growth pattern make it stand out. In time the plant produces green, upright cones. Plants may be sold either grafted or rooted from cuttings.

VARIETY	FOLIAGE COLOR	HEIGHT/WIDTH	HARDINESS
Abies lasiocarpa			
(Alpine Fir)			
var. *arizonica* 'Compacta'***	Blue	8'/4'	−30°F
'Green Globe'****	Dark green	3'/3'	−30°F
'Silberzwerg'***	Green	2'/2'	−30°F

'Compacta' is a grafted plant commonly known as "Cork Bark Fir" because it has unusual cream-colored bark. Its foliage is dense with an excellent blue coloration. It has an attractive conical shape. 'Green Globe' displays dense, dark green needles. While typically short and rounded, it will form a rather tall, upright specimen if leaders are not removed. The photo in this section represents that type of *atypical* growth. 'Silberszwerg' is rounded. Its needles are green on top and silver on the bottom. This globe has horizontal branches that show off the silver coloration of the needles.

Acer ginnala

ACER

(AY-sir)

MAPLE

The varieties of Maples chosen are large shrubs or small trees that are quite adaptable to a wide range of conditions. Their spring flowers are delicate and relatively inconspicuous. Their foliage is clean and especially interesting when contrasted to the winged fruits (samaras), often tinged a light pink to intense red as they mature. The samaras contain seeds that appeal to wildlife. However, the most outstanding feature of these Maples is their fall color. In addition, all have an interesting branching pattern in winter and are quite insect and disease free.

How Maples Grow

The roots of these select Maples are coarse and wide-spreading, but not particularly deep. By nature, they tend to be multistemmed, although some can be trained into single-stemmed trees. The stems are a bit brittle. The leaves have a fine texture and look. All of the Maples produce winged fruits in mid- to late summer. These mature over a period of weeks. The tip of the fruit is a flat seed. Some of these Maples can be quite invasive in that they self-sow freely, which can be desirable in naturalized areas.

Where to Plant

Site and Light Maples prefer full sun but will grow quite well in partial shade. As mentioned, they are adaptable.

Soil and Moisture Maples thrive in well-drained soils. The pH of the soil can be important in that Maples often grow poorly if it is overly alkaline. They prefer consistent moisture, but will tolerate fairly dry conditions once mature.

Spacing When planting Maples, always take into consideration their potential width at maturity. What may look like a twig at planting can become a large shrub or small tree in a relatively short time.

Landscape Use

These Maples are prized for their fall color, making them excellent specimen plants. Many home gardeners plant them closely to create an attractive screen or trim them into hedges. On large properties they make good mass plantings. These are also good trees for wildlife plantings since the seeds in the winged fruits attract birds. If used in shrub borders, place them in the back. They combine well with shrubs or other small trees that have interesting fall foliage color or berries, including *Amelanchier* (Serviceberry), *Aronia* (Chokeberry), *Euonymus* (Euonymus), *Hamamelis* (Witch Hazel), and *Viburnum trilobum* (Highbush Cranberry). Many of the Maples listed have extremely graceful winter forms, especially spreading, multistemmed specimens.

Planting

Bare Root Get bare root plants into the garden as soon as the ground can be worked in spring. Remove plants from their shipping package immediately on arrival. Soak them in room temperature water for no fewer than 3 hours before planting. Place a small amount of superphosphate in the base of the hole and cover with 3 inches (7.5 cm) of soil. Spread roots out over a cone of well-prepared soil. Make sure the crown is level with the surrounding soil surface. Fill the hole with soil, firm it with your fingers, and water immediately. Dissolve water-soluble fertilizer in a gallon (about 4 liters) of water following the directions on the label. Pour ½ cup (about 120 ml) of this starter solution around the base of each plant. If you prefer organic fertilizer, use fish emulsion instead.

Containerized Plants Plant Maples as early in the season as possible. If the soil in the container is dry, soak it and let it drain overnight before planting. Carefully remove the plant from the container so as not to break the root ball. Plant at the same depth as in the container after preparing the hole in a similar manner as that for a bare root plant. Fill the hole with well-prepared soil, firm with your fingers, and water immediately. Pour ½ cup (about 120 ml) of starter solution around the base of the plant.

Balled and Burlapped Plant as you would a containerized plant with these added precautions: Place the plant in the hole making sure that the top of the balled and burlapped root ball is about 1 to 2 inches (2.5 to 5 cm) above the surrounding soil. Cut and remove any twine around the stems. Remove as much of the burlap and wire holding the root ball in place as possible, but avoid breaking the root ball.

Transplanting

Transplant Maples in early spring before new growth emerges. Keep the soil moist at all times. Also mist them frequently as they bud out to encourage quick and healthy recovery from the move. Avoid transplanting them in fall as they tend to dry out and may die because of water loss through their very thin bark. Naturally, as Maples get larger, they get increasingly difficult to move.

How to Care for Maples

Water Keep the soil evenly moist from spring until the soil freezes in fall. Consistent watering is especially important during the first 2 years. Always saturate the soil deeply with each watering. When the top 2 inches (5 cm) of soil dry out, water. Once mature, these shrubs can withstand dry conditions.

Mulch Apply a 2- to 4-inch (5- to 10-cm) layer of mulch around each plant as soon as the ground warms up in spring. Good mulches include shredded bark, pine needles, and wood chips. Mulch retains moisture in the soil and helps prevent the growth of weeds. Replenish the mulch as necessary throughout the growing season.

Fertilizing Maples vary in their nutritional needs as outlined in the chart at the end of this section. After initial planting, many do not need any fertilizer at all, while others do better if fertilized lightly.

If a specific Maple prefers fertile soil, fertilize in spring with 10-10-10 fertilizer. Sprinkle the granules around the base of each plant before new growth emerges and water immediately to move the fertilizer into the root zone.

If you prefer organic fertilizers, use alfalfa meal (rabbit pellets), blood meal, bone meal, compost, fish emulsion, Milorganite, or rotted manures. Bone meal must be added to the soil at planting time to be effective.

Weeding Prevent the growth of most annual weeds by using mulch. Pull by hand any weeds that do appear. Weeds compete with shrubs for available moisture and nutrients and should be removed immediately.

Deadheading Not necessary.

Pruning At any time of year cut off any dead, damaged, or diseased portion of the shrub or tree.

Pruning is also recommended to make a tree from a multistemmed shrub, to shape multistemmed trees into a desired form, or to create a hedge.

For a tree with a single trunk, keep the most upright stem and remove all others immediately after purchasing the plant. Cut the unwanted stems back to the base. The various species as well as *Acer ginnala* 'Embers' and 'Flame' all make good single-trunked trees. Their branching is quite irregular, giving them architectural interest.

As mentioned, a number of the multitrunked plants are lovely in winter. Careful pruning accents the architectural form of these.

Acer ginnala (Amur Maple) and its named varieties make good hedges and screens. For a formal hedge, buy a number of plants about 12 inches (30 cm) tall. Plant them about 24 inches (60 cm) apart. Let them grow undisturbed for the first year. In the second year after new growth has emerged, start to trim the plants to the desired shape. Trimming induces more stems to grow from the base of the plant. The plants are quite fast growing and should be trimmed every year until they reach the desired height and shape.

To create a screen, let the plants grow naturally but plant them 36 to 48 inches (90 to 120 cm) apart. Prune out only those stems that grow in an undesirable pattern. Almost no pruning will be required.

Winter Protection Not needed.

Problems

Insects Aphids, tiny insects that suck juices from the plant, often cluster on new growth and can be a problem. Usually, many of them can be sprayed off with a strong stream of water. If this doesn't work and they begin to spread, then spray them with an insecticide. Aphids are generally killed by relatively mild insecticidal soaps. In rare instances, a product such as Orthene may be needed. The latter is absorbed by plant tissue and kills the insects as they feed on the new growth.

Leafhoppers are an occasional problem. These insects cause foliage to turn yellow and appear stunted. While this is not aesthetically pleasing, the problem is not usually serious enough to warrant spraying. If the problem persists or does get severe, use Orthene as for aphid infestations.

Diseases If you plant Maples in soil that drains freely, you rarely have problems with disease. If the soil is compacted or overly wet, verticillium wilt can occur. Signs of the disease vary somewhat by the time of year. Typically, leaves will discolor, shrivel, and die, and the tree appears scorched and defoliates. Unfortunately, this disease is fatal. Dig up and destroy the tree by burning it. Plant a different shrub in that area.

Marauders None.

Propagation

Suckers These shrubs do not sucker.

Cuttings Propagate Maples from softwood, not hardwood, cuttings. Take cuttings in early summer to midsummer just as new growth begins to harden (true softwood and greenwood). Cut off 4- to 6-inch (10- to 15-cm) cuttings from this new growth. Cuttings should have no fewer than three sets of leaves. Many stems on Maples are quite thin. You will increase your success rate by choosing only the most vigorous, moderate-size stems for cuttings. For additional information, see pages 406–8.

Seed Soak seed for no less than 24 and no more than 48 hours. Place the seed in a container filled with moist peat at room temperature for at least 60 days. Press the seed gently into the peat. Seed germinates best if exposed to light. If the seed is extremely fresh, there is a chance the seeds will sprout quickly. If the seed does not germinate, moist chill it for no less than 60 days and up to 120 days, if possible. Germination is highly erratic and you may have to wait up to a year for it to occur. For additional information, see pages 409–12.

Special Uses

None.

Sources

Bergeson Nursery, 4177 Cty Hwy 1, Fertile, MN 56540, (218) 945-6988

Bloom River Gardens, 39744 Deerhorn Rd., Springfield, OR 97478, (541) 726-8997

Burnt Ridge Nursery, Inc., 432 Burnt Ridge Rd., Onalaska, WA 98570, (360) 985-2873

Camellia Forest Nursery, 620 Hwy 54 W, Chapel Hill, NC 27516, (919) 968-0504

Colvos Creek Nursery, 1904 Third Ave., Suite 415, Seattle, WA 98101, (206) 749-9508

Dave's Nursery, 818 Amwell Rd., Hillsborough, NJ 08844, (908) 369-0267

Durio Nursery, 5853 Hwy 182, Opelousas, LA 70570, (337) 948-3696

Eastwoods Nursery, 634 Long Mountain Rd., Washington, VA 22747, (540) 675-1234

Essence of the Tree, P.O. Box 323, Potter Valley, CA 95469, (888) 489-1886

Fantastic Plants, 5865 Steeplechase, Bartlett, TN 38134, (800) 967-1912

Farmer Seed & Nursery, 818 NW 4th St., Faribault, MN 55021, (507) 334-1623

ForestFarm, 990 Tetherow Rd., Williams, OR 97544, (541) 846-7269

Fragrant Path, P.O. Box 328, Fort Calhoun, NE 68023, (no phone by request)

Fraser's Thimble Farms, 175 Arbutus Rd., Salt Spring Island, BC V8K 1A3 Canada, (250) 537-5788

Fritz Creek Gardens, P.O. Box 15226, Homer, AK 99603, (907) 235-4969

Greer Gardens, 1280 Goodpasture Island Rd., Eugene, OR 97401, (541) 686-8266

Hortico, Inc., 723 Robson Rd., RR# 1, Waterdown, ON L0R 2H1 Canada, (905) 689-6984

Mason Hollow Nursery, 47 Scripps Lane, Mason, NH 03048, (603) 878-4347

McKay Nursery Co., P.O. Box 185, Waterloo, WI 53594, (920) 478-2121

Meadowbrook Nursery/We-Du Natives, 2055 Polly Spout Rd., Marion, NC 28752, (828) 738-8300

Plant & Gnome, P.O. Box 5344, Charleston, WV 25361, (304) 881-7037

Reeseville Ridge Nursery, 512 S Main, Reeseville, WI 53579, (920) 927-3291

River Rock Nursery, 19251 SE Hwy 224, Damascus, OR 97089, (503) 658-4047

St. Lawrence Nurseries, 325 Ste Hwy 345, Potsdam, NY 13676, (315) 265-6739

Venero Gardens, 5985 Seamans Dr., Shorewood, MN 55331, (952) 474-8550

Wavecrest Nursery, 2509 Lakeshore Dr., Fennville, MI 49408, (888) 869-4159

Whitman Farms, 3995 Gibson Rd. NW, Salem, OR 97304, (503) 585-8728

Whitney Gardens & Nursery, P.O. Box 170, Brinnon, WA 98320, (360) 796-4411

Wildwood Farm, 10300 Sonoma Hwy, Kenwood, CA 95452, (888) 833-4181

VARIETIES

VARIETY	FALL FOLIAGE COLOR	HEIGHT/WIDTH	HARDINESS
Acer ginnala***			
(Amur Maple)	Yellow to orange scarlet	20'/25'	−40°F
'Bailey Compact' ('Compactum')***	Yellow to orange scarlet	15'/20'	−40°F
'Embers'***	Scarlet to purple red	20'/25'	−40°F
'Flame'***	Yellow to orange scarlet	20'/25'	−40°F

The species is a graceful small tree with spreading branches. Its lightly scented, pale creamy yellow flowers are not showy, but the winged fruit is lovely in mid growth when it glows pink to red against green summer foliage. Fall foliage is exceptional, offering varied colors from yellow to orange to brilliant red. Although all are good as hedges, 'Bailey Compact' stands out for this use. 'Embers' has colorful winged fruit, green early in the season, turning bright red by mid summer before turning brown in late summer. 'Flame' is noted for its uniform fall coloration even when grown from seed. All grow well in infertile soils and can be invasive in that they self-sow freely. For this reason some states prohibit the sale of these Maples to protect natural habitat.

Acer japonicum			
(Full Moon Maple)			
'Vitifolium'	Brilliant red/orange/yellow	10'/6'	−20°F

Cold climate gardeners report success growing this variety. It has a nice, rounded silhouette. Its large green leaves turn brilliant colors in fall. The reddish purple flowers in spring and winged seeds are also showy. The beauty of this plant makes it worth a gamble. Further field testing is needed before this plant can be rated.

Acer palmatum****			
(Greenleaf Japanese Maple)	Yellow red	15'/15'	−20°F
var. *atropurpureum*****	Reddish purple	15'/15'	−20°F
'Bloodgood'*****	Reddish purple	15'/15'	−20°F
'Mikawa Yatsubusa'	Red	5'/5'	−20°F
'Yasemin'	Scarlet	15'/15'	−20°F

The species is usually rounded with wide leaves, that are indented (lobed) but not deeply. The purplish flowers are relatively insignificant. Fruits are rather rare. If they do appear on isolated specimens they are similar to those of other species. With its numerous, airy branches, it has wonderful winter form. The var. *atropurpureum* commonly known as Redleaf Japanese Maple, has somewhat smaller leaves but a rich reddish coloration. 'Bloodgood' is noted for wonderful form and coloration. However, these require extreme winter protection in colder areas.

Acer ginnala (flowers)

Acer ginnala (seeds aka. samaras)

Acer ginnala

Acer palmatum 'Bloodgood'

One method is to mound soil around the base of the stem, cover the entire plant with leaves, then add a tarp just as the ground permanently freezes. Or, plant them in containers moved and stored in protected but cool areas during winter. A number of Maples in this group may be hardier, including 'Mikawa Yatdubusa' with pointy green foliage that turns red in fall and 'Yasemin' with toothed foliage that is a rich red throughout the entire season. Further field testing is needed before these two plants can be rated.

VARIETY	FALL FOLIAGE COLOR	HEIGHT/WIDTH	HARDINESS
Acer pseudosieboldianum****			
(Purplebloom or Korean Maple)	Variable	15'/15'	−30°F

This tree has an attractive, spreading form. Since it is presently grown from seed, the fall foliage of individual plants varies dramatically in color, from mostly yellow to an enticing reddish tone. This is the cold climate gardener's answer to growing a look alike to the popular but not so hardy *Acer palmatum* (Japanese Maple). Foliage also varies dramatically in seedling-grown shrubs. Leaf indentations may be deep or not so deep. This tree is unlikely to be invasive. It prefers highly fertile soils.

Acer shirasawanum			
(Golden Full Moon Maple)			
'Aureum'	Red yellow	12'/12'	−20°F

This is another borderline hardy Maple that cold climate gardeners are finding worth the gamble. Its form is quite open and airy. Its leaves tend to be pale yellow in spring, yellow green in summer, and a deeper yellow edged red in fall. It grows best in slightly shaded area protected from prevailing winds. Not yet rated.

Acer tataricum***			
(Tatarian Maple)	Yellow	25'/20'	−40°F
Hot Wings® ('GarAnn')****	Yellow red	20'/20'	−40°F

This species tends to be the most tree-like of this group. It crosses readily with *Acer ginnala* (Amur Maple) so that foliage is often tinged red on some plants sold under this name. A true Tatarian Maple is yellow to pink in fall. It produces lovely red fruit for weeks in late summer. All in all it makes an excellent specimen plant and has the advantage of being more tolerant of alkaline soils than other members of this group. It is also the most drought tolerant, but it can be invasive as it self sows readily. It prefers relatively infertile soil.

Acer triflorum****			
(Three-flower Maple) .	Yellow to orange red	20'/15'	−30°F

This species makes an attractive small tree with nice fall color and interesting tan to brown exfoliating bark. Since it's slow growing, it's easy to control and is not at all invasive. It's a fine specimen plant typically grown as a small single-trunked tree that tolerates slightly shadier locations than the other species. This tree thrives in moist, well-drained soil that is slightly acidic and fertile.

Amelanchier laevis 'Rogers' (Lustre™)

AMELANCHIER

(am-uh-LANG-keer)

SERVICEBERRY, JUNEBERRY, SARVIS TREE, SARVISBERRY, SASKATOON BERRY, SHADBLOW, SHADBUSH, PETITES POIRES

Serviceberries are native to much of the United States and make excellent plants for naturalized settings where their berries will attract varied wildlife. Some are quite valuable in that they tolerate shade well. The flowers on all types are white, fairly attractive, and rather short-lived. All types produce purplish blue to black edible fruits. These shrubs and small trees are particularly noted for excellent fall color, often rich red, orange, or yellow. Many of the plants have interesting winter form with smooth gray bark. They are fairly disease and insect resistant.

How Serviceberries Grow

Serviceberries can be divided into two major groups: low types that spread by underground runners and tall types that resemble trees. The low types often form thickets by sending off suckers to the side of the mother plant. Serviceberries have shallow, rather coarse roots. It is best to buy plants grown on their own roots. Plants tend to be multistemmed by nature. The grayish bark may be lightly striped on some types. Plants vary from upright to horizontal in form. All bloom in spring with white flowers. On some types these are similar to those of wild blackberries. Leaves are generally oval and medium green with a whitish underside. Many emerge tinted red. Berries are edible and technically not berries at all. They should be called *pomes,* as are apples and pears. They vary in size from that of a small pea up to ½ inch (1.25 cm) or more on some named varieties. They are formed in clusters of six to twelve berries, which change color as they mature, going from green to red and then to purple black. Plants have a moderate growth rate and may self-sow.

Where to Plant

Site and Light This group of plants is highly variable in its light needs. Some plants do best in full sun, while others prefer partial shade. The light needs of specific plants are covered in the chart at the end of this section. They do not tolerate air pollution well. However, they are fairly salt tolerant.

Soil and Moisture All Serviceberries do best in well-drained soils, preferably ones that are mildly acidic. The correct amount of water varies considerably by type of shrub grown and is covered in the chart at the end of this section. However, most prefer consistently moist soil.

Spacing Space according to the potential size of mature plants. Note that these plants can get quite wide, and it is a common mistake to plant them too close together. For hedgerows, place plants roughly 2 yards (1.8 meters) apart.

Landscape Use

Serviceberries make excellent specimen plants and are also ideal for naturalized settings. Tree forms are ideally suited for patios and entryways. Selections of *Amelanchier alnifolia* (Saskatoon Berry) produce an edible fruit that makes an excellent replacement for Blueberries in the far north. These shrubs are also good for hedgerows, providing protection and food for wildlife, especially birds. Serviceberries

combine well with other spring flowering trees such as *Cercis* (Redbud), *Malus* (Crabapple), and *Prunus* (Flowering Almond, Plum). Spring-blooming bulbs planted underneath these trees and shrubs create wonderful contrasting color.

Planting

Bare Root Get bare root plants into the garden as soon as the ground can be worked in spring. Remove plants from their shipping package immediately on arrival. Soak them in room temperature water for no less than 3 hours before planting. Place a small amount of superphosphate in the base of the hole and cover with 3 inches (7.5 cm) of soil. If you're an organic gardener, simply replace superphosphate with bone meal. Spread roots out over a cone of well-prepared soil. Make sure the crown is level with the surrounding soil surface. Fill the hole with soil, firm it with your fingers, and water immediately. Dissolve water-soluble fertilizer in a gallon (about 4 liters) of water following the directions on the label. Pour ½ cup (about 120 ml) of this starter solution around the base of each plant. If you prefer organic fertilizer, use fish emulsion instead.

Containerized Plants Plant Serviceberries as early in the season as possible. If the soil in the container is dry, soak it and let it drain overnight before planting. Carefully remove the plant from the container so as not to break the root ball. Plant at the same depth as in the container after preparing the hole in a similar manner as that for a bare root plant. Fill the hole with well-prepared soil, firm with your fingers, and water immediately. Pour ½ cup (about 120 ml) of starter solution around the base of the plant.

Balled and Burlapped Plant as you would a containerized plant with these added precautions: Place the plant in the hole making sure that the top of the balled and burlapped root ball is about 1 to 2 inches (2.5 to 5 cm) above the surrounding soil. Cut and remove any twine around the stems. Remove as much of the burlap and wire holding the root ball in place as possible, but avoid breaking the root ball.

Transplanting

Transplant in early spring before new growth emerges. For types that grow into trees this is only practical when they are still young.

How to Care for Serviceberries

Water Keep the soil evenly moist from spring until the soil freezes in fall. Consistent watering is especially important during the first 2 years. Always saturate the soil deeply with each watering. When the top 2 inches (5 cm) of soil dry out, water. Some Serviceberries tolerate drought better than others.

Mulch Apply a 2- to 4-inch (5- to 10-cm) layer of mulch around each plant as soon as the ground warms up in spring. Good mulches include shredded bark, pine needles, and wood chips. Mulch retains moisture in the soil and helps prevent the growth of weeds. Replenish the mulch as necessary throughout the growing season.

Fertilizing Fertilizing is optional, but if Serviceberries are being grown for fruit, it is recommended. Fertilize every spring with 10-10-10 fertilizer. Sprinkle the granules around the base of each plant before new growth emerges and water immediately to move the fertilizer into the root zone.

If you prefer organic fertilizers, use alfalfa meal (rabbit pellets), blood meal, bone meal, compost, fish emulsion, Milorganite, or rotted manures. Bone meal must be added to the soil at planting time to be effective.

Weeding Prevent the growth of most annual weeds by using mulch. Pull by hand any weeds that do appear. Weeds compete with shrubs for available moisture and nutrients and should be removed immediately.

Staking In general, staking small trees is not recommended (see page 384). However, a number of gardeners do stake tree types of *Amelanchier* × *grandiflora* (Apple Serviceberry) and *Amelanchier laevis* (Sarvis Tree). The best way to do this is by driving three stakes into the ground outside the root zone of the trees. Then run wires to each of the stakes from the tree, making sure that the wires run through a pad around the trunk of the tree. Remove these supports as soon as the trees have rooted well, generally after the first year.

Deadheading Not necessary.

Pruning Remove dead, damaged, or diseased branches at any time of year. After several years it's fine to remove weak stems or branches and open up the center of the plant somewhat with judicious pruning in late winter. If growing plants for fruit, remove a few older stems each year since younger ones tend to produce more berries. Also, if growing plants for fruit, keep the plants at a height of about 6 feet (1.8 meters) to make picking berries easier. Again, pruning to control size should be done in late winter.

Winter Protection Not needed.

Problems

Insects None serious.

Diseases Serviceberries may develop leaf spots, caused by a number of different diseases. Since these rarely affect the long-term health of the plant, there is generally no need to spray.

Marauders Birds are a major problem if these shrubs are being raised for edible fruit. The only practical way to stop birds from stripping branches bare is to cover the entire shrub with netting. Make sure that the base of the netting is firmly anchored. Get netting into place at the first sign of the fruit changing color from green to red.

Propagation

Suckers If small plantlets appear off to the side of the mother plant, dig them up in early spring before new growth emerges and plant them immediately as you would a bare root plant. All of the Serviceberries have a tendency to sucker, and this is one of the easiest ways to propagate them.

Layering Bend over and wound very pliable stems at a point where they touch the ground. Follow the detailed instructions outlined on page 405.

Softwood Cuttings In summer cut off 4 to 6 inches (10 to 15 cm) of new growth from the tips of the stems just as they begin to harden (greenwood) and just after they become quite hard (semihardwood). Plant these as outlined on pages 406–408. This method of propagating Serviceberries is difficult even for commercial growers, so don't be discouraged if you have trouble with it. Hardwood cuttings are even more difficult, if not next to impossible, with which to work.

Seed Start all but named varieties from seed. Sow seed in a starting mixture. Keep at room temperature for about 60 days. Then moist chill for at least 60 to 90 days. Bring into room temperature. Seed may take months to germinate. For additional information, see pages 409–412.

Special Uses

Berries Serviceberries produce edible fruit similar to a Blueberry. These are excellent for jams, jellies, pies, and wine. Native Americans dried the berries; mixed them with dried, pulverized meat and melted fat; and then pressed them into cakes called *pemmican*.

Sources

Blackfoot Native Plants Nursery, P.O. Box 761, Bonner, MT 59823, (406) 244-5800

Burnt Ridge Nursery, Inc., 432 Burnt Ridge Rd., Onalaska, WA 98570, (360) 985-2873

Colvos Creek Nursery, 1904 Third Ave., Suite 415, Seattle, WA 98101, (206) 749-9508

Corn Hill Nursery Ltd., 2700 Rte 890, Corn Hill, NB E4Z 1M2 Canada, (506) 756-3635

Digging Dog Nursery, 31101 Middle Ridge Rd., Albion, CA 95410, (707) 937-1130

Eastern Plant Specialties, 660 A Berrys Mill Rd., West Bath, ME 04530, (207) 504-4405

Edible Landscaping, 361 Spirit Ridge Lane, Afton, VA 22920, (800) 524-4156

Elk Mountain Nursery, P.O. Box 599, Asheville, NC 28802, (828) 683-9330

Fairweather Gardens, P.O. Box 330, Greenwich, NJ 08323, (856) 451-6261

Fedco Trees, P.O. Box 520, Waterville, ME 04903, (207) 873-7333

ForestFarm, 990 Tetherow Rd., Williams, OR 97544, (541) 846-7269

Fraser's Thimble Farms, 175 Arbutus Rd., Salt Spring Island, BC V8K 1A3 Canada, (250) 537-5788

Hortico, Inc., 723 Robson Rd., RR# 1, Waterdown, ON L0R 2H1 Canada, (905) 689-6984

Mason Hollow Nursery, 47 Scripps Lane, Mason, NH 03048, (603) 878-4347

McKay Nursery Co., P.O. Box 185, Waterloo, WI 53594, (920) 478-2121

Meadowbrook Nursery/We-Du Natives, 2055 Polly Spout Rd., Marion, NC 28752, (828) 738-8300

Missouri Wildflowers Nursery, 9814 Pleasant Hill Rd., Jefferson City, MO 65109, (573) 496-3492

Musser Forests, Inc., 1880 Route 119 Hwy N, Indiana, PA 15701, (724) 465-5685

Oikos Tree Crops, P.O. Box 19425, Kalamazoo, MI 49019, (269) 624-6233

Out Back Nursery, Inc., 15280 110th St. S, Hastings, MN 55033, (651) 438-2771

Prairie Moon Nursery, 32115 Prairie Lane, Winona, MN 55987, (507) 452-1362

Prairie Restorations, Inc., P.O. Box 327, Princeton, MN 55371, (800) 837-5986

Raintree Nursery, 391 Butts Rd., Morton, WA 98356, (360) 496-6400

RareFind Nursery, 957 Patterson Rd., Jackson, NJ 08527, (732) 833-0613

Reeseville Ridge Nursery, 512 S Main, Reeseville, WI 53579, (920) 927-3291

River Rock Nursery, 19251 SE Hwy 224, Damascus, OR 97089, (503) 658-4047

St. Lawrence Nurseries, 325 Ste Hwy 345, Potsdam, NY 13676, (315) 265-6739

The Sandy Mush Herb Nursery, 316 Surrett Cove Rd., Leicester, NC 28748, (828) 683-2014

South Meadow Fruit Gardens, P.O. Box 211, Baroda, MI 49101, (269) 422-2411

Whitman Farms, 3995 Gibson Rd. NW, Salem, OR 97304, (503) 585-8728

VARIETIES

VARIETY	FLOWER	FALL COLOR	HEIGHT/WIDTH	HARDINESS
Amelanchier alnifolia***				
(Saskatoon Berry)	White	Red orange	5'/5'	−45°F
'Obelisk'***	White	Red orange	15'/4'	−45°F
'Regent'***	White	Red orange	5'/5'	−45°F
'Smoky' ('Smokey')***	White	Red orange	5'/5'	−45°F

These low-growing, upright shrubs or small trees produce one of the main fruit crops in parts of Canada. The plants are very easy to grow. Flowers are formed in upright clusters. The foliage is bluish green on top, gray green on the bottom. The plants need full sun to produce well and do tolerate dry conditions once mature. 'Regent' and 'Smoky' will sucker and are recommended only for their large purplish black fruit, not their ornamental value. 'Obelisk' (First Editions® Standing Ovation) has an upright columnar form and can be used as a hedge.

VARIETY	FLOWER	FALL COLOR	HEIGHT/WIDTH	HARDINESS
Amelanchier arborea***				
(Downy Serviceberry)	White	Yellow orange	30'/15'	−30°F

This multistemmed small tree is commonly mixed up with *Amelanchier canadensis* in the trade, but it is not the same plant.

VARIETY	FLOWER	FALL COLOR	HEIGHT/WIDTH	HARDINESS
Amelanchier canadensis***				
(Juneberry or Serviceberry)	White	Yellow to orange	15'/10'	−30°F
'Prince William'****	White	Yellow to orange	10'/6'	−30°F
Rainbow Pillar® ('Glenn's Upright')***	White	Varied	15'/6'	−30°F

These multistemmed shrubs blossom freely with upright clusters in spring. Foliage varies from silvery green to medium green as it matures. The plants produce edible, if very seedy, dark purple fruits that are particularly attractive to birds. The fall color of Rainbow Pillar® is usually a combination of yellow, orange, and red. The shrubs are quite interesting in winter since they have silvery gray bark and a fine branching pattern. The plants need full sun to do well and will tolerate dry sites once mature.

Amelanchier canadensis

Amelanchier × grandiflora 'Autumn Brilliance'

Amelanchier laevis

Amelanchier fruits

VARIETY	FLOWER	FALL COLOR	HEIGHT/WIDTH	HARDINESS
Amelanchier × grandiflora				
(Apple Serviceberry)				
Autumn Brilliance®*****	White	Red orange	25'/20'	−30°F
'Princess Diana'****	White	Brilliant red	25'/20'	−30°F

Both of these hybrids can be grown as single- or multistemmed small trees. They are noted for producing purple fruit attractive to birds. The fruit is larger than that produced by many other members of this group. Flowers are in between upright and hanging in form. They may have a slightly pinkish tinge before fading to white. Foliage of Autumn Brilliance® is outstanding, usually orange red. All named varieties have an interesting branching growth pattern. As they mature, the bark turns a lovely, smooth, silvery gray color. Plants in this group prefer partial shade but tolerate full sun. They need moist but well-drained soil high in organic matter to thrive.

VARIETY	FLOWER	FALL COLOR	HEIGHT/WIDTH	HARDINESS
*Amelanchier laevis****				
(Sarvis Tree)	White	Variable	30'/15'	−30°F
'Cumulus'****	White	Red orange	20'/15'	−30°F
Lustre™ ('Rogers')****	White	Red orange	20'/15'	−30°F
'Snowcloud'***	White	Red orange	20'/15'	−30°F

This group contains single- or multistemmed small trees ideal for naturalizing and very good for producing purple fruit for wildlife. Place them on the edge of woods, if possible. The green to dark green foliage emerges with a distinctive red coloration that contrasts nicely with the white flowers that follow. The deep purple fruit is similar to that of *Amelanchier canadensis* (Juneberry), but considered juicier and sweeter. Fall foliage color varies from year to year. In good years, it's a red orange. These shrubs thrive in partial shade but do tolerate full sun. They need moist but well-drained soil high in organic matter to thrive.

VARIETY	FLOWER	FALL COLOR	HEIGHT/WIDTH	HARDINESS
*Amelanchier × lamarckii***				
(Lamarck Serviceberry)	White	Variable	20'/15'	−30°F

This hybrid is very similar to *Amelanchier canadensis* (Juneberry). However, the purple fruits are larger. And the plant is somewhat more vigorous in growth, which makes it an excellent selection for wildlife planting. This plant does well in full sun, tolerates partial shade, and can withstand dry spells once mature.

Aronia melanocarpa 'Autumn Magic'

ARONIA

(uh-ROWN-knee-uh)

CHOKEBERRY

Chokeberries are tough, dependable shrubs with excellent, multiseasonal interest. All of these shrubs produce white flowers in spring. The deep green foliage turns brilliant red in fall and can be breathtaking. The shrubs produce astringent red or black berries that draw in wildlife. One of the Chokeberries produces a significant fruit crop in Canada and parts of Europe. The shrubs are quite disease and insect resistant. Foliage does tend to be a bit sparse around the base of the plant. Since Chokeberries tend to sucker, they can be somewhat invasive—a plus in naturalized areas.

How Chokeberries Grow

Chokeberries have a shallow root system, slightly more coarse than fibrous. Plants produce numerous stems that are fairly thin and pliable. Foliage is dark green and finely toothed. Most leaves are about 2 inches (5 cm) long. The white flowers with contrasting black anthers are conspicuous but not as showy as shrubs such as *Spiraea* (Spirea). Different types produce fleshy berries of varying colors, with the red berries being about half the size of the black ones. The shrubs grow at a moderate rate, but do produce plantlets (suckers) to the side of the mother plant. In this way the shrub will spread out in size over a period of years. Berries contain seed and can self-sow.

Where to Plant

Site and Light Chokeberries grow best in full sun. Lots of light encourages vigorous growth and good fruiting. However, the plants tolerate partial shade. Although the stems are relatively thin, they seem to stand up to wind well, and the plant can certainly be placed in exposed sites.

Soil and Moisture Chokeberries tolerate a wide range of soil types as long as they drain freely. They are very adaptable plants, but prefer even moisture throughout the season. They will tolerate some drought once mature.

Spacing Space the plants according to the potential width of the branches. They do send out suckers and will take up much more space than you might think at initial planting.

Landscape Use

Chokeberries may attract some birds. They thrive in naturalized settings as long as they have adequate moisture. Use them for mass plantings as they spread freely. They are best placed in the back of borders since they tend to be somewhat bare at their bases. However, their rich green foliage combines well with perennials such as *Coreopsis* (Tickseed), *Leucanthemum*-Superbum Group (Shasta Daisy), and *Rudbeckia fulgida* 'Goldsturm.'

Planting

Bare Root Get bare root plants into the garden as soon as the ground can be worked in spring. Remove plants from their shipping package immediately on arrival. Soak them in room temperature water for no less than 3 hours before planting. Place a small amount of superphosphate in the base of the hole and cover with 3 inches (7.5 cm) of soil. Spread the roots

out over a cone of well-prepared soil. Make sure the crown is level with the surrounding soil surface. Fill the hole with soil, firm it with your fingers, and water immediately. Dissolve water-soluble fertilizer in a gallon (about 4 liters) of water following the directions on the label. Pour ½ cup (about 120 ml) of this starter solution around the base of each plant. If you prefer organic fertilizer, use fish emulsion instead.

Containerized Plants Plant Chokeberries as early in the season as possible. If the soil in the container is dry, soak it and let it drain overnight before planting. Carefully remove the plant from the container so as not to break the root ball. Plant at the same depth as in the container after preparing the hole in a similar manner as that for a bare root plant. Fill the hole with well-prepared soil, firm with your fingers, and water immediately. Pour ½ cup (about 120 ml) of starter solution around the base of the plant.

Balled and Burlapped Chokeberries are rarely sold in this manner.

Transplanting

Chokeberries are quite easy to transplant. Dig up the plant in early spring before it begins to bud out. Get as many roots as possible, trying to keep the soil around them in place. Plant immediately. Saturate the soil at once.

How to Care for Chokeberries

Water Keep the soil evenly moist from spring until the soil freezes in fall. Consistent watering is especially important during the first 2 years, but helpful throughout the shrub's entire life cycle. Always saturate the soil deeply with each watering. When the top 2 inches (5 cm) of soil dry out, water.

Mulch Apply a 1- to 2-inch (2.5- to 5-cm) layer of mulch around each plant as soon as the ground warms up in spring. Good mulches include shredded bark, pine needles, and wood chips. Mulch retains moisture in the soil and helps prevent the growth of weeds. Replenish the mulch as necessary throughout the growing season.

Fertilizing Fertilize every other spring with 10-10-10 fertilizer. Sprinkle the granules around the base of each plant before new growth emerges and water immediately to move the fertilizer into the root zone.

If you prefer organic fertilizers, use alfalfa meal (rabbit pellets), blood meal, bone meal, compost, fish emulsion, Milorganite, or rotted manures. Bone meal must be added to the soil at planting time to be effective.

Weeding Prevent the growth of most annual weeds by using mulch. Pull by hand any weeds that do appear. Weeds compete with shrubs for available moisture and nutrients and should be removed immediately.

Deadheading Not necessary.

Pruning Cut out any dead or diseased stem tissue immediately, cutting the stem back to a live, healthy bud or leaf. Avoid trying to control potential height through trimming, since the plants do much better if left untrimmed. Chokeberries have been recommended as a hedge in some references, but these shrubs are not particularly suited for this use since they tend to have sparse foliage around the lower portion of their stems.

Winter Protection Not needed.

Problems

Insects None serious.

Diseases None serious.

Marauders Occasionally, larger animals feeding on berries may snap branches or stems. Simply snip these off to healthy stem tissue below the break.

Propagation

Suckers If small plantlets appear off to the side of the mother plant, dig them up in early spring and plant them as you would bare root plants. This is simple to do. Plants will hardly notice being moved as long as the work is done quickly and the roots never dry out.

Layering Bend over and wound very pliable stems at a point where they touch the ground. Follow the detailed instructions outlined on page 405.

Softwood Cuttings Snip off 4 to 6 inches (10 to 15 cm) of this year's growth just as it begins to harden (greenwood) or gets quite woody (semihard). Plant these as outlined on pages 406–8. Avoid hardwood cuttings. They are extremely difficult to root.

Seed Place the radish-like seed in moist peat and cold chill for at least 90 days. Then bring out into room temperature and keep moist until germination. See pages 409–12 for further information.

Special Uses

Berries The berries can be quite interesting in wreaths and floral arrangements. Use them fresh or dried.

The black berries are used for jams and jellies in extremely cold areas where other fruiting shrubs and small trees are unlikely to survive. Birds are not much of a problem with these berries. It's unlikely these berries will need protection as required with more tasty fruits.

Sources

Arrowhead Alpines, P.O. Box 857, Fowlerville, MI 48836, (541) 223-3581
Burnt Ridge Nursery, Inc., 432 Burnt Ridge Rd., Onalaska, WA 98570, (541) 985-2873
Colvos Creek Nursery, 1904 Third Ave., Suite 415, Seattle, WA 98101, (206) 749-9508
Digging Dog Nursery, 31101 Middle Ridge Rd., Albion, CA 95410, (707) 937-1130

Elk Mountain Nursery, P.O. Box 599, Asheville, NC 28802, (828) 683-9330

Fedco Trees, P.O. Box 520, Waterville, ME 04903, (207) 873-7333

ForestFarm, 990 Tetherow Rd., Williams, OR 97544, (877) 846-7269

Fraser's Thimble Farms, 175 Arbutus Rd., Salt Spring Island, BC V8K 1A3 Canada, (250) 537-5788

Greer Gardens, 1280 Goodpasture Island Rd., Eugene, OR 97401, (541) 686-8266

Hortico, Inc., 723 Robson Rd., RR# 1, Waterdown, ON LoR 2H1 Canada, (905) 689-6984

McKay Nursery Co., P.O. Box 185, Waterloo, WI 53594, (920) 478-2121

Meadowbrook Nursery/We-Du Natives, 2055 Polly Spout Rd., Marion, NC 28752, (828) 738-8300

Musser Forests, Inc., 1880 Rte 119 Hwy N, Indiana, PA 15701, (724) 465-5685

Oikos Tree Crops, P.O. Box 19425, Kalamazoo, MI 49019, (269) 624-6233

One Green World, 28696 S Cramer Rd., Molalla, OR 97038, (877) 353-4028

Out Back Nursery, Inc., 15280 110th St. S, Hastings, MN 55033, (732) 438-2771

Plant & Gnome, P.O. Box 5344, Charleston, WV 25361, (304) 881-7037

Prairie Restorations, P.O. Box 327, Princeton, MN 55371, (503) 389-4342

Raintree Nursery, 391 Butts Rd., Morton, WA 98356, (920) 391-8892

Reeseville Ridge Nursery, 512 S Main, Reeseville, WI 53579, (920) 927-3291

Aronia melanocarpa

Aronia melanocarpa var. *elata*

St. Lawrence Nurseries, 325 Ste Hwy 345, Potsdam, NY 13676, (304) 265-6739

Shooting Star Nursery, 160 Soards Rd., Georgetown, KY 40324, (732) 867-7979

Whitman Farms, 3995 Gibson Rd. NW, Salem, OR 97304, (503) 585-8728

Woodlanders, Inc., 1128 Colleton Ave., Aiken, SC 29801, (803) 648-7522

VARIETIES

VARIETY	FLOWER COLOR	BERRY COLOR	HEIGHT/WIDTH	HARDINESS
Aronia arbutifolia				
(Red Chokeberry)				
'Brilliantissima'****	White	Red	5'/4'	−20°F

'Brilliantissima' and the species are sometimes confused by nurseries, so you may be getting either one or the other. The true 'Brilliantissima' is more free flowering and produces more and showier fruit than the species, and, therefore, is the shrub you really want. Both, however, have lovely red to purplish fall foliage. Fruit may persist into the winter. The species suckers freely.

VARIETY	FLOWER COLOR	BERRY COLOR	HEIGHT/WIDTH	HARDINESS
*Aronia melanocarpa***				
(Black Chokeberry)	White	Black	5'/4'	−40°F
'Autumn Magic'****	White	Black	5'/4'	−40°F
Iroquois Beauty™ ('Morton')****	White	Black	4'/4'	−40°F
var. *elata***	White	Black	5'/4'	−40°F
'Viking'***	White	Black	5'/4'	−40°F

The natural form of these plants is upright and mounded with Iroquois Beauty™ being more compact. 'Autumn Magic' and var. *elata* have glossier green foliage than the species. 'Autumn Magic' and Iroquois Beauty™ are noted for rich mahogany to wine red fall color. Unless eaten by wildlife, their small astringent, black berries persist through the winter. 'Viking' has larger fruit that can be used for jams and jellies. 'Nero' (not listed) is also very good for this use; common in Canada and northern Europe, but not yet in the United States.

VARIETY	FLOWER COLOR	BERRY COLOR	HEIGHT/WIDTH	HARDINESS
*Aronia × prunifolia***				
(Purple Chokeberry)	White	Purple black	5'/4'	−30°F

This is very similar to *Aronia melanocarpa* (Black Chokeberry), but certainly not superior. It, too, has lovely red fall foliage.

Berberis thunbergii 'Crimson Pygmy'

BERBERIS

(BURR-burr-us)

BARBERRY

Barberries are a varied group of shrubs. Several have showy yellow flowers. Most of the Barberries have interesting summer and fall foliage as well as brightly colored berries attractive to wildlife and the eye. Most Barberries are quite thorny, and this can either be good or bad depending upon your point of view and the purpose for which they are planted. Overall, Barberries are tough, dependable plants rarely bothered by insects and disease.

stems that are quite pliable when young but more brittle as they mature. Most of the Barberries have very thorny stems. The summer foliage is highly variable in color depending upon the named variety as indicated in the chart at the end of this section. Flowers appear in early spring and are rather inconspicuous with several notable exceptions. Berries appear in late summer and are always red. Some of the Barberries sucker readily, while others don't. Barberries may self-sow.

How Barberry Grows

Barberries have a fibrous root system that penetrates fairly deeply into the soil. Plants produce numerous

Where to Plant

Site and Light Most Barberries prefer full sun but will tolerate partial shade. Plant the golden-leaved types in partial shade for best coloration. These are tough plants requiring no protection from winds.

Soil and Moisture Barberries need well-drained soil to grow properly. They prefer consistent moisture throughout the growing season. This is especially important during the first 2 years when they are getting established. Once mature, they tolerate some drought.

Spacing Take the potential width into consideration when planting Barberries. Note that some of them do sucker. If you do not plan on removing suckers, give the plants even more space than the potential width listed in the varietal chart.

Landscape Use

Barberries are ideal shrubs for barriers and hedges. Most are so spiny that they steer traffic in whatever direction you desire. Since these shrubs produce lots of berries, they are excellent for wildlife. The berries provide excellent fall color and early winter interest. A few of the more handsome Barberries make eye-catching specimen plants with stunning summer and fall foliage. 'Crimson Pygmy' is an excellent choice in foundation plantings next to evergreens, including low-growing forms of *Juniperus* (Juniper) and globe forms of *Thuja* (Arborvitae). This Barberry is tidy, and the contrast between its foliage and that of evergreens is especially interesting.

Planting

Bare Root Get bare root plants into the garden as soon as the ground can be worked in spring. Remove plants from their shipping package immediately on arrival. Soak them in room temperature water for no less than 3 hours before planting. Place a small amount of superphosphate in the base of the hole and cover with 3 inches (7.5 cm) of soil. Spread roots out over a cone of well-prepared soil. Make sure the crown is level with the surrounding soil surface. Fill the hole with soil, firm it with your fingers, and water

immediately. Dissolve water-soluble fertilizer in a gallon (about 4 liters) of water following the directions on the label. Pour ½ cup (about 120 ml) of this starter solution around the base of each plant. If you prefer organic fertilizer, use fish emulsion instead.

Containerized Plants Plant Barberries as early in the season as possible. If the soil in the container is dry, soak it and let it drain overnight before planting. Carefully remove the plant from the container so as not to break the root ball. Plant at the same depth as in the container after preparing the hole in a similar manner as that for a bare root plant. Fill the hole with well-prepared soil, firm with your fingers, and water immediately. Pour ½ cup (about 120 ml) of starter solution around the base of the plant.

Balled and Burlapped Barberries are rarely sold this way.

Transplanting

Barberries are easy to transplant. Dig up the plants before new growth emerges in early spring, getting as much of the root system as possible. Try to keep soil around the roots. Plant the shrubs immediately as you would a bare root plant.

How to Care for Barberries

Water Keep the soil evenly moist during the active growing season. This is especially important during the first 2 years. Always saturate the soil deeply with each watering. When the top 2 inches (5 cm) of soil dry out, water. Keep watering on a regular schedule until the ground freezes late in the fall. This is especially important if there is a dry spell, quite common at this time of year.

Mulch Apply a 1- to 2-inch (2.5- to 5-cm) layer of mulch around each plant as soon as the ground warms up in spring. Good mulches include shredded bark, pine needles, and wood chips. Mulch retains moisture in the soil and helps prevent the growth of weeds.

Replenish the mulch as necessary throughout the growing season.

Fertilizing Fertilize every spring with 10-10-10 fertilizer. Sprinkle the granules around the base of each plant before new growth emerges and water immediately to move the fertilizer into the root zone. Yearly fertilizing is critical for good summer foliage color on the red and yellow leaved varieties.

If you prefer organic fertilizers, use alfalfa meal (rabbit pellets), blood meal, bone meal, compost, fish emulsion, Milorganite, or rotted manures. Bone meal must be added to the soil at planting time to be effective.

Weeding Prevent the growth of most annual weeds by using mulch. Pull by hand any weeds that do appear. Weeds compete with shrubs for available moisture and nutrients and should be removed immediately.

Deadheading Not necessary.

Pruning Barberries may suffer dieback during the winter. Let the plant leaf out in spring, then snip off any portion of stem not producing buds or leaves. Occasionally, an entire stem may die back. Cut it off at the base. Otherwise, Barberries need no pruning to remain healthy. To shape the plant, prune immediately after blooming. The plant flowers on old wood, and it is important to give it plenty of time to form new flower buds in the current growing season.

Many of the Barberries make good hedges. Let the plants grow during the first year with minimal pruning. The second year begin to prune more heavily. With regular pruning over a period of years, a superb hedge should grow. When choosing plants for a hedge, take the potential height of any given variety into consideration.

Winter Protection It is not unusual for Barberries to suffer some dieback in severe winters. While winter protection might prevent this, it's simply not practical.

Problems

Insects None serious.

Diseases Barberries are quite disease resistant. However, some of them can act as alternate hosts for black stem rust, a serious threat to wheat. Wheat-producing states often have tight regulations in regard to the sale of Barberries. One reason the Barberries listed in the chart at the end of this section have been selected is they do not act as hosts for black stem rust disease. Barberries themselves suffer few problems with disease. However, they will suffer root rot if soil does not drain freely.

Marauders Not a problem.

Propagation

Suckers Small plantlets form readily off to the sides of *Berberis koreana* (Korean Barberry). Dig these up in early spring before new growth emerges and plant immediately as you would a bare root plant.

Layering Bend over and wound very pliable stems at a point where they touch the ground. Follow the detailed instructions outlined on page 405.

Softwood Cuttings Take softwood cuttings in early summer (semihard). Cuttings should be 2 to 3 inches (5 to 7.5 cm) long for dwarf types and twice as long for taller types. All cuttings should have at least three sets of leaves. Taking cuttings from branches that include a small portion of the main stem (heel cuttings) also is highly recommended. Plant these as outlined on pages 406–408. Hardwood cuttings are difficult to root and best avoided, although they are used in commercial production of some types.

Seed Moist chill seed for a minimum of 8 weeks. Press the seed into the surface of a moist peat and perlite mixture. Seed tends to germinate best if exposed to light. Keep at 50°F to 65°F (10°C to 18°C) until germination occurs, generally within 180 days. For additional information, see pages 409–12.

Special Uses

Fall Foliage and Fruit The combination of fall foliage and fruit makes the prickly stems desirable in late-season floral arrangements. Remove all leaves that will end up underwater in the final arrangement.

Sources

Colvos Creek Nursery, 1904 Third Ave., Suite 415, Seattle, WA 98101, (542) 749-9508

Corn Hill Nursery Ltd., 2700 Rte 890, Corn Hill, NB E4Z 1M2 Canada, (542) 756-3635

Deer-resistant Landscape Nursery, 3200 Sunstone Ct., Clare, MI 48617, (800) 595-3650

ForestFarm, 990 Tetherow Rd., Williams, OR 97544, (878) 846-7269

Gossler Farms Nursery, 1200 Weaver Rd., Springfield, OR 97478, (541) 746-3922

Greer Gardens, 1280 Goodpasture Island Rd., Eugene, OR 97401, (541) 686-8266

Hortico, Inc., 723 Robson Rd., RR# 1, Waterdown, ON L0R 2H1 Canada, (829) 689-6984

Klehm's Song Sparrow Perennial Farms, 13101 E Rye Rd., Avalon, WI 53505, (800) 553-3715

McKay Nursery Co., P.O. Box 185, Waterloo, WI 53594, (270) 478-2121

Variegated Foliage Nursery, 245 Westford Rd., Eastford, CT 06242 , (733) 974-3951

Wavecrest Nursery, 2509 Lakeshore Dr., Fennville, MI 49408, (269) 543-4175

Well-Sweep Herb Farm, 205 Mount Bethel Rd., Port Murray, NJ 07865, (908) 852-5390

VARIETIES

VARIETY	SUMMER FOLIAGE	FALL FOLIAGE	HEIGHT/WIDTH	HARDINESS
Berberis koreana***				
(Korean Barberry)	Medium green	Red purple	5'/5'	−40°F

This extremely hardy Barberry has unusual and striking golden yellow flowers in spring and attractive light to medium green foliage in summer that turns purple red in the fall. It produces an abundance of red fruits in fall that often persist into winter. While often recommended as a hedge, this Barberry tends to sucker. For this reason you may not want it for this purpose unless there is enough space for the plants to ramble.

Berberis koreana × *thunbergii*				
(Hybrid Barberries)				
Emerald Carousel® ('Tara')****	Glossy green	Red	5'/5'	−30°F
Golden Carousel® ('Bailsel')**	Golden yellow	Golden red	4'/4'	−30°F

Emerald Carousel® is probably the showiest Barberry in flower. Summer foliage is glossy green. The combination of lovely fall foliage and fruit is equally exceptional. Golden Carousel® is particularly attractive for its golden yellow summer foliage, but the plant must be placed in the right spot. Afternoon sun tends to burn the foliage while too much shade turns it pale green. These plants rarely sucker.

Berberis 'Tara' (Emerald Carousel®)

Berberis 'Tara' (Emerald Carousel®)

Berberis thunbergii var. *atropurpurea*

Berberis thunbergii Golden Nugget® ('Monlers')

VARIETY	SUMMER FOLIAGE	FALL FOLIAGE	HEIGHT/WIDTH	HARDINESS
Berberis thunbergii (Japanese Barberry)***				
'Admiration'****	Dark red/yellow edge	Red	1½'/2'	−25°F
'Aurea'**	Yellow green to green	Yellow/red	3'/4'	−25°F
var. *atropurpurea***	Reddish purple	Reddish purple	4'/4'	−25°F
'Bagatelle'****	Red purple	Reddish purple	1½'/1½'	−25°F
Bonanza Gold® ('Bogozam')***	Yellow to gold	Yellow	1½'/2'	−25°F
Burgundy Carousel® ('Bailtwo')***	Reddish purple	Purple	3'/4'	−25°F
'Concorde'****	Reddish purple	Reddish purple	1½'/2'	−25°F
'Crimson Pygmy' ('Atropurpurea Nana')*****	Reddish purple	Reddish purple	1½'/2'	−25°F
First Editions®Cabernet® ('Moretti')*****	Red to purple red	Orange scarlet	2'/2'	−25°F
Golden Nugget® ('Monlers')***	Yellow to gold	Greenish	1½'/2'	−25°F
'Golden Rocket'***	Gold yellow	Orange red	4'/2'	−25°F
Golden Ruby™***	Red edged gold	Orange red	1½'/2'	−25°F
'Harlequin'**	Red pink white green	Reddish purple	3'/4'	−25°F
'Helmond Pillar'****	Reddish purple	Purple to red	6'/2'	−25°F
Jade Carousel® ('Bailgreen')***	Bright green	Reddish purple	3'/4'	−25°F
'Kobold'****	Glossy dark green	Greenish	1½'/2'	−25°F
'Orange Rocket'***	Orange red	Ruby red orange	4'/2'	−25°F
'Rose Glow' ('Rosy Glow')****	Mottled pink purple	Reddish purple	4'/4'	−25°F
'Rosy Rocket'***	Mottled pink purple	Red	4'/1½'	−25°F
Royal Burgundy® ('Gentry')****	Deep red purple	Reddish purple	1½'/2'	−25°F
Ruby Carousel® ('Bailone')***	Reddish purple	Reddish purple	4'/4'	−25°F
Sunsation® ('Monry')***	Yellow to gold	Gold	3'/4'	−25°F
Sunjoy™Gold Pillar™ ('Maria')***	Yellow to gold	Orange red yellow	4'/4'	−25°F

This is a group of very adaptable shrubs noted for sharp thorns. Plants have very nice form, varying from upright to arching or rounded. Foliage tends to be finely textured and dense. Plants do flower, but this is not an outstanding characteristic. Flowers are generally whitish to yellowish green and inconspicuous. However, foliage coloration is wonderful, especially if plants are grown in full sun. 'Rose Glow' stands out for its reddish purple foliage mottled with streaks of rose pink. Barberries may produce limited bright red fruit that may persist throughout the winter and can be invasive, especially Golden Ruby® and 'Helmond Pillar.' The plants in this group are excellent for hedges, mass plantings, specimen plants, and barriers because they do not sucker.

Buxus microphylla var. *koreana* 'Wintergreen'

BUXUS

(BUCK-suhs)

BOXWOOD

oxwood is an evergreen shrub that many cold-climate gardeners would like to grow. Those that have the best chance to survive and seem to grow quite well are included in the chart at the end of this section. While the recommended plants do emit a distinctive fragrance on still, warm days, they do not have the intense scent of more tender Boxwoods grown in warmer climates. They also tend to burn in severe winters, meaning that the outer leaves and stem tips dry out in blustery winter winds and under intense winter sun. They do best if winter protected. Yet, these Boxwoods are neat, tidy, and lovely plants if grown properly. The varieties chosen here are rarely bothered by disease or insects.

How Boxwood Grows

Boxwoods have a fibrous root system that is very close to the soil surface. They produce numerous stems with small, glossy light to deep green leaves. The plants appear twiggy. The flowers, both male and female, are barely noticeable. The fruits are tiny ¼-inch (.635-cm) horned capsules that split open early in the season. Although these capsules do produce seed, plants do not self-sow.

Where to Plant

Site and Light In cold climates Boxwoods thrive in full sun, but tolerate partial shade. Winter winds and winter sun can damage these sensitive plants by drying out foliage; therefore, plant them in a sheltered location. Plant them on the north or east side of your home to reduce the risk of winter burn. Keep them away from areas that could be salted during the winter as well.

Soil and Moisture Boxwoods do best in very loose soil that drains freely. Avoid planting them in acidic soils since they prefer neutral to slightly alkaline conditions. Consistent moisture throughout the season is highly recommended.

Spacing Space according to the potential height and width of the plants. Proper spacing for hedges is covered in the section on pruning.

Landscape Use

Boxwoods make good formal hedges. They can also be used for small, rounded specimen plants and are quite effective in Japanese or Oriental-type gardens. They can even grow in containers, although this is not recommended. While they are commonly shaped into whimsical forms (topiary) in warmer areas, this is less common in colder climates. They do, however, blend nicely into mixed shrub and perennial borders, providing an interesting color and textural contrast.

Planting

Bare Root Boxwoods are not commonly sold this way.

Containerized Plants Plant Boxwoods as early in the season as possible. If the soil in the container is dry, soak it and let it drain overnight before planting. Carefully remove the plant from the container so as not to break the root ball. Place a small amount of superphosphate in the base of the planting hole.

Cover it with 3 inches (7.5 cm) of soil. Plant the root ball at the same depth as in the container. Fill the hole with well-prepared soil, firm with your fingers, and water immediately. Dissolve water-soluble fertilizer in a gallon (about 4 liters) of water following the directions on the label. Pour ½ cup (about 120 ml) of this starter solution around the base of each plant. If you prefer organic fertilizer, use fish emulsion instead.

Balled and Burlapped Plant as you would a containerized plant with these added precautions: Place the plant in the hole making sure that the top of the balled and burlapped root ball is about 1 to 2 inches (2.5 to 5 cm) above the surrounding soil. Cut and remove any twine around the stems. Remove as much of the burlap and wire holding the root ball in place as possible, but avoid breaking the root ball.

Clay Pots Boxwoods planted in clay pots are popular with garden designers. Use a 12-inch (30-cm) or larger clay pot with drain holes in the bottom. Use a professional potting mix when planting Boxwoods in pots. The soil in pots tends to dry out quickly, so pay special attention to keeping it moist throughout the growing season.

Transplanting

Boxwoods transplant well. Dig up individual plants in early spring before any new growth emerges. Keep as much soil around the roots as possible. Plant immediately as you would a balled and burlapped plant.

How to Care for Boxwoods

Water Keep the soil evenly moist during the active growing season. This is important for the plant's entire life cycle. Always saturate the soil deeply with each watering. When the top 2 inches (5 cm) of soil dry out, water. Keep watering on a regular schedule until the ground freezes late in the fall. This is especially important if there is a dry spell, quite common at this time of year. Saturate the soil thoroughly just before the first expected freeze. This step is highly recommended for all evergreens whose leaves dry out in winter.

Mulch Apply a 1- to 2-inch (2.5- to 5-cm) layer of mulch around each plant as soon as the ground warms up in spring. Good mulches include shredded bark, pine needles, and wood chips. Mulch retains moisture in the soil and helps prevent the growth of weeds. Boxwoods react especially well to mulch because it keeps roots moist and cool. Replenish the mulch as necessary throughout the growing season.

Fertilizing Fertilize every spring with 10-10-10 fertilizer. Sprinkle the granules around the base of each plant before new growth emerges and water immediately to move the fertilizer into the root zone.

If you prefer organic fertilizers, use alfalfa meal (rabbit pellets), blood meal, bone meal, compost, fish emulsion, Milorganite, or rotted manures. Bone meal must be added to the soil at planting time to be effective.

Weeding Prevent the growth of most annual weeds by using mulch. Pull by hand any weeds that do appear. Weeds compete with shrubs for available moisture and nutrients and should be removed immediately. Never hoe around these plants since this often results in damage to the plant's shallow root system.

Deadheading Not necessary.

Pruning Some dieback of the tips of stems is common in severe winters. It is easy to tell which portion of the stem has died as it is usually discolored, brittle, or wrinkled. Live stem tissue will begin to show signs of new growth early in the season. Prune out any dead stem tissue with pruning shears. Cut back to a live bud. At the same time, pick out any dead leaves from inside the branches and stems to clean up all debris.

The Boxwoods recommended here make excellent hedges. Space young plants about 12 inches (30 cm) apart. Prune little, if at all, during the first year. Once plants are growing well in the second year, begin to shear off a small portion of new growth in early spring. This will encourage additional branching from the base of the plant. Keep the hedge trimmed to a height of about 30 inches (75 cm) or less for best results. Trimming should not be severe.

Winter Protection There is no practical or aesthetically pleasing way to protect a large number of these sensitive plants other than to plant them in a sheltered location from the start. Do not expose them to winter winds and sun. If you have only a plant or two, then you can certainly help them survive by watering them well until the first freeze. Pound stakes into the ground around the plant. Once the ground freezes, attach burlap to the stakes as a shield around the plant and fill in the space with whole leaves.

Plants grown in containers need special attention. At the end of the season, just before the first expected hard freeze, dig a hole wide and deep enough to hold the root ball of the plant. Dig the hole in a spot well protected from winter sun and winds. Remove the plant from the container. The easiest way is to place the pot on its side and pull the shrub gently out. Place the root ball in a perforated plastic bag. Soak the root ball. Immediately place it in the hole. Mound soil around the base of the plant, but do not cover any foliage. Keep the soil evenly moist until it freezes. Surround the plant with burlap after the first freeze to protect the evergreen foliage from winter burn. Remove the plant from the hole and repot as soon as it warms up in spring. See page 371 for additional information.

Problems

Insects None serious.

Diseases None serious.

Marauders Normally not a problem.

Propagation

Suckers These shrubs do not sucker.

Division Possible, but rarely done.

Softwood Cuttings In midsummer, cut off 2 to 3 inches (5 to 7.5 cm) on the present year's growth (semihard with heel). Plant as outlined on pages 406–8. Hardwood cuttings are extremely difficult to root and not recommended, although they are used in commercial production.

Seed Not recommended. The seeds of the named varieties chosen here will not produce plants identical to their parents. Furthermore, seeds may take up to 2 years to germinate.

Special Uses

None.

Sources

Bluestone Perennials, 7211 Middle Ridge Rd., Madison, OH 44057, (800) 852-5243

Colvos Creek Nursery, 1904 Third Ave., Suite 415, Seattle, WA 98101, (206) 749-9508

Durio Nursery, 5853 Hwy 182, Opelousas, LA 70570, (337) 948-3696

ForestFarm, 990 Tetherow Rd., Williams, OR 97544, (541) 846-7269

Girard Nurseries, P.O. Box 428, Geneva, OH 44041, (543) 466-2881

Greer Gardens, 1280 Goodpasture Island Rd., Eugene, OR 97401, (541) 686-8266

Hortico, Inc., 723 Robson Rd., RR# 1, Waterdown, ON LoR 2H1 Canada, (905) 689-6984

Buxus microphylla var. *koreana* 'Wintergreen'

Buxus microphylla var. *koreana* 'Wintergreen'

McKay Nursery Co., P.O. Box 185, Waterloo, WI 53594, (543) 478-2121

Musser Forests, Inc., 1880 Rte 119 Hwy N, Indiana, PA 15701, (879) 465-5685

Plant & Gnome, P.O. Box 5344, Charleston, WV 25361, (830) 881-7037

RareFind Nursery, 957 Patterson Rd., Jackson, NJ 08527, (271) 833-0613

Reeseville Ridge Nursery, 512 S Main, Reeseville, WI 53579, (920) 927-3291

The Sandy Mush Herb Nursery, 316 Surrett Cove Rd., Leicester, NC 28748, (734) 683-2014

Shrub Source, 248 N Colonial St., Zeeland, MI 49464, (800) 530-2969

Venero Gardens, 5985 Seamans Dr., Shorewood, MN 55331, (952) 474-8550

VARIETIES

VARIETY	FOLIAGE COLOR	HEIGHT/WIDTH	HARDINESS
Buxus microphylla var. *koreana*			
(Korean or Littleleaf Boxwood)			
'Winter Gem' (possibly same as 'Wintergreen')			
'Wintergreen'***	Light green	2'/3'	−30°F

This broadleaved evergreen has a compact and rounded form and, technically, falls under the name *Buxus sinica* var. *insularis*. Its small, rounded leaves are very appealing in summer and tend to turn coppery to bronze in fall and remain that color throughout the winter. Expect stem tip dieback in severe winters.

VARIETY	FOLIAGE COLOR	HEIGHT/WIDTH	HARDINESS
Buxus sempervirens			
(Common Box)			
Northstar™ ('Katerberg')***	Dark green	3'/3'	−20°F
'Vardar Valley'***	Dark green	3'/3'	−20°F

Most plants in this group are not hardy in cold climates. Northstar™ forms a lovely mound of shiny dark green foliage and can be found in some garden centers in cold-climate areas. It and 'Vardar Valley' are marginally hardy but worth a gamble on the southern edge of the cold-climate region.

VARIETY	FOLIAGE COLOR	HEIGHT/WIDTH	HARDINESS
Buxus (Hybrids)			
'Chicagoland Green' ('Glencoe')****	Dark green	3'/3'	−25°F
'Green Gem'***	Dark green	1½'/1½'	−25°F
'Green Mound'****	Dark green	3'/3'	−25°F
'Green Mountain'****	Dark green	5'/3'	−25°F
'Green Velvet'****	Dark green	3'/3'	−25°F
Northern Charm™ ('Wilson')***	Emerald green	4'/5'	−25°F
'Saskatoon'****	Medium green	2'/2'	−25°F

'Chicagoland Green' is quite similar to 'Green Velvet,' but tends to grow more rapidly and often has better winter coloration. 'Green Gem' has glossy dark green foliage requiring little pruning. 'Green Mound' gets its name from its overall shape. 'Green Mountain' has a more upright, rather oval form. Its foliage tends to be a bronzy green in winter. 'Green Velvet' is an excellent choice for colder climates. Though still rounded, its form is more upright than 'Wintergreen.' Its leaves are also larger. Foliage tends to hold its color throughout the winter with a slightly darkish cast. The height of Northern Charm™ makes it ideal for formal hedges. 'Saskatoon' grows slowly, but it has tight growth and makes an excellent low hedge. It may be slightly hardier than the others. Expect dieback in severe winters.

Caragana frutex

CARAGANA

(care-uh-GAIN-uh)

PEASHRUB

Peashrubs are hardy plants that can withstand tough conditions—drought, wind, cold, varying soils. The flowers on some are fairly ornamental. The forms of the plants vary greatly, but some stand out for fine-textured foliage. In general, this group of shrubs is informal rather than refined. All Peashrubs are disease resistant but commonly plagued by insects. Foliage can become quite unattractive early in the season.

How Peashrubs Grow

The root system of Peashrubs falls somewhere between fibrous and coarse. Plants are multistemmed with forms varying from upright to weeping. The stems range in thickness and appearance by variety. Peashrubs will form a large clump in time, but only *Caragana frutex* (Russian Peashrub) suckers mildly. The shrubs bloom in spring with pea-like yellow blossoms, varying in richness of color and overall size. The foliage is generally comprised of smaller leaflets. The shrubs form 1½- to 2-inch (3- to 5-cm) green pods that turn deep brown late in the season. Inside are three to five radish-like seeds. The plant rarely self-sows.

Where to Plant

Site and Light Peashrubs demand full sun and do very poorly in shade. They can withstand any amount of wind and are one of the toughest plants.

Soil and Moisture Peashrubs do best in slightly alkaline to neutral soils. They do not tolerate acidic soils well nor do they need soil high in organic matter. Peashrubs are ideally suited to dryland sites, although they tolerate moist soils well. Since Peashrubs fix nitrogen in the soil, they thrive in soils low in nutrients.

Spacing Space plants according to their potential size. Small types used for hedges should be planted 18 to 24 inches (45 to 60 cm) apart.

Landscape Use

Peashrubs make ideal windbreaks and can also be clipped lightly to form informal hedges. They are excellent barriers as well, blocking out traffic, noise, dust, and snow. A few of the Peashrubs are suitable for use as specimen plants or mixed into the perennial border. Combine these durable plants with equally tough shrubs and perennials. Highly recommended are combinations with *Potentilla* (Shrub Cinquefoil) and *Rosa rugosa* (Rugosa Shrub Roses). Tough perennials that can withstand the same abuse as Peashrubs include *Echinacea* (Purple Coneflower) and *Rudbeckia* (Coneflower).

Planting

Bare Root Get bare root plants into the garden as soon as the ground can be worked in spring. Remove plants from their shipping package immediately on arrival. Soak them in room temperature water for no less than 3 hours before planting. Place a small amount of superphosphate in the base of the hole and cover with 3 inches (7.5 cm) of soil. Spread roots out over a cone of well-prepared soil. Make sure the crown is level with the surrounding soil surface. Fill the hole with soil, firm it with your fingers, and water immediately. Dissolve water-soluble fertilizer in a gallon (about 4 liters) of water following the directions on the label. Pour ½ cup (about 120 ml) of this starter solution around the base of each plant. If you prefer organic fertilizer, use fish emulsion instead.

Containerized Plants Plant Peashrubs as early in the season as possible. If the soil in the container is dry, soak it and let it drain overnight before planting. Carefully remove the plant from the container so as not to break the root ball. Plant at the same depth as in the container after preparing the hole in a similar manner as that for a bare root plant. Fill the hole with well-prepared soil, firm with your fingers, and water immediately. Pour ½ cup (about 120 ml) of starter solution around the base of the plant.

Balled and Burlapped Peashrubs are rarely sold this way.

Transplanting

Dig up plants in early spring before any new growth emerges. Plant them immediately as you would a bare root plant. Peashrubs transplant well, but if they are large, this is backbreaking work.

How to Care for Peashrubs

Water During the first month after planting, water the plant well at least once a week. After that let nature take its course unless there is a severe drought in the first season. Always saturate the soil deeply with each watering. In hot, dry periods spray the foliage off forcefully with water to discourage the formation of spider mite colonies.

Mulch Apply a 2- to 4-inch (5- to 10-cm) layer of mulch around each plant as soon as the ground warms up in spring. Good mulches include shredded bark, pine needles, and wood chips. Mulch retains moisture in the soil and helps prevent the growth of weeds. Replenish the mulch as necessary throughout the growing season.

Fertilizing Peashrubs are adapted to poor soils and fix nitrogen in the soil. They require no fertilization at all.

Weeding Prevent the growth of most annual weeds by using mulch. Pull by hand any weeds that do appear.

Weeds compete with shrubs for available moisture and nutrients and should be removed immediately.

Deadheading Not necessary.

Pruning Always remove damaged, dead, or diseased stems at any time of year. Most Peashrubs make good informal hedges, screens, and windbreaks. Prune only to control size and shape. Very little pruning is generally required. If a screen or windbreak from the larger Peashrubs is desired, simply let the plants mature to the desired height and trim back to keep them from getting any taller.

Winter Protection Not needed.

Problems

Disease Foliage may have spots on it in late summer. Defoliation may occur, especially in humid areas. In such extreme cases use an appropriate fungicide. If spotting is merely cosmetic, do not spray.

Insects Leafhoppers are a problem on Peashrubs. These insects cause foliage to turn yellow and appear stunted. While this is not aesthetically pleasing, the problem is not serious enough to warrant spraying. Leafhoppers are very unlikely to cause the death of these superhardy shrubs.

Spider mites do show up during hot, dry periods. They too cause leaves to turn yellow. Spray foliage forcefully with water, concentrating on the undersides of leaves. If forceful spraying several days in a row does not stop the mites from colonizing, spray with a miticide.

Marauders None serious.

Propagation

Suckers Only *Caragana frutex* (Russian Peashrub) produces small plantlets off to the side of the mother plant. In early spring before new growth emerges, dig these up and plant them immediately as you would bare root plants.

Softwood Cuttings Two to 4 weeks after bloom cut off 4 to 6 inches (10 to 15 cm) from the tips of stems (greenwood). Plant these as outlined on pages 406–8. Do not bother with hardwood cuttings.

Seed Place seed in water just hot enough for you to keep your hand in it. Let the seed soak as the hot water cools down over a period of no less than 24 hours. Plant any seed that begins to swell. Change water daily if necessary. Plant seed in spring by pressing it into a moist mixture of peat and perlite without any moist chilling period. Seed germinates best if exposed to light at temperature of approximately 70°F (21°C). Seed generally germinates within 3 weeks. Follow the instructions as outlined on pages 409–12.

Special Uses

The seeds with their pods can be ground into feed for poultry. They are extremely high in protein.

Caragana arborescens 'Walker'

Sources

Bergeson Nursery, 4177 Cty Hwy 1, Fertile, MN 56540, (218) 945-6988

ForestFarm, 990 Tetherow Rd., Williams, OR 97544, (541) 846-7269

Hortico, Inc., 723 Robson Rd., RR# 1, Waterdown, ON L0R 2H1 Canada, (544) 689-6984

McKay Nursery Co., P.O. Box 185, Waterloo, WI 53594, (544) 478-2121

St. Lawrence Nurseries, 325 Ste Hwy 345, Potsdam, NY 13676, (315) 265-6739

Whitman Farms, 3995 Gibson Rd. NW, Salem, OR 97304, (503) 585-8728

VARIETIES

VARIETY	COLOR	HEIGHT	HARDINESS
*Caragana arborescens***			
(Siberian Peashrub)	Deep yellow	20'/12'	−50°F
'Lorbergii'***	Light yellow	5'/3'	−50°F
'Pendula'***	Deep yellow	4'/3'	−50°F
'Sutherland'**	Deep yellow	10'/10'	−50°F
'Walker'****	Light yellow	4'/3'	−50°F

The species is an excellent choice in windy areas as a hedge, screen, or windbreak. The multistemmed shrub with shiny bark looks like an upright vase. Its foliage is dark green and nearly eliptical in shape. A popular specimen tree is made by grafting the weeping named variety 'Pendula' onto the rootstock of *Caragana arborescens*. It has foliage similar to that of the species. 'Sutherland' is an upright form, also with foliage similar to the species. 'Walker,' another weeping form, is also grafted onto rootstock of the species. If not grafted, it simply spreads out along the ground. It is prized for its fine-textured, ferny, light green foliage. 'Walker' makes an excellent accent or specimen tree.

*Caragana frutex***			
(Russian Peashrub)	Gold yellow	8'/6'	−50°F
'Globosa'***	Not applicable	3'/3'	−50°F

The species is an upright shrub. 'Globosa' rarely flowers, but makes a nice hedge. The deep bluish green foliage usually remains attractive throughout the entire growing season because this plant is quite resistant to leafhoppers.

*Caragana pygmaea***			
(Pygmy Peashrub)	Light yellow	2½'/4'	−50°F

This is a low, mounded plant with finely textured, silvery green foliage and yellowish bark. It is very nice at the front of a shrub border and rarely has problems with leafhoppers.

*Caragana rosea***			
(Red Flower Pea Shrub)	Yellow red	3'/3'	−40°F

This low, mounded plant is noted primarily for the red to purplish tints in its flowers. It is very drought tolerant once mature.

Cercis canadensis

CERCIS

(SIR-suhs)

REDBUD

Redbuds, among our finest native plants, are noted for their beautiful and long-lasting spring bloom. The purplish pink or white color of the tiny flowers is rich and eye-catching against bare branches. The trees are noted for their architectural form with branches having a lovely layered feel. The large heart-shaped leaves are attractive all summer long and may develop a pleasing yellow color in the fall. Some gardeners also find the seed pods attractive late in the season. These pods persist through the winter. Redbuds are relatively insect resistant but prone to damage from disease. They also require a sheltered location in colder climates to reach their full potential.

How Redbuds Grow

Redbuds have a fairly shallow, coarse root system. Typically, the tree is multistemmed, but singlestemmed trees are sold. Individual stems get quite large with a smooth and dark gray bark. The bark on older trees peels away from the stem and often has an orangish coloration. In early spring branches are covered with striking purplish pink buds that open into tiny, pea-like flowers before leaves appear. Once mature, the heart-shaped leaves are large and deep green, although they may go through a series of color changes from early spring to midsummer depending upon the variety. The flattened seed pods are roughly 3 inches (7.5 cm) long and brownish to brownish black once dry. Inside are small, tan seeds. However, Redbuds rarely self-seed, although most varieties are best grown from seed. The source of seed is extremely important because it affects the mature plant's ability to tolerate cold. Commercial growers must be extremely careful in buying seed from the right source. 'Alba' can be grown from seed, but may also be grafted onto rootstock of *Cercis canadensis* (Eastern Redbud).

Where to Plant

Site and Light Redbuds prefer partial shade, but tolerate full sun and even full shade.

Soil and Moisture Redbuds grow best in well-drained soils high in organic matter. The pH of the soil is not a major concern. They do like consistent moisture throughout the growing season as long as conditions are not wet or boggy. Boggy soils can lead to problems with disease.

Spacing Redbuds can become quite large, so give them plenty of space at initial planting. This is one plant that you do not want to transplant later.

Landscape Use

Redbuds make wonderful specimen plants. They also blend beautifully into naturalized settings. One of the finest combinations is a Redbud in front of large conifers. The color contrast of purplish pink against a dark green to blue green background is unbeatable. Redbuds can also be placed in the back of a shrub border. Combine these exquisite trees wth other spring flowering shrubs and small trees, including *Amelanchier* (Serviceberry), *Chionanthus* (Fringe Tree), *Cornus* (Dogwood), *Malus* (Crabapple), and *Rhododendron* (Azalea).

Planting

Bare Root Preferably, Redbuds should not be purchased this way, but if they are, follow any planting instructions provided to the letter. Because the trees are slow to leaf out, home gardeners tend to overwater the plants in hopes of stimulating growth. This damages the plants. While they can be grown this way, you should buy containerized plants instead.

Containerized Plants Plant Redbuds as early in the season as possible. If the soil in the container is dry, soak it and let it drain overnight before planting. Carefully remove the plant from the container so as not to break the root ball. Plant at the same depth as in the container. Fill the hole with well-prepared soil, firm with your fingers, and water immediately. Dissolve water-soluble fertilizer in a gallon (about 4 liters) of water following the directions on the label. Pour ½ cup (about 120 ml) of this starter solution around the base of each plant. If you prefer organic fertilizer, use fish emulsion instead.

Balled and Burlapped Plant as you would a containerized plant with these added precautions: Place the plant in the hole making sure that the top of the balled and burlapped root ball is about 1 to 2 inches (2.5 to 5 cm) above the surrounding soil. Cut and remove any twine around the stems. Remove as much of the burlap and wire holding the root ball in place as possible, but avoid breaking the root ball. **Note:** Redbuds resent being dug from fields as they get larger. They grow poorly and often die if transplanted when too mature. For this reason, buy smaller shrubs or trees only. Since the trees have a moderate growth rate, you'll have a nice specimen in a few years.

Transplanting

Redbuds can be transplanted relatively easily when they are young. However, as they get larger it's not practical or advised. It is wiser to buy a new plant. If you do transplant the shrub, do it in very early spring before new growth emerges. Keep as much soil around the root ball as possible. Replant immediately as you would a balled and burlapped plant.

How to Care for Redbuds

Water Keep the soil evenly moist from spring until the soil freezes in fall. Consistent watering is critical during the first 2 years and extremely helpful throughout the plant's entire life cycle. Always saturate the soil deeply with each watering. When the top 2 inches (5 cm) of soil dry out, water.

Mulch Apply a 2- to 4-inch (5- to 10-cm) layer of mulch around each plant as soon as the ground warms up in spring. Good mulches include shredded bark, pine needles, and wood chips. Mulch retains moisture in the soil and helps prevent the growth of weeds. Replenish the mulch as necessary throughout the growing season.

Fertilizing Fertilize every other spring with 10-10-10 fertilizer. Sprinkle the granules around the base of each plant before new growth emerges and water immediately to move the fertilizer into the root zone.

If you prefer organic fertilizers, use alfalfa meal (rabbit pellets), blood meal, bone meal, compost, fish emulsion, Milorganite, or rotted manures. Bone meal must be added to the soil at planting time to be effective.

Weeding Prevent the growth of most annual weeds by using mulch. Pull by hand any weeds that do appear. Weeds compete with shrubs for available moisture and nutrients and should be removed immediately.

Deadheading Not necessary.

Pruning Remove any dead or diseased stems or branches immediately at any time of year. Do not try to create a multistemmed tree through pruning. If you want a tree with several stems, buy one that has the number of stems you want. If you want a tree with a single trunk, buy a plant with only one stem.

Winter Protection There is no practical form of winter protection other than to plant Redbuds in sheltered locations where they will not be battered by winter winds.

Problems

Insects Although Redbuds have been known to be attacked by borers, this is rare in cold areas.

Diseases Cankers, caused by either bacterial or fungal infections, are a threat to Redbuds. If cankers kill older stems, the plant tends to send out new growth from its base. Remove the dead stem or trunk and let nature take its course. Researchers are presently trying to develop plants resistant to this problem.

The following practices may help prevent cankers from developing in the first place: (1) Buy plants grown from seed produced in a northern area. (2) Take good care of Redbuds, following all of the recommendations in this section to reduce stress. Trees growing poorly are far more susceptible to infection. (3) Never injure the tree with lawn mowers or weed whips. (4) Accept the reality that Redbuds are fairly short-lived. They normally begin to decline between the ages of 20 and 30 years. If they begin to die back at this stage, cut them back to ground level just after they flower in early spring. They often resprout, creating a new and vigorous plant.

Marauders None.

Propagation

Suckers These trees do not sucker.

Cuttings Possible but not recommended.

Seed This form of growing Redbuds is highly recommended for cold-climate gardeners. Seed collected in the north has a much better chance of producing shrubs or small trees that will survive. While it may take years to get a sizeable tree, the process is enjoyable and the rewards well worth the effort. Grow the species, 'Alba,' and the strains from seed. The seed from 'Alba' will only come true if the tree is isolated. If 'Alba' is grown near other Redbuds, then its seed will produce shrubs or trees with pink blossoms.

Gather the bean-like pods before they become completely dry in fall. Early gathering reduces the chance that the pods will have already been damaged by insects. Remove the smooth brown to black seeds and sow them immediately outdoors in a moist medium following the instructions on pages 409–10. To grow the seed indoors, break (scarify) the seed coat in a blender, barely cover the seed in a mixture of moist peat and perlite for 90 days at room temperature, then moist chill it in the refrigerator for another 90 days. Finally, bring the seed back out into room temperature. Seed should germinate within 90 days. Note that you can also break down the seed coat by pouring boiling water over the seeds and letting them cool down overnight before placing them in the starting mix. See pages 410–12 for further instructions.

Special Uses

None.

Sources

Arrowhead Alpines, P.O. Box 857, Fowlerville, MI 48836, (517) 223-3581

Durio Nursery, 5853 Hwy 182, Opelousas, LA 70570, (545) 948-3696

Eastern Plant Specialties, 660 A Berrys Mill Rd., West Bath, ME 04530, (207) 504-4405

Fairweather Gardens, P.O. Box 330, Greenwich, NJ 08323, (856) 451-6261

Fedco Trees, P.O. Box 520, Waterville, ME 04903, (207) 873-7333

ForestFarm, 990 Tetherow Rd., Williams, OR 97544, (541) 846-7269

Greer Gardens, 1280 Goodpasture Island Rd., Eugene, OR 97401, (541) 686-8266

Heronswood Nursery, 300 Park Ave., Warminster, PA 18974, (877) 674-4714

Hortico, Inc., 723 Robson Rd., RR# 1, Waterdown, ON L0R 2H1 Canada, (545) 689-6984

Klehm's Song Sparrow Perennial Farm, 13101 E Rye Rd., Avalon, WI 53505, (800) 553-3715

Mason Hollow Nursery, 47 Scripps Lane, Mason, NH 03048, (603) 878-4347

McKay Nursery Co., P.O. Box 185, Waterloo, WI 53594, (920) 478-2121

Meadowbrook Nursery/We-Du Natives, 2055 Polly Spout Rd., Marion, NC 28752, (880) 738-8300

Musser Forests, Inc., 1880 Rte 119 Hwy N, Indiana, PA 15701, (831) 465-5685

RareFind Nursery, 957 Patterson Rd., Jackson, NJ 08527, (272) 833-0613

Reeseville Ridge Nursery, 512 S Main, Reeseville, WI 53579, (735) 927-3291

River Rock Nursery, 19251 SE Hwy 224, Damascus, OR 97089, (503) 658-4047

Shooting Star Nursery, 160 Soards Rd., Georgetown, KY 40324, (504) 867-7979

Tripple Brook Farm, 37 Middle Rd., Southampton, MA 01073, (413) 527-4626

Wavecrest Nursery, 2509 Lakeshore Dr., Fennville, MI 49408, (888) 869-4159

Cercis canadensis

Cercis canadensis Minnesota Strain

VARIETIES

VARIETY	FLOWER COLOR	HEIGHT/WIDTH	HARDINESS
Cercis canadensis****			
(Eastern Redbud)	Rosy pink	20'/25'	−30°F
'Alba' (var. *alba*)***	White	20'/25'	−25°F
Columbus Wisconsin Strain****	Rosy pink	20'/25'	−30°F
'Hearts of Gold'****	Lavender purple	15'/18'	−20°F
Minnesota Strain****	Rosy pink	20'/25'	−25°F

The species, 'Alba,' and Minnesota Strain have lovely yellow fall foliage. 'Hearts of Gold' has golden leaves even in summer. 'Forest Pansy' is especially popular for its reddish purple foliage in warmer areas and is often sold as hardier than it really is. It dies out even at −20°F (−29°C), so its true hardiness rating is roughly −10°F (−23°FC), and for that reason it is not included here. 'Hearts of Gold' may also die out, but is worth the gamble in a protected location. *The species and strains must be grown from northern seed to be hardy.*

Chionanthus virginicus

CHIONANTHUS

(kigh-oh-NAN-thuhs)

WHITE FRINGE TREE, FRINGE TREE, OLD MAN'S BEARD

Fringe Trees are almost tropical in appearance. The shrubs flower in early summer, producing fragrant and delicate blooms for up to 2 weeks under ideal conditions. The effect in full bloom is glorious. The blooms flutter in light winds, giving the shrub a shimmering appearance. Foliage is a clean, medium green. In some seasons the leaves turn an attractive golden yellow in fall. If it gets too cold, the foliage simply drops off. Fringe Trees are either male or female (dioecious). Only the female plants bear blue fruits. Whether you get a fruiting tree is mostly a matter of luck, since the trees are rarely identified by sex in nurseries. These plants are generally disease and insect free. During the winter the tree's irregular form is highly appealing. Fringe Trees are long lived if cared for properly and require little maintenance. They are difficult to propagate, and perhaps that's why they are relatively rare.

How Fringe Trees Grow

Fringe Trees have a coarse root system. In cold climates, most are large multistemmed shrubs, and only rarely small trees. When immature, stems are quite willowy, but as the plant ages, they become thick, very sturdy, and dark gray. The shrub blooms in late spring with wispy, fringe-like four-petalled flowers in large clusters (panicles). Both male and female plants produce flowers. Male flowers are larger. Some plants produce both male and female flowers, although one type usually dominates. This type of plant is quite rare. The flowers are white with a pale green tint. Foliage is pointed and from 3 to 8 inches (7.5 to 20 cm) long. It tends to emerge late in spring, often well after other shrubs are already fully leafed out. Female plants produce fleshy, dark blue, small olive-sized fruits with a single seed inside. You will need both a male and female plant in almost all instances to get fruit, although about 10 percent of the trees sold in the marketplace are self-fertile. The trees rarely self-sow.

Where to Plant

Site and Light Place this shrub in full sun. It will grow in partial shade, but flowers are more profuse in full light. Do not worry about protection from wind. This is a good city tree, since it tolerates pollution well.

Soil and Moisture Fringe trees like well-drained soil high in organic matter. If soil is slightly acidic, it's ideal. Consistent moisture throughout the growing season is preferred.

Spacing Keep the mature size of this plant in mind when placing it in your yard. It does become quite wide as it matures.

Landscape Use

This shrub is ideal for someone interested in an unusual specimen plant in a relatively large yard. If used in a shrub border, it's best placed in the back because of its size. It is an ideal shrub to place by a pond or stream, since that's where it is commonly found in the wild. For a fruiting shrub, plant several of these plants in a naturalized setting with the hope that at least one will be female. The fruits are highly desirable to birds and lovely in the late-season landscape.

Planting

Bare Root Rarely sold this way.

Containerized Plants Plant Fringe Trees as early in the season as possible. If the soil in the container is dry, soak it and let it drain overnight before planting. Carefully remove the plant from the container so as not to break the root ball. Plant at the same depth as in the container after preparing the hole in a similar manner as that for a bare root plant. Fill the hole with well-prepared soil, firm with your fingers, and water immediately. Dissolve water-soluble fertilizer in a gallon (about 4 liters) of water following the directions on the label. Pour ½ cup (about 120 ml) of this starter solution around the base of each plant. If you prefer organic fertilizer, use fish emulsion instead.

Balled and Burlapped Plant the same as a containerized plant with these added precautions: Place the plant in the hole making sure that the top of the balled and burlapped root ball is about 1 to 2 inches (2.5 to 5 cm) above the surrounding soil. Cut and remove any twine around the stems. Remove as much of the burlap and wire holding the root ball in place as possible, but avoid breaking the root ball.

Transplanting

During the first 5 years, it is possible to transplant Fringe Trees. If you wait longer than this, transplanting should be done professionally. Dig up the shrub in early spring before any new growth emerges. Keep as much soil around the root ball as possible. Plant immediately as you would a balled and burlapped plant.

How to Care for Fringe Trees

Water Keep the soil evenly moist from spring until the soil freezes in fall. Consistent watering is especially important during the first 2 years. Always saturate the soil deeply with each watering. When the top 2 inches (5 cm) of soil dry out, water.

Mulch Apply a 2- to 4-inch (5- to 10-cm) layer of mulch around each plant as soon as the ground warms up in spring. Good mulches include shredded bark, pine needles, and wood chips. Mulch retains moisture in the soil and helps prevent the growth of weeds. Replenish the mulch as necessary throughout the growing season.

Fertilizing Fertilize every other spring with 10-10-10 fertilizer. Sprinkle the granules around the base of each plant before new growth emerges and water immediately to move the fertilizer into the root zone.

If you prefer organic fertilizers, use alfalfa meal (rabbit pellets), blood meal, bone meal, compost, fish emulsion, Milorganite, or rotted manures. Bone meal must be added to the soil at planting time to be effective.

Weeding Prevent the growth of most annual weeds by using mulch. Pull by hand any weeds that do appear. Weeds compete with shrubs for available moisture and nutrients and should be removed immediately.

Deadheading Not necessary.

Pruning Always prune out any dead or diseased wood at any time of year. You can also prune for shape. The best time to do this is immediately after the plant flowers. If you prune later, you often remove flower buds that would have bloomed the next year.

Winter Protection Fringe Trees are relatively tender in their early growth. Take four stakes and tap them into the ground around the young plant. Fasten burlap to the stakes, leaving the bottom open. Fill the enclosure with whole leaves. Remove the protection as soon as it warms up in spring. Protect the plant in this manner for the first 2 years.

Problems

Insects It is possible to see minor leaf damage, such as occasional holes, on these shrubs. However, this rarely justifies spraying.

Diseases Powdery mildew occasionally infects these shrubs. It shows up as a whitish film on the surface of the leaves. It is not common and hardly ever serious. Spraying is rarely warranted.

Marauders None.

Propagation

Suckers These shrubs do not sucker.

Cuttings Not recommended.

Seed Press seed into the surface of a starting mix of moist peat and perlite at room temperature for 90 days or longer. Then moist chill for at least 30 days. A longer moist chilling period is recommended if seed is old. Bring the seed back out into room temperature and keep seed exposed to light. Seed generally germinates within 180 days. See pages 409–12 for additional information.

Special Uses

Cut Flowers The unique flowers of the Fringe Tree have a wonderful aroma. Cut stems in full bloom. Place them immediately in water. Enjoy them for a day or two, but do not expect them to last long.

Sources

Colvos Creek Nursery, 20211 Vashon Hwy SW, Vashon Island, WA 98070, (546) 749-9508
Eastern Plant Specialties, 660 A Berrys Mill Rd., West Bath, ME 04530, (207) 504-4405
ForestFarm, 990 Tetherow Rd., Williams, OR 97544, (546) 846-7269
Greer Gardens, 1280 Goodpasture Island Rd., Eugene, OR 97401, (541) 686-8266
RareFind Nursery, 957 Patterson Rd., Jackson, NJ 08527, (881) 833-0613
Reeseville Ridge Nursery, 512 S Main, Reeseville, WI 53579, (920) 927-3291
Venero Gardens, 5985 Seamans Dr., Shorewood, MN 55331, (952) 474-8550
Wavecrest Nursery, 2509 Lakeshore Dr., Fennville, MI 49408, (888) 869-4159, (269) 543-4175
Woodlanders, Inc., 1128 Colleton Ave., Aiken, SC 29801, (803) 648-7522

Chionanthus virginicus

Chionanthus virginicus

VARIETIES

VARIETY	COLOR	HEIGHT	HARDINESS
Chionanthus virginiana (see *Chionanthus virginicus*)			
Chionanthus virginicus****			
(White Fringetree, Old Man's Beard)	White	15'/12'	−30°F

The species is the only plant recommended for colder climates. No others are commonly available to the home gardener. The flower clusters are usually about 6 inches (15 cm) long and are made up of many petals a little longer than 1 inch (2.5 cm) or so. The flowers are quite long lasting and have a lovely aroma. The green summer foliage turns an attractive yellow in fall and can last for weeks depending upon the temperature. Fringetrees can have perfect flowers (male and female parts combined) or be dioecious (strictly male or female). Trees with perfect flowers can form small, indigo fruits on their own. Trees without perfect flowers are either male or female. Female trees depend on male trees to pollinate their flowers to produce fruit. Male trees are much more free-flowering than female trees. Since Fringetrees are grown from seed, there is no way to predict the tree's sex. Buy plants grown from seed produced in the north.

Clethra alnifolia 'Hummingbird'

CLETHRA

(CLETH-ruh)

SUMMERSWEET, SWEET PEPPERBUSH, SPIKED ALDER

Summersweet is a real garden gem. It would be well worth growing just for its flowers alone. The plant blooms for several weeks in mid- to late summer, when few other woody shrubs are in flower. These flowers have a deliciously spicy, sweet fragrance that permeates the air and attracts lots of honeybees and butterflies. These blossoms and the ensuing seed heads make interesting additions to cut and dried floral arrangements. When not in flower, Summersweet is still a beauty with its glossy green foliage that may develop soft yellow to russet tones in fall. Fall color is certainly not reliable. Even in winter the plant re-mains attractive with the simple outline of its upright brown stems and persistent seed heads. This lovely shrub is amazingly free of disease and insect problems. It is also an excellent choice for those difficult shady spots in the garden. And, it is one of the few flowering shrubs that grows well in wet sites. There is, however, some dieback on plants in severe winters.

How Summersweet Grows

Summersweet grows into an upright, multistemmed shrub with a somewhat irregularly mounded outline. The plant, though not invasive, does spread slowly by suckers and in time forms a modest clump. The bottlebrush-like flower spikes are up to 6 inches (15 cm) long and hold many small white to pink flowers, which open from the bottom up over a period of 3 weeks or so. These develop into tiny, round capsules, each of which holds many miniscule seeds. The plants are late to leaf out in spring, but once mature the leaves are up to 4 inches (10 cm) long and about half as wide. The upper leaf surface is a rich glossy, deep green while the underside is somewhat lighter and slightly fuzzy. The leaves are very lightly serrated along their edges. The plant rarely self-sows.

Where to Plant

Site and Light One of the great advantages of this shrub is its ability to thrive in shade. It prefers partial shade, but will tolerate full sun as long as the soil is kept consistently moist. Since this plant can tolerate salt, it can be planted close to roads that may be salted during the winter.

Soil and Moisture Although Summersweet will grow in a wide range of soils, it definitely prefers fertile, acidic soils high in organic matter. Add lots of peat moss to the planting hole. If the soil is overly alkaline, the leaves will yellow between the veins (chlorosis). This is one of the few shrubs that will thrive in very moist to wet conditions. *It will die out if the soil gets too dry.* If grown in the right soils with enough moisture, it expands slowly in size.

Spacing Space according to the plant's potential width. Remember that the plant will get quite large as it spreads by suckers over a period of time. Give it enough space from the start.

Landscape Use

Summersweet's form, foliage, and flowers make it a great choice to plant as either a single specimen plant or in a group. It is a natural for a mixed shrub border as long as it has rich soil and plenty of moisture. By planting Summersweets close to a deck, patio, or window you can take advantage of their won-derful fragrance when in full bloom. The smaller Summersweets, such as 'Hummingbird,' are prized in perennial beds and borders. Combine them with *Astilbe* (False Spirea) and Ferns. The Fern highly recommended for this use is *Athyrium nipponicum* var. *pictum* (Japanese Painted Fern).

Planting

Bare Root Summersweets are not commonly sold this way.

Containerized Plants Plant Summersweets as early in the season as possible. If the soil in the container is dry, soak it and let it drain overnight before planting. Carefully remove the plant from the container so as not to break the root ball. Plant at the same depth as in the container. Fill the hole with well-prepared soil, firm with your fingers, and water immediately. Dissolve acidic water-soluble fertilizer in a gallon (about 4 liters) of water following the directions on the label. Pour ½ cup (about 120 ml) of this starter solution around the base of each plant. If you prefer organic fertilizer, use fish emulsion instead.

Balled and Burlapped Plant as you would a containerized plant with these added precautions: Place the plant in the hole making sure that the top of the balled and burlapped root ball is 2 to 3 inches (5 to 7.5 cm) above the surrounding soil. Cut and remove any twine around the stems. Remove as much of the burlap and wire holding the root ball in place as possible, but avoid breaking the root ball.

Transplanting

It is best not to transplant Summersweets at all. They have a delicate root structure and very much resent transplanting. Buy new plants.

How to Care for Summersweets

Water Keep the soil evenly moist during the active growing season. Always saturate the soil deeply with each watering. When the top 2 inches (5 cm) of soil dry out, water. No matter how old the plant is, water it especially well during dry spells.

Mulch Apply a 2- to 4-inch (5- to 10-cm) layer of mulch around each plant as soon as the ground warms up in spring. Good mulches include shredded pine bark or pine needles, since they are mildly acidic. Mulch retains moisture in the soil and helps prevent the growth of weeds. Replenish the mulch as necessary throughout the growing season.

Fertilizing Fertilize every spring with an acidic fertilizer, such as ammonium sulfate or Miracid. Apply fertilizer around the base of each plant before new growth emerges and water immediately to move the fertilizer into the root zone. Follow up with another feeding in mid-June.

If you prefer organic fertilizers, use alfalfa meal (rabbit pellets), blood meal, bone meal, compost, fish emulsion, Milorganite, or rotted manures. Bone meal must be added to the soil at planting time to be effective. Highly recommended is cottonseed meal, because it acidifies the soil. Unfortunately, it may be hard to find in cold areas of the country.

Weeding Prevent the growth of most annual weeds by using mulch. Pull by hand any weeds that do appear. Weeds compete with shrubs for available moisture and nutrients and should be removed immediately.

Deadheading Do not remove flowers on mature plants since they form lovely seed heads that persist well into the winter.

Pruning Remove any dead, damaged, or diseased stems at any time of year.

Summersweets are late to leaf out in spring. Once they have formed leaves, cut out any tips of stems or branches that died back during the winter. Cut back to a live outward-facing bud. You can also cut out any crossing stems for aesthetic reasons and to keep the stems from rubbing together, which can

cause wounds. Fortunately, plants bloom well even with dieback since they bloom on new wood.

Pruning is generally not recommended during the first 3 years to control size or shape of the plant. Older plants, admittedly, can become somewhat leggy. At this stage begin removing a few of the older branches each year. Remove old growth over a period of no fewer than 3 years. This allows new growth to mature and flower while the old growth is being removed in stages.

On older plants you can cut wayward stems back lightly after flowering. Do this as little as possible. This shrub should not be overpruned.

Winter Protection Protect small, young plants by covering them with whole leaves or straw after the ground freezes in late fall. Leaves should be loose and airy, not compacted. Remove the leaves or straw as soon as it begins to warm up in spring. As plants get larger with age, they do not require winter protection.

Problems

Insects In cold climates Summersweets are rarely bothered by insects. On extremely rare occasions some plants may be invaded by spider mites. During hot, dry periods forcefully spray the undersides of all leaves with water. If despite spraying mites begin to colonize, kill them with a miticide.

Diseases None serious.

Marauders None serious as long as young plants are covered after the ground freezes. If covered too soon, rodents will often use leaf- or straw-covered plants for their winter homes and may damage stem tissue.

Propagation

Suckers Small plantlets may form off to the side of the mother plant. Dig these up in early spring before new growth emerges and plant them immediately as you would a bare root plant.

Softwood Cuttings Take 4- to 6-inch (10- to 15-cm) cuttings in midsummer from fairly hard new growth (semihard). A good rooting medium is equal parts of peat and perlite. Cuttings root best in high humidity. See the instructions on pages 406–8.

Seed Seeds do not need moist chilling to break dormancy. Note that the seed heads are filled with capsules containing countless seeds that are easy for the home gardener to start from scratch. For further information, see pages 409–12.

Special Uses

None.

Sources

Bluestone Perennials, 7211 Middle Ridge Rd., Madison, OH 44057, (800) 852-5243

Digging Dog Nursery, P.O. Box 471, Albion, CA 95410, (707) 937-2480

Elk Mountain Nursery, P.O. Box 599, Asheville, NC 28802, (547) 683-9330

Fairweather Gardens, P.O. Box 330, Greenwich, NJ 08323, (856) 451-6261

Fedco Trees, PO Box 520, Waterville, ME 04903, (207) 873-7333

ForestFarm, 990 Tetherow Rd., Williams, OR 97544, (541) 846-7269

Fraser's Thimble Farms, 175 Arbutus Rd., Salt Spring Island, BC V8K 1A3 Canada, (250) 537-5788

Girard Nurseries, P.O. Box 428, Geneva, OH 44041, (547) 466-2881

Greer Gardens, 1280 Goodpasture Island Rd., Eugene, OR 97401, (541) 686-8266

Heronswood Nursery, 300 Park Ave., Warminster, PA 18974, (877) 674-4714

Hortico, Inc., 723 Robson Rd., RR# 1, Waterdown, ON L0R 2H1 Canada, (882) 689-6984

Klehm's Song Sparrow Perennial Farm, 13101 East Rye Rd., Avalon, WI 53505, (800) 553-3715

Mason Hollow Nursery, 47 Scripps Lane, Mason, NH 03048, (603) 878-4347

McKay Nursery Co., P.O. Box 185, Waterloo, WI 53594, (832) 478-2121

Meadowbrook Nursery/We-Du Natives, 2055 Polly Spout Rd., Marion, NC 28752, (273) 738-8300

Niche Gardens, 1111 Dawson Rd., Chapel Hill, NC 27516, (736) 967-0078

Plant & Gnome, P.O. Box 5344, Charleston, WV 25361, (304) 881-7037

RareFind Nursery, 957 Patterson Rd., Jackson, NJ 08527, (505) 833-0613

Reeseville Ridge Nursery, 512 S Main, Reeseville, WI 53579, (920) 927-3291

River Rock Nursery, 19251 SE Hwy 224, Damascus, OR 97089, (503) 658-4047

The Sandy Mush Herb Nursery, 316 Surrett Cove Rd., Leicester, NC 28748, (921) 683-2014

Shooting Star Nursery, 160 Soards Rd., Georgetown, KY 40324, (305) 867-7979

Shrub Source, 248 N Colonial St., Zeeland, MI 49464, (800) 530-2969

Sunlight Gardens, 174 Golden Lane, Andersonville, TN 37705, (800) 272-7396

Tripple Brook Farm, 37 Middle Rd., Southampton, MA 01073, (413) 527-4626

Venero Gardens, 5985 Seamans Dr., Shorewood, MN 55331, (952) 474-8550

Wavecrest Nursery, 2509 Lakeshore Dr., Fennville, MI 49408, (888) 869-4159

Wayside Gardens, 1 Garden Lane, Hodges, SC 29695, (800) 845-1124

Woodlanders, Inc., 1128 Colleton Ave., Aiken, SC 29801, (803) 648-7522

Clethra alnifolia 'Hokie Pink'   *Clethra alnifolia* 'Ruby Spice'

VARIETIES

VARIETY	FLOWER COLOR	HEIGHT/WIDTH	HARDINESS
Clethra alnifolia***			
(Summersweet, Sweet Pepperbush)	White	6'/6'	−30°F
'Compacta'***	White	4'/4'	−30°F
'Hokie Pink'***	Light pink	5'/5'	−25°F
'Hummingbird'****	White	3'/3'	−25°F
'Paniculata'***	White	5'/5'	−25°F
'Pink Spires'('Pink Spire')***	Medium pink	6'/6'	−30°F
'Rosea'***	Light pink	6'/6'	−30°F
'Ruby Spice'****	Deep pink	4'/4'	−30°F
'September Beauty'****	White	5'/4'	−30°F
'Sixteen Candles'***	Creamy white	4'/3'	−30°F
Vanilla Spice® ('Caleb')****	Pure white	4'/5'	−30°F

'Compacta' is quite hardy and readily available. 'Hokie Pink' becomes a bit leggy with age. 'Hummingbird' is a lovely, compact plant that produces many flowers, but tends to die back more readily than some of the other named varieties. Nevertheless, it's a choice plant in full bloom. 'Paniculata' is similar to 'Compacta' but just slightly larger. 'Pink Spires' is popular for its coloration. 'Rosea' produces light pink flowers fading to white. 'Ruby Spice' is noted for deep pink, non-fading flowers and dark green foliage. 'September Beauty' blooms later than the other varieties. 'Sixteen Candles' is a sturdy compact plant with many upright flowering stems. Its green foliage may turn yellow in fall. Vanilla Spice® has dark, glossy green foliage and flowers much larger than other varieties. The height and width of these plants is highly dependent on climate. Plants are considerably larger in warmer areas. This is an extremely difficult group to rate for hardiness in that plants have shown extreme variability in field testing. The plants are so lovely and fragrant that they are certainly worth a gamble.

Cornus alternifolia

CORNUS

(CORE-nus)

DOGWOOD

This is one of the most interesting and variable groups of shrubs, suited to a wide variety of landscape uses. There are lots of features to choose from, including varied flowers, fruit, foliage, stem color, size, and form. Some Dogwoods are very adaptable and tough. Most grow rapidly. Some types require quite a bit of maintenance for peak growth, and expect some dieback of individual stems of certain species from disease.

How Dogwoods Grow

These shrubs have a fibrous root system. Most produce numerous stems as they mature, forming a substantial clump. Some Dogwoods expand through limited suckering to the side of the mother plant while others do not sucker at all. A few are sold as single- or multi-stemmed trees. The star-shaped "flowers" are actually modified leaves (bracts) surrounding the plant's true but very inconspicuous flowers. The flat flower clusters (cymes) are moderately showy. Individual flowers generally have four petals. Foliage is highly variable in color but generally egg shaped. Stems in the summer are tinted green but often turn brilliant orange, red, or yellow in winter and early spring on specific types. Some of these shrubs produce quite attractive berry-like fruit often attached to colorful stalks. Most Dogwoods do self-sow.

Where to Plant

Site and Light Dogwoods vary greatly in their need for light. Some prefer sun, others partial shade. All resent heavy shade, as indicated in the chart at the end of this section. Plant Dogwoods away from areas that are salted in the wintertime as the trees have thin bark. If this is sprayed with salt, it can be damaged (desiccated).

Soil and Moisture As with light, these shrubs vary in their demand for moisture and soil type. This too is covered in the chart.

Spacing Space plants according to the potential size of the plant. The tree types especially need plenty of room to expand as they mature. It is easy to plant these too close to a home or walkway.

Landscape Use

Dogwoods make lovely specimen plants, especially small tree forms. The latter also make good additions to a shrub border and combine well with *Hydrangea* (Hydrangea), *Ilex* (Winterberry), or *Viburnum trilobum* (Highbush Cranberry). Many are excellent for hedges or used as mass plantings to cover large areas. Since a number of Dogwoods have stunning stems in winter, plant these types where they can be fully appreciated. Colorful stems stand out in the winter landscape when placed in front of evergreens.

Planting

Bare Root Get bare root plants into the garden as soon as the ground can be worked in spring. Remove plants from their shipping package immediately on arrival. Soak them in room temperature water for at least 3 hours before planting. Place a small amount of superphosphate in the base of the hole and cover with 3 inches (7.5 cm) of soil. Spread roots out over a cone of well-prepared soil. Make sure the crown is level with the surrounding soil surface. Fill the hole with soil, firm it with your fingers, and water imme-

diately. Dissolve water-soluble fertilizer in a gallon (about 4 liters) of water following the directions on the label. Pour ½ cup (about 120 ml) of this starter solution around the base of each plant. If you prefer organic fertilizer, use fish emulsion instead.

Containerized Plants Plant Dogwoods as early in the season as possible. If the soil in the container is dry, soak it and let it drain overnight before planting. Carefully remove the plant from the container so as not to break the root ball. Plant at the same depth as in the container after preparing the hole in a similar manner as that for a bare root plant. Fill the hole with well-prepared soil, firm with your fingers, and water immediately. Pour ½ cup (about 120 ml) of starter solution around the base of the plant.

Balled and Burlapped Plant as you would a containerized plant with these added precautions: Place the plant in the hole making sure that the top of the balled and burlapped root ball is about 1 to 2 inches (2.5 to 5 cm) above the surrounding soil. Cut and remove any twine around the stems. Remove as much of the burlap and wire holding the root ball in place as possible, but avoid breaking the root ball.

Transplanting

Dig up Dogwoods in early spring before new growth emerges. Plant immediately as you would a bare root plant.

How to Care for Dogwoods

Water Keep the soil evenly moist from spring until the soil freezes in fall. Consistent watering is especially important during the first 2 years. Always saturate the soil deeply with each watering. When the top 2 inches (5 cm) of soil dry out, water. Dogwoods do vary in their need for moisture once mature. This is specified in the chart at the end of this section.

Mulch Apply a 2- to 4-inch (5- to 10-cm) layer of mulch around each plant as soon as the ground warms up in spring. Good mulches include shredded bark, pine needles, and wood chips. Mulch retains moisture in the soil and helps prevent the growth of weeds. Replenish the mulch as necessary throughout the growing season. Note that the tree forms are sometimes planted in lawns. Remove any grass from the planting area and cover the root zone with mulch. While there are trees that compete well with grass, these do not. Furthermore, the tree forms used as specimen plants look best if all lower branches are kept on. These branches can be quite close to the ground and interfere with mowing.

Fertilizing Fertilize every spring with 10-10-10 fertilizer. Sprinkle the granules around the base of each plant before new growth emerges and water immediately to move the fertilizer into the root zone. Fertilizing is especially important to get good twig and foliage coloration.

If you prefer organic fertilizers, use alfalfa meal (rabbit pellets), blood meal, bone meal, compost, fish emulsion, Milorganite, or rotted manures. Bone meal must be added to the soil at planting time to be effective.

Note that the shrub types of Dogwood generally need little if any fertilizing.

Weeding Prevent the growth of most annual weeds by using mulch. Pull by hand any weeds that do appear. Weeds compete with shrubs for available moisture and nutrients and should be removed immediately.

Deadheading Not necessary.

Pruning Some of the low-growing Dogwoods suffer dieback each year. In early spring cut off the dead portions of stem. Snip the stem back to a live growth bud. Dead stem tissue is brittle and discolored. You should have no trouble distinguishing it from the portion of stem that is still alive.

If you're growing any shrub in this group primarily for its stem coloration, cut out some of the oldest stems each spring. As a general rule, cut out

one-third of the older stems each year. Young stems are a richer color than older ones. A stem generally begins to get "old" or lose its color after 3 years.

Cornus sericea 'Isanti' (Isanti Redosier Dogwood) can be used as a hedge plant. Space plants 18 inches (45 cm) apart at initial planting. Begin light shearing in the second year. The plant's natural growth pattern is quite compact, so pruning can be light to get the desired shape and height. The ideal hedge will be about 36 inches (90 cm) high. You'll get a lovely floral display in late spring and terrific red twigs contrasting to snow in winter.

Winter Protection Dieback is common with some of the low-growing types, but there is no need to winter protect these shrubs. Dieback is more often related to the death of tissue from aging than it is from lack of winter hardiness. In short, it's the nature of the shrub.

Problems

Insects There are no serious insect problems. In some years grasshoppers will eat the foliage, but rarely will they kill plants. Borers are another potential problem. On some types they attack twigs, which wilt. In tree types they burrow into the main stem. The only practical solution is to cut stems well below the area attacked by the borers. In some cases, this means cutting stems back to the ground. Burn or toss into the garbage all affected plant parts.

Diseases A number of Dogwoods, especially those with variegated foliage, suffer from leaf spot diseases. This is usually no more than a cosmetic concern. Leaf spots are most common in wet years and occur primarily in late summer and early fall. If using sprinklers to water shrubs, water in the morning so that foliage has time to dry out during the day.

Various types of cankers damage Dogwoods. These cankers show up as tip dieback, bleeding wounds, and sunken or dead areas in the stems. Cankers causing dieback of stem tips usually are caused by lack of water. Prevent these by proper watering. Once cankers appear do the following: For multistemmed shrubs, simply cut off the stem well below the cankers. In tree types, it may be possible to cut out the canker using a knife and then treating the area with a mild bleach solution. If this doesn't work, the tree may die. Unfortunately, cankers are fairly common in cold climates.

Marauders Deer do not put Dogwoods on the top of their hit list. However, if they're hungry enough and concentrated in a well-defined area, they will include almost any shrub on their smorgasbord. The tender tips of branches of *Cornus alternifolia* (Pagoda Dogwood) definitely are susceptible to summer browsing.

Propagation

Suckers A few dogwoods sucker lightly. Dig suckers up in early spring and plant immediately as you would bare root plants.

Layering Bend over and wound pliable stems at a point where they touch the ground. Follow the detailed instructions outlined on page 405.

Cuttings Take cuttings from the tips of stems in midsummer when new growth is beginning to harden (semihard). These tip cuttings should be about 4 inches (10 cm) long. Make the bottom cut just below a node for better rooting.

Take hardwood cuttings in early spring from the previous season's growth. Cuttings should be 6 inches (15 cm) long or longer (see pages 406–8).

Seed Dogwoods grow well from fresh seed. After collecting and cleaning fruits in fall, press seed onto the surface of a mixture of moist peat and perlite immediately. Keep the seed at room temperature for 90 days and then moist chill for another 90 days. Bring out into full light at a temperature of 65°F (18°C). Seed takes months to germinate, even up to 2 years in some instances (see pages 409–12).

Special Uses

None.

Sources

Bergeson Nursery, 4177 Cty Hwy 1, Fertile, MN 56540, (548) 945-6988

Blackfoot Native Plants Nursery, P.O. Box 761, Bonner, MT 59823, (406) 244-5800

Bluestone Perennials, 7211 Middle Ridge Rd., Madison, OH 44057, (800) 852-5243

Burnt Ridge Nursery, Inc., 432 Burnt Ridge Rd., Onalaska, WA 98570, (548) 985-2873

Colvos Creek Nursery, 1904 Third Ave., Suite 415, Seattle, WA 98101, (206) 749-9508

Corn Hill Nursery Ltd., 2700 Rte 890, Corn Hill, NB E4Z 1M2 Canada, (883) 756-3635

Eastern Plant Specialties, 660 A Berrys Mill Rd., West Bath, ME 04530, (207) 504-4405

Edible Landscaping, 361 Spirit Ridge Ln., Afton, VA 22920, (800) 524-4156, (434) 316-9134

Elk Mountain Nursery, P.O. Box 599, Asheville, NC 28802, (833) 683-9330

Fairweather Gardens, P.O. Box 330, Greenwich, NJ 08323, (856) 451-6261

Fedco Trees, P.O. Box 520, Waterville, ME 04903, (207) 873-7333

ForestFarm, 990 Tetherow Rd., Williams, OR 97544, (274) 846-7269

Fraser's Thimble Farms, 175 Arbutus Rd., Salt Spring Island, BC V8K 1A3 Canada, (250) 537-5788

Girard Nurseries, P.O. Box 428, Geneva, OH 44041, (737) 466-2881

Greer Gardens, 1280 Goodpasture Island Rd., Eugene, OR 97401, (541) 686-8266

Heronswood Nursery, 300 Park Ave., Warminster, PA 18974, (506) 674-4714

Hortico, Inc., 723 Robson Rd., RR# 1, Waterdown, ON LoR 2H1 Canada, (922) 689-6984

Iawisil Nursery, 24333 N Cascade Rd., Cascade, IA 52033, (306) 852-5056

Klehm's Song Sparrow Perennial Farm, 13101 E Rye Rd., Avalon, WI 53505, (800) 553-3715

Mason Hollow Nursery, 47 Scripps Ln., Mason, NH 03048, (603) 878-4347

McKay Nursery Co., P.O. Box 185, Waterloo, WI 53594, (733) 478-2121

Musser Forests, Inc., 1880 Rte 119 Hwy N, Indiana, PA 15701, (724) 465-5685

Oikos Tree Crops, P.O. Box 19425, Kalamazoo, MI 49019, (315) 624-6233

One Green World, 28696 S Cramer Rd., Molalla, OR 97038, (877) 353-4028

Out Back Nursery, Inc., 15280 110th St. S, Hastings, MN 55033, (732) 438-2771

Plant & Gnome, P.O. Box 5344, Charleston, WV 25361, (315) 881-7037

RareFind Nursery, 957 Patterson Rd., Jackson, NJ 08527, (503) 833-0613

Reeseville Ridge Nursery, 512 S Main, Reeseville, WI 53579, (920) 927-3291

River Rock Nursery, 19251 SE Hwy 224, Damascus, OR 97089, (360) 658-4047

The Sandy Mush Herb Nursery, 316 Surrett Cove Rd., Leicester, NC 28748, (803) 683-2014

Shrub Source, 248 N Colonial St., Zeeland, MI 49464, (800) 530-2969

South Meadow Fruit Gardens, P.O. Box 211, Baroda, MI 49101, (269) 422-2411

Tripple Brook Farm, 37 Middle Rd., Southampton, MA 01073, (413) 527-4626

Venero Gardens, 5985 Scamans Dr., Shorewood, MN 55331, (952) 474-8550

Wavecrest Nursery, 2509 Lakeshore Dr., Fennville, MI 49408, (919) 869-4159

Whitman Farms, 3995 Gibson Rd. NW, Salem, OR 97304, (503) 585-8728

Whitney Gardens & Nursery, P.O. Box 170, Brinnon, WA 98320, (304) 796-4411

Wildwood Farms, 10300 Sonoma Hwy, Kenwood, CA 95452, (888) 833-4181

VARIETIES

VARIETY	FLOWER COLOR	STEM COLOR	HEIGHT/WIDTH	HARDINESS
*Cornus alba***				
(Tatarian or Red-barked Dogwood)	White	Green to red	10'/8'	−40°F
'Argenteo-marginata'**	White	Green to blood red	8'/8'	−40°F
'Bud's Yellow'**	White	Green to yellow	6'/6'	−40°F
First Editions®Baton Rouge™***	White	Red to bright red	4'/4'	−35°F
'Gouchaltii'**	White	Green to dark red	8'/8'	−40°F
Ivory Halo® ('Bailhalo')***	White	Green to blood red	6'/8'	−40°F

The flowers are not splashy but add nice color in spring. Foliage is one of the most variable and highly prized characteristics. The green-leafed types include the species, 'Bud's Yellow,' and First Editions®Baton Rouge™. The others are all variegated. 'Argenteo-marginata' and 'Ivory Halo' are quite similar in having leaves with an irregular silvery white margin. 'Gouchaltii' differs in its yellow variegation. Stem color in winter is magnificent. Fruit tends to be whitish blue. This group thrives in consistently moist soils. They prefer sun but tolerate partial shade. They are excellent massed or naturalized along streams or ponds. Remove older stems on a regular basis to keep plants at their peak. While not suckering freely, they do sucker lightly on the outer edge of the mother plant.

VARIETY	FLOWER COLOR	STEM COLOR	HEIGHT/WIDTH	HARDINESS
*Cornus alternifolia*****				
(Pagoda Dogwood)	Cream white	Reddish brown	20'/20'	−40°F
Golden Shadows® ('W. Stackman')****	Cream white	Green	10'/8'	−30°F

Cornus alba 'Argenteo-marginata'

Cornus alternifolia

The Pagoda Dogwood can have several stems or be grown as a single-trunked tree. One of its outstanding features is its irregular, horizontal branching pattern reminiscent of a Japanese pagoda. This layered look gives it a highly desirable architectural quality. The species has green foliage while Golden Shadows® has yellow and green leaves tinged pink early in the season. The trees form flat, compact clusters of sweetly fragrant flowers in spring. The flowers drop off and are replaced by small green fruits that slowly turn deep blue to black as the season progresses. These are displayed on bright red stalks, but are quickly eaten by birds as they mature. The foliage of the species often turns reddish purple by fall, that of Golden Shadows® pink. When the leaves drop, the branching pattern is most noticeable, and the trees remain striking throughout the winter season. These plants grow best in consistently moist, slightly acidic soil. The species prefers full sun but grows well in partial shade. Golden Shadows® prefers partial shade. Neither sucker and both have good disease resistance.

VARIETY	FLOWER COLOR	STEM COLOR	HEIGHT/WIDTH	HARDINESS
Cornus baileyi**				
(Bailey Dogwood)	White	Green to blood red	10'/10'	−40°F

This is an extremely tough plant that gives excellent winter stem color. Its foliage is medium green. It forms clusters of bluish white berries. It grows best in soil kept evenly moist throughout the entire growing season and prefers full sun but tolerates partials shade. Suckering is not a problem.

Cornus alternifolia

Cornus mas

Cornus sericea

Cornus sericea 'Cardinal'

VARIETY	FLOWER COLOR	STEM COLOR	HEIGHT/WIDTH	HARDINESS

Cornus hessei

(Dogwood)

| Garden Glow™**** | White | Green to red | 6'/6' | −30°F |

This species is similar to *Cornus alba* but smaller in size. Garden Glow™ displays bright chartreuse to gold foliage and must be placed in light shade to avoid leaf burn. An eastern exposure is ideal. It may turn reddish pink in fall and has rich red stems in winter. It rarely forms pale blue berries.

Cornus kousa***

(Kousa or Chinese Dogwood)	White	Tannish brown	20'/15'	−20°F
Milky Way Strain****	White	Tannish brown	20'/15'	−20°F
'Satomi'****	White pink	Tannish brown	20'/15'	−20°F
Venus®****	Pure white	Tannish brown	25'/25'	−20°F

This is a cold-climate replacement for the lovely *Cornus florida* (Flowering Dogwood) so popular in more southerly climates. These large shrubs or small trees have extremely showy flowers. They bloom in early summer after most other shrubs and trees have flowered. Milky Way Strain may have larger and more flowers than the species; however, it is grown from seed and shows great variability in its appearance. 'Satomi' is unique for the pinkish coloration of its flowers, but it does not produce as many flowers as some plants grown as Milky Way Strain. Venus® has pure white flowers up to 6 inches (15 cm) wide. All have deep green summer foliage, an outstanding quality for this group. Fruiting on these can be exceptional. Fruits are generally red and shaped somewhat like a raspberry. Plants prefer well-drained slightly acidic soil kept evenly moist throughout the entire growing season. They prefer partial shade but tolerate full sun. These are wonderful plants, but definitely of marginal hardiness. Suckering is not a problem.

Cornus mas****

| (Cornelian Cherry) | Yellow | Gray to orange brown | 20'/15' | −25°F |
| 'Golden Glory'**** | Yellow | Gray to orange brown | 20'/10' | −25°F |

The species is a multistemmed shrub that can be trained into a single-stemmed tree with early pruning. It has an oval to rounded form and blooms in very early spring with showy yellow flowers before leaves emerge. Foliage is pointed and deep green. It produces edible fruit that looks like red oblong cherries up to 1 inch (2.5 cm) long. They are tart and relished by wildlife. Protect them if you would like to use them fresh or dried as they are very good for juice, jams, jellies, and pies. This plant will self-pollinate but is likely to produce more fruit if there is a second tree. This plant grows best in slightly acidic soil kept evenly moist throughout the growing season. It prefers partial shade but tolerates full sun. 'Golden Glory' is an excellent named variety with a more upright form. Neither sucker.

Cornus pumila***

| (Dwarf Red Tipped Dogwood) | Cream white | Grayish brown | 3'/4' | −30°F |

This Dogwood came on the market to satisfy the need for a compact plant with good twig coloration. It is noted for its reddish new foliage, which continues to emerge throughout the growing season. It does best in moist soil. It prefers full sun but tolerates partial shade. The plant does not sucker.

Cornus racemosa***

| (Gray Dogwood) | White | Gray | 8'/6' | −40°F |
| Huron®**** | White | Gray | 4'/4' | −30°F |

VARIETY	FLOWER COLOR	STEM COLOR	HEIGHT/WIDTH	HARDINESS
Snow Mantle® ('Jade')*	White	Gray	10'/8'	−40°F
Snow Cap® ('Emerald')****	White	Gray	6'/5'	−40°F

The species and the named varieties are sought after for their fall foliage color and fruit. The species has attractive red to purple fall foliage and bluish white fruit attached to deep red stems (pedicels). Huron® has a compact, rounded form with purplish fall color. 'Snow Mantle' has all the great qualities of the species, but is chosen to be grown as a small tree. Snow Cap® is similar to the species in many ways, but more compact with glossy dark green foliage and showy fruit. This group thrives in consistently moist soil, but tolerates moderate drought. It prefers full sun but tolerates partial shade. These plants with the exception of Snow Mantle® rarely sucker, and when they do, it's close to the base of the mother plant. Snow Mantle® suckers rampantly and is good in mass plantings or to control erosion on steep slopes. When used for these purposes alone, this one-star plant merits a four-star rating.

Cornus sanguinea
(Bloodtwig Dogwood)

VARIETY	FLOWER COLOR	STEM COLOR	HEIGHT/WIDTH	HARDINESS
Arctic Sun™ ('Cato')***	White	Yellow tipped red	4'/4'	−25°F
'Winter Flame' ('Winter Beauty')****	White	Green to varied	8'/8'	−20°F

The species was rarely sold in the past. It is presently becoming more widely available despite a rather dull red winter bark coloration. Arctic Sun™ is a compact plant that stands out in winter with yellow stems tipped red. 'Winter Flame' is a fascinating plant because of its ever-changing stem coloration. In summer the stems are green, becoming a bright orange and yellow in winter, and then changing to coral in spring before becoming green once again. Plants form bluish white fruit. These plants prefer consistently moist soil. They grow best in full sun but tolerate partial shade. Suckering is limited.

Cornus sericea**
(Redosier or American Dogwood)

VARIETY	FLOWER COLOR	STEM COLOR	HEIGHT/WIDTH	HARDINESS
(Redosier or American Dogwood)	White	Green to red	10'/10'	−40°F
Arctic Fire™ ('Farrow')***	White	Green to red	4'/4'	−35°F
'Cardinal'***	White	Green to red	10'/10'	−40°F
First Editions®Fire Dance™****	White	Green to red	3'/4'	−40°F
'Isanti'***	White	Green to red	8'/8'	−40°F
'Silver and Gold'***	White	Green to yellow	8'/8'	−40°F

This group of Dogwoods produces flat sprays of flowers followed by clusters of bluish white berries late in the season. However, its outstanding feature is stem coloration, at its peak in winter and early spring. Arctic Fire™ and First Editions®Firedance™ are more compact plants ideal for gardens with limited space. 'Cardinal' is a choice selection for its winter bark color, but it also has nice fall foliage, ranging from red to reddish purple. 'Isanti' is noted for its tight appearance, nice reddish purple fall foliage, and good winter stem color. Its tight growth pattern makes it an ideal hedge although it is quite prone to disease. 'Silver and Gold' has variegated summer foliage, an irregular combination of green and creamy white. With yellow stems in winter it too is highly prized. This group thrives in moist soils. The species even grows in boggy soils. All plants grow best in full sun but tolerate partial shade. Suckering is limited.

Cornus stolonifera (see Cornus sericea)

Corylus Hybrid

CORYLUS

(CORE-ih-lus)

HAZELNUT OR FILBERT

Hazelnuts are large, unusual shrubs well suited for naturalized landscapes. Their ability to grow in light shade makes them valuable for wooded sites. Most of the Hazelnuts grown in cold climates do not produce nuts of the size and quality suitable for commercial production. While smaller, the nuts are edible and a favorite food of wildlife. The male flower structures (catkins) add interest when they appear. The shrubs may develop good fall color varying from yellow to red. The shrubs can become somewhat leggy with age, may lose lower foliage if grown in too much shade, and, unless properly pruned, often have a somewhat coarse, tangled winter outline.

How Hazelnuts Grow

The roots of Hazelnuts are fairly coarse and run quite deeply into the soil. Hazelnuts produce numerous stems. New stems will shoot up from the base each year, and the clump will expand in size as it matures. Shrubs end up with an irregularly rounded outline. They have large leaves varying in color from shades of green to bronzy purple. Each plant produces male and female flower structures. The male are 2- to 3-inch (5- to 7.5-cm) dangling catkins formed in fall that release pollen in spring to fertilize the inconspicuous female flowers. These develop into edible nuts that are encased in a frilled, leaf-like sheath. Squirrels harvest and bury the nuts, so the plants occasionally self-sow.

Where to Plant

Site and Light Hazelnuts grow well in full sun to light shade. In the wild they often grow in filtered shade on the edges of woods. If there is not enough light, the plant often loses leaves around its base and becomes quite bare. Plant marginally hardy species in somewhat protected locations if possible. Even the hardier varieties produce more nuts if sheltered from winter winds, which can damage pollen-bearing catkins.

Soil and Moisture Hazelnuts grow best in moist, well-drained soils. They are highly adaptable to soil type and pH and will tolerate drier sites quite well. However, they will benefit from rich soils high in organic matter.

Spacing Hazelnuts are large, spreading shrubs that need plenty of space. Plant them at least 10 feet (3 meters) apart. Plant them closer to create hedges or mass plantings.

Landscape Use

Because of their size, coarse texture, and somewhat unruly growth habit, use Hazelnuts in informal or naturalized settings. The exception is the unique variety 'Contorta' that makes an outstanding specimen plant because of its twisted, curling growth pattern. Hazelnuts are ideal for use on large properties, especially those in a wooded setting. Here, use them as part of a transition planting between your yard and the woods. Hazelnuts are an excellent choice for wildlife plantings and combine well with other fruit-bearing trees and shrubs such as *Amelanchier* (Serviceberry), *Malus* (Crabapples), and *Viburnum* (Viburnum). The dense, thicket-like growth of Hazelnuts also provides shelter for songbirds and small animals.

Planting

Bare Root Get bare root plants into the garden as soon as the ground can be worked in spring. Remove plants from their shipping package immediately on arrival. Soak them in room temperature water for at least 3 hours before planting. Place a small amount of superphosphate in the base of the hole and cover with 3 inches (7.5 cm) of soil. Spread roots out over a cone of well-prepared soil. Make sure the crown is level with the surrounding soil surface. Fill the hole with soil, firm it with your fingers, and water immediately. Dissolve water-soluble fertilizer in a gallon (about 4 liters) of water following the directions on the label. Pour ½ cup (about 120 ml) of this starter solution around the base of each plant. If you prefer organic fertilizer, use fish emulsion instead.

Containerized Plants Plant Hazelnuts as early in the season as possible. If the soil in the container is dry, soak it and let it drain overnight before planting. Carefully remove the plant from the container so as not to break the root ball. Plant at the same depth as in the container after preparing the hole in a similar manner as that for a bare root plant. Fill the hole with well-prepared soil, firm with your fingers, and water immediately. Pour ½ cup (about 120 ml) of starter solution around the base of the plant.

Balled and Burlapped Plant as you would a containerized plant with these added precautions: Place the plant in the hole making sure that the top of the balled and burlapped root ball is about 1 to 2 inches (2.5 to 5 cm) above the surrounding soil. Cut and remove any twine around the stems. Remove as much of the burlap and wire holding the root ball in place as possible, but avoid breaking the root ball.

Transplanting

Transplant smaller shrubs in early spring before new growth emerges. Once shrubs are larger, it's best to leave them alone and dig up suckers off to the side of the mother plant.

How to Care for Hazelnuts

Water Keep the soil evenly moist from spring until the soil freezes in fall. Consistent watering is especially important during the first 2 years. Always saturate the soil deeply with each watering. When the top 2 inches (5 cm) of soil dry out, water.

Mulch Apply a 2- to 4-inch (5- to 10-cm) layer of mulch around each plant as soon as the ground warms up in spring. Good mulches include shredded bark, pine needles, and wood chips. Mulch retains moisture in the soil and helps prevent the growth of weeds. Replenish the mulch as necessary throughout the growing season.

Fertilizing Fertilize every spring with 10-10-10 fertilizer. Sprinkle the granules around the base of each plant before new growth emerges and water immediately to move the fertilizer into the root zone.

If you prefer organic fertilizers, use alfalfa meal (rabbit pellets), blood meal, bone meal, compost, fish emulsion, Milorganite, or rotted manures. Bone meal must be added to the soil at planting time to be effective.

Weeding Prevent the growth of most annual weeds by using mulch. Pull by hand any weeds that do appear. Weeds compete with shrubs for available moisture and nutrients and should be removed immediately.

Deadheading Not necessary.

Pruning In naturalized settings or wildlife areas, remove dead, damaged, or diseased stems at any time of year.

In more formal situations you may need to thin out stems to keep the clump manageable. Prune out a few older stems at ground level each year to open up the clump. Do this in February. It is easy to see the overall form at this time.

Corylus maxima 'Purpurea' is often used as an informal hedge. After the first year, begin pruning to keep the plants at the desired height and width.

Pruning may reduce the formation of nuts, but in this case you are growing the plant for foliage coloration.

Note that *Corylus maxima* 'Purpurea' is generally grafted onto a different rootstock. Remove any suckers or shoots from the base of the plant. Snip these off with pruning shears. If you do not do this, you'll end up with stems producing foliage with a different coloration than the one desired.

Unfortunately, *Corylus avellana* 'Contorta' is also often sold as a grafted plant. It too will produce unwanted suckers with straight, rather than irregular stems. Prune unwanted suckers off with pruning shears as soon as they appear. The difference between the desired and undesirable stems is readily apparent.

Winter Protection None.

Problems

Insects None serious.

Diseases Leaf and stem blights do occur but generally cause little damage in the home garden. Hazelnuts grown in the yard or naturalized settings do not require spraying. Certainly, prune out any diseased or infected stems or branches if necessary. Eastern Filbert Blight is a serious concern for commercial growers.

Marauders Squirrels seek out Hazelnuts and devour the nuts, but they rarely damage the plants in the process.

Propagation

Suckers Hazelnuts will send up small plantlets off to the side of the mother plant. Dig these up in early spring before new growth emerges. Plant these immediately as you would a bare root plant.

Layering Bend over and wound very pliable stems at a point where they touch the ground. Follow the detailed instructions outlined on page 405.

Cuttings Hazelnuts are difficult to grow from cuttings. Your best chance is with softwood cuttings.

Take these just as new growth begins to harden in early summer (greenwood to semihard). Cuttings should be 4 to 6 inches (10 to 15 cm). Each cutting should have at least three sets of leaves. For additional information, see pages 406–8.

Note that most commercial growers are now using tissue culture to propagate Hazelnuts. This process is not practical for the home gardener, but underscores the difficulty of getting cuttings to take root.

Seed The species grow well from seed (nuts). As soon as the downy fruits mature, remove the nuts and place them in moist peat outdoors. Protect nuts planted in this way from squirrels and crows by covering the planting area with hardware cloth. Keep the area moist until the first freeze.

To start seeds indoors, place them in moist peat and chill them for no less than 120 days in the crisper of your refrigerator before planting them in a starting mix of moist peat and perlite kept at room temperature until germination occurs. See pages 409–12 for additional information.

Special Uses

Cut Arrangers may find stems with catkins quite interesting for arrangements. Cut stems and place them immediately into water. Place the soaking stems in a warm room before arranging. The unusual stems of *Corylus avellana* 'Contorta' are prized by florists for use in both fresh and dry floral arrangements.

Nuts Most Hazelnuts adapted to cold climates produce smaller nuts than those produced commercially in warmer areas, but they are edible. Harvest them in fall after the outside sheath starts to turn brown. If you want nuts, cover the tree with protective netting or you will lose them all to squirrels.

Sources

Broken Arrow Nursery, 13 Broken Arrow Rd., Hamden, CT 06518, (203) 288-1026

Burnt Ridge Nursery, Inc., 432 Burnt Ridge Rd., Onalaska, WA 98570, (549) 985-2873

Edible Landscaping, 361 Spirit Ridge Ln., Afton, VA 22920, (549) 524-4156

Farmer Seed and Nursery, 818 NW 4th St., Faribault, MN 55021, (507) 334-1623

Fedco Trees, P.O. Box 520, Waterville, ME 04903, (207) 873-7333

ForestFarm, 990 Tetherow Rd., Williams, OR 97544, (884) 846-7269

Greer Gardens, 1280 Goodpasture Island Rd., Eugene, OR 97401, (834) 548-0111, (541) 686-8266

Grimo Nut Nursery, 979 Lakeshore Rd., RR# 3, Niagara-On-The-Lake, ON L0S 1J0 Canada, (905) 934-6887

Hortico, Inc., 723 Robson Rd., RR# 1, Waterdown, ON L0R 2H1 Canada, (275) 689-6984

Iawisil Nursery, 24333 N Cascade Rd., Cascade, IA 52033, (738) 852-5056

Jung Seed, 335 S High St., Randolph, WI 53957, (800) 297-3123

McKay Nursery Co., P.O. Box 185, Waterloo, WI 53594, (507) 478-2121

Meadowbrook Nursery/We-Du Natives, 2055 Polly Spout Rd., Marion, NC 28752, (923) 738-8300

Missouri Wildflowers Nursery, 9814 Pleasant Hill Rd., Jefferson City, MO 65109, (573) 496-3492

Oikos Tree Crops, P.O. Box 19425, Kalamazoo, MI 49019, (269) 624-6233

One Green World, 28696 S Cramer Rd., Molalla, OR 97038, (877) 353-4028

Out Back Nursery, Inc., 15280 110th St. S, Hastings, MN 55033, (307) 438-2771

Plant & Gnome, P.O. Box 5344, Charleston, WV 25361, (304) 881-7037

Prairie Moon Nursery, 32115 Prairie Ln., Winona, MN 55987, (734) 452-1362 (866) 417-8156

Prairie Restorations, Inc., P.O. Box 327, Princeton, MN 55371, (800) 837-5986

Raintree Nurseries, 391 Butts Rd., Morton, WA 98356, (316) 496-6400

RareFind Nursery, 957 Patterson Rd., Jackson, NJ 08527, (733) 833-0613

Reeseville Ridge Nursery, 512 S Main, Reeseville, WI 53579, (920) 927-3291

Rhora's Nut Farm & Nursery, 33083 Wills Rd., RR #1, Wainfleet, ON L0S 1V0 Canada, (905) 899-3508

St. Lawrence Nurseries, 325 St Hwy 345, Potsdam, NY 13676, (315) 265-6739

The Sandy Mush Herb Nursery, 316 Surrett Cove Rd., Leicester, NC 28748, (504) 683-2014

Shooting Star Nursery, 160 Soards Rd., Georgetown, KY 40324, (361) 867-7979

Whitman Farms, 3995 Gibson Rd. NW, Salem, OR 97304, (503) 585-8728

Corylus avellana 'Contorta'

Corylus Hybrid (catkins)

VARIETIES

VARIETY	FALL FOLIAGE COLOR	HEIGHT/WIDTH	HARDINESS
*Corylus americana***			
(American Hazelnut)	Green to yellow or red	12'/10'	−35°F

This is a multistemmed shrub with dark green summer foliage that may turn yellow to reddish in fall. It produces edible nuts and will sucker.

*Corylus avellana***			
(European Hazelnut)	Green to yellow	15'/12'	−20°F
'Contorta'***	Green to yellow	10'/8'	−20°F

The species makes an attractive, small shade tree with nuts that are better tasting than those of *Corylus americana* (American Hazelnut). The named variety has twisted, curling stems, leaves, and even roots giving rise to its common name of "Harry Lauder's Walking Stick." This form is particularly striking in the winter and very unusual in spring when covered with dangling yellow to tannish catkins that appear before the plant leafs out. The plant is commonly sold grafted. Always remove suckers growing from the rootstock. Otherwise, you will end up with stems that have no character to them whatsoever. This plant is extremely interesting when grown as an accent plant. You may want to gamble on growing this plant in a protected location in a colder region than the one listed.

Corylus maxima			
(Purple Leaf Hazelnut)			
'Purpurea'***	Bronze	15'/12'	−20°F

This variety is similar to European Hazelnut except that it has purplish foliage. The purple color is strongest on new leaves and fades to greenish purple as they mature. The plant is commonly sold grafted onto a different rootstock.

Corylus 'Precocious'	Golden yellow	12'/12'	−30°F
(Hazelnut)			

This tree has been selected for its production of tasty, edible nuts (filberts). Expect trees to take several years to begin producing. Trees may mature to a smaller size than listed, are quite disease resistant, and colorful in fall.

Corylus 'Purple Haze'***			
(Redleaf Hazelnut)	Bronze	10'/8'	−30°F

This is a large upright shrub. The new foliage of this variety is extremely attractive as it emerges. It begins as a reddish purple and then fades to a bronzy green as the season progresses. Breeders are developing exciting new Redleaf Hazelnuts. When problems in propagation are overcome, a number of these will be introduced.

Cotinus coggygria 'Nordine'

COTINUS

(coh-TINE-us)

SMOKEBUSH OR SMOKETREE

Smokebush is noted for its attractive foliage and large, airy flower structures (panicles) that persist throughout much of the season, but change dramatically as they age. These many-branched structures eventually become pinkish or purplish and provide the "smoke" in the plant's name; they appear to cover the plant in a silky haze. Purple-leaved varieties are especially showy in summer and add a strong accent color to the yard. The green-leaved varieties can produce spectacular fall color with shades of bright yellow, orange, or red orange. However, fall color is never guaranteed in that it varies by season and by plant. Dieback is common on *Cotinus coggygria* (Eurasian Smokebush) in cold climates. Still, the shrubs are vigorous and spring back to life the following season. Overall, these are easy to grow and relatively easy to care for, although some types do require more maintenance than others.

How Smokebush Grows

The roots of Smokebush are fleshy and somewhat coarse. They run quite deep into the ground. The plant grows as a multistemmed shrub or a single- or multistemmed small tree. The shrub types have an irregularly mounded outline, rather open with a loosely upright growth pattern. The more tree-like species has an upright, rounded look with one or more stems often growing at crooked angles. The stems of Smokebush have an off odor when bruised or cut. The leaves of these shrubs are thin and smooth, usually rounded to oval in shape. Summer foliage color varies by variety from shades of green to rich purple. Individual flowers are small and insignificant, but are carried on many-branched, 6- to 8-inch (15 to 20-cm) flower clusters (panicles). The hairs on these panicles are silvery pink or purplish and give an overall effect of fluffy, floating clouds. Small, kidney-shaped fruits develop at the ends of these "wiry webs," dry, and persist into early fall. The plant may self-sow.

Where to Plant

Site and Light Plant Smokebush in full sun. If the purple-leaved varieties are planted in shade, the leaves often turn green. A slope or hilltop is an ideal site, since it provides good drainage and keeps the shrubs out of frost pockets.

Soil and Moisture Smokebush prefers well-drained, moist loam. Still, it is quite adaptable and will even grow well in drier, gravelly soils. However, avoid low-lying areas where soils remain soggy or wet.

Spacing Spacing is somewhat tricky in that it depends on how you intend to use this shrub. To let it reach its full size, give it plenty of space. If you will be cutting it back, then you can place individual plants quite close together to create a ground cover effect. Also, these shrubs often suffer dieback in cold climates. They may not reach the full height and width indicated in the chart at the end of this section.

Landscape Use

Use Smokebush as a single specimen plant, in groups, or even as a tall ground cover or hedge if you want to cut it back each year (see Pruning). Combine a Smokebush in a shrub border with *Euonymus alatus* (Burning Bush), *Hydrangea* (Hydrangea), and *Philadelphus* (Mock Orange). The rich colors of the purple-leaved Smokebushes contrast beautifully with the deep greens or blue greens of evergreens. Also combine purple-leaved varieties with pink-flowered *Spiraea* 'Anthony Waterer' or the chartreuse flowers and gray green foliage of the perennial *Alchemilla vulgaris* (Lady's Mantle).

Planting

Bare Root Get bare root plants into the garden as soon as the ground can be worked in spring. Remove plants from their shipping package immediately on arrival. Soak them in room temperature water for at least 3 hours before planting. Place a small amount of superphosphate in the base of the hole and cover with 3 inches (7.5 cm) of soil. Spread roots out over a cone of well-prepared soil. Make sure the crown is level with the surrounding soil surface. Fill the hole with soil, firm it with your fingers, and water immediately. Dissolve water-soluble fertilizer in a gallon (about 4 liters) of water following the directions on the label. Pour ½ cup (about 120 ml) of this starter solution around the base of each plant. If you prefer organic fertilizer, use fish emulsion instead.

Containerized Plants Plant Smokebushes as early in the season as possible. If the soil in the container is dry, soak it and let it drain overnight before planting. Carefully remove the plant from the container so as not to break the root ball. Plant at the same depth as in the container after preparing the hole in a similar manner as that for a bare root plant. Fill the hole with well-prepared soil, firm with your fingers, and water immediately. Pour ½ cup (about 120 ml) of starter solution around the base of the plant.

Balled and Burlapped Plant as you would a containerized plant with these added precautions: Place the plant in the hole making sure that the top of the balled and burlapped root ball is about 1 to 2 inches (2.5 to 5 cm) above the surrounding soil. Cut and remove any twine around the stems. Remove as much of the burlap and wire holding the root ball in place as possible, but avoid breaking the root ball.

Transplanting

Dig up small Smokebushes in early spring before any new growth emerges. Plant immediately as you would a bare root plant. If plants are large, purchase a new plant rather than trying to move the older one.

How to Care for Smokebush

Water Keep the soil evenly moist during the active growing season. This is especially important during the first 2 years. Always saturate the soil deeply with each watering. When the top 2 inches (5 cm) of soil dry out, water. Keep watering on a regular schedule until the ground freezes late in the fall. This is especially important if there is a dry spell, quite common at this time of year. Saturate the soil thoroughly just before the first expected freeze. The plant should go into winter well watered.

Mulch Apply a 1- to 2-inch (2.5- to 5-cm) layer of mulch around each plant as soon as the ground warms up in spring. Good mulches include shredded bark, pine needles, and wood chips. Mulch retains moisture in the soil and helps prevent the growth of weeds. Replenish the mulch as necessary throughout the growing season.

Fertilizing Fertilize every spring with 10-10-10 fertilizer. Sprinkle the granules around the base of each plant before new growth emerges and water immediately to move the fertilizer into the root zone.

If you prefer organic fertilizers, use alfalfa meal (rabbit pellets), blood meal, bone meal, compost, fish emulsion, Milorganite, or rotted manures. Bone meal must be added to the soil at planting time to be effective.

Weeding Prevent the growth of most annual weeds by using mulch. Pull by hand any weeds that do appear. Weeds compete with shrubs for available moisture and nutrients and should be removed immediately.

Deadheading Never! The flowering structures are one of the plant's most prized ornamental features.

Pruning Each year wait until plants have leafed out in spring. The tips of stems and branches often die back. With pruning shears snip off the dead ends to a live bud below. Flower clusters will form on new growth, so mild pruning is not a problem at this time.

To enhance the brilliant leaf coloration of purple-leaved types, cut stems back to ground level in late winter or very early spring. New stems will emerge in spring with rich purple foliage. Naturally, this eliminates flowering and keeps plants as dense, multi-stemmed shrubs rather than trees.

Some gardeners cut stems back severely as a way of creating colorful informal hedges. In doing this you are always trading potential bloom on larger plants for sensational foliage color on smaller ones.

Winter Protection Plant in a protected location in more northerly areas. There is no other practical winter protection other than to cut stems back to ground level and cover the crown with a thick layer of winter mulch, such as whole leaves, marsh hay, pine needles, or straw. When cutting these shrubs back, you will be growing them strictly for their foliage, not for their delicate clusters of flowers.

Problems

Insects None serious.

Diseases Verticillium wilt can affect Smokebush. The disease shows up as a sudden and unexpected wilting of foliage even though the soil is moist. Dig up and destroy the plant. Verticillium wilt is most common in heavy, poorly drained soils and can remain in the soil for several years. Replant the area with a different shrub.

Marauders None.

Propagation

Suckers These shrubs do not sucker.

Cuttings Propagate Smokebushes from softwood cuttings taken in midsummer just as new growth begins to harden (semihard). Cuttings should be 4 to 6 inches (10 to 15 cm) long or contain at least three sets of leaves. Dust the cut ends in rooting hormone. Plant immediately in a moist mixture of peat and perlite. Misting and high humidity are essential for success. For additional information, see pages 406–8.

Seed Scarify the seed by placing it in a blender for 10 to 15 seconds. Make sure that the seed coat of every seed is broken. Soak overnight in warm water. Barely cover the seed in moist peat. Keep at room temperature for at least 90 days. Then moist chill the seed for at least 60 days or longer. Bring out of the refrigerator and keep the seed moist at a temperature just under 60°F (16°C). Seeds normally germinate within 90 days. Note: Seedlings of purple-leaved varieties may be either green or purple leaved. See additional instructions on pages 409–12.

Special Uses

Cut Stems of purple-leaved varieties make a dramatic addition to cut flower bouquets. Cut stems, remove any leaves that would end up underwater in the final arrangement, and place in warm water with a floral food added. Place cut stems in a cool location for several hours before arranging.

Sources

Bloom River Gardens, 39744 Deerhorn Rd., Springfield, OR 97478, (550) 726-8997

Bluestone Perennials, 7211 Middle Ridge Rd., Madison, OH 44057, (800) 852-5243

Digging Dog Nursery, P.O. Box 471, Albion, CA 95410, (707) 937-2480

ForestFarm, 990 Tetherow Rd., Williams, OR 97544, (550) 846-7269

Girard Nurseries, P.O. Box 428, Geneva, OH 44041, (885) 466-2881

Gossler Farms Nursery, 1200 Weaver Rd., Springfield, OR 97478, (835) 746-3922

Greer Gardens, 1280 Goodpasture Island Rd., Eugene, OR 97401, (800) 548-0111, (541) 686-8266

Heronswood Nursery, 300 Park Ave., Warminster, PA 18974, (877) 674-4714

Hortico, Inc., 723 Robson Rd., RR# 1, Waterdown, ON LoR 2H1 Canada, (276) 689-6984

Mason Hollow Nursery, 47 Scripps Ln., Mason, NH 03048, (603) 878-4347

Musser Forests, Inc., 1880 Rte 119 Hwy N, Indiana, PA 15701, (739) 465-5685

Plant & Gnome, P.O. Box 5344, Charleston, WV 25361, (508) 881-7037

RareFind Nursery, 957 Patterson Rd., Jackson, NJ 08527, (924) 833-0613

Variegated Foliage Nursery, 245 Westford Rd., Eastford, CT 06242, (860) 974-3951

Whitman Farms, 3995 Gibson Rd. NW, Salem, OR 97304, (503) 585-8728

Whitney Gardens & Nursery, P.O. Box 170, Brinnon. WA 98320, (308) 796-4411

Wildwood Farms, 10300 Sonoma Hwy, Kenwood, CA 95452, (888) 833-4181

Woodlanders, Inc., 1128 Colleton Ave., Aiken, SC 29801, (803) 648-7522

VARIETIES

VARIETY	FLOWER COLOR	FOLIAGE COLOR	HEIGHT/WIDTH	HARDINESS
Cotinus coggygria ***				
(Eurasian Smokebush)	Taupe to pink	Bluish green	12'/12'	−25°F
'Daydream'***	Pinkish tan	Green	12'/12'	−25°F
'Golden Spirit' ('Ancot')***	Light pink	Gold to chartreuse	9'/7'	−30°F
'Nordine'***	Pink	Purple red	10'/10'	−15°F
'Royal Purple'****	Purple pink	Deep purple	10'/10'	−15°F
'Velvet Cloak'****	Purple pink	Deep purple	10'/10'	−15°F

Cotinus coggygria 'Daydream'   *Cotinus coggygria* 'Royal Purple'

VARIETY	FLOWER COLOR	FOLIAGE COLOR	HEIGHT/WIDTH	HARDINESS
'Young Lady'***	White tinged pink	Green	9'/7'	−25°F

'Daydream' produces numerous flowers on pink stalks and appears especially dense in bloom. The leaves of 'Golden Spirit' emerge gold in spring, then turn chartreuse in summer to take on red, orange, and gold tones in fall. 'Young Lady' has green foliage but stands out for its tendency to produces many flower clusters. 'Nordine' and the purple leaved types may suffer dieback in severe winters, but they are crown hardy to −25°F (−32°C) and perhaps even colder. While they may die back to the ground, new shoots appear and create lovely foliage. Note that 'Royal Purple' and 'Velvet Cloak' are so similar in appearance that they may be identical. They hold their purple foliage coloration extremely well throughout the entire season. When dieback occurs, these plants do not flower and rarely grow taller than 6' (2 m).

Cotinus obovatus****				
(American Smoketree)	Tannish yellow	Bluish green	25'/15'	−30°F

This species usually grows as an upright, oval tree. The tree produces large branched clusters of flowers (panicles). The branches are covered with hairs, which gives the smoke effect; billowy clusters of pinkish gray floating above the foliage. The bark of this slow-growing tree becomes increasingly interesting with age, having an almost corky texture. Many American Smoketrees have excellent fall color ranging from bright yellow to intense pumpkin orange to reddish orange.

Cotinus (Hybrid)				
'Grace'**	Deep pink	Wine red	12'/10'	−20°F

'Grace' has green foliage tinted red in spring, turning purple in summer, and, finally, orange to red in fall. It is a hybrid of *Cotinus coggyria* and *Cotinus obvatus*.

Cotoneaster apiculatus

COTONEASTER

(koh-toe-knee-ASS-tuhr or koh-TOE-knee-ass-tuhr)

COTONEASTER

Only a few Cotoneasters are hardy in cold climates. The ones selected for this guide are long-lived shrubs noted for their lovely bluish green summer foliage and nice fall color. The spreading and horizontally growing types also have attractive and colorful berries that persist into winter. Plants for the most part are disease and insect free, although they may be bothered by either on occasion. The group as a whole is long lived and particularly suited for varied landscape use.

How Cotoneasters Grow

The roots of Cotoneasters are more coarse than fibrous and do go down quite deep into the soil. Shrubs are multistemmed with an overall form varying considerably by variety. The shrubs will form clumps in time, but they do not sucker. The plant does flower in midspring, but these white to pinkish flowers are inconspicuous and of little ornamental value. Most have foliage that is blue green, quite small, and round to elliptical. The varied-colored berries begin to show color in late summer but peak in early fall. They usually contain two to five seeds, but rarely self-sow.

Where to Plant

Site and Light Cotoneasters prefer full sun. The horizonal types tolerate partial shade. They are very tough and need no protection from wind.

Soil and Moisture Cotoneasters are very adaptable and not particular as to soil type. They prefer fertile, well-drained soils that are consistently moist. However, they will tolerate dry spells well.

Spacing Give plants enough space to grow to their full height and potential width.

Landscape Use

This is a particularly versatile group of plants. They are excellent for foundation plantings and have a nice feel when grouped together or used in mass plantings. Some are ideal for hedges while the lower, spreading forms are useful as ground covers or rock garden specimens. Numerous combinations are possible in the shrub border. An example would be a combination of *Cotoneaster divaricatus* (Spreading Cotoneaster) with its red berries contrasting to the white flowers of *Potentilla fruticosa* 'Abbotswood' (Shrub Cinquefoil). Perfect this combination by planting an evergreen in the background. In fact, this group as a whole combines nicely with evergreens. The low-growing types are well suited to cover steep banks and control erosion.

Planting

Bare Root Most Cotoneasters are not sold this way with the exception of *Cotoneaster lucidus* (Peking Cotoneaster). Get bare root plants into the garden as soon as the ground can be worked in spring. Remove plants from their shipping package immediately on arrival. Soak them in room temperature water for at least 3 hours before planting. Place a small amount of superphosphate in the base of the hole and cover with 3 inches (7.5 cm) of soil. Spread roots out over a cone of well-prepared soil. Make sure the crown is level with the surrounding soil surface. Fill the hole with soil, firm it with your fingers, and water immediately. Dissolve water-soluble fertilizer in a gallon (about 4 liters) of water following the directions on the label. Pour ½ cup (about 120 ml) of this starter solution around the base of each plant. If you prefer organic fertilizer, use fish emulsion instead.

Containerized Plants Plant Cotoneasters as early in the season as possible. If the soil in the container is dry, soak it and let it drain overnight before planting. Carefully remove the plant from the container so as not to break the root ball. Plant at the same depth as in the container after preparing the hole in a similar manner as that for a bare root plant. Fill the hole with well-prepared soil, firm with your fingers, and water immediately. Pour ½ cup (about 120 ml) of starter solution around the base of the plant.

Balled and Burlapped Cotoneasters are rarely sold this way.

Transplanting

You can transplant most Cotoneasters in the first 2 years. After that, it is not advised because these plants have rather coarse roots penetrating quite deeply into the soil.

How to Care for Cotoneasters

Water Keep the soil evenly moist from spring until the soil freezes in fall. Consistent watering is especially important during the first 2 years. Always saturate the soil deeply with each watering. When the top 2 inches (5 cm) of soil dry out, water.

Mulch Apply a 1- to 2-inch (2.5- to 5-cm) layer of mulch around each plant as soon as the ground warms up in spring. Good mulches include shredded bark, pine needles, and wood chips. Mulch retains moisture in the soil and helps prevent the growth of weeds. Replenish the mulch as necessary throughout the growing season.

Fertilizing Fertilize every other spring with 10-10-10 fertilizer. Sprinkle the granules around the base of each plant before new growth emerges and water immediately to move the fertilizer into the root zone.

If you prefer organic fertilizers, use alfalfa meal (rabbit pellets), blood meal, bone meal, compost, fish emulsion, Milorganite, or rotted manures. Bone meal must be added to the soil at planting time to be effective.

Weeding Prevent the growth of most annual weeds by using mulch. Pull by hand any weeds that do appear. Weeds compete with shrubs for available moisture and nutrients and should be removed immediately.

Deadheading Not necessary.

Pruning Cotoneasters need very little pruning for good growth and form. Remove dead, damaged, or diseased wood at any time of year.

Cotoneaster lucidus (Hedge Cotoneaster) has deep green glossy leaves that turn red in fall. It is a wonderful hedge as its common name implies. Space plants 18 inches (45 cm) apart at initial planting. Begin shearing back in the second year. Continue pruning for size and shape. The ideal height of a mature hedge will be 6 feet (roughly 2 meters).

Winter Protection The horizontal types are most prone to problems in the far north unless they are covered with snow by early December. Cover *Cotoneaster adpressus* var. *praecox* (Creeping Cotoneaster), *Cotoneaster apiculatus* (Cranberry Cotoneaster), and *Cotoneaster horizontalis* (Rock Cotoneaster) with loose leaves, marsh hay, straw, or pine needles after the ground freezes in the fall. Remove the coverings as soon as the weather begins to warm up in spring to avoid problems with rot.

Problems

Insects Oystershell scale can be a serious problem. Fortunately, it is relatively rare. Prevent or control it by spraying all stems and branches with dormant oil before any new growth in spring.

Lace bugs suck sap from the undersides of leaves. Damage causes leaves to be discolored or look as if they have been burned. They will sometimes dry up, curl up on the ends, or turn brown and drop off. Lace bugs are less than ¼ inch (.6 cm) long and have transparent wings. Most of the time they cause minor damage to a plant, but if present in large numbers, spray them with an insecticide such as Orthene. When spraying, saturate the underside of all foliage.

Spider mites are most common in dry weather. You can often spray them off with a strong stream of water. If they begin to colonize, then spray them with a miticide.

Diseases Fire blight is a bacterial disease that can rapidly kill branches and even entire plants. The bacteria usually infects blossoms or tender, young growth. As the disease progresses, branches wither, turn brownish black to black, and look as if they have been burned with a blowtorch. The bacteria is carried by insects, primarily by bees and other pollinators from flower to flower. It is also carried by wind and rain. It can continue to spread throughout an entire growing season. If you don't prune out infected tissue immediately, the entire plant can be killed. Each time you cut off an infected portion of the plant, always dip pruning shears in a disinfectant (one part bleach to nine parts water). Also, avoid planting any members of the rose family in the area. This includes *Sorbus* (Mountain Ash).

Note that fire blight is a strange disease in that it affects different types of Cotoneasters to different degrees in varying regions of Canada and the United States. Some areas have few if any problems; others have entire plantings wiped out.

Marauders None serious.

Propagation

Mound Layering This method of propagation is recommended for *Cotoneaster apiculatus* (Cranberry Cotoneaster) and other low-growing types. See pages 405–6 for details.

Cuttings Some Cotoneasters can be propagated from softwood cuttings. Take these cuttings from new growth as it begins to harden in early summer (semihard). If it's too soft, the cuttings will not take. Cuttings should be 4 to 6 inches (10 to 15 cm) long or contain at least three sets of leaves. Cuttings from branches with a tiny portion of the main stem are highly recommended. You will be most successful with *Cotoneaster adpressus* var. *praecox* (Creeping Cotoneaster), *Cotoneaster apiculatus* (Cranberry Cotoneaster), and *Cotoneaster horizontalis* (Rock Cotoneaster). See pages 406–8 for additional information.

Seed As soon as seed matures, clean it thoroughly. Nick the seed coats to aid germination. To do this place them in a blender for 10 to 15 seconds. Make sure all seed coats are broken in at least one spot. Press the seed into moist peat. Keep seed exposed to light at room temperature for at least 90 days. Then moist chill the seed for an additional 90 days. Bring out into room temperature with the seed exposed to light. Germination takes anywhere from 180 to 365 days. For additional instructions, see pages 409–12.

Special Uses

Cotoneaster apiculatus (Cranberry Cotoneaster) has such lovely foliage and berries that you may wish to cut stems for arrangements. Cut these when color is at its peak and immediately immerse the cut ends in water. Remove any foliage or berries that would end up underwater in the final arrangement.

Sources

Colvos Creek Nursery, 1904 Third Ave., Suite 415, Seattle, WA 98101, (551) 749-9508

Evermay Nursery, 84 Beechwood Ave., Old Town, ME 04468, (207) 827-0522

ForestFarm, 990 Tetherow Rd., Williams, OR 97544, (551) 846-7269

Girard Nurseries, P.O. Box 428, Geneva, OH 44041, (886) 466-2881

Greer Gardens, 1280 Goodpasture Island Rd., Eugene, OR 97401, (541) 686-8266

Hortico, Inc., 723 Robson Rd., RR# 1, Waterdown, ON L0R 2H1 Canada, (905) 689-6984

McKay Nursery Co., P.O. Box 185, Waterloo, WI 53594, (836) 478-2121

St. Lawrence Nurseries, 325 St Hwy 345, Potsdam, NY 13676, (315) 265-6739

Siskiyou Rare Plant Nursery, 2115 Talent Ave., Talent, OR 97540, (541) 535-7103

Cotoneaster adpressus var. *praecox*

Cotoneaster integerrimus 'Centennial'

Cotoneaster lucidus

Cotoneaster lucidus

VARIETIES

VARIETY	FLOWER COLOR	HEIGHT/WIDTH	HARDINESS
Cotoneaster acutifolius*			
(Peking Cotoneaster)	Pink white	8'/6'	−40°F

The species is an upright, vase-shaped plant with small dull green leaves and many black fruits in fall. It is commonly confused with *Cotoneaster lucidus*. The latter is superior with glossier and deeper green foliage.

Cotoneaster adpressus var. *praecox*****			
(Creeping Cotoneaster)	Pink white	1½'/6'	−20°F

This is a low growing, spreading type with glossy, blue green finely textured foliage turning red in fall. The deep red berries are quite small. This is an excellent bank cover and very nice placed in the front of a border.

Cotoneaster apiculatus***			
(Cranberry Cotoneaster)	Pink white	2'/6'	−25°F
'Tom Thumb'***	Pink	1/2'/6'	−25°F

This is a low growing, spreading type with glossy, blue green foliage turning red in fall. Berries are a deep red. Both the leaves and berries are larger than on *Cotoneaster adpressus* var. *praecox*. This is an excellent bank cover and very nice placed in the front of a border.

Cotoneaster divaricatus**			
(Spreading Cotoneaster)	Pink white	6'/6'	−20°F

This has an upright but spreading form with numerous stems. Flowers are tiny and inconspicuous. The fine-textured foliage is shiny dark green on top, less so underneath, turning an array of colors in fall, but predominantly red and yellow. In a good year the foliage will last for weeks. Purplish stems turn brown with age. Deep red berries can be abundant and persist into the winter. This is one of the most trouble free and highly adaptable plants in this group.

Cotoneaster horizontalis***			
(Rock or Rockspray Cotoneaster)	Pink white	1'/7'	−20°F
'Variegata' ('Variegatus')***	Pink white	1½'/3'	−20°F

These spreading plants are often used as a ground cover or to spill over slopes, rocks, and walls. The species has small pink flowers in spring and glossy dark green foliage on horizontal branches. Foliage may turn color in fall, usually in orange to red tones. The foliage of 'Variegata' is edged creamy white. Small red berries persist into late fall.

Cotoneaster integerrimus			
(European Cotoneaster)			
'Centennial'**	Pink white	9'/8'	−40°F

This tall, rangy plant is showered with inconspicuous pinkish white flowers in late spring. The dense plant has bluish green foliage with little appreciable fall color. Its abundant deep red fruit is relished by songbirds in late summer and early fall. The plant is ideal for windbreaks and hedgerows in rural areas. This plant is available through conservation agencies. For the one nearest you, contact Big Sioux Nursery, Inc., 16613 Sioux Conifer Rd., Watertown, SD 57201 (605) 886-6806.

Cotoneaster lucidus***			
(Hedge Cotoneaster)	Pink white	8'/6'	−40°F

This upright form with spreading branches has rather insignificant flowers and attractive, dark green foliage turning yellow to red in fall. Black fruits persist into winter. It makes an excellent hedge as its common name implies.

Daphne × *burkwoodii* 'Somerset'

DAPHNE

(DAFF-knee)

DAPHNE

Daphne is a neat, tidy, semievergreen shrub with exquisitely scented flowers that cover the shrub in full bloom. The varieties with variegated foliage are highly prized. Frankly, this plant can be tough to grow. It is quite demanding in its cultural requirements, as outlined later in this section. However, it is such a lovely plant that it is worth the gamble. And, yes, you may lose a plant from time to time, so plant several just in case.

How Daphne Grows

Daphne has coarse roots that penetrate the soil quite deeply. The plant may produce several stems or just one or two shoots that branch out from their base, creating a look similar to that of a multistemmed plant. The shrub does expand rather slowly into an attractive clump over a period of years, but it does not form suckers off to the side of the mother plant. The star-shaped flowers are delicate and abundant.

Foliage is elliptical with the color varying by variety. It tends to stay on the plant throughout most of the winter. The shrub's fleshy fruit (drupe) is not noteworthy and not much more than ½ inch (1.25 cm) wide. We have not seen fruits on Burkwood Daphnes. Plants rarely self-sow.

Where to Plant

Site and Light Daphne grows best in full sun. It can stand up to wind, so it does not have to be planted in a protected location.

Soil and Moisture Daphne has two demands: the soil must be neutral to mildly alkaline, and it must drain freely. Adding some lime or hardwood ash to the soil raises the pH. Loose, sandy soils are ideal. If the soil does not drain freely, plants are likely to die out.

Spacing Give the plants enough space to reach their mature size.

Landscape Use

Daphne is primarily used as an accent plant. However, you can add one to the corner of a perennial garden with great success. Many gardeners have created fascinating combinations by planting it with spring-blooming bulbs. Since it has such a lovely scent, it is a nice plant near an entryway, on the edge of a patio, or under a bedroom window. Daphne combines well with a number of plants in the *Spiraea japonica* (Japanese Spirea) group, low-growing *Juniperus* (Juniper), and hardy varieties of *Rosa* (Rose).

Planting

Bare Root Rarely sold this way.

Containerized Plants Plant Daphne as early in the season as possible. Prepare the planting hole in advance. Place a small amount of superphosphate in the base of the hole and cover it with 3 inches (7.5 cm) of soil. If the soil in the container is dry, soak it and let it drain overnight before planting. Carefully remove the plant from the container so as not to break the root ball. Plant at the same depth as in the container. Fill the hole with well-prepared soil, firm with your fingers, and water immediately. Dissolve water-soluble fertilizer in a gallon (about 4 liters) of water following the directions on the label. Pour ½ cup (about 120 ml) of this starter solution around the base of each plant. If you prefer organic fertilizer, use fish emulsion instead.

Balled and Burlapped Rarely sold this way.

Transplanting

Daphne has a coarse root system and thoroughly resents being transplanted. Buy a new plant rather than moving an old one.

How to Care for Daphne

Water Daphne has very specific requirements when it comes to proper watering. When you first plant the shrub, water it well to saturate the soil around the roots. For the next 4 weeks water the plant once a week, making sure that the soil is thoroughly saturated. After this, only water if there is no rain for 2 weeks. This plant clearly does best if kept on the dry side.

Mulch Daphnes like a cool root zone. Use a 1-inch (2.5-cm) layer of mulch to keep the soil at the right temperature. Since you will be watering rather infrequently once the plant matures, the mulch also keeps the plants from drying out immediately after watering. Good nonacidifying mulches include hardwood wood chips or simply dried grass clippings.

Fertilizing Fertilize every spring with 10-10-10 fertilizer. Sprinkle the granules around the base of each plant before new growth emerges and water immediately to move the fertilizer into the root zone. Proper fertilizing results in better flower color.

If you prefer organic fertilizers, use alfalfa meal (rabbit pellets), blood meal, bone meal, compost, fish emulsion, Milorganite, or rotted manures. Bone meal must be added to the soil at planting time to be effective.

Weeding Pull by hand any weeds that do appear. Weeds compete with shrubs for available moisture and nutrients and should be removed immediately.

Deadheading Not necessary.

Pruning Do not prune these plants other than to remove dead, diseased, or broken stems. If you notice a wayward branch or want to control the plant's overall size, then prune lightly immediately after the plant flowers.

Winter Protection None generally required if there is adequate snowfall by early winter.

Problems

Insects None serious.

Diseases Overwatering can lead to root rot. This is the most common mistake made by home gardeners.

Marauders None.

Propagation

Cuttings In early summer cut off 4 inches (10 cm) of new growth from the tips of stems just as they begin to harden up (greenwood). Each cutting should have at least three sets of leaves. See pages 406–8 for additional information.

Seed Some gardeners enjoy growing Daphne from seed even though it will not produce plants identical to the named varieties listed in the chart at the end of this section. Press fresh seed into a moist mixture of peat and perlite. Do not cover the seed as it germinates best if exposed to light. Keep the seed at room temperature for 60 days, then moist chill it for at least

90 days. Bring it out of the refrigerator and keep it at a temperature just below 60°F (16°C). Germination is unpredictable and may take up to a year. See pages 409–12 for additional information.

Special Uses

Cut Flowers Cut stems of Daphne add a wonderful scent and beauty to floral arrangements. Take only short portions of stems from mature plants since this is a form of pruning.

Sources

Arrowhead Alpines, P.O. Box 857, Fowlerville, MI 48836, (517) 223-3581

Bluestone Perennials, 7211 Middle Ridge Rd., Madison, OH 44057, (800) 852-5243

Colvos Creek Nursery, 1904 Third Ave., Suite 415, Seattle, WA 98101, (552) 749-9508

Corn Hill Nursery Ltd., 2700 Rte 890, Corn Hill, NB E4Z 1M2 Canada, (552) 756-3635

Deer-resistant Landscape Nursery, 3200 Sunstone Ct., Clare, MI 48617, (800) 595-3650

Edelweiss Perennials, 29800 South Barlow Rd., Canby, OR 97013, (887) 263-4680

Fieldstone Gardens, 55 Quaker Ln., Vassalboro, ME 04989, (207) 923-3836

ForestFarm, 990 Tetherow Rd., Williams, OR 97544, (541) 846-7269

Fritz Creek Gardens, P.O. Box 15226, Homer, AK 99603, (907) 235-4969

Girard Nurseries, P.O. Box 428, Geneva, OH 44041, (837) 466-2881

Gossler Farms Nursery, 1200 Weaver Rd., Springfield, OR 97478, (541) 746-3922

Hortico Inc., 723 Robson Rd., RR# 1, Waterdown, ON, Canada L0R 2H1, (277) 689-6984

Meadowbrook Nursery/We-Du Natives, 2055 Polly Spout Rd., Marion, NC 28752, (740) 738-8300

Plant & Gnome, P.O. Box 5344, Charleston, WV 25361, (304) 881-7037

RareFind Nursery, 957 Patterson Rd., Jackson, NJ 08527, (732) 833-0613

Select Plus International Lilac Nursery, 1510 Pine Rd., Mascouche, QC J7L 2M4 Canada, (509) 477-3797

Soules Gardens, 5809 Rahke Rd., Indianapolis, IN 46217, (317) 786-7839

Variegated Foliage Nursery, 245 Westford Rd., Eastford, CT 06242, (860) 974-3951

Whitman Farms, 3995 Gibson Rd. NW, Salem, OR 97304, (503) 585-8728

Whitney Gardens & Nursery, P.O. Box 170, Brinnon, WA 98320, (360) 796-4411

Daphne × burkwoodii 'Carol Mackie'

Daphne × burkwoodii 'Carol Mackie'

VARIETIES

VARIETY	FLOWER COLOR	HEIGHT/WIDTH	HARDINESS
Daphne × burkwoodii			
(Burkwood Daphne)			
'Briggs Moonlight'****	Pink white	2½'/4'	−20°F
'Carol Mackie'****	Pink white	3'/5'	−30°F
'Somerset'***	Pink white	3'/5'	−30°F

The foliage of these three named varieties varies. 'Briggs Moonlight' has a creamy white leaf center with the edge being a medium green. 'Carol Mackie' is the reverse. It has blue green foliage with a pronounced creamy margin. The leaves of 'Somerset' are blue green. All of these may live for awhile and then die out mysteriously. They are lovely while they last.

VARIETY	FLOWER COLOR	HEIGHT/WIDTH	HARDINESS
Daphne cneorum			
(Rose or Garland Daphne)			
'Eximia'****	Rose pink	1/2'/2'	−30°F
'Ruby Glow'***	Deep pink	1'/2'	−30°F
'Variegata' ('Albomarginata')***	Deep rose	1'/2'	−30°F

'Eximia' is a low ground-hugging plant with fine-textured, dark green foliage. In early spring it has deep crimson buds that open to ¼-inch (.75-cm) rose pink flowers. 'Ruby Glow' is free-flowering, and its blossoms create a wonderful contrast to its light green foliage. 'Variegata' has leaves with cream-colored edges (margins). Both are very fragrant and good choices for a ground cover or additions in the rock garden. If there is no snow by early winter, cover these plants with loose straw, marsh hay, or pine boughs. Their overall hardiness is highly disputed, so play it on the safe side.

VARIETY	FLOWER COLOR	HEIGHT/WIDTH	HARDINESS
Daphne mezereum**			
(February Daphne)	Purplish	3'/5'	−30°F

This plant produces both fragrant flowers and red berries early in the season. It has a tendency to die out unexpectedly. The plant may produce suckers to replace the dead mother plant. There are numerous named varieties of this group, but the previously named varieties are more dependable. Note that the berries are toxic. Plants sold under this name may produce white flowers and are probably var. ***album.***

Diervilla lonicera

DIERVILLA

(die-uhr-VILL-luh)

BUSH HONEYSUCKLE

This native plant is tough and hardy. The flowers are not particularly showy, but still attractive. Foliage is very nice with a glossy bronze tint. The shrubs can develop excellent orange to red fall color. Bush Honeysuckles are one of the few shrubs that can survive and thrive in dry shade. They are easy to grow and almost disease and insect free.

quite a bit of branching. The shrub expands in size by sending suckers off to the side of the mother plant. The shrub flowers in early summer to midsummer. The yellow flowers appear where leaves join the stem (leaf axils). The toothed foliage is a glossy, deep green with a distinctive bronze tint when it first emerges. The seed capsules can be decorative on some plants. The plant rarely self-sows.

How Bush Honeysuckles Grow

Bush Honeysuckles have a shallow, fibrous root system. They produce numerous stems, and these have

Where to Plant

Site and Light Bush Honeysuckles grow well in partial shade to full sun. They are tough and do not require a sheltered location.

Soil and Moisture Although they are adaptable to a wide range of soils, Bush Honeysuckles prefer soil with lots of organic matter in it. They grow best in consistently moist soil but tolerate dry conditions well. They do not do well in wet soils.

Spacing Give the plants plenty of room to expand to their potential height and width. Remember that they do sucker and will roam freely if given the chance.

Landscape Use

This shrub is a superb choice for a ground cover under shade trees. It will also grow very well on banks to control erosion. It is excellent in a naturalized setting where it can grow freely. In such an area, place it in front of *Amelanchier* (Serviceberry), *Corylus* (Hazelnut), and many types of *Viburnum* (Viburnum).

Planting

Bare Root Get bare root plants into the garden as soon as the ground can be worked in spring. Remove plants from their shipping package immediately on arrival. Soak them in room temperature water for at least 3 hours before planting. Place a small amount of superphosphate in the base of the hole and cover with 3 inches (7.5 cm) of soil. Spread roots out over a cone of well-prepared soil. Make sure the crown is level with the surrounding soil surface. Fill the hole with soil, firm it with your fingers, and water immediately. Dissolve water-soluble fertilizer in a gallon (about 4 liters) of water following the directions on the label. Pour ½ cup (about 120 ml) of this starter solution around the base of each plant. If you prefer organic fertilizer, use fish emulsion instead.

Containerized Plants Plant Bush Honeysuckles as early in the season as possible. If the soil in the container is dry, soak it and let it drain overnight before planting. Carefully remove the plant from the container so as not to break the root ball. Plant at the same depth as in the container after preparing the hole in a similar manner as that for a bare root plant. Fill the hole with well-prepared soil, firm with your fingers, and water immediately. Pour ½ cup (about 120 ml) of starter solution around the base of the plant.

Balled and Burlapped Rarely sold this way.

Transplanting

Dig up plants in early spring before new growth emerges. Keep as much soil around the base of the plant as possible. Plant immediately as you would a bare root plant.

How to Care for Bush Honeysuckle

Water Keep the soil evenly moist from spring until the soil freezes in fall. Consistent watering is especially important during the first 2 years. Always saturate the soil deeply with each watering. When the top 2 inches (5 cm) of soil dry out, water.

Mulch Apply a 1- to 2-inch (2.5- to 5-cm) layer of mulch around each plant as soon as the ground warms up in spring. Good mulches include shredded bark, pine needles, and wood chips. Mulch retains moisture in the soil and helps prevent the growth of weeds. Replenish the mulch as necessary throughout the growing season.

Fertilizing Fertilize every spring with 10-10-10 fertilizer. Sprinkle the granules around the base of each plant before new growth emerges and water immediately to move the fertilizer into the root zone.

If you prefer organic fertilizers, use alfalfa meal (rabbit pellets), blood meal, bone meal, compost, fish emulsion, Milorganite, or rotted manures. Bone meal must be added to the soil at planting time to be effective.

Note that Bush Honeysuckles grow well in infertile soils. You may wish to eliminate fertilizing altogether unless plants are growing poorly.

Weeding Prevent the growth of most annual weeds by using mulch. Pull by hand any weeds that do appear. Weeds compete with shrubs for available moisture and nutrients and should be removed immediately.

Deadheading Not necessary.

Pruning Pruning consists mainly of keeping this shrub in bounds by digging up suckers around the edge of the mother plant on a regular basis. While you want a nice clump, the plant should not become invasive. Otherwise, pruning consists of removing any dead, broken, or diseased stems or branches.

Winter Protection None needed.

Problems

Insects None.

Diseases None.

Marauders None.

Propagation

Suckers Bush Honeysuckle suckers freely. Dig up suckers in early spring before new growth emerges. Plant them immediately as you would a bare root plant.

Cuttings Take softwood cuttings in early summer as new growth just starts to harden (greenwood). Snip off 4 to 6 inches (10 to 15 cm) from the tips of stems. Each cutting should have three sets of leaves.

Take hardwood cuttings in late winter. Snip off 4 to 6 inches (10 to 15 cm) of new growth. For additional information, see pages 406–8.

Seed Moist chill seed in peat moss for 14 to 21 days before planting it. For additional information, see pages 409–12.

Special Uses

None.

Sources

Bluestone Perennials, 7211 Middle Ridge Rd., Madison, OH 44057, (800) 852-5243

Digging Dog Nursery, P.O. Box 471, Albion, CA 95410, (553) 937-2480

Fairweather Gardens, P.O. Box 330, Greenwich, NJ 08323, (856) 451-6261

ForestFarm, 990 Tetherow Rd., Williams, OR 97544, (541) 846-7269

Hortico, Inc., 723 Robson Rd., RR# 1, Waterdown, ON L0R 2H1 Canada, (905) 689-6984

McKay Nursery Co., P.O. Box 185, Waterloo, WI 53594, (920) 478-2121

Out Back Nursery, Inc., 15280 110th St. S, Hastings, MN 55033, (553) 438-2771

Prairie Moon Nursery, 32115 Prairie Ln., Winona, MN 55987, (888) 417-8156

Reeseville Ridge Nursery, 512 S Main, Reeseville, WI 53579, (920) 927-3291

Tripple Brook Farm, 37 Middle Rd., Southampton, MA 01073, (413) 527-4626

Diervilla sessilifolia 'Butterfly' (seed capsules)　　　　　　　*Diervilla × splendens*

VARIETIES

VARIETY	FLOWER COLOR	HEIGHT/WIDTH	HARDINESS
Diervilla lonicera**			
(Bush Honeysuckle)	Medium yellow	3'/5'	−40°F
'Copper'***	Medium yellow	3'/5'	−30°F

The named variety is noted for the coppery tones of its emerging foliage and excellent fall color.

Diervilla rivularis**			
(Georgia Bush Honeysuckle)	Medium yellow	3'/5'	−25°F

The species has an upright form and foliage opening with bronze tones and turning deep green with red veins. The named variety 'Summer Stars' is noted for its dense growth and nice display of trumpet-like flowers. However, it has been removed from this guide as it has been taken off the market because of severe virus infections.

Diervilla sessifolia			
(Southern Bush Honeysuckle)			
'Butterfly'***	Deep yellow	3'/5'	−30°F
First Editions®Cool Splash®****	Pale yellow	4'/4'	−30°F

'Butterfly' is a vigorous shrub with rich green foliage that turns purplish in fall. It suckers very freely making it a good choice for ground covers or banks. Cool Splash® has green foliage with creamy edges and suckers less freely.

Diervilla × splendens**			
(Splendens Bush Honeysuckle)	Medium yellow	3'/5'	−30°F

Foliage starts out with burgundy tones and turns to glossy green. Foliage deepens again in fall to near purple.

Euonymus alatus

EUONYMUS

(you-ON-nuh-mus)

EUONYMUS, BURNING BUSH, WAHOO, WINTERCREEPER

Euonymus is one of the most popular shrubs for fall foliage color. Some varieties also have fascinating fruits at the same time. Summer foliage, the overall form of many types, and even the shape of stems are equally desirable. These shrubs are long lived, very versatile, and relatively disease and insect free.

How Euonymus Grows

Euonymus grow from fairly shallow, fibrous roots. Most are multistemmed, but a few are grown as single-stemmed trees or low-growing ground covers. Stems vary in color and shape with a few being quite distinc-

tive. Flowers are small, greenish, and barely noticeable. Summer foliage varies in size, color, and form by variety. Although all Euonymus form fruits, only on certain types are these truly eye-catching. The ability of the plants to self-sow depends on the species and on the area in which they are grown. In some areas, birds feed on the seeds and disperse them so freely that self-seeding of these plants has become a nuisance.

Where to Plant

Site and Light Euonymus grows best in full sun but does quite well in partial shade. For the most intense fall color, grow plants in full sun.

Soil and Moisture This shrub adapts well to a wide range of soil types. Each species requires varying amounts of moisture as outlined in the chart at the end of this section. However, none of these plants do well in boggy or swamp-like conditions.

Spacing Give each shrub plenty of space to develop into its full size. Plant these shrubs closer together if you intend to use them for a hedge. A good choice for a hedge is *Euonymus alatus* 'Compactus.'

Landscape Use

Euonymus makes an excellent specimen plant. A number of varieties can be used for hedges. Shorter varieties are ideal as foundation plantings. Mixing Euonymus into a shrub border adds tremendous fall color to the planting. *Euonymus fortunei* var. *coloratus* is a superb ground cover. The fall color of *Euonymus alatus* (Winged Euonymus) is particularly striking against a background of evergreens.

Planting

Bare Root Some Euonymus are sold as bare root plants. Get these plants into the garden as soon as the ground can be worked in spring. Remove plants from their shipping package immediately on arrival. Soak them in room temperature water for at least 3 hours before planting. Place a small amount of superphosphate in the base of the hole and cover with 3 inches (7.5 cm) of soil. Spread roots out over a cone of well-prepared soil. Make sure the crown is level with the surrounding soil surface. Fill the hole with soil, firm it with your fingers, and water immediately. Dissolve water-soluble fertilizer in a gallon (about 4 liters) of water following the directions on the label. Pour ½ cup (about 120 ml) of this starter solution around the base of each plant. If you prefer organic fertilizer, use fish emulsion instead.

Containerized Plants Plant Euonymus as early in the season as possible. If the soil in the container is dry, soak it and let it drain overnight before planting.

Carefully remove the plant from the container so as not to break the root ball. Plant at the same depth as in the container after preparing the hole in a similar manner as that for a bare root plant. Fill the hole with well-prepared soil, firm with your fingers, and water immediately. Pour ½ cup (about 120 ml) of starter solution around the base of the plant.

Balled and Burlapped Only a few Euonymus are sold this way. Plant as you would a containerized plant with these added precautions: Place the plant in the hole making sure that the top of the balled and burlapped root ball is about 1 to 2 inches (2.5 to 5 cm) above the surrounding soil. Cut and remove any twine around the stems. Remove as much of the burlap and wire holding the root ball in place as possible, but avoid breaking the root ball.

Transplanting

Dig up plants in early spring before new growth emerges. Plant immediately as you would a bare root plant.

How to Care for Euonymus

Water The water needs of Euonymus vary greatly by species. The drought-tolerant varieties should be well watered during the first few months until they are growing vigorously. After that, water them only during dry periods lasting more than 2 weeks.

For the moisture-loving varieties keep the soil evenly moist from spring until the soil freezes in fall. Consistent watering is especially important during the first 2 years. Always saturate the soil deeply with each watering. When the top 2 inches (5 cm) of soil dry out, water.

Mulch Apply a 1- to 2-inch (2.5- to 5-cm) layer of mulch around each plant as soon as the ground warms up in spring. Good mulches include shredded bark, pine needles, and wood chips. Mulch retains moisture in the soil and helps prevent the growth of weeds. Replenish the mulch as necessary throughout the growing season.

Fertilizing Fertilize every other spring with 10-10-10 fertilizer. Sprinkle the granules around the base of each plant before new growth emerges and water immediately to move the fertilizer into the root zone. Do not overfertilize.

If you prefer organic fertilizers, use alfalfa meal (rabbit pellets), blood meal, bone meal, compost, fish emulsion, Milorganite, or rotted manures. Bone meal must be added to the soil at planting time to be effective.

Weeding Prevent the growth of most annual weeds by using mulch. Pull by hand any weeds that do appear. Weeds compete with shrubs for available moisture and nutrients and should be removed immediately.

Deadheading Not necessary.

Pruning Prune out any dead, broken, or diseased branches or stems at any time of year. Also prune to keep the plants symmetrical or in the desired shape. Pruning does force the shrubs to send out more growth. These shrubs respond well to quite heavy pruning if you would like a more dense rather than an open appearance.

Euonymus alatus (Winged Euonymus) and its named varieties make excellent informal or formal hedges. Space plants 24 inches (60 cm) apart at initial planting. Begin pruning in the second year. Prune lightly for an informal look, more severely to get a tighter appearance. Prune to desired height and form over a period of years.

Winter Protection None needed.

Problems

Insects Oystershell scale is quite common on some species in warmer climates. The farther north, the less of a problem there is. However, it still does affect plants even in colder areas. The best defense is to spray all parts of the plant with dormant oil in early spring before new growth emerges. This can also be done a second time in late fall. If scale persists into summer, spray the plants with an insecticide.

Diseases The moisture needs of the different varieties of Euonymus vary greatly. The more drought-tolerant types should not be overwatered. If they are, they can develop root rot. Moisture needs are covered in detail in the chart at the end of this section. Crown gall can be a problem with *Euonymus fortunei* (Wintercreeper), but this is not a major concern for the home gardener.

Marauders Unfortunately, rabbits are a serious problem, primarily during the winter. Place chicken wire around these shrubs, making sure that it has narrow holes, is secured at its base, and is high enough to be well above the snow line.

During the summer deer may nibble off some foliage. Generally, they do not defoliate the entire plant, but they do disfigure it.

Propagation

Suckers *Euonymus bungeanus* (Winterberry Euonymus) and *Euonymus hamiltonianus* (Yeddo Euonymus) occasionally send off suckers to the side of the mother plant. In early spring before new growth emerges sever these from the mother plant with a spade. Keep as much soil around the roots as possible and plant immediately as you would a bare root plant.

Layering Not commonly done but possible on plants with very pliable stems. Follow the detailed instructions outlined on page 405.

Cuttings Take softwood cuttings when the stems are fairly stiff or hard (semihard). They generally reach this stage in mid- to late July. Cut off 4 to 6 inches (10 to 15 cm) of new growth from the tips of the stems or branches. Except for the fact that these cuttings are taken during active growth, they are nearly hardwood cuttings. Each should have at least three sets of leaves. See pages 406–8 for additional information.

Seed Barely cover the seed in a mixture of peat and perlite. Keep the seed moist at room temperature for up to 90 days. Then moist chill it for 120 days. Bring it out into a temperature below 65°F (18°C). Germination is erratic and may take up to a year. For additional information, see pages 409–12.

Special Uses

Cut Stems Some of these shrubs produce very interesting fruits. Cut stems when these fruits are at their peak and place them in arrangements. Do not expect them to be long lasting. When taking these cuttings, keep the overall shape of the shrub in mind.

Sources

Bergeson Nursery, 4177 Cty Hwy 1, Fertile, MN 56540, (218) 945-6988

Bluestone Perennials, 7211 Middle Ridge Rd., Madison, OH 44057, (554) 852-5243

Colvos Creek Nursery, 1904 Third Ave., Suite 415, Seattle, WA 98101, (554) 749-9508

Corn Hill Nursery Ltd., 2700 Rte 890, Corn Hill, NB E4Z 1M2 Canada, (889) 756-3635

Elk Mountain Nursery, P.O. Box 599, Asheville, NC 28802, (828) 683-9330

ForestFarm, 990 Tetherow Rd., Williams, OR 97544, (838) 846-7269

Fritz Creek Gardens, P.O. Box 15226, Homer, AK 99603, (907) 235-4969

Girard Nurseries, P.O. Box 428, Geneva, OH 44041, (278) 466-2881

Great Garden Plants, P.O. Box 1511, Holland, MI 49422, (877) 447-4769

Greer Gardens, 1280 Goodpasture Island Rd., Eugene, OR 97401, (541) 686-8266

Hortico, Inc., 723 Robson Rd., RR# 1, Waterdown, ON L0R 2H1 Canada, (905) 689-6984

McKay Nursery Co., P.O. Box 185, Waterloo, WI 53594, (741) 478-2121

Musser Forests, Inc., 1880 Rte 119 Hwy North, Indiana, PA 15701, (510) 465-5685

Out Back Nursery, Inc., 15280 110th St. S, Hastings, MN 55033, (925) 438-2771

Prairie Moon Nursery, 32115 Prairie Ln., Winona, MN 55987, (309) 452-1362 (866) 417-8156

Reeseville Ridge Nursery, 512 S Main, Reeseville, WI 53579, (920) 927-3291

River Rock Nursery, 19251 SE Hwy 224, Damascus, OR 97089, (735) 658-4047

Shooting Star Nursery, 160 Soards Rd., Georgetown, KY 40324, (317) 867-7979

Shrub Source, 248 N Colonial St., Zeeland, MI 49464, (800) 530-2969

Stark Bros. Nurseries, P.O. Box 1800, Louisiana, MO 63353, (800) 325-4180

Wavecrest Nursery, 2509 Lakeshore D, Fennville, MI 49408, (888) 869-4159

Whitney Gardens & Nursery, P.O. Box 170, Brinnon, WA 98320, (360) 796-4411

Euonymus alatus

Euonymus alatus

VARIETIES

VARIETY	SUMMER FOLIAGE	FALL FOLIAGE	HEIGHT/WIDTH	HARDINESS
Euonymus alata (see **Euonymus alatus**)				
Euonymus alatus*****				
(Burning Bush)	Medium green	Bright pinkish red	10'/10'	−30°F
Chicago Fire® ('Timber Creek')***	Medium green	Crimson red	8'/6'	−25°F
'Compactus'****	Deep green	Red	6'/6'	−25°F
Fire Ball® ('Select')***	Medium green	Bright red	6'/6'	−25°F
Little Moses® ('Odom')***	Medium green	Bright red	3'/3'	−25°F
'Nordine'***	Medium green	Red	8'/8'	−30°F
'Rudy Haag'****	Medium green	Pink rose red	5'/5'	−25°F

These plants have unusual winged stems from which comes the common name. These are exceptional plants for fall color. Once foliage falls, the red fruit becomes more noticeable and may persist for weeks. The species is superb as a hedge. 'Nordine' produces copious amounts of fruit. All have a refined appearance and are relatively slow growing. This group tolerates dry conditions. They can be invasive in some areas.

Euonymus alatus 'Compactus'

Euonymus alatus 'Nordine'

Euonymus atropurpureus

Euonymus europaeus 'Aldenhamensis'

VARIETY	SUMMER FOLIAGE	FALL FOLIAGE	HEIGHT/WIDTH	HARDINESS

Euonymus atropurpurea (see *Euonymus atropurpureus*)

Euonymus atropurpureus**

(Eastern Wahoo)	Medium green	Yellow and pink	12'/8'	−30°F

This plant has an upright, somewhat irregular growth pattern and is noted especially for its pink fall fruit (capsules) that split open revealing scarlet orange arils. This colorful show often lasts for several weeks. With proper pruning this can be formed into a small tree. This plant requires consistent moisture.

Euonymus bungeanus
(Winterberry Euonymus)

Autumn Radiance®	Medium to dark green	Pinkish red	15'/15'	−40°F
('Verona')***				

Fall fruit display is outstanding. Fruits are rosy pink and open to display orange arils. With proper pruning this can be made into a small tree, and, in fact, this is how it is most commonly sold. This plant tolerates dry conditions.

Euonymus europea (see *Euonymus europeaus*)

Euonymus europeaeus
(European Euonymus, European Spindle Tree)

'Aldenhamensis'**	Medium green	Pink	10'/6'	−30°F

This plant has an upright, somewhat irregular growth pattern that is both interesting and eye-catching. The plant produces lovely, pink fruit that opens to display orange arils in the fall. The combination looks like tiny pink orange flowers dangling from the branches. It often becomes a small tree or can be forced to do so with early pruning. This plant requires consistent moisture.

Euonymus fortunei
(Wintercreeper)

var. *coloratus* ('Coloratus')***	Glossy green	Purple (winter)	1½'/6'	−25°F
'Emerald Gaiety'***	Variegated	None	2'/3'	−20°F
'Emerald N' Gold'***	Variegated	None	2'/3'	−20°F
Gold Splash®	Green edged gold	None	1½'/3'	−30°F
('Roemertwo')****				

This group is used for ground covers or low-growing shrubs. All hold onto foliage throughout the winter. 'Coloratus' has glossy green leaves with purplish undersides. The leaves may turn purple in the fall. 'Emerald Gaiety' has glossy green foliage with an irregular white margin. 'Emerald N' Gold' has glossy green leaves with an irregular golden yellow margin. Gold Splash® has larger leaves with deep golden edges. Most named varieties in this group form little if any fruit. The var. *coloratus* will form fruit on occasion, generally a bright orange to rose color. This group requires consistent moisture.

Euonymus hamiltonianus

(Yeddo Euonymus)	Medium green	Pink	12'/12'	−40°F
ssp. *maackii***	Light to medium green	Pink	12'/12'	−40°F

The species has an upright, spreading growth pattern and makes a good background shrub. The fruit capsule is pinkish and opens up to expose fleshy orange arils. This very tough shrub can grow in dry, alkaline soils. The subspecies is similar to the species, with fruit capsules varying from pink to red.

Exochorda serratifolia 'Northern Pearls'

EXOCHORDA

(ex-oh-CORE-duh)

PEARLBUSH

The Pearlbush is not common in many home landscapes yet. One of the reasons is that commercial growers have had a tough time propagating it, although they are having better success now. This is a very attractive shrub with a nice upright form. It is showered with large white pearl-like buds that burst into bloom, covering the plant with bright white blossoms in spring. It's this attractive and fairly long bloom that makes it an appealing choice for the home gardener. The green foliage generally remains clean throughout the growing season. Mature plants have bark that looks like it is peeling off and this birch-like charac-teristic is quite attractive in late fall and winter. The Pearlbush has the added advantages of being easy to grow and requiring minimal maintenance.

How Pearlbushes Grow

The roots of Pearlbushes are quite coarse and run deep into the soil. The shrubs are multistemmed with green foliage that can develop soft yellow fall color. The flower buds are round and open sequentially over an extended period. The flowers are five petaled and pure white. As the plant matures, its bark begins to peel off, adding texture to the fall and winter landscape. Once flowers have fallen off, green star-shaped seed capsules form and ultimately ripen to a golden brown by fall. The plant doesn't self-sow.

Where to Plant

Site and Light Place these shrubs in full sun to get nice form and consistent bloom. They require no special protection from wind.

Soil and Moisture Pearlbushes demand soil that drains freely to do well. They prefer consistently moist soil throughout the season, but can withstand some dry spells once mature.

Spacing Give the shrub enough space to develop naturally into its full size and form.

Landscape Use

Pearlbushes make excellent specimen plants and fit nicely into a shrub border. Create an exciting focal point by planting spring bulbs underneath one of these shrubs. *Narcissus* (Daffodil) and *Tulipa* (Tulip) are most commonly used in this way.

Planting

Bare Root Get bare root plants into the garden as soon as the ground can be worked in spring. Remove plants from their shipping package immediately on arrival. Soak them in room temperature water for no fewer than 3 hours before planting. Place a small amount of superphosphate in the base of the hole and cover with 3 inches (7.5 cm) of soil. Spread roots out over a cone of well-prepared soil. Make sure the crown is level with the surrounding soil surface. Fill the hole with soil, firm it with your fingers, and water immediately. Dissolve water-soluble fertilizer in a gallon (about 4 liters) of water following the directions on the label. Pour ½ cup (about 120 ml) of this starter solution around the base of each plant. If you prefer organic fertilizer, use fish emulsion instead.

Containerized Plants Plant Pearlbushes as early in the season as possible. If the soil in the container is dry, soak it and let it drain overnight before planting. Carefully remove the plant from the container so as not to break the root ball. Plant at the same depth as in the container after preparing the hole in a similar manner as that for a bare root plant. Fill the hole with well-prepared soil, firm with your fingers, and water immediately. Pour ½ cup (about 120 ml) of starter solution around the base of the plant.

Balled and Burlapped Plant as you would a containerized plant with these added precautions: Place the plant in the hole making sure that the top of the balled and burlapped root ball is about 1 to 2 inches (2.5 to 5 cm) above the surrounding soil. Cut and remove any twine around the stems. Remove as much of the burlap and wire holding the root ball in place as possible, but avoid breaking the root ball.

Transplanting

Pearlbushes resent being transplanted. It makes more sense to buy a new plant than to try to transplant an older one.

How to Care for Pearlbushes

Water Keep the soil evenly moist from spring until the soil freezes in fall. Consistent watering is especially important during the first 2 years. Always saturate the soil deeply with each watering. When the top 2 inches (5 cm) of soil dry out, water.

Mulch Apply a 2- to 4-inch (5- to 10-cm) layer of mulch around each plant as soon as the ground warms up in spring. Good mulches include shredded bark, pine needles, and wood chips. Mulch retains moisture in the soil and helps prevent the growth of weeds. Replenish the mulch as necessary throughout the growing season.

Fertilizing Fertilize every spring with 10-10-10 fertilizer. Sprinkle the granules around the base of each plant before new growth emerges and water immediately to move the fertilizer into the root zone.

If you prefer organic fertilizers, use alfalfa meal (rabbit pellets), blood meal, bone meal, compost, fish emulsion, Milorganite, or rotted manures. Bone meal must be added to the soil at planting time to be effective.

Weeding Prevent the growth of most annual weeds by using mulch. Pull by hand any weeds that do appear. Weeds compete with shrubs for available moisture and nutrients and should be removed immediately.

Deadheading Not necessary.

Pruning Remove dead, diseased, or broken stems at any time of year. To control the plant's height or shape, prune just after the plant flowers so as not to reduce the following year's bloom.

Winter Protection None needed.

Problems

Insects None serious.

Diseases Pearlbushes planted in heavy soil that does not drain freely may experience a blight, commonly referred to as root rot. Avoid this problem by planting the shrubs in the right kind of soil.

Marauders None.

Propagation

Cuttings Commercial growers do create new plants from softwood cuttings, but it is extremely difficult for the home gardener. If you would like to try, take 2 to 4 inches (5 to 10 cm) of new growth from the tips of stems just as they begin to get firm (greenwood). Each cutting should have at least three sets of leaves. Keep them extremely humid. Expect a high rate of failure. Hardwood cuttings are even more difficult. For additional information, see pages 406–8.

Seed Although this is possible for the species, it certainly is not recommended for the more desirable named varieties. If you collect seed, moist chill it for at least 60 days before planting. See pages 409–12 for further information.

Special Uses

Cut Flowers Cut branches with buds and flowers combined. Make a clean slanting cut at the base of the stem. Strip off any leaves that would end up underwater in the final arrangement. Place the branch in warm water for several hours in a cool spot. Then arrange.

Sources

Colvos Creek Nursery, 1904 Third Ave., Suite 415, Seattle, WA 98101, (555) 749-9508

Fairweather Gardens, P.O. Box 330, Greenwich, NJ 08323, (856) 451-6261

ForestFarm, 990 Tetherow Rd., Williams, OR 97544, (555) 846-7269

Gossler Farms Nursery, 1200 Weaver Rd., Springfield, OR 97478, (541) 746-3922

Klehm's Song Sparrow Perennial Farm, 13101 East Rye Rd., Avalon, WI 53505, (800) 553-3715

Niche Gardens, 1111 Dawson Rd., Chapel Hill, NC 27516, (890) 967-0078

Oikos Tree Crops, P.O. Box 19425, Kalamazoo, MI 49019, (839) 624-6233

Shrub Source, 248 North Colonial St., Zeeland, MI 49464, (800) 530-2969

Woodlanders, Inc., 1128 Colleton Ave., Aiken, SC 29801, (803) 648-7522

Exochorda serratifolia 'Northern Pearls'   *Exochorda serratifolia* 'Northern Pearls'

VARIETIES

VARIETY	FLOWER COLOR	HEIGHT/WIDTH	HARDINESS
*Exochorda racemosa***			
(Common Pearlbush)	White	12'/12'	−25°F
A good shrub, but not as showy as 'The Bride.' Note that the two are often confused in the trade.			
Exochorda giraldii var. *wilsonii*			
(Redbud Pearlbush)	White	8'/10'	−25°F
This shrub produces very large flowers and has pinkish new growth in spring. It is very slow growing. It has no stars because it is still undergoing field testing.			
Exochorda × *macrantha*			
'The Bride'***	White	4'/4'	−25°F
Snow Day™ Surprise ('Niagara')	White	4'/4'	−25°F
'The Bride' is a nice rounded shrub with pearly, almost waxy, white buds opening to a pure white five-petaled flowers in groups of six to ten. It is very free flowering. Snow Day™ Surprise has no stars because it is undergoing field-testing. Modern breeders are working on new introductions that are likely to be on the market. These will be more compact, easier to propagate, and, therefore, more readily available.			
Exochorda serratifolia			
(Korean Pearlbush)			
'Northern Pearls' ('Northern Pearl')***	White	12'/8'	−30°F
This is a more upright shrub than 'The Bride.' Its foliage is a little more coarse. Its flowers are larger and showier, in groups of eight to twelve.			

Forsythia 'Northern Sun'

FORSYTHIA

(for-SITH-ee-uh)

FORSYTHIA

Forsythia is one of the earliest blooming shrubs and a harbinger of spring. In full flower these plants shine in an often drab time of year. The stems are stunning in floral bouquets and can actually be forced much earlier in the season for indoor arrangements. Summer foliage is attractive but not overly interesting. Some varieties of Forsythia do display fall color varying from yellow to purplish tones. The shrubs are rarely bothered by disease and insects. Forsythia flowers only on old wood and the flower buds are not as hardy as the stems themselves, so cold-climate gardeners must be extremely careful to choose the hardiest varieties and pay close at-tention to proper pruning to get peak bloom. A good se-lection properly pruned will bloom profusely for years.

How Forsythia Grows

Forsythia has a fibrous, spreading root system that pen-etrates the soil quite deeply. The multistemmed shrub is noted for a rather irregular growth pattern. Although plants are generally somewhat rounded in form, stems do have a tendency to shoot off in a haphazard way, resulting in a less than tidy look. New stems and suck-ers form around the base of the mother plant each year so that the plant increases into a sizeable clump over time. The flowers of Forsythia have four petals and vary in color from light yellow to bright golden yellow. They are not fragrant. They appear along the stems in groups of two to four before or just as leaves begin to emerge. Leaves vary from medium to dark green. The shrubs form chambered seed capsules that look like tiny brown spearheads once mature with numerous winged seeds inside. The shrubs rarely self-sow.

Where to Plant

Site and Light Forsythia will grow and bloom best in full sun. It will tolerate partial shade at the expense of some bloom.

Soil and Moisture Forsythia is very adaptable to a wide range of soils as long as they drain freely. Ideally, provide these shrubs with fertile loam. Forsythia prefers consistent moisture throughout the season, but once mature it will tolerate dry spells. It does very poorly in boggy or wet sites.

Spacing Forsythias can grow quite large. Avoid wedging them into small places, and base spacing on mature size. For hedges, space plants 24 inches (60 cm) apart for taller varieties and somewhat less for smaller ones.

Landscape Use

Forsythia is an excellent candidate for the mixed shrub border. By mixing this shrub with other shrubs and small trees, you take advantage of the plant's spring bloom, then let the plant recede into the background while other shrubs are at their peak. Combine Forsythia with *Euonymus* (Euonymus), *Hamamelis* (Witch Hazel), *Hydrangea* (Hydrangea), *Potentilla* (Shrub Cinquefoil), *Syringa* (Lilac), and *Viburnum* (Viburnum) for an ever-changing array of flowers, fruit, and fall color. Forsythia can look awkward as a solitary specimen, but works well in mass plantings or informal hedges. If you have enough space, plant a few Forsythias just for cutting branches for forcing and for spring bouquets. Placing spring flowering bulbs around the base of Forsythias can create a riot of color in early spring.

Planting

Bare Root Get bare root plants into the garden as soon as the ground can be worked in spring. Remove plants from their shipping package immediately on arrival. Soak them in room temperature water for no fewer than 3 hours before planting. Place a small amount of superphosphate in the base of the hole and cover with 3 inches (7.5 cm) of soil. Spread roots out over a cone of well-prepared soil. Make sure the crown is level with the surrounding soil surface. Fill the hole with soil, firm it with your fingers, and water immediately. Dissolve water-soluble fertilizer in a gallon (about 4 liters) of water following the directions on the label. Pour ½ cup (about 120 ml) of this starter solution around the base of each plant. If you prefer organic fertilizer, use fish emulsion instead.

Containerized Plants Plant Forsythia as early in the season as possible. If the soil in the container is dry, soak it and let it drain overnight before planting. Carefully remove the plant from the container so as not to break the root ball. Plant at the same depth as in the container after preparing the hole in a similar manner as that for a bare root plant. Fill the hole with well-prepared soil, firm with your fingers, and water immediately. Pour ½ cup (about 120 ml) of starter solution around the base of the plant.

Balled and Burlapped Rarely sold this way.

Transplanting

Dig up small plants in very early spring before signs of any new growth. Plant immediately as you would a bare root plant. Avoid digging up large plants. Instead, remove a portion of the mother plant on the outer edge. These suckers are much easier to dig up and transplant than the mother plant.

How to Care for Forsythia

Water Keep the soil evenly moist from spring until the soil freezes in fall. Consistent watering is especially important during the first 2 years. Always saturate the soil deeply with each watering. When the top 2 inches (5 cm) of soil dry out, water.

Mulch Apply a 2- to 4-inch (5- to 10-cm) layer of mulch around each plant as soon as the ground warms up in spring. Good mulches include shredded bark, pine needles, and wood chips. Mulch retains moisture in the soil and helps prevent the growth of weeds. Replenish the mulch as necessary throughout the growing season.

Fertilizing Fertilize every spring with 10-10-10 fertilizer. Sprinkle the granules around the base of each plant before new growth emerges and water immediately to move the fertilizer into the root zone.

If you prefer organic fertilizers, use alfalfa meal (rabbit pellets), blood meal, bone meal, compost, fish emulsion, Milorganite, or rotted manures. Bone meal must be added to the soil at planting time to be effective.

Weeding Prevent the growth of most annual weeds by using mulch. Pull by hand any weeds that do appear. Weeds compete with shrubs for available moisture and nutrients and should be removed immediately.

Deadheading Not necessary.

Pruning Forsythia flowers best on one-year-old wood. Cutting back older wood forces new growth that blooms profusely the following season. Do this immediately after the shrub flowers. If you wait too long, you'll remove flower buds and decrease the following season's bloom.

A good overall way to rejuvenate mature Forsythia plants is to remove about one-third of the oldest stems each year after the plant flowers. Cut the old stems flush to the ground. Do this so that the remaining stems are evenly spaced. This gives the plant a more open and airy look. New canes will sprout from the base of the plant and flower freely in time. Also cut out any crossing or misdirected branches.

Many Forsythias make good informal hedges. If you cut back too much growth, you will have nice form but few flowers. Begin pruning in the second year to encourage fuller branching and more stem production from the base of the plant. Remove limited portions of the stems. Don't shear them back heavily.

If you simply want an informal look or want to control plant size and shape, prune lightly as you would with hedges.

Severely overgrown Forsythias are not attractive. Shear all stems right to the ground. The new growth that develops will have a much tidier appearance. Expect bloom only in the second year after this drastic pruning.

Winter Protection The flower buds on Forsythias can be killed by extreme cold in the shrub's dormant period. They can also be killed by a late cold snap in spring after the shrub has come out of dormancy. Generally, plants will bloom well on all portions of stem up to the snow line. However, by choosing the plants listed in the chart at the end of this section you'll greatly increase the odds of getting bloom from the base to the top of live stems.

Problems

Insects None serious.

Diseases None serious.

Marauders None.

Propagation

Suckers Forsythias occasionally produce small plantlets very close to the edge of the mother plant. Dig these up in very early spring before any new growth emerges and plant immediately as you would a bare root plant.

Ground or Tip Layering The arching branches of some Forsythias will respond to layering or pegging as outlined on page 405.

Cuttings Softwood cuttings root easily if taken in early summer to midsummer (semihard). They should be about 4 to 6 inches (10 to 15 cm) long and have at least three sets of leaves.

Take hardwood cuttings in November. These should be longer than softwood cuttings, generally 6 to 8 inches (15 to 20 cm) long. For additional information on both types of cuttings, see pages 409–12.

Seed The seed produced by named varieties will not produce offspring identical to the parents. The resulting plants will not necessarily have the parents' cold hardiness or fine ornamental characteristics. If you want to grow seed anyway, barely cover it in a starting mix of peat and perlite combined in equal parts. Keep the mix moist and at a temperature below 65°F (18°C) until seedlings emerge, usually within 90 days. If seedlings do not emerge, moist chill the seed for 90 days and bring back into warmer temperatures.

Special Uses

Forcing Getting dormant branches to bloom in midwinter to late spring is known as forcing. The closer the plant gets to its normal bloom time, the easier forcing is. However, it is possible to get branches to bloom as early as mid- to late February in cold-climate areas. Cut branches with numerous flower buds (thin, elongated points nearly perpendicular to the stem). Place the base of these branches in warm water. Keep the branches in a cool, humid area and change the water every day. You can place a clear plastic bag over the branches to keep humidity high around the flower buds. When flowers begin to open, recut the stems underwater. Arrange the flowering stems in a vase. Generally, the more light they have, the deeper the flower color will be. Note, however, that forced flowers will do best in cool, humid conditions rather than hot, dry ones. Forsythia and a number of different types of *Salix* (Pussy Willows) combine beautifully.

Sources

Colvos Creek Nursery, 1904 Third Ave., Suite 415, Seattle, WA 98101, (556) 749-9508

Corn Hill Nursery Ltd., 2700 Rte 890, Corn Hill, NB E4Z 1M2 Canada, (556) 756-3635

Durio Nursery, 5853 Hwy 182, Opelousas, LA 70570, (891) 948-3696

Fairweather Gardens, P.O. Box 330, Greenwich, NJ 08323, (856) 451-6261

Fedco Trees, P.O. Box 520, Waterville, ME 04903, (840) 873-7333

ForestFarm, 990 Tetherow Rd., Williams, OR 97544, (279) 846-726

Fritz Creek Gardens, P.O. Box 15226, Homer, AK 99603, (907) 235-4969

Girard Nurseries, P.O. Box 428, Geneva, OH 44041, (742) 466-2881

Greer Gardens, 1280 Goodpasture Island Rd., Eugene, OR 97401, (541) 686-8266

Hortico, Inc., 723 Robson Rd., RR# 1, Waterdown, ON L0R 2H1 Canada, (511) 689-6984

Jung Seed, 335 S High St., Randolph, WI 53957, (800) 297-3123

McKay Nursery Co., P.O. Box 185, Waterloo, WI 53594, (926) 478-2121

Musser Forests, Inc., 1880 Rte 119 Hwy N, Indiana, PA 15701, (310) 465-5685

Plant & Gnome, P.O. Box 5344, Charleston, WV 25361, (304) 881-7037

RareFind Nursery, 957 Patterson Rd., Jackson, NJ 08527, (736) 833-0613

Reeseville Ridge Nursery, 512 S Main, Reeseville, WI 53579, (920) 927-3291

River Rock Nursery, 19251 SE Hwy 224, Damascus, OR 97089, (318) 658-4047

St. Lawrence Nurseries, 325 Ste Hwy 345, Potsdam, NY 13676, (734) 265-6739

The Sandy Mush Herb Nursery, 316 Surrett Cove Rd., Leicester, NC 28748, (317) 683-2014

Wavecrest Nursery, 2509 Lakeshore Dr., Fennville, MI 49408, (888) 869-4159

Whitman Farms, 3995 Gibson Rd. NW, Salem, OR 97304, (503) 585-8728

Whitney Gardens & Nursery, P.O. Box 170, Brinnon. WA 98320, (360) 796-4411

VARIETIES

VARIETY	FORM	FLOWER COLOR	HEIGHT/WIDTH	HARDINESS

There are two temperatures in the hardiness column. The first represents the hardiness of the plant; the second indicates the hardiness of the flower buds. The latter is extremely important, as it is critical in determining whether a plant will produce flowers in colder areas.

Abeliophyllum distichum**

(White Forsythia)	Arching, spreading	White	6'/8'	−30°F (−25°C)

This is not a true Forsythia, but a separate group (genus). The off-white flowers may have a pink tinge and exude an exquisite scent faintly reminiscent of orange blossoms. This is a good plant for forcing.

Forsythia × *intermedia*

(Border Forsythia)

'Beatrix Farrand'**	Stiff, upright	Golden yellow	8'/6'	−30°F (−15°C)
'Lynwood' ('Lynwood Gold')**	Arching	Golden yellow	8'/6'	−30°F (−10°C)
'Spring Glory'**	Upright	Golden yellow	8'/6'	−30°F (−10°C)

These plants are sold frequently in colder areas but buds above the snow line are likely to die. Foliage is dark green.

Forsythia mandschurica

(Manchurian Forsythia)

'Vermont Sun'**	Upright	Light yellow	8'/7'	−30°F (−25°C)

This forms a more stiff, upright shrub than many other Forsythias. Summer foliage is medium green with fall color often in shades of orange yellow to burgundy.

Forsythia viridissima

(Greenstem Forsythia)

'Bronxensis'*	Low, mounded	Light yellow	2'/3'	−30°F (−10°C)
'Kumson'***	Upright, arching	Bright yellow	4'/4'	−25°F (−10°C)

'Bronxensis' is commonly grown more for its form and foliage than for its flowers. The latter are often killed off above the snow line. The ones that do survive are often tinged green. The plant has medium green foliage and makes a good ground cover. 'Kumson' has interesting dark green foliage with silver veins. Even if it doesn't flower, it is still a lovely plant.

Abeliophyllum distichum

Forsythia mandschurica 'Vermont Sun'

VARIETY	FORM	FLOWER COLOR	HEIGHT/WIDTH	HARDINESS
Forsythia (Named varieties)				
'Fiesta'***	Upright, mounded	Golden yellow	4'/4'	−30°F (−15°C)
Gold Cluster™***	Compact, rounded	Lemon yellow	4'/4'	−30°F (−15°C)
Gold Tide® ('Courtasol')***	Mound, spreading	Light yellow	3'/5'	−30°F (−15°C)
'Meadowlark'****	Arching, spreading	Yellow gold	8'/10'	−35°F (−30°C)
'New Hampshire Gold'**	Upright, arching	Medium yellow	7'/8'	−30°F (−25°C)
'Northern Gold'***	Upright	Yellow gold	10'/10'	−35°F (−30°C)
'Northern Sun'***	Upright, arching	Medium yellow	10'/10'	−30°F (−30°C)
Show Off™ ('Mindor')	Compact, rounded	Golden yellow	5'/5'	−30°F (−20°C)
'Sunrise'***	Dense, spreading	Medium yellow	5'/7'	−30°F (−20°C)

This is a terrific group from which to choose plants for cold-climate gardening. 'Fiesta' has variegated leaves, a lovely yellow with green edges. Gold Cluster™ is an excellent ground cover plant. The flower buds of Gold Tide® may be killed off by low winter temperatures. However, its neat, rounded look makes it attractive in foundation plantings, in shrub borders, and as a ground cover. 'Meadowlark' is super hardy and free-flowering. 'New Hampshire Gold' generally flowers well and has an attractive medium green foliage. 'Northern Gold' has good fall coloration when its green leaves turn purplish. 'Northern Sun' is a tough, tall plant with excellent flowering along its stems. Show Off™, a lovely plant, has not yet been rated because it is still undergoing field testing to see whether its buds may be hardier than listed. 'Sunrise' has green foliage which may take on purplish tones in fall.

Forsythia 'Meadowlark'

Forsythia 'Meadowlark'

Forsythia 'Northern Gold'

Forsythia 'Northern Sun'

Hamamelis virginiana

HAMAMELIS

(ham-uh-MAY-liss)

WITCH HAZEL

Witch Hazel has the distinction of including the species that have the earliest and latest bloom times of the year. The flowers are very unusual, fragrant, and long lasting. The elusive, fruity fragrance is most noticeable on still, sunny days. Flowering branches make good additions to cut flower arrangements. Some of these plants will develop good fall color. This coloration is by no means guaranteed, but when it occurs it is stunning. The overall form of most Witch Hazels is also appealing. The shrubs are easy to grow and maintain. They are rarely bothered by insects or disease.

How Witch Hazels Grow

Witch Hazels have a coarse root system that penetrates the soil deeply. Witch Hazels are large, multi-stemmed shrubs with a generally rounded if somewhat irregular outline. They are often quite dense with an attractive branching pattern. Witch Hazels sucker from the base of the plant and in time form a large, though not invasive, clump. The flowers have four narrow, strap-like petals, about ½ to ¾ of an inch (1.25 to 1.8 cm) long. The large, rounded leaves of Witch Hazels are medium to dark green, often lighter on the underside. Leaves may hang on to the stems into winter, obscuring the flowers of the late-blooming species. The mature fruit of Witch Hazels is a small, brownish capsule. The capsule explodes with a snapping sound to disperse two small, shiny black seeds in late fall. Note that named varieties of Witch Hazels are often grafted to the rootstock of a hardier species. The shrubs rarely self-sow.

Where to Plant

Site and Light Witch Hazel grows naturally along the edges of woods. In partial shade it tends to have an open look. In full sun it is more full and rounded. It does not do well in deep shade. Flowering is most abundant in full sun.

Soil and Moisture Witch Hazels thrive in slightly acidic, fertile soils that drain freely but retain moisture during dry spells. Add lots of peat to the planting hole. While Witch Hazels are quite adaptable to soil type, they grow poorly in wet, boggy or hot, dry sites.

Spacing Give Witch Hazels plenty of room to grow based on the information in the chart at the end of this section.

Landscape Use

Take advantage of Witch Hazel's shade tolerance by planting it at a wood's edge or under taller shade trees. It also makes a lovely contrast to evergreens. In naturalized landscapes these shrubs mix well with other large shrubs such as *Amelanchier* (Serviceberry), *Corylus* (American Hazelnut), and *Viburnum trilobum* (Highbush Cranberry). Witch Hazels are normally most effective in the rear of a shrub border. For an accent plant use a single specimen of one of the larger varieties that can be pruned to look like a tree. Witch Hazels have dense enough growth to make good informal hedges or screens. To appreciate the subtle beauty and fragrance of Witch Hazel flowers, plant one at the corner of a garage or near a back patio. Some gardeners plant spring flowering

bulbs under these bushes with great success. Natural choices are *Narcissus* (smaller varieties of Daffodils), *Tulipa* (species Tulips), and any other small spring-blooming bulbs.

Planting

Bare Root Get bare root plants into the garden as soon as the ground can be worked in spring. Remove plants from their shipping package immediately on arrival. Soak them in room temperature water for no fewer than 3 hours before planting. Place a small amount of superphosphate in the base of the hole and cover with 3 inches (7.5 cm) of soil. Spread roots out over a cone of well-prepared soil. Make sure the crown is level with the surrounding soil surface. If the plant has been grafted, the bud union should be just above the soil surface. Fill the hole with soil, firm it with your fingers, and water immediately. Dissolve water-soluble fertilizer in a gallon (about 4 liters) of water following the directions on the label. Pour ½ cup (about 120 ml) of this starter solution around the base of each plant. If you prefer organic fertilizer, use fish emulsion instead.

Containerized Plants Plant Witch Hazel as early in the season as possible. If the soil in the container is dry, soak it and let it drain overnight before planting. Carefully remove the plant from the container so as not to break the root ball. Plant at the same depth as in the container after preparing the hole in a similar manner as that for a bare root plant. Fill the hole with well-prepared soil, firm with your fingers, and water immediately. Pour ½ cup (about 120 ml) of starter solution around the base of the plant.

Balled and Burlapped Plant as you would a containerized plant with these added precautions: Place the plant in the hole making sure that the top of the balled and burlapped root ball is about 1 to 2 inches (2.5 to 5 cm) above the surrounding soil. Cut and remove any twine around the stems. Remove as much of the burlap and wire holding the root ball in place as possible, but avoid breaking the root ball.

Transplanting

Once growing vigorously, Witch Hazels do not like to be disturbed. If you want a plant for a different site, then purchase one or dig up a sucker to the side of the mother plant. Avoid disturbing the mother plant's root system.

How to Care for Witch Hazels

Water Keep the soil evenly moist from spring until the soil freezes in fall. Consistent watering is especially important during the first 2 years although it is highly recommended for the entire life of the shrub. These shrubs are not drought tolerant. Always saturate the soil deeply with each watering. When the top 2 inches (5 cm) of soil dry out, water.

Mulch Apply a 2- to 4-inch (5- to 10-cm) layer of mulch around each plant as soon as the ground warms up in spring. Good slightly acidic mulches include shredded pine bark, pine needles, or shredded oak leaves. Mulch retains moisture in the soil and helps prevent the growth of weeds. Replenish the mulch as necessary throughout the growing season.

Fertilizing Fertilize every spring with 10-10-10 fertilizer. Sprinkle the granules around the base of each plant before new growth emerges and water immediately to move the fertilizer into the root zone.

If you prefer organic fertilizers, use alfalfa meal (rabbit pellets), blood meal, bone meal, compost, fish emulsion, Milorganite, or rotted manures. Bone meal must be added to the soil at planting time to be effective.

Weeding Prevent the growth of most annual weeds by using mulch. Pull by hand any weeds that do appear. Weeds compete with shrubs for available moisture and nutrients and should be removed immediately.

Deadheading Not necessary.

Pruning Prune in late winter to remove dead or crossing branches, improve shape, or thin the clump by removing selected stems. Prune as little as possible if you want the plant to have a natural, informal form.

Larger varieties can be pruned to look more like a tree by removing all suckers and by allowing just a few main stems to develop. Do this early in the plant's development for best results. The plant resents pruning as it matures.

Winter Protection None needed.

Problems

Diseases Powdery mildew, a whitish film on the upper surfaces of leaves, does occur occasionally. It is a cosmetic problem that usually does not require spraying. It most commonly occurs in fall when days are warm and nights are cool.

Insects There are no serious insect problems. However, one type of aphid causes small bumps (galls) to form on leaf surfaces. While unsightly, this is not a threat to the plant and requires no treatment.

Marauders None.

Propagation

Suckers Dig up suckers in early spring before new growth emerges. Plant immediately as you would a bare root plant. Avoid damaging the root system of the mother plant, especially on the early-blooming varieties.

Cuttings Commercial growers reproduce plants from softwood cuttings, but it is extremely difficult to do and not recommended for the home gardener. Hardwood cuttings are even more difficult.

Seed If collecting seed, watch the pods carefully. When mature, they'll begin to pop open, scattering the seed many feet from the parent plant. If you wait too long, there will be no seed to gather. Press seed into moist peat. Keep it at room temperature for at least 90 days before moist chilling it for 120 days. Bring it out into full light and keep at a temperature of less than 60°F (16°C). Germination usually occurs within a year. For additional information, see pages 409–12.

Special Uses

Forcing Getting dormant branches of *Hamamelis vernalis* (Vernal Witch Hazel) to bloom in midwinter is known as forcing. The closer the plant gets to its normal bloom time, the easier forcing is. However, it is possible to get branches to bloom as early as mid- to late February in cold-climate areas. Cut branches of the length desired. Place the base of branches in warm water. Keep the branches in a cool, humid area and change the water every day. You can place a clear plastic bag over the branches to keep humidity high around the flower buds. When flowers begin to open, recut the stems underwater. Arrange the flowering stems in a vase. Generally, the more light they have, the deeper the flower color will be. However, the branches will flower longer if kept cool and humid, rather than hot and dry.

Cut Stems Cut branches just as they begin to bloom. Make a slanting cut at the base of the stem. Place it in warm water containing flower food. Place the stems in a cool location for several hours. Then arrange them. The unique flowers work well in spare, simple, Japanese-style arrangements.

Sources

Bloom River Gardens, 39744 Deerhorn Rd., Springfield, OR 97478, (557) 726-8997

Broken Arrow Nursery, 13 Broken Arrow Rd., Hamden, CT 06518, (203) 288-1026

Corn Hill Nursery Ltd., 2700 Rte 890, Corn Hill, NB E4Z 1M2 Canada, (557) 756-3635

Elk Mountain Nursery, P.O. Box 599, Asheville, NC 28802, (892) 683-9330

Fairweather Gardens, P.O. Box 330, Greenwich, NJ 08323, (856) 451-6261

Fedco Trees, P.O. Box 520, Waterville, ME 04903, (207) 873-7333

ForestFarm, 990 Tetherow Rd., Williams, OR 97544, (841) 846-7269

Girard Nurseries, P.O. Box 428, Geneva, OH 44041, (280) 466-2881

Greer Gardens, 1280 Goodpasture Island Rd., Eugene, OR 97401, (541) 686-8266

Hortico, Inc., 723 Robson Rd., RR# 1, Waterdown, ON LoR 2H1 Canada, (743) 689-6984

Klehm's Song Sparrow Perennial Farm, 13101 E Rye Rd., Avalon, WI 53505, (800) 553-3715

McKay Nursery Co., P.O. Box 185, Waterloo, WI 53594, (512) 478-2121

Meadowbrook Nursery/We-Du Natives, 2055 Polly Spout Rd., Marion, NC 28752, (927) 738-8300

Musser Forests, Inc., 1880 Rte 119 Hwy N, Indiana, PA 15701, (724) 465-5685

Out Back Nursery, Inc., 15280 110th St. S, Hastings, MN 55033, (311) 438-2771

Plant & Gnome, P.O. Box 5344, Charleston, WV 25361, (304) 881-7037

Prairie Moon Nursery, 32115 Prairie Ln., Winona, MN 55987, (507) 452-1362 (866) 417-8156

RareFind Nursery, 957 Patterson Rd., Jackson, NJ 08527, (737) 833-0613

Reeseville Ridge Nursery, 512 S Main, Reeseville, WI 53579, (920) 927-3291

River Rock Nursery, 19251 SE Hwy 224, Damascus, OR 97089, (503) 658-4047

The Sandy Mush Herb Nursery, 316 Surrett Cove Rd., Leicester, NC 28748, (319) 683-2014

Tripple Brook Farm, 37 Middle Rd., Southampton, MA 01073, (413) 527-4626

Wavecrest Nursery, 2509 Lakeshore Dr., Fennville, MI 49408, (735) 869-4159

Well-Sweep Herb Farm, 205 Mount Bethel Rd., Port Murray, NJ 07865, (908) 852-5390

Whitman Farms, 3995 Gibson Rd. NW, Salem, OR 97304, (503) 585-8728

Whitney Gardens & Nursery, P.O. Box 170, Brinnon, WA 98320, (360) 796-4411

Woodlanders, Inc., 1128 Colleton Ave., Aiken, SC 29801, (803) 648-7522

Hamamelis vernalis

Hamamelis virginiana

VARIETIES

VARIETY	FLOWER COLOR	FALL FOLIAGE	HEIGHT/WIDTH	HARDINESS
Hamamelis × intermedia				
(Hybrid Witch Hazel)				
'Arnold Promise'****	Yellow/red	Yellow	15'/15'	−20°F
'Diane'****	Orange red	Varied	15'/15'	−20°F
'Jelena'****	Coppery orange	Orange red	15'/15'	−20°F
'Pallida'***	Sulfur yellow	Yellow	12'/12'	−20°F
'Ruby Glow'***	Copper red	Red	15'/15'	−20°F

These upright, spreading trees flower in very early spring. The twisted, unusual flowers are just under 1 inch (2.5 cm) long and appear before the heart-shaped foliage. They have a mild, spicy fragrance. The flowers of 'Diane' vary from yellow to orange red. The summer foliage is deep green. These are superb choices for gardeners living along the southern edge of the cold-climate range. They are commonly grafted onto the rootstock of *Hamamelis virginiana*.

*Hamamelis vernalis***				
(Vernal Witch Hazel)	Yellow to red orange	Yellow	10'/15'	−25°F
Autumn Embers™***	Orange	Red to plum	8'/10'	−25°F
'Sandra'***	Yellow	Orange red to plum	10'/15'	−25°F

These shrubs have an upright form. They are noted for extremely early bloom. The yellow to orange very fragrant flowers look like thin ribbons or strings. They appear before the foliage, even at times when snow may still be on the ground. New foliage often has an attractive bronze or reddish cast when it first unfolds. These shrubs sucker freely and will form a thicket in time.

*Hamamelis virginiana***				
(Common Witch Hazel)	Yellow	Yellow gold	20'/20'	−30°F

This large shrub has an upright spreading form with an open, loose feel. Its leaves are 3 to 6 inches (7.5 to 15 cm) long, turning from medium green in summer to splendid gold in fall. Fragrant, pale yellow flowers about ¾ inches (1.8 cm) long appear late in the season, usually just as leaves begin to fall. These delicate ribbons are only noticeable once leaves drop off. The fruit is about ½ inch (1.25 cm) long and insignificant. It looks like a dark, chambered pod and is mildly ornamental once it pops open. It takes two years to form and so appears next to the current year's bloom. The shrub's pliable branches have been used for "witching" or dowsing water for centuries. Many parts of the tree have been used in traditional medicines.

Hydrangea macrophylla 'All Summer Beauty'

HYDRANGEA

(high-DRANGE-uh)

HYDRANGEA

Hydrangeas are valued for their showy summer blooms. Most cold-hardy Hydrangeas produce white flowers in billowy drifts or lacey cones. Blooming in mid- to late summer, these lovely flowers add a cool, sparkling note to a hot landscape. In late summer and early fall these flowers usually age to an inviting tan or pink and will persist through the winter to the following spring. While blue- and pink-flowered Hydrangeas are prized, they require a great deal of effort to overwinter successfully. All Hydrangeas make excellent cut or dried flowers.

How Hydrangeas Grow

The roots of Hydrangeas are quite fibrous and wide spreading, but they do not penetrate the soil deeply. Most Hydrangeas are rounded, multistemmed shrubs, though one species grows as a clinging woody vine with short, horizontal branches. Some shrub forms can be pruned as small trees. Depending upon the species, Hydrangeas are upright to rounded shrubs. Branches may die back on some while on others they will survive cold well. As they mature, the majority of Hydrangeas form an ever-wider clump. Hydrangeas have flower clusters composed of large sterile flowers, small fertile flowers, or a combination of both. Hydrangeas bloom on new growth or the previous year's growth depending upon the species. In cold climates it's far easier to grow Hydrangeas that bloom on the current season's growth. Leaves tend to be large and medium to dark green, sometimes with a lighter green or silvery underside. Fall leaf color may be yellow, although more often than not leaves remain green or turn brown with the onset of winter. The plants rarely self-sow.

Where to Plant

Site and Light Hydrangeas vary in their light needs. Some flower better in full sun, others somewhat better in partial shade. This is covered in detail in the chart at the end of this section. The less hardy shrub and vining varieties of Hydrangea need a protected site to survive in colder climates. A protected site is one where the plant will not be exposed to cold, drying winter winds. It's also a spot where you can easily cover the crown of the plant with a winter mulch or snow. Note that while *Hydrangea macrophylla* (Bigleaf Hydrangea) stands up poorly to winter winds, it is quite salt tolerant.

Soil and Moisture Hydrangeas adapt well to a wide range of soil types. However, they prefer moist, well-drained soil high in organic matter. Avoid very dry sites, since plants will wilt quickly if they dry out. Some Hydrangeas have blue or pink flowers. Coloration is directly related to the availability of aluminum. This in turn depends on soil pH. If the soil is acidic, then the flowers will be blue. If it is alkaline, they turn pink. It is not uncommon to see bushes with both pink and blue blossoms combined. This indicates that the soil is neither acidic enough for purely blue flowers, nor alkaline enough for purely pink ones.

Spacing Space Hydrangeas with their mature size in mind. Plant Hydrangeas used for hedges or mass plantings closer together.

Landscape Use

Take advantage of Hydrangeas' shade tolerance by planting them under trees or on the north side of buildings. Remember if they are planted under trees, they will need to be watered regularly since trees compete with them for available moisture. The lower-growing Hydrangeas are excellent as low hedges, as borders, and as screens to hide building foundations or the edges of decks and porches. Larger Hydrangeas make nice dense informal hedges or small groupings. Because of their summer bloom, Hydrangeas are a great addition to a mixed shrub border. They provide flowering interest in the time between spring bloom and fall foliage color. 'Annabelle' planted with pink shrub roses makes a lovely old-fashioned combination. Pink Elf® is a good choice for growing a small Hydrangea in a large container.

Planting

Bare Root Get bare root plants into the garden as soon as the ground can be worked in spring. Remove plants from their shipping package immediately on arrival. Soak them in room temperature water for no fewer than 3 hours before planting. Place a small amount of superphosphate in the base of the hole and cover with 3 inches (7.5 cm) of soil. Spread roots out over a cone of well-prepared soil. Make sure the crown is level with the surrounding soil surface. Fill the hole with soil, firm it with your fingers, and water immediately. Dissolve water-soluble fertilizer in a gallon (about 4 liters) of water following the directions on the label. Pour ½ cup (about 120 ml) of this starter solution around the base of each plant. If you prefer organic fertilizer, use fish emulsion instead.

Containerized Plants Plant Hydrangeas as early in the season as possible. If the soil in the container is dry, soak it and let it drain overnight before planting. Carefully remove the plant from the container so as not to break the root ball. Plant at the same depth as in the container after preparing the hole in a similar manner as that for a bare root plant. Fill the hole with well-prepared soil, firm with your fingers, and water immediately. Pour ½ cup (about 120 ml) of starter solution around the base of the plant.

Balled and Burlapped Hydrangeas are only rarely sold this way. Plant as you would a containerized plant with these added precautions: Place the plant in the hole making sure that the top of the balled and burlapped root ball is about 1 to 2 inches (2.5 to 5 cm) above the surrounding soil. Cut and remove any twine around the stems. Remove as much of the burlap and wire holding the root ball in place as possible, but avoid breaking the root ball.

Transplanting

You can dig up small Hydrangeas fairly easily in early spring before new growth emerges. Plant immediately as you would a bare root plant. Larger Hydrangeas are very difficult to transplant. However, you can divide these large plants (see Propagation).

How to Care for Hydrangeas

Water Keep the soil evenly moist from spring until the soil freezes in fall. Consistent watering is especially important during the first 2 years. However, even mature plants can be stressed if allowed to wilt during dry periods. Hydrangeas are among the first shrubs to show signs of water stress by wilting. Wise gardeners use them to gauge the moisture content of their soil. Always saturate the soil deeply with each watering. When the top 2 inches (5 cm) of soil dry out, water.

Mulch Apply a 2- to 4-inch (5- to 10-cm) layer of mulch around each plant as soon as the ground warms up in spring. Good mulches include shredded bark, pine needles, and wood chips. Mulch retains moisture in the soil and helps prevent the growth of weeds. Replenish the mulch as necessary throughout the growing season.

Fertilizing Fertilize once in mid-June with 10-10-10 fertilizer. Sprinkle the granules around the base of each plant and water immediately to move the fertilizer into the root zone.

If you prefer organic fertilizers, use alfalfa meal (rabbit pellets), blood meal, bone meal, compost, fish emulsion, Milorganite, or rotted manures. Bone meal must be added to the soil at planting time to be effective.

Weeding Prevent the growth of most annual weeds by using mulch. Pull by hand any weeds that do appear. Weeds compete with shrubs for available moisture and nutrients and should be removed immediately.

Deadheading Whether to remove spent blossoms is strictly a matter of personal choice. If you do not like the appearance of flower heads as they turn color and dry out, simply snip them off to a leaf below.

However, most gardeners feel that these flower heads are a wonderful addition to the winter landscape. Removing the flower heads or leaving them on has no effect on the plant's health and is not related to the next season's flowering.

Pruning At any time of year remove dead, diseased, or broken stems or branches. Some Hydrangeas will have significant dieback after winter. Cut stems back to live wood.

If you want to improve the form or control the size of a plant, prune it back in late winter or early spring. Since *Hydrangea arborescens* (Smooth Hydrangea) blooms on new wood, stems can be cut right back to the ground. *Hydrangea anomala* ssp. *petiolaris* (Climbing Hydrangea) should only be pruned to remove dead, broken, or diseased plant parts.

Winter Protection The less hardy varieties of Hydrangeas listed in the chart at the end of this section benefit from winter protection. *Hydrangea anomala* ssp. *petiolaris* (Climbing Hydrangea) is particularly prone to winter damage during the first few years of its growth. As soon as the ground freezes, cover its base with whole leaves, marsh hay, pine needles, or straw to a depth of 12 inches (30 cm).

Hydrangea macrophylla (Bigleaf Hydrangea) demands good winter protection. Some gardeners simply place varieties from this group in a protected location and cover them with snow throughout the winter.

However, if these plants are exposed, they need additional protection. Unfortunately, this group is slow to go dormant in the fall. In late fall before temperatures drop below 20°F (–7°C), encircle the shrub with chicken wire at least 4 feet (over a meter) tall and 2 feet (61 cm) outside the outer perimeter of the plant. If the plant is 3 feet (1 meter) wide, then the fencing would be 7 feet (2 meters) in diameter. Fill the cage with dry leaves so that the entire plant is covered with at least 12 inches (30 cm) of leaves. Then cover the leaves with a 4-ml-thick sheet of white plastic, tucking the edges of the plastic down to the ground on the inside of the fencing. Now cover the plastic with additional leaves until the entire cage is filled up. Finally, cover this additional layer of leaves with another sheet of plastic that goes over the wire and to the ground where you can anchor it in place. Begin removing this intricate covering in spring as soon as it starts to warm up.

Alternatively, consider growing smaller varieties of Bigleaf Hydrangea as container plants. The containers must be at least a 10-gallon (about 40-liter) size and will have to be moved each fall into a protected location. Any area where it stays cold but does not drop below freezing is ideal. If the area could drop below freezing, then place the container in a large plastic bag, and surround the container and the plant with a thick layer of whole leaves or straw. The goal is to stop the soil from freezing in the container.

Problems

Insects Aphids do attack Hydrangeas on occasion, although they are not a common problem. These tiny insects come in a range of colors and damage the plant by sucking out juices from its tissue. As soon as you see them, spray them off the foliage with a force-

ful jet of water. Concentrate the spray on new growth and the undersides of leaves. Do this several days in a row. If aphids continue to be a problem, try an insecticidal soap. Only use more potent insecticides, such as Orthene, as a last resort.

Diseases None serious.

Marauders None.

Propagation

Division *Hydrangea arborescens* (Smooth Hydrangea) and *Hydrangea macrophylla* (Bigleaf Hydrangea) are quite easy to divide. In early spring, cut through the outer edge of the clump with a spade. Dig down as far as possible keeping as many roots with the stems as feasible. Plant immediately as you would a bare root plant.

Mound Layering This method can be used to propagate *Hydrangea arborescens* (Smooth Hydrangea) and *Hydrangea macrophylla* (Bigleaf Hydrangea). See page 405 for additional information.

Cuttings Take softwood cuttings in early to midsummer when new growth is just becoming firm (greenwood) or quite hard (semihard). Cuttings should be 4 to 6 inches (10 to 15 cm) long and have no fewer than two sets of leaves.

Take hardwood cuttings in November. These should be 8 inches (20 cm) long. For additional information, see pages 406–8.

Seed The named varieties will not come true from seed. However, the species can be grown from seed. Collect the seed and plant it immediately at room temperature in a moist starting mix. For additional information, see pages 409–12.

Special Uses

Cut Flowers Most Hydrangea flowers make excellent cut flowers, both fresh and dried. Cut fresh flowers while still green or just as they reach peak coloration. Remove any foliage that will end up underwater in the final arrangement. Flowers cut while they are still green make a wonderful foil to the bold colors of other flowers. The light, muted tones and unusual form are both highly desirable.

Flowers can be dried at any stage. Remove all foliage from the stems. Hang individual stems upside down in a warm, dry, airy place until they dry out completely. Some gardeners wrap them in tissue paper before hanging them. Do not expect colors, especially blues, to remain bright.

Another easy and effective method to dry Hydrangeas is to place the defoliated stems in a large vase with the flower heads spread apart. The vase should have 2 inches (5 cm) of water in the bottom. The stems will absorb the water quickly and then dry out gradually. Do not add more water as they dry. The advantage of this method is that you can enjoy the flowers throughout the drying process.

Finally, you can let flowers fade and dry right on the plant. These dried flowers may be tannish brown to pinkish to almost purple. They are often just as attractive as flowers cut and dried earlier in the season. In some cases the tones in fall are exquisite. Snip the stems off, remove the leaves, and use the already partially to fully dried flowers in an arrangement.

Sources

Bloom River Gardens, 39744 Deerhorn Rd., Springfield, OR 97478, (558) 726-8997

Bluestone Perennials, 7211 Middle Ridge Rd., Madison, OH 44057, (558) 852-5243

Colvos Creek Nursery, P.O. Box 1512, Vashon Island, WA 98070, (893) 749-9508

Corn Hill Nursery Ltd., 2700 Rte 890, Corn Hill, NB E4Z 1M2 Canada, (842) 756-3635

Digging Dog Nursery, P.O. Box 471, Albion, CA 95410, (281) 937-2480

Durio Nursery, 5853 Hwy 182, Opelousas, LA 70570, (337) 948-3696

Elk Mountain Nursery, P.O. Box 599, Asheville, NC 28802, (744) 683-9330

Fairweather Gardens, P.O. Box 330, Greenwich, NJ 08323, (856) 451-6261

Fedco Trees, P.O. Box 520, Waterville, ME 04903, (207) 873-7333

Fieldstone Gardens, Inc., 620 Quaker Ln., Vassalboro, ME 04989, (207) 923-3836

ForestFarm, 990 Tetherow Rd., Williams, OR 97544, (513) 846-7269

Girard Nurseries, P.O. Box 428, Geneva, OH 44041, (928) 466-2881

Gossler Farms Nursery, 1200 Weaver Rd., Springfield, OR 97478, (312) 746-3922

Great Garden Plants, P.O. Box 1511, Holland, MI 49422, (877) 447-4769

Greer Gardens, 1280 Goodpasture Island Rd., Eugene, OR 97401, (541) 686-8266

Heronswood Nursery, 300 Park Ave., Warminster, PA 18974, (877) 674-4714

Hortico, Inc., 723 Robson Rd., RR# 1, Waterdown, ON L0R 2H1 Canada, (738) 689-6984

Hydrangea Farm Nursery, 86 Madaket Rd., Nantucket, MA 02554, (508) 228-6493

Hydrangeas Plus, P.O. Box 389, Aurora, OR 97002, (320) 651-2887

Joy Creek Nursery, 20300 NW Watson Rd., Scappoose, OR 97056, (736) 543-7474

Klehm's Song Sparrow Perennial Farm, 13101 E Rye Rd., Avalon, WI 53505, (318) 553-3715

Mason Hollow Nursery, 47 Scripps Ln., Mason, NH 03048, (603) 878-4347

McKay Nursery Co., P.O. Box 185, Waterloo, WI 53594, (505) 478-2121

Meadowbrook Nursery/We-Du Natives, 2055 Polly Spout Rd., Marion, NC 28752, (362) 738-8300

Musser Forests, Inc., 1880 Rte 119 Hwy N, Indiana, PA 15701, (804) 465-5685

Nantucket Hydrangeas, P.O. Box 3402, 76 Hummock, Nantucket, MA 02554, (508) 292-1528

Niche Gardens, 1111 Dawson Rd., Chapel Hill, NC 27516, (920) 967-0078

Plant & Gnome, P.O. Box 5344, Charleston, WV 25361, (305) 881-7037

RareFind Nursery, 957 Patterson Rd., Jackson, NJ 08527, (732) 833-0613

Reeseville Ridge Nursery, 512 S Main, Reeseville, WI 53579, (920) 927-3291

River Rock Nursery, 19251 SE Hwy 224, Damascus, OR 97089, (503) 658-4047

The Sandy Mush Herb Nursery, 316 Surrett Cove Rd., Leicester, NC 28748, (828) 683-2014

Shooting Star Nursery, 160 Soards Rd., Georgetown, KY 40324, (502) 867-7979

Shrub Source, 248 N Colonial St., Zeeland, MI 49464, (800) 530-2969

Sunlight Gardens, 174 Golden Ln., Andersonville, TN 37705, (800) 272-7396

Variegated Foliage Nursery, 245 Westford Rd., Eastford, CT 06242, (860) 974-3951

Venero Gardens, 5985 Scamans Dr., Shorewood, MN 55331, (952) 474-8550

Vintage Gardens, 4130 Gravenstein Hwy N, Sebastapol, CA 95462, (707) 829-2035

Wavecrest Nursery, 2509 Lakeshore Dr., Fennville, MI 49408, (888) 869-4159

Wayside Gardens, 1 Garden Ln., Hodges, SC 29695, (800) 845-1124

White Flower Farm, P.O. Box 50, Litchfield, CT 06759, (800) 503-9624

Whitman Farms, 3995 Gibson Rd. NW, Salem, OR 97304, (503) 585-8728

Whitney Gardens & Nursery, P.O. Box 170, Brinnon, WA 98320, (360) 796-4411

Wilkerson Mill Garden, 9595 Wilkerson Mill Rd., Palmetto, GA 30268, (770) 463-2400

Woodlanders, Inc., 1128 Colleton Ave., Aiken, SC 29801, (803) 648-7522

VARIETIES

VARIETY	FLOWER COLOR	HEIGHT/WIDTH	HARDINESS
Hydrangea anomala			
(Climbing or Vining Hydrangea)			
ssp. *petiolaris*****	White	30'/10'	−25°F

This plant blooms on old wood. This beautiful, woody vine has many short horizontal branchlets that give the plant more depth and architectural form than many other woody vines. This vine attaches itself to vertical surfaces with aerial root-like holdfasts and can grow on buildings, over arbors and fences, or along the ground. It may take up to 2 years before the vine clings well to a flat surface, but once the tiny holdfasts develop, the vine grows more rapidly. It produces 6- to 8- inch (15- to 20- cm) flat clusters of scented flowers. It has glossy, dark green foliage. Peeling stems have a nice cinnamon color and interesting texture. In colder areas where it may die back, it still makes an excellent ground cover or low vine and looks especially nice growing along low rock walls. Plant it in full sun for best results.

VARIETY	FLOWER COLOR	HEIGHT/WIDTH	HARDINESS
Hydrangea arborescens**			
(Smooth Hydrangea)	White	5'/7'	−40°F
'Annabelle'****	White	5'/5'	−40°F
Endless Summer® Bella Anna™****	Dark magenta pink	3'/3'	−40°F
'Bounty'****	White	3/3'	−40°F
'Grandiflora' ('Hills of Snow')***	White	5'/6'	−40°F
Invincibelle™ Spirit***	Deep pink to pink	4'/4'	−40°F
Incrediball™***	Light pink	5'/6'	−40°F

These plants bloom on new wood. The species sends up many stems with few side branches. 'Annabelle' has many large, rounded flower heads held erect by strong stems and blooms a week or two later than 'Grandiflora.' The latter has somewhat smaller flower clusters than 'Annabelle' creating a more open and less heavy appearance. Bella Anna™ has the richest flower color in this group, as well as dark green foliage. 'Bounty' is a sturdy plant with flowers made up of smaller petals (sepals) than 'Annabelle.' Invincibelle Spirit™ has an extended bloom period and lovely pink flowers. Incrediball™ has strong stems that can support its massive blooms. These plants thrive in partial shade and have a deeper green foliage in such a location, but will also grow well in full sun if kept watered.

VARIETY	FLOWER COLOR	HEIGHT/WIDTH	HARDINESS
*Hydrangea macrophylla***			
(Bigleaf Hydrangea)	Blue or pink	6'/6'	−20°F
'All Summer Beauty'***	Blue or pink blue	4'/5'	−20°F
Endless Summer® Blushing Bride™***	White with pink blush	4'/4'	−25°F
'Glowing Embers'****	Deep pink red	3'/3'	−20°F
First Editions® Light-O-Day®***	Blue to pink	4'/4'	−25°F
'Nikko Blue'***	Blue	5'/5'	−20°F
Pink Elf® ('Pia')***	Pink	3'/3'	−20°F
Endless Summer® The Original****	Blue to pink	5'/5'	−25°F
Endless Summer® Twist-n-Shout®*****	Blue to pink	4'/4'	−30°F
'Variegata'***	Blue	4'/4'	−20°F

These plants bloom almost entirely on old wood with the exception of the new reblooming Endless Summer® series. These Hydrangeas have been grown in areas where winter temperatures drop below −30°F (−34°C), but always in highly protected areas where they are often covered by drifts of snow and protected from drying winds. Some gardeners will have severe dieback even at the temperatures listed. Again, with the exception of the Endless Summer® series, these Hydrangeas bloom on wood from the previous season's growth, so that if they do die back, you will have no bloom, just deep green foliage. This is fine for Light-O-Day® and 'Variegata' since they have lovely leaves with attractive white to creamy yellow margins, but for the other varieties is not at all acceptable. Flower color in this group is affected by the availability of aluminum in the soil, which in turn depends on soil acidity. In acidic soils with a pH below 5.5, flowers are usually blue and on slightly less acidic soils with a pH ranging from 6 to 6.5, flowers are usually pink. The flowers appear either as globes (a clump of sterile flowers) or as lace caps (small fertile flowers surrounded by larger sterile flowers). The globular forms are called Hortensias or Mopheads. All of the named varieties above are Hortensias with the exception of Light-O-Day®, Twist-n-Shout®, and 'Variegata' which have lace cap flowers. All of these plants do better in partial to full shade than in full sun.

VARIETY	FLOWER COLOR	HEIGHT/WIDTH	HARDINESS
*Hydrangea paniculata***			
(Panicle Hydrangea)	Ivory	10'/10'	−35°F
'Grandiflora' ('Pee Gee Hydrangea')***	Ivory	10'/10'	−35°F
First Editions® Great Star®****	White	7'/8'	−35°F
'Kyushu'***	Ivory	8'/8'	−35°F
'Limelight'****	White to lime green	8'/7'	−35°F
'Little Lamb'***	White to lime green	6'/6'	−35°F
Little Lime™ ('Jane')***	White to lime green	4'/4'	−35°F
'Phantom'	White tinged pink	10'/8'	−35°F
'Pink Diamond'***	Ivory	9'/9'	−35°F
Pinky Winky™****	White turning pink	7'/7'	−35°F
Quick Fire™ ('Bulk')****	White to deep pink red	7'/7'	−35°F
'Silver Dollar'	White tinged pink	8'/6'	−35°F
'Tardiva'****	Ivory	9'/9'	−35°F
First Editions® Tickled Pink™****	White to rose pink	4'/5'	−35°F
'Unique'****	Ivory	10'/10'	−35°F

Hydrangea anomala ssp. *petiolaris*

Hydrangea arborescens 'Annabelle'

Hydrangea macrophylla

Hydrangea paniculata 'Tardiva'

VARIETY	FLOWER COLOR	HEIGHT/WIDTH	HARDINESS
First Editions® Vanilla Strawberry™****	White to red	6'/5'	−35°F
First Editions® White Diamonds®****	White to green	4'/5'	−35°F

These plants bloom on new wood. The species is rounded to upright spreading in shape and has many well-branched stems. The long-lasting, upright conical flower clusters (panicles) consist of many small ivory and a scattering of larger white flowers. The flowers turn pink to dark rose as they age. 'Grandiflora' produces large, conical clusters of flowers that are so heavy they bend branches down in an arching form. Great Star® produces flower clusters with some of the individual flowers flaring out like shooting stars. 'Kyushu' has a nice upright form and produces many flowers, some small, others larger. 'Limelight' has abundant white to lime green flower clusters that take on pinkish tones in fall. 'Little Lamb' is a compact plant with small flower clusters and small petals. Little Lime™ resembles a dwarf 'Limelight.' 'Phantom' has a strong upright appearance and very large, dense flower clusters. 'Pink Diamond' has very long flower clusters that turn deep pink to pinkish purple as they age. Pinky Winky™ has flower clusters that turn from white to pink. The pink clusters are in turn tipped white. Quick Fire™ has very early bloom and turns pink well before fall. 'Silver Dollar' has numerous, dense, creamy white flowers flushed pink as they age. 'Tardiva' stands out for prolific late summer to early fall bloom. Its flowers have a very open, airy look. Tickled Pink™ has large flower heads. 'Unique' is similar to 'Tardiva' but has flower clusters up to 12 inches (30 cm) in length. Vanilla Strawberry™ produces large clusters of flowers that change from cream, to pink, to red as the season progresses. White Diamonds® is an ideal choice for gardeners with limited space. Its flowers take on a pinkish tone late in the season. These plants have medium green foliage that may be slightly deeper green in partial shade. However, they seem to grow best in full sun. All can be pruned into tree form. Note that we have not given stars to 'Phantom' and 'Silver Dollar' because these European introductions have not yet been fully field tested.

Ilex verticillata 'Red Sprite'

ILEX

(EYE-lex)

WINTERBERRY, INKBERRY, HOLLY, POSSUM HAW

This group is made up of both deciduous and evergreen plants. The deciduous species are far hardier. Plants in this group are noted for their glossy green summer foliage and brilliantly colored fall fruits. The latter are attractive to birds as they mature. Branches with berries are highly decorative in floral arrangements. Winterberries are one of the few shrubs that will grow in wet soils. Although these shrubs lack fall color, the evergreen varieties do retain foliage through the winter months. Unfortunately, the evergreen types are only marginally hardy in colder climates.

How Winterberries Grow

Winterberries have fibrous roots that penetrate quite deeply into the soil. They are multistemmed shrubs. Stems tend to be gray and are overshadowed by the rich, deep green foliage. Some types produce suckers off to the side of the mother plant. Flowers are inconspicuous, usually white or greenish. Plants are either male or female (dioecious). Female plants have flowers with a green central knob (pistil). Male plants have flowers with numerous protrusions (stamens). These are yellowish when covered with ripe pollen. A male pollinator is needed to fertilize the flowers of the female plants if you want to get berries. The berries (drupes) on all Winterberries are usually about ⅜ of an inch (1 cm) wide and contain several seeds. The plants rarely self-sow.

Where to Plant

Site and Light Winterberries prefer full sun but grow quite well in partial shade. The evergreen types need protection from winter wind and sun. Placing them in sheltered locations on the east or north side of your home is highly recommended.

Soil and Moisture These shrubs need mildly acidic soil to grow well. A pH of 5 to 6 is ideal. Overly alkaline soil often leads to yellowing of leaves. These shrubs thrive in well-drained soil as long as it is kept consistently moist throughout the growing season. They will even grow well in wet to boggy conditions. Add lots of organic matter to the soil for best results. Note that while they prefer consistently moist conditions, they will tolerate short dry spells but not a prolonged drought.

Spacing Give shrubs enough space to reach their full height and width upon maturity. If using Winterberries as an informal hedge, plant them more tightly together than you would otherwise. Place female plants, the ones that produce berries, in the most conspicuous areas with the male in the background.

Landscape Use

Winterberries make good informal hedges and specimen plants. They can be mixed into the shrub border or used as screens if tall enough. The smallest forms are ideal in front of shrubs that lose foliage around the lower portions of their stems. These "facing" plants with their dense foliage cover the bare area during the growing season. If soil is acidic enough and drains freely, these plants combine nicely with *Rhododendron* (Azalea and Rhododendron). The red-fruited female plants are stunning when placed in front of evergreens.

Planting

Bare Root Get bare root plants into the garden as soon as the ground can be worked in spring. Remove plants from their shipping package immediately on arrival. Soak them in room temperature water for no fewer than 3 hours before planting. Place a small amount of superphosphate in the base of the hole and cover with 3 inches (7.5 cm) of soil. Spread roots out over a cone of well-prepared soil. Make sure the crown is level with the surrounding soil surface. Fill the hole with soil, firm it with your fingers, and water immediately. Dissolve acidic water-soluble fertilizer in a gallon (about 4 liters) of water following the directions on the label. Pour ½ cup (about 120 ml) of this starter solution around the base of each plant. If you prefer organic fertilizer, use fish emulsion instead.

Containerized Plants Plant Winterberries as early in the season as possible. If the soil in the container is dry, soak it and let it drain overnight before planting. Carefully remove the plant from the container so as not to break the root ball. Plant at the same depth as in the container after preparing the hole in a similar manner as that for a bare root plant. Fill the hole with well-prepared soil, firm with your fingers, and water immediately. Pour ½ cup (about 120 ml) of starter solution around the base of the plant.

Balled and Burlapped Plant as you would a containerized plant with these added precautions: Place the plant in the hole making sure that the top of the balled and burlapped root ball is about 1 to 2 inches (2.5 to 5 cm) above the surrounding soil. Cut and remove any twine around the stems. Remove as much of the burlap and wire holding the root ball in place as possible, but avoid breaking the root ball.

Transplanting

Dig up shrubs in early spring before new growth emerges. Keep as much soil around the roots as possible. Plant immediately as you would a bare root plant.

How to Care for Winterberries

Water Keep the soil evenly moist from spring until the soil freezes in fall. Consistent watering is especially important during the first 2 years, although these plants should never be allowed to suffer through drought at any stage of growth. Always saturate the soil deeply with each watering. When the top 2 inches (5 cm) of soil dry out, water.

Mulch Apply a 2- to 4-inch (5- to 10-cm) layer of mulch around each plant as soon as the ground warms up in spring. Good slightly acidic mulches include shredded pine bark, pine needles, and shredded oak leaves. Mulch retains moisture in the soil and helps prevent the growth of weeds. Replenish the mulch as necessary throughout the growing season.

Fertilizing Fertilize every spring with 10-10-10 fertilizer. Sprinkle the granules around the base of each plant before new growth emerges and water immediately to move the fertilizer into the root zone. If soil is not acidic, then use Miracid, iron sulfate, or sulfur to keep the pH down.

If you prefer organic fertilizers, use alfalfa meal (rabbit pellets), blood meal, bone meal, compost, fish emulsion, Milorganite, or rotted manures. Bone meal must be added to the soil at planting time to be effective. To acidify the soil use cottonseed meal if it is available.

Weeding Prevent the growth of most annual weeds by using mulch. Pull by hand any weeds that do appear. Weeds compete with shrubs for available moisture and nutrients and should be removed immediately.

Deadheading Not necessary.

Pruning Remove dead, broken, or diseased stems at any time of year. You may also prune these shrubs to keep them at a specific height or to shape them. Very little pruning is usually required to keep them in an attractive, natural form. The best time to do this is in early spring. You can also pinch or cut off growing tips to encourage side branching. Naturally, pruning for hedges must be more severe. Again, do this in spring.

Winter Protection None needed.

Problems

Insects Winterberries are not seriously threatened by insects in general, although spider mite infestations do occur on rare occasions. Keep plants well watered and spray them down during hot, dry spells to ward off mites. If the mites colonize, use a miticide.

Diseases Winterberries are prone to leaf spots, especially in rainy years. These are mainly a cosmetic concern and do not require spraying. Powdery mildew, a whitish film on the leaf surfaces, does occur occasionally as well. As with many other shrubs, this rarely endangers the plant and does not require treatment.

Chlorosis If soil is too alkaline, the leaves on Winterberries may turn yellow between the veins. Lower the soil pH by using an acidic fertilizer each year. This will make iron more readily available to the plant. Over time the leaves will regain their deep green coloration.

Marauders Not usually.

Propagation

Suckers Winterberries will often sucker. Dig up the sucker to the side of the mother plant in early spring before new growth emerges on the plant. Plant it immediately as you would a bare root plant.

Cuttings Just as new growth begins to harden, cut off 4 to 6 inches (10 to 15 cm) from the tips of stems (semihard). Each cutting should contain at least three sets of leaves. These softwood cuttings are much easier to root than hardwood. Avoid hardwood cuttings altogether. For additional information, see pages 406–8.

Seed Place seed in moist peat moss for no less than 3 and up to 18 months if you have the patience. Then moist chill the seed for 3 to 4 months. Bring out into room temperature after this period and keep the starting mix moist until germination occurs. Note that success with seeds often requires varying the periods of warmth and cold dramatically. Even commercial growers are sometimes unsuccessful getting seed to germinate. For additional information, see pages 409–12.

Special Uses

The wood of various species has been used for everything from walking sticks to the black keys on pianos. *Ilex glabra* (Ink Berry) got its common name from its strong color used in making inks and dyes.

Cut Stems When berries reach maturity, cut off stems and use them in arrangements. Unless plants are mature and quite dense, do this sparingly to avoid ruining the shape of the plant. Note that cut stems often last just as well without water in the vase.

Sources

Bluestone Perennials, 7211 Middle Ridge Rd., Madison, OH 44057, (559) 852-5243

Colvos Creek Nursery, 1904 Third Ave., Suite 415, Seattle, WA 98101, (559) 749-9508

Corn Hill Nursery Ltd., 2700 Rte 890, Corn Hill, NB E4Z 1M2 Canada, (894) 756-3635

Eastern Plant Specialties, 660 A Berrys Mill Rd., West Bath, ME 04530, (207) 504-4405

Elk Mountain Nursery, P.O. Box 599, Asheville, NC 28802, (843) 683-9330

Fairweather Gardens, P.O. Box 330, Greenwich, NJ 08323, (282) 451-6261

Fedco Trees, P.O. Box 520, Waterville, ME 04903, (207) 873-7333

ForestFarm, 990 Tetherow Rd., Williams, OR 97544, (541) 846-7269

Girard Nurseries, P.O. Box 428, Geneva, OH 44041, (745) 466-2881

Greer Gardens, 1280 Goodpasture Island Rd., Eugene, OR 97401, (541) 686-8266

Hartmann's Plant Company, P.O. Box 100, Lacota, MI 49063, (269) 253-4281

Hortico, Inc., 723 Robson Rd., RR# 1, Waterdown, ON L0R 2H1 Canada, (905) 689-6984

Mason Hollow Nursery, 47 Scripps Ln., Mason, NH 03048, (603) 878-4347

McKay Nursery Co., P.O. Box 185, Waterloo, WI 53594, (514) 478-2121

Musser Forests, Inc., 1880 Rte 119 Hwy N, Indiana, PA 15701, (929) 465-5685

Plant & Gnome, P.O. Box 5344, Charleston, WV 25361, (304) 881-7037

Out Back Nursery, Inc., 15280 110th St. S, Hastings, MN 55033, (313) 438-2771

RareFind Nursery, 957 Patterson Rd., Jackson, NJ 08527, (739) 833-0613

Reeseville Ridge Nursery, 512 S Main, Reeseville, WI 53579, (321) 927-3291

St. Lawrence Nurseries, 325 Ste Hwy 345, Potsdam, NY 13676, (315) 265-6739

The Sandy Mush Herb Nursery, 316 Surrett Cove Rd., Leicester, NC 28748, (737) 683-2014

Shooting Star Nursery, 160 Soards Rd., Georgetown, KY 40324, (319) 867-7979

Shrub Source, 248 N Colonial St., Zeeland, MI 49464, (800) 530-2969

Southmeadow Fruit Gardens, P.O. Box 211, Baroda, MI 49101, (269) 422-2411

Wavecrest Nursery, 2509 Lakeshore Dr., Fennville, MI 49408, (506) 869-4159

Woodlanders, Inc., 1128 Colleton Ave., Aiken, SC 29801, (803) 648-7522

Ilex verticillata 'Shaver'   *Ilex verticillata* 'Winter Red'

VARIETIES

VARIETY	FOLIAGE COLOR	BERRY COLOR	HEIGHT/WIDTH	HARDINESS

The species (wild) plants can either be male or female. The named varieties are either male or female exclusively. Only female plants produce berries.

Ilex glabra **

(Inkberry)	Dark green	Black or no berries	6'/6'	−20°F
'Compacta'***	Dark green	Black	4'/4'	−20°F
'Nigra'***	Dark green	Black	3'/3'	−20°F
'Nordic'**	Dark green	No berries	4'/4'	−25°F
'Shamrock'****	Dark green	Black	3'/3'	−20°F

These evergreen shrubs are easily damaged by winter sun and should be planted in a sheltered location on the east or north side of your home. Branches are also prone to breakage from the weight of snow. Leaves are quite small and rounded. The fruit is about the size of a pea and not particularly showy, but a favorite of birds. Plants tolerate quite wet soils. They sucker freely. Be sure to plant 'Nordic' along with several of the females to get berry production.

VARIETY	FOLIAGE COLOR	BERRY COLOR	HEIGHT/WIDTH	HARDINESS
Ilex × *meserveae*				
(The Meserve Hybrid Hollies, Hybrid Blue Hollies)				
'Blue Prince'**	Dark blue green	No berries	10'/10'	−20°F
'Blue Princess'***	Dark blue green	Red	10'/10'	−20°F
Castle Spire™***	Green	No berries	6'/3'	−20°F
Castle Wall™***	Green	Red	9'/2'	−20°F
China Boy® ('Mesbob')**	Dark blue green	No berries	10'/8'	−20°F
China Girl® ('Mesog')***	Dark blue green	Red	10'/10'	−20°F

These evergreen shrubs are very prone to winter burn in colder climates. Place them on the east or north side of your home in a sheltered location to avoid damage from winter winds and sun. Use a male pollinator to get berry production from the females. You only need one male for a number of females. For example, China Boy® would be used to pollinate China Girl®. This group represents the best of evergreen Hollies for cold-climate gardeners. They do not sucker.

*Ilex verticillata***				
(Winterberry)	Dark green	No berries or red	8'/8'	−40°F
'Afterglow'****	Dark green	Bright red	6'/5'	−30°F
'Aurantiaca'***	Dark green	Orange	6'/6'	−30°F
'Cacapon'***	Dark green	Bright red	6'/5'	−30°F
'Jim Dandy'**	Dark green	No berries	6'/6'	−30°F
'Red Sprite'****	Dark green	Bright red	4'/5'	−30°F
'Shaver'****	Dark green	Bright red to red orange	5'/5'	−30°F
'Southern Gentlemen'**	Dark green	No berries	8'/8'	−30°F
'Winter Gold'****	Dark green	Yellow orange	8'/8'	−30°F
Winter Red®***	Dark green	Bright red	8'/8'	−30°F

The species of this deciduous group can either be male or female, but both sexes are needed to get berries. Named varieties are either exclusively male or female. The females need males for proper pollination. The greenish white flowers are inconspicuous. Foliage is quite shiny and attractive, but drops off in fall. Use 'Jim Dandy' to pollinate 'Aferglow,' 'Auriantiaca,' 'Cacapon,' 'Red Sprite,' and 'Shaver.' Use 'Southern Gentleman' to pollinate 'Winter Red.' It will also pollinate 'Christmas Cheer' and 'Sparkleberry' listed in the next grouping. This group produces berries in profusion. The berry-laden branches are highly sought after for cut flower arrangements, but you'll have to cut them before the birds devour the fruit. Berries do tend to blacken as winter sets in and then drop unless already eaten by birds. The latter is highly likely. This group grows well in very moist soils and suckers lightly.

Ilex verticillata × *serrata* (named varieties)				
(Winterberry)				
'Christmas Cheer'***	Dark green	Red	5'/5'	−30°F
'Sparkleberry'***	Dark green	Red	12'/12'	−20°F

These deciduous plants need pollinators to produce berries. 'Southern Gentleman' is a good choice. These plants prefer moist, slightly acidic soils. They may occasionally sucker.

Juniperus chinensis 'Maney'

JUNIPERUS

(june-IP-purr-us)

JUNIPER

Junipers are extremely popular and widely used because they are among the finest evergreen shrubs available to cold-climate gardeners. Their wonderful textures and foliage colors add year-round interest to the landscape. Their wide variety of shapes, widths, and heights make them especially desirable in landscape design. They do require some pruning and attention to disease and insects, but overall they are durable and dependable plants.

How Junipers Grow

Junipers have rather coarse roots. The upright forms have roots that dig deep into the soil. Spreading types are more shallow rooted. While these shrubs do expand steadily with age, they do not send off suckers from the mother plant. Needles (leaves) vary in color, texture, and shape. The leaves may look like needles or appear more like small scales. Junipers are either male or female (dioecious). Male plants produce inconspicuous yellow catkin-like cones, while females produce berry-like cones. Shades of these blue cones vary by the variety. Some of the berries are covered with a whitish film (bloom) that gives them a unique look. If both male and female plants are present, the female Junipers may produce berries. However, nurseries do not "sex" plants and it can be difficult to get correct combinations if berries are one of your goals. Most Junipers rarely self-sow.

Where to Plant

Site and Light Plant all Junipers in full sun. They thrive in bright light and heat. If planted in shade, they will have sparse foliage. They need no special protection from winds. Keep them away from areas that could be sprayed with highway salt. If you plant them under eaves, make sure they get enough water throughout the growing season and especially before winter. Avoid planting them directly under drip lines since snow falling off in winter can damage branches.

Soil and Moisture Junipers adapt well to a wide variety of soils as long as they drain freely. They prefer neutral to slightly acidic soil with some organic matter in it. This keeps the soil consistently moist. Once mature, they tolerate soils on the dry side. If the soil gets too wet, the plants are likely to be infected with disease. Junipers grow particularly well on slopes where runoff from rains is common and keeps the soil just the way they like it.

Spacing Spacing is very important for Junipers since they need enough space for good air circulation to prevent juniper blight. Initial planting may seem sparse, but correct spacing from the start is much easier than digging up plants at a later date.

Landscape Use

The upright Junipers are excellent as accent plants at the corners of buildings. They also make good windbreaks. Some gardeners use them for informal or formal hedges with great success. *Juniperus virginiana* is popular for naturalizing. Low-growing Junipers are favored for foundation plantings and ground covers. They are also excellent in rock gardens and perennial borders, and when used as small specimen plants. Their foliage texture and coloration can be used to provide contrast in such settings.

Planting

Bare Root Rarely sold this way.

Containerized Plants Plant Junipers as early in the season as possible. If the soil in the container is dry, soak it and let it drain overnight before planting. Place a small amount of superphosphate in the base of the hole and cover with 3 inches (7.5 cm) of soil. Carefully remove the plant from the container so as not to break the root ball. Fill the hole with well-prepared soil, firm with your fingers, and water immediately. Dissolve water-soluble fertilizer in a gallon (about 4 liters) of water following the directions on the label. Pour ½ cup (about 120 ml) of this starter solution around the base of each plant. If you prefer organic fertilizer, use fish emulsion instead.

Balled and Burlapped Plant as you would a containerized plant with these added precautions: Place the plant in the hole making sure that the top of the balled and burlapped root ball is about 1 to 2 inches (2.5 to 5 cm) above the surrounding soil. Cut and remove any twine around the stems. Remove as much of the burlap and wire holding the root ball in place as possible, but avoid breaking the root ball.

Transplanting

The spreading types are much easier to transplant by hand than the upright forms, as long as they are still relatively immature. The latter should be transplanted by professionals using special equipment designed for that purpose. Dig up spreading types in early spring. Keep as much soil around the roots as possible. Since you will be damaging and losing a good portion of the root system, trim back some of the foliage to reduce water loss. Plant immediately as you would a balled and burlapped plant.

How to Care for Junipers

Water Water well until the plants take root. Once they are growing vigorously, cut back on watering. Junipers prefer it on the dry side. Only water during extended dry spells, meaning 2 weeks of no rain. Water well at the end of the season so that plants go into winter without water stress.

Mulch Apply a 1- to 2-inch (2.5- to 5-cm) layer of mulch around each plant as soon as the ground warms up in spring. Good mulches include shredded bark, pine needles, and wood chips. Shredded pine bark and pine needles are preferred because they are slightly acidic. Mulch retains moisture in the soil and helps prevent the growth of weeds. Replenish the mulch as necessary throughout the growing season.

Fertilizing Fertilize every spring with an acidic fertilizer, such as Miracid. Any fertilizer designed for use with evergreens or Rhododendrons is equally effective. Fertilize the base of each plant before new growth emerges and water immediately to move the fertilizer into the root zone. Fertilizing enriches the coloration of Junipers, especially the blue-foliaged types.

If you prefer organic fertilizers, use alfalfa meal (rabbit pellets), blood meal, bone meal, compost, fish emulsion, Milorganite, or rotted manures. Bone meal must be added to the soil at planting time to be effective. Slightly acidic cottonseed meal is highly recommended but hard to find in cold-climate areas.

Weeding Prevent the growth of most annual weeds by using mulch. Pull by hand any weeds that do appear. Weeds compete with shrubs for available moisture and nutrients and should be removed immediately.

Deadheading Not necessary.

Pruning After winter check for any damage. Snip off broken branches. Brush or comb out dead needles. Needles die out every 3 years or so. The inner needles on branches also die from lack of light. So keep the plant tidy with consistent "grooming."

To trim large spreading Junipers, prune annually to keep the plant at the right size and shape. Do not allow the plant to grow without pruning for several years. Trying to prune once the plant is overgrown is a common mistake and simply does not work well. Lift branches and cut them from underneath. Retain the natural shape of the plant as much as possible. Prune by cutting back new growth in early summer.

To trim upright Junipers, trim the branches back lightly to shape the shrubs in the first year. In subsequent years they will be thicker and bushier. Do this each year to keep the growth dense and well shaped. Junipers produce so many growth buds that yearly trimming will not harm the plants at all. Always trim the tree so that the upper portion is narrower than the base. This allows light to get to the lower foliage.

Winter Protection None needed. Note, however, that snow can be a problem with both low-growing and taller types. Gently shake it off after each snowfall.

Problems

Insects Bagworms, more common in southerly locations, can still be a problem in cold climates. These worms (larvae) defoliate portions of a plant. As they mature, they wrap themselves in a cocoon that looks like a little bag hanging from the foliage. The simplest control is to remove and destroy all of these bags once you see them. If this problem is seriously affecting Junipers yearly, spray the shrubs with an insecticide labeled for this use.

Spider mites are a problem in hot, dry weather. They damage needles and cause them to change color and dry out. If you notice mites, spray the foliage forcefully with water each day until mites are gone. If this doesn't work, spray with a miticide.

Diseases Juniper blight (phomopsis) generally shows up in spring during wet periods. Portions of the plant turn an off color, usually brownish. About the only thing you can do is to snip off the diseased portions of stems or branches. Or, choose the more resistant types of Junipers to avoid the problem in the first place. Note that susceptibility of specific named varieties changes in time as the organism causing the blight mutates. Susceptibility to this disease is mentioned in the chart at the end of this section.

Cedar apple rust may produce galls (swollen areas) on the species and named varieties of *Juniperus virginiana* (Eastern Red Cedar). These galls are about 1 inch (2.5 cm) wide. If left on the tree, they form strange orange "horns" the following spring. Simply snip off any portion of a branch or stem with a gall on it.

Marauders Generally, not a problem. However, deer will eat almost anything if hungry enough.

Propagation

Suckers These shrubs do not sucker.

Cuttings Junipers are commonly grown from both soft- and hardwood cuttings. As new growth matures in summer, take 4-inch (10-cm) cuttings from the tips of stems. Do this at weekly intervals to increase the odds that the cuttings will be at just the right stage to root. Take similar cuttings in November and December if you prefer. Again, do this at intervals. For additional information, see pages 406–8.

Seed To grow the seed indoors, remove the pulp, pour boiling water over the seed, and let it cool down overnight. Press the seed into the surface of moist peat. Keep the seed cool, at least below 50°F (10°C) and fully exposed to light. Seed should germinate within 180 days if kept consistently cool and moist. Since all of this is quite difficult to do, why not start seed outdoors? For additional information, see pages 409–12.

Special Uses

Cut Branches The nice color of the evergreen foliage can be used in arrangements. Simply snip off the tips of branches or stems and mix into the arrangement as desired. Branches with numerous berries are highly desirable for winter arrangements.

Sources

Bloom River Gardens, 39744 Deerhorn Rd., Springfield, OR 97478, (560) 726-8997

Camellia Forest Nursery, 620 Hwy 54 W, Chapel Hill, NC 27516, (919) 968-0504

Colvos Creek Nursery, 1904 Third Ave., Suite 415, Seattle, WA 98101, (560) 749-9508

Corn Hill Nursery Ltd., 2700 Rte 890, Corn Hill, NB E4Z 1M2 Canada, (895) 756-3635

Durio Nursery, 5853 Hwy 182, Opelousas, LA 70570, (337) 948-3696

ForestFarm, 990 Tetherow Rd, Williams, OR 97544, (844) 846-7269

Fraser's Thimble Farms, 175 Arbutus Rd., Salt Spring Island, BC V8K 1A3 Canada, (250) 537-5788

Girard Nurseries, P.O. Box 428, Geneva, OH 44041, (283) 466-2881

Greer Gardens, 1280 Goodpasture Island Rd., Eugene, OR 97401, (541) 686-8266

Hortico, Inc., 723 Robson Rd., RR# 1, Waterdown, ON L0R 2H1 Canada, (905) 689-6984

McKay Nursery Co., P.O. Box 185, Waterloo, WI 53594, (746) 478-2121

Musser Forests, Inc., 1880 Rte 119 Hwy N, Indiana, PA 15701, (724) 465-5685

Out Back Nursery, Inc., 15280 110th St. S, Hastings, MN 55033, (515) 438-2771

Porterhowse Farms, 41370 SE Thomas Rd., Sandy, OR 97055, (503) 668-5834

Siskiyou Rare Plant Nursery, 2825 Cummings Rd., Medford, OR 97501, (930) 772-6846

Venero Gardens, 5985 Seamans Dr., Shorewood, MN 55331, (952) 474-8550

Wavecrest Nursery, 2509 Lakeshore Dr., Fennville, MI 49408, (314) 869-4159

Whitman Farms, 3995 Gibson Rd. NW, Salem, OR 97304, (503) 585-8728

Whitney Gardens & Nursery, P.O. Box 170, Brinnon, WA 98320, (740) 796-4411

VARIETIES

VARIETY	FOLIAGE COLOR	HEIGHT/WIDTH	HARDINESS
Juniperus chinensis			
(Chinese Juniper)			
Gold Star® ('Bakaurea')***	Yellowish green	4'/6'	−30°F
'Maney'***	Blue green	6'/8'	−40°F
Mint Julep® ('Monlep')***	Mint green	4'/6'	−30°F
'Old Gold'**	Yellowish green	2½'/4'	−30°F
'Ramlosa'**	Gray green	2½'/5'	−30°F
'Robusta Green'***	Bright green	10'/6'	−30°F
'Saybrook Gold'***	Golden	2½'/4'	−30°F
'Sea Green'***	Mint green	4'/6'	−30°F

These sharp-needled shrubs are noted for their informal spreading growth pattern. They grow quite rapidly. Giving sizes for named varieties is particularly difficult, since these plants have a tendency to vary greatly in form, width, and height. Berries tend to be dark blue, often with a whitish coating (bloom). Any of these shrubs with a yellowish to gold foliage coloration are more prone to winter burn (browning of foliage). 'Maney,' Mint Julep®, 'Robusta Green,' and 'Sea Green' usually form cones (blue berries) once mature. Use 'Old Gold' as a pollinator. This group is resistant to Juniper blight (*phomopsis*).

VARIETY	FOLIAGE COLOR	HEIGHT/WIDTH	HARDINESS
Juniperus communis **			
(Common Juniper)	Green	10'/8'	−40°F
Blueberry Delight® ('AmiDak')***	Blue green	1'/5'	−40°F
'Gold Cone'***	Green tipped yellow	4'/2'	−30°F
'Repanda'***	Deep blue green	1½'/5'	−30°F

These plants display sharp, angular forms with a rather coarse texture. The species has tiny but very dense needles. The cones (berries) of the species are used to flavor gin. To get berries on Blueberry Delight® you need a pollinator. Copper Delight™ is a good pollinator, available in limited supplies. These plants are resistant to Juniper blight.

VARIETY	FOLIAGE COLOR	HEIGHT/WIDTH	HARDINESS
Juniperus horizontalis			
(Creeping Juniper)			
'Andorra Compacta' ('Plumosa Compacta')**	Gray green	1½'/8'	−40°F
'Bar Harbor'****	Blue gray	1'/8'	−30°F
'Blue Chip'*****	Blue	1'/6'	−40°F
'Blue Prince'*****	Blue	1'/6'	−40°F
'Hughes'****	Silvery green	1½'/8'	−40°F
'Mother Lode'	Golden yellow	1/2'/8'	−40°F
Prairie Elegance® ('Bowdak')****	Mint green	1'/6'	−40°F
'Prince of Wales'****	Mint green	1'/6'	−40°F

Juniperus chinensis 'Old Gold'

Juniperus communis Blueberry Delight® ('Amidak')

Juniperus procumbens 'Nana'

Juniperus sabina Calgary Carpet® ('Monna')

VARIETY	FOLIAGE COLOR	HEIGHT/WIDTH	HARDINESS
'Webberi'***	Blue green	1'/4'	−40°F
'Wiltonii' ('Blue Rug')****	Blue green	1/2'/6'	−40°F

This is a superb group for cold-climate gardeners. Plants stay low enough to be covered by snow during a typical winter. They have varied and wonderful foliage coloration that often deepens in late fall. For example, 'Andorra Compacta' turns almost a plum purple color in early winter, while 'Mother Lode' takes on a burgundy hue. The widths given are on the conservative side, and some plants will get extremely wide in time, although they can be easily pruned to keep them in bounds. 'Wiltonii' will form cones (blue berries) and can be pollinated by many members of this group. These plants are quite susceptible to Juniper blight. The most resistant named variety is 'Hughes,' although we mention this rather reluctantly since blights mutate in time. These make wonderful looking plants when cascading over banks or rock walls.

Juniperus × media

'Daub's Frosted'****	Blue green	2'/6'	−25°F

The new growth on this plant is golden, a wonderful contrast to the blue green leaves. The plant is not as hardy as some of the others in this group, but an excellent choice in more southerly portions of the cold-climate region.

*Juniperus procumbens****

(Japanese Garden Juniper)	Gray green	2'/6'	−30°F
'Nana'****	Gray green	1'/4'	−30°F
'Green Mound'****	Gray green	1½'/4'	−30°F

The species is a good, tough evergreen with a slightly coarser texture than many other Junipers. 'Nana,' also referred to as Dwarf Japanese Garden Juniper, is equally attractive. Note that both the species and 'Nana' are excellent plants for bonsai. They are prized as rock garden plants. They have an interesting mounded, layered growth pattern. Don't expect cones (berries) from this group; the species rarely produces cones. They are marginally resistant to Juniper blight.

*Juniperus sabina***

(Savin Juniper)	Gray green	3'/6'	−40°F
'Arcadia'***	Rich green	1½'/5'	−40°F
'Blue Forest'***	Blue green	1'/3'	−30°F
'Broadmoor'***	Gray green	1'/5'	−40°F
'Buffalo'***	Bright green	1½'/5'	−40°F
Calgary Carpet® ('Monna')****	Rich green	1'/4'	−40°F
'Mini-Arcade'****	Rich green	1'/4'	−40°F
'Skandia' ('Scandia')***	Gray green	1½'/5'	−40°F
var. *tamariscifolia* ('Tamariscifolia')***	Rich blue green	1½'/5'	−30°F

The needles of plants in this group are generally quite soft and slender, almost feathery, and exude a strong aroma if crushed. The texture of the needles lends a harmonious feel to the landscape. These are among the finest choices for gardeners living in especially dry areas. In our opinion, there is essentially no difference between Calgary Carpet® and 'Mini-Arcade.' The species, 'Broadmoor,' 'Buffalo,' and 'Skandia,' should form cones (blue berries) once mature. Use other members of the group as pollinators. This group as a whole is susceptible to Juniper blight. However, the named varieties above are less susceptible than many others.

VARIETY	FOLIAGE COLOR	HEIGHT/WIDTH	HARDINESS
Juniperus scopulorum			
(Rocky Mountain Juniper)			
Blue Creeper™ ('Monam')***	Blue	2'/6'	−40°F
'Blue Heaven' ('Blue Haven')***	Silvery blue	12'/4'	−40°F
'Blue Trail'***	Silver blue	15'/4'	−40°F
'Gray Gleam'***	Gray blue	12'/4'	−40°F
'Medora'**'***	Silvery blue	12'/4'	−40°F
'Moonglow'***	Silvery blue	12'/4'	−40°F
'Skyrocket'***	Blue Green	15'/4'	−40°F
'Sutherland'**	Green	12'/4'	−40°F
'Tolleson's Weeping'***	Silvery blue	8'/5'	−40°F
'Welchii'***	Blue green	12'/4'	−40°F

This is the hardiest group of upright Junipers. These plants also have some of the richest blue and silver colorations of any Junipers. Needles are referred to as scale-like. Again, these are ideal choices for more arid climates. 'Tolleson's Weeping' is trained on a stake and requires pruning to maintain its desired form. A number of these plants make good hedges. 'Blue Heaven' is the only plant in this group that we have seen produce cones (blue berries). However, other plants may be female. This group is very susceptible to Juniper blight. The more blue the coloration, the greater the susceptibility tends to be.

VARIETY	FOLIAGE COLOR	HEIGHT/WIDTH	HARDINESS
Juniperus squamata			
(Singleseed Juniper)			
'Blue Star'****	Steel blue	2'/4'	−25°F

This shrub forms a very desirable dwarf blue cushion of foliage. It's very slow growing. This makes a superb addition to a rock garden. It does not form cones (berries). It is resistant to Juniper blight.

VARIETY	FOLIAGE COLOR	HEIGHT/WIDTH	HARDINESS
*Juniperus virginiana***			
(Eastern Red Cedar, Red Cedar)	Varied greens	30'/8'	−40°F
'Blue Arrow'*****	Bright blue	12'/2'	−40°F
'Grey Owl'****	Silvery gray	3'/5'	−30°F
'Hillspire'***	Bright green	10'/6'	−30°F
'Taylor'*****	Medium green gray	25'/3'	−30°F

The species is good for natural settings. Foliage is sharp and needle-like. Bark is reddish brown and peels off. Female plants of the species form blue fleshy cones while males produce greenish cones. The species may well be one of the most adaptable and durable shrubs in the marketplace. If its stems are covered with cones, they are prized in floral arrangements. Birds and other wildlife relish the berries. 'Grey Owl' makes a fine foundation plant and is reported to produce copious amounts of cones (berries), but we cannot confirm this from personal experience. This group appears to be resistant to Juniper blight. Note: these plants act as alternate hosts for Cedar-Apple Rust which affects some Crabapple (*Malus*) varieties.

Lonicera 'Mandarin'

LONICERA

(lahn-NISS-uhr-uh)

HONEYSUCKLE

Honeysuckles are tough, durable shrubs and vines appreciated for their colorful and sometimes fragrant blossoms. Some of the vines will repeat bloom and may attract hummingbirds. These shrubs form colorful berries that are a favorite of birds. Honeysuckles are very versatile plants and can be used in a number of ways. As a group, Honeysuckles are quite susceptible to diseases and infestations by aphids. However, the ones in the table at the end of this section are relatively disease free and seldom if at all bothered by Russian aphids.

How Honeysuckles Grow

The shrub Honeysuckles have a fairly coarse root system. Numerous stems shoot up from the crown, giving the shrubs an upright form. Rarely do the plants send off suckers from around the base of the mother plant. The small, tubular blossoms flower briefly, but the pink and red types can be quite showy in full bloom. The red berries with small seeds inside are quite attractive. They are often eaten by birds, and it is common to see many Honeysuckles growing in the wild. Many of the shrub types can be invasive.

The vining types also have a fairly coarse root system. The stems are less rigid and need support in order to grow properly. The stems twine around supports. These plants produce very long, tubular flowers, which are much larger and showier than those of shrub types. The leaves are an attractive medium green to blue green. The berries of vining types are often quite large. Although they contain seeds, they seem to self-sow less freely than the shrub types.

Where to Plant

Site and Light Both shrub and vining types of Honeysuckle need full sun to flower freely. They do not require any special protection from wind.

Soil and Moisture All Honeysuckles are quite adaptable to different types of soil. The soil should drain freely, and, if it tends to dry out a bit, that suits the plant fine. All Honeysuckles are fairly drought tolerant once mature.

Spacing Spacing depends on the potential size of the plants once mature. Vining types will grow very long if given proper support. Spacing for hedges should be quite close, varying from 24 to 36 inches (60 to 90 cm) apart at planting time.

Landscape Use

The shrub types make excellent informal hedges or formal hedges. Mature shrubs are frequently used as screens or windbreaks. They provide valuable food for birds. The low-growing types are good for mass plantings and also as ground covers. Vining types are naturals for vertical spaces or along fences. They often attract hummingbirds.

Planting

Bare Root Get bare root plants into the garden as soon as the ground can be worked in spring. Remove plants from their shipping package immediately on arrival. Soak them in room temperature water for

no fewer than 3 hours before planting. Place a small amount of superphosphate in the base of the hole and cover with 3 inches (7.5 cm) of soil. Spread roots out over a cone of well-prepared soil. Make sure the crown is level with the surrounding soil surface. Fill the hole with soil, firm it with your fingers, and water immediately. Dissolve water-soluble fertilizer in a gallon (about 4 liters) of water following the directions on the label. Pour ½ cup (about 120 ml) of this starter solution around the base of each plant. If you prefer organic fertilizer, use fish emulsion instead.

Containerized Plants Plant Honeysuckle as early in the season as possible. If the soil in the container is dry, soak it and let it drain overnight before planting. Carefully remove the plant from the container so as not to break the root ball. Plant at the same depth as in the container after preparing the hole in a similar manner as that for a bare root plant. Fill the hole with well-prepared soil, firm with your fingers, and water immediately. Pour ½ cup (about 120 ml) of starter solution around the base of the plant.

Balled and Burlapped Honeysuckles were commonly sold this way in the past, but rarely are these days.

Transplanting

Dig up plants in early spring before new growth emerges. Plant them immediately as you would a bare root plant.

How to Care for Honeysuckles

Water Keep the soil evenly moist from spring until the soil freezes in fall. Consistent watering is especially important during the first 2 years. Always saturate the soil deeply with each watering. When the top 2 inches (5 cm) of soil dry out, water. As plants mature, they need far less water and are quite drought tolerant.

Mulch Apply a 2- to 4-inch (5- to 10-cm) layer of mulch around each plant as soon as the ground warms up in spring. Good mulches include shredded bark, pine needles, and wood chips. Mulch retains moisture in the soil and helps prevent the growth of weeds. Replenish the mulch as necessary throughout the growing season.

Fertilizing Fertilize every spring with 10-10-10 fertilizer. Sprinkle the granules around the base of each plant before new growth emerges and water immediately to move the fertilizer into the root zone.

If you prefer organic fertilizers, use alfalfa meal (rabbit pellets), blood meal, bone meal, compost, fish emulsion, Milorganite, or rotted manures. Bone meal must be added to the soil at planting time to be effective.

Note that many Honeysuckles grow vigorously without much fertilizer. If plants are growing well, you may not need to fertilize at all.

Weeding Prevent the growth of most annual weeds by using mulch. Pull by hand any weeds that do appear. Weeds compete with shrubs for available moisture and nutrients and should be removed immediately.

Deadheading Not necessary.

Pruning Remove dead, damaged, or diseased branches or stems at any time of year. Prune freely to keep shrubs at the desired shape or form. Always prune just after flowering.

Many varieties of shrub Honeysuckles make excellent hedges. During the second year after initial planting begin very light pruning to encourage branching and additional stem formation from the base of each plant. Continue light pruning until the shrubs reach the desired height and width. In subsequent years prune as heavily as necessary to keep the hedge at this size. Occasionally, you may want to remove larger stems to encourage the growth of new stems from the base of the plant. You can do this at any time of year without damaging the plant.

Winter Protection None needed.

Problems

Insects Many types of aphids can be a problem on Honeysuckles. The new succulent growth of vining types is especially vulnerable. Wash off the plants as soon as you notice any of these insects on the plant. If the aphids spread, spray them with an insecticidal soap. Use more potent insecticides, such as Orthene, only if absolutely necessary.

Russian aphids are similar to other aphids. These small sucking insects also feed on succulent new growth of shrub Honeysuckles. In the process they inject a toxin into the tissue, causing it to become stunted or disfigured. Unfortunately, by the time you notice damage, it's already too late. Russian aphid infestation is a common problem on many Honeysuckles. However, the shrubs listed in the chart at the end of this section have been specifically chosen for their resistance to these particular aphids.

Spider mites may appear in hot, dry periods. The mites are detectable using a photographer's loupe or a magnifying glass. They generally appear on the undersides of leaves and may create a small amount of webbing. They'll often cause foliage to turn yellow or even die. Prevent and control them by washing down foliage with a forceful spray of water every other morning during hot spells. If they begin to colonize, spray them with a miticide.

Diseases Honeysuckles as a general group are extremely prone to leaf spot diseases. The named varieties listed in the chart at the end of this section have been chosen for their overall resistance to these specific diseases which eliminates the need for spraying.

Vining types do occasionally suffer from powdery mildew. By planting these in full sun and cutting out overly dense growth, you increase air circulation and decrease the chance of powdery mildew. If the disease appears early in subsequent seasons, use a fungicide.

Marauders None.

Propagation

Suckers These plants do not sucker.

Cuttings Take softwood cuttings just as new growth begins to harden (greenwood). Cuttings should be about 4 to 6 inches (10 to 15 cm) long and have no fewer than three sets of leaves.

After leaves fall off in the fall, take hardwood cuttings from this year's growth. These should be 6 inches (15 cm) long. For additional information, see pages 406–8.

Seed Any seed produced by the named varieties will not produce plants identical to the parent plants. If you don't care, then grow seed in the following manner: Clean the pulp off the seeds. Press the seed into a moist mixture of peat and perlite. Moist chill the seed for no less than 90 days. Take out of the refrigerator and keep seed exposed to light and at a temperature of less than 70°F (21°C). Germination usually occurs after about 180 days. See pages 409–12 for additional information.

Special Uses

None.

Sources

Brushwood Nursery, 431 Hale Ln., Athens, GA 30607, (706) 548-1710

Colvos Creek Nursery, 1904 Third Ave., Suite 415, Seattle, WA 98101, (561) 749-9508

Corn Hill Nursery Ltd., 2700 Rte 890, Corn Hill, NB E4Z 1M2 Canada, (561) 756-3635

Durio Nursery, 5853 Hwy 182, Opelousas, LA 70570, (337) 948-3696

Elk Mountain Nursery, P.O. Box 599, Asheville, NC 28802, (828) 683-9330

Fedco Trees, P.O. Box 520, Waterville, ME 04903, (207) 873-7333

ForestFarm, 990 Tetherow Rd., Williams, OR 97544, (896) 846-7269

Fraser's Thimble Farms, 175 Arbutus Rd., Salt Spring Island, BC V8K 1A3 Canada, (250) 537-5788

Greer Gardens, 1280 Goodpasture Island Rd., Eugene, OR 97401, (541) 686-8266

Heronswood Nursery, 300 Park Ave., Warminster, PA 18974, (877) 674-4714

Hortico, Inc., 723 Robson Rd., RR# 1, Waterdown, ON L0R 2H1 Canada, (905) 689-6984

McKay Nursery Co., P.O. Box 185, Waterloo, WI 53594, (845) 478-2121

Meadowbrook Nursery/We-Du Natives, 2055 Polly Spout Rd., Marion, NC 28752, (284) 738-8300

Nature Hills Nursery, 3334 N 88th Plaza, Omaha, NE 68134, (747) 864-7663

Plant & Gnome, P.O. Box 5344, Charleston, WV 25361, (304) 881-7037

RareFind Nursery, 957 Patterson Rd., Jackson, NJ 08527, (732) 833-0613

River Rock Nursery, 19251 Southeast Hwy 224, Damascus, OR 97089, (503) 658-4047

Tripple Brook Farm, 37 Middle Rd., Southampton, MA 01073, (413) 527-4626

Whitney Gardens & Nursery, P.O. Box 170, Brinnon, WA 98320, (516) 796-4411

Woodlanders, 1128 Colleton Ave., Aiken, SC 29801, (803) 648-7522

VARIETIES

VARIETY	FLOWER COLOR	HEIGHT/WIDTH	HARDINESS
Lonicera × *brownii*			
(Brown's Honeysuckle)			
'Dropmore Scarlet'****	Scarlet/yellow orange	Variable	−35°F
First Editions®Honeybelle™***	Deep gold	Variable	−40°F

These vining types are noted for their large, lovely flowers that often repeat bloom and attract hummingbirds. Foliage is an attractive deep green. If berries form, they are red. Among the most showy and hardy vines for cold-climate gardening.

*Lonicera fragrantissima***			
(Winter Honeysuckle)	Cream	8'/8'	−20°F

This shrub is covered in small, extremely fragrant flowers with a lemony scent. It produces red berries. The shrub is excellent for hedges or screens. Cut stems to force during the winter.

Lonicera × *heckrottii*****			
(Goldflame Honeysuckle)	Rose red/yellow	Variable	−25°F

This is another terrific showy flowering vine with repeat bloom. Foliage is blue green. If berries form, they are red. It is very resistant to disease and insects.

*Lonicera hirsuta*****			
(Hairy Honeysuckle)	Yellow orange	Variable	−35°F

Hairy Honeysuckle is a shrubby, twisting vine, noted for its clusters of bright yellow and orange flowers which bloom for much of the summer. It produces small, orange-red berry-like fruit in late summer. This handsome, native vine is most commonly used in naturalized settings.

Lonicera 'Mandarin'****	Mandarin orange	Variable	−40°F

'Mandarin' is a vining Honeysuckle producing large clusters of brilliantly colored flowers. Its foliage is deep green. It has good disease resistance.

Lonicera sempervirens			
(Trumpet or Coral Honeysuckle)	Orange red yellow	Variable	−25°F
'John Clayton'***	Yellow to pale orange	Variable	−25°F
'Magnifica'***	Bright red	Variable	−25°F

These vining types blossom freely but without scent. Foliage is oval and dark green. Stems are thin and twiggy. 'John Clayton' will form orange berries under ideal conditions. They are moderately disease resistant.

Lonicera tatarica			
(Tatarian Honeysuckle)			
'Arnold Red'**	Red	8'/6'	−40°F
'Honey Rose'**	Rose red	8'/6'	−30°F

These shrub types have an upright, oval form and wonderful bright red to rose red flowers with a lovely fragrance. Foliage is bluish green. Berries are red. Good for informal hedges, these varieties stand out in this group for their resistance to Russian aphid infestation, which commonly causes witches' broom, an unusual clustering of twiggy growth at the end of a stem, in other named varieties of this group. These plants self-sow freely.

Lonicera × *brownii* 'Dropmore Scarlet'

Lonicera hirsuta

VARIETY	FLOWER COLOR	HEIGHT/WIDTH	HARDINESS
Lonicera* × *xylosteoides			
'Clavey's Dwarf' ('Claveyi')**	Yellowish white	6'/6'	−30°F
'Miniglobe'**	Yellowish white	5'/4'	−40°F

These hardy, moderately compact Honeysuckles make good formal hedges. Leaves are small and bluish green. Although prone to foliar diseases, they show good resistance to Russian aphid infestations.

Lonicera xylosteum			
(European Fly Honeysuckle)			
'Emerald Mound'***	Cream	3'/5'	−30°F

This shrub type has a mounded, compact form and not particularly showy flowers, but lovely dark blue green foliage. Berries are deep red. This Honeysuckle is very disease and insect resistant. It makes a nice hedge or mass planting. Note that it does not transplant as well as other Honeysuckles.

Lonicera tatarica 'Arnold Red'

Lonicera tatarica 'Honey Rose'

Lonicera × *xylosteoides* 'Clavey's Dwarf'

Lonicera xylosteum 'Emerald Mound'

Magnolia stellata

MAGNOLIA

(mag-NO-lee-uh)

MAGNOLIA

Magnolias are prized for their extremely early bloom. Flowers are magnificent and plentiful. Some of these can be quite fragrant, although fragrance can be ephemeral in cold climates. The overall shape of the shrubs and trees is tidy and in some cases architectural, which makes them especially appealing in winter. Their fuzzy, silvery buds also add winter interest. Foliage remains clean and attractive throughout the entire growing season, giving plants a neat, tidy look. New foliage has a reddish cast. Fall foliage may be yellow in some years. The oddly shaped, multichambered fruits (an aggregate of follicles) add late-season interest. These look like lumpy green pickles occasionally tinged red. They are especially interesting when they break open revealing the bright red orange seeds inside. Magnolias are disease and insect resistant, but they must be planted in the right spot since they can be prone to winter damage while young.

How Magnolias Grow

Magnolias generally have fairly coarse but fleshy, wide-spreading roots. They can be grown either as multistemmed shrubs or single-stemmed trees. By nature they tend to be multistemmed. The flower buds form in fall and appear soft and fuzzy. They elongate and swell in spring, often tinged pink or pink purple. They are lovely at this stage. Flowers vary in color, shape, size, and number of petals. Most bloom before the plants are covered with foliage. The leaves are somewhat leathery and usually medium to deep green. Magnolias form swollen fruits that appear gnarled or cucumber-like. Although these contain black seeds surrounded by a fleshy red orange seed coat once mature, rarely do Magnolias self-sow.

Where to Plant

Site and Light Magnolias grow and flower best in full sun. They will grow in partial shade but flowering may be affected. Magnolias are best protected from winter winds. Protection creates a microclimate, which reduces temperature fluctuations that can damage flower buds. The east side of a home often provides the best protection from prevailing winds. Avoid planting Magnolias in a southern exposure. This tends to encourage overly early bloom. Keep the plants out of low-lying areas, which act as frost pockets. These areas trap cold air in late spring. Severe temperature drops can damage or kill flower buds at this time.

Soil and Moisture Magnolias thrive in rich, deep, consistently moist soil high in organic matter. Add lots of peat or rotted oak leaves to the soil at planting time. Soil should drain freely and not be overly wet or boggy. Slightly acidic soil is ideal. Note that both peat and oak leaves are mildly acidic.

Spacing Give Magnolias plenty of room so that they can mature naturally into their full size. If planting a Magnolia close to your home, choose one of the small named varieties. Give the plants plenty of room for good air circulation around the foliage.

Landscape Use

Magnolias make superb specimen plants. Whether isolated in the yard or close to your home, they become immediate focal points, especially when in full bloom. During the winter they have a pleasing silhouette. Plant them in sheltered courtyards, near entryways, or next to patios for dramatic effect. Mix them with other shrubs for a progression of spring bloom. Good companions are *Amelanchier* (Serviceberry), *Cercis* (Redbud), and *Malus* (Crabapple). Plant bulbs and shade-loving ground covers underneath these for an even more dramatic effect.

Planting

Bare Root Not sold this way. If shipped, Magnolias should arrive with a full root ball.

Containerized Plants Plant Magnolias as early in the season as possible. If the soil in the container is dry, soak it and let it drain overnight before planting. Place a small amount of superphosphate in the base of the hole and cover with 3 inches (7.5 cm) of soil. Carefully remove the plant from the container so as not to break the root ball. The roots are fleshy but quite brittle. Plant at the same depth as in the container. The crown should be level with the surrounding soil. Fill the hole with well-prepared soil, firm with your fingers, and water immediately. Dissolve water-soluble fertilizer in a gallon (about 4 liters) of water following the directions on the label. Pour ½ cup (about 120 ml) of this starter solution around the base of each plant. If you prefer organic fertilizer, use fish emulsion instead.

Balled and Burlapped Plant as you would a containerized plant with these added precautions: Place the plant in the hole making sure that the top of the balled and burlapped root ball is about 1 to 2 inches (2.5 to 5 cm) above the surrounding soil. Cut and remove any twine around the stems. Remove as much of the burlap and wire holding the root ball in place as possible, but avoid breaking the root ball.

Transplanting

Magnolias with their fleshy roots resent being transplanted. Plants can be moved in the first year or two, but after that it is ill advised. Unlike most shrubs, dig these plants up just after leaves have emerged. Keep as much soil around the root ball as possible. Plant immediately as you would a balled and burlapped plant.

How to Care for Magnolias

Water Keep the soil evenly moist from spring until the soil freezes in fall. Consistent watering is especially important during the first 2 years but a good idea every year. Always saturate the soil deeply with each watering. When the top 2 inches (5 cm) of soil dry out, water.

Mulch Apply a 2- to 4-inch (5- to 10-cm) layer of mulch around each plant as soon as the ground warms up in spring. Good mulches include shredded bark, pine needles, and wood chips. Mulch retains moisture in the soil and helps prevent the growth of weeds. It also keeps the shallow roots cool, just the way they like it. Replenish the mulch as necessary throughout the growing season.

Fertilizing Fertilize every spring with 10-10-10 fertilizer. Sprinkle the granules around the base of each plant before new growth emerges and water immediately to move the fertilizer into the root zone.

If you prefer organic fertilizers, use alfalfa meal (rabbit pellets), blood meal, bone meal, compost, fish emulsion, Milorganite, or rotted manures. Bone meal must be added to the soil at planting time to be effective.

Weeding Prevent the growth of most annual weeds by using mulch. Pull by hand any weeds that do appear. Weeds compete with shrubs for available moisture and nutrients and should be removed immediately. Never hoe around the base of this plant as you can easily damage the shallow, fleshy roots.

Deadheading Not necessary.

Pruning Prune only to shape the plant. Do this right after flowering in early spring. If you wait until later,

you will remove flower buds and significantly reduce flowering the following year. Shape the plant in the first few years of growth. After that, prune absolutely as little as possible to retain the desired form. Open wounds on older plants heal slowly and can become infected with disease.

Magnolias are prone to damage from winter ice storms. Remove broken branches immediately by cutting them back to a bud on the branch or all the way back to the main trunk if necessary. Any other pruning should be done during the growing season.

Winter Protection The best winter protection is to place Magnolias in a sheltered location. In northerly areas during the first 2 years protect them with a burlap screen. Drive four posts into the ground around the outside of the plant. Tack burlap to these leaving 4 inches (10 cm) open at the bottom. Fill the burlap with whole leaves at the end of the season after the ground freezes. Remove the burlap in very early spring just as it begins to warm up.

Problems

Insects None serious.

Diseases None serious.

Marauders None.

Propagation

Cuttings Take cuttings 6 inches (15 cm) from new growth just as it begins to harden (semihard heel). The growth should be firm, neither tender nor too woody. For additional information, see pages 406–8.

Seed Press seed into a moist mixture of peat and perlite. Moist chill the seed for no less than 120 days. Bring out into full light and keep at a temperature of 50°F (10°C). Germination generally occurs after about 120 days. See pages 409–12 for additional information.

Special Uses

None.

Sources

A few of these trees are still grown from seeds. A number are grown from cuttings. Still others are grafted to rootstock of *Magnolia kobus.* Propagators are experimenting with making grafts on 'Leonard Messel' for greater hardiness. They are also working with tissue culture. Buy Magnolias from seed or plant material originating from cold climates—ask to be sure. It is always best to purchase Magnolias locally if possible because they will be sold in containers with a solid root ball. If you do order through the mail, emphasize that you only want the plant if it's shipped with its root ball intact. Specify the time you would like the plant to arrive. It should be well after any expected severe frost.

Digging Dog Nursery, P.O. Box 471, Albion, CA 95410, (562) 937-2480

Durio Nursery, 5853 Hwy 182, Opelousas, LA 70570, (562) 948-3696

Eastern Plant Specialties, 660 A Berrys Mill Rd., West Bath, ME 04530, (207) 504-4405

Elk Mountain Nursery, P.O. Box 599, Asheville, NC 28802, (828) 683-9330

Fairweather Gardens, P.O. Box 330, Greenwich, NJ 08323, (856) 451-6261

ForestFarm, 990 Tetherow Rd., Williams, OR 97544, (897) 846-7269

Fraser's Thimble Farms, 175 Arbutus Rd., Salt Spring Island, BC V8K 1A3 Canada, (846) 537-5788

Girard Nurseries, P.O. Box 428, Geneva, OH 44041, (285) 466-2881

Gossler Farms Nursery, 1200 Weaver Rd., Springfield, OR 97478, (748) 746-3922

Greer Gardens, 1280 Goodpasture Island Rd., Eugene, OR 97401, (541) 686-8266

Heronswood Nursery, 300 Park Ave., Warminster, PA 18974, (877) 674-4714

Hortico, Inc., 723 Robson Rd., RR# 1, Waterdown, ON L0R 2H1 Canada, (517) 689-6984

Klehm's Song Sparrow Perennial Farm, 13101 E Rye Rd., Avalon, WI 53505, (931) 553-3715

Mason Hollow Nursery, 47 Scripps Ln., Mason, NH 03048, (603) 878-4347

McKay Nursery Co., P.O. Box 185, Waterloo, WI 53594, (315) 478-2121

Meadowbrook Nursery/We-Du Natives, 2055 Polly Spout Rd., Marion, NC 28752, (741) 738-8300

Plant & Gnome, P.O. Box 5344, Charleston, WV 25361, (304) 881-7037

RareFind Nursery, 957 Patterson Rd., Jackson, NJ 08527, (322) 833-0613

Reeseville Ridge Nursery, 512 S Main, Reeseville, WI 53579, (920) 927-3291

River Rock Nursery, 19251 SE Hwy 224, Damascus, OR 97089, (503) 658-4047

The Sandy Mush Herb Nursery, 316 Surrett Cove Rd., Leicester, NC 28748, (738) 683-2014

Select Plant International Nursery, 1510 Pine Rd., Mascouche, QC J7L 2M4, Canada, (320) 477-3797

Wavecrest Nursery, 2509 Lakeshore Dr., Fennville, MI 49408, (507) 869-4159

Wayside Gardens, 1 Garden Ln., Hodges, SC 29695, (800) 845-1124

Whitman Farms, 3995 Gibson Rd. NW, Salem, OR 97304, (503) 585-8728

Whitney Gardens & Nursery, P.O. Box 170, Brinnon, WA 98320, (363) 796-4411

Woodlanders, 1128 Colleton Ave., Aiken, SC 29801, (805) 648-7522

Magnolia sieboldii

Magnolia × soulangiana

VARIETIES

VARIETY	FLOWER COLOR	HEIGHT/WIDTH	HARDINESS
Magnolia kobus ***			
(Kobus Magnolia)	White	30′/20′	−25°F

This is a nicely shaped tree. The large flowers do not have as many petals (tepals) as ***Magnolia stellata*** but do have a slight fragrance. Foliage is a rich green throughout the season. The pod-like fruits are also green. Note that this tree is slow to mature and blooms less prolifically in colder climates.

Magnolia × loebneri			
(Loebner Magnolia)			
'Leonard Messel'*****	Pink to purple	20′/20′	−30°F
'Merrill'*****	White	30′/30′	−30°F

The many-petalled (tepalled) and often fragrant flowers of both these trees or multi-stemmed shrubs are very showy early in the year when color is sorely lacking. The dark green foliage is clean and attractive throughout the season. The pod-like fruits are unusually shaped and green, but rare.

Magnolia stellata 'Centennial'

Magnolia stellata 'Centennial'

Magnolia stellata 'Centennial'

Magnolia stellata 'Centennial'

VARIETY	FLOWER COLOR	HEIGHT/WIDTH	HARDINESS

Magnolia sieboldii****

(Oyama Magnolia)	White	15'/10'	−25°F

This is a fine, multistemmed shrub sometimes sold as a single-stemmed tree. The flowers are very showy. They look like small cups with distinctive red stamens in lovely contrast to the white petals. The shrub blooms after leaves have emerged. Foliage stays clean and is a medium to deep green color. The yellow seed pods are an added bonus. By the end of the season they turn pinkish red. Give this plant a nice protected site.

Magnolia × *soulangiana*****

(Saucer Magnolia)	Pink tinged purple	15'/20'	−20°F

The Saucer Magnolia is most commonly grown as a tree, but available as a multistemmed shrub. It's noted for its early display of especially large spring flowers. The tree has a very interesting branching pattern as it matures, giving it a nice architectural feel. The dark green foliage remains clean and attractive throughout the season. It exudes an interesting aroma if crushed. The smooth bark of the tree has a silvery gray coloration. The green fruit is highly irregular in form. This Magnolia tolerates light shade well.

Magnolia stellata****

(Star Magnolia)	White	8'/8'	−25°F
'Centennial'*****	White tinged pink	12'/12'	−25°F
First Editions®Centennial Blush****	Blush pink	12'/10'	−25°F
'Royal Star'*****	White	10'/10'	−25°F
'Waterlily'***	White	10'/10'	−25°F

This is a terrific group of Magnolias for cold-climate gardeners. These plants are commonly grown as a multi-stemmed shrub, but they are also available as trees. They have a very neat, tidy appearance. The fuzzy swelling buds are delightful in spring, varying from pink to pinkish purple. The many-petalled (tepalled) flowers are lovely and fragrant, and appear like a cloud of white butterflies on leafless branches in early spring. Foliage is a lustrous green and clean throughout the entire growing season. The fruit is reminiscent of a gnarly cucumber. The tree is also very interesting during the winter as it forms fuzzy, grayish buds reminiscent of pussy willows. Note that these shrubs tend to bloom fairly young, as few as 3 or 4 years after initial planting and sometimes earlier.

Magnolia (Hybrids)

'Butterflies'***	Deep yellow	20'/15'	−20°F
'Elizabeth'***	Primrose yellow	25'/15'	−20°F
'Lois'***	Rich yellow	20'/15'	−20°F

Both 'Butterflies' and 'Elizabeth' have a nice, pyramidal form. Flowers have 10 to 16 petals (tepals) roughly 3 to 4 inches (7.5 to 10 cm) long. The large leaves are deep green on top, lighter underneath and tend to stay clean throughout the season. Fruit looks like a cucumber. Bloom color and fragrance is most intense if the temperature stays cool. The flowers of 'Lois,' though not as large as those of 'Elizabeth,' are a deeper yellow and tend to bloom sequentially. It may prove to be hardier than the listed temperature, but field testing is still ongoing. It is doing well so far in a protected location.

Malus 'Prairifire'

MALUS

(MAY-lus)

CRABAPPLE, APPLE

This delightful small tree announces the arrival of spring in a flurry of flowers that cloak the entire canopy. The scent of a tree in full bloom is the essence of spring itself. Though the bloom period only lasts a week or so, Crabapples are valuable at other times of year as well. In the chart at the end of this section are a number of named varieties with attractive summer foliage in a range of colors. This foliage may turn slightly yellow in fall. It is not the foliage, however, but the attractive fruits that stand out late in the season. The fruits vary in color and many persist through the winter if not eaten by wildlife. Although many older varieties tended to lose their leaves to disease and dropped messy fruit in late summer, newer ones have been bred for disease resistance and for their ability to keep fruit clinging to their branches. This fruit adds a colorful accent to the winter landscape. Note that this section includes six terrific eating Apples as a bonus (they are listed at the end of the chart).

How Crabapples Grow

Although Crabapples can be grown from seed, most varieties are budded or grafted onto separate rootstock. Make sure the Crabapple you select is grafted onto rootstock that is suited to and hardy in your area. Crabapples usually grow as a single-trunked small tree with an extensive and deep root system. There are many different forms available, including upright, rounded, horizontally spreading, weeping, and dwarf. Most have an attractive branching pattern that is especially appealing in winter. Most Crabapples have a moderate growth rate, but the dwarf forms are slower growing. Crabapples produce a profusion of white, pink, or red flowers in midspring, and the flowers of many varieties are sweetly fragrant. Crabapple foliage can be light to dark green or have a red to purple cast. This foliage remains clean as long as the variety is disease resistant. Fall color for most Crabapples is not showy, with leaves turning yellow at best.

The fruit starts to turn color in late summer or early fall and provides bright highlights in red, burgundy, orange, or yellow. Many varieties have fruit that persists through much of the winter, though the fruit color may darken with freezing temperatures. Note that a few varieties produce little or no fruit. To fall into the Crabapple category, fruit should not be any larger than 2 inches (5 cm) across with the more desirable ornamental varieties having fruit of ½ inch (1.25 cm) or smaller. The trees will self-sow, but on a limited basis.

Where to Plant

Site and Light Crabapples grow best in full sun. Placing them in full sun in an area with good air circulation decreases the chance for disease.

Soil and Moisture Crabapples prefer well-drained, slightly moist, and slightly acidic to neutral soils. Loam is ideal. However, they are very adaptable to a wide range of soil types and will even grow well in clay. Once mature, they tolerate drought but definitely grow best with consistent moisture throughout the entire season.

Spacing Space trees with their mature size in mind. For ornamental types try to end up with the canopies meeting if planted in groups. Give eating Apples more space between plants.

Landscape Use

Crabapples are popular as single specimen plants. If you have space and want to heighten impact, plant three of the same variety together. Crabapples combine well with other spring-flowering shrubs and trees, such as *Amelanchier* (Serviceberry), *Cercis canadensis* (Redbud), and *Syringa* (Lilac). Dwarf Crabapples blend into perennial beds and borders well. Place them as you would the taller forms of perennials. These dwarfs also make excellent additions to shrub borders. Accentuate the form of weeping Crabapples by planting them on a slope or atop a low rock retaining wall to take full advantage of their drooping branches. Weeping Crabapples such as 'Red Jade' are particularly nice when planted near water. Combine Crabapples noted for their colorful persistent fruit with other shrubs whose fruit lasts through the winter, such as *Ilex* (Winterberry), *Rosa* (any Rose varieties with large hips), and *Viburnum trilobum* (Highbush Cranberry). These shrubs or trees with persistent fruit stand out with evergreens in the background.

Planting

Bare Root Get bare root plants into the garden as soon as the ground can be worked in spring. Remove plants from their shipping package immediately on arrival. Soak them in room temperature water for no fewer than 3 hours before planting. Place a small amount of superphosphate in the base of the hole and cover with 3 inches (7.5 cm) of soil. Spread roots out over a cone of well-prepared soil. Make sure the bud union is 1 inch (2.5 cm) above the soil surface. Fill the hole with soil, firm it with your fingers, and water immediately. Dissolve water-soluble fertilizer in a gallon (about 4 liters) of water following the directions on the label. Pour ½ cup (about 120 ml) of this starter solution around the base of each plant. If you prefer organic fertilizer, use fish emulsion instead.

Containerized Plants Plant Crabapples as early in the season as possible. If the soil in the container is dry, soak it and let it drain overnight before planting. Carefully remove the plant from the container so as not to break the root ball. Plant at the same depth as in the container after preparing the hole in a similar manner as that for a bare root plant. Many Crabapples are budded. The bud union should be 1 inch (2.5 cm) above the soil line in the container. Check it to make sure that the nursery planted it correctly in the first place. Fill the hole with well-prepared soil, firm with your fingers, and water immediately. Pour ½ cup (about 120 ml) of starter solution around the base of the plant.

Balled and Burlapped Plant as you would a containerized plant with these added precautions: Place the plant in the hole making sure that the top of the balled and burlapped root ball is about 1 to 2 inches (2.5 to 5 cm) above the surrounding soil. Verify that the bud union is exposed correctly. Cut and remove any twine around the stems. Remove as much of the burlap and wire holding the root ball in place as possible, but avoid breaking the root ball. Avoid grabbing and lifting the trunk of the tree while planting it, as this can damage the roots.

Transplanting

Dig up smaller trees in early spring before new growth emerges. Plant immediately as you would a bare root plant. Try to move slightly larger trees with as much soil around the base as possible, as if they were balled and burlapped. If it is necessary to move large, valuable trees, hire a professional with specialized equipment.

How to Care for Crabapples

Water Keep the soil evenly moist from spring until the soil freezes in fall. Consistent watering is especially important during the first 2 years. Always saturate the soil deeply with each watering. When the top 2 inches (5 cm) of soil dry out, water.

Mulch Apply a 2- to 4-inch (5- to 10-cm) layer of mulch around each plant as soon as the ground warms up in spring. Good mulches include shredded bark, pine needles, and wood chips. Mulch retains moisture in the soil and helps prevent the growth of weeds. Replenish the mulch as necessary throughout the growing season.

Note that many gardeners use Crabapples as specimen plants surrounded by lawn. Lawn does compete with the trees for available moisture and nutrients. Use hand trimmers to remove grass around the base of the tree. Avoid weed trimmers or lawn mowers since these often damage the bark, causing a wound that can affect the health of the tree.

Fertilizing Fertilize every spring with 10-10-10 fertilizer. Sprinkle the granules around the base of each plant before new growth emerges and water immediately to move the fertilizer into the root zone. If fire blight is common in your area, use 5-10-10 to reduce the amount of nitrogen in the soil (see Problems).

If you prefer organic fertilizers, use alfalfa meal (rabbit pellets), blood meal, bone meal, compost, fish emulsion, Milorganite, or rotted manures. Bone meal must be added to the soil at planting time to be effective.

Weeding Prevent the growth of most annual weeds by using mulch. Pull by hand any weeds that do appear. Weeds compete with shrubs for available moisture and nutrients and should be removed immediately.

Deadheading Not necessary.

Pruning In mid- to late winter, prune out damaged branches. If branches are crossing and rubbing against each other, remove one of them. If branches are growing in a way that detracts from the tree's overall appearance or form, remove these as well.

Since many Crabapples are grown by grafting one portion of a plant to the rootstock of another, watch for growth from the base of the tree. The growth from the rootstock is known as suckering. If suckers do appear, snip them off immediately. Suckering varies greatly by the type of rootstock used and becomes less of a problem as the tree ages. Fortunately, as the years go by, commercial growers have begun using rootstocks that sucker less frequently than ones used in the past.

Also, remove water sprouts. These are thin stems shooting straight up from the trunk or branches. Snip them off with pruners. They often resprout. Simply snip them off again.

Winter Protection None required.

Problems

Insects Relatively few insects attack Crabapples in cold climates. Japanese beetles have been spreading into northern areas in recent years, and these can cause damage. Kill them using biological or chemical controls in your lawn area. This control is a form of prevention, rather than a cure. It is highly effective if these insects are present in your locale.

Borers, insects which tunnel into the trunk of the tree, have also been reported but are relatively rare in healthy Crabapples. They seem to be drawn to trees under stress. If you take good care of your trees, you'll rarely have a problem with borers.

Admittedly, there are other insects, including scale, that do occasionally bother Crabapples, but these are neither prevalent nor particularly serious. Disease is much more of a threat overall.

However, insects are a problem with the eating Apples listed in the chart at the end of this section. Apple maggots, codling moths, and plum curculio are common. Prevent problems by regular spraying with a home orchard spray available from a local garden center.

Diseases Unfortunately, Crabapples are prone to a number of diseases. *Your best defense against these is to buy disease-resistant varieties in the first place.* The ones listed in the chart at the end of this section generally fall into this category. The most common diseases are

apple scab, cedar apple rust, fire blight, and powdery mildew.

Apple scab is a fungal disease affecting both leaves and fruits. Unsightly spots on the leaves are usually black, almost sooty in appearance. You will notice lesions on fruits. The infection can cause partial to complete defoliation of the tree. While this may not kill the tree, it affects its vigor and is aesthetically unpleasant. Control with fungicides is simply not practical for the home gardener. Scab is most common in extremely humid periods.

Cedar apple rust is also a fungal disease that attacks native Crabapple varieties. It shows up as yellowish to orange spots on leaves that turn yellow and may drop off. The fungus relies on the presence of *Juniperus virginiana* (Eastern Red Cedar) to complete its life cycle. Control with fungicides is not practical. The varieties listed in this guide are of Oriental origin and resistant to this disease.

Fire blight is an insect- and wind-borne bacterial disease that can devastate susceptible plants. It shows up as blackened stem tissue that looks like it has been burned with a blowtorch. The disease can kill branches or in some instances entire trees. The presence of fire blight varies considerably by region. There is virtually nothing you can do about it once it infects a tree except to prune out infected branches immediately. Dip pruning shears in a disinfectant (one part bleach to nine parts water) after each cut. A number of the Crabapples listed in the chart are quite resistant to fire blight and have been chosen for that reason. Note there is some evidence suggesting that the overuse of nitrogen in fertilizing trees may increase their susceptibility to fire blight.

Powdery mildew is a fungal disease. The tops of leaves are covered with a whitish film. The disease is only serious if it shows up early in the season when it can cause poor flowering. Generally, it shows up late and is simply unsightly. Planting trees in full sun and having good air circulation around the plant cuts down on this problem. Powdery mildew is most common during periods of high humidity. If the disease persists from one year to the next and begins early in the year, use a fungicide to control it. If it shows up late, simply accept it as a nuisance.

Marauders Deer can be a problem with Crabapples. Bucks may use the tree as a place where they rub velvet off their antlers. In one night they can scrape off all the bark on the side of the tree. Placing protective covers around the trunk of young trees in midfall is about the only solution. Strangely, hanging a can from a low branch also discourages deer from using the tree as a rub, but nothing could be less attractive.

Deer will also feed on twigs and fruit any time of the year, but particularly late in the season. Commercial repellents are on the market, but they are quite expensive, have to be applied more than once, and often do not work.

Rodents Rodents, including rabbits, voles, and moles, may gnaw on bark at the base of young trees during the winter. This can kill the tree if the trunk is completely girdled. Use trunk guards or fine mesh hardware cloth collars to prevent damage. Also, when applying mulch, keep it several inches away from the trunk. Pull it even farther back during the winter, since smaller rodents may use it for their winter homes.

Propagation

Suckers See Pruning page 159.

Cuttings Most Crabapple varieties are budded or grafted on hardy understock. Although it is possible to propagate these trees from softwood cuttings, it is not recommended. Hardwood cuttings are next to impossible to get to root.

Seed Seed of the named varieties will not produce plants identical to the parents. Most will be inferior to the parent plants and likely to be more prone to disease. Nevertheless, for diehards who simply enjoy growing plants from seed, soak seed for 24 hours. Press the seed into moist peat. Moist chill for no less than 150 days. Bring out into full light and keep at 50°F (10°C) until germination occurs, generally within 365 days. See pages 409–12 for additional information.

Special Uses

Cut Flowers Cut stems as the first flowers on a branch begin to open up. The branches are delightful because of the wonderful fragrance but are very short-lived. Branches bearing colorful fruit also make excellent additions to fall arrangements and last much longer. Remember that removing branches at any time is a form of pruning, so be careful which branches you remove to retain the beauty and form desired.

Sources

Adams County Nursery, 26 Nursery Rd., Aspers, PA 17304, (563) 677-8105

Bay Laurel Nursery, 2500 El Camino Real, Atascadero, CA 93422, (563) 466-3406

Cummins Nursery, 1408 Trumansburg Rd., Ithaca, NY 14850, (898) 592-2801

Edible Forest Nursery, E7946 Upper Maple Dale Rd., Viroqua, WI 54665 (no phone)

Edible Landscaping, 361 Spirit Ridge Ln., Afton, VA 22920, (847) 524-4156

Fedco Trees, P.O. Box 520, Waterville, ME 04903, (207) 873-7333

ForestFarm, 990 Tetherow Rd., Williams, OR 97544, (286) 846-7269

Fritz Creek Gardens, P.O. Box 15226, Homer, AK 99603, (749) 235-4969

Greenmantle Nursery, 3010 Ettersburg Rd., Garberville, CA 95542, (707) 986-7504

Greer Gardens, 1280 Goodpasture Island Rd., Eugene, OR 97401, (541) 686-8266

Hortico, Inc., 723 Robson Rd., RR# 1, Waterdown, ON L0R 2H1 Canada, (518) 689-6984

Jung Seed, 335 S High St., Randolph, WI 53957, (932) 297-3123

Klehmn's Song Sparrow Perennial Farm, 13101 E Rye Rd., Avalon, WI 53505, (800) 553-3715

McKay Nursery Co., P.O. Box 185, Waterloo, WI 53594, (316) 478-2121

Musser Forests, Inc., 1880 Rte 119 Hwy N, Indiana, PA 15701, (742) 465-5685

One Green World, 28696 S Cramer Rd., Molalla, OR 97038, (877) 353-4028

Raintree Nurseries, 391 Butts Rd., Morton, WA 98356, (360) 496-6400

St. Lawrence Nurseries, 325 Ste Hwy 345, Potsdam, NY 13676, (323) 265-6739

Stark Bros. Nurseries, P.O. Box 1800, Louisiana, MO 63353, (800) 325-4180

South Meadow Fruit Gardens, P.O. Box 211, Baroda, MI 49101, (269) 422-2411

Venero Gardens, 5985 Seamans Dr., Shorewood, MN 55331, (739) 474-8550

Woodstock Nursery, N1831 Ste Rd 95, Neillsville, WI 54456, (888) 803-8733

VARIETIES

There are hundreds of varieties of Crabapples on the market. The following were selected on these criteria: prolific spring bloom with good flower color; abundant fruit with nice coloration that attracts birds in the fall or persists through the winter; distinctive overall form and branching patterns for both summer and winter interest; and resistance to disease and insect infestations. All of the Crabapples in this list have single flowers with the exception of Brandywine®, Coralburst®, 'Doubloons,' and 'Spring Bride' which have double flowers.

VARIETY	FLOWER COLOR	FRUIT	HEIGHT/WIDTH	HARDINESS
Malus baccata				
(Siberian Crab)				
'Jackii'***	White	Dark red	25'/25'	−45°F

This tough tree has a rounded form. Its buds are white. Foliage is a clean, dark green. The tree is disease resistant, especially to scab. Fruits are glossy and about ½ inch (1.25 cm) wide. They are moderately persistent.

Malus floribunda				
(Japanese Flowering Crabapple)***	White	Yellow to orange	20'/20'	−25°F

Broad, rounded form with interesting branching pattern. Red buds burst into white flowers tinged pink. Wonderful floral display. The green foliage offers good disease resistance. The abundant pea-size fruit is a favorite of birds and wildlife. The fruit is not highly persistent and so can be messy if it falls on paved surfaces.

Malus sargentii				
(Sargent or Sargent's Crabapple)****	White	Bright red	8'/15'	−25°F
Firebird® ('Select A')****	White	Bright red	10'/8'	−30°F

The species has a dense, mounded form with nice horizontal branching. Red buds open to 1" (2.5 cm) flowers. Foliage is dark green and quite disease resistant although scab can be a problem in some areas. Fruit ranges up to ½ inch (1.25 cm) across and is relished by wildlife. It will be long gone before winter. This Crabapple does have a tendency to flower more prolifically in alternate years. Firebird® is quite similar to the species, but with smaller size and fruit that often persists into winter. It may be grafted on a different rootstock to keep its size in check. When grafted, it has a lovely globe shape. Very disease resistant.

Malus (Named Crabapple varieties)				
'Adams'***	Purplish pink	Dark red	20'/20'	−35°F

Dense, rounded form. Dark reddish pink buds open to medium purplish pink flowers. The dark green foliage has a slight reddish cast and is disease resistant. Fruit is about ⅝ inch (1.35 cm) across and persistent.

VARIETY	FLOWER COLOR	FRUIT	HEIGHT/WIDTH	HARDINESS
'Adirondack'****	White	Bright coral red	18'/10'	−30°F

Dense, upright form, similar to an ice cream cone. Dark pink buds open to large white flowers. Foliage is dark green and highly disease resistant. Fruits are about ½ inch (1.25 cm) across and persist well into the winter.

Anne E.® ('Manbeck Weeper')***	White	Red	10'/12'	−30°F

Horizontal, semi-weeping form. The bright red buds open to white flowers with reddish margins which then fade to pure white. Foliage is a glossy, medium green and disease resistant. Fruit is about ⅜ inch (1 cm) across and persistent.

Brandywine® ('Scbrazam')***	Rose pink	Yellow green	15'/15'	−30°F

Attractive, symmetrical form. The tree appears in spring as being draped in rose buds. The buds burst into fragrant double pink flowers. The foliage is dark reddish green with resistance to apple scab but susceptible to cedar-apple rust. The fruit is about the size of a large cherry and can create litter.

Camelot® ('Camzam')****	White/pink	Dark burgundy	10'/8'	−30°F

Compact, rounded form. Flower buds are red opening to two-toned white and pink flowers. The disease resistant foliage is dark green with a purplish cast. Fruits are about ⅜ inch (1 cm) across and moderately persistent.

'Candymint'***	Medium pink	Purplish red	10'/15'	−25°F

Horizontal, spreading form. Deep pink buds open to medium pink flowers with a reddish pink margin around each petal, giving a two-toned effect. Foliage emerges with a purplish cast and fades to bronzy green. It is disease resistant. The fruit is about ⅜ inch (1 cm) across and persists fairly well into winter.

'Cardinal'***	Red	Dark red	15'/15'	−20°F

Horizontal, spreading form. Purple buds open into delightful rose to red flowers. Glossy, reddish foliage is highly disease resistant. Small ½-inch (1.25-cm) glossy red fruits typically persist into winter.

Centurion®***	Rose red	Cherry red	25'/15'	−30°F

Columnar when young, maturing into a more rounded form. Rich pink red buds open into dark pink red flowers. Foliage is reddish in spring turning into bronze green and is quite disease resistant. Small glossy red fruit may persist into winter.

Coralburst® ('Coracole')***	Coral pink	Orange brown	15'/15'	−30°F

Extremely dense, this tree has a rounded form. It is usually grafted to a tall stem (42 inches or 105 cm high) to form a small tree. If not, it makes a lovely shrub with compact growth and fine textured foliage. The coral pink flowers are double and produce few fruits about ½ inch (1.25 cm) across. Foliage is medium green. It is slightly susceptible to apple scab.

'David'****	White	Red	15'/15'	−30°F

Compact, rounded form. The white flowers are followed by an abundance of ⅜ inch (1 cm) fruits. These persist into winter. Foliage is glossy, light green and generally disease resistant, but somewhat susceptible to fire blight. This tree tends to flower more heavily in alternate years.

'Dolgo'***	White	Crimson red	20'/30'	−50°F

Upright, spreading form. Pink buds burst into white flowers. Foliage is medium green and fairly disease resistant. The tree is noted for its delicious fruit up to 1½ inches (4.25 cm) in diameter. It is one of the very best fruits for making jelly. However, the fruit will litter the ground if left unpicked. Note that fruits do not last long once picked.

Malus Camelot® ('Camzam')   *Malus* 'David'

VARIETY	FLOWER COLOR	FRUIT	HEIGHT/WIDTH	HARDINESS
'Donald Wyman'****	White	Bright red	20'/25'	−35°F

Rounded to broadly horizontal form. Light pink buds open to pure white flowers. The medium green foliage has good disease resistance overall but is becoming vulnerable to one strain of apple scab. The fruit is outstanding, a glossy, bright red. It's about ⅜ inch (1 cm) in diameter, persists to spring, and keeps its color well.

'Doubloons'****	White	Yellow	15'/12'	−30°F

Dense, rounded form. Dark pink buds open to double white flowers, followed by nice ⅜ inch (1 cm) fruits that persist well into winter. Its medium green foliage shows good disease resistance.

Golden Raindrops® ('Schmidtcutleaf')*****	White	Golden yellow	15'/20'	−30°F

The overall form of this tree is rounded with an attractive horizontal branching pattern. Pink buds open to white petals. Leaves are deeply cut and deep green. They stay clean throughout the season. Fruits are about ¼ inch (.6 cm) across and persist well into winter. This tree is susceptible to fire blight.

Harvest Gold® ('Hargozam')****	White	Golden	20'/15'	−30°F

Upright, vase form. Pink buds opening to pure white. Foliage is dark green and quite disease resistant. It may turn yellow to orange red in fall. Fruit roughly the size of marbles persists into winter.

Malus 'Donald Wyman'

Malus 'Donald Wyman'

Malus 'Prairifire'

Malus 'Red Jade'

VARIETY	FLOWER COLOR	FRUIT	HEIGHT/WIDTH	HARDINESS
'Indian Magic'***	Dark pink	Red orange	15'/15'	−30°F

Upright, spreading form. Lovely dark pink flowers are followed by an abundance of oval red orange fruits about ½ inch (1.25 cm) across. Fruit does not persist into the winter since wildlife relish it. Though the dark green foliage is moderately susceptible to apple scab, the early leaf drop actually makes it easier to see the beautiful fruit. This tree has a tendency to bloom more profusely in alternate years.

VARIETY	FLOWER COLOR	FRUIT	HEIGHT/WIDTH	HARDINESS
'Indian Summer'****	Rose red	Bright red	18'/18'	−30°F

Evenly rounded form. Rosy red flowers are followed by great quantities of persistent, bright red fruit about ½ inch (1.25 cm) across that provide color throughout the winter. The bronzy green foliage has good disease resistance.

VARIETY	FLOWER COLOR	FRUIT	HEIGHT/WIDTH	HARDINESS
'Jewelberry'****	White	Bright red	8'/12'	−20°F

Dense, low growing, spreading form. It has a shrubby, irregular branching pattern. Bright pink buds open to white flowers. Foliage is medium green and highly disease resistant. It produces many ½ inch (1.25 cm) fruits which persist only into early winter.

VARIETY	FLOWER COLOR	FRUIT	HEIGHT/WIDTH	HARDINESS
Lancelot® ('Lanzam')****	White	Yellow gold	10'/8'	−20°F

Upright, oval form. Dark pink buds open to white flowers. The medium green foliage turns a lovely yellow in fall and is disease resistant. Fruit is about ⅜ inch (1 cm) across and darkens from yellow gold to a rich cider color as it matures. The fruit persists through winter.

VARIETY	FLOWER COLOR	FRUIT	HEIGHT/WIDTH	HARDINESS
'Liset'***	Deep red	Dark red	20'/15'	−30°F

Upright, spreading form with an open branching pattern. It has deep red buds. Foliage is purplish in spring and matures into green with red tones. It is disease resistant. The smallish glossy red fruit generally does not persist into winter.

VARIETY	FLOWER COLOR	FRUIT	HEIGHT/WIDTH	HARDINESS
Lollipop® ('Lollizam')****	White	Golden amber	10'/10'	−30°F

This tree is grafted on a standard, typically 'Dolgo.' It has a lovely round lollipop shape that can be kept uniform with regular pruning. Its red flower buds burst into fragrant white flowers that turn into golden fruit about the size of peas generally eaten by wildlife before winter sets in. Foliage is dark green with good disease resistance.

VARIETY	FLOWER COLOR	FRUIT	HEIGHT/WIDTH	HARDINESS
'Louisa'****	Medium pink	Deep yellow/red	15'/15'	−25°F

This tree has a wonderful, weeping form. Red buds open into medium pink flowers. Foliage is dark green with good disease resistance. Fruit is about ⅜ inch (1 cm) across and often persists into winter.

VARIETY	FLOWER COLOR	FRUIT	HEIGHT/WIDTH	HARDINESS
'Luwick'***	Pale pink	Bright red	7'/12'	−30°F

Gracefully weeping form. Dark pink flower buds open to full, pale pink flowers. Fruit is about ⅜ inch (1 cm) across and not abundant. Its medium green leaves are narrow and reported to be disease resistant.

VARIETY	FLOWER COLOR	FRUIT	HEIGHT/WIDTH	HARDINESS
'Mary Potter'****	White	Bright red	10'/15'	−25°F

Low, wide spreading form. Dark pink buds that open to white flowers. Flowering is generally heavy every other year. The glossy, dark green foliage is relatively disease resistant, although fire blight of the tree itself can be a problem. Fruit is about ⅜ inch (1 cm) across and persistent.

VARIETY	FLOWER COLOR	FRUIT	HEIGHT/WIDTH	HARDINESS
Molten Lava® ('Molizam')****	White	Reddish orange	12'/15'	−30°F

Unique, informal, spreading to somewhat weeping form with branches growing irregularly and downward. Dark pink buds open to pure white flowers. Fruits are ⅜ inch (1 cm) across and moderately persistent. Foliage is dark green and fairly disease resistant.

VARIETY	FLOWER COLOR	FRUIT	HEIGHT/WIDTH	HARDINESS
'Morning Princess'***	Pinkish red	Purple	10'/8'	−50°F

An extremely cold hardy weeper for frigid regions. Reddish buds open into pinkish red flowers. Foliage is burgundy shaded green and very disease resistant. Fruits are ½ inch (1.25-cm) wide and persist into winter.

'Orange Crush'****	Deep red	Bright red	15'/15'	−30°F

Spreading, but compact form. Deep red buds open into rich red flowers. Foliage is green turning to yellow in fall and disease resistant. Bright red fruit, sometimes with orange tones, persists into winter.

'Pink Princess' ('Parrsi')***	Medium pink	Dark red	15'/15'	−25°F

Spreading form. Dark pink buds open to clear medium pink flowers. New foliage is reddish purple, turning purplish green as it matures and moderately disease resistant. The fruit is tiny, about ¼ inch (.65 cm) wide and somewhat persistent.

Pink Sparkles® ('Malusquest')***	Pink to white	Cherry red	15'/12'	−30°F

Compact, upright form. Crimson pink buds open into pink flowers that age to white. Glossy deep green foliage that is disease resistant. Small fruits are cherry red deepening to burgundy in fall and persist into winter.

'Prairifire'*****	Dark pink	Burgundy	20'/20'	−35°F

Upright-spreading to rounded form with an irregular, but very attractive branching pattern. Flowers are a clear dark pink, not muddied by any purple tones. Fruit is about ½ inch (1.25 cm) across and persistent. Additionally, the bark is a lovely reddish brown, reminiscent of cherry trees. Foliage has a slight purplish cast and is disease resistant.

'Professor Sprenger'*****	White	Orange	20'/20'	−30°F

Upright, spreading form. White flowers are followed by an abundance of ½ inch (1.25 cm) fruits that persist through the winter. The foliage is bright green and very disease resistant.

'Purple Prince'***	Purple pink	Purple	20'/20'	−30°F

Rounded form. The dark purplish pink flowers are followed by distinctly purple fruits, which are moderately persistent. The tree's dark, cherry-like bark adds greatly to its appeal. It is prized for its purple green foliage and is disease resistant. It makes an excellent substitute for 'Royalty,' a purple leaved Crabapple that is extremely susceptible to disease.

'Red Jade'****	White	Bright red	10'/12'	−35°F

Weeping form with branches reaching to the ground. It can be trained to grow especially low, giving a cascading effect over walls. Pink flower buds burst open into lovely clear white flowers. The oval fruit is about ½ inch (1.25 cm) long and is somewhat persistent, though frequently eaten by birds in the fall. The medium green foliage is moderately susceptible to apple scab.

Red Jewel® ('Jewelcole')*****	White	Bright red	15'/12'	−30°F

Upright, oval form. Pinkish red buds burst into white flowers. The dark green foliage is very attractive and generally disease resistant. Fruits are abundant, about ⅜ inch (1 cm) across, and persist well into winter.

'Robinson'***	Deep pink	Dark red	25'/25'	−30°F

Upright, spreading form. Crimson buds open into deep pink flowers. Attractive green foliage with purplish hues and good disease resistance. Fruit varies in size and is persistent if not eaten first by wildlife or picked for jelly.

Royal Raindrops®****	Magenta pink	Glossy red	20'/15'	−30°F

Upright, spreading form. Red buds burst into bright reddish pink flowers. Wonderful red leaves, almost purple. Cut-leaf foliage often red orange by fall and disease resistant. Small red fruits persist into winter.

VARIETY	FLOWER COLOR	FRUIT	HEIGHT/WIDTH	HARDINESS
First Editions® Ruby Tears™ ('Bailears')*****	Medium pink	Dark red	10'/15'	−30°F

A weeping Crabapple. Red buds open into pink flowers. Foliage emerges red and turns to burgundy green and has excellent disease resistance. The dark red fruit persists until eaten by wildlife.

'Snowdrift'***	White	Orange	20'/20'	−30°F

Dense, upright-spreading to rounded form. Pink buds open to white flowers. The small ⅓ inch (.85 cm) fruits are somewhat persistent, but often stripped off by birds in the fall. The bright green foliage is often disease-free, but, the tree is susceptible to fire blight.

'Spring Bride'***	White	Orange yellow	20'/20'	−40°F

Upright, oval form at maturity. Pink red buds open into double white fragrant flowers. Dark green foliage tends to turn yellow by fall. The tree produces little or no fruit. Its disease resistance is fair.

Sugar Tyme® ('Sutyzam')****	White	Red	18'/15'	−25°F

This is a dense, upright oval tree. Buds are pink and open to white fragrant blossoms. Foliage is medium green. The abundant fruit is roughly ½ inch (1.25 cm) across, bright red in fall, and deep red into January. This tree is very disease resistant.

'Tina'****	White	Bright red	Variable	−25°F

Low growing, rounded form. The plant is usually grafted onto a short stem about 42 inches (105 cm) high. The small white flowers are followed by many bright red fruits about ¼ inch (.6 cm) across. The small, medium green leaves add to this plant's delicate appearance and are disease resistant. If the plant is not grafted to a different rootstock, it will only get about 3 feet (1 meter) tall.

White Cascade® ('Cascole')***	White	Lemon yellow	15'/15'	−25°F

Cascading form, but not as weeping as 'Red Jade.' Lovely deep pink buds burst open into small, white flowers. Foliage is medium green with good disease resistance. Abundant but small fruit may persist into winter if not eaten by birds.

Malus (named Apple varieties)				
'Honeycrisp'*****	White	Striped red	Variable	−30°F
'Honeygold'***	White	Golden yellow	Variable	−30°F
'Regent'****	White	Yellow/red	Variable	−25°F
SnowSweet®***	White	Bronze red	Variable	−30°F
'Sweet Sixteen'****	White	Greenish red	Variable	−35°F
Zestar!®*****	White	Striped red	Variable	−30°F

These varieties are suitable to cold climates and vary in height from 10 to 30 feet (3 to 9.1 meters) depending upon the rootstock. The latter can have a dwarfing effect ranging from 20 to 80 percent. The dwarfing rootstock Malling 7 will reduce the overall size of a tree by 40 percent while Malling 26 reduces the size by up to 60 percent. Dwarf trees have several advantages. They can produce Apples earlier, often within 2 years, and their smaller size makes care and picking much easier. Dwarf trees fit nicely into yards with limited space. Therefore, when purchasing these trees ask on what rootstock they have been grafted. It is best to buy 2-year old certified trees. Following are the taste, texture, and season of the Apples: 'Honeycrisp' (sweet tart, very crisp, very juicy—mid-season), 'Honeygold' (sweet, crisp, mildly juicy—late-season), 'Regent' (sweet tart, crisp, juicy—late-season), SnowSweet® (sweet tart, crisp, mildly juicy—late season), 'Sweet Sixteen' (sweet, crisp, mildly juicy—mid-season), and Zestar!® (sweet tart, crisp, juicy—early season). SnowSweet™ will store well for up to two months and will stay white long after being cut. All of these trees require routine spraying with a home orchard spray if you want perfect fruit. Note that the Japanese and some ardent organic gardeners cover individual Apples with paper bags to protect them instead of using sprays.

Microbiota decussata

MICROBIOTA

(meye-crow-bye-OH-tuh)

RUSSIAN CYPRESS, SIBERIAN CARPET CYPRESS, RUSSIAN ARBORVITAE

Russian Cypress is one of the few low-spreading evergreens that will thrive in shade as well as sun. That in itself makes it a valuable landscape plant. It is extremely tough and can withstand severe winters. Its soft, lacy foliage is bright green in summer and turns bronze to purplish or even brown in early fall and winter. This plant likes cold climates and does poorly in more southerly areas. It is a low-maintenance plant, almost disease and insect free, and likely to live for your lifetime if taken care of properly. The plant is slow to green up in spring, and gardeners should not mistake this for dieback or winter burn.

How Russian Cypress Grows

The root system of Russian Cypress is coarse but spreading. The shrub has many low, wide-spreading branches radiating from a short central stem. These horizontal branches lengthen each year and a single plant will eventually cover a large area. Each branch has many flat, fan-like smaller side branches that are covered with scale-like needles. The needles are smoothly pressed to the branchlets so there are no prickly needle tips with which to contend. Although the shrub is a conifer and self-fertile (monoecious), it does not have pine or spruce-like cones. Instead, the minute cones consist of a single seed held within a cluster of scales. The cone apparently turns from green to brown at maturity, although we have never seen one. In fact, the formation of cones is extremely rare.

Where to Plant

Site and Light Russian Cypress grows well in full sun as long as it is watered frequently. It thrives in partial to almost full shade where it's a bit cooler. It does not do well in dense shade. There it grows slowly, but more importantly tends to have sparser foliage. Place this shrub on flat or gently sloping ground. Its root system is not strong enough to hold it in place on steep slopes or banks. This is one shrub that thrives in areas with cool summers. If you live where it gets quite hot, place the plant in partial shade and water frequently.

Soil and Moisture Russian Cypress needs well-drained soil to survive. If soil is compacted, the plant often gets root rot and dies out. Prepare soil well. If you have clay or rocky soil, replace it or build a raised bed. Keep the soil consistently moist and cool.

Spacing Give these evergreens plenty of space to roam. They can be planted about 48 inches (120 cm) apart to get faster coverage of an exposed area, but eventually the plants will get wider than this space. At that time transplant some of the original plantings and allow the remaining plants to expand in size.

Landscape Use

Russian Cypress makes an excellent low evergreen ground cover. It is particularly useful in lightly shaded areas where spreading junipers will not thrive. Its ferny foliage makes it an appealing choice for planting along walkways or the entrances to homes. The shrub is superb when planted in retaining wall terraces where its spreading branches can trail over the walls, softening the edge of the brick-, stone-, or woodwork. As a ground cover, Russian Cypress also

makes a good transition planting between lawns and taller shrubs.

Planting

Bare Root Rarely sold this way.

Containerized Plants Plant Russian Cypress as early in the season as possible. If the soil in the container is dry, soak it and let it drain overnight before planting. Prepare the planting hole in advance. Place a small amount of superphosphate in the base of the hole and cover it with 3 inches (7.5 cm) of soil. Carefully remove the plant from the container so as not to break the root ball. Plant at the same depth as in the container. Fill the hole with well-prepared soil, firm with your fingers, and water immediately. Dissolve water-soluble fertilizer in a gallon (about 4 liters) of water following the directions on the label. Pour ½ cup (about 120 ml) of this starter solution around the base of each plant. If you prefer organic fertilizer, use fish emulsion instead.

Balled and Burlapped Rarely sold this way.

Transplanting

This is such a wide-spreading shrub that it is difficult to transplant once mature. However, while still relatively young, you can move it. Dig it up in early spring. Keep as much soil around the root ball as possible. Plant it immediately as you would a containerized plant.

How to Care for Russian Cypress

Water Keep the soil evenly moist from spring until the soil freezes in fall. Consistent watering is especially important during the first 2 years. However, this shrub does not tolerate drought even when mature. Always saturate the soil deeply with each watering. When the top 2 inches (5 cm) of soil dry out, water.

Mulch Apply a 1- to 2-inch (2.5- to 5-cm) layer of mulch around each plant as soon as the ground warms up in spring. Good mulches include shredded bark, pine needles, and wood chips. Mulch retains moisture in the soil and helps prevent the growth of weeds. Replenish the mulch as necessary throughout the growing season.

Fertilizing Fertilize every spring with 10-10-10 fertilizer. Sprinkle the granules around the base of each plant before new growth emerges and water immediately to move the fertilizer into the root zone.

If you prefer organic fertilizers, use alfalfa meal (rabbit pellets), blood meal, bone meal, compost, fish emulsion, Milorganite, or rotted manures. Bone meal must be added to the soil at planting time to be effective.

Weeding Prevent the growth of most annual weeds by using mulch. Pull by hand any weeds that do appear. Weeds compete with shrubs for available moisture and nutrients and should be removed immediately.

Deadheading Not necessary.

Pruning Prune out only dead or broken stems. These evergreens look best if they are allowed to spread freely and reach their maximum width without trimming. For this reason, if you plant them close together initially for quick coverage, you may have to transplant or remove some at a later date rather than pruning them back severely.

Winter Protection Although it is in the nature of these plants to turn brown in winter, their foliage can be damaged by winter sun and drying winter winds. So plant them in a sheltered spot or in an area where they are likely to be covered by lots of snow.

Problems

Insects None serious.

Diseases Russian Cypress is nearly disease free. However, in poorly drained soils it will often rot out. Avoid this by preparing soil properly.

Marauders These plants are typically covered by snow in winter. If not covered, deer may nibble off some of the foliage.

Propagation

Suckers These shrubs do not sucker.

Cuttings Take hardwood cuttings in early spring from the previous season's growth. Cuttings should be 4 to 6 inches (10 to 15 cm) long. For additional information, see pages 406–8.

Seed Rarely produces seed at all.

Special Uses

None.

Sources

Arrowhead Alpines, P.O. Box 857, Fowlerville, MI 48836, (517) 223-3581
Bluestone Perennials, 7211 Middle Ridge Rd., Madison, OH 44057, (800) 852-5243
Colvos Creek Nursery, 1904 Third Ave., Suite 415, Seattle, WA 98101, (564) 749-9508
Fedco Trees, P.O. Box 520, Waterville, ME 04903, (564) 873-7333
Great Garden Plants, P.O. Box 1511, Holland, MI 49422, (877) 447-4769
Greer Gardens, 1280 Goodpasture Island Rd., Eugene, OR 97401, (541) 686-8266
Hortico Nurseries Inc., 723 Robson Rd., RR #1, Waterdown, ON L0R 2H1 Canada, (905) 689-9323
Mason Hollow Nursery, 47 Scripps Ln., Mason, NH 03048, (603) 878-4347
McKay Nursery Co., P.O. Box 185, Waterloo, WI 53594, (899) 478-2121
RareFind Nursery, 957 Patterson Rd., Jackson, NJ 08527, (848) 833-0613

Microbiota decussata

River Rock Nursery, 19251 SE Hwy 224, Damascus, OR 97089, (503) 658-4047

Siskiyou Rare Plant Nursery, 2825 Cummings Rd., Medford, OR 97501, (541) 772-6846

Wavecrest Nursery, 2509 Lakeshore Dr., Fennville, MI 49408, (287) 869-4159

VARIETIES

VARIETY	FOLIAGE COLOR	HEIGHT/WIDTH	HARDINESS
Microbiota decussata***			
(Russian Cypress)	Medium green	1'/6'	−50°F
'Northern Pride'***	Medium green	1'/6'	−50°F

This evergreen has foliage similar to that of *Thuja* (Arborvitae). During the summer, foliage coloration varies from light to medium green often with bronze to purple tones in fall. The plant has been known to spread twice as wide as the width given above, but the latter is typical. 'Northern Pride' is similar to the species and has been sold as both a ground cover and a tree. The tree form has not done well without winter protection. 'Fuzzball' is a vase-shaped, upright version with foliage more like a Juniper. 'Jacobsen' is a little more upright and slower growing than the species. Its Juniper-like foliage is commonly described as "fluffy. We do not have personal experience with them, but they are available.

Paeonia 'Luoyang Hong'

PAEONIA

(pay-OWN-knee-uh)

TREE PEONY

Discovered in China more than 1,600 years ago, Tree Peonies are noted for their exotic blooms and are often referred to as the "King of Flowers." The huge, silky flowers are indeed spectacular, and they stay in bloom for up to a week or longer depending upon sunlight and temperature. Many of these are highly scented. If you have a variety of plants that come into bloom at different times, you can extend the bloom season to many weeks. The flowers come in a wide range of colors. Individual blossoms may be a blend of colors and often have crimson or maroon flares (anglets or blotches) radiat-ing out from the center of the flower. These brilliant colors may surround a prominent center, often a distinctly different color than the petals.

The foliage remains attractive and clean throughout the season, and on some varieties it can be quite striking in fall. The unusual seed pods are interesting for cut and dried flower arrangements. Tree Peonies commonly take 4 or 5 years to bloom well. They have a reputation of being difficult to grow. If purchased young, they can indeed be finicky even for the most experienced grower. If purchased at least 3 years old, they are much easier to grow. They are susceptible to dieback in severe winters, but are crown hardy to a much lower temperature than is commonly believed. Note that blossoms tend to be unattractive after rain.

How Tree Peonies Grow

Tree Peonies really should be called "Shrub Peonies." While it is possible to grow these plants from seed, all named varieties are taken as divisions, branch layered, or grafted onto rootstock of a wide variety of herbaceous Peonies. Tree Peonies are generally no more than 6 feet (1.8 m) tall and equally wide or wider while many are considerably smaller. Their form is quite erect. The woody stems and side branches (laterals) generally have one flower, but may have several on some named varieties.

The flowers are up to 10 inches (25 cm) wide, but more commonly about 6 to 8 inches (15 to 20 cm) across. The flowers are composed of eight or more petals. The centers (anthers) of the flowers are often a distinctly different color. Depending upon the number of petals, the flowers are classified as single, semidouble, or double. Some doubles have in excess of three hundred petals. The flowers themselves may face up, down, or off to the side of the plant. The flower petals may appear crinkled, frilly, ruffled, satiny, silky, smooth, twisted, velvety, wavy, or wispy. It is their distinctive texture, form, and vivid lustrous color that make the blossoms so magical. Blossoms have varied scents, reminiscent of citrus fruits, pine, roses, and various spices.

Tree Peonies bloom in spring. The stems and branches are rather coarse with attractive foliage, often deeply cut toward the center of the leaf. The leaves are often whitish underneath. The plant is deciduous, and all of its leaves drop off at the end of the season or should be removed. Over the summer the plants will form seed pods (carpels) if blossoms are not removed. These light green pods are multichambered and contain one to fifty seeds, depending upon the variety. Some varieties are fertile and will self-sow.

Intersectional (Itoh) Hybrids are a cross between herbaceous Peonies, the type with stems that die back to the ground each year, and Tree Peonies. These Hybrids combine the hardiness of herbaceous Peonies with the beauty and form of the Tree Peonies. Additional tips on these special plants are included in the chart.

Where to Plant

Site and Light Intersectional (Itoh) Hybrids (see the varietal chart) grow well in full sun. So do Tree Peonies, but their flowers may last no more than a day in intense light. Since Tree Peonies grow well in partial shade and flowers last longer there, place them along the edge of woods or in filtered light. Tree Peonies do not flower well in deep shade. Planting them where they will be covered with snow in winter is highly recommended, as is placing them on the upper portion of a slope for good drainage.

Soil and Moisture Tree Peonies grow well in a wide range of soils as long as they drain freely. *If the soil remains soggy, the plants will die out.* If your soil is compacted, replace it or build a raised bed. Add lots of organic matter to the soil at planting time. These shrubs grow most vigorously in rich, fertile soil that retains moisture without being compacted and wet. Dig a large planting hole in advance, one at least 24 inches (60 cm) deep and doubly wide. Fill it with rich loam amended with peat moss, compost, or well-rotted leaves. Organic matter should make up at least one-fourth of the soil. Tree Peonies tolerate a range of pH from mildly acidic to mildly alkaline (roughly 6.5 to 7.2). In overly alkaline soils they may suffer from chlorosis.

Spacing These shrubs can grow quite wide. Since they need good air circulation around the foliage, give them plenty of space in which to mature. This is especially important to keep in mind if you're planting them next to a fence or wall. Typically, in colder climates the largest Tree Peonies can get up to 6 feet (1.8 meters) wide after years of proper nurturing.

Landscape Use

Tree Peonies are superb specimen plants, but they also make good focal points in perennial and shrub borders because they have fine-textured leaves and occasionally good fall color. Place them where they can be fully appreciated. In the early years some gardeners interplant spring bulbs and annuals with Tree Peonies. As the Tree Peony matures, interplanting becomes increasingly less important. Tree Peonies combine particularly well with a background of *Syringa* (Lilac). If these shrubs bloom simultaneously, the results are breathtaking. Tree Peonies also make lovely informal hedges. The foliage is striking in summer; the stems are interesting silhouettes in winter.

Planting

Bare Root Bare root plants are sold either grafted or on their own roots. Plant these as soon as they are available in the fall. Buy bare root plants at least 3 years old. Remove plants from their shipping package immediately on arrival. You'll see a ridge where the graft is. On grafted plants you'll notice that the lower portion of the plant (understock or rootstock) looks quite different from the grafted upper portion (scion). The understock will have quite thick and swollen tuberous roots. If the plant is already growing on its own roots, you'll see fibrous roots growing from the base of the stem. If the tuberous roots are not firm, soak the plant in room temperature water for no fewer than 3 hours before planting. Mix roughly ⅛ cup (25 grams) of 5-10-10 into the soil in the base of the hole. Other sources of phosphorus and potassium are fine. Now add 3 inches (7.5 cm) of soil. Place or spread roots on or over a cone of well-prepared soil. If the plant is grafted, place the graft 5 to 8 inches (12.5 to 20 cm) below the soil surface.

This deep planting encourages roots to grow from the upper grafted portion (scion) of the stem in most instances and also protects the roots from freezing in severe winters. Many growers place a tag or band near the proper planting level. If the bare root plant is small, simply plant it in a hole so that you can fill in around the stem as it matures. Alternatively, you can lay the plant on its side under the soil. Fill the hole with soil, firm it with your fingers, and water immediately. Dissolve water-soluble fertilizer in a gallon (about 4 liters) of water following the directions on the label. Pour ½ cup (about 120 ml) of this starter solution around the base of each plant. If you prefer organic fertilizer, use fish emulsion instead. Surround and cover the plant with 2 to 4 inches (5 to 7.5 cm) of bark mulch. (See Winter Protection for additional tips.)

Containerized Plants Buy 3-year-old plants. Plant them as early in the season as possible. You can often buy them in early spring. If the soil in the container is dry, soak and let it drain overnight before planting. Carefully remove the plant from the container so as not to break the root ball. Plant the root ball 2 to 3 inches (5 to 15 cm) deeper than it was in the container after preparing the hole in a similar manner as that for a bare root plant. Fill the hole with well-prepared soil, firm with your fingers, and water immediately. Pour ½ cup (about 120 ml) of starter solution around the base of the plant.

Balled and Burlapped Rarely sold this way.

Transplanting

Transplanting Tree Peonies once they are mature is a chore, so choose the correct planting site from the start. If you must move a plant, dig it up in the fall. Get as much of the root system as possible. If you can keep soil around the roots, so much the better. Trim stems back by half. Plant the shrub immediately as you would a bare root plant.

How to Care for Tree Peonies

Water Water well at planting time. From then on water only in dry periods. Plants may need watering before and during the bloom period. Excessive watering in soils that do not drain freely often causes premature death in Tree Peonies. This is why planting Tree Peonies on slopes or in raised beds is so highly recommended.

Mulch If planted in fall, apply a 4-inch (10-cm) layer of mulch around each plant. Then place 2 inches (5 cm) of mulch directly over the plant. This keeps the soil at an even temperature and prevents any chance of the newly planted shrub from heaving out of the soil. The best mulch is shredded bark. Pine needles and shredded leaves are also fine. In the spring the stems will shoot up through the mulch.

If you plant in the spring, place mulch around the plant. Mulch retains moisture in the soil and helps prevent the growth of weeds. Replenish the mulch as necessary throughout the growing season.

Fertilizing Fertilize every spring with 10-10-10 or 5-10-10 fertilizer. Sprinkle the granules around the base of each plant before new growth emerges and water immediately to move the fertilizer into the root zone. Fertilize again 2 weeks after the plant blooms, preferably with a fertilizer high in phosphorus such as 12-24-24. The latter is commonly found in co-ops or feed stores. Match the amount of fertilizer to the size of the shrub. This second fertilizing stimulates root growth and the formation of new growth buds or "eyes."

If you prefer organic fertilizers, use alfalfa meal (rabbit pellets), blood meal, bone meal, compost, fish emulsion, or Milorganite. Processed chicken and cow manures are also highly recommended. Nonprocessed manures are equally fine as long as they are allowed to rot before being used. Bone meal must be added to the soil at planting time to be effective.

Weeding Prevent the growth of most annual weeds by using mulch. Pull by hand any weeds that do appear. Weeds compete with shrubs for available moisture and nutrients and should be removed immediately.

Deadheading Removing spent blossoms is strictly optional. Leave some spent blossoms on each plant since they form seed pods that add late-season interest to the garden. Pick up petals as they fall. They can stick to leaves and be a potential source of disease. Keep the area around the plant clean.

Pruning Stems may die back somewhat in severe winters. Occasionally, a stem may also snap from heavy snows. Cut off dead or broken stems in spring after new growth emerges. This is the easiest time to tell what portion of a stem has died and what is still alive. Generally, stems die back naturally to a node. The dead portion will often drop off with a gentle swipe of your hand. If dieback is not to a node, then just snip it back to that spot with pruning shears.

Some gardeners snip off small portions of stem immediately after the plant flowers to keep the plant at the size and shape desired. In cold climates do this sparingly, if at all.

Do not cut the plant back in fall the way you would herbaceous Peonies. A few gardeners snip stems on mature plants back to a height of 12 inches (30 cm) if the plant is not forming enough new stems from its base, but this is rarely required and rarely advisable in cold climates. (See the introduction to Intersectional Hybrids in the chart for an exception to this rule.)

If the plant is grafted, the rootstock can send up undesirable stems (suckers) from below the soil surface. These suckers have leaves that are quite different from those produced by the Tree Peony. Remove suckers immediately. Dig down carefully to where they are sprouting and snip them off. Do not confuse suckers from the rootstock with newly developing Tree Peony stems! Never remove the latter. If the Tree Peony is planted correctly, suckering is extremely rare.

Winter Protection Winter protection is absolutely critical for young plants in northerly areas. As soon as the soil is frozen, cover the shrub with 5 to 9 inches (12.5 to 27 cm) of loose straw, marsh hay, or whole leaves. The cover should be light and airy but as thick as possible. Light netting or wire anchored in place around the plant is helpful in keeping winter mulch in place and rabbits away from the plants. Remove the winter protection only after the weather warms up in spring. Moisture and heat buildup at that time can damage the stems and invite disease.

While mature plants may survive relatively severe winters unprotected, it's best to provide them with winter protection anyway. Begin by supporting the woody stems with stakes. Tie the stems to the stakes with fabric or soft ties in a figure-eight knot. The best protection is deep snow. A snow fence or some sort of block to cause snow to drift over the Tree Peonies is one of the simplest and most effective ways of protecting them. Another method that works fairly well is to encircle the shrub with chicken wire after the ground freezes. The wire should be 12 inches (30 cm) outside the outermost portion of the plant for best protection. Fill the enclosure with straw, marsh hay, or whole leaves. These should be loose and airy. Chicken wire also keeps rabbits away from the plants during the winter when they are most vulnerable to attack.

Remove the protection about 6 weeks before you'd expect the plant to bloom. Timing the removal can be tricky. Late freezes can damage flower buds, yet you don't want to leave the winter cover on too long since heat buildup can damage stems and invite disease.

Commercial growers emphasize that if a plant dies back, even all the way to the ground, do not give up on the plant. It almost always springs back to life, creates new stems, and produces a few flowers the first year. While flowers may be few, they are often much larger than those produced by an older plant.

Problems

Insects Scale can be a problem in some years. If noticed early enough, you can push off the little insects with your fingernail. If scale spreads, use an insecticidal soap or a stronger pesticide.

Carpenter bees are black to bluish green and about ½ inch (1.25 cm) long. The insects bore into the tips of stems, especially those that are open, to lay eggs. These mature into yellowish, curved maggots that eat their way down the stems. Inspect the bare stems in fall or early spring. Look for holes in the stems. Just straighten out a paper clip and push it into the hole. If you find and destroy the maggot, cover the hole with clear glue. Otherwise, cut off the infested stem to a healthy bud below the hole as soon as you notice it. Spraying plants with insecticides has not proven effective in controlling adult carpenter bees or borers themselves.

Diseases You can avoid many problems with disease if you plant your Tree Peonies in well-drained soil. At the end of the season remove dead leaves from the shrub and pick up all debris from around the base of the plant.

Stem wilts and botrytis (a fungal disease) are more of a problem with herbaceous Peonies, but they can infect Tree Peonies on occasion. Botrytis shows up as wilted and darkened stems and damaged foliage and buds. Cut infected stems off immediately below the soil line. Removing and replacing the topsoil may also be helpful. If problems recur, spray plants early in the season with a product registered for botrytis control on Peonies.

If you're an organic gardener, ask the supplier which plants tend to be most resistant to botrytis. Among the plants listed in this chapter, there is a wide range of susceptibility. Some of the interspecies hybrids are almost disease free. Organic gardeners report success preventing botrytis by combining the use of sea kelp, copper and zinc sprays, and sprays made from horsetail. These products are offered in organic publications.

No Bloom As with a number of shrubs, the flower buds of Tree Peonies can be damaged by a late frost or cold spell after it initially warms up in spring. (See Winter Protection.) Little or no bloom may also be caused by lack of fertilizer, too little light, or competition with other plants for available moisture and nutrients.

Marauders Some gardeners report problems with rabbits, especially with younger plants. This is most common during the winter. The method outlined for winter protection keeps rabbits away from the stems.

Propagation

Grafting Most commercial growers propagate Tree Peonies by grafting. While grafting is not considered extremely complex, it does require matching the correct rootstock to cuttings (scions) from the named varieties. It is best left in the hands of professional growers who have been doing this for years.

Seed The seed of species Tree Peonies is available and a fun way to start plants if you're extraordinarily patient. Seed produced by named varieties rarely produces plants similar to the parent plant and takes 4 to 7 years to produce bloom. Collect seed as it hardens and is just about to drop off the plant. Place seed 2 inches (5 cm) deep in a moist mixture of peat and perlite in a cold frame. Keep it evenly moist until it freezes. With luck, the seed will sprout the following year, but don't be discouraged if it doesn't. Keep the starting mix moist for yet another year. See pages 409–12 for additional information.

Pegging (Layering) Some of the low-growing, spreading types of Tree Peonies can be layered. When 1-year-old stems become long enough so that you can bend them to the ground without breaking them, then layering becomes possible. Let plants root for at least 2 years before cutting stems. For additional information, see page 405.

Division The true beauty of these plants comes with maturity. The most valuable plant is the one that has remained undisturbed for years. Older plants bloom the most freely. Therefore, division is not recommended although certainly possible in the fall.

Intersectional (Itoh) Hybrids are propagated through division. Do this in early fall approximately 6 to 8 weeks before the ground is expected to freeze. The root system is so woody that commercial growers commonly use power saws to cut through the tissue. Each division should have several eyes and a healthy system of roots attached. Plant immediately as you would a bare root plant.

Special Uses

Cut Flowers Take cut flowers when buds are about as soft as a marshmallow. Remove as little of the stem as possible. You can also simply remove the blossom and float it in a bowl of water. This is lovely and does no damage to the plant.

Dry Flowers and Seed Pods The unusual seed pods make interesting additions to fresh and dried floral arrangements. Cut them at whatever stage of maturity most appeals to you. Cut them off with as little of the stem as possible. Then create a stem with wire available from floral shops.

Drying flowers is not easy, but it is possible. Singles do not dry well. Use semidouble or double flowers only. Cut the blooms just as they reach their peak and dry them in a desiccant, such as Scoop Away cat litter or silica.

Sources

All of the varieties in this chapter are available from one or more sources listed below. The number of Tree Peonies available today is remarkable as demand for them has soared. Intersectional (Itoh) Hybrids were once hard to find, but that is no longer the case.

A & D Nursery, P.O. Box 2338, Snohomish, WA 98291, (565) 668-9690

Adelman Peony Gardens, 5690 Brooklake Rd. NE, Salem, OR 97305, (503) 393-6185

André Viette Farm & Nursery, P.O. Box 1109, Fishersville, VA 22939, (565) 575-5538

Brothers Herbs and Peonies, P.O. Box 1370, Sherwood, OR 97140, (503) 625-7548

Callies Beaux Jardins, W6658 Sunset Ln., Fort Atkinson, WI 53538, (900) 563-2927

Countryside Gardens, 10602 Fenner Ave. SE, Delano, MN 55328, (952) 955-2283

Cricket Hill Garden, 670 Walnut Hill Rd., Thomaston, CT 06787, (860) 283-1042

ForestFarm, 990 Tetherow Rd., Williams, OR 97544, (849) 846-7269

Fraser's Thimble Farms, 175 Arbutus Rd., Salt Spring Island, BC V8K 1A3, (288) 537-5788

Greer Gardens, 1280 Goodpasture Island Rd., Eugene, OR 97401, (541) 686-8266

Hollingsworth Nursery, 28747 290 St., Maryville, MO 64468, (660) 562-3010

Idlewild Farm, Inc., 278 Stottsville Rd., Parkesburg, PA 19365, (800) 559-9768

Klehm's Song Sparrow Perennial Farm, 13101 E Rye Rd., Avalon, WI 53505, (750) 553-3715

La Pivoinerie d'Aoust, P.O. Box 220, Hudson Heights, Quebec J0P 1J0, (519) 458-2759

Peony's Envy, P.O. Box 114, Bernardsville, NJ 07924, (933) 578-3032

Reath's Nursery, N-195 Cty Rd. 577, Vulcan, MI 49892, (317) 563-9777

Swenson Gardens, P.O. Box 209, Howard Lake, MN 55349, (763) 350-2051

White Flower Farm, P.O. Box 50, Litchfield, CT 06759-0050, (800) 503-9624

VARIETIES

Following are the main considerations in purchasing Tree Peonies: the hardiness of the plant; its age; its potential size; the color, form, size, and fragrance of the flower; the plant's tendency to bloom freely; the time of bloom; the foliage color and shape; its disease resistance; whether blooms float above the foliage or are tucked into it; and the overall growth pattern and vigor of the plant. Plants come primarily from China and Japan. Most Japanese plants are either single or semi-double with little fragrance, while Chinese plants have traditionally had more varied forms and scents. The latter vary from mild to strong to spicy or sweet. The following list was compiled with the help of Kasha and David Furman (Cricket Hill Garden), Kathy Gagan (Peony's Envy), Roy Klehm (Klehm's Song Sparrow Perennial Farm), Scott Reath (Reath's Nursery), and Rick Rogers (Brothers Tree Peonies, Inc.). In this list there are two American Peony Society gold medal winners: 'Age of Gold' and 'Garden Treasure,' the latter an Itoh hybrid. The single, semi-double, and double forms indicate an increasing number of petals in each flower. A particular variety may have both single and semi-double flowers on the same or different plants. For this reason sources often vary in how they list the flower form of any given plant. The Chinese Peony Society and other groups may label flowers by form and shape. But, to keep things simple, only the three forms already mentioned are used here. Summer foliage is usually green. 'Tiger Tiger,' if planted in sun, has a dramatic purple foliage color, while in shade the leaves are green. None of the plants listed in this varietal chart have been given stars since the information is based primarily on outside advice rather than personal experience. **The hardiness rating given in the following chart is for exposed, not underground stem tissue. Most of these plants will survive temperatures approximately 10°F colder than those given in the chart.**

VARIETY	COLOR	FORM	HEIGHT/WIDTH	HARDINESS
Paeonia delavayi				
(Maroon Tree Peony)	Crimson	Single	6'/4'	−20°F

This species produces abundant 3-inch (7.5 cm) blossoms. Leaves are bronzy purple as they emerge, turning a deep green during the summer. This plant spreads by underground stems (stolons) to form an ever-widening clump. It does well in moist soil and tolerates relatively shady areas.

Paeonia lutea var. *delavayi* (see *Paeonia delavayi*)

Paeonia 'Age of Gold'

Paeonia 'Anna Marie'

VARIETY	COLOR	FORM	HEIGHT/WIDTH	HARDINESS
Paeonia rockii				
(Rock's Variety)	White	Single	5'/5'	−30°F

Although sold under a number of different names, this species is outstanding. The true species is single and has a blackish purple blotch in the center of the blossom, as if someone poured ink into it. This is a very hardy and highly desirable plant. It deserves a place in your landscape. Note that there are semi-double and double forms of this plant. They are technically not the same plant, but are certainly as beautiful, desirable, and hardy.

Paeonia suffruticosa subsp. **rockii** (see **Paeonia rockii**)				
Paeonia suffruticosa var. **rocks** (see **Paeonia rockii**)				
Paeonia (Named varieties)				
'Age of Gold'	Gold yellow	Semi-double	3½'/3'	−25°F
'Alhambra'	Golden yellow	Semi-double	5'/3'	−25°F
'Anna Marie'	Orchid lavender	Single	4'/3½'	−25°F
'Ambrose Congreve'	Pink/deeper flares	Single	4½'/4'	−25°F
'Aphrodite'	White	Semi-double	4'/4'	−25°F

Paeonia 'Bartzella'

Paeonia 'First Arrival'

Paeonia 'Shan Hu Tai'

Paeonia 'Shimane Otone Mai'

VARIETY	COLOR	FORM	HEIGHT/WIDTH	HARDINESS
'Ariadne'	Yellow red blush	Semi-double	4'/4'	−25°F
'Bai Bi Lan Duan'	White	Single	6'/4'	−25°F
'Banquet'	Red blend	Single/Semi-double	3½'/3½'	−25°F
'Baron Thyssen Bornemisza'	Mauve/purple flares	Semi-double	4'/3'	−25°F
'Black Panther'	Dark red maroon	Semi-double	3½'/3½'	−25°F
'Boreas'	Burgundy red	Semi-double	4'/6'	−25°F
'Budding Beauty' ('Dou Kou Nian Hua')	White/purple flares	Double	3'/3'	−25°F
'Center Stage'	White/dark flares	Single	3'/3'	−25°F
'Cherry Blossoms'	Soft pink	Semi-double	4'/4'	−25°F
'Chinese Dragon'	Crimson red	Single/Semi-double	3'/4'	−25°F
'Cinnabar Ramparts' ('Zhu Sha Lei')	Medium pink	Semi-double	5'/4'	−25°F
'Companion of Serenity'	Soft pink	Single	3'/4'	−20°F
'Gosling Yellow' ('Chu E Huang')	Cream yellow	Double	3'/3'	−25°F
'Guardian of the Monastery'	Pink purple/gold	Single	3'/3'	−25°F
'Gauguin'	Yellow red blend	Single	4'/4'	−25°F
'Goldfinch'	Bright yellow	Single	4'/4'	−25°F
'High Noon'	Lemon yellow	Semi-double	5'/4'	−25°F
'Joseph Rock' (see *Paeonia rockii*)				
'Kishu Caprice'	Silver rose pink	Semi-double	3'/3'	−25°F
'Leda'	Orchid pink/purple	Semi-double	3'/3'	−25°F
'Luoyang Hong' ('Luoyang Red')	Magenta red	Double	6'/4'	−25°F
'Luster of Jade' ('Jing Yu')	White	Double	3'/3'	−25°F
'Marchioness'	Yellow rose	Single/Semi-double	3'/3'	−25°F
'Mystery'	Ivory lilac	Single	3'/3'	−25°F
'Nike'	Peachy pink/gold	Semi-double	5'/4'	−25°F
'Pink Jade of Bright Radiance'	Pink/purple flares	Double	3'/3'	−25°F
'Pink Scarf' ('Feng Jin Yu')	White/magenta flares	Semi-double/double	3'/3'	−25°F
'Renkaku'	White	Semi-double	4'/3½'	−25°F
'Savage Splendor'	Ivory/rose purple	Single/Semi-double	4'/3'	−25°F
'Shan Hu Tai'	Pink coral	Semi-double/double	5'/4'	−25°F
'Shima Daijin'	Purple red	Semi-double	4'/3'	−25°F
'Shimane Otone Mai'	Rose pink	Semi-double	4'/3'	−25°F

VARIETY	COLOR	FORM	HEIGHT/WIDTH	HARDINESS
'Snow Lotus'	White	Single	5'/4'	−25°F
'Sunrise'	Yellow rose	Semi-double	4'/3'	−25°F
'Themis'	Lavender pink	Single	3½'/4'	−25°F
'Thunderbolt'	Deep crimson	Single	3½'/3½'	−25°F
'Tiger Tiger'	Red pink/dark flares	Single	4'/4'	−25°F
'Tria'	Yellow	Single	3'/3'	−25°F
'Vesuvian'	Black red	Double	2'/3'	−25°F
'Yachiyo Tsubaki'	Coral pink	Semi-double	4'/4'	−25°F
'Zephyrus'	Pink peach	Semi-double	3½'/3½'	−25°F

Intersectional (Itoh) Hybrids

The stems of these Peonies do die back each fall. Unlike herbaceous Peonies, do not cut the stems to ground level. Instead, snip each stem approximately 1 inch (2.5 cm) above the ground after foliage dies back in fall. This preserves growth buds at the base of the plant which increase flower production the following year. Expect these plants to emerge later in spring than herbaceous Peonies. These very hardy plants produce foliage and flowers similar to Tree Peonies, have a nice upright form, will stand up to wind and heavy rain, are very disease resistant, and produce many flowers once mature. The flowers also last longer than those of standard Tree Peonies. Most of the Intersectional Hybrids have a light, pleasing fragrance. However, 'Bartzella' stands out for its distinctive lemon scent, most noticeable in early bloom. 'Garden Treasure' is a gem with a main bud surrounded by many side buds. Thanks to Roger Anderson and Laverne Dunsmore in the selection of these plants, including some of Don Hollingsworth's finest introductions.

VARIETY	COLOR	FORM	HEIGHT/WIDTH	HARDINESS
'Bartzella'	Sulphur yellow	Semi-double/double	3½'/4'	−40°F
'Brianna Irene'	Light pink	Double	2½'/3½'	−40°F
'Cat Whiskers'	Lavender pink	Semi-double	2½'/3'	−40°F
'Cora Louise'	White/purple flares	Semi-double	2½'/3'	−40°F
'First Arrival'	Lavender pink	Semi-double	2½'/3'	−40°F
'Garden Treasure'	Light gold yellow	Semi-double	1½'/3'	−40°F
'Gordon E. Simonson'	Pink lavender tones	Double	2½'/3½'	−40°F
'Hillary'	Red yellow blend	Semi-double/double	2½'/2½'	−40°F
'Love Affair'	White	Semi-double	2'/3'	−40°F
'Mercedes Renée'	Reddish lavender	Semi-double/double	2½'/3½'	−40°F
'Morning Lilac'	Lavender	Single/semi-double	3'/4'	−40°F
'New Millenium'	Coral pink	Semi-double/double	2½'/3'	−40°F
'Old Rose Dandy'	Yellow purplish rose mix	Single	2'/2½'	−40°F
'Prairie Charm'	Clear yellow/red purple flares	Semi-double	3'/3'	−40°F
'Pastel Splendor'	White to yellow	Single	2½'/2½'	−40°F
'Prairie Sunshine'	Brilliant clear yellow	Semi-double	2'/3'	−40°F
'Scarlet Heaven'	Scarlet red	Single/semi-double	2½'/3'	−40°F
'Sequestered Sunshine'	Lemon yellow	Semi-double	3'/3'	−40°F

Perovskia atriplicifolia

PEROVSKIA

(purr-RAHV-skee-yuh)

RUSSIAN SAGE

Russian Sage is commonly sold as a perennial. Since its stems often survive winters, it acts more like a subshrub. It blooms later in the season than most shrubs and is especially valuable for color at that time. The plant is quite dramatic once mature, forming an impressive clump of tall stems covered with clouds of tiny blue to blue lavender blossoms for weeks on end. It is a durable, low-maintenance plant that rarely is bothered by insects or disease. Once fully mature, it is certainly one of the most drought-tolerant plants listed in this guide. When working with Russian Sage, you'll notice an aromatic scent that permeates the air.

How Russian Sage Grows

Russian Sage grows into a multistemmed plant with a dense crown and fibrous roots. Each year as the plant matures it forms an ever-widening clump of tall, silvery stems with numerous branches. Tiny light blue to blue lavender blossoms swirl around the upper portions of the stems creating a hazy blue cloud from a distance. Foliage is rather sparse and tinted silver. The shallowly toothed leaves are rarely longer than 1½ inches (3.25 cm). The plant is reported to form nutlets (seeds). We have never seen them in our region.

Where to Plant

Site and Light Russian Sage thrives in intense sunlight. Place it in full sun in a highly exposed location. The spot can be hot as well without harming the plant at all. If planted in shady areas, Russian Sage often becomes sparse and sprawling.

Soil and Moisture Russian Sage does well in most soils, but prefers any soil that drains freely. If soil is compacted, replace it or build a raised bed. Russian Sage will die out in winter if the soil remains soggy. Russian Sage is extremely heat and drought tolerant once mature, but it still prefers consistent moisture throughout the growing season.

Spacing Russian Sage will become quite large over the years, often spreading much wider than it is tall. Give it plenty of space, especially if combining it with perennials in a bed or border. To speed up the process of getting a bold effect, place three plants 24 inches (60 cm) apart in a triangle. These plants will meld together and look almost like a single shrub.

Landscape Use

As long as it has plenty of space and lots of light, Russian Sage does very well in a perennial bed or border. There it is especially effective between bold, dominant colors of *Monarda* (Bee Balm) and *Phlox*-Paniculata Group (Garden Phlox). Other good perennial combinations are made with *Coreopsis* (Tickseed), *Echinacea* (Purple Coneflower), ornamental Grasses, and *Rudbeckia* (Coneflower). Russian Sage combines well with pink varieties of *Spiraea* (Spirea) and white, pink, and yellow flowered varieties of *Rosa* (Shrub Roses). Use it as well in an isolated grouping, particularly with evergreens as a background. Its form is upright and graceful, not at all overpowering but still dramatic. The silvery gray foliage remains attractive after bloom and persists for winter interest. Some gardeners use Russian Sage in mass plantings where space allows.

Planting

Bare Root Get bare root plants into the garden as soon as the ground can be worked in spring. Remove plants from their shipping package immediately on arrival. Soak them in room temperature water for no fewer than 3 hours before planting. Place a small amount of superphosphate in the base of the hole and cover with 3 inches (7.5 cm) of soil. Spread roots out over a cone of well-prepared soil. Make sure the crown is level with the surrounding soil surface. Fill the hole with soil, firm it with your fingers, and water immediately. Dissolve water-soluble fertilizer in a gallon (about 4 liters) of water following the directions on the label. Pour ½ cup (about 120 ml) of this starter solution around the base of each plant. If you prefer organic fertilizer, use fish emulsion instead.

Containerized Plants Plant Russian Sage as early in the season as possible. If the soil in the container is dry, soak it and let it drain overnight before planting. Carefully remove the plant from the container so as not to break the root ball. Plant at the same depth as in the container after preparing the hole in a similar manner as that for a bare root plant. Fill the hole with well-prepared soil, firm with your fingers, and water immediately. Pour ½ cup (about 120 ml) of starter solution around the base of the plant.

Balled and Burlapped Rarely sold this way.

Transplanting

The plant really is more like a perennial than a shrub, although a mature clump gets quite large. You can dig a portion of the clump from the crown or dig up the entire plant in early spring before new growth starts. Get the plant up and out of the ground and into its new site as quickly as possible. Treat it with as much care as you would a bare root plant. Keep it well watered until it is growing vigorously.

How to Care for Russian Sage

Water Keep the soil evenly moist from spring until the soil freezes in fall. Consistent watering is especially important during the first 2 years. Always saturate the soil deeply with each watering. When the top 2 inches (5 cm) of soil dry out, water. Once the plant is mature, it can withstand hot, dry conditions better than most plants listed in this guide. The plant is drought tolerant, but it does better when watered regularly.

Mulch Apply a 1- to 2-inch (2.5- to 5-cm) layer of mulch around each plant as soon as the ground warms up in spring. Good mulches include dried grass clippings, shredded leaves, and pine needles. Mulch retains moisture in the soil and helps prevent the growth of weeds. Replenish the mulch as necessary throughout the growing season.

Fertilizing Sprinkle 10-10-10 fertilizer around the base of the plant every other year in early spring just as new growth starts. Increase the dosage as the plant matures, even to the point of fertilizing once each year. Water immediately to move the fertilizer into the root zone.

If you prefer organic fertilizers, use alfalfa meal (rabbit pellets), blood meal, bone meal, compost, fish emulsion, Milorganite, or rotted manures. Bone meal must be added to the soil at planting time to be effective.

If Russian Sage becomes spindly or sprawly when grown in full sun, cut back on fertilizing the following year. Or, don't fertilize at all. Too much nitrogen sometimes results in lax growth.

Weeding Prevent the growth of most annual weeds by using mulch. Pull by hand any weeds that do appear. Weeds compete with shrubs for available moisture and nutrients and should be removed immediately.

Deadheading Not necessary.

Pruning Other than removing any portion of an individual stem that dies back over winter, no pruning is required. Occasionally, in severe winters all of the stems die back to the ground. Snip them off at ground level in spring. The plant will produce new growth quickly from its base and bloom prolifically despite the apparent setback. Note that some gardeners cut the plant to the ground each year, claiming that this produces more stems. Either method is fine.

Winter Protection Covering the plant with 4 to 6 inches (10 to 15 cm) of whole leaves, marsh hay, straw, or pine needles is recommended only in the first year. After that, the plant normally will survive even the harshest winters without protection. Always remove this winter mulch in early spring as soon as the weather warms up to prevent rot.

Problems

Insects None serious.

Diseases None serious.

Marauders Rabbits will eat standing stems in winter. Since the plant regenerates so quickly in spring, protection rarely is worth any effort.

Propagation

Division In early spring before new growth begins, dig up the plant and divide it into sections with several stems per division. Plant immediately as you would a bare root plant. Division works well, but taking stem cuttings is preferred if you would like to save the mother plant. Note that the plant sometimes produces growth (offshoots) to the side of the mother plant. It is easy to cut these off and plant them as if they were bare root plants without damaging the main crown.

Softwood Cuttings This is the easiest and most highly recommended way to increase stock. Cut 3- to 4-inch (7.5- to 10-cm) tips off the main stems when they reach a height of 24 inches (60 cm). Strip off leaves from the bottom 2 inches (5 cm). Dip the cut end in rooting hormone. Plant cuttings in a mixture of equal parts peat and perlite. Keep the mixture consistently moist and the humidity high by covering the cuttings with plastic until they begin to root. If humidity gets too high or the rooting mixture is soggy, cuttings may rot out. Once the cuttings take root, remove the plastic covering immediately. Cuttings often take root in less than 3 weeks.

Basal Cuttings When stems are about 4 inches (10 cm) high cut them off the mother plant, taking a little portion of the crown with each one. Treat these as you would softwood cuttings. For additional information, see pages 406–8.

Seed The species can be grown from seed. Place the seed just under the surface of sterile starting mix. Keep it evenly moist at room temperature until it germinates, generally within 30 to 160 days. For additional information, see pages 409–12.

Soil Layering Bend a mature stem to the ground. Make a shallow cut into the stem about 6 inches (15 cm) from the tip. Cover the wounded stem with moist soil amended with peat moss and keep in place with a rock or pin. Keep the ground consistently moist until roots form at the cut. Sever the newly created plant from the main stem at that time. Plant immediately as you would a bare root plant.

Special Uses

Cut Flowers After being cut the flower tends to drop petals rather quickly. Still, when in peak bloom, long stems are impressive all by themselves in a large vase. The scent is also quite attractive, although some gardeners find it a bit strong.

Sources

Ambergate Gardens, 8730 Cty Rd. 43, Chaska, MN 55318, (566) 211-9769

Busse Gardens, 17161 245th Ave., Big Lake, MN 55309, (800) 544-3192

Deer-resistant Landscape Nursery, 3200 Sunstone Ct., Clare, MI 48617, (800) 595-3650

Earthly Pursuits, 2901 Kuntz Rd., Windsor Mill, MD 21244, (410) 496-2523

Fieldstone Gardens, Inc., 620 Quaker Ln., Vassalboro, ME 04989, (207) 923-3836

Fraser's Thimble Farms, 175 Arbutus Rd., Salt Spring Island, BC, Canada V8K 1A3, (250) 537-5788

Goodness Grows, Inc., P.O. Box 311, Lexington, GA 30648, (706) 743-5055

Goodwin Creek Gardens, P.O. Box 83, Williams, OR 97544, (566) 846-7357

High Country Gardens, 2902 Rufina St., Santa Fe, NM 87507, (800) 925-9387

Joy Creek Nursery, 20300 NW Watson Rd., Scappoose, OR 97056, (503) 543-7474

Plant Delights Nursery, Inc., 9241 Sauls Rd., Raleigh, NC 27603, (901) 772-4794

The **Sandy Mush Herb Nursery,** 316 Surrett Cove Rd., Leicester, NC 28748, (850) 683-2014

Well-Sweep Herb Farm, 205 Mount Bethel Rd., Port Murray, NJ 07865, (289) 852-5390

White Flower Farm, P.O. Box 50, Litchfield, CT 06759, (800) 503-9624

Perovskia atriplicifolia

Perovskia atriplicifolia

VARIETIES

VARIETY	FLOWER COLOR	HEIGHT/WIDTH	HARDINESS
Perovskia atriplicifolia****			
(Russian Sage)	Deep lavender blue	4'/4'	−30°F
'Blue Spire'****	Deep lavender blue	4'/4'	−20°F
'Filagran' ('Filigrin')****	Deep lavender blue	3'/4'	−30°F
'Little Spire'****	Lavender blue	2'/2'	−30°F
'Longin'****	Light lavender blue	3'/4'	−30°F

The species is noted for its strongly scented, gray green foliage that has an attractive, lacy appearance. The plant tends to be somewhat floppy, especially if not grown in full sun. This is fine plant for open areas or naturalized settings. The intensity of its flower color is relatively strong. 'Blue Spire' may be a cross or simply another name for the species. Their similarity is striking. 'Filagran' is very popular because it tends to have a more upright growth pattern and rather lacy, silvery green foliage similar to that of the species. 'Little Spire' is a potentially low-growing form ideally suited to urban settings where gardeners often have limited space. It often grows taller than the height listed but not as tall as the species. It tends to stay smaller in areas with cool summers. 'Longin,' like 'Filagran,' has an attractive upright appearance. The differences between these plants is quite subtle. Even sophisticated growers can have a hard time telling them apart.

Philadelphus 'Buckley's Quill'

PHILADELPHUS

(fill-uh-DELL-fuss)

MOCKORANGE

Mockorange is noted for its abundant bloom, and, most of all, for its wonderful fragrance reminiscent of orange blossoms. While in bloom, it's a magnificent plant. The rest of the year it has little to offer. Although this shrub has fallen out of favor in recent years, the introduction of smaller plants with exquisite double blooms is bringing it back to life. It is certainly one of the toughest and most durable shrubs on the market and very easy to grow. It does require regular pruning for maximum beauty.

How Mockorange Grows

The roots of this shrub are coarse and penetrate the soil quite deeply. Each shrub forms numerous stems. Most shrubs tend to be somewhat lanky and irregular with the exception of the more compact forms. The blossoms are single (four petals) or double (twenty to thirty petals). Inside the petals are striking golden anthers. Leaves are generally dark green with the exception of 'Aureus,' noted for its light green to golden coloration. Plants form seed capsules with small brown seeds, but the shrubs rarely self-sow.

Where to Plant

Site and Light Mockoranges bloom best if placed in full sun. They will tolerate partial shade, but the amount of bloom will be reduced.

Soil and Moisture Mockoranges are very adaptable to a wide range of soils as long as they drain freely. Fertile soils are ideal. Although these shrubs tolerate dry spells once mature, they prefer consistent moisture throughout the entire growing season.

Spacing Space according to the potential height and width of the mature plant.

Landscape Use

Place your Mockorange in the back of a shrub border or in a spot where it can be left in obscurity after its initial bloom is over. Smaller plants fit nicely into the corner of a large perennial garden or shrub border. Mix Mockorange with other shrubs that bloom at different times of the year or have good fall color to provide a progression of seasonal interest. Plants that fit into this pattern nicely are *Euonymus* (Euonymus), hardy varieties of *Rosa* (Rose), *Spiraea* (Spirea), and *Syringa* (Lilac).

Planting

Bare Root Get bare root plants into the garden as soon as the ground can be worked in spring. Remove plants from their shipping package immediately on arrival. Soak them in room temperature water for no fewer than 3 hours before planting. Place a small amount of superphosphate in the base of the hole and cover with 3 inches (7.5 cm) of soil. Spread roots out over a cone of well-prepared soil. Make sure the crown is level with the surrounding soil surface. Fill the hole with soil, firm it with your fingers, and water immediately. Dissolve water-soluble fertilizer in a gallon (about 4 liters) of water following the directions on the label. Pour ½ cup (about 120 ml) of this starter solution around the base of each plant. If you prefer organic fertilizer, use fish emulsion instead.

Containerized Plants Plant Mockorange as early in the season as possible. If the soil in the container is dry, soak it and let it drain overnight before planting. Carefully remove the plant from the container so as not to break the root ball. Plant at the same depth as in the container after preparing the hole in a similar manner as that for a bare root plant. Fill the hole with well-prepared soil, firm with your fingers, and water immediately. Pour ½ cup (about 120 ml) of starter solution around the base of the plant.

Balled and Burlapped Rarely sold this way.

Transplanting

Dig up plants early in the season before new growth emerges. Plant immediately as you would a bare root plant.

How to Care for Mockoranges

Water Keep the soil evenly moist from spring until the soil freezes in fall. Consistent watering is especially important during the first 2 years. Always saturate the soil deeply with each watering. When the top 2 inches (5 cm) of soil dry out, water. Note that once established these shrubs are relatively drought tolerant, but prefer consistent moisture.

Mulch Apply a 2- to 4-inch (5- to 10-cm) layer of mulch around each plant as soon as the ground warms up in spring. Good mulches include shredded bark, pine needles, and wood chips. Mulch retains moisture in the soil and helps prevent the growth of weeds. Replenish the mulch as necessary throughout the growing season.

Fertilizing Fertilize every spring with 10-10-10 fertilizer. Sprinkle the granules around the base of each plant before new growth emerges and water immediately to move the fertilizer into the root zone.

If you prefer organic fertilizers, use alfalfa meal (rabbit pellets), blood meal, bone meal, compost, fish emulsion, Milorganite, or rotted manures. Bone meal must be added to the soil at planting time to be effective.

Weeding Prevent the growth of most annual weeds by using mulch. Pull by hand any weeds that do appear. Weeds compete with shrubs for available moisture and nutrients and should be removed immediately.

Deadheading Not necessary.

Pruning These shrubs do have a tendency to die back somewhat each year. Since they flower on old wood, cut back the dead portions of the stems to the closest outward-facing bud on live stem tissue. The less wood removed, the better. The time to do this is just after new growth emerges. At this time you can easily tell the difference between live and dead portions of stem.

Immediately after flowering, prune the shrub to control its size and shape. If you do not do this right away and do it later in the season, you will be removing flower buds. It is common for these shrubs to have one or two long, wayward branches. Simply snip them off where appropriate to keep a natural contour.

Note that older plants can be quite scraggly. Some gardeners cut a portion of older stems right down to the ground each year over a period of years to rejuvenate an older plant. Thinning out stems from a mature clump does give a plant a less-crowded look and does result in new stems emerging from the base of the plant. Do this immediately after the plant flowers.

Winter Protection If you're trying to grow a plant marginally hardy for your area, the only realistic way to protect it is to plant it in a sheltered location where much of the plant will be covered with snow.

Problems

Insects None serious.

Diseases None serious.

Marauders Rabbits can be a problem during the winter. They eat the stems right down to the snow line. The only feasible way to protect these shrubs is to surround them with chicken wire in late fall. Take the potential height of snowfall into mind when deciding how high the protection must be.

Propagation

Division Not recommended.

Suckers These shrubs rarely sucker.

Layering Bend over and wound very pliable stems at a point where they touch the ground. Follow the detailed instructions outlined on page 405.

Cuttings Take softwood cuttings from the tips of stems in midsummer when new growth is beginning to harden (semihard). These tip cuttings should be about 4 inches (10 cm) long and have no fewer than three sets of leaves. Make the bottom cut just below a node for better rooting.

Take hardwood cuttings any time during the dormant season. For most home gardeners the easiest time to do this is in late fall or very early spring. Cuttings should be 6 inches (15 cm) long. For additional information, see pages 406–8.

Seed Seed from the named varieties in the chart at the end of this section will not produce plants identical to the parents. Barely cover seed of the species in a mixture of moist peat and perlite. Keep at room temperature until germination occurs, generally within 60 days. See pages 409–12 for additional information.

Special Uses

Cut Flowers Cut stems just as blooms begin to unfurl. Strip off all leaves that will end up underwater in the final arrangement. Although these flowers have a very short vase life, the scent is so wonderful that the ephemeral nature of the blooms is secondary.

Sources

Blackfoot Native Plants Nursery, P.O. Box 761, Bonner, MT 59823, (406) 244-5800

Burnt Ridge Nursery, Inc., 432 Burnt Ridge Rd., Onalaska, WA 98570, (567) 985-2873

Colvos Creek Nursery, 1904 Third Ave., Suite 415, Seattle, WA 98101, (567) 749-9508

Corn Hill Nursery Ltd., 2700 Rte 890, Corn Hill, NB E4Z 1M2 Canada, (506) 756-3635

Digging Dog Nursery, P.O. Box 471, Albion, CA 95410, (902) 937-2480

Durio Nursery, 5853 Hwy 182, Opelousas, LA 70570, (337) 948-3696

Elk Mountain Nursery, P.O. Box 599, Asheville, NC 28802, (851) 683-9330

Fedco Trees, P.O. Box 520, Waterville, ME 04903, (207) 873-7333

ForestFarm, 990 Tetherow Rd., Williams, OR 97544, (541) 846-7269

Fraser's Thimble Farms, 175 Arbutus Rd., Salt Spring Island, BC V8K 1A3 Canada, (250) 537-5788

Gossler Farms Nursery, 1200 Weaver Rd., Springfield, OR 97478, (290) 746-3922

Greer Gardens, 1280 Goodpasture Island Rd., Eugene, OR 97401, (541) 686-8266

Heronswood Nursery, 300 Park Ave., Warminster, PA 18974, (877) 674-4714

High Country Gardens, 2902 Rufina St., Santa Fe, NM 87507, (751) 925-9387

Philadelphus coronarius 'Aureus'

Philadelphus lewisii

Hortico, Inc., 723 Robson Rd., RR# 1, Waterdown, ON
L0R 2H1 Canada, (905) 689-6984

Joy Creek Nursery, 20300 NW Watson Rd., Scappoose,
OR 97056, (520) 543-7474

Mail-Order Natives, P.O. Box 9366, Lee, FL 32059,
(850) 973-6830

McKay Nursery Co., P.O. Box 185, Waterloo, WI 53594,
(934) 478-2121

Plant & Gnome, P.O. Box 5344, Charleston, WV 25361,
(318) 881-7037

The Sandy Mush Herb Nursery, 316 Surrett Cove Rd.,
Leicester, NC 28748, (743) 683-2014

VARIETIES

VARIETY	FLOWER COLOR	FRAGRANCE	HEIGHT/WIDTH	HARDINESS
*Philadelphus coronarius***				
(Sweet Mockorange)	White single	Strong	10'/8'	−30°F
'Aureus'**	White single	Strong	5'/4'	−30°F

The species is loosely upright in form. It has lovely four-petalled flowers with a delicious aroma and bright yellow center. Its foliage is deep green. 'Aureus' has similar flowers but its foliage is golden to yellowish green.

*Philadelphus lewisii***				
(Lewis Mockorange)	White single	Moderate	8'/5'	−40°F
'Blizzard'***	White single	Moderate	5'/3'	−40°F

The species is loosely upright in form. It also has lovely four-petalled flowers with a less intense aroma and a less pronounced yellow center. 'Blizzard' blooms far more profusely. Both have deep green foliage.

Philadelphus × *virginalis***				
(Virginal Mockorange)	White double	Strong	8'/5'	−30°F
'Minnesota Snowflake'**	White double	Strong	8'/5'	−30°F

The species is loosely upright in form. It has lovely eight-petalled flowers with great scent but not much coloration in the center. 'Minnesota Snowflake' is quite upright and leggy but very free flowering. Both have deep green foliage.

Philadelphus (Named varieties)				
'Buckley's Quill'***	White double	Strong	5'/5'	−30°F
'Miniature Snowflake'***	White double	Strong	4'/3'	−30°F
'Natchez'***	White single	Mild	8'/5'	−25°F
'Snow Dwarf'**	White double	Moderate	3'/3'	−30°F
'Snowgoose'***	White double	Strong	4'/3'	−30°F
'Snowbelle'***	White double	Moderate	3'/4'	−30°F
Snow White Sensation™***	White single	Moderate	5'/4'	−30°F

This group is noted for excellent flowering and lovely scents. Foliage of all plants is deep green. 'Natchez' stands out in an already free-flowering group for its abundance of large flowers. Note that 'Miniature Snowflake' is sometimes sold as 'Dwarf Minnesota Snowflake.'

Physocarpus opulifolius 'Snowfall'

PHYSOCARPUS

(feye-so-CAR-pus)

NINEBARK

Ninebark, native to cold climates, is a tough and very hardy shrub. Most of these shrubs bloom prolifically. The summer foliage on some varieties is yellow or purple. The bark on the stems can also be attractive if the plant is pruned in such a way to expose that area. The bark often peels off and is somewhat similar to that of a birch. Once mature, these shrubs are quite drought tolerant. Overall, they are relatively disease and insect free. They can become somewhat coarse if left unpruned, but pruning is simple and has the side benefit of lovely cut stems for floral arrangements.

How Ninebark Grows

Ninebarks have roots that vary from fibrous to coarse. They penetrate the soil quite deeply but are not particularly wide spreading. The form of the shrub is upright spreading. Each shrub forms many stems, and these tend to arch over unless pruned for a more upright appearance. The leaves look like those of ***Ribes alpinum*** (Alpine Currant), but are considerably larger. Foliage color varies by variety. Clusters (umbels) of tiny white or pale pink flowers appear in early summer. The flowers are followed by fruits (follicles), similar to the seed heads of ***Spiraea*** (Spirea) but more pronounced and showy. They are reddish before turning brown. Each contains three to five shiny yellowish seeds. The plant occasionally self-sows.

Where to Plant

Site and Light Place Ninebarks in full sun. They need no protection from prevailing winds.

Soil and Moisture Ninebarks adapt well to a wide range of soil types as long as they drain freely. While young plants should be kept well watered, this is one shrub that actually prefers it somewhat on the dry side once mature.

Spacing Space according to the shrub's potential height and width.

Although a number of Ninebarks are suitable for hedging, one of the best is *Physocarpus opulifolius* 'Nanus' (Dwarf Ninebark). Space young plants about 24 inches (60 cm) apart for a tight, bushy appearance.

Landscape Use

Ninebarks make excellent hedges, screens, and windbreaks. Combine any of them with *Berberis* (Barberry) to create a solid barrier but also to take advantage of contrasting foliage colorations. Varieties with yellow or purple foliage add an interesting accent in shrub borders. Ninebarks are good in naturalized settings since they make good cover for wildlife.

Planting

Bare Root Get bare root plants into the garden as soon as the ground can be worked in spring. Remove plants from their shipping package immediately on arrival. Soak them in room temperature water for at least 3 hours before planting. Place a small amount of superphosphate in the base of the hole and cover with 3 inches (7.5 cm) of soil. Spread roots out over a cone of well-prepared soil. Make sure the crown is

level with the surrounding soil surface. Fill the hole with soil, firm it with your fingers, and water immediately. Dissolve water-soluble fertilizer in a gallon (about 4 liters) of water following the directions on the label. Pour ½ cup (about 120 ml) of this starter solution around the base of each plant. If you prefer organic fertilizer, use fish emulsion instead.

Containerized Plants Plant Ninebark as early in the season as possible. If the soil in the container is dry, soak it and let it drain overnight before planting. Carefully remove the plant from the container so as not to break the root ball. Plant at the same depth as in the container after preparing the hole in a similar manner as that for a bare root plant. Fill the hole with well-prepared soil, firm with your fingers, and water immediately. Pour ½ cup (about 120 ml) of starter solution around the base of the plant.

Balled and Burlapped Rarely sold this way.

Transplanting

These plants have a heavy root system. Transplant them only during the first 3 years of growth. Do this in early spring before new growth emerges.

How to Care for Ninebarks

Water Keep the soil evenly moist until the plants are growing vigorously. After that only water after 2 weeks without rain. These plants like it on the dry side. Always saturate the soil deeply with each watering. When the top 2 inches (5 cm) of soil dry out, water.

Mulch Apply a 2- to 4-inch (5- to 10-cm) layer of mulch around each plant as soon as the ground warms up in spring. Good mulches include shredded bark, pine needles, and wood chips. Mulch retains moisture in the soil and helps prevent the growth of weeds. Replenish the mulch as necessary throughout the growing season.

Fertilizing Fertilize every spring with 10-10-10 fertilizer. Sprinkle the granules around the base of each plant before new growth emerges and water immediately to move the fertilizer into the root zone. Once plants are growing vigorously, you can often get by with fertilization every other year.

If you prefer organic fertilizers, use alfalfa meal (rabbit pellets), blood meal, bone meal, compost, fish emulsion, Milorganite, or rotted manures. Bone meal must be added to the soil at planting time to be effective.

Weeding Prevent the growth of most annual weeds by using mulch. Pull by hand any weeds that do appear. Weeds compete with shrubs for available moisture and nutrients and should be removed immediately.

Deadheading Not necessary.

Pruning Remove any portion of the plant that is dead, damaged, or diseased at any time of year. Prune as needed to control the overall form and size of the plant. Always prune immediately after the plant flowers. Cut back to an outward-facing bud. Many gardeners thin the shrubs to a few stems for an airy, open look.

To create a lovely hedge, begin light pruning in the first year. As plants become more vigorous, prune more heavily. You want to create thick, bushy growth by consistent pruning from year to year. Hedges will produce limited bloom.

Winter Protection None needed.

Problems

Insects None serious.

Diseases Disease is quite rare on free-standing shrubs. However, if the shrub is used as a hedge, there is a chance that it will be bothered occasionally by powdery mildew. The latter shows up as a white film on scattered portions of the hedge. Snip out the infected areas with a pruning shears. Burn or toss the infected tissue into the garbage. Leaf spots also occur, but are rarely of any major concern.

Marauders None serious.

Propagation

Division Not recommended.

Cuttings Take softwood cuttings from new growth just as it begins to harden (semihard). Cuttings should be 4 to 6 inches (10 to 15 cm) long and have no fewer than three sets of leaves.

Hardwood cuttings taken any time during the dormant season are preferred. These should be at least 6 inches (15 cm) long. For additional information, see pages 406–8.

Seed This is not recommended as the named varieties will not come true from seed.

Special Uses

Cut Foliage Ninebarks are vigorous shrubs. Snip off foliage for fresh floral arrangements. The foliage combines beautifully with any number of flowers. Always cut back to just above an outward-facing bud since removing stems for cut flower use amounts to pruning. Consider cutting stems just as fruit (seed heads) form. Hang the stems upside down in a warm, dry, shaded area with excellent air circulation. Let the stems dry out completely. The rich reddish browns will make excellent additions to fall arrangements. Or just let the seed heads mature and dry on the shrub.

Sources

Bluestone Perennials, 7211 Middle Ridge Rd., Madison, OH 44057, (800) 852-5243

Corn Hill Nursery Ltd., 2700 Route 890, Corn Hill, NB E4Z 1M2 Canada, (568) 756-3635

Digging Dog Nursery, P.O. Box 471, Albion, CA 95410, (707) 937-2480

Physocarpus opulifolius (seed heads)

Physocarpus opulifolius 'Dart's Gold'

Physocarpus opulifolius Diabolo®/'Monlo'

Physocarpus opulifolius 'Nanus'

ForestFarm, 990 Tetherow Rd., Williams, OR 97544, (568) 846-7269

Fritz Creek Gardens, P.O. Box 15226, Homer, AK 99603, (907) 235-4969

Greer Gardens, 1280 Goodpasture Island Rd., Eugene, OR 97401, (541) 686-8266

Hortico, Inc., 723 Robson Rd., RR# 1, Waterdown, ON L0R 2H1 Canada, (903) 689-6984

Klehm's Song Sparrow Perennial Farm, 13101 E Rye Rd., Avalon, WI 53505, (800) 553-3715

Mason Hollow Nursery, 47 Scripps Ln., Mason, NH 03048, (603) 878-4347

McKay Nursery Co., P.O. Box 185, Waterloo, WI 53594, (852) 478-2121

Out Back Nursery, Inc., 15280 110th St. S, Hastings, MN 55033, (291) 438-2771

RareFind Nursery, 957 Patterson Rd., Jackson, NJ 08527, (752) 833-0613

Shrub Source, 248 N Colonial St., Zeeland, MI 49464, (800) 530-2969

Venero Gardens, 5985 Seamans Dr., Shorewood, MN 55331, (952) 474-8550

Wavecrest Nursery, 2509 Lakeshore Dr., Fennville, MI 49408, (888) 869-4159

VARIETIES

VARIETY	FLOWER COLOR	FOLIAGE COLOR	HEIGHT/WIDTH	HARDINESS
Physocarpus opulifolius				
(Common Ninebark)				
Center Glow™****	White	Burgundy red yellow	7'/4'	−40°F
'Coppertina'****	Rose	Red orange bronze	7'/5'	−40°F
'Dart's Gold'***	White	Golden	6'/6'	−50°F
Diabolo® ('Monlo')***	Pinkish white	Purple aging bronze	8'/6'	−40°F
First Editions®Little Devil™***	Creamy white	Dark purple	4'/4'	−40°F
'Nanus'**	Greenish white	Deep green	6'/6'	−50°F
'Nugget'***	White	Greenish yellow	6'/6'	−40°F
'Snowfall'**	White	Medium green	7'/8'	−50°F
Summer Wine® ('Seward')****	Pinkish white	Dark purple wine	5'/5'	−40°F

The spring foliage of Center Glow™ is golden yellow. It matures into red burgundy as the season progresses. 'Coppertina' has peachy yellow orange new growth that matures into a lime green. 'Dart's Gold' makes a lovely hedge. It thrives when sheared back at a height of about 3 feet (1 meter) and shines in the summer sun with its golden leaves. Diabolo® with its distinctive purple foliage is an excellent replacement for *Prunus* × *cistena* (Purple Leaf Sand Cherry). The purple foliage may turn purplish green or bronze by mid summer. Little Devil™ is a nice, compact plant with small purple leaves. 'Nanus' has smaller leaves and, like 'Dart's Gold,' makes an excellent low-growing hedge. 'Nugget' has nicely textured foliage that changes color with the season, having more golden tones early in spring and later in fall. For good flowering choose 'Snowfall,' since it flowers somewhat more freely than the other varieties. Summer Wine® is a tough plant with lovely white flowers often tinged pink that contrast beautifully with its burgundy foliage.

Picea abies 'Nidiformis'

PICEA

(pie-SEE-uh)

SPRUCE

Spruce trees are among the most popular evergreens. They are not only attractive, but long lived if properly cared for. The compact or dwarf forms of these trees require relatively little maintenance and can be used in a wide variety of ways to add texture and year-round color to the yard. Overall, they are relatively disease and insect free.

How Spruce Grows

Each tree produces many coarse, shallow roots. The upright types have a main stem while the dwarf types often have numerous branches instead. Foliage consists of needles rarely more than ¾ inch (1.8 cm) long.

They are quite stiff. New growth (candles) has a different coloration from old growth. Needles often turn a deeper color in cold winter months. Spruce trees produce cones once mature. Cones are made up of many scales and produce winged seeds. The seeds pop out of the base of the cone scales. Only one of the plants included in the chart at the end of this section is likely to form cones in the home landscape. Trees will occasionally self-sow.

Where to Plant

Site and Light Spruce grow best in full sun. They do tolerate partial shade, but their foliage is reduced by lack of light. Dense shade results in nearly bare branches. In general, it's best to keep these plants away from areas where they may be damaged by salt. They also grow best if protected from drying winter winds.

Soil and Moisture Spruce are adaptable to a wide range of soils although they need good drainage. They prefer soil slightly on the acidic side with some organic matter mixed in. Even moisture throughout the season is ideal. They do poorly in overly wet conditions and do not tolerate drought.

Spacing Give each plant plenty of space to grow to its full height and width. Spruce will begin to drop needles if branches overlap or if they are not exposed to enough light.

Landscape Use

The dwarf and compact forms of Spruce trees make excellent specimen or accent plants. Their neat, tidy appearance and in many cases attractive blue foliage add year-round interest to the landscape and are especially prized in rock gardens. They are also good evergreen additions to foundation plantings. *Picea abies* 'Acrocona' is a very unusual plant with fascinating cones. Place it where this unusual trait is most likely to be appreciated. Keep in mind that while it grows very slowly, it does become quite large once mature.

Planting

Bare Root Not sold this way.

Containerized Plants Plant Spruce as early in the season as possible. If the soil in the container is dry, soak it and let it drain overnight before planting. Carefully remove the plant from the container so as not to break the root ball. Place a small amount of superphosphate in the base of the planting hole and cover it with 3 inches (7.5 cm) of soil. Plant at the same depth as in the container. Fill the hole with well-prepared soil, firm with your fingers, and water immediately. Dissolve acidic water-soluble fertilizer

in a gallon (about 4 liters) of water following the directions on the label. Pour ½ cup (about 120 ml) of this starter solution around the base of each plant. If you prefer organic fertilizer, use fish emulsion instead.

Balled and Burlapped Plant as you would a containerized plant with these added precautions: Place the plant in the hole making sure that the top of the balled and burlapped root ball is about 1 to 2 inches (2.5 to 5 cm) above the surrounding soil. Cut and remove any twine around the stems. Remove as much of the burlap and wire holding the root ball in place as possible, but avoid breaking the root ball.

Transplanting

During the first 3 years these shrubs can be transplanted. Dig them up early in the season before new growth emerges. Keep as much soil around the roots as possible. Plant immediately as you would a balled and burlapped plant. If a plant is older, it is very difficult to transplant successfully. Have it moved professionally with specialized equipment.

How to Care for a Spruce

Water Keep the soil evenly moist from spring until the soil freezes in fall. Consistent watering is especially important during the first 2 years. Always saturate the soil deeply with each watering. When the top 2 inches (5 cm) of soil dry out, water. In subsequent years water deeply whenever there is a prolonged dry spell.

Mulch Apply a 1- to 2-inch (2.5- to 5-cm) layer of mulch around each plant as soon as the ground warms up in spring. Good mulches include shredded bark, pine needles, and wood chips. Shredded pine bark and pine needles are preferred since they are mildly acidic. Mulch retains moisture in the soil and helps prevent the growth of weeds. Replenish the mulch as necessary throughout the growing season.

Fertilizing Fertilize every spring with an acidic fertilizer, such as Miracid. Proper fertilization is especially important to help trees produce abundant new growth that has much deeper blue coloration than older needles.

Any acidic fertilizers designed for use with evergreen and Rhododendron (Azalea) plants are recommended. Follow the directions on the labels as to recommended dosage. If using any granular fertilizer, saturate the soil to dissolve the particles and carry nutrients into the root zone.

If you prefer organic fertilizers, use alfalfa meal (rabbit pellets), blood meal, bone meal, compost, fish emulsion, Milorganite, or rotted manures. Bone meal must be added to the soil at planting time to be effective. Cottonseed meal is excellent because it is mildly acidic, but it is becoming difficult to find in cold climates.

Weeding Prevent the growth of most annual weeds by using mulch. Pull by hand any weeds that do appear. Weeds compete with shrubs for available moisture and nutrients and should be removed immediately.

Deadheading Not applicable.

Pruning Some of the plants in this group require little if any pruning. A light annual pruning in early summer just as new growth begins to harden off helps define size and shape. With a pruning shears snip off one-third of each new shoot.

Winter Protection Winter protection is not necessary. Note, however, that some of these plants are prone to damage by heavy snow on their branches. Shake off snow gently to stop branches from breaking off and downward where they connect to the main stem. Avoid tossing snow onto them during the winter.

Problems

Insects The larvae of sawflies show up early in the year. These tiny, pale yellow insects nibble on needles, leaving bare spots on the plant. If you look in these areas, you will see them. Pick them off by hand (wear gloves). Try spraying them off with water. Or, use Orthene immediately if these methods don't work. If left unchecked, they defoliate plants rapidly.

In hot, dry weather spider mites can be a problem. You can often spray mites off foliage by hosing it down with a forceful stream of water. If the spider mite population begins to explode, use a miticide.

Occasionally, there is distorted growth on the tips of branches. This is caused by spruce gall aphids. Snip off and burn the branch tip immediately. These galls are usually no more than a nuisance.

Diseases Cankers show up as wounds on trees and branches. Branches may appear discolored and begin to lose their needles. Prevent cankers by taking good care of trees; proper watering is especially important. Once cankers appears, there is little you can do.

Needle cast, similar to canker, is again best prevented with good care. It generally shows up as purplish discoloration of needles, which may turn brown before falling off. It often affects older branches first. Control of the disease is difficult. Spraying the trees early in the season with a fungicide (Daconil) and a few weeks later may provide limited control.

Marauders None.

Propagation

Suckers These shrubs do not sucker.

Cuttings In October and November take cuttings from the previous season's growth of *Picea abies* 'Nidiformis' or 'Pumila.' Cuttings should be 2 to 4 inches (5 to 10 cm) long. Take cuttings from *Picea glauca* 'Conica' at the same stage. These should be no longer than 2 inches (5 cm). Getting these cuttings to root is difficult despite what other sources say. For additional information, see pages 406–8.

Seed Recommended only for the species, none of which are listed.

Special Uses

None.

Sources

Bloom River Gardens, 39744 Deerhorn Rd., Springfield, OR 97478, (569) 726-8997

Camellia Forest Nursery, 620 Hwy 54 W, Chapel Hill, NC 27516, (919) 968-0504

Corn Hill Nursery Ltd., 2700 Rte 890, Corn Hill, NB E4Z 1M2 Canada, (569) 756-3635

Eastwoods Nursery, 634 Long Mountain Rd., Washington, VA 22747, (540) 675-1234

Evermay Nursery, 84 Beechwood Ave., Old Town, ME 04468, (904) 827-0522

Fantastic Plants, 5865 Steeplechase, Bartlett, TN 38134, (800) 967-1912

ForestFarm, 990 Tetherow Rd., Williams, OR 97544, (853) 846-7269

Fritz Creek Gardens, P.O. Box 15226, Homer, AK 99603, (907) 235-4969

Girard Nurseries, P.O. Box 428, Geneva, OH 44041, (292) 466-2881

Greer Gardens, 1280 Goodpasture Island Rd., Eugene, OR 97401, (541) 686-8266

Hortico, Inc., 723 Robson Rd., RR# 1, Waterdown, ON LoR 2H1 Canada, (753) 689-6984

Joy Creek Nursery, 20300 NW Watson Rd., Scappoose, OR 97056, (521) 543-7474

Klehm's Song Sparrow Perennial Farm, 13101 E Rye Rd., Avalon, WI 53505, (800) 553-3715

Musser Forests, Inc., 1880 Rte 119 Hwy N, Indiana, PA 15701, (724) 465-5685

Porterhowse Farms, 41370 SE Thomas Rd., Sandy, OR 97055, (935) 668-5834

River Rock Nursery, 19251 SE Hwy 224, Damascus, OR 97089, (503) 658-4047

Venero Gardens, 5985 Seamans Dr., Shorewood, MN 55331, (952) 474-8550

Whitney Gardens & Nursery, P.O. Box 170, Brinnon, WA 98320, (319) 796-4411

VARIETIES

VARIETY	FOLIAGE COLOR	HEIGHT/WIDTH	HARDINESS
Picea abies			
(Norway Spruce)			
'Acrocona'****	Medium green	15'/12'	−40°F
'Little Gem'****	Medium green	1½'/6'	−40°F
'Mucronata'***	Deep green	8'/6'	−40°F
'Nidiformis'***	Gray green	3'/5'	−30°F
'Pendula'***	Gray green	6'/variable	−40°F
'Pumila'****	Medium green	4'/5'	−40°F

'Acrocona' is a slow-growing tree with distinctive cones that point skyward and change color with the seasons. They begin as a soft green, then turn purplish red, and finally brown by late summer. 'Asselyn' and 'Clanbrazillian' and 'Compacta Asselyn' grow slowly into conical shaped trees. 'Compacta Asselyn' has showy buds. 'Little Gem' grows slowly, has dense foliage, and makes a good rock garden plant. 'Mucronata' is a tidy, upright tree with pyramidal form and dense growth. 'Nidiformis' is commonly known as "Bird's Nest Spruce." This plant forms a neat spreading mound of seemingly soft needles with an indentation in the middle. Indeed, it does look somewhat like a nest. It is popular for both its form and color. It does suffer mild dieback or winter burn. Simply snip off brown growth in spring and keep removing the interior branches that die out from lack of light. 'Pendula' is a weeping form with slender branches. 'Pumila' is commonly called "Dwarf Norway Spruce." It is even a little more rounded than 'Nidiformis' and has very dense growth less susceptible to winter burn. It is excellent for bonsai.

Picea abies 'Acrocona'

Picea abies 'Mucronata'

Picea glauca 'Conica'

Picea omorika 'Nana'

VARIETY	FOLIAGE COLOR	HEIGHT/WIDTH	HARDINESS
Picea glauca			
(Dwarf Alberta Spruce)			
var. ***albertiana*** 'Conica' (see 'Conica')			
'Conica'	Light green	10'/4'	−25°F
'Rainbow's End'***	Yellowish green	10'/4'	−25°F

'Conica' is a compact and extremely slow growing tree. It has fine-textured, fragrant foliage. 'Rainbow's End' is similar in form but its new growth is a buttery yellow. Foliage turns to yellow green and then green as the season progresses. The foliage of both trees is susceptible to winter burn. Plant them on the east side of your home and protect them from strong winds for best results. If grown properly, they are gems.

Picea omorika			
(Dwarf Serbian Spruce)			
'Nana'****	Dark green	8'/8'	−40°F

This spruce is a compact mound when young, a cone when mature. It is slow growing, compact, and dense. White bands run along the underside of the needles, giving the plant an interesting two-toned effect. New foliage is light; older foliage is deep green.

Picea pungens			
(Colorado Spruce)			
'Fat Albert'****	Blue	15'/10'	−40°F
'Glauca Globosa'*****	Blue	3'/4'	−40°F
'Montgomery'****	Blue	5'/3'	−40°F
'Procumbens'***	Blue	1'/6'	−40°F

'Fat Albert' is a grafted plant and shows great uniformity in its stunning blue foliage. 'Glauca Globosa' is a low, mounded plant and grows slowly. Its foliage coloration, form, and size make it a popular plant. 'Montgomery' starts off looking like 'Glauca Globosa' but ends up forming a strong central stem (leader) and expanding in size to a broad conical evergreen. 'Procumbens' produces branches that may either hang down or remain horizontal to the ground. This unusual, undulating plant is often placed on top of a rock wall where its branches can hang down for a dramatic effect.

Pinus mugo var. *mugo*

PINUS

(PIE-nus)

PINE

P ines are delightful evergreen plants favored for their texture, year-round color, and lovely scent. Pines require little maintenance and are relatively disease and insect free. Pines listed here are dwarf or compact forms, not large trees.

How Pines Grow

Pines have a fairly coarse, shallow root system. The Pines in this guide are multistemmed shrubs with numerous branches. The named varieties are grafted on the species' rootstock. Foliage consists of slender needles 1 to 3 inches (2.5 to 7.5 cm) long and varying in color. These are usually formed in bundles (fascicles) of two to five needles. Some of the plants listed in this section will produce seed-bearing cones once mature. They occasionally self-sow.

Where to Plant

Site and Light Pines grow best in full sun. A few tolerate very light shade. They require no protection from winds. However, it is wise to plant them away from areas where they may be exposed to salt. In general, they do not tolerate air pollution well.

Soil and Moisture Pines adapt to a wide range of soils as long as they drain freely. They do prefer acidic soils. Consistent moisture throughout the growing season is highly recommended, although mature Pines certainly tolerate dry spells well.

Spacing Plant Pines with their full height and width in mind. Some can be pruned quite severely to form nice, uniform mounds.

Landscape Use

The Pines listed here make excellent specimen plants. They combine well with other evergreens as well as with deciduous shrubs that have reddish purple or yellow foliage such as *Prunus* × *cistena* (Purple Leaf Sand Cherry) and *Physocarpus* Diabolo® (Ninebark). Many are good for foundation plantings. *Pinus mugo* (Mugo Pine) is a superb choice for raised planters or for growing in a container. One fine combination is *Pinus mugo* (Mugo Pine) with *Potentilla fruticosa* 'Goldfinger' (Shrub Cinquefoil) and *Berberis* 'Crimson Pygmy.' The colors and textures of these very different shrubs create a vibrant focal point.

Planting

Bare Root Rarely sold this way.

Containerized Plants Plant Pines as early in the season as possible. If the soil in the container is dry, soak it and let it drain overnight before planting. Place a small amount of superphosphate in the base of the planting hole and cover it with 3 inches (7.5 cm) of soil. Carefully remove the plant from the container so as not to break the root ball. Plant at the same depth as in the container. Fill the hole with well-prepared soil, firm with your fingers, and water immediately. Dissolve acidic water-soluble fertilizer in a gallon (about 4 liters) of water following the directions on the label. Pour ½ cup (about 120 ml) of this starter solution around the base of each plant. If you prefer organic fertilizer, use fish emulsion instead.

Balled and Burlapped Plant as you would a containerized plant with these added precautions: Place the plant in the hole making sure that the top of the balled and burlapped root ball is about 1 to 2 inches (2.5 to 5 cm) above the surrounding soil. Cut and remove any twine around the stems. Remove as much of the burlap and wire holding the root ball in place as possible, but avoid breaking the root ball.

Transplanting

Transplant these shrubs only during the first 3 years. Dig them up in early spring before new growth (candles) emerges. Keep as much soil around the roots as possible. Plant them immediately as you would a balled and burlapped plant. If plants are older, have them moved professionally with specialized equipment.

How to Care for Pines

Water Keep the soil evenly moist from spring until the soil freezes in fall. Consistent watering is especially important during the first 2 years. Always saturate the soil deeply with each watering. When the top 2 inches (5 cm) of soil dry out, water. Once mature, Pines can tolerate dry spells quite well. However, during drought, water the plants regularly.

Mulch Apply a 1- to 2-inch (2.5- to 5-cm) layer of mulch around each plant as soon as the ground warms up in spring. Good mulches include shredded bark, pine needles, and wood chips. Shredded pine bark, pine needles, and shredded oak leaves are most highly recommended because they are mildly acidic. Mulch retains moisture in the soil and helps prevent the growth of weeds. Replenish the mulch as necessary throughout the growing season.

Fertilizing Fertilize every spring with an acidic fertilizer, such as Miracid. Any acidic fertilizers designed for use with evergreen and Rhododendron (Azalea) plants are recommended. Follow the directions on the labels as to correct dosage. If using any granular fertilizer, saturate the soil to dissolve the particles and carry nutrients into the root zone.

If you prefer organic fertilizers, use alfalfa meal (rabbit pellets), blood meal, bone meal, compost, fish emulsion, Milorganite, or rotted manures. Bone meal must be added to the soil at planting time to be effective. Cottonseed meal, which can be quite difficult to find in cold-climate areas, is highly recommended because it is mildly acidic.

Weeding Prevent the growth of most annual weeds by using mulch. Pull by hand any weeds that do appear. Weeds compete with shrubs for available moisture and nutrients and should be removed immediately.

Deadheading Not applicable.

Pruning Pruning is highly recommended to control the size of the larger varieties of Pines listed in the chart at the end of this section. Pruning also creates much denser growth. Each spring plants will form new growth at the tips of their stems. The new growth is commonly referred to as candles. The candles are often distinctly different in color from the old growth. Just as the candles begin to harden off in early summer, cut them back by one-third with pruning shears.

Winter Protection None.

Problems

Insects The larvae of pine shoot moths bore into the tips of new shoots and buds, killing them in the process. You'll notice the problem just as new growth occurs in spring. Snip off the tips and destroy them immediately. This is generally more common on tree types and very rarely affects more than a few shoots. Spray with an insecticide, such as Orthene (Acephate) only if borers are affecting many new shoots and buds.

The larvae of sawflies also cause problems in spring. They nibble on needles, causing bare patches on shrubs or small trees. The pale yellow larvae are small, visible, and voracious. Pick them off by hand or spray them immediately with Orthene before they spread and do extensive damage.

The adults of pine needle scale show up as $\frac{1}{10}$-inch (roughly 3-mm) whitish flecks on needles. In cold climates mature insects generally lay eggs once. These overwinter and hatch the following spring into crawlers (reddish nymphs). These immature insects suck juice from the needles, causing them to turn yellow and eventually die off. Scale can weaken trees, making them susceptible to cankers and borer infestations. Kill eggs by spraying plants with dormant oil or lime sulfur solution in late fall or early spring before new growth starts. Kill crawlers with insecticidal soap. If that doesn't control them, use Malathion or any product containing Acephate. Spraying Pines with chemicals is usually most effective during or just after Lilacs are in full bloom.

Diseases *Pinus strobus* (White Pine) is very susceptible to white-pine blister rust that shows up as a powdery red rust on the bark. The alternate hosts to this disease are specific varieties of the *Ribes* group (Currant or Gooseberry). The two should not be planted in the same area.

Marauders If deer become a problem, surround plants with fencing or spray them with repellents to keep damage down.

Propagation

The varieties listed in the chart at the end of this section are grafted onto rootstock of varying species. The process is not practical for the home gardener. *Pinus mugo* (Mugo Pine) is an exception and can be grown from seed.

Special Uses

Cones In theory, all Pines will produce cones once fully mature. We have been observing *Pinus strobus* 'Nana' (Dwarf White Pine) for more than 40 years and have yet to see a single cone. You may see cones on *Pinus mugo* (Mugo Pine) or *Pinus banksiana* 'Uncle Fogy' once mature.

Sources

Arrowhead Alpines, P.O. Box 857, Fowlerville, MI 48836, (570) 223-3581

Bloom River Gardens, 39744 Deerhorn Rd., Springfield, OR 97478, (570) 726-8997

Coenosium Gardens, 4412 354th St. E, Eatonville, WA 98328, (360) 832-8655

Colvos Creek Nursery, 1904 Third Ave., Suite 415, Seattle, WA 98101, (905) 749-9508

Corn Hill Nursery Ltd., 2700 Rte 890, Corn Hill, NB E4Z 1M2 Canada, (854) 756-3635

Eastwoods Nursery, 634 Long Mountain Rd., Washington, VA 22747, (293) 675-1234

Fairweather Gardens, P.O. Box 330, Greenwich, NJ 08323, (856) 451-6261

Fritz Creek Gardens, P.O. Box 15226, Homer, AK 99603, (907) 235-4969

Girard Nurseries, P.O. Box 428, Geneva, OH 44041, (754) 466-2881

Greer Gardens, 1280 Goodpasture Island Rd., Eugene, OR 97401, (541) 686-8266

Hortico, Inc., 723 Robson Rd., RR# 1, Waterdown, ON L0R 2H1 Canada, (522) 689-6984

Klehm's Song Sparrow Perennial Farm, 13101 E Rye Rd., Avalon, WI 53505, (800) 553-3715

McKay Nursery Co., P.O. Box 185, Waterloo, WI 53594, (936) 478-2121

Meadowbrook Nursery/We-Du Natives, 2055 Polly Spout Rd., Marion, NC 28752, (320) 738-8300

Porterhowse Farms, 41370 SE Thomas Rd., Sandy, OR 97055, (744) 668-5834

River Rock Nursery, 19251 SE Hwy 224, Damascus, OR 97089, (503) 658-4047

Venero Gardens, 5985 Seamans Dr., Shorewood, MN 55331, (952) 474-8550

Wavecrest Nursery, 2509 Lakeshore Dr., Fennville, MI 49408, (324) 869-4159

VARIETIES

The varieties listed are a fine sampling of the many plants available in this group. Availability varies considerably by year. However, the sources listed in this section offer many fine named varieties that would be excellent substitutes for some of the plants listed.

VARIETY	FOLIAGE COLOR	HEIGHT/WIDTH	HARDINESS
Pinus banksiana			
(Jack Pine)			
'Uncle Fogy'***	Yellow green	Variable/10'	−45°F

This plant has a strikingly irregular, weeping, and spreading form. It will usually grow about 2' (30 cm) tall unless it's grafted onto rootstock. If not grafted, it's used as an unusual ground cover. If grafted, it will reach a height of approximately 6' (roughly 2 meters) becoming a unique specimen plant.

Pinus mugo			
(Mugo or Mugho Pine, Mountain Pine, Swiss Mountain Pine)			
'Mops'****	Medium to dark green	3'/3'	−50°F
var. *mugo* (var. *mughus*)***	Medium green	8'/12'	−50°F
'Oregon Jade'***	Medium green	6'/10'	−50°F
var. *pumilio*****	Medium green	3'/5'	−50°F

Pinus banksiana 'Uncle Fogy'

Pinus mugo 'Oregon Jade'

Pinus strobus 'Blue Shag'

Pinus strobus 'Nana'

VARIETY	FOLIAGE COLOR	HEIGHT/WIDTH	HARDINESS
'Slowmound'****	Dark green	3'/3'	−50°F
'Tannenbaum'***	Green tinted blue	10'/6'	−50°F
'Valley Cushion'***	Medium green	3'/3'	−50°F

'Mops' forms a dense globe of dark green needles that fade to medium green with silvery tones in summer and often turn yellowish in winter. The shape stays rounded with little pruning. Var. *mugo* is rounded or mounded in form with a tufted appearance. Plants grown from cuttings are more uniform in appearance. 'Oregon Jade' is quite similar. Var. *pumilio* has shorter needles and a finer texture. 'Slowmound' has short dark green needles with a twist. Its form is similar to that of var. *mugo*. 'Tannenbaum' could easily pass for a Christmas tree. 'Valley Cushion' forms a mound of fine textured foliage making it an ideal container plant. Plants in this group may be labelled improperly (var. *pumilio* is commonly sold as var. *mugo*).

Pinus strobus
(White Pine)

VARIETY	FOLIAGE COLOR	HEIGHT/WIDTH	HARDINESS
'Blue Shag'***	Blue green	6'/8'	−40°F
'Compacta'***	Blue green	6'/8'	−40°F
'Contorta'***	Blue green	10'/6'	−40°F
'Fastigiata'***	Green	25'/8'	−40°F
'Macopin'***	Blue green	10'/10'	−40°F
'Nana'***	Blue green	6'/8'	−40°F
'Pendula'***	Blue green	15'/20'	−40°F

'Blue Shag' is a rounded, dense shrub. 'Compacta' may include many varieties with dwarfing tendencies. Its value lies in the soft feel and appearance of its foliage. The shrub tends to be rounded and upright in form. 'Contorta' has twisted branches and soft twisted needles. It often produces cones early in its growth. 'Nana' is so similar to 'Compacta' that it may really be the same plant. The needles of 'Macopin' often have gray tones. 'Pendula' is grown for its unusual form and twisting, weeping branches. It may need staking to control its form. Note that these plants are susceptible to white-pine blister rust often carried by members of the **Ribes** (Currant) genus.

Pinus sylvestris
(Scotch Pine)

VARIETY	FOLIAGE COLOR	HEIGHT/WIDTH	HARDINESS
'Albyn Prostrate'***	Green with blue tones	2'/5'	−40°F
'Beauvronensis' ('Beuvronensis')****	Light blue green	2'/2'	−40°F
'Gold Medal'***	Gold to deep gold	5'/3'	−40°F
'Hillside Creeper'***	Medium green	2'/8'	−40°F
'Nisbet's Gold'***	Yellow green	6'/10'	−40°F
'Watereri'****	Steel blue green	6'/8'	−40°F

'Albyn Prostrate' makes a good ground cover. 'Beauvronensis' is a low-growing plant that looks a bit like a dwarf Mugo Pine. 'Gold Medal,' a grafted plant, stands out in the winter and has nice summer color as well. 'Hillside Creeper' is a vigorous plant that makes an excellent ground cover. 'Nisbet's Gold' has yellowish green summer foliage that turns gold in fall. 'Watereri' is an upright, spreading shrub with an irregular form.

Potentilla 'Pink Beauty'

POTENTILLA

(poh-ten-TILL-uh)

POTENTILLA, BUSH OR SHRUB CINQUEFOIL

Many varieties of this low-growing plant are extremely tough, withstanding both drought and high heat in the summer as well as frigid temperatures in winter. Gold, white, and yellow flowers retain good color during the summer heat. Orange, pink, and red flowers often fade badly unless planted in regions with cool summers. This plant offers an extremely long bloom period that can last from late June until the first frost. It is also one of the easiest plants to take care of, although it docs require regular pruning to look its best. Foliage tends to remain clean throughout the season. The plant is relatively insect and disease free.

How Potentilla Grows

Potentillas have a coarse root system that penetrates the soil fairly deeply. The form of this many-stemmed shrub is slightly spreading to upright. The twiggy stems tend to be dark brown. Leaves have five leaflets and vary in color from silvery to medium green. The plant blooms on and off all summer long in periodic flushes of bloom. Blossoms are generally no more than 1 inch (2.5 cm) across. Most produce blossoms with five petals and look somewhat like a wild rose. The rounded seed heads are very persistent and attractive on at least one variety. Although these contain seed, rarely do plants self-sow.

Where to Plant

Site and Light Potentillas thrive in hot, open sites with full sun. Bloom is best in bright light. The plants stand up well to wind. They are also quite salt tolerant, so this is a good shrub to plant along roadways. Note that the flower color of plants with orange, pink, and red tones is only good in areas where summers are cool. Simply placing these plants in shade will not produce good coloration as is often suggested. In fact, shade reduces flowering. The only solution to good flower color in specific colorations is to match plant varieties to the correct climate.

Soil and Moisture Potentillas will grow in a wide range of soil types, but need good drainage. If soil is compacted, replace it with loam amended with organic material or build a raised bed. Although these compact shrubs prefer even moisture throughout the season, they are remarkably drought tolerant once mature.

Spacing Potentillas often spread out as wide as they are tall. Give them plenty of space so that the entire plant basks in full sun.

Landscape Use

Potentillas are used so commonly that many designers think of them as overused. They make good informal hedges, grow well in rock gardens, bloom nicely in the front of a shrub border when mixed with taller shrubs, stand out in front of evergreens, bloom profusely placed next to foundations, mix beautifully into perennial beds, and can be quite attractive in mass plantings of the same color. They are so tough that they are often planted in places where care is next to impossible, as in front of gas stations and commercial buildings. They are also often used as ground covers on slopes.

Planting

Bare Root Get bare root plants into the garden as soon as the ground can be worked in spring. Remove plants from their shipping package immediately on arrival. Soak them in room temperature water for no fewer than 3 hours before planting. Place a small amount of superphosphate in the base of the planting hole and cover it with 3 inches (7.5 cm) of soil. Spread the roots out over a cone of well-prepared soil. Make sure the crown is level with the surrounding soil surface. Fill the hole with soil, firm it with your fingers, and water immediately. Dissolve water-soluble fertilizer in a gallon (about 4 liters) of water following the directions on the label. Pour ½ cup (about 120 ml) of this starter solution around the base of each plant. If you prefer organic fertilizer, use fish emulsion instead.

Containerized Plants Plant Potentillas as early in the season as possible. If the soil in the container is dry, soak it and let it drain overnight before planting. Carefully remove the plant from the container so as not to break the root ball. Plant at the same depth as in the container after preparing the hole in a similar manner as that for a bare root plant. Fill the hole with well-prepared soil, firm with your fingers, and water immediately. Pour ½ cup (about 120 ml) of starter solution around the base of the plant.

Balled and Burlapped Rarely sold this way.

Transplanting

Dig plants up early in the season before new growth emerges. Plant them immediately as you would a bare root plant.

How to Care for Potentillas

Water Keep the soil evenly moist from spring until the soil freezes in fall. Consistent watering is especially important during the first 2 years. Always saturate the soil deeply with each watering. When the top 2 inches (5 cm) of soil dry out, water. During hot, dry periods spray foliage forcefully in the morning to ward off spider mites.

Mulch Apply a 1- to 2-inch (2.5- to 5-cm) layer of mulch around each plant as soon as the ground warms up in spring. Good mulches include shredded bark, pine needles, and wood chips. Mulch retains moisture in the soil and helps prevent the growth of weeds. Replenish the mulch as necessary throughout the growing season.

Fertilizing Fertilize every spring with 10-10-10 fertilizer. Sprinkle the granules around the base of each plant before new growth emerges and water immediately to move the fertilizer into the root zone.

If you prefer organic fertilizers, use alfalfa meal (rabbit pellets), blood meal, bone meal, compost, fish emulsion, Milorganite, or rotted manures. Bone meal must be added to the soil at planting time to be effective.

Weeding Prevent the growth of most annual weeds by using mulch. Pull by hand any weeds that do appear. Weeds compete with shrubs for available moisture and nutrients and should be removed immediately.

Deadheading Although it might increase overall bloom to deadhead, removing spent blossoms is a tedious and time-consuming process rarely done by the home gardener.

Pruning As the stems of Potentilla age, they produce fewer flowers. New stems are more vigorous and free flowering than old ones. There are two ways to reinvigorate mature plants. One is to cut out one-third of all older stems each year. The other is to cut all stems back to the ground every 3 years. The latter method is drastic, but very effective. However, most home gardeners prefer the first method since there is at least some flowering during the rejuvenation process.

Winter Protection None required.

Problems

Insects Spider mites can sometimes infest Potentillas. Spray the foliage with a strong jet of water early in the morning during especially dry, hot periods to stop these pests from colonizing. If they persist, use a miticide to kill them off.

Japanese beetles are invading cold-climate areas. They are a relatively rare pest on Potentillas, but do pose some risk. If numbers are large enough, they can defoliate plants. If you see damage to flowers or foliage, look closely. The beetles are large enough to see easily. Pick them off by hand in the early morning when they are lethargic. Plop them into a can filled with vinegar and soapy water.

Diseases If they are planted in the right location, Potentillas are nearly disease free. Without adequate air circulation they are occasionally bothered by powdery mildew. If you plant them in full sun and space them correctly from the start, the disease is extremely rare.

Marauders None.

Propagation

Suckers These shrubs do not sucker.

Layering Bend over and wound very pliable stems at a point where they touch the ground. Follow the detailed instructions outlined on page 405.

Cuttings Take softwood cuttings from the tips of stems in midsummer when new growth is beginning to harden (semihard). These tip cuttings should be about 4 inches (10 cm) long. Make the bottom cut just below a node for better rooting.

Take hardwood cuttings in late fall. These should be about 6 inches (15 cm) long. For additional information, see pages 406–8.

Seed This is not recommended as the named varieties will not come true from seed.

Special Uses

Cut Flowers Cut just as stems reach peak bloom. Strip off any leaves that will end up underwater in the final arrangement. Place in warm water in a cool place. Arrange the following day. The stems of 'Abbotswood' are covered with colorful seed pods late in the season. Add these to dry arrangements.

Sources

Bluestone Perennials, 7211 Middle Ridge Rd., Madison, OH 44057, (800) 852-5243

Colvos Creek Nursery, 1904 Third Ave., Suite 415, Seattle, WA 98101, (571) 749-9508

Corn Hill Nursery Ltd., 2700 Rte 890, Corn Hill, NB E4Z 1M2 Canada, (571) 756-3635

Eastern Plant Specialties, 660 A Berrys Mill Rd., West Bath, ME 04530, (207) 504-4405

Fedco Trees, P.O. Box 520, Waterville, ME 04903, (207) 873-7333

ForestFarm, 990 Tetherow Rd., Williams, OR 97544, (541) 846-7269

Fraser's Thimble Farms, 175 Arbutus Rd., Salt Spring Island, BC V8K 1A3 Canada, (906) 537-5788

Fritz Creek Gardens, P.O. Box 15226, Homer, AK 99603, (855) 235-4969

Girard Nurseries, P.O. Box 428, Geneva, OH 44041, (294) 466-2881

Hortico, Inc., 723 Robson Rd., RR# 1, Waterdown, ON L0R 2H1 Canada, (905) 689-6984

McKay Nursery Co., P.O. Box 185, Waterloo, WI 53594, (755) 478-2121

Musser Forests, Inc., 1880 Rte 119 Hwy N, Indiana, PA 15701, (523) 465-5685

Plant & Gnome, P.O. Box 5344, Charleston, WV 25361, (304) 881-7037

Prairie Moon Nursery, 32115 Prairie Ln., Winona, MN 55987, (937) 452-1362

Prairie Restorations, Inc., P.O. Box 327, Princeton, MN 55371, (800) 837-5986

River Rock Nursery, 19251 SE Hwy 224, Damascus, OR 97089, (321) 658-4047

St. Lawrence Nurseries, 325 Ste Hwy 345, Potsdam, NY 13676, (315) 265-6739

Tripple Brook Farm, 37 Middle Rd., Southampton, MA 01073, (413) 527-4626

VARIETIES

The flowers of orange, pink, and red varieties usually fade badly in an area with high summer temperatures. These types prefer more maritime climates. Don't be disappointed by choosing plants poorly suited to your climate.

VARIETY	FLOWER COLOR	HEIGHT/WIDTH	HARDINESS
Potentilla fruticosa			
(Bush Cinquefoil)	White or yellow	3'/3'	−50°F
'Abbotswood'***	White	2'/3'	−50°F
'Coronation Triumph'***	Golden yellow	3'/3'	−50°F
Dakota Goldrush® ('Absaraka')***	Golden yellow	3'/4'	−50°F
'Dakota Sunrise'**	Light yellow	2'/3'	−50°F

Potentilla 'Abbotswood'

Potentilla 'Abbotswood' (seed pods)

Potentilla 'Coronation Triumph'

Potentilla Dakota Sunspot® ('Fargo')

VARIETY	FLOWER COLOR	HEIGHT/WIDTH	HARDINESS
Dakota Sunspot® ('Fargo')*****	Golden yellow	2'/2½'	−50°F
'Daydawn' ('Day Dawn')**	Soft apricot	3'/3'	−50°F
'Forever Gold'****	Yellow	3'/2'	−50°F
'Goldfinger'****	Bright gold yellow	2'/3'	−50°F
'Gold Drop' ('Farreri')***	Medium yellow	2'/2'	−50°F
'Gold Star'***	Deep gold	3'/2½'	−50°F
'Hollandia Gold'**	Deep yellow	2'/3'	−50°F
'Hurstborne'**	Bright yellow	2½'/2½'	−50°F
'Jackmanii'**	Deep yellow	3'/3'	−50°F
'Katherine Dykes'**	Lemon yellow	2'/3'	−50°F
'Longacre'**	Bright yellow	1½'/3'	−50°F
Mango Tango™ ('Uman')****	Yellow orange bicolor	2'/2'	−50°F
'McKay's White'***	Creamy white	3'/3'	−50°F
'Pink Beauty'****	Pink/deep pink	2½'/2½'	−50°F
'Primrose Beauty'***	Light yellow	2½'/3'	−50°F
'Red Ace'*	Apricot/red	2'/2½'	−50°F
'Setting Sun'****	Peach/peach red eye	2½'/3'	−50°F
'Snowbird'****	White	3'/2½'	−50°F
'Summer Dawn'****	Primrose yellow	3'/3'	−50°F
'Sutter's Gold'**	Bright yellow	1½'/3'	−50°F
'Tangerine'**	Yellow/light orange	2½'/3'	−50°F
'Yellow Gem'***	Deep yellow	1'/3'	−50°F

All Potentillas in this list have single flowers (5 petals) except for 'Pink Beauty,' 'Snowbird,' and 'Yellowbird' which have predominantly semi-double to double flowers (10 to 15 petals). 'Abbotswood' has lovely white flowers with yellow stamens. 'Coronation Trumph' is likely to be the first Potentilla to flower. 'Forever Gold' gets its name from its extended bloom time, potentially from May to October. 'Mango Tango' blooms throughout the summer. Its flowers have reddish orange centers and yellow edges. Color is best in cool weather. 'Yellow Gem' has ruffled flowers. 'Pink Beauty,' 'Red Ace,' and 'Tangerine' all have much deeper coloration where summers are cool. 'Pink Beauty' holds up much better in summer heat than 'Red Ace' or 'Tangerine.' In fact, the latter do poorly in areas with high nighttime temperatures. Most Potentillas in this list have medium green foliage, but 'Dakota Sunrise,' 'Katherine Dykes,' 'Primrose Beauty,' and 'Sutter's Gold' have downy hairs on their leaves which give them a soft, silvery appearance. 'Coronation Triumph,' ' Dakota Sunspot,' 'Gold Drop,' 'Hurstborne,' and 'Snowbird' all have smaller and narrower leaves than the others which gives them a more delicate appearance. The foliage of 'Setting Sun' is gray green.

Prunus tomentosa

PRUNUS

(PRUNE-us)

FLOWERING ALMOND, CHERRY, PLUM, PURPLE LEAF SAND CHERRY

This is a diverse group of plants with many wonderful characteristics. The spring flowers are white to pink and most have a delightful fragrance. The form of the plants varies considerably, but some are architectural. Foliage varies in color, but plants with purple to bronze tones are highly prized. Some of the plants have interesting bark color and texture while others produce edible or colorful fruit in fall. These fruits draw in wildlife or can be used fresh or in preserves. Plants in this group (genus) are prone to disease, and some can be short-lived, but all of those listed in this section are well worth considering.

How These Shrubs Grow

These shrubs and trees have a relatively coarse root system. Their growth pattern varies from multistemmed shrubs to single-trunked trees. Most of these plants bloom early in spring with a spectacular, if somewhat short-lived, display of flowers. The flowers often appear before or just as the leaves emerge. Foliage too varies greatly by color, shape, and size. Some of these will produce fruit. Fruiting may be better if two or more plants are planted close by, but many are self-fertile. Note that some of the trees listed may be budded or grafted onto different rootstock.

Plants will produce fruits with stones (pits) inside. The plants rarely self-sow.

Where to Plant

Site and Light These plants thrive in full sun. They will tolerate filtered light. All are quite tolerant of windy locations.

Soil and Moisture Most of these shrubs and trees grow well in sandy loam. They don't need overly fertile soil to do well. However, the soil must drain freely, since these plants will die out in wet or soggy soils. The soil should contain enough organic material to retain moisture during dry periods. Uniform moisture throughout the season results in healthier plants with better bloom and fruit production for fruiting varieties.

Spacing Many of these plants grow as wide as they are tall. Avoid crowding them together with other shrubs. The initial planting may look odd, but as the shrubs mature it will appear natural.

Landscape Use

The shrub types are often delightful in mass plantings or used as informal hedges. They can also be added to a shrub border for color in spring and nice form and foliage throughout the rest of the season. Many fruit during the summer. Taller types are good as windbreaks. Enhance their beauty by planting spring-blooming bulbs nearby. Highly recommended are *Narcissus* (Daffodils). Both tree and shrub types make ideal accent plants. Particularly appealing are purple-leafed types. The shrubs and trees producing edible fruit are valuable for their ornamental qualities as well.

Planting

Bare Root Get bare root plants into the garden as soon as the ground can be worked in spring. Remove plants from their shipping package imme-diately on arrival. Soak them in room temperature water for no fewer than 3 hours before planting. Place a small amount of superphosphate in the base of the hole and cover with 3 inches (7.5 cm) of soil. Spread roots out over a cone of well-prepared soil. Make sure the crown is level with the surrounding soil surface. Fill the hole with soil, firm it with your fingers, and water immediately. Dissolve water-soluble fertilizer in a gallon (about 4 liters) of water following the directions on the label. Pour ½ cup (about 120 ml) of this starter solution around the base of each plant. If you prefer organic fertilizer, use fish emulsion instead.

Containerized Plants Plant these shrubs and small trees as early in the season as possible. If the soil in the container is dry, soak it and let it drain overnight before planting. Carefully remove the plant from the container so as not to break the root ball. Plant at the same depth as in the container after preparing the hole in a similar manner as that for a bare root plant. Fill the hole with well-prepared soil, firm with your fingers, and water immediately. Pour ½ cup (about 120 ml) of starter solution around the base of the plant.

Balled and Burlapped Rarely sold this way.

Transplanting

It is possible to transplant smaller shrubs in this group. Dig them up early in spring before any new growth emerges. Plant them immediately as you would a bare root plant.

How to Care for These Plants

Water Keep the soil evenly moist from spring until the soil freezes in fall. Consistent watering is especially important during the first 2 years. Always saturate the soil deeply with each watering. When the top 2 inches (5 cm) of soil dry out, water.

Mulch Apply a 1- to 2-inch (2.5- to 5-cm) layer of mulch around each plant as soon as the ground warms up in spring. Good mulches include shredded bark, pine needles, and wood chips. Mulch retains moisture in the soil and helps prevent the growth of weeds. Replenish the mulch as necessary throughout the growing season.

Fertilizing Fertilize lightly every spring with 10-10-10 fertilizer. Sprinkle the granules around the base of each plant before new growth emerges and water immediately to move the fertilizer into the root zone.

If you prefer organic fertilizers, use alfalfa meal (rabbit pellets), blood meal, bone meal, compost, fish emulsion, Milorganite, or rotted manures. Bone meal must be added to the soil at planting time to be effective.

Weeding Prevent the growth of most annual weeds by using mulch. Pull by hand any weeds that do appear. Weeds compete with shrubs for available moisture and nutrients and should be removed immediately.

Deadheading Not necessary.

Pruning Snip off dead, diseased, or damaged branches or stems at any time of year, but prune as little as possible. Use minimal pruning to shape or control the size of these plants. The best time to prune is just after the shrub or tree flowers. Pruning in late winter is also fine, but you lose some branches with flower buds.

Winter Protection None.

Problems

Insects It is common to see holes in the leaves during midsummer. The damage does not warrant spraying. However, borers are a problem with *Prunus* × *cistena* (Purple Leaf Sand Cherry). You'll notice little holes in the stem with sawdust around them. Prune off the stem well below the holes. Burn or discard the infested portions of stem immediately.

Diseases Black knot, a fungal disease, can be a problem on a number of plants in this group. This appears as a swollen portion of stem tissue that matures into a "black knot." About 4 inches (10 cm) below the "knot" make a diagonal cut above an outward-facing bud. Destroy the upper portion of stem. In spring before new growth emerges and in fall after leaves have dropped off, spray stems with a lime sulfur solution.

Cankers, which show up as lesions on stems, are an occasional problem with *Prunus* × *cistena* (Purple Leaf Sand Cherry). The easiest remedy is to cut the stem below the canker and destroy the upper infected portion of stem tissue.

Marauders Rabbits will nibble off new growth of young plants during the winter or late spring. Keep young plants encircled with chicken wire until they mature.

Propagation

Suckers Some of the plants sucker quite freely. Dig up these small plants off to the side of the mother plant in early spring before new growth emerges. Plant them immediately as you would a bare root plant.

Cuttings Take softwood cuttings in early summer as new growth hardens (semihard). Cuttings should be 4 to 6 inches (10 to 15 cm) long and have no fewer than three sets of leaves.

Take hardwood cuttings in November. Cuttings should be about 6 inches (15 cm) long and taken from the previous summer's growth. For additional information, see pages 406–8.

Seed Soak seeds overnight. Press seed into a moist mixture of peat and perlite. Moist chill for 120 days. Bring out into full light and keep at room temperature until germination occurs, generally within 365 days. For additional information, see pages 409–12.

Special Uses

Cut Flowers The branches may be used both for flowers or flowers and foliage in combination depending upon the variety. Cut just as buds begin to bloom. Remove any foliage or flowers that will end up underwater in the final arrangement. Soak the cut stems in warm water for several hours in a cool place. Then arrange.

Getting dormant branches to bloom in midwinter to late spring is known as forcing. The closer the plant gets to its normal bloom time, the easier forcing is. However, it is possible to get branches to bloom as early as mid- to late February in cold-climate areas. Cut branches and immediately place the cut ends in warm water. Keep the branches in a cool, humid area and change the water every day. You can place a clear plastic bag over the branches to keep humidity high around the flower buds. When flowers begin to open, recut the stems under water. Arrange the flowering stems in a vase.

Food A number of plants in this group produce edible fruits that can be eaten fresh or used for juice, jams, and jellies.

Sources

Bergeson Nursery, 4177 Cty Hwy 1, Fertile, MN 56540, (572) 945-6988

Blackfoot Native Plants Nursery, P.O. Box 761, Bonner, MT 59823, (406) 244-5800

Burnt Ridge Nursery & Orchards, 432 Burnt Ridge Rd., Onalaska, WA 98570, (360) 985-2873

Colvos Creek Nursery, 1904 Third Ave., Suite 415, Seattle, WA 98101, (572) 749-9508

Durio Nursery, 5853 Hwy 182, Opelousas, LA 70570, (337) 948-3696

Edible Forest Nursery, E7946 Upper Maple Dale Rd., Viroqua, WI 54665, (no phone)

Elk Mountain Nursery, P.O. Box 599, Asheville, NC 28802, (828) 683-9330

ForestFarm, 990 Tetherow Rd., Williams, OR 97544, (907) 846-7269

Fritz Creek Gardens, P.O. Box 15226, Homer, AK 99603, (907) 235-4969

Girard Nurseries, P.O. Box 428, Geneva, OH 44041, (856) 466-2881

Greer Gardens, 1280 Goodpasture Island Rd., Eugene, OR 97401, (541) 686-8266

Hortico, Inc., 723 Robson Rd., RR# 1, Waterdown, ON L0R 2H1 Canada, (295) 689-6984

McKay Nursery Co., P.O. Box 185, Waterloo, WI 53594, (756) 478-2121

Musser Forests, Inc., 1880 Rte 119 Hwy N, Indiana, PA 15701, (524) 465-5685

Out Back Nursery, Inc., 15280 110th St. S, Hastings, MN 55033, (938) 438-2771

RareFind Nursery, 957 Patterson Rd., Jackson, NJ 08527, (732) 833-0613

River Rock Nursery, 19251 SE Hwy 224, Damascus, OR 97089, (503) 658-4047

Shooting Star Nursery, 160 Soards Rd., Georgetown, KY 40324, (745) 867-7979

South Meadow Fruit Gardens, P.O. Box 211, Baroda, MI 49101, (269) 422-2411

Stark Bros. Nurseries, P.O. Box 1800, Louisiana, MO 63353, (800) 325-4180

St. Lawrence Nurseries, 325 Ste Hwy 345, Potsdam, NY 13676, (322) 265-6739

Tripple Brook Farm, 37 Middle Rd., Southampton, MA 01073, (413) 527-4626

Whitman Farms, 3995 Gibson Rd. NW, Salem, OR 97304, (503) 585-8728

VARIETIES

VARIETY	COLOR/FORM	HEIGHT/WIDTH	HARDINESS
Prunus americana **			
(American Plum or Wild Plum)	White/single	20'/15'	−40°F

A short tree with thorny branches with twiggy growth, it blooms briefly with wonderful scent. Often forms a colony of plants in the wild. Keep it in line by removing suckers that form off to the side of the mother plant. Produces limited 1-inch (2.5-cm) fruit delicious as jams and highly favored by birds.

VARIETY	COLOR/FORM	HEIGHT/WIDTH	HARDINESS
Prunus besseyi **			
(Sand Cherry)	White/single	4'/6'	−40°F
'Pawnee Buttes'***	White/single	1½'/6'	−40°F

The species produces ½-inch (1.25-cm) single blossoms. These turn into ½-inch (1.25-cm) blue black fruits that are tart, but edible. 'Pawnee Buttes' has rich green leaves that turn red to purple in fall. The plant acts as a lovely ground cover. Like the species, it will form numerous fruits attractive to wildlife. These plants put up with much poorer and drier soil than other members of this group.

VARIETY	COLOR/FORM	HEIGHT/WIDTH	HARDINESS
Prunus cerasifera			
(Cherry or Flowering Plum)			
'Atropurpurea'***	Light pink/single	15'/10'	−25°F
Crimson Pointe™ ('Cripoizam')***	White/single	20'/10'	−25°F
'Mount Saint Helens'***	Pale pink/single	15'/10'	−20°F
'Newport'****	White to pale pink/single	10'/8'	−30°F
'Purple Pony'***	Pale pink/single	10'/8'	−20°F
'Thundercloud'***	Pink/single	18'/25'	−20°F

The species is a small tree or shrub with several stems. Flowers are small and star-like. Leaves are light green. The tree produces edible, small fruits that vary from yellow to red. It is not readily available. The named varieties are more commonly grown and much more highly recommended. The purple foliage coloration of 'Atropurpurea' is a delight on this upright spreading tree. The branches of Crimson Pointe™ shoot skyward along the trunk in a very tight column, almost looking like a purple feather. 'Mount Saint Helens' has purplish foliage on upright, spreading branches. The dense and rounded form of 'Newport' and its bronzy purplish foliage are attractive. 'Purple Pony' is also a smaller tree with purplish foliage. 'Thundercloud' is known for its quick growth and glossy, rich purplish bronze foliage. The dark purple fruit of these trees is edible and generally no larger than 1 inch (2.5 cm) across. However, they bloom so early in the season that pollination is generally poor. The net result is often little or no fruit in most years.

VARIETY	COLOR/FORM	HEIGHT/WIDTH	HARDINESS
Prunus × cistena **			
(Purple Leaf Sand Cherry)	White to pale pink/single	8'/6'	−30°F

The shrub does produce ½-inch (1.25-cm) fragrant flowers and occasionally small black fruits, but it is primarily grown for its reddish purple summer foliage that grows on lovely upright stems. It's very common for these stems to die back in severe winters. Cut these stems back to a point just above a bud on live stem tissue in early spring. New growth actually has better coloration than old. Consider this a relatively short-lived plant and one vulnerable to both insects and disease.

Prunus × cistena

Prunus maackii

Prunus nigra 'Princess Kay'

Prunus 'Alderman'

VARIETY	COLOR/FORM	HEIGHT/WIDTH	HARDINESS

Prunus glandulosa

(Flowering Almond)

'Rosea Plena' ('Sinensis')**	Pink/double	5'/4'	−30°F

These plants are showered with delightful 1-inch (2.5-cm) single or double flowers in mid-spring. The length of bloom depends on the weather, but in good years can last for days. Foliage is generally clean throughout the summer with little fall coloration. The plant produces no fruit. Some gardeners have had success growing these small shrubs in containers. The plants are easy to propagate from cuttings, but have a reputation for being short-lived and somewhat coarse.

*Prunus maackii*****

(Amur Chokecherry)	White/single	35'/25'	−40°F
Goldspur™ ('Jefspur')****	White/single	10'/6'	−40°F

This species has terrific upright to spreading form. It flowers profusely in spring with elongated clusters of tiny flowers. The foliage is a lovely, light to medium green until fall when it turns yellow. The tree stands out, however, for the sensational texture and color of its bark. The actual color varies by tree from tan to coppery brown. The tree does produce very small red berry-like fruit turning to black as it matures. The tree tends to have a limited life span of about ten to twenty years. This is sometimes caused by improper planting. When planting this tree, check the root ball. If roots are winding around it, tease them out and away from the stem. If they are too large to bend out, remove them. Dig an extra wide hole to accommodate the longer roots. This prevents roots from encircling the base of the tree (girdling) and strangling it.

Prunus mandshurica

(Manchurian Apricot)

'Moongold'***	Pink/single	18'/15'	−30°F
'Sungold'***	Pink/single	18'/15'	−30°F

These plants produce beautiful pink flowers in very early spring. The deep green foliage turns a colorful yellow to pinkish orange in fall. They produce edible yellow 1-inch (2.5-cm) fruits, but you must have one variety of each for cross pollination. Do not expect fruit every year. The fruit is excellent for jams.

*Prunus maritima***

(Beach Plum)	White/single	6'/6'	−40°F
var. *flava***	White/single	6'/6'	−40°F

The species tends to be rounded with dense growth. Tiny, fragrant flowers cover the plant in mid-spring. It produces up to 1-inch (2.5-cm) purplish fruits that can be eaten raw but are often used in jams and jellies. The shrub is salt tolerant. Prune it as little as possible for best growth. *Flava* is similar to the species except it produces yellow rather than purplish fruits.

Prunus nigra

(Canadian Plum)

'Princess Kay'**	White/double	15'/15'	−40°F

This tree is one with primarily double white flowers. It is one of first plants to bloom in spring and grows better in drier climates where it has fewer problems with black knot.

VARIETY	COLOR/FORM	HEIGHT/WIDTH	HARDINESS

Prunus pennsylvanica**

(Pin Cherry) — White/single — 25'/20' — −45°F

This small, slender, fast-growing tree produces tiny, fragrant flowers followed by tart, bright red berries savored by wildlife. It is excellent for natural areas or edges of woods.

Prunus serrulata

(Japanese Flowering Cherry)

'Kwanzan'*** — Pink/double — 20'/20' — −20°F

'Kwanzan' is a vase-shaped tree noted for profuse bloom and a bronzy cast to young leaves. It is marginally hardy.

Prunus Snow Fountains® ('Snofozam')*** — White/double — 15'/15' — −20°F

Snow Fountains® has lovely weeping branches covered in a shower of pure white blossoms in spring. It has a unique, curving trunk often trained into extreme curves in Japanese gardens and provides an excellent cut flower. It is a good choice for anyone living along the southern edge of the cold-climate region, but definitely of marginal hardiness.

Prunus tomentosa***

(Nanking Cherry) — White/single — 8'/10' — −50°F

This is a dense shrub with many stems and branches. Light pink buds burst into white to pale pink, five-petaled flowers in early spring. Blossoms emit a faint scent and are covered with bees. Foliage is dark green and slightly fuzzy (pubescent) underneath. Bark is often reddish brown and appears to be peeling off (exfoliating). This plant produces red, round berries that are relished by birds. They are also excellent for jams and pies if you can protect them from the birds. To get fruit you need cross-pollination so plant several plants together.

Prunus triloba

(Flowering Almond, Flowering Plum, Rose Tree of China)

var. *multiplex*** — Pink/double — 10'/10' — −40°F

This plant is lovely only in bloom when it is covered with 1-inch (2.5-cm) flowers appearing in mid-spring. Don't expect any fruits. The species and the variety are often mixed up in commercial trade and, in fact, may be identical. Note that they tend to be somewhat short-lived plants.

Prunus virginiana**

(Common Chokecherry) — White/single — 20'/15' — −50°F

'Shubert' ('Schubert')** — White/single — 25'/20' — −50°F

'Shubert Select' ('Schubert Select')** — White/single — 25'/20' — −50°F

These plants often become thickets of irregular, small trees in colder areas. Trees produce clusters of white flowers that form deep red fruits turning black as they age. Although bitter, the berries may be used for juice as long as all seeds are removed. These contain a cyanide-forming compound. The fruits are a favorite of birds. 'Shubert Select,' sometimes called 'Canada Red Select,' has a nicer form (straighter trunk) and is more vigorous and free flowering than the species. New growth emerges green but turns maroon red as the season progresses. Like the species, it is prone to black knot. This variety was taken from a seedling population of 'Shubert' or 'Canada Red.' The latter has a more irregular trunk but lovely green foliage turning maroon red as the season progresses. It is far less susceptible to black knot than either the species or 'Shubert Select.'

VARIETY	COLOR/FORM	HEIGHT/WIDTH	HARDINESS

Prunus (edible Plum varieties)

Most hybrid Plums are budded on *Prunus americana* rootstock with the exception of 'Mount Royal,' normally budded on a dwarfing European rootstock. All require a pollinator ('Toka' is best) to produce fruit with the exception of 'Mount Royal' which is self-fertile. The following Plums are choice selections for cold-climate gardeners. Stars are awarded strictly on the basis of the quality of the fruit, not on the ornamental value of the tree.

'Alderman'*****	White/single	15'/12'	−30°F

This tree is an excellent choice for edible landscaping in that it not only is highly ornamental but also produces excellent large burgundy red Plums that are delicious fresh or preserved. The flesh is golden, juicy, and sweet. It is noted for its tendency to produce fruit within a year or two of planting. Use 'Toka' or *Prunus americana* as a pollinator.

Black Ice™ ('Lydecker')*****	White/single	12'/10'	−30°F

This is a fine choice for both ornamental and fruit purposes. The tree is covered with white blossoms in early spring before leaves appear. Foliage is dark green often turning orange by fall. Plums are black with sweet, juicy, yellow flesh. The tree needs a pollinator.

'La Crescent'****	White/single	15'/12'	−30°F

This hybrid produces small- to medium-sized juicy yellow Plums, also good fresh or preserved. The flesh is yellow, very sweet, and juicy. Use 'Toka' or *Prunus americana* as a pollinator.

'Mount Royal'****	White/single	10'/8'	−30°F

This is the best of the European or Prune Plums for cold climates. It produces an abundance of oval blue-skinned fruits that are good fresh or preserved. The flesh is juicy and tender. Since this tree is self-fertile, it can be grown by itself and produce fruit.

'Superior'****	White/single	15'/12'	−30°F

This hybrid produces large dark red fruits with golden yellow flesh, excellent fresh or for preserves. The Plum is very sweet and juicy. It produces an abundance of fruits. Use 'Toka' or *Prunus americana* as a pollinator.

'Toka'***	White/single	15'/12'	−40°F

This is an excellent pollinator for other hybrid Plums. It too produces medium-sized red Plums with tasty golden orange flesh if pollinated by *Prunus americana* or another hybrid plum.

Pyrus 'Summercrisp'

PYRUS

(PIE-russ)

PEAR

Different varieties of Pears can be grown either for their delicious fruit or for their lovely flowers and foliage. In early spring, all Pear trees are covered with white flowers—nice to look at, not so nice to smell. The bloom period is relatively brief but quite spectacular. Most Pears have glossy green foliage throughout the summer, and some varieties develop outstanding fall color in shades of orange, red, and purple. The edible-fruited types are prized for their juicy, succulent late-summer fruits. Many Pears have an upright growth pattern and branches tend to have narrow crotch angles, which can make them susceptible to damage from storms and heavy snowfalls. Growing Pears for fruits also poses risks in cold areas. Since Pears bloom fairly early in the spring, either just before or as leaves are forming, the blossoms may be damaged by late frosts or may not be pollinated properly if cold hinders bee activity. These Pears are only fertile for a short time. Pear blossoms have a low sugar content, and even if bees are present, they are not drawn to these flowers as readily as to other flowering plants. Still, many gardeners will get fruit in most years.

How Pears Grow

Most Pears are small- to medium-sized single-stemmed trees, though one very hardy species grows more like a large shrub. Many Pear species have stout, spur-like thorns, though most named varieties have been selected for their lack of thorns. Most ornamental Pears and edible-fruited types are grafted on rootstocks. The hardiest (–40°F/–40°C) rootstock is *Pyrus ussuriensis* (Ussurian Pear). Less hardy (–30°F/–34°C) but commonly used is *Pyrus communis* (Common Pear) and 'Old Home.' For dwarf Pears the most common rootstock is 'OH × F333' (a cross between 'Old Home' and 'Farmingdale'). Edible Pears need two different varieties for cross-pollination, and these must bloom at the same time for pollination to be effective. The chart at the end of this section suggests which Pears to plant together for success. Most Pears take from 4 to 8 years to produce fruit. The dwarf Pears may come in a bit earlier.

Where to Plant

Site and Light Plant Pears in full sun. While they tolerate partial shade, this decreases flowering, fruiting, and good fall color. Plant Pears in a sheltered location where they'll get lots of sun in summer but less sun early in the season. Avoid planting Pears in low-lying areas, as these act as frost pockets. The ideal location is just below the top of a north-facing hill.

Soil and Moisture Pears grow best in fertile, moist, well-drained soils. They even do quite well in clay soils, which can retard the growth of many fruit-bearing trees. Pears, especially the ornamental types, can also tolerate moderate dry spells once mature. Edible Pears demand consistent moisture throughout the entire growing season for good fruit production.

Spacing Space Pears according to the potential size of the mature tree. Give the edible types plenty of space for good sun exposure and air circulation.

Landscape Use

Both ornamental and edible-fruited Pears have a high landscape value. Ornamental Pears are most often used as single specimen plants or in small groups. *Pyrus fauriei* (Korean Pear) makes an excellent informal hedge. Accent this plant's early spring flowering by surrounding the tree with spring flowering bulbs like *Crocus* (Crocus), *Narcissus* (Daffodils), and *Scilla* (Squill). The bright colors of early flowering shrubs like *Forsythia* (Forsythia) and *Rhododendron mucronulatum* (Korean Rhododendron) combine well with this tree's white blossoms. Edible-fruited Pears combine nicely with hardy varieties of *Prunus* (Plum). The fiery fall foliage of some varieties looks stunning against a backdrop of evergreens.

Planting

Bare Root Get bare root plants into the garden as soon as the ground can be worked in spring. Remove plants from their shipping package immediately on arrival. Soak them in room temperature water for no fewer than 3 hours before planting. Place a small amount of superphosphate in the base of the hole and cover it with 3 inches (7.5 cm) of soil. Spread roots out over a cone of well-prepared soil. On dwarf varieties do not bury the bud union, or the budded or grafted top portion of the tree will grow, losing the dwarfing effect. On regular-sized trees bury the bud union up to 4 inches (10 cm) below the soil surface. This results in the plant being hardier. Fill the hole with soil, firm it with your fingers, and water immediately. Dissolve water-soluble fertilizer in a gallon (about 4 liters) of water following the directions on the label. Pour ½ cup (about 120 ml) of this starter solution around the base of each plant. If you prefer organic fertilizer, use fish emulsion instead.

Containerized Plants Plant Pears as early in the season as possible. If the soil in the container is dry, soak it and let it drain overnight before planting.

Carefully remove the plant from the container so as not to break the root ball. Plant at the same depth as in the container after preparing the hole in a similar manner as that for a bare root plant. Many Pears are budded or grafted. The bud union should be at the correct level as for bare root plants. Check it to make sure that the nursery planted it correctly in the first place. Fill the hole with well-prepared soil, firm with your fingers, and water immediately. Pour ½ cup (about 120 ml) of starter solution around the base of the plant.

Balled and Burlapped Plant as you would a containerized plant with these added precautions: Place the plant in the hole making sure that the top of the balled and burlapped root ball is about 1 to 2 inches (2.5 to 5 cm) above the surrounding soil. Make sure the bud union is properly buried or exposed. Cut and remove any twine around the stems. Remove as much of the burlap and wire holding the root ball in place as possible, but avoid breaking the root ball. Avoid grabbing and lifting the trunk of the tree while planting it, as this can damage the roots.

Transplanting

Dig up smaller trees in very early spring before new growth emerges. Plant immediately as you would a bare root plant. Larger trees are next to impossible to transplant so place them in the right spot from the start.

How to Care for Pears

Water Keep the soil evenly moist from spring until the soil freezes in fall. Consistent watering is especially important during the first 2 years. Always saturate the soil deeply with each watering. When the top 2 inches (5 cm) of soil dry out, water. Ornamental Pears can withstand dry periods once mature, but edible Pears need consistent moisture all season long to produce good fruit.

Mulch Apply a 2- to 4-inch (5- to 10-cm) layer of mulch around each plant as soon as the ground warms up in spring. Good mulches include shredded bark, pine needles, and wood chips. Mulch retains moisture in the soil and helps prevent the growth of weeds. Replenish the mulch as necessary throughout the growing season.

Fertilizing Do not fertilize Pears unless they are not growing well. They should put out at least 6 inches (15 cm) of new growth each year. If they are not growing vigorously with good leaf coloration, fertilize lightly the following spring before new growth emerges. Sprinkle 10-10-10 granules around the base of each plant and water immediately to move the fertilizer into the root zone. The use of too much nitrogen can encourage overly lush foliage growth that is most susceptible to fire blight.

If you prefer organic fertilizers, use alfalfa meal (rabbit pellets), blood meal, bone meal, compost, fish emulsion, Milorganite, or rotted manures. Bone meal must be added to the soil at planting time to be effective.

Weeding Prevent the growth of most annual weeds by using mulch. Pull by hand any weeds that do appear. Weeds compete with shrubs for available moisture and nutrients and should be removed immediately.

Deadheading This is generally not required. However, the removal of some fruit may be necessary if branches become too heavily weighed down. Otherwise, the branches may break off.

Pruning Both ornamental and edible Pears tend to produce suckers (shoots from the base of the plant) and water sprouts (upright shoots from the trunk or branches). Cut these off as soon as they appear. On either type, always remove dead, damaged, or diseased branches immediately at any time of year. If a branch is diseased, cut it back at least 6 inches (15 cm) below the infected area.

Ornamental Pears only need to be pruned to improve form and remove crossing branches that may rub against each other, causing wounds easily infected by disease.

Edible Pears require more extensive pruning. Growth on these trees tends to be upright and relatively dense. As the plant matures, keep the central stem or trunk (leader) and six to eight branches. Cut off all other branches back to the trunk. The branches should be evenly spaced along the trunk. Unfortunately, the branches often grow nearly straight up and close to the main stem. When the tree is young, use a clothespin on each branch to push it down and away from the main stem. This opens up the crotch, or the angle between the branch and the main stem. The more open the crotch, the stronger the branch becomes. As the tree matures, replace clothespins with spacers or spreaders. These are just pieces of wood with a "V" notch cut into the base. Slide the spreaders between the trunk and set the "V" notch against the branch. This again pushes the branch down and away from the main stem.

Each year over a period of years you may have to create longer spreaders until you've achieved your goal—a tree with limited branches spreading out and away from the main stem or trunk of the tree. Forcing the plant to have horizontal branches allows more sun to get to the fruit, creates better air circulation that may help prevent disease, and makes for much stronger branches that can withstand wind and heavy snows.

An alternate method of growing Pears is to let the tree form multiple leaders and cut these off at the top (head back) when they reach about 10 feet (3 meters). Some gardeners insist that this is a good way of growing Pears because if one of the leaders gets infected with fire blight, it can be cut off completely, leaving a number of main stems to produce fruit.

No matter which method you choose, you'll increase fruit production by cutting the thin branches off the main branches back to three to four buds in midwinter. If you do this at any other time of year, you increase the chance of the tree being infected by fire blight.

Winter Protection None required.

Problems

Insects Ornamental types are rarely disturbed by insects. Edible Pears are bothered by a number of pests. Whether to spray for these depends on the extent of the yearly damage. A few potential pests are the larvae of codling moths, pear midge, and pear psylla.

The pinkish white larvae of codling moths can do quite a bit of damage to fruit of edible types. Woodpeckers are excellent allies in controlling this problem. Place suet in the yard to draw them in. Spraying trees with home orchard sprays is effective, but follow directions on the container exactly.

The pear midge lays eggs in blossoms. The eggs produce grubs that penetrate and destroy fruit. Early application of a home orchard spray is recommended if this problem persists for more than a year.

Pear psylla are primarily a problem in the East and West. With a magnifying glass you can often see yellow eggs at the base of leaf buds in early spring. Control this pest by spraying trees with dormant oil in late fall and early spring just as buds begin to emerge. Insecticidal soaps are also recommended. If the insects are not killed early, they will suck sap from the plant, spreading disease in the process, and excrete honeydew. The latter promotes the growth of a fungus that turns the honeydew black. The telltale sign of infestation is blackened leaves and fruit.

Diseases Fire blight is a bacterial disease that can rapidly kill branches and even entire plants. The bacteria usually infect blossoms or tender, young growth. As the disease progresses, branches wither and turn brownish black to black as if burned with a blowtorch. The bacteria are carried by insects, primarily bees and other pollinators, from flower to flower. They're also carried by wind and rain. Fire blight can continue to spread throughout an entire growing season. If infected tissue isn't pruned out immediately, the entire plant can be killed. Each time you cut off an infected portion of the plant, always dip your pruning shears in a disinfectant (one part bleach to nine parts water). Also, you may wish to avoid planting any members of the rose family in the area. This includes *Sorbus* (Mountain Ash).

Leaf Scorch Leaf scorch is occasionally confused with fire blight. Leaves curl up, turn brown, and drop off. Fruits develop but are small and distorted. This is caused by a lack of potassium in the soil. If you fertilize regularly, this will not be a problem.

Marauders None serious.

Propagation

Suckers See Pruning page 228.

Cuttings Too difficult to recommend.

Seed The seed of named varieties will not produce plants identical to the parents. The species can be started from seed. Press the seed into moist peat and chill for 90 days. Bring out and keep at room temperature until germination occurs. See pages 409–12 for additional information.

Special Uses

Cut Flowers While these flowers are lovely outdoors, they have an unpleasant smell.

Fruit Getting the best taste and texture from Pears is quite tricky and varies greatly by variety and region. The Pears listed in this guide should be picked before they are fully mature. The longer the fruit is allowed to ripen on the tree, the grittier it gets. Harvest the Pears just as the green coloration begins to lighten but

before much yellow appears. 'Summercrisp' is unique in that it must be picked when still firm and green with just a blush of red. Pears continue to ripen after harvesting. Handle them carefully as they bruise easily. You can place them in the refrigerator to delay ripening. Or, keep them at a temperature no higher than 65°F (18°C) until fully ripe.

Sources

Burnt Ridge Nursery & Orchards, 432 Burnt Ridge Rd., Onalaska, WA 98570, (360) 985-2873

Colvos Creek Nursery, 1904 Third Ave., Suite 415, Seattle, WA 98101, (573) 749-9508

Edible Forest Nursery, E7946 Upper Maple Dale Rd., Viroqua, WI 54665, (no phone by request)

Fedco Trees, P.O. Box 520, Waterville, ME 04903, (207) 873-7333

ForestFarm, 990 Tetherow Rd., Williams, OR 97544, (573) 846-7269

Fritz Creek Gardens, P.O. Box 15226, Homer, AK 99603, (907) 235-4969

Greer Gardens, 1280 Goodpasture Island Rd., Eugene, OR 97401, (541) 686-8266

Hortico, Inc., 723 Robson Rd., RR# 1, Waterdown, ON L0R 2H1 Canada, (905) 689-6984

McKay Nursery Co., P.O. Box 185, Waterloo, WI 53594, (908) 478-2121

RareFind Nursery, 957 Patterson Rd., Jackson, NJ 08527, (732) 833-0613

Stark Bros. Nurseries, P.O. Box 1800, Louisiana, MO 63353, (296) 325-4180

St. Lawrence Nurseries, 325 Ste Hwy 345, Potsdam, NY 13676, (857) 265-6739

Woodstock Nursery, N1831 Ste Rd 95, Neillsville, WI 54456, (888) 803-8733

VARIETIES

VARIETY	FLOWER COLOR	FRUIT	HEIGHT/WIDTH	HARDINESS
Pyrus calleryana				
(Callery Pear)				
'Aristocrat'****	White	Variable	30'/20'	−20°F
'Autumn Blaze'****	White	Variable	30'/20'	−25°F
'Bradford'**	White	Variable	30'/30'	−20°F
'Cleveland Select' (Chanticleer®)****	White	Variable	25'/15'	−20°F
Jack® ('Jaczam')***	White	Variable	15'/10'	−20°F
'Redspire'***	White	Variable	25'/20'	−25°F

The Callery Pears have dense, pyramidal forms. Trees are showered in small white flowers in early spring. Their glossy, dark green leaves turn scarlet to purple to wine red in fall. The trees produce an inedible russet to blackish fruit about ⅜ inch (1 cm) across. These plants have some resistance to fire blight, but this varies greatly not only by named variety but by individual plant. In general, these plants are good choices for suburban areas because they tolerate pollution well. Note that 'Bradford' has a very tight branching pattern. Prune out stems for good spacing. Even with proper pruning, the branches on older trees commonly break off during heavy snows. Jack®'s small size makes it highly desirable.

*Pyrus fauriei*****				
(Korean Pear)	White	Black	15'/12'	−30°F
Korean Sun™ ('Westwood')****	White	Black	15'/12'	−30°F

The species is an upright, rounded shrub. that is very dense and twiggy. It is showered with blossoms each spring well after foliage has emerged. The leaves are small, glossy green, with excellent fall color varying from yellow to orange to red. Fruit is inedible and about ⅜ inch (1 cm) across. This species makes an excellent informal hedge. Individual plants can be pruned into small trees. It has good tolerance to fire blight. Note: There is a Callery Pear variety named 'Fauriei' that should not be confused with this species. 'Korean Sun' grows as a small tree rather than as a shrub. It is noted for its red to reddish purple fall coloration.

Pyrus salicifolia				
(Willow-Leaved Pear)				
'Pendula'***	White	Brown	15'/15'	−20°F

This weeping tree is grown for its lovely willowy form and silvery to gray green foliage. It produces white pink buds in spring that burst into abundant white flowers. Regular pruning can keep it to any desired height and width. It is susceptible to fire blight.

Pyrus 'Silver Ball'***	White	Brown	12'/12'	−25°F

This is a compact tree noted for its silvery green leaves that are quite small. Their size gives the plant a unique texture. Flowers are small. The green leaves often turn yellow to orange by fall.

*Pyrus ussuriensis***				
(Ussurian Pear or Siberian Pear)	White	Green	25'/25'	−40°F
Mountain Frost® ('Bailfrost')***	White	Green	20'/15'	−40°F
Prairie Gem® ('Mordak')***	White	Green	20'/20'	−40°F

Pyrus calleryana 'Cleveland Select' (Chanticleer®)

Pyrus fauriei

Pyrus fauriei

Pyrus ussuriensis Mountain Frost® ('Bailfrost')

The species is a small- to medium-sized tree with an oval to rounded form that is covered with flowers in spring. Nice glossy, green leaves develop yellow, red, or purple fall color. The tree produces inedible fruits up to 1½ inches (4.25 cm) across that can be a nuisance when they drop in late summer or seen as a benefit to wildlife. It is resistant to fire blight. Mountain Frost® is a vigorous, upright variety of Ussurian Pear. Although it blooms heavily, it produces only a light crop of inedible green fruit about ¾ inch (1.8 cm) across. Its leaves are dark green and develop good yellow fall color. Prairie Gem® is another attractive tree with a rather rounded form. It is noted for its thick, glossy, dark green leaves that turn orange yellow in fall. It too produces a very light crop of ornamental fruit.

VARIETY	FLOWER COLOR	FRUIT	HEIGHT/WIDTH	HARDINESS

Pyrus (edible Pear varieties)

This group is made up of edible Pears, the most well-known being 'Bartlett' and 'Bosc' that unfortunately are hardy only to –15°F (–26°C). Most of the varieties listed here can be purchased on dwarf rootstock that keeps them a manageable size and also results in earlier fruiting. All of these trees have a nice, upright form. The star rating is related only to the quality of the fruit, not to any given tree's ornamental value.

VARIETY	FLOWER COLOR	FRUIT	HEIGHT/WIDTH	HARDINESS
'Golden Spice'****	White	Yellow	20'/15'	–40°F

Foliage is dark green. Fruit is just under 2 inches (5 cm). It is a lovely mid yellow blushed red when ripe. Fruits are good for canning and spicing, fair for fresh eating. Nice fall color and good disease resistance.

VARIETY	FLOWER COLOR	FRUIT	HEIGHT/WIDTH	HARDINESS
'Gourmet'***	White	Greenish yellow	20'/15'	–30°F

Foliage is leathery green. Medium sized greenish yellow to yellow Pears that are crisp, sweet, and juicy. Ripens in early fall. This tree is slightly resistant to fire blight. Do not use this variety as a pollinator since it produces little viable pollen.

VARIETY	FLOWER COLOR	FRUIT	HEIGHT/WIDTH	HARDINESS
'Luscious'***	White	Bright yellow	20'/15'	–30°F

Foliage is leathery green, turning a nice red in fall. Small- to medium-sized bright yellow fruit is tender, sweet, and juicy. Ripens in early fall. The plant has good resistance to fire blight. Do not use this variety as a pollinator since it produces little viable pollen.

VARIETY	FLOWER COLOR	FRUIT	HEIGHT/WIDTH	HARDINESS
'Parker'***	White	Yellow tan	20'/15'	–30°F

Foliage is leathery green. Large yellow tan fruit is tender, mildly sweet, and juicy. Fruit deteriorates rapidly if left on the tree too long. Ripens late summer. This tree is susceptible to fire blight.

VARIETY	FLOWER COLOR	FRUIT	HEIGHT/WIDTH	HARDINESS
'Patten'**	White	Green	20'/15'	–30°F

Foliage is leathery green. Large fruit is tender, mildly sweet, and juicy. Ripens early fall. Fairly susceptible to fire blight.

VARIETY	FLOWER COLOR	FRUIT	HEIGHT/WIDTH	HARDINESS
'Summercrisp'****	White	Green red	20'/15'	–30°F

Foliage is leathery green. Medium to large greenish Pears are crisp, sweet, and juicy. Ripens in late summer. Fruit deteriorates rapidly if left on the tree too long. The tree is resistant to fire blight.

VARIETY	FLOWER COLOR	FRUIT	HEIGHT/WIDTH	HARDINESS
'Ure'**	White	Yellow green	20'/15'	–40°F

Foliage is leathery green. Small, rounded yellow green fruit is tender, sweet, and very juicy. Ripens in late summer. Fruit deteriorates rapidly if left on the tree too long. The plant is very hardy but not in the same league in regards to fruit quality as the previous named varieties. It is fairly resistant to fire blight.

Rhododendron 'Rosy Lights'

RHODODENDRON

(row-doe-DEN-druhn)

AZALEA AND RHODODENDRON

These shrubs are particularly noted for gorgeous and abundant spring bloom. Colors are rich and striking even at great distances. The bloom period can be quite long and will be extended by cool, humid weather. Many varieties have scented blossoms that add to their value as cut flowers. Summer foliage is particularly attractive on the evergreen types. The deciduous varieties are not particularly attractive when out of bloom, looking somewhat coarse. Some deciduous and evergreen types have good fall color. Although prone to specific diseases, the group is quite insect resistant. Both evergreen and deciduous types are demanding in their soil requirements. They are also prone to flower bud damage if temperatures get too low in midwinter or if planted in an exposed location.

How Azaleas and Rhododendrons Grow

Throughout this section plants will be referred to as deciduous or evergreen types. The deciduous types drop their leaves and are generally known as Azaleas, although two species of true Rhododendrons also drop their leaves. The evergreen types are commonly called Rhododendrons. Both deciduous and evergreen types have a shallow, fibrous, but wide-spreading root system. They may produce one or more stems with numerous branches and side branches. Flower buds form at the tips of stems or branches and bloom the following season. The mainly deciduous types (Azaleas) have flowers with five stamens. The primarily evergreen types (Rhododendrons) have flowers with ten stamens. The leaves of evergreen types are usually more attractive than those of deciduous types. If temperatures get too low in the winter, flower buds formed in the previous season can be damaged and will not produce the spectacular spring bloom desired. After bloom, plants will form elongated narrow seedpods that split along the edges, revealing tiny tan seeds inside. The plants rarely self-sow.

Where to Plant

Site and Light In cold climates the deciduous types of Rhododendron do well in full sun or partial shade. The evergreen shrubs grow best in cool, partially shaded areas. If possible, plant them on the north or east side of your home where they will not be exposed to intense winter sun but will get good morning sun and reflected light in the summer. The evergreen types do especially well under oaks or along the edges of woods. Oaks have deep roots so that the shrubs and trees do not compete for moisture. Avoid planting them in deep shade. Plant them in protected areas, especially ones not battered by winter winds. Never plant them under eaves since they need to be covered by snow in winter and drenched in rain in summer.

Soil and Moisture Ninety percent of success with these shrubs depends on soil preparation. Both deciduous and evergreen types have two basic soil requirements: the right pH (soil acidity) and loose soil with lots of organic matter in it. Soil must drain freely but retain moisture during dry periods. *If soil does not drain freely, these shrubs may die out.*

The right pH: These shrubs demand a pH of 4.5 to 5.5. If the pH is higher than this, the plants will not survive or will do extremely poorly. The lower acidity helps roots take in iron and magnesium. A lack of these often results in yellowing between leaf veins. It's critical to test the soil before planting these shrubs.

Contact county extension offices for locations of soil testing laboratories and have a soil test done.

When ordering this test, tell the lab that you want to grow Azaleas and Rhododendrons. The lab will return the test with exact instructions on how to prepare the soil. Most tests will indicate that you have to lower the soil pH.

There are two products to do this. Both are excellent. One is sulfur. Most products sold as sulfur are 88 percent to 100 percent sulfur and take about 3 to 4 months to lower soil pH. The other product is iron sulfate (ferrous sulfate). You will usually have to apply iron sulfate at a higher rate to get the same results. However, it does work more rapidly than sulfur, reducing pH in about 2 to 3 weeks. It also contains iron, an element essential to the good growth of these shrubs. If you use iron sulfate, wear a dusk mask, protective goggles, and old clothing. The dust is fine and does stain clothes with rusty blotches or streaking.

If you add sulfur or iron sulfate to the soil in the fall, have the soil tested again in the spring. If these chemicals are added in the spring, test again later in the season. The tests may indicate the need for an additional application of sulfur or iron sulfate.

Important: Avoid the use of aluminum sulfate, sometimes recommended as a product to reduce soil pH. While it does make soil more acidic, it also retards root growth. Equally important: Do not add lime to the soil. Although it contains nutrients, it increases the soil pH. Wood ash also increases soil pH and should be avoided.

The right soil: These shrubs thrive in rich, well-drained soils high in organic matter. If soil is rocky or compacted, consider building a raised bed.

Since these shrubs like consistent moisture throughout the growing season, add lots of organic matter to the soil or loam. Acidic peat moss and rotted oak leaves are highly recommended soil amendments, since they are acidic. Organic matter should make up roughly 50 percent of the soil.

You can either prepare a large bed for a number of plants or a single planting hole. For the latter dig a hole at least five times as wide as the root ball and about 6 inches (15 cm) deeper than you plan to place it. Amend the soil with peat moss or rotted oak leaves as already indicated.

You can't get around the fact that these plants demand acidic, fertile, and well-drained soil to thrive. But you can simplify the planting method. Dig a hole and amend the soil exactly as outlined. Plant your shrub and fertilize regularly with an acidic fertilizer throughout the entire growing season. If the foliage on your plants remains green and vibrant, your gamble pays off. If leaves turn yellowish, then you have a problem. Most gardeners are successful with this highly simplified planting method, but it is certainly not as reliable as the more complex process of soil preparation.

Spacing Space according to the potential height and width of the plant. Give enough space from walls or other structures for good air circulation.

Landscape Use

Rhododendrons and Azaleas make excellent specimen plants and are wonderful in mass plantings on larger properties. The evergreen types are ideal for foundation plantings. Since Rhododendrons and *Vaccinium* (Blueberry) thrive in similar conditions, plant the latter in front of these shrubs for berries and wonderful red fall color. Plant evergreen Rhododendrons in front of *Taxus* (Yew) on the east or north side of your home. The dark green foliage of these evergreens is an excellent foil for the bright blossoms of Rhododendrons. Other good plants to consider with this group are *Clethra* (Summersweet) and *Ilex* (Winterberry) since both thrive in acidic soils. Consider placing a bed of Azaleas in front of a group of small spring-blooming trees, such as *Amelanchier* (Serviceberry) and *Cercis* (Redbud).

Planting

Bare Root Best not sold in this fashion. Plants are removed from containers and the root ball wrapped in plastic or other materials, then shipped to the con-

sumer. Plant immediately as you would a containerized plant.

Containerized Plants If the soil in the pot is dry, soak and let it drain overnight. Plant at the same depth as in the pot, but loosen and spread out the roots at the base of the plant with your fingers. If drainage is questionable, elevate the plant slightly 1 to 2 inches (2.5 to 5 cm) above the surrounding soil. Fill the hole in with soil amended with organic matter, firm with your fingers, and water immediately. Dissolve acidic water-soluble fertilizer in a gallon (about 4 liters) of water following the directions on the label. Pour ½ cup (about 120 ml) of this starter solution around the base of each plant. If you prefer organic fertilizer, use fish emulsion instead.

Balled and Burlapped Plant these as soon as the ground can be worked in spring. Plant as you would a containerized plant with these added precautions: Place the plant in the hole making sure that the top of the balled and burlapped root ball is about 1 to 2 inches (2.5 to 5 cm) above the surrounding soil. Cut and remove any twine around the stems. Remove as much of the burlap and wire holding the root ball in place as possible, but avoid breaking the root ball.

Transplanting

Dig plants up in very early spring before any signs of new growth. Plant them immediately as you would a containerized plant. Do not remove plants from the wild. They need to be conserved in their native habitat. Plant immediately as you would a balled and burlapped plant.

How to Care for Azaleas and Rhododendrons

Water Keep the soil evenly moist during the active growing season. This is critical during the first 2 years, but almost as important in the years to follow. Always saturate the soil deeply with each watering. When the top 2 inches (5 cm) of soil dry out, water. During hot, dry periods spray foliage in the morning with a strong stream to knock off spider mites, wash off dust, and cool plants down. Continue watering, especially if there is a dry spell late in the season. This is common in cold climates. Saturate the soil in late fall just before the first expected freeze. This is especially important for the evergreen types that should go into winter with moisture around their roots.

Mulch Place 1 to 2 inches (2.5 to 5 cm) of organic mulch around the base of the plant as soon as the ground warms up in spring. Use pine needles, shredded oak leaves, shredded pine bark, or cedar chips. Keep mulch back from the stems. Mulch keeps the soil moist and cool while preventing annual weed growth. Since these shrubs demand acidic conditions, the best mulches are pine needles or pine bark. Shredded oak leaves are a good alternative in that they are mildly acidic. Replace the mulch as necessary throughout the growing season. Mulch in fall is especially important for evergreen types in that their leaves will continue to lose moisture until the following spring.

Fertilizer Fertilize every spring with an acidic fertilizer before buds emerge. Ammonium sulfate is the most highly recommended. Miracid and comparable water-soluble fertilizers used to acidify the soil are also fine. Follow the directions on the labels as to recommended dosage. If using any granular fertilizer, saturate the soil to dissolve the particles and carry nutrients into the root zone.

In areas where the soil tends to be alkaline, so does the water. Each watering increases the pH. Since Rhododendrons need acidic conditions, fertilize them regularly with an acidic fertilizer even after reducing the soil pH at initial planting time. Fertilize in early spring, then fertilize again after plants bloom. Do not fertilize any later than 2 months before the first expected frost in your region.

If you prefer organic fertilizers, use alfalfa meal (rabbit pellets), blood meal, bone meal, compost, fish emulsion, Milorganite, or rotted manures. Bone meal must be added to the soil at planting time to be effective. In colder areas cottonseed meal may be hard to find, but it's highly recommended because it's quite acidic. Manures are only recommended if they have been allowed to decompose over a period of time. Fresh manures contain soluble salts which can damage Rhododendrons.

Weeding Kill all perennial weeds before planting. Mulch inhibits the growth of most annual weeds. If a few pop up, pull them out of the moist ground by hand. Weeds compete with the shrubs for valuable nutrients and moisture. Never use a hoe around the base of these plants. The roots are quite shallow and can easily be damaged by the blade.

Deadheading The value of removing spent blossoms is questionable, but commonly done on large-leafed varieties. It is not believed to cause more blooms the following year, although some gardeners disagree, insisting that stopping seed formation keeps plants more vigorous. They argue that this in turn results in much better flowering the following season. This argument clearly is made more commonly regarding Rhododendrons than Azaleas. Seed heads are not particularly attractive, so if you have the time and patience, there is no reason not to remove spent flowers.

If you do choose to remove the spent blossoms on Rhododendrons, gently bend them down with your fingers. This mild motion breaks them off with little effort. When doing this, be careful not to disturb the buds right below the spent blossoms. If you're careless, you can pull off shoots that produce flower buds later in the season and thereby reduce flowering the following spring.

Pruning Always remove any dead or damaged branches at any time of year. Additional pruning is strictly optional. Generally, these plants need very little pruning at all. This is especially true of evergreen types.

Deciduous types can be pruned to get bushier growth. Just after plants finish flowering, cut each stem back by one-third. Cut back to a growth bud that looks like a swollen ring around the stem. This encourages lateral branching and a fuller look. If done later than indicated, this kind of pruning may reduce the number of flowers in the following year. Only begin this type of pruning when a plant is at least 3 years old. Note that you may want to experiment on one stem to see the results before attempting this on an entire plant the following season. If you get good branching, prune the next year. If results are poor, then don't prune at all. Frankly, these plants are slow growing in cold areas, so this type of pruning is mentioned rather reluctantly.

Winter Protection Protect evergreen varieties for at least 2 years with winter protection consisting of burlap or similar material wrapped around four stakes tapped into the ground around the outside of the plant. Leave about a 4-inch (10-cm) opening at the base of the burlap. After the ground freezes, fill in around the shrub with whole leaves. This helps protect young plants from drying winter winds. It also protects the leaves of evergreen varieties from exposure to direct winter sun which can dry out, damage, or discolor them.

Placing plants where they'll receive filtered light during the winter also prevents damage, as does protecting them from strong winter winds as outlined earlier.

Problems

Insects The grubs of black vine weevil damage Rhododendrons badly. Notches in leaves are a sign of adult weevils feeding at night. To kill them before they lay eggs, treat plants late in the day with a product containing acephate. Do this two times three weeks apart. Several week later treat the soil with a product containing Imidacloprid.

Lace bugs suck sap from the undersides of leaves. Damage causes leaves to be discolored or look as if they have been burned. They will sometimes dry up, curl up on the ends, or turn brown and drop off. Lace bugs are less than ¼ inch (.6 cm) long and have transparent wings. Most of the time they cause minor damage to a plant, but if present in large numbers, spray them with an insecticide. When spraying, saturate the underside of all foliage.

Spider mites are almost invisible. They thrive in drought and high heat. Their feeding causes leaves to turn spotty and yellow. Discourage spider mite infestations by forcefully spraying your plants down during dry weather. Spray with a miticide in severe cases. Generally, spider mites are only a problem with deciduous types.

Disease If soil is not prepared properly so that it drains freely, you may have problems with root rot.

Powdery mildew, a whitish film on leaves, can be a problem in humid periods. Treat plants with a fungicide only if plants are clearly being damaged by the disease. Usually, this is more a cosmetic than a health problem. Also, ask about a plant's resistance to powdery mildew when buying it in the first place. For example, 'Spicy Lights' (not in the book) is commonly infected with powdery mildew in late summer.

Iron Chlorosis In many areas water is quite alkaline. Proper watering increases the pH of the soil. If the pH gets too high, leaves may turn yellow between the veins. Solve the problem by reducing the pH with acidic fertilizers used regularly every year.

Marauders The only effective way to protect shrubs is by surrounding them with wire so that animals cannot get to them in the dormant season. Rabbits are a particular nuisance in cold areas.

Propagation

Suckers These shrubs do not sucker.

Softwood Cuttings In late June or early July, remove 4-inch (10-cm) cuttings from the tip of branches showing new growth (semihard). Do this early in the morning. Treat them as outlined on pages 406–8. Note that getting cuttings of these shrubs to root is extremely difficult for the home gardener.

Hardwood Cuttings Evergreen types can be propagated in this manner quite successfully. Take cuttings in late fall or early winter. Follow the steps outlined on pages 406–8.

Seed Only species come true from seed. Start seed 12 weeks before the last expected frost in spring. Use an acidic starting mix consisting of sand mixed with peat or rotted oak leaves and covered with a thin layer of moist, pulverized sphagnum moss. Press the seed into the moss. Seeds germinate best in diffused light and high humidity. Keep the seed consistently moist at 45°F (7°C) to 50°F (10°C) until germination occurs, usually within 50 to 90 days. You may need a temperature-controlled greenhouse or heated outdoor cold frame to provide these conditions. Increase the temperature slowly once seedlings emerge, but always keep them in diffused, never in direct, light. Feed them with ammonium sulfate diluted at the rate of ⅓ teaspoon (2 g) per gallon (about 4 liters) of water. Don't expect flowering plants for 3 years or longer. See pages 409–12 for additional information.

Layering Just after the shrub flowers, bend a long branch to the ground. About 18 inches (46 cm) from the tip of the branch, make a diagonal cut about 1 inch (2.5 cm) long and one-third of the way through the stem just under a leaf. Remove leaves on both sides of the cut. Then follow the instructions for layering on page 405. This method is usually easier for the home gardener than taking cuttings.

Special Uses

Cut Flowers Stems of these shrubs are stunning in floral arrangements both for color and scent. Cut stems just as they reach peak bloom. Strip off any leaves or flowers that would end up below water in the final arrangement. Place the stems in warm water for several hours in a cool place. Use floral food in the water. Change the water daily.

Sources

Bluestone Perennials, 7211 Middle Ridge Rd., Madison, OH 44057, (574) 852-5243

Broken Arrow Nursery, 13 Broken Arrow Rd., Hamden, CT 06518, (203) 288-1026

Carlson's Gardens, P.O. Box 305, South Salem, NY 10590, (914) 763-5958

Colvos Creek Nursery, 1904 Third Ave., Suite 415, Seattle, WA 98101, (574) 749-9508

Down's Rhododendrons, 11736 Little Rock Rd. SW, Olympia, WA 98512, (909) 943-5199

Eastern Plant Specialties, 660 A Berrys Mill Rd., West Bath, ME 04530, (207) 504-4405

Fairweather Gardens, P.O. Box 330, Greenwich, NJ 08323, (858) 451-6261

ForestFarm, 990 Tetherow Rd., Williams, OR 97544, (297) 846-7269

Fritz Creek Gardens, P.O. Box 15226, Homer, AK 99603, (907) 235-4969

Girard Nurseries, P.O. Box 428, Geneva, OH 44041, (757) 466-2881

Gossler Farms Nursery, 1200 Weaver Rd., Springfield, OR 97478, (541) 746-3922

Greer Gardens, 1280 Goodpasture Island Rd., Eugene, OR 97401, (541) 686-8266

Jung Seed Company, 335 S High St., Randolph, WI 53957, (800) 297-3123

Mason Hollow Nursery, 47 Scripps Ln., Mason, NH 03048, (525) 878-4347

McKay Nursery Co., P.O. Box 185, Waterloo, WI 53594, (939) 478-2121

Meadowbrook Nursery We-Du Natives, Polly Spout Rd., Marion, NC 28752, (740) 738-8300

Musser Forests, Inc., 1880 Rte 119 Hwy N, Indiana, PA 15701, (323) 465-5685

RareFind Nursery, 957 Patterson Rd., Jackson, NJ 08527, (746) 833-0613

Reeseville Ridge Nursery, 512 S Main, Reeseville, WI 53579, (920) 927-3291

Rhododendron Species Foundation, 2225 S 336th St., Federal Way, WA 98001, (321) 661-9377

River Rock Nursery, 19251 SE Hwy 224, Damascus, OR 97089, (503) 658-4047

Shooting Star Nursery, 160 Soards Rd., Georgetown, KY 40324, (325) 867-7979

Tripple Brook Farm, 37 Middle Rd., Southampton, MA 01073, (413) 527-4626

Whitney Gardens & Nursery, P.O. Box 170, Brinnon, WA 98320, (508) 796-4411

Woodlanders, Inc., 1128 Colleton Ave., Aiken, SC 29801, (803) 648-7522

VARIETIES

These varieties represent a wide range of possible choices based on these characteristics: overall form of the plant; flower color, form, and fragrance; foliage form, summer color, and fall color; time of bloom from very early season to late season for an extended show of color; and hardiness. Always take into account that hardiness is related not just to a plant's genetic background, but also to soil preparation, good drainage, and correct placement in the landscape to provide proper light and protection from drying winds. The named varieties can withstand the temperatures listed when cared for properly. The species (wild varieties) should be grown from seeds or tissue taken from plants proven to thrive in cold-climate regions. Heights and widths represent the typical size of a plant grown for 10 years. Rhododendrons take a few years to bloom well, so it is often worth the extra expense to buy older plants. Catalogs may list Rhododendrons as Lepidotes (scaly, small-leafed plants) or Elepidotes (smooth, large-leafed plants). For help in this section our special thanks to Betty Ann Addison, Ann Haines, Stan Hokanson, Diane Johnson, Dr. Harold Pellett, John and Sally Perkins, and Patrick Vettling.

VARIETY	FLOWER COLOR	TYPE (LEAF SIZE)	HEIGHT/WIDTH	HARDINESS
Rhododendron catawbiense***				
(Catawba Rhododendron)	Lilac purple	Evergreen (large)	8'/6'	−25°F

This shrub forms large clusters of lavender flowers, often with green to brown toned spots. Flower color may vary from pink to purple to white. Its leaves are dark green and leathery. Mid season bloom.

Rhododendron carolinianum × *dauricum*				
(Hybrids)				
'Aglo'****	Light pink/red throat	Evergreen (small)	4'/5'	−25°F
'Molly Fordham'****	White	Evergreen (small)	4'/4'	−20°F
'Olga Mezitt'****	Bright pink	Evergreen (small)	5'/4'	−25°F
'PJM'****	Lavender	Evergreen (small)	5'/4'	−30°F
'PJM Compact'****	Lavender pink	Evergreen (small)	4'/4'	−30°F

These are relatively compact plants with rather small leaves. With the exception of 'Molly Fordham' their dark green foliage takes on a bronzy, reddish, or purplish cast in winter. 'Olga Mezitt' tolerates winter sun better than the others. Small-leaved Rhododendrons are generally very hardy. Early season bloom.

Rhododendron dauricum**				
(Dahurian Rhododendron)	Rosy purple	Semi-evergreen (small)	4'/4'	−30°F
'Arctic Pearl'**	White	Evergreen (small)	3'/3'	−30°F
'Madison Snow'**	White	Evergreen (small)	3'/3'	−30°F

The species is erect, very open, and loose looking. The blossoms are typically rose purple but can have pink and white tones. Its green foliage has a purple cast. The purplish color deepens in the fall when some, but not all, of the leaves drop off. 'Arctic Pearl' and 'Madison Snow' don't turn purplish. The leaves that drop off 'Madison Snow' have a lovely yellowish fall color. Otherwise, both plants have green foliage throughout the winter. Plant these shrubs in a protected area where they will not be exposed to winter winds. Very early season bloom.

VARIETY	FLOWER COLOR	TYPE (LEAF SIZE)	HEIGHT/WIDTH	HARDINESS
Rhododendron				
(Lights Series Hybrid Azalea)				
Candy Lights™****	Pink streaked yellow	Deciduous	4'/4'	−30°F
'Golden Lights'****	Coppery gold	Deciduous	5'/4'	−30°F
'Lemon Lights'****	Lemon yellow	Deciduous	4'/4'	−30°F
Lilac Lights™****	Pinkish purple	Deciduous	4'/4'	−45°F
'Mandarin Lights'****	Deep orange	Deciduous	4'/4'	−30°F
'Northern Hi-Lights'*****	Cream white/yellow	Deciduous	5'/5'	−30°F
'Northern Lights'***	Varied pinks	Deciduous	5'/5'	−40°F
'Rosy Lights'***	Rose pink	Deciduous	5'/5'	−40°F
'Tri-Lights'****	White yellow pink	Deciduous	4'/3'	−30°F
'White Lights'*****	White/pink	Deciduous	4'/5'	−30°F

These shrubs are among the finest for cold-climate gardeners. The plants themselves are rather open and informal. They flower freely in a wide range of colors. These Azaleas grow well in full sun as long as soil is prepared properly and drains freely. Choose 'Candy Lights,' 'Golden Lights,' and 'Northern Lights' for fragrance; 'Golden Lights' and 'Northern Hi-Lights' for disease resistance; 'Rosy Lights' and White Lights' for abundant bloom; and Candy Lights™, 'Northern Hi-Lights,' and 'Tri-Lights' for possible fall color. 'Lemon Lights' will sometimes rebloom in fall. Mid season bloom.

VARIETY	FLOWER COLOR	TYPE (LEAF SIZE)	HEIGHT/WIDTH	HARDINESS
Rhododendron × marjatta				
(Marjatta Hybrid Rhododendron)				
'Haaga'*****	Deep pink	Evergreen (large)	6'/4'	−30°F
'Helsinki University'*****	Medium pink	Evergreen (large)	5'/4'	−30°F

The buds on these plants are stunning. The form of the plant and the beauty of of the deep green, leathery foliage is so striking that some gardeners would grow them for these characteristics alone. Plants must be mature before the blooms begin to float above the foliage. Mid season bloom.

VARIETY	FLOWER COLOR	TYPE (LEAF SIZE)	HEIGHT/WIDTH	HARDINESS
Rhododendron mucronulatum				
(Korean Rhododendron)				
'Cornell Pink'***	Clear pink	Deciduous	4'/3'	−30°F

This loose, upright plant has numerous, delicate flowers covering leafless branches in spring. The green leaves may have a yellow to bronze to red hue in fall. Very early season bloom.

VARIETY	FLOWER COLOR	TYPE (LEAF SIZE)	HEIGHT/WIDTH	HARDINESS
Rhododendron vaseyi				
(Pink Shell Azalea)				
'White Find'***	White/green throat	Deciduous	7'/5'	−25°F

This is an open and loose-looking shrub with an irregular, delicate branching pattern. It produces lightly fragrant flowers. Its dark green leaves turn into a colorful mix of orange, pink, red, and yellow shades in fall. This is an excellent choice for woodland settings. It does not tolerate road salt nor inorganic fertilizers. Organic fertilizers in moderation are fine. It responds well to a heavy mulch around its base. Very early season bloom.

Rhododendron 'PJM'

Rhododendron × *marjatta* 'Haaga'

VARIETY	FLOWER COLOR	TYPE (LEAF SIZE)	HEIGHT/WIDTH	HARDINESS
Rhododendron viscosum***				
(Swamp Azalea)	White	Deciduous	6'/5'	−25°F
This rather loose, open shrub is ideal for mass plantings. Its small flowers exude an exquisite clove-like scent. Its green leaves may turn bright red in fall. Even moisture throughout the season is critical to good performance. These plants will tolerate soggy soils as the common name would imply. Late season bloom.				
Rhododendron				
(Weston Hybrids)				
'Weston's Firecracker' ('Firecracker')****	Rose red	Deciduous	5'/5'	−25°F
'Weston's Innocence'*****	White	Deciduous	4'/3'	−25°F
'Weston's Lemon Drop' ('Lemon Drop')***	Light buttery yellow	Deciduous	4'/4'	−25°F
'Weston's Lollipop'****	Light pink	Deciduous	5'/4'	−25°F

Rhododendron 'Lemon Lights'

Rhododendron 'Mandarin Lights'

Rhododendron 'Northern Hi-Lights'

Rhododendron 'White Lights'

VARIETY	FLOWER COLOR	TYPE (LEAF SIZE)	HEIGHT/WIDTH	HARDINESS
'Weston's Millenium' ('Millenium')****	Dark pink red	Deciduous	5'/5'	−25°F
'Weston's Popsicle'****	Dark pink/orange flare	Deciduous	4'/3'	−25°F

These plants are known for their late June and July bloom in colder areas. 'Weston's Firecracker' displays rich red tubular flowers and wonderful blue green foliage. 'Weston's Innocence' has funnel-shaped, fragrant flowers and glossy foliage that turns red in fall. The peach buds of 'Weston's Lemon Drop' open into trumpet-shaped flowers with a light lemon scent. The blue green leaves turn shades of pink, red, and yellow in fall. 'Weston's Lollipop' has deep pink buds that open into light pink fragrant flowers that turn silvery pink as they mature. Foliage is medium green with red orange coloration in fall. 'Weston's Millenium' has fragrant flowers with a wavy edge and bluish tones to its foliage which may turn bronze red in fall. The flowers of 'Weston's Popsicle' are fragrant and its foliage burgundy in fall. These multistemmed shrubs are disease resistant. Late season bloom.

Rhododendron yakushimanum (*Rhododendron degronianum* ssp. *yakushimanum*)

VARIETY	FLOWER COLOR	TYPE (LEAF SIZE)	HEIGHT/WIDTH	HARDINESS
'Crete'***	Pink to white	Evergreen (large)	3'/4'	−20°F
'Ken Janeck'***	Pink to white	Evergreen (large)	3'/4'	−20°F
'Mist Maiden'***	Pink to white	Evergreen (large)	3'/4'	−20°F

Although borderline hardy in cold climates, these plants are so lovely that they are worth a gamble. The abundant flowers and dark green foliage with silvery hairs make them gems. They demand excellent drainage and will die out unless protected from winter sun and wind. Mid season bloom.

Rhododendron (Hybrids)

VARIETY	FLOWER COLOR	TYPE (LEAF SIZE)	HEIGHT/WIDTH	HARDINESS
'April Mist'****	White tinged lavender (D)	Evergreen (small)	3'/3'	−20°F
'April Rose'****	Raspberry red (D)	Evergreen (small)	3'/3'	−25°F
'April Snow'***	White (D)	Evergreen (small)	3'/3'	−25°F
'Bluenose'***	Lavender blue	Evergreen (small)	3'/3'	−20°F
'Henry's Red'****	Dark red	Evergreen (large)	4'/4'	−25°F
'Jane Abbott'****	Red pink	Deciduous	5'/5'	−30°F
'Karin Seleger'****	Vibrant violet	Evergreen (small)	2½'/3'	−25°F
'Landmark'****	Reddish pink	Evergreen (small)	5'/4'	−20°F
'Narcissiflora'****	Light yellow (D)	Deciduous	4'/4'	−20°F
'Purple Gem'****	Purplish blue	Evergreen (small)	2'/3'	−25°F
'Windbeam'****	Mid to light pink	Evergreen (small)	2'/2'	−25°F

These hybrids represent a fine cross section of the hundreds of Rhododendrons on the market today. 'April Mist,' 'April Rose,' and 'April Snow' are lovely doubles (D) prized for their long bloom season. 'Blue Nose' has exquisite, delicate flowers. The flowers of 'Henry's Red' are almost wine colored. 'Jane Abbott' is free-flowering with slightly more intense color than 'Rosy Lights.' 'Karin Seleger' is a compact plant with wavy edged blossoms. The blossoms of 'Landmark' are abundant and breathtaking. 'Narcissiflora' is an extremely fragrant double that flowers at an early age. 'Purple Gem' is a compact plant showered with blossoms at peak bloom. The wavy edged flowers of 'Windbeam' open mid pink turning light pink with age. Early season bloom for most. Mid season bloom for 'Henry's Red,' 'Jane Abbott,' 'Narcissiflora,' and 'Windbeam.'

Rhus glabra

RHUS

(ROOSE)

SUMAC

Sumac is one of the easiest shrubs to grow and requires very little maintenance. The fact that it is so common somehow detracts from its overall desirability in the marketplace. If it were rare, it would be highly prized. Those familiar with the many varieties and their multiple uses understand that this plant is, indeed, highly desirable. When the plant first begins to grow in spring, the new growth has an intriguing pink tinge. The foliage varies in color, shape, and texture, but is very clean and attractive throughout the summer season. This shrub is one of the earliest to show fall color, turning a range of colors, including intense, fiery reds that glow in the afternoon sun. This colorful red theme is continued in Sumac's seed heads, which start to turn red in mid- to late summer and remain showy through much of the winter and often into the following spring. These seed heads are lovely fresh or dried in arrangements. The taller shrub types have a unique angled branching pattern and thickets of these present a very interesting crisscrossing architecture, most noticeable in winter. These plants are effectively insect and disease free. Most Sumacs sucker freely, and this can be seen as a plus or a minus depending upon their intended use. **Note:** Poison Sumac (**Rhus vernix**) grows in swamps and is rarely found in cold climates. Like its cousins, it has brilliant fall foliage, but forms hanging clusters of yellowish white rather than upright clusters of red berries.

How Sumac Grows

Sumacs have a somewhat thick, fibrous to coarse root system with rather fleshy roots. Depending upon the species and the variety, Sumacs can be low-spreading shrubs, upright irregularly rounded shrubs, or trained as small trees. All spread vigorously by suckers and can form large thickets. The stems are quite pithy and easy to snap. Most branch freely and are covered with medium to deep green leaves, often quite glossy. These leaves are arranged either in clusters of three (trifoliate) or as many leaflets along a central leaf stalk (pinnate). The branches themselves are usually smooth, but one species has velvety hairs on new growth. Most Sumacs produce either male or female flowers on different plants (dioecious). Male flowers are either yellow or greenish yellow. They may look either like catkins or large pyramidal clusters. Female flowers are quite similar in color and form but turn into dense clusters of small velvety red berry-like fruits with seeds inside. The plants will self-sow since the seeds are often scattered by birds.

Where to Plant

Site and Light Sumacs prefer full sun but tolerate partial shade. Most varieties like hotter rather than cooler sites. They will grow just about anywhere if given enough light, even on the steepest slope. They need no protection from winter winds.

Soil and Moisture Sumacs tolerate a wide variety of soil types as long as they drain freely. Their preferred soil would be sand or loam. Soil does not have to be overly fertile. In fact, plants do well in rather lean soils. Plants tolerate quite dry conditions once mature. They will also tolerate a limited amount of salt if planted along roadways. Avoid planting them in constantly wet or boggy sites.

Spacing Space according to the mature size of the plant. If you want the plant to colonize, allow suckers to form off to the side of the mother plant. Within a few years you'll have a lovely clump of Sumac under ideal conditions.

Landscape Use

Because of their fibrous, suckering root system and tolerance to poor soils, Sumacs are highly valuable for planting on slopes and rough terrain. Their ability to form dense thickets also makes Sumacs a good choice for low ground covers, informal hedges, and mass plantings. Though better suited to large areas, Sumacs can be used in smaller spots if the planting space is confined by paved areas or located where suckers can simply be mowed off regularly. Sumacs are generally most attractive in groups. If you desire a single specimen, then the cutleaf varieties are the best choice. For naturalized areas they combine well with *Acer ginnala* (Amur Maple), *Amelanchier* (Serviceberry), *Aronia* (Chokeberry), *Hamamelis* (Witch Hazel), and *Viburnum* (Viburnum). The combination of these can create a riot of fall color.

Planting

Bare Root Get bare root plants into the garden as soon as the ground can be worked in spring. Remove plants from their shipping package immediately on arrival. Soak them in room temperature water for no fewer than 3 hours before planting. Place a small amount of superphosphate in the base of the hole and cover with 3 inches (7.5 cm) of soil. Spread roots out over a cone of well-prepared soil. Make sure the crown is level with the surrounding soil surface. Fill the hole with soil, firm it with your fingers, and water immediately. Dissolve water-soluble fertilizer in a gallon (about 4 liters) of water following the directions on the label. Pour ½ cup (about 120 ml) of this starter solution around the base of each plant. If you prefer organic fertilizer, use fish emulsion instead.

Containerized Plants Plant Sumacs as early in the season as possible. If the soil in the container is dry, soak it and let it drain overnight before planting. Carefully remove the plant from the container so as not to break the root ball. Plant at the same depth as in the container after preparing the hole in a similar manner as that for a bare root plant. Fill the hole with well-prepared soil, firm with your fingers, and water immediately. Pour ½ cup (about 120 ml) of starter solution around the base of the plant.

Balled and Burlapped Rarely sold this way.

Transplanting

Young Sumac plants are extremely easy to transplant. Dig them up in early spring before new growth emerges. Plant immediately as you would a bare root plant. Older plants are difficult to transplant. Simply dig up suckers off to the side of these in early spring and plant immediately as you would a bare root plant.

How to Care for Sumac

Water Keep the soil evenly moist from spring until the soil freezes in fall. Consistent watering is especially important during the first 2 years. Always saturate the soil deeply with each watering. When the top 2 inches (5 cm) of soil dry out, water.

Mulch Apply a 1- to 2-inch (2.5- to 5-cm) layer of mulch around each plant as soon as the ground warms up in spring. Good mulches include shredded bark, pine needles, and wood chips. Mulch retains moisture in the soil and helps prevent the growth of weeds. Replenish the mulch as necessary throughout the growing season.

Fertilizing Note that Sumacs in general do not require rich soils to grow well. Watch for fall color. If fall color is poor, reduce or eliminate any fertilizer around these plants altogether. Fall color is certainly dependent on other considerations, but this is one you can control.

Weeding Prevent the growth of most annual weeds by using mulch. Pull by hand any weeds that do appear. Weeds compete with shrubs for available moisture and nutrients and should be removed immediately. Note, however, that Sumac does grow quite well in grassy areas.

Deadheading Not recommended at all. The seed heads are one of the plant's most ornamental and interesting features.

Pruning In general, Sumacs need very little pruning. To create a tree from a Sumac, choose a plant with a strong, straight, upward stem. Remove all but the top branches and continue pruning for form. These make quite unusual specimen plants.

If a Sumac thicket is getting out of control, consider shearing plants back in midwinter to ground level. New plants are usually quite attractive within two seasons and a much more manageable size. This step is most common with the larger Sumacs.

Also, to keep thickets within bounds, remove suckers each spring. Note that the suckering habit of Sumacs is highly desirable if you're trying to cover a steep bank with plants.

Winter Protection None needed.

Problems

Insects None serious.

Diseases None serious.

Marauders The only problem with Sumac is that deer sometimes rub their antlers against the stems, which wounds the stem tissue.

Propagation

Suckers Many Sumacs sucker profusely and this is certainly an easy way to increase stock. Dig up the suckers off to the side of the mother plant in very early spring before any new growth starts. Plant immediately as you would a bare root plant.

Root Cuttings Dig up the side of a large plant in early spring to expose one or more long roots. Sever these from the mother plant and cut into sections about 4 inches (10 cm) long. Plant these immediately in rooting medium. For additional information, see pages 408–9.

Layering Layering is possible with *Rhus aromatica* (Fragrant Sumac) and *Rhus trilobata* (Three-Lobe Sumac). Bend over and wound very pliable stems at a point where they touch the ground. Follow the detailed instructions outlined on page 405.

Seed The seed of the named varieties will not produce plants identical to the parents. To grow the species, nick the seed by placing it in a blender for 10 to 15 seconds. Or, soak the seed for 24 hours until it swells. If the seed does not swell, poke it with a pin and place it in fresh water for another 24 hours. Then place the seed into a moist mixture of peat and perlite. Barely cover it. Keep the seed at room temperature until it germinates, usually within 90 days. If the seed does not germinate, moist chill it for 90 days before bringing it out to room temperature to try again. See pages 409–12 for additional information.

Special Uses

Fresh Seed Heads The foliage of Sumacs is not good in fresh floral arrangements. However, the seed heads are excellent. Cut them as they reach peak color, remove all foliage, and place immediately in water.

Dried Seed Heads Cut seed heads as they reach peak coloration. Hang them upside down in a dry, warm, dark area until they dry thoroughly. They'll lose some of their brilliant coloration, but are still attractive in dried arrangements.

Drinks Cut off the fresh, ripe seed heads of *Rhus glabra* (Smooth Sumac) or *Rhus typhina* (Staghorn Sumac) and steep them in cold water. Strain the fruit from the water and sweeten to taste. This makes a tart, lemonade-like drink.

Sources

Bergeson Nursery, 4177 County Highway 1, Fertile, MN 56540, (575) 945-6988

Blackfoot Native Plants Nursery, P.O. Box 761, Bonner, MT 59823, (406) 244-5800

Colvos Creek Nursery, 1904 Third Ave., Suite 415, Seattle, WA 98101, (575) 749-9508

Fairweather Gardens, P.O. Box 330, Greenwich, NJ 08323, (856) 451-6261

ForestFarm, 990 Tetherow Rd., Williams, OR 97544, (541) 846-7269

Greer Gardens, 1280 Goodpasture Island Rd., Eugene, OR 97401, (541) 686-8266

High Country Gardens, 2902 Rufina St., Santa Fe, NM 87507, (800) 925-9387

Hortico, Inc., 723 Robson Rd., RR# 1, Waterdown, ON LoR 2H1 Canada, (905) 689-6984

McKay Nursery Co., P.O. Box 185, Waterloo, WI 53594, (910) 478-2121

Musser Forests, Inc., 1880 Route 119 Highway N, Indiana, PA 15701, (859) 465-5685

Nature Hills Nursery, 3334 North 88th Plaza, Omaha, NE 68134, (888) 864-7663

Out Back Nursery, Inc., 15280 110th St. S, Hastings, MN 55033, (298) 438-2771

Reeseville Ridge Nursery, 512 S Main, Reeseville, WI 53579, (920) 927-3291

River Rock Nursery, 19251 SE Hwy 224, Damascus, OR 97089, (503) 658-4047

Shooting Star Nursery, 160 Soards Rd., Georgetown, KY 40324, (526) 867-7979

St. Lawrence Nurseries, 325 Ste Hwy 345, Potsdam, NY 13676, (758) 265-6739

Wavecrest Nursery, 2509 Lakeshore Dr., Fennville, MI 49408, (888) 869-4159

Woodlanders, Inc., 1128 Colleton Ave., Aiken, SC 29801, (803) 648-7522

VARIETIES

VARIETY	FLOWER COLOR	FALL FOLIAGE	HEIGHT/WIDTH	HARDINESS
Rhus aromatica **				
(Fragrant Sumac)	Pale yellow	Orange, purple, red	6′/10′	−35°F
'Gro-Low'****	Greenish yellow	Orange, red, yellow	2′/8′	−35°F

The species forms a dense mound of branches covered in three-lobed, softly fuzzy leaves. Flowers are small and tinged yellow. Fuzzy, red, berry-like fruits form at the tips of some of the branches if the plant is grown in full sun. The species varies from dull to brilliant red and yellow in fall. It grows quite well in light shade and is drought tolerant when mature. It also grows rapidly and suckers freely. The foliage and stems emit a strong, somewhat pungent aroma when bruised. 'Gro-Low' is another tough plant with glossy medium to dark green leaves. It's a superb ground cover. It, too, is very drought tolerant when mature.

VARIETY	FLOWER COLOR	FALL FOLIAGE	HEIGHT/WIDTH	HARDINESS
Rhus copallinum ***				
(Shining Sumac)	Yellow green	Orange, red	15′/15′	−20°F

Shining Sumac is noted for its lustrous dark green foliage that turns scarlet red to brilliant orange in fall. The plant creates spikes of tiny yellow green flowers in spring. Female plants form fairly compact clusters of red, hairy berry-like fruit. This plant has a somewhat finer leaf and stem texture than other tall growing Sumacs. It spreads readily to form large thickets. It is possible to grow this plant in a container by keeping it at a small size with consistent pruning.

VARIETY	FLOWER COLOR	FALL FOLIAGE	HEIGHT/WIDTH	HARDINESS
Rhus copallinum var. *latifolia*				
(Prairie Flame Sumac)				
Prairie Flame® ('Morton')***	Yellow green	Mahogany, orange, red	5′/6′	−20°F

This male plant produces no fruit. It is highly regarded because of its compact form, lustrous dark green foliage, and fiery red fall color. It is a superb selection for someone with limited space.

VARIETY	FLOWER COLOR	FALL FOLIAGE	HEIGHT/WIDTH	HARDINESS
Rhus glabra ***				
(Smooth Sumac)	White to green	Maroon, orange, red	15′/15′	−40°F
'Laciniata'***	White to green	Orange, red, yellow	10′/10′	−40°F

Smooth, medium to dark green leaves turn vivid orange, purple, red, or yellow in fall. The most prized fall coloration is bright red or dark purple red. The smooth stems and twigs have a slightly bluish cast. Floral spires on female plants are usually whitish green and up to 8 inches (20 cm) long. These produce lovely, velvety red berries. The species spreads rapidly by suckers, forming a large colony in time. Since whole colonies may be either male or female, you'll find entire clumps with or without berries. The plants are both salt and drought tolerant. 'Laciniata,' known as Cutleaf Smooth Sumac, has very decorative, finely cut, fern-like foliage. This named variety is female and produces showy, upright clusters of red fruit.

Rhus aromatica

Rhus aromatica 'Gro-Low'

Rhus glabra

Rhus typhina

Rhus typhina

Rhus typhina

Rhus typhina 'Laciniata'

Rhus typhina 'Laciniata'

VARIETY	FLOWER COLOR	FALL FOLIAGE	HEIGHT/WIDTH	HARDINESS

Rhus trilobata**

(Three Lobe Sumac)	Greenish yellow	Orange, red	6'/10'	−30°F

This western species is very similar to *Rhus aromatica* (Fragrant Sumac) with slightly smaller leaves that have a pungent, skunky smell when crushed. It spreads rapidly into a dense thicket. Female plants produce small clusters of red fruits. These are tart and edible, although most gardeners grow them as wildlife plantings. There are male plants, but they do not produce berries. This species thrives in exposed sites in dry, sandy soil. It is prone to foliar diseases unless grown in relatively arid areas.

Rhus typhina***

(Staghorn Sumac)	White to green	Maroon, orange, red	15'/15'	−35°F
'Laciniata' ('Dissecta')****	White to green	Orange, red, yellow	8'/8'	−35°F
First Editions®Tiger Eyes®*****	Insignificant	Yellow, orange, red	6'/6'	−30°F

The species can either be shrub- or tree-like depending on how it is pruned. It has dense, velvety hairs on its stems. The common name of the species may come from this velvety layer resembling the seasonal velvet on stag's antlers or from the crisscrossing pattern of its branches, which look like antlers. The light to medium green leaves with whitish undersides are hairy and finely cut with a somewhat fern-like appearance. They turn orange, purple, red, or yellow in fall. Female plants send up green spikes of flowers in late spring or early summer. In fall these become showy, upright clusters of red fruit and persist through the winter standing up like red velvety candles. The berries can be made into a fruity drink. The species spreads rapidly by root suckers forming a colony in time. Gardeners vary in their opinion of the overall appearance of the shrub; some insist its branching habit is architectural while others find it coarse. The plants are effective in mass plantings in natural settings. The plant may suffer severe dieback in winter. Prune off dead portions of stem in spring, and the plant recuperates quickly. 'Laciniata,' or Cutleaf Staghorn Sumac, is strictly a female plant as is 'Dissecta,' which may be the same plant or only slightly different. Tiger Eyes® is noted for its chartreuse to bright yellow leaves and lovely purplish stems. Fall foliage takes on pink and red hues. It is a knockout and has become one of the most popular cold-climate plants.

Ribes aureum

RIBES

(REYE-bees)

CURRANT

Currants are useful both for ornamental and culinary purposes. The ornamental Currants make excellent informal and formal hedges. They leaf out very early in spring, providing welcome greenery after a long winter. The flowers of Clove Currant are quite lovely and have a wonderful aroma that perfumes the air in spring. Currants produce berries that attract birds as they mature in mid- to late summer. The berries of edible Currants are prized for jellies. Plants do require quite a bit of maintenance to perform at their best. They are relatively disease resistant except for leaf spot diseases that can plague some species.

How Currants Grow

Currants have a fibrous root system that spreads quite widely. They produce numerous stems and the edible types often produce suckers off to the side of the mother plant. If stems of the ornamental types touch the ground, they will often take root and form a new plant. Stems grow quickly and multiply each year to form an increasingly larger shrub. Flowers vary in color and size by variety. Some are quite showy, others rather inconspicuous. The berries may be black, green, red, or white and contain seeds, but rarely self-sow.

Where to Plant

Site and Light Ornamental types do well in full sun to partial shade. Edible types prefer full sun but produce decent crops in light shade. They do not require protection from winter winds. However, some of the edible types do spread, and you may wish to place them in a corner of a garden where this will not be a problem. Avoid low-lying areas, which act as frost pockets in the spring.

Soil and Moisture Currants grow vigorously in rich loam, which drains freely. Add some organic matter to the soil at planting time. This helps the soil stay consistently moist, which these plants like. However, they do not like overly wet or boggy soils.

Spacing For ornamental types of Currants, space them with mature height and width in mind.

For hedges, place plants about 18 inches (45 cm) apart. This tight planting results in a more dense appearance. It does require consistent pruning and more attention to care.

Plant edible Currants roughly 36 to 48 inches (90 to 120 cm) apart.

Landscape Use

The ornamental types are primarily used for informal and formal hedges. They are neat and tidy and grow rapidly. They define spaces beautifully and make excellent backdrops for perennial gardens. Since they will grow well in full sun and partial shade, they are particularly versatile for this use. Any ornamental type with significant flowers can be combined with spring flowering bulbs or placed in the perennial garden. The edible types are valuable for their fruit used for jellies or juice.

Planting

Bare Root Numerous plants are needed to create hedges. The most economical way to do this is with bare root plants. Check locally to see where these will be available and reserve the number you need well in advance. Pick them up as soon as they arrive and get them into the garden as soon as the ground can be worked in spring. If ordered through the mail, remove plants from their shipping package immediately on arrival. Soak them in room temperature water for no fewer than 3 hours before planting. Place a small amount of superphosphate in the base of the hole and cover with 3 inches (7.5 cm) of soil. Spread roots out over a cone of well-prepared soil. Make sure the crown is level with the surrounding soil surface. Fill the hole with soil, firm it with your fingers, and water immediately. Dissolve water-soluble fertilizer in a gallon (about 4 liters) of water following the directions on the label. Pour ½ cup (about 120 ml) of this starter solution around the base of each plant. If you prefer organic fertilizer, use fish emulsion instead.

Containerized Plants Plant Currants as early in the season as possible. If the soil in the container is dry, soak it and let it drain overnight before planting. Carefully remove the plant from the container so as not to break the root ball. Plant at the same depth as in the container after preparing the hole in a similar manner as that for a bare root plant. Fill the hole with well-prepared soil, firm with your fingers, and water immediately. Pour ½ cup (about 120 ml) of starter solution around the base of the plant.

Balled and Burlapped Rarely sold this way.

Transplanting

Currants are relatively easy to transplant even when mature. Dig up the plants in early spring before buds begin to break. Get as much of the fibrous root system as possible. Immediately plant these as you would bare root plants.

How to Care for Currants

Water Keep the soil evenly moist from spring until the soil freezes in fall. Consistent watering is especially important during the first 2 years. Always saturate the soil deeply with each watering. When the top 2 inches (5 cm) of soil dry out, water. Water early in the day to allow foliage to dry out by the evening. Currants are more prone to leaf spot diseases if foliage is wet at night.

Mulch Apply a 2- to 4-inch (5- to 10-cm) layer of mulch around each plant as soon as the ground warms up in spring. Good mulches include shredded bark, pine needles, and wood chips. Mulch retains moisture in the soil and helps prevent the growth of weeds. Replenish the mulch as necessary throughout the growing season.

Fertilizing Fertilize every spring with 10-10-10 fertilizer. Sprinkle the granules around the base of each plant before new growth emerges and water immediately to move the fertilizer into the root zone.

If you prefer organic fertilizers, use alfalfa meal (rabbit pellets), blood meal, bone meal, compost, fish emulsion, Milorganite, or rotted manures. Bone meal must be added to the soil at planting time to be effective.

Weeding Prevent the growth of most annual weeds by using mulch. Pull by hand any weeds that do appear. Weeds compete with shrubs for available moisture and nutrients and should be removed immediately.

Deadheading Not necessary.

Pruning If using *Ribes alpinum* (Alpine Currant) for a hedge, begin trimming back lightly in the second year. As the hedge gets larger, cut off both the sides and the top if a formal look is desired. Keep the top of the hedge narrower than the bottom so that light can get to the base of the plant. Shearing the plants causes dense growth by forcing each plant to create more branches and more new stems from the base. Rarely will you have to trim mature hedges more than once in early spring and once again in midsummer. Do not prune late in the season as this encourages new growth, which is likely to die off in winter.

It is common for a few older branches or stems in hedges to die off each year. In early spring these are most noticeable by a total lack of foliage or by partial defoliation. Move your hand down to the bottom of these stems and push on the stem. It will often snap off at the base if it is completely dead. Then snip off any remaining portion with lopping or pruning shears. Sometimes the latter are needed to snip off the stem if it is not brittle. Do not let these dead stems remain in the hedge. Remove them in the spring to allow for new growth to fill in the gap.

Pruning out older stems on a regular basis also encourages the growth of new stems from the base of the shrub. Cut out some of the stems older than 3 years each spring before new growth emerges. A nice balanced shrub will have from nine to twelve stems varying in age from one to three years old.

Winter Protection None needed.

Problems

Insects Currants are occasionally bothered by aphids. If they become a regular problem, spray them with insecticidal soaps or more potent insecticides such as Orthene. Other insects do occasionally cause difficulties, but none stand out as major problems.

Diseases Leaf spots can be a problem in some years. If one or two branches have yellowing leaves, simply snip them off at their bases. These are often stressed and will die out anyway. This problem may also be an indication of poor drainage. Do not remove stems simply because leaves have some spotting. This is generally no more than a cosmetic concern. Consistent watering throughout the season keeps plants vigorous and able to ward off most diseases.

Anthracnose, a fungal infection, can cause serious problems with Currants in wet seasons. It shows up as spots on leaves that look as if they are water soaked. If severe enough, the foliage drops off completely. For the home gardener there is no practical cure except patience. Simply wait until the following season to see whether the plants spring back to life without additional problems. If the disease is present 2 or 3 years in a row, plants are severely weakened. At that point prune the plants back severely. If that doesn't work, you may have to replace them with a different type of hedge.

White-pine blister rust does infect a number of edible Currants, mainly ones with black fruit. If severe enough, it causes leaves to drop off early in the season. The Currants act as a host for the disease, which can spread to *Pinus strobus* (White Pine). The latter can be severely damaged by the disease. Some states do not allow any Currants to be mailed into the state. European Black Currant is one definitely to avoid, since it is a common carrier of this disease.

Marauders During the winter rabbits commonly eat a few stems if no better food is available. Rarely do they do much damage to a mature hedge. They also like the shelter the hedge provides and may use it as winter protection. Deer do not seem to be a common problem, although they'll eat almost any shrub if hungry enough.

Propagation

Suckers Some of the Currants sucker freely. Simply cut off the small plantlet from the side of the mother plant in early spring before new growth emerges. Plant immediately as you would a bare root plant.

Layering (Pegging) The ornamental Currants will often take root where side stems touch the ground. Once roots have formed on these suckers, cut them off in spring and plant immediately as you would a bare root plant. See Pegging on page 405 for additional information.

Layering (Mound) Cut a mature plant down to the ground. Cover it with 6 inches of soil amended generously with peat and keep moist. New growth will emerge through the mound. When the individual stems form roots at their bases, snip them off. Plant them immediately as you would a bare root plant.

Cuttings Take softwood cuttings just as new growth begins to harden (semihard). Cuttings should be about 4 to 6 inches (10 to 15 cm) long.

Take hardwood cuttings any time from late fall to late winter. These cuttings should be 6 inches (15 cm) long. For additional information, see pages 406–8.

Seed Moist chill and sow seed indoors or outdoors following the standard procedures on pages 409–12.

Special Uses

Berries The fruit of 'Red Lake' and other edible varieties is excellent for juice, jam, or jelly. It can also be fermented into wine. If used to make jam or jelly, pick fruit just as it ripens. At this stage it should have its highest concentration of pectin.

Sources

Bergeson Nursery, 4177 Cty Hwy 1, Fertile, MN 56540, (576) 945-6988

Blackfoot Native Plants Nursery, P.O. Box 761, Bonner, MT 59823, (406) 244-5800

Burnt Ridge Nursery & Orchards, 432 Burnt Ridge Rd., Onalaska, WA 98570, (360) 985-2873

Corn Hill Nursery Ltd., 2700 Rte 890, Corn Hill, NB E4Z 1M2 Canada, (576) 756-3635

Edible Landscaping, 361 Spirit Ridge Ln., Afton, VA 22920, (434) 316-9134

ForestFarm, 990 Tetherow Rd., Williams, OR 97544, (911) 846-7269

Fritz Creek Gardens, P.O. Box 15226, Homer, AK 99603, (907) 235-4969

Greer Gardens, 1280 Goodpasture Island Rd., Eugene, OR 97401, (541) 686-8266

Hortico, Inc., 723 Robson Rd., RR# 1, Waterdown, ON L0R 2H1 Canada, (860) 689-6984

Indiana Berry and Plant Co., 2811 US 31, Plymouth, IN 46563, (299) 295-2226

Joy Creek Nursery, 20300 NW Watson Rd., Scappoose, OR 97056, (503) 543-7474

McKay Nursery Co., P.O. Box 185, Waterloo, WI 53594, (759) 478-2121

Nourse Farms, Inc., 41 River Rd., South Deerfield, MA 01373, (413) 665-2658

Oikos Tree Crops, P.O. Box 19425, Kalamazoo, MI 49019, (527) 624-6233

One Green World, 28696 S Cramer Rd., Molalla, OR 97038, (940) 353-4028

Reeseville Ridge Nursery, 512 S Main, Reeseville, WI 53579, (920) 927-3291

River Rock Nursery, 19251 SE Hwy 224, Damascus, OR 97089, (324) 658-4047

Shooting Star Nursery, 160 Soards Rd., Georgetown, KY 40324, (747) 867-7979

South Meadow Fruit Gardens, P.O. Box 211, Baroda, MI 49101, (269) 422-2411

St. Lawrence Nurseries, 325 Ste Hwy 345, Potsdam, NY 13676, (315) 265-6739

Whitman Farms, 3995 Gibson Rd. NW, Salem, OR 97304, (503) 585-8728

Ribes alpinum

Ribes 'Red Lake'

VARIETIES

VARIETY	FOLIAGE COLOR	HEIGHT/WIDTH	HARDINESS
Ribes alpinum***			
(Alpine Currant)	Dark green	5'/4'	−50°F
Green Jeans™ ('Spreg')***	Dark green	5'/4'	−50°F
'Green Mound'***	Dark green	3'/4'	−50°F

The species is one of the most commonly used plants for low hedges. Properly pruned, these plants live for years and form a dense, deep green barrier. If you're lucky, you'll have both male and female plants for reddish orange berry production. The fruit is not that noticeable, but wildlife likes it. 'Green Jeans' is noted for its resistance to disease. 'Green Mound' is an ideal choice for gardeners who want a much lower, compact, but still tidy hedge. This named variety will not form any berries.

Ribes aureum**			
(Golden Currant)	Medium green	5'/5'	−50°F

This plant, often sold as "Clove Currant," produces lovely yellow flowers in spring. These have an extraordinary scent. The bark is somewhat reddish brown. Frankly, the plant's form is rather gangly or sprawling, which limits its use. Place it in the back of a perennial garden where you can enjoy both its color and fragrance in spring but have it screened by the perennials the rest of the season. Note that "Golden Currant" is a western species that seems to have more problems with foliar disease the farther east you go. Don't confuse it with *Ribes alpinum* 'Aureum.' The latter is not even listed as a desirable plant in this guide.

Ribes odoratum**			
(Clove Currant)	Medium green	5'/5'	−30°F

The true "Clove Currant" is almost identical to "Golden Currant." However, it does not have its extreme hardiness. On the other hand, it's more resistant to foliar disease. It produces purple fruit in the fall. Its foliage also turns purplish as well, giving it added interest late in the season.

Ribes rubrum			
(Red Currant)			
'Red Lake'	Medium green	4½'/3'	−30°F
'Jonkheer Van Tets'	Medium green	5'/4'	−30°F
'Redstart'	Green tinted red	4½'/3'	−30°F
'Rovada'	Pale green	4½'/3'	−30°F

Edible Currants can be eaten fresh, but are more commonly made into delicious brightly colored jams and jellies. 'Jonkheer Van Tets' has been highly recommended, but it has a tendency to flower early. If you have a spring warmup followed by a quick dip in temperature, you can lose your crop. For this reason it is best used in the southern range of the cold-climate region. 'Red Lake' is a long-time favorite and is widely available in the marketplace. In some areas the plant is prone to powdery mildew. But it has been tested for years and is an excellent plant. 'Redstart' is another highly rated variety and more disease resistant than 'Red Lake.' It's noted for producing lots of fruit. 'Rovada' is highly recommended for both the size and taste of its fruit. Edible Currants are best placed on gentle slopes. If placed in full sun, avoid a southern exposure. Buy one- to two-year-old bare root plants. Note that there are dozens of edible Currants on the market. These four were the most highly recommended by a breeder.

Ribes uva-crispa			
(Gooseberry)			
'Pixwell'	Medium green	4'/4'	−30°F

Nearly thornless with green to purplish pink fruit, this Gooseberry gets its name from the tendency of its fruit to hang down making it easy to pick.

Salix purpurea 'Nana'

SALIX

(SAY-licks)

WILLOW

Willows are very easy to grow and are one of the few plants that thrive in moist, even wet conditions. They grow very rapidly. The stems, branches, and foliage of many Willows are favored by florists for both dry and fresh floral arrangements. Such arrangements highlight the Willow's catkins, stem and foliage color, or unique contorted growth pattern. The numerous forms, foliage colors, shapes, stem colors, and textures of Willows available in the market today provide many potential uses. A few of the large Willows have rich golden fall color. If Willows have a drawback, it is their susceptibility to disease and insects. However, grown and cared for properly, they will often live for years, providing interest from spring through winter.

How Willows Grow

The roots of Willows are fairly coarse and penetrate the soil quite deeply. Most Willows are multistemmed shrubs or small trees with wispy, whip-like stems and branches. The multistemmed Willows send up new stems from the base each year, expanding in size over time. Some spread by suckers to create a larger mass. The stems vary greatly in color but are often one of the plant's most interesting features. Willows bloom very early in the spring with male and female flowers on different plants (dioecious). The male catkins are usually soft, fuzzy, and gray to silvery white in color. The species with the longest catkins are commonly known as Pussy Willows. Female flowers are small and inconspicuous and mature into small capsules that contain many seeds, each with a bit of cotton-like fluff, or small hairs, that allow them to float effortlessly in the wind.

Willows are also very early to leaf out in spring and retain leaves well into the fall. The leaves of Willows vary in shape from long and narrow to oblong. Leaf color ranges from light green to dark blue green with some leaves having silvery undersides. Leaves on some types turn an attractive yellow in fall. Mature Willows rarely self-sow.

Where to Plant

Site and Light Most Willows thrive in full sun. They tolerate partial shade, but you'll get best growth and color in high-light conditions. Some varieties with variegated foliage may retain better leaf color if planted in light shade. The more tender varieties will have less dieback if placed in a protected location. Note that the roots of Willows are extremely aggressive and should be kept away from septic tanks.

Soil and Moisture Willows do extremely well in consistently moist sites. Some will even tolerate poor drainage and seasonal flooding. This is a quality rare among shrubs. However, most Willows grow well in soils that drain freely as long as they are watered frequently during the growing season.

Spacing Space plants appropriately according to their potential size. Some of the smaller varieties will not need a lot of space between plants, but the larger ones should not be crowded unless trimmed back severely. A number of Willows make good hedges and mass plantings. Closer spacing makes sense in these instances.

Landscape Use

Willows grow where many other small trees and shrubs won't. Place them close to ponds or standing water or plant them in poorly drained sites.

Willows that sucker freely are excellent for stopping erosion on banks routinely buffeted by waves or flowing water. These same Willows are suitable as plantings to control erosion on steep banks or slopes, even if not near water.

Willows with especially attractive bark or stem coloration combine well in the winter landscape with any red-stemmed varieties of *Cornus* (Dogwood), *Ilex verticillata* (Winterberry), and *Viburnum trilobum* (American Cranberrybush Viburnum). During the winter they also stand out if planted in front of evergreens.

The Willows with the most attractive catkins are normally best suited to naturalized areas because their overall form is not as appealing as others. They also tend to be a little messier.

The weeping form of Pussy Willow when grafted to a standard makes a lovely specimen plant.

A loose line of trimmed Arctic Willows creates an extremely interesting hedge-like effect. In fact, many Willows make good informal or formal hedges depending upon how they are trimmed. Some of these can be cut back to ground level each year and still make good hedges.

Planting

Bare Root Get bare root plants into the garden as soon as the ground can be worked in spring. Remove plants from their shipping package immediately on arrival. Soak them in room temperature water for no fewer than 3 hours before planting. Place a small amount of superphosphate in the base of the hole and cover with 3 inches (7.5 cm) of soil. Spread roots out over a cone of well-prepared soil. Make sure the crown is level with the surrounding soil surface. Fill the hole with soil, firm it with your fingers, and water immediately. Dissolve water-soluble fertilizer in a gallon (about 4 liters) of water following the directions on the label. Pour ½ cup (about 120 ml) of this starter solution around the base of each plant. If you prefer organic fertilizer, use fish emulsion instead.

Containerized Plants Plant Willows as early in the season as possible. If the soil in the container is dry, soak it and let it drain overnight before planting. Carefully remove the plant from the container so as not to break the root ball. Plant at the same depth as in the container after preparing the hole in a similar manner as that for a bare root plant. Fill the hole with well-prepared soil, firm with your fingers, and water immediately. Pour ½ cup (about 120 ml) of starter solution around the base of the plant.

Balled and Burlapped Rarely sold this way.

Transplanting

It is quite easy to transplant Willows as long as they are of manageable size. Do this early in the year before new growth emerges. If a Willow is large but suckers freely, dig up the suckers off to the side of the mother plant. Plant any of these young plants or suckers immediately as you would a bare root plant.

How to Care for Willows

Water Keep the soil evenly moist from spring until the soil freezes in fall. Consistent watering is especially important during the first 2 years. Always saturate the soil deeply with each watering. When the top 2 inches (5 cm) of soil dry out, water. During hot, dry periods spray the foliage forcefully to knock off aphids.

Mulch Apply a 2- to 4-inch (5- to 10-cm) layer of mulch around each plant as soon as the ground warms up in spring. Good mulches include shredded bark, pine needles, and wood chips. Mulch retains moisture in the soil and helps prevent the growth of weeds. Replenish the mulch as necessary throughout the growing season.

Fertilizing Fertilize every spring with 10-10-10 fertilizer. Sprinkle the granules around the base of each plant before new growth emerges and water immediately to move the fertilizer into the root zone. Once plants are growing vigorously, stop fertilizing altogether. Most Willows need little fertilizer to grow well.

If you prefer organic fertilizers, use alfalfa meal (rabbit pellets), blood meal, bone meal, compost, fish emulsion, Milorganite, or rotted manures. Bone meal must be added to the soil at planting time to be effective.

Weeding Prevent the growth of most annual weeds by using mulch. Pull by hand any weeds that do appear. Weeds compete with shrubs for available moisture and nutrients and should be removed immediately.

Deadheading Not necessary.

Pruning Prune Willows to remove damaged, dead, or crossing branches that are rubbing against each other and to improve the plant's overall form. A number of Willows respond well to severe pruning. You can cut these right back to the ground, which controls their size and produces more stems. The same is highly recommended for Willows noted for colorful bark. Young bark often is the most attractive. By cutting plants back in late winter you encourage lots of new growth and a greater number of stems, adding to the plant's beauty the following winter.

Many Willows make good hedges and these can be either informal or formal depending upon how they are pruned. Willows are versatile and easy to work with to create the form, width, and height desired.

Winter Protection None required.

Problems

Insects Aphids will cluster on new growth. Wash these off with a strong stream of water several days in a row. If this doesn't work, spray them with an insecticidal soap. Use more potent insecticides only if absolutely necessary.

Lace bugs sometimes can be a nuisance. Like aphids, they suck sap from the plant and can cause damage to leaves. Spray them with an insecticidal soap before their numbers increase.

Scale may infest stems and leaves. These tiny insects are best controlled by spraying plants with dormant oil in both late fall and early spring. If they begin to form colonies, spray them with an insecticide.

Stem borers are attracted to stressed plants. Prevent attacks by growing plants properly in the first place. If borers do invade a plant, cut the stems back well below the hole created by the borer. In some instances, you may have to remove the entire stem. Burn or toss the infected stems into the garbage.

Willow leaf beetles are small, shiny blue black insects that chew holes in leaves and can actually defoliate entire trees if not sprayed. Spray first with insecticidal soap. If that doesn't stop the population from ballooning, resort to a more formidable insecticide such as Orthene or Sevin.

Diseases Willows are susceptible to a number of canker diseases, which cause dead spots on twigs and stems. In severe cases the canker encircles the entire stem and kills it. Prevent cankers by growing healthy plants and avoiding any injury to the bark. Weed trimmers and mowers cutting into stems are the most common cause of wounds. If cankers do show up, cut off the twigs or stems to a point well below the lesion. Burn or toss the infected stems into the garbage. No chemical treatment is recommended.

Marauders None serious.

Propagation

Suckers *Salix elaeagnos* (Rosemary Willow) and *Salix purpurea* (Purpleosier Willow) produce suckers. Dig up small plants to the side of the mother plant in early spring before new growth emerges. Plant these immediately as you would a bare root plant.

Cuttings Willows are one of the easiest plants to grow from cuttings. Cut 24 inches (60 cm) off the ends of actively growing branches. Place them in water. Just change the water regularly and wait until the roots have reached 2 inches (5 cm) before planting as you would a bare root plant.

Take softwood cuttings from this year's growth. Cut off 4 to 6 inches (10 to 15 cm) from the tips of stems just as they begin to harden (greenwood) or just after they are becoming somewhat woody (semihard).

Take hardwood cuttings in midwinter. Each cutting should be roughly 6 inches (15 cm) long. For additional information, see pages 406–8.

Seed Willows are so easy to grow from cuttings that starting them from seed is strictly for the hybridizer or ardent seed grower. The seed must be planted as soon as it ripens. Do not store it as old seed is extremely difficult to germinate. Plant seed immediately after you collect it in damp peat moss. Note that seeds may germinate in as little as one day if collected ripe and planted immediately.

Special Uses

Cut The showy catkins of *Salix caprea* and *Salix discolor* (Pussy Willows) make lovely additions to fresh flower arrangements, especially when combined with *Narcissus* (Daffodils) or other early-blooming flowers. Cut stems once catkins have emerged. Strip off only those catkins that will end up underwater. Note that these can be left to dry and used in other arrangements. The catkins will remain attractive.

Stems of Willows with dark green or variegated leaves are a wonderful addition to summer bouquets. Cut them as desired, removing leaves that will end up underwater in the final arrangement. If you change the water regularly, the stems will often begin to form roots and can later be planted as cuttings to form new plants.

Dried Cut stems once catkins are at the desired size. Place them upright in a dry vase. Over a period of time the stems will dry out. Note that the catkins are easily knocked off. To keep them in place once fully dried, spray them with a fixative.

Also, the dried branches and new stems of *Salix* 'Golden Curls' and *Salix matsudana* 'Tortuosa' are commonly used by florists in arrangements. The stems placed alone in a colorful basket make a simple but stunning statement.

Baskets Willow stems are very flexible and have long been used in weaving baskets. Bark can either be stripped off or left on. To strip it off, cut stems in early spring when bark slides off easily.

Sources

Bergeson Nursery, 4177 Cty Hwy 1, Fertile, MN 56540, (218) 945-6988

Bluestone Perennials, 7211 Middle Ridge Rd., Madison, OH 44057, (800) 852-5243

Burnt Ridge Nursery & Orchards, 432 Burnt Ridge Rd., Onalaska, WA 98570, (577) 985-2873

Colvos Creek Nursery, 1904 Third Ave., Suite 415, Seattle, WA 98101, (577) 749-9508

Corn Hill Nursery Ltd., 2700 Rte 890, Corn Hill, NB E4Z 1M2 Canada, (912) 756-3635

Digging Dog Nursery, P.O. Box 471, Albion, CA 95410, (861) 937-2480

Durio Nursery, 5853 Hwy 182, Opelousas, LA 70570, (337) 948-3696

Elk Mountain Nursery, P.O. Box 599, Asheville, NC 28802, (828) 683-9330

Fedco Trees, P.O. Box 520, Waterville, ME 04903, (207) 873-7333

Forestfarm, 990 Tetherow Rd., Williams, OR 97544, (300) 846-7269

Fritz Creek Gardens, P.O. Box 15226, Homer, AK 99603, (760) 235-4969

Great Garden Plants, P.O. Box 1511, Holland, MI 49422, (877) 447-4769

Greer Gardens, 1280 Goodpasture Island Rd., Eugene, OR 97401, (541) 686-8266

Hortico, Inc., 723 Robson Rd., RR# 1, Waterdown, ON L0R 2H1 Canada, (905) 689-6984

McKay Nursery Co., P.O. Box 185, Waterloo, WI 53594, (528) 478-2121

Out Back Nursery, Inc., 15280 110th St. S, Hastings, MN 55033, (941) 438-2771

Plant & Gnome, P.O. Box 5344, Charleston, WV 25361, (304) 881-7037

Prairie Moon Nursery, 32115 Prairie Ln., Winona, MN 55987, (325) 452-1362 (866) 417-8156

Prairie Restorations, Inc., P.O. Box 327, Princeton, MN 55371, (748) 837-5986

Reeseville Ridge Nursery, 512 S Main, Reeseville, WI 53579, (920) 927-3291

River Rock Nursery, 19251 SE Hwy 224, Damascus, OR 97089, (326) 658-4047

St. Lawrence Nurseries, 325 Ste Hwy 345, Potsdam, NY 13676, (315) 265-6739

Wavecrest Nursery, 2509 Lakeshore Dr., Fennville, MI 49408, (888) 869-4159

Whitney Gardens & Nursery, P.O. Box 170, Brinnon, WA 98320, (360) 796-4411

Woodlanders, Inc., 1128 Colleton Ave., Aiken, SC 29801, (803) 648-7522

VARIETIES

VARIETY	STEM COLOR	FALL FOLIAGE	HEIGHT/WIDTH	HARDINESS
*Salix caprea***				
(Pussy or Goat Willow)	Yellow brown	Green yellow	20'/15'	−25°F
'Pendula'***	Yellow brown	Green yellow	6'/8'	−25°F

With an upright, oval form, the species is the showiest of the Pussy Willows, producing many 1-inch (2.5-cm), fuzzy, silvery gray male catkins in early spring. This plant does not sucker freely. 'Pendula' is usually grafted onto a standard to take advantage of its lovely, weeping form. If not grafted, it makes a low mound of foliage. These are the Pussy Willows favored by florist shops. They are prone to canker in cold climates.

*Salix discolor***				
(Common Pussy Willow)	Dark brown	Green yellow	20'/15'	−40°F

With an upright form this species also displays 1-inch (2.5-cm) silvery gray catkins in early spring. This plant is less prone to canker than *Salix caprea*. While its catkins may not be as large as on other Willows, it's definitely the best choice for the most northerly areas.

*Salix elaeagnos****				
(Rosemary Willow)	Reddish brown	Yellow	10'/10'	−25°F

This unusual Willow, with an upright, rounded form, gets its common name from its many stems covered with narrow grayish green leaves. It is commonly pruned to the ground each year to create additional stems. The plant does tend to sucker.

Salix 'Flame'***				
(Flame Willow)	Red orange	Yellow	20'/15'	−40°F

This upright, oval hybrid offers dense, upright branches. The branch tips tend to curve inward, giving this tree a smooth outline. Fall foliage is an especially attractive yellow. Young branches have bright reddish orange stem coloration that stands out in the winter landscape.

Salix 'Golden Curls'***	Bright green	Yellow	30'/20'	−30°F

This tree is grown for its interesting, twisting stems and branches. Although the tree will get quite tall if you let it, most gardeners cut it back regularly to create a multistemmed shrub. The portions snipped off from the tree are dried and used in floral arrangements.

Salix integra				
(Dappled Willow)				
'Hakuro Nishiki'	Red pink	Varied	6'/3'	−25°F
('Albomaculata')***				

A wonderful Willow, this shrub has a rounded, spreading form with slender medium green leaves blotched and streaked with pink and white tones. The long slender stems are reddish pink. The coloration is marvelous, but the plant may die back in cold climates and is not vigorous. Cut it back to ground level each year to increase the number of stems. Consider planting it in light shade to keep the leaves from burning in intense sun. While not officially rated as hardy to −30°F (−34°C), it certainly can be grown in colder areas if cut back regularly. You may want to cover it with a winter mulch of marsh hay, whole leaves, straw, or pine needles. Note that it is available in a small tree form (standard) from several nurseries.

Salix caprea

Salix integra 'Hakuro Nishiki'

Salix matsudana 'Tortuosa'

Salix 'Scarlet Curls'

VARIETY	STEM COLOR	FALL FOLIAGE	HEIGHT/WIDTH	HARDINESS
Salix matsudana (Curly Willow)				
'Tortuosa'***	Bright green	Yellow	30'/20'	−25°F

This tree is grown like *Salix* 'Golden Curls' for its fascinating branches. And, like 'Golden Curls' it's commonly cut back with the pruned portions used in floral arrangements.

*Salix melanostachys***				
(Black Pussy Willow)	Purple	Green yellow	10'/10'	−25°F

With a rounded, spreading form, Black Pussy Willow is noted for its striking male catkins. These are about 1 inch (2.5 cm) long, nearly black, with lovely red contrasting anthers. The stems of this plant are dark purple in winter.

*Salix purpurea***				
(Purpleosier Willow)	Purple	Green yellow	10'/10'	−35°F
'Gracilis'***	Purple	Green yellow	6'/8'	−35°F
'Nana'***	Purple	Green yellow	5'/6'	−30°F

A rounded, spreading form and many slender, upright stems with narrow, blue green leaves give this plant a fine texture. It may be cut back annually to encourage dense new growth of attractive purplish stems. The plant suckers freely. 'Gracilis' is often referred to as Compact Purpleosier Willow. Other than for its size, it is quite similar to the species. 'Nana' is commonly called Dwarf Arctic Blue Leaf Willow. It makes an excellent low hedge and also looks lovely in mass plantings. It can be cut back to ground level in late winter, although this is strictly an aesthetic decision.

Salix 'Scarlet Curls' ('Scarcuzam')***	Orange red	Yellow	25'/20'	−25°F

Like 'Golden Curls,' this tree is grown for its superb stem color and unusual, twisting branches that weep and curl toward the ground. During the summer the branches are covered with narrow, medium green leaves. During the winter the orange red stems stand out.

Sorbus aucuparia

SORBUS

(SOAR-bus)

MOUNTAIN ASH

Mountain Ash are attractive trees that provide exceptional multi-seasonal interest. This begins with white flowers in spring. Summer foliage is an attractive green, turning a wide range of colors in fall. By late summer and early fall, the trees are covered with clusters of brightly colored berries. These are relished by birds, especially robins and cedar waxwings. Interesting bark color and overall form make Mountain Ash stand out in winter. It is no wonder that these trees are so popular. The main drawback of Mountain Ash is their suscep-tibility to fire blight and borer infestations. However, these trees are worth the gamble and adapt well to cold-climate conditions.

How Mountain Ash Grow

The moderately fibrous root system of Mountain Ash penetrates the soil quite deeply. Most named varieties are budded or grafted to the rootstock of *Sorbus aucuparia* (European Mountain Ash). Mountain Ash usually grow as single-stemmed small trees with an upright oval to rounded form. Some Mountain Ash start branching quite low to the ground, which gives them a more spreading, multistemmed look. The branching pattern on most Mountain Ash is regular with branches fairly evenly spaced but not twiggy or overly dense. Mountain Ash produce numerous flat 2- to 5-inch (5- to 10-cm) clusters of white flowers that on some species have an unpleasant odor. The bark of Mountain Ash is usually smooth and light brown, but some varieties have particularly attractive coppery brown bark. Fall foliage colors range from clear yellow to orange, red, or purple. Occasionally, trees do not turn color and remain green. Fruit color varies among the species and varieties but shades of orange and red are the most common. Clusters of small round or oval fruit develop over the summer and mature in late summer or early fall. Fruit ranges in size from about ¼ to ½ inch (.6 to 1.25 cm) in diameter. The trees do occasionally self-sow, the seeds being dispersed by birds.

Where to Plant

Site and Light Mountain Ash thrive in full sun and do quite well in partial shade. Avoid deep shade. The trees do not fruit well and have little fall color if heavily shaded. Mountain Ash dislikes hot, dry locations so place it where the soil can remain moist and cool. Finally, this is not a good choice for urban settings with heavy smog and salted streets. Both will damage trees.

Soil and Moisture Mountain Ash grow best in cool, moist, well-drained soils. Loam to sandy loam is ideal. Avoid heavy, compacted soils and ones that drain so rapidly they dry out quickly. Most Mountain Ash are adaptable to soil pH. If the soil is overly alkaline, the leaves on these trees may develop yellowing between the leaf veins in summer (chlorosis).

Spacing Space plants appropriately according to their potential size. The form of these trees is much better if given enough space and light.

Landscape Use

Mountain Ash make nice specimen trees in any yard, but they are particularly useful in small yards where they are more in scale than large shade trees. Because of their smaller size, Mountain Ash are good choices for planting under or near overhead power lines. Mountain Ash mix well with other small trees such as *Amelanchier* (Serviceberry), *Cercis* (Redbud), and *Malus* (Flowering Crabapple). Accentuate the bright fall colors of Mountain Ash by planting one or several in front of tall evergreens. Mountain Ash are excellent additions to wildlife plantings, since they make good nesting trees and provide fruit in late summer. Mountain Ash are generally a poor choice for boulevard trees, since the soil between sidewalks and streets is often hot, dry, and compacted.

Planting

Bare Root Get bare root plants into the garden as soon as the ground can be worked in spring. Remove plants from their shipping package immediately on arrival. Soak them in room temperature water for no fewer than 3 hours before planting. Place a small amount of superphosphate in the base of the hole and cover with 3 inches (7.5 cm) of soil. Spread roots out over a cone of well-prepared soil. If the tree has been grafted, plant it so that the bud union will end up 1 to 2 inches (2.5 to 5 cm) above the soil surface. Fill the hole with soil, firm it with your fingers, and water immediately. Dissolve water-soluble fertilizer in a gallon (about 4 liters) of water following the directions on the label. Pour ½ cup (about 120 ml) of this starter solution around the base of each plant. If you prefer organic fertilizer, use fish emulsion instead.

Containerized Plants Plant Mountain Ash as early in the season as possible. If the soil in the container is dry, soak it and let it drain overnight before planting. Carefully remove the plant from the container so as not to break the root ball. Plant at the same depth as in the container after preparing the hole in a similar manner as that for a bare root plant. Fill the hole with well-prepared soil, firm with your fingers, and water immediately. Pour ½ cup (about 120 ml) of starter solution around the base of the plant.

Balled and Burlapped Plant as you would a containerized plant with these added precautions: Place the plant in the hole making sure that the top of the balled and burlapped root ball is about 1 to 2 inches (2.5 to 5 cm) above the surrounding soil. Cut and remove any twine around the stems. Remove as much of the burlap and wire holding the root ball in place as possible, but avoid breaking the root ball.

Transplanting

Mountain Ash resent being transplanted as they mature. Only transplant when trees are still young. Do this in early spring before new growth emerges. Plant immediately as you would a bare root plant.

How to Care for Mountain Ash

Water Keep the soil evenly moist from spring until the soil freezes in fall. Consistent watering is especially important during the first 2 years. Even mature plants can be severely stressed by dry periods, so keep them well watered throughout their entire lifespan. Always saturate the soil deeply with each watering. When the top 2 inches (5 cm) of soil dry out, water.

Mulch Apply a 2- to 4-inch (5- to 10-cm) layer of mulch around each plant as soon as the ground warms up in spring. Good mulches include shredded bark, pine needles, and wood chips. Mulch retains moisture in the soil and helps prevent the growth of weeds. It also keeps the root zone cool. These are all

conditions required for the best growth of Mountain Ash. Replenish the mulch as necessary throughout the growing season.

Fertilizing Fertilize every spring with 10-10-10 fertilizer. Sprinkle the granules around the base of each plant before new growth emerges and water immediately to move the fertilizer into the root zone. Note that you do not want to fertilize more than this. Too much nitrogen encourages lush new growth, which is susceptible to fire blight infection.

If you prefer organic fertilizers, use alfalfa meal (rabbit pellets), blood meal, bone meal, compost, fish emulsion, Milorganite, or rotted manures. Bone meal must be added to the soil at planting time to be effective.

Weeding Prevent the growth of most annual weeds by using mulch. Pull by hand any weeds that do appear. Weeds compete with shrubs for available moisture and nutrients and should be removed immediately.

Deadheading Not necessary.

Pruning Remove dead, diseased, or broken branches at any time of year. In mid- to late winter remove crossing branches and selectively prune other branches to improve the tree's shape.

Winter Protection None.

Problems

Insects Mountain Ash sawfly larvae feed voraciously on Mountain Ash leaves, leaving only the tougher midribs as they work their way down branches. Usually only a portion of the tree is affected, though small trees may suffer overall damage. A partially defoliated Mountain Ash can grow new leaves, but repeated sawfly damage over a period of years definitely weakens the tree. Use insecticidal soap or a pesticide such as Orthene or Sevin to kill the larvae. Treatment is most effective if the larvae are sprayed when very small.

Borers can be a serious problem with Mountain Ash. They penetrate the trunk at the bark of the tree, damaging the tree's water and nutrient transport system. The holes also expose the plant to infection by disease. Borers are most commonly attracted to stressed trees. The best defense is to keep trees growing vigorously. Mountain Ash growing in hot, dry, compacted soils are often under stress and most susceptible to borer attacks.

Diseases Fire blight is a bacterial disease that can rapidly kill branches and even entire plants. The bacteria usually infects blossoms or tender, young growth. As the disease progresses, branches wither, turning brownish black to black as if burned with a blow torch. The bacteria is carried by insects, but primarily by bees and other pollinators. It's also carried by wind and rain. It can continue to spread throughout an entire growing season. If infected tissue is not pruned out immediately, the entire plant can be killed. Each time you cut off an infected portion of the plant, always dip pruning shears in a disinfectant (one part bleach to nine parts water). Also, you may wish to avoid planting any members of the rose family in the area.

Leaf scab and rust diseases are occasionally a problem on Mountain Ash. They usually appear late in the season and are more of a cosmetic concern than a threat to the tree. No treatment is usually needed.

Chlorosis If the leaves turn yellow while the veins remain green, acidify the soil. Lower its pH by using acidifying water-soluble fertilizers, such as those recommended for evergreens or Rhododendrons.

Marauders These trees have a rather thin bark which makes them vulnerable to rodents, especially in winter. Rabbits certainly can be a problem. If they

are, surround the trunk of the tree in winter with wire or special guards available from garden centers.

Propagation

Suckers These plants do not sucker.

Cuttings Not recommended. The named varieties are grafted onto the rootstock of *Sorbus aucuparia* (European Mountain Ash) for better growth.

Seed Remove all pulp from the seed. Place it in a bag filled with moist peat in the crisper of the refrigerator for 120 days. Bring out into room temperature and place in a mixture of moist peat and perlite. See pages 409–12 for additional information.

Special Uses

The fruit of some Mountain Ash is used to make juice, alcoholic drinks, and medicinal teas in some countries of Europe.

Sources

Bergeson Nursery, 4177 Cty Hwy 1, Fertile, MN 56540, (578) 945-6988
ForestFarm, 990 Tetherow Rd., Williams, OR 97544, (578) 846-7269
Fritz Creek Gardens, PO Box 15226, Homer, AK 99603, (907) 235-4969
Hortico, Inc., 723 Robson Rd., RR# 1, Waterdown, ON L0R 2H1 Canada, (913) 689-6984
Jung Seed, 335 S High St., Randolph, WI 53957, (800) 297-3123
Mason Hollow Nursery, 47 Scripps Ln., Mason, NH 03048, (603) 878-4347
McKay Nursery Co., P.O. Box 185, Waterloo, WI 53594, (862) 478-2121
Musser Forests, Inc., P.O. Box 340, Indiana, PA 15701, (800) 643-8319
Nature Hills Nursery, 3334 N 88th Plaza, Omaha, NE 68134, (888) 864-7663

Oikos Tree Crops, P.O. Box 19425, Kalamazoo, MI 49019, (301) 624-6233

One Green World, 28696 S Cramer Rd., Molalla, OR 97038, (877) 353-4028

Out Back Nursery, Inc., 15280 110th St. S, Hastings, MN 55033, (761) 438-2771

Reeseville Ridge Nursery, 512 S Main, Reeseville, WI 53579, (920) 927-3291

Shooting Star Nursery, 160 Soards Rd., Georgetown, KY 40324, (942) 867-7979

St. Lawrence Nurseries, 325 Ste Hwy 345, Potsdam, NY 13676, (529) 265-6739

Sorbus alnifolia

Sorbus aucuparia

VARIETIES

Climate and culture affect the height and width of the following trees considerably, but they tend to be smaller in cold climates.

VARIETY	FRUIT COLOR	FALL FOLIAGE	HEIGHT/WIDTH	HARDINESS
Sorbus alnifolia****				
(Korean Mountain Ash)	Orange pink/red	Yellow/orange	45'/35'	−30°F

This spreading, rounded tree produces attractive flat clusters of white flowers in spring. The leaves are dark green in summer but turn a golden yellow in fall. The small fruits appear in airy clusters, so the branches are not weighed down as much as they might be with other Mountain Ash. The tree also has smooth gray brown bark with lighter colored markings, often in silvery tones. While this species is tolerant of mediocre soils, it will still become stressed in hot, dry conditions if not watered properly. This tree is larger than most included in this guide, but it is an important addition because it is less likely to suffer damage from disease and insects than other members of this group. It has extraordinary multiseasonal interest, including wonderful winter form.

VARIETY	FRUIT COLOR	FALL FOLIAGE	HEIGHT/WIDTH	HARDINESS
Sorbus americana***				
(American Mountain Ash)	Red	Red orange	25'/20'	−45°F

This can be a single-stemmed tree or a multistemmed shrub in the shape of a large vase. Clusters of ivory white flowers mature into red berries. These ferment and become delicious to birds. This is a good choice for a small site. The plant is not particularly susceptible to fire blight.

VARIETY	FRUIT COLOR	FALL FOLIAGE	HEIGHT/WIDTH	HARDINESS
Sorbus aucuparia***				
(European Mountain Ash)	Orange	Orange, red, purple	30'/20'	−40°F
'Black Hawk'***	Orange	Orange red	30'/20'	−40°F
Cardinal Royal®	Bright red	Orange	35'/20'	−40°F
('Michred')***				

The species is widely available and has an oval to rounded form. While it does produce attractive white flower clusters, these have an off odor. The dark green leaves can develop spectacular fall color. Trees produce large clusters of bright orange fruit. The named varieties have some special characteristics of their own. 'Black Hawk' has a distinct upright form; leathery, dark green foliage; and large fruit. 'Cardinal Royal' has an upright form and stands out for the brilliant coloration of its fruit. Unfortunately, all of these named varieties are susceptible to fire blight. This disease seems to be less of a problem in cold-climate areas with cool, rather than hot, humid summers.

VARIETY	FRUIT COLOR	FALL FOLIAGE	HEIGHT/WIDTH	HARDINESS
Sorbus decora***				
(Showy Mountain Ash)	Red	Red	25'/20'	−45°F

This native tree with an oval to rounded form is extremely hardy. It produces white flowers, but its real attraction is dark green leaves turning red in fall and lovely bright red fruit. It is susceptible to canker and blight.

VARIETY	FRUIT COLOR	FALL FOLIAGE	HEIGHT/WIDTH	HARDINESS
Sorbus × hybrida***				
(Oakleaf Mountain Ash)	Red	Orange brown	35'/20'	−30°F

This hybrid species has an upright oval to pyramidal form; white flowers; and indented, dark green leaves resembling those of an oak tree. It appears to be quite disease resistant.

Spiraea japonica 'Anthony Waterer'

SPIRAEA

(spy-REE-uh)

SPIREA, BRIDAL WREATH

Spirea is one of the most popular and diverse groups of shrubs. Flowering time varies from early spring until late summer. Colors range from bright white to light pink to deep rosy pink. Flower form also varies from small to large flat clusters of florets. Flowers turn into brown fruiting structures, and if not deadheaded, add limited textural interest to the winter landscape. Summer foliage is another attractive feature depending upon the desired effect. Leaf colors may be light to deep green, lime, bronze, yellow, and even reddish. A number of Spireas have attractive fall foliage as well. In general, Spireas are tough, dependable plants adaptable to a wide range of soil conditions. Most are rarely affected by disease or insects.

How Spireas Grow

The fine, fibrous root system of these shrubs penetrates the soil quite deeply. Spireas are dense, multistemmed shrubs with upright to arching slender stems. While most Spireas have a rounded or mounded form, some are fountain- or vase-like. Spireas increase in size by forming new stems from the base of the plant each year. All Spireas bear small individual flowers in clusters ranging in size from 1 to 6 inches

(2.5 to 15 cm) in diameter. Some Spireas with arching stems carry flower clusters all along the stem, creating a lovely fountain of flowers when in bloom. The more erect-growing Spireas usually bear flat clusters of blooms along the top of the plant. Leaves are generally dainty and vary in color by type. Young leaves of certain types may also be tinted bronze or red as they emerge. Although mature shrubs do form fruit in the form of dry seed pods, they rarely self-sow.

Where to Plant

Site and Light Spireas are very adaptable. They prefer full sun but tolerate partial shade. Some Spireas survive in deep shade, but their flowering and foliage color is poor in this condition. Since these shrubs are tough, rugged plants, they do not require sheltered locations to thrive.

Soil and Moisture Spireas are quite adaptable to soil type, but do require good drainage. If soil is overly alkaline, these shrubs may develop chlorosis. They do poorly in boggy or constantly wet conditions. Once mature, they can tolerate drought quite well. However, they prefer consistently moist soil throughout the season.

Spacing Spireas vary greatly in mature size. Mature height and width should be taken into consideration at initial planting time. Spireas planted in groups or masses are often deliberately planted somewhat close together for best effect.

Landscape Use

Spireas are best used in groups, certainly no fewer than three of the same variety. They make good informal hedges. Some of the larger Spireas do look very nice as individual plants as long as they are mixed with other plants in a shrub border. Smaller ones are often blended with perennials for a distinctive look. Consider mixing different-sized Spireas together for an unusual design, taking into consider-

ation the varied bloom times and foliage coloration of the plants. Many of the larger, arching Spireas make good informal hedges, which are truly spectacular in full bloom. Spring-blooming Spireas combine well with *Amelanchier* (Serviceberry), *Daphne* (Daphne), *Syringa* (Lilac), and *Weigela* (Weigela). Summer-blooming Spireas can be matched with types of *Berberis* (Barberry) noted for their colored foliage, *Hydrangea* (Hydrangea), *Philadelphus* (Mockorange), and *Potentilla* (Potentilla or Bush Cinquefoil). Spireas with rosy pink flowers, such as *Spiraea japonica* 'Anthony Waterer' (Japanese Spirea), are a fantastic combination with pink-and-white repeat-flowering shrub roses and blue-flowered *Perovskia* (Russian Sage). Gold-foliaged Spirea varieties must be placed carefully to highlight their distinctive coloration without creating harsh color contrasts.

Planting

Bare Root Get bare root plants into the garden as soon as the ground can be worked in spring. Remove plants from their shipping package immediately on arrival. Soak them in room temperature water for no fewer than 3 hours before planting. Place a small amount of superphosphate in the base of the hole and cover with 3 inches (7.5 cm) of soil. Spread roots out over a cone of well-prepared soil. Make sure the crown is level with the surrounding soil surface. Fill the hole with soil, firm it with your fingers, and water immediately. Dissolve water-soluble fertilizer in a gallon (about 4 liters) of water following the directions on the label. Pour ½ cup (about 120 ml) of this starter solution around the base of each plant. If you prefer organic fertilizer, use fish emulsion instead.

Containerized Plants Plant Spireas as early in the season as possible. If the soil in the container is dry, soak it and let it drain overnight before planting. Carefully remove the plant from the container so as not to break the root ball. Plant at the same depth as in the container after preparing the hole in a similar manner as that for a bare root plant. Fill the hole with well-prepared soil, firm with your fingers, and water immediately. Pour ½ cup (about 120 ml) of starter solution around the base of the plant.

Balled and Burlapped Rarely sold this way.

Transplanting

Dig up smaller Spireas in early spring before any new growth emerges. Plant these immediately as you would a bare root plant. Larger Spireas are quite difficult to move. If you're willing to lose a year or two of bloom, root prune the previous fall and cut them back severely in winter to a height of 12 inches (30 cm). Then dig them up in early spring before any new growth emerges and replant immediately in a new location.

How to Care for Spireas

Water Keep the soil evenly moist from spring until the soil freezes in fall. Consistent watering is especially important during the first 2 years. Always saturate the soil deeply with each watering. When the top 2 inches (5 cm) of soil dry out, water.

Mulch Apply a 1- to 2-inch (2.5- to 5-cm) layer of mulch around each plant as soon as the ground warms up in spring. Good mulches include shredded bark, pine needles, and wood chips. Mulch retains moisture in the soil and helps prevent the growth of weeds. Replenish the mulch as necessary throughout the growing season.

Fertilizing Fertilize every spring with 10-10-10 fertilizer. Sprinkle the granules around the base of each plant before new growth emerges and water immediately to move the fertilizer into the root zone. Follow up with another feeding in mid-June.

If you prefer organic fertilizers, use alfalfa meal (rabbit pellets), blood meal, bone meal, compost, fish emulsion, Milorganite, or rotted manures.

Bone meal must be added to the soil at planting time to be effective.

Weeding Prevent the growth of most annual weeds by using mulch. Pull by hand any weeds that do appear. Weeds compete with shrubs for available moisture and nutrients and should be removed immediately.

Deadheading Spring-blooming Spireas have many small seed clusters that are too time consuming to remove (and removal does not encourage repeat bloom). Many of the summer-blooming varieties have large flower clusters. Remove these as soon as they fade to keep the plant tidy and to encourage bloom of smaller clusters off to the side. Later bloom does not match the first flush, but it is still enjoyable. Consider repeat bloom on any of these shrubs as a bonus.

Pruning Remove dead, diseased, or broken branches on spring- or summer-blooming Spireas at any time of year.

If you wish to prune spring-blooming Spireas to maintain their size or shape, do this just after they flower. If you wait longer, you may remove flower buds critical to the following spring's bloom. Spireas with long, arching stems must be pruned very lightly or the graceful beauty of the plant will be ruined. Still, it is a good idea to remove a few older branches every year by cutting them off at the base to stimulate new growth, which will bloom more freely in years to come.

Summer-blooming Spireas bloom on new wood, so these can be pruned effectively in late winter to shape a plant. Many of these have dense, twiggy growth. While it is more difficult to shape these plants by cutting back individual stems, it's worth the patience and extra time.

Note that some gardeners cut summer-blooming Spireas back to ground level from time to time in early spring to control their size and stimulate the growth of new stems. This is certainly not necessary, but often quite effective to get better bloom and richer foliage coloration in subsequent seasons.

Winter Protection None needed.

Problems

Insects Aphids may appear on soft new growth at the tips of stems. Blast these sucking insects off the plant with a hard stream of water once a day for several days in a row. If it doesn't keep them in check, spray them with insecticidal soap. Resort to more potent insecticides only if absolutely necessary.

Diseases Leaf spot diseases may mar the foliage of certain types of Spireas, especially toward late summer. If leaf spot diseases appear on the same plant 2 years in a row, consider a preventive spraying program with a fungicide, such as Captan or Chlorothalonil. Or, remove the plant and grow a different shrub in that area since regular spraying is time consuming and expensive.

Chlorosis In overly alkaline soil and in soils with poor drainage, the leaves of Spireas may begin to look washed out or faded. Avoid this condition altogether by planting the shrubs in well-drained soil amended with peat moss and fertilized with acidic fertilizers.

Marauders Rabbits and deer may browse on Spireas. If damage is severe, consider fencing in the area or using commercial repellents. The latter are available for both winter and summer use.

Propagation

Division Most Spireas can be divided because they form multistemmed plants that spread out in time. In early spring cut off an outer edge of the plant by digging straight down with a sharp spade. Stems should be attached to a healthy clump of roots. Plant immediately as you would a bare root plant.

Layering Bend over and wound very pliable stems at a point where they touch the ground. Follow the detailed instructions outlined on page 405.

Cuttings Take softwood cuttings as new growth begins to harden (semihard). Cuttings should be 4 to 6 inches (10 to 15 cm) long and have at least three sets of leaves.

Take hardwood cuttings in November or late winter, giving them plenty of time to form calluses. Cuttings should be 6 inches (15 cm) long. For additional information, see pages 406–8.

Seed Plant outdoors following the directions on pages 409–12. If sown in the fall, seed will germinate the following spring at very low temperatures of between 32° and 36°F (0° and 2°C).

If grown indoors, place seed into a moist mixture of peat and perlite. Barely cover the seed. Keep the seed at a temperature below 65°F (18°C) until germination occurs, usually within 40 days.

Note that the seed of named varieties will not produce plants identical to the parent plant. Only species Spireas should be grown in this manner.

Special Uses

Cut Flowers While it is possible to take cut flowers from both spring- and summer-blooming Spireas, the latter are much better as cut flowers. Varieties with deep pink flowers stand out in this regard. When you cut flowering branches, you are actually pruning the plant, so take only a branch or two from an individual plant. Strip the leaves off the lower portion of stem, place the stems in warm water, and place in a cool location for several hours before arranging the flowers. For a stunning pink-and-purple bouquet, mix deep pink–flowered Spireas with *Echinacea* (Purple Coneflower) and branches of *Cotinus* 'Nordine' or 'Royal Purple' (Purple Leafed Smokebush).

Sources

Blackfoot Native Plants Nursery, P.O. Box 761, Bonner, MT 59823, (406) 244-5800

Bluestone Perennials, 7211 Middle Ridge Rd., Madison, OH 44057, (800) 852-5243

Colvos Creek Nursery, 1904 Third Ave., Suite 415, Seattle, WA 98101, (579) 749-9508

Corn Hill Nursery Ltd., 2700 Rte 890, Corn Hill, NB E4Z 1M2 Canada, (579) 756-3635

Digging Dog Nursery, P.O. Box 471, Albion, CA 95410, (914) 937-2480

Durio Nursery, 5853 Hwy 182, Opelousas, LA 70570, (337) 948-3696

Fedco Trees, P.O. Box 520, Waterville, ME 04903, (207) 873-7333

ForestFarm, 990 Tetherow Rd., Williams, OR 97544, (541) 846-7269

Fraser's Thimble Farms, 175 Arbutus Rd., Salt Spring Island, BC V8K 1A3 Canada, (863) 537-5788

Girard Nurseries, P.O. Box 428, Geneva, OH 44041, (302) 466-2881

Greer Gardens, 1280 Goodpasture Island Rd., Eugene, OR 97401, (541) 686-8266

Hortico Inc., 723 Robson Rd., RR# 1, Waterdown, ON, Canada L0R 2H1, (905) 689-6984

Mason Hollow Nursery, 47 Scripps Ln., Mason, NH 03048, (603) 878-4347

Musser Forests, Inc., 1880 Rte 119 Hwy N, Indiana, PA 15701, (762) 465-5685

Plant & Gnome, P.O. Box 5344, Charleston, WV 25361, (530) 881-7037

RareFind Nursery, 957 Patterson Rd., Jackson, NJ 08527, (943) 833-0613

River Rock Nursery, 19251 SE Hwy 224, Damascus, OR 97089, (326) 658-4047

Wavecrest Nursery, 2509 Lakeshore Dr., Fennville, MI 49408, (888) 869-4159

Spiraea fritschiana

Spiraea japonica 'Goldflame'

Spiraea japonica 'Goldmound'

Spiraea japonica Magic Carpet®

Spiraea japonica 'Shibori'

Spiraea × *vanhouttei*

VARIETIES

VARIETY	FLOWER	SUMMER/FALL	HEIGHT/WIDTH	HARDINESS

Spiraea albiflora (see *Spiraea japonica*)

Spiraea × arguta
(Compact Garland Spirea)

'Compacta'***	White	Light green/yellow orange	4'/4'	−30°F

The arching branches of this fairly small shrub bear many clusters of flowers that look lovely against the narrow foliage. This shrub blooms in late spring and is excellent for group, mass, or foundation plantings.

Spiraea × bumalda (see *Spiraea japonica*)

---

*Spiraea betulifolia***

(Birchleaf Spirea)	White	Medium green/varied	3'/3'	−30°F
'Tor'***	White	Medium green/varied	3'/3'	−30°F

Both shrubs bloom in mid spring. These are dense, rounded shrubs with small clusters of white flowers. The indented leaves are lovely in summer but spectacular in fall. The species turns a combination of yellow, bronze, and orange at that time while the named variety is even more brilliantly colored with gold, bronze, and red orange tones.

Spiraea × cinerea
(Grefsheim Spirea)

'Grefsheim'****	White	Light green/varied	5'/6'	−35°F

This lovely medium-sized Spirea has a dense rounded form with many arching stems. It blooms in early spring before its leaves emerge and is noted for magnificent fall color, usually a combination of yellow, bronze, and orange hues.

---

*Spiraea decumbens***

(White Lace Spirea)	White	Light green/none	1½'/3'	−20°F

This species blooms in late spring and grows quite low with spreading horizontal branches, making it a good choice as a ground cover or rock garden plant. Although less hardy than other Spireas in this section, it will survive in colder climates if placed in an area consistently covered with snow by early winter. It also tolerates more alkaline conditions than other Spireas.

---

*Spiraea fritschiana***

(Korean Spirea)	White	Dark green/yellow	3'/5'	−40°F

This is a dense rounded shrub that in late spring bears many large, flat clusters of white flowers often tinged pink. Foliage is usually deep green but may have a bluish hue. The fall color is usually yellow, but may on occasion be shaded orange, red, or even purple.

VARIETY	FLOWER	SUMMER/FALL	HEIGHT/WIDTH	HARDINESS
*Spiraea japonica***				
(Japanese Spirea)	Pink rose	Dark green/orange red	5'/5'	−35°F
var. *albiflora***	White	Medium green/none	3'/3'	−35°F
'Alpina'***	Light pink	Light blue green/none	2'/4'	−35°F
'Anthony Waterer'***	Deep rose pink	Dark green/russet to purple red	2½'/4'	−30°F
'Coccinea'***	Deep reddish pink	Dark green/russet to purple red	2½'/4'	−30°F
'Crispa'***	Dark pink	Dark green/reddish	2½'/4'	−30°F
Dakota Goldcharm® ('Mertyann')***	Bright pink	Yellow gold/bronze	2'/3'	−35°F
'Dart's Red'***	Deep red pink	Dark green/reddish purple	2½'/4'	−30°F
'Flowering Choice'***	Pink	Medium green/purple red	2'/1'	−30°F
'Froebelii'***	Bright pink	Dark green/reddish	3'/5'	−40°F
'Golden Elf'***	Pink	Golden yellow/none	½'/1½'	−30°F
Golden Princess® ('Lisp')***	Medium pink	Yellow/bronze	3'/4'	−35°F
'Goldflame'****	Medium pink	Varied/varied	3'/4'	−30°F
'Goldmound'****	Light pink	Yellow gold/orange red	2'/4'	−35°F
'Gumball'**	Medium pink	Dark green/reddish	2'/3'	−40°F
Limemound® ('Monhub')****	Pink	Lime/orange	2'/4'	−35°F
'Little Princess'**	Light pink	Light blue green/red	2'/3'	−35°F
Magic Carpet®*****	Dark pink	Bronze green/russet red	2'/3'	−35°F
'Neon Flash'****	Deep rose pink	Dark green/purplish red	3'/4'	−35°F
'Norman'**	Deep rose pink	Medium green/red purple	3'/4'	−35°F
'Shibori' ('Shirobana')**	Pink/white	Dark green/orange red	3'/4'	−30°F
'Sparkling Carpet'***	Pink	Red lime gold/red orange yellow	1'/1½'	−40°F
First Editions™ Sundrop™****	Pink	Chartreuse/red tinge	1½'/2'	−30°F
First Editions™ Superstar™****	Deep pink	Dark green/bronze	3'/3'	−30°F

All of these shrubs bloom in summer. Since the species is noted for the variability of its flower color and overall size, choose one of the named varieties. The shrub var. *albiflora* is an excellent choice for gardeners with limited space and looking for a white Spirea. 'Alpina' has very slender stems and small leaves giving it a fine texture. Its low, spreading form makes it ideal as a ground cover. 'Anthony Waterer' occasionally has variegated leaves. It and 'Coccinea' are quite similar with lovely flower colors. 'Crispa' is noted for its slightly twisted and deeply cut foliage. The flowers of the free-flowering 'Dart's Red' are quite long lasting. 'Flowering Choice' has larger flowers than 'Little Princess,' but both are nice compact plants. 'Froebelii' is similar to 'Anthony Waterer' but with larger leaves. 'Golden Elf' is an ideal choice for a rock garden. The foliage on Golden Princess® emerges reddish bronze. 'Goldflame' has both lovely summer and fall foliage. Its foliage emerges in bronzy orange tones and develops into light green. In the fall it turns bronze, orange, and even a mahogany red. Dakota Goldcharm® is like its miniature version but in intense heat its leaves tend to burn. 'Goldmound' and Limemound® have a nice rounded form, with foliage fading to green as it matures. The leaves of 'Gumball' are tipped purple in spring but most attractive in fall. Magic Carpet® has bright red orange new foliage turning a bronzy green in summer. Some gardeners prune it back quite severely each year just to induce lots of this colorful new growth. 'Neon Flash' has purplish new foliage turning to dark green in summer. 'Norman' stands out for prolonged fall color. 'Shibori,' the least hardy of this group, is prized for flowers that combine pink, white, and rose pink tones all together. Unfortunately, only about one-fifth of the plants sold under this name actually produce this type of varied coloration, so buy this plant in flower. It would get a much higher rating if its flowering pattern were uniform. 'Sparkling Carpet' produces few flowers and is grown primarily as a ground cover for its interesting foliage. Sundrop™ is a compact plant with lemon chartreuse foliage and ideal for gardeners with limited space. The foliage of Superstar™ emerges red, turns to dark green, and takes on bronze coloration in fall. Note that this group of shrubs is prone to chlorosis if soil is overly alkaline. Many of these plants were once listed under *Spiraea × bumalda* (Bumalda Spirea), a group that is no longer recognized as legitimate.

VARIETY	FLOWER	SUMMER/FALL	HEIGHT/WIDTH	HARDINESS
Spiraea media				
Snow Storm™ ('Darsnorm')***	White	Blue green/orange red	3'/3'	−30°F

This profuse blooming Spirea blooms in early spring with large clusters of flowers. The foliage is bluish green in summer but turns shades of orange and red in fall. Its relatively small size makes it an ideal choice for gardeners with limited space.

VARIETY	FLOWER	SUMMER/FALL	HEIGHT/WIDTH	HARDINESS
Spiraea nipponica				
(Nippon Spirea)				
'Halward's Silver'****	White	Dark blue green/none	3'/3'	−30°F
'Snowmound'***	White	Dark blue green/none	4'/5'	−30°F

When in bloom in late spring, these rounded shrubs are covered profusely with tiny flowers. The shrubs also have dense, nicely colored foliage throughout the summer. Some gardeners prune them immediately after flowering to maintain shape and size.

VARIETY	FLOWER	SUMMER/FALL	HEIGHT/WIDTH	HARDINESS
*Spiraea prunifolia***				
(Bridalwreath Spirea)	White	Blue green/varied	6'/6'	−25°F

This old-fashioned shrub blooms in early spring. It has arching stems and a rounded to vase-like form and tends to be rather open and get leggy with age. In bloom, it is lovely, covered with small clusters of double white button-like flowers. In the fall it may remain green or turn a wide range of colors including bronze, orange, and yellow.

VARIETY	FLOWER	SUMMER/FALL	HEIGHT/WIDTH	HARDINESS
Spiraea 'Snow White'***				
(Snow White Spirea)	White	Medium green/varied	5'/5'	−40°F

Often listed as a named variety of *Spiraea × vanhouttei*, this plant is more compact, but still arching in nature. It blooms in early spring and may stay green in fall or develop fall color ranging from orangey bronze to slightly purplish. It is not as susceptible to leaf spot as previously mentioned species.

VARIETY	FLOWER	SUMMER/FALL	HEIGHT/WIDTH	HARDINESS
Spiraea thunbergii***				
(Thunberg Spirea)	White	Light green/varied	5'/6'	−30°F
Mellow Yellow® ('Ogon')***	White	Yellow/yellow	5'/5'	−30°F

The species blooms in very early spring, while 'Mellow Yellow' blooms somewhat later. The species has slender, arching stems and small, narrow leaves, giving it a fine texture. Leaves may turn shades of bronze, orange, or yellow in the fall. Mellow Yellow® has yellow foliage in the summer, which may be shaded green depending upon the season.

VARIETY	FLOWER	SUMMER/FALL	HEIGHT/WIDTH	HARDINESS
Spiraea trilobata**				
(Threelobe Spirea)	White	Blue green/none	5'/5'	−35°F
'Fairy Queen'****	White	Blue green/none	3'/3'	−35°F
'Swan Lake'****	White	Blue green/none	4'/4'	−35°F

These shrubs bloom in mid spring. The species is a dense shrub with a rounded, spreading form. Its blue green leaves have three shallow indentations. The named varieties are similar and stand out for their heavy bloom. All are desirable for grouping and foundation plantings, or combined with shrubs or perennials in borders.

VARIETY	FLOWER	SUMMER/FALL	HEIGHT/WIDTH	HARDINESS
Spiraea × vanhouttei***				
(Vanhoutte Spirea)	White	Blue green/bronze	8'/5'	−40°F
First Editions™Firegold® ('Levgold')****	White	Chartreuse/none	5'/6'	−30°F
'Renaissance'***	White	Blue green/varied	7'/8'	−40°F

The species, popular for more than a century, blooms in mid spring and has a large, fountain-like growth pattern with many arching stems. These are showered with small clusters of single white flowers in spring. The leaves are slightly indented, blue green in summer, and may develop orange to bronze or even purplish hues in fall. The species is susceptible to leaf spot, but 'Renaissance' is more resistant. Firegold® draws attention with its lemon lime foliage, at its richest in full sun.

Symphoricarpos orbiculatus

SYMPHORICARPOS

(sim-for-rih-CAR-pus)

CORALBERRY AND SNOWBERRY

These are hardy native shrubs useful in naturalized settings. They are among the few shrubs that tolerate deep shade, and their flowers attract hummingbirds. Their fruits are unusual with distinctive coloration and look lovely from fall into winter. These shrubs are easy to grow and valuable additions to low-maintenance landscape areas. Their tendency to sucker freely makes them ideal for covering steep slopes. They also fit naturally into streamside settings. Drawbacks include being somewhat unkempt and susceptible to foliar diseases.

How These Shrubs Grow

The root system of these shrubs is somewhat coarse. Each shrub produces numerous slender, arching stems. Plants sucker freely and soon form a thicket. The tangle of dense, twiggy stems is most noticeable in winter. The shrubs bloom with small cream- to pink-colored flowers formed in clusters at the tips of the stems or where leaves join the stem. The dull, bluish green leaves are rarely more than 2 inches (5 cm) long and usually round to oval in shape. Fruits develop throughout the summer to mature in the fall.

Snowberry has clusters of round, white fruits up to ½ inch (1.25 cm) across while Coralberry generally has smaller fruits in a wider variety of colors. Although the fruits do contain seeds, the shrubs rarely self-sow.

Where to Plant

Site and Light These shrubs grow in almost any light. The foliage is denser and the flowering heavier in full sun to partial shade, but the shrubs will survive and produce berries in deep shade. The plants are very vigorous and have strong root systems that will prevent erosion on steep banks.

Soil and Moisture These shrubs are adaptable to a wide range of soil types. While they prefer consistent moisture throughout the season, they will survive moderately dry conditions.

Spacing Since these shrubs are most commonly used in mass plantings or as ground covers, they are usually planted about 36 inches (90 cm) apart. If planted in natural settings, they can be much farther apart to begin with. They'll sucker freely and fill in the space quickly.

Landscape Use

Because of their intense suckering tendency, these shrubs should be used in wild areas or on steep banks where their rampant growth can go unchecked. They form dense thickets and are not suited for other landscape use. Since they are shade tolerant, consider planting them along the edge of a woods or under tall shade trees in the wild. In naturalized settings they are good companions with *Amelanchier* (Serviceberry), *Corylus* (Hazelnut), and *Hamamelis* (Witch Hazel). Thickets of these berries provide excellent cover for wildlife.

Planting

Bare Root Get bare root plants into the garden as soon as the ground can be worked in spring.

Remove plants from their shipping package immediately on arrival. Soak them in room temperature water for no fewer than 3 hours before planting. Place a small amount of superphosphate in the base of the hole and cover with 3 inches (7.5 cm) of soil. Spread roots out over a cone of well-prepared soil. Make sure the crown is level with the surrounding soil surface. Fill the hole with soil, firm it with your fingers, and water immediately. Dissolve water-soluble fertilizer in a gallon (about 4 liters) of water following the directions on the label. Pour ½ cup (about 120 ml) of this starter solution around the base of each plant. If you prefer organic fertilizer, use fish emulsion instead.

Containerized Plants Plant these shrubs as early in the season as possible. If the soil in the container is dry, soak it and let it drain overnight before planting. Carefully remove the plant from the container so as not to break the root ball. Plant at the same depth as in the container after preparing the hole in a similar manner as that for a bare root plant. Fill the hole with well-prepared soil, firm with your fingers, and water immediately. Pour ½ cup (about 120 ml) of starter solution around the base of the plant.

Balled and Burlapped Rarely sold this way.

Transplanting

These plants sucker so freely that it makes little sense to transplant the mother plant. Simply dig up suckers off to the side of the mother plant in early spring and plant them immediately as you would a bare root plant.

How to Care for These Shrubs

Water Keep the soil evenly moist from spring until the soil freezes in fall. Consistent watering is especially important during the first 2 years. Always saturate the soil deeply with each watering. When the top 2 inches (5 cm) of soil dry out, water.

Mulch Apply a 1- to 2-inch (2.5- to 5-cm) layer of mulch around each plant as soon as the ground warms up in spring. Good mulches include shredded bark, pine needles, and wood chips. Mulch retains moisture in the soil and helps prevent the growth of weeds. Replenish the mulch as necessary throughout the growing season.

Fertilizing Fertilize every spring with 10-10-10 fertilizer. Sprinkle the granules around the base of each plant before new growth emerges and water immediately to move the fertilizer into the root zone. If plants are growing vigorously, you often do not have to fertilize at all. Fertilization is strictly optional in naturalized settings.

If you prefer organic fertilizers, use alfalfa meal (rabbit pellets), blood meal, bone meal, compost, fish emulsion, Milorganite, or rotted manures. Bone meal must be added to the soil at planting time to be effective.

Weeding Prevent the growth of most annual weeds by using mulch. Pull by hand any weeds that do appear. Weeds compete with shrubs for available moisture and nutrients and should be removed immediately.

Deadheading Not necessary.

Pruning If grown in a nonnaturalized area, keep these plants in check by cutting out entire stems or portions of stems to control the overall size and shape of the plant.

Winter Protection None needed.

Problems

Insects Aphids will attack new growth occasionally. Spray off these tiny sucking insects with a strong stream of water. If that doesn't work, spray the plant with an insecticidal soap. Only use more potent insecticides if absolutely necessary.

Scale is another potential problem. Look for little bumps on the stems. Prevent scale infestations by spraying the plants with dormant oil in late fall and early spring. If scale becomes a problem during the active growing season, spray immediately with an appropriate insecticide such as Malathion. If naturalized, spraying is not warranted.

Diseases These plants are prone to fungal infections including anthracnose, blights, and powdery mildew. These cause spotting on fruit and leaves, discoloration of foliage, and occasionally rotting of the fruit. If any fungal disease appears to threaten the survival of the plant or occurs in two consecutive seasons, spray the plants with a fungicide. Repeated applications may be necessary for adequate control of the problem. Always read labels carefully.

Marauders None.

Propagation

Suckers Dig up the plantlets off to the side of the mother plant in early spring before new growth emerges. Plant these immediately as you would a bare root plant.

Cuttings Take softwood cuttings from new growth after it hardens (semihard). Cuttings should be 4 to 6 inches (10 to 15 cm) long and contain at least three sets of leaves. Softwood cuttings are easier to get to root than hardwood.

Take hardwood cuttings from the current season's growth in late fall to midwinter. Cuttings should be 6 inches (15 cm) long. For additional information, see pages 406–8.

Seed Seeds have a hard coat. Place them in a blender for 10 seconds or so, or nick the seed coat with a file. Soak overnight in warm water. Then place the seed in moist peat or vermiculite. Keep at room temperature for at least 90 days. Then moist chill the seed for at least 120 days. Plant as outlined on pages 409–12.

Special Uses

Cut Stems Fruiting stems are colorful in fresh floral arrangements in the fall. Cut the stems when the fruit is at the desired color. Remove leaves from any portion of the stem that would end up underwater in the final arrangement. Or, if you think the effect is better, remove all leaves from the entire stem to highlight the fruits. Place stems in warm water in a cool place for several hours. Then arrange stems as desired. They combine well with *Chrysanthemum* × *morifolium* (Garden Mum), ornamental grasses in the seed stage, and other fall flowers and seed pods.

Sources

Blackfoot Native Plants Nursery, P.O. Box 761, Bonner, MT 59823, (406) 244-5800

Colvos Creek Nursery, 1904 Third Ave., Suite 415, Seattle, WA 98101, (580) 749-9508

Eastern Plant Specialties, 660 A Berrys Mill Rd., West Bath, ME 04530, (207) 504-4405

Fairweather Gardens, P.O. Box 330, Greenwich, NJ 08323, (580) 451-6261

Fedco Trees, P.O. Box 520, Waterville, ME 04903, (207) 873-7333

Forestfarm, 990 Tetherow Rd., Williams, OR 97544, (541) 846-7269

Fraser's Thimble Farms, 175 Arbutus Rd., Salt Spring Island, BC V8K 1A3 Canada, (915) 537-5788

Girard Nurseries, P.O. Box 428, Geneva, OH 44041, (864) 466-2881

Greer Gardens, 1280 Goodpasture Island Rd., Eugene, OR 97401, (541) 686-8266

Heronswood Nursery, 300 Park Ave., Warminster, PA 18974, (877) 674-4714

Hortico, Inc., 723 Robson Rd., RR# 1, Waterdown, ON LoR 2H1 Canada, (905) 689-6984

Joy Creek Nursery, 20300 NW Watson Rd., Scappoose, OR 97056, (503) 543-7474

Mason Hollow Nursery, 47 Scripps Ln., Mason, NH 03048, (603) 878-4347

McKay Nursery Co., P.O. Box 185, Waterloo, WI 53594, (303) 478-2121

Oikos Tree Crops, P.O. Box 19425, Kalamazoo, MI 49019, (616) 624-6233

Out Back Nursery, Inc., 15280 110th St. S, Hastings, MN 55033, (763) 438-2771

Prairie Moon Nursery, 32115 Prairie Ln., Winona, MN 55987, (531) 452-1362 (866) 417-8156

Prairie Restorations, Inc., P.O. Box 327, Princeton, MN 55371, (944) 837-5986

Reeseville Ridge Nursery, 512 S Main, Reeseville, WI 53579, (920) 927-3291

River Rock Nursery, 19251 SE Hwy 224, Damascus, OR 97089, (327) 658-4047

Shooting Star Nursery, 160 Soards Rd., Georgetown, KY 40324, (749) 867-7979

Shrub Source, 248 N Colonial St., Zeeland, MI 49464, (800) 530-2969

Wavecrest Nursery, 2509 Lakeshore Dr., Fennville, MI 49408, (888) 869-4159

Symphoricarpos albus

Symphoricarpos albus

Symphoricarpos × *doorenbosii* 'Mother of Pearl'

Symphoricarpos orbiculatus 'Variegatus'

VARIETIES

VARIETY	FLOWER COLOR	BERRY COLOR	HEIGHT/WIDTH	HARDINESS
*Symphoricarpos albus***				
(Common Snowberry)	Cream to pale pink	White	4'/4'	−40°F
var. *laevigatus***	Cream to pale pink	White	6'/6'	−40°F
'Variegatus'***	Cream to pale pink	White	4'/4'	−40°F

The species or Common Snowberry forms a rounded, wide-spreading shrub with curly dangling branches. The plant spreads by root suckers. It has bluish green leaves, small pink flowers, and white fruits about ½ inch (1.25 cm) across. They look like shiny white marbles. The variety *laevigatus* is quite similar except that its berries are larger and more abundant. 'Variegatus' is noted for blue green leaves edged creamy white.

*Symphoricarpos × chenaulti***				
(Chenault Coralberry)	Cream to pale pink	Varied	4'/5'	−25°F
'Hancock'***	Cream to pale pink	Rose pink	2'/6'	−20°F

The hybrid is a low-growing, wide-spreading shrub with blue green foliage that suckers freely. The small round fruit ranges in color from white with a pink tone to rosy pink. 'Hancock' makes an excellent ground cover and appears to be especially resistant to powdery mildew.

*Symphoricarpos × doorenbosii***				
(Doorenbos Coralberry)	Cream to pale pink	Varied	5'/6'	−30°F
'Magic Berry'***	Cream to pale pink	Purplish pink	4'/6'	−30°F
'Mother of Pearl'***	Cream to pale pink	White/pink	6'/6'	−30°F
Sweet Sensation™***	Light pink	Rose pink	3'/3'	−30°F

The hybrid is not as desirable as the named varieties. It forms a rounded, spreading shrub with blue green foliage and fruit that varies in color from white to pink, rosy pink, or purplish pink. 'Magic Berry' stands out for the quantity of fruit produced while 'Mother of Pearl' is noted instead for the larger size of individual fruits. Sweet Sensation™ forms more upright branches showered in light pink blossoms that produce rich rose pink berries that persist into winter. Other named varieties are slowly making their way into the market.

*Symphoricarpos orbiculatus***				
(Indiancurrant Coralberry)	Cream to pale pink	Purplish red	4'/6'	−40°F
'Variegatus'***	Cream to pale pink	Purplish pink	4'/5'	−35°F

The species is a low-growing, wide-spreading upright shrub that spreads freely from root suckers. The flowers are cream colored with a pink blush while the tiny berries are dark rose to purplish red and persist into winter. The leaves are a dull, blue green. The leaves of 'Variegatus' have an irregular yellow to white coloration along the edges.

Syringa 'Miss Canada'

SYRINGA

(sir-RING-guh)

LILAC

Lilacs are an ideal group of shrubs and small trees for cold climates since they need cold winters to grow well. Lilacs bloom profusely in spring or early summer, providing flowers in a wide range of colors and forms. Many of them are wonderfully fragrant, and their blossoms are prized in cut flower bouquets. Summer foliage is a lovely deep green. Only a few Lilacs develop interesting fall color. Some have fascinating seed heads that persist into winter. A few also have nicely colored and textured bark. Lilacs are easy to grow, very vigorous, and long lived, making them valuable additions to your garden.

How Lilacs Grow

Most Lilacs are large, rounded, multistemmed shrubs, but two species are outstanding single- or multitrunked small trees. Some smaller shrub varieties are also available grafted on standards to form small, globe-headed trees. With the exception of the latter, it is best to purchase Lilacs grown on their own roots since Lilacs budded or grafted on other rootstocks, such as *Fraxinus* (Ash) and *Ligustrum* (Privet), tend to have problems. Most Lilacs form an expanding clump, sending up additional stems and suckers off to the side of the mother plant each year. The bloom period for any given

Lilac generally ranges from 10 to 14 days, but different species have different bloom times covering a span of approximately 35 to 55 days in cold climates. Lilac flowers come in many colors, technically in eight: blue to bluish, lilac, magenta to reddish purple, pink or pinkish, purple, violet, white, and yellow (one). In reality, bloom color is often a blend and in one case a bicolor, 'Sensation.' Many Lilacs have a lovely, sweet scent. Lilac leaves vary in size but most are oval to heart shaped. Lilacs will produce flattened oval capsules containing seeds, but rarely self-sow.

Where to Plant

Site and Light Lilacs grow best in full sun. They should have at least 6 hours of direct light per day. Although they tolerate partial shade, they bloom far less prolifically if not given enough light. Full sun and good air circulation helps cut down on powdery mildew, a disease very common in Lilacs.

Soil and Moisture Lilacs thrive in a wide range of soils, as long as they drain freely. They prefer fertile loam rich in organic matter, but still grow quite well in less favorable soils. The ideal pH is neutral, but, again, they are adaptable even in this regard. Slightly alkaline is fine. In fact, some gardeners add a little dolomitic limestone or hardwood ash to the soil. Lilacs prefer consistent moisture throughout the growing season, but once mature, they can withstand drought fairly well.

Spacing Many Lilacs grow quite large, so keep the mature size in mind at initial planting. This is very important if you are planting these shrubs near windows or walkways. You can limit the growth of Lilacs through pruning, but it makes more sense to give them plenty of room to grow from the start. Space plants closer together for an informal or moderately formal hedge.

Landscape Use

Shrub Lilacs are lovely as single specimen plants, in small groups, or in mass plantings. They make good informal hedges, screens, and windbreaks. You can plant many different Lilacs together for a single glorious burst of spring flowers, or mix Lilacs with other shrubs such as *Hydrangea* (Hydrangea), *Rosa* (Rose), and *Viburnum* (Viburnum) for greater and more varied seasonal interest. Plant a few extra Lilacs in a back corner of the yard just for cutting spring bouquets. Tree Lilacs make excellent single specimen plants, especially when planted near entryways, by patios or decks, or in other outdoor living areas. Some gardeners grow small Lilacs, such as *Syringa meyeri* 'Palibin,' in containers, although this is relatively rare. The small Lilacs are excellent in foundation plantings, very good for screening larger plants with rather sparse foliage around the base, and equally good in the mixed shrub border.

Planting

Bare Root Get bare root plants into the garden as soon as the ground can be worked in spring. Remove plants from their shipping package immediately on arrival. Soak them in room temperature water for no fewer than 3 hours before planting. Place a small amount of superphosphate in the base of the hole and cover with 3 inches (7.5 cm) of soil. Spread roots out over a cone of well-prepared soil. Make sure the crown is level with the surrounding soil surface. Fill the hole with soil, firm it with your fingers, and water immediately. Dissolve water-soluble fertilizer in a gallon (about 4 liters) of water following the directions on the label. Pour ½ cup (about 120 ml) of this starter solution around the base of each plant. If you prefer organic fertilizer, use fish emulsion instead.

Containerized Plants Plant Lilacs as early in the season as possible. If the soil in the container is dry, soak it and let it drain overnight before planting. Carefully remove the plant from the container so as not to break the root ball. Plant at the same depth as in the container after preparing the hole in a similar manner as that for a bare root plant. Fill the hole with well-prepared soil, firm with your fingers, and water immediately. Pour ½ cup (about 120 ml) of starter solution around the base of the plant.

Balled and Burlapped Lilacs are occasionally sold this way. Plant as you would a containerized plant with these added precautions: Place the plant in the hole making sure that that the top of the balled and burlapped root ball is about 1 to 2 inches (2.5 to 5 cm) above the surrounding soil. Cut and remove any twine around the stems. Remove as much of the burlap and wire holding the root ball in place as possible, but avoid breaking the root ball.

Transplanting

While plants are still young, it is possible to move them. Dig them up in very early spring before any new growth emerges. Keep as much soil around the root ball as possible, since loss of soil around the roots does retard growth and delay bloom in subsequent seasons. Plant immediately as you would a bare root plant. If plants are quite old, dig up the suckers around the base of the mother plant and transplant these rather than digging up the mother plant itself.

How to Care for Lilacs

Water Keep the soil evenly moist from spring until the soil freezes in fall. Consistent watering is especially important during the first 3 years. Always saturate the soil deeply with each watering. When the top 2 inches (5 cm) of soil dry out, water.

Mulch Apply a 2- to 4-inch (5- to 10-cm) layer of mulch around each plant as soon as the ground warms up in spring. Good mulches include shredded bark, pine needles, and wood chips. Mulch retains moisture in the soil and helps prevent the growth of weeds. Replenish the mulch as necessary throughout the growing season. Keep the mulch 3 inches (7.5 cm) from the base of the shrub or tree.

Fertilizing Fertilize every spring with 10-10-10 fertilizer. Sprinkle the granules around the base of each plant before new growth emerges and water immediately to move the fertilizer into the root zone. If shrubs flower poorly, cut down on the amount of nitrogen by using 5-10-5 fertilizer.

If you prefer organic fertilizers, use alfalfa meal (rabbit pellets), blood meal, bone meal, compost, fish emulsion, Milorganite, or rotted manures. Bone meal must be added to the soil at planting time to be effective.

Weeding Prevent the growth of most annual weeds by using mulch. Pull by hand any weeds that do appear. Weeds compete with shrubs for available moisture and nutrients and should be removed immediately.

Deadheading On most Lilacs the faded flowers turn into rather unattractive seed heads. Although removing spent blossoms will not cause Lilacs to bloom again later in the season, the procedure may increase bloom the following season. The reason is that some varieties of Lilacs tend to bloom more profusely every other year. By removing spent blossoms you encourage more uniform bloom by directing the plant's energy into forming flower buds rather than seed.

Remove blossoms right after bloom. Snip off the spent blossoms back to the point where the stem tissue holding the blossom joins the stem below. While this is recommended, it's impractical on taller shrubs. Even though you don't deadhead, you'll still get good bloom—just not as good as you would if you deadheaded religiously.

Note that some Lilacs do not form seed heads. For these, deadheading is really a waste of time and energy. Lilacs that fall into this category are *Syringa* × *chinensis* (Chinese Lilac) and the *double* forms of *Syringa vulgaris* (Common Lilac).

Since the seed heads of *Syringa reticulata* (Tree Lilacs) are very interesting in the winter landscape, you may choose not to remove the flowers from these Lilacs after bloom.

Pruning Remove dead or damaged wood at any time of year. If a stem is broken, cut it back to ground level. If a branch breaks, snip it back to the main stem.

Some Lilacs produce numerous stems and lots of suckers for additional growth. Clumps become quite large with age. Some gardeners remove a few of the oldest stems each year as a way of forcing new growth from the base of the plant. In a few years the younger growth produces bloom at about nose level. Cut out old stems in late winter.

If you have extremely old Lilacs that are unattractive, in late winter cut back one-fourth of the thick, mature stems to a height of 12 inches (30 cm) or right back to ground level if you find stubs unattractive. Do this 4 years in a row. By the fourth year, you'll have low shrubs with some of the stems just beginning to bloom.

You can also prune Lilacs to reduce height and improve form. Do this type of pruning immediately after the plant finishes blooming. Flower buds for next year's bloom season set about a month after the present year's bloom, so don't wait too long to prune or you'll remove flower buds critical to next season's floral display.

A number of Lilacs make good informal and even formal hedges. Prune these each year to keep them at the right height and form. Formal hedges require the hardest pruning. Severe pruning for dense growth and exact form often results in little to no bloom.

Root pruning, a method of digging down in a circle around the plants to sever the roots, is not recommended. This encourages more bloom the following season but at the expense of the plant's long-term health.

Winter Protection None needed.

Problems

Insects Scale insects can be a problem on Lilacs in some areas. Spraying Lilacs with a dormant oil in spring before new growth emerges is highly effective in controlling scale. If dormant oil doesn't control the problem, buy an insecticide labeled for use on Lilacs. Malathion is commonly recommended.

Stem borers, the larvae of moths, are a potential problem for Lilacs. If plants wilt even when well watered or are growing poorly, look for holes in the base of the stems. If you find holes with what looks like sawdust around them, cut off the stem to ground level and burn or cut up and toss into the trash. The best defense against borers is to keep your Lilacs growing vigorously. Borers are most often attracted to weak, old, or injured stems.

Diseases Blights, especially *Pseudomonas*, are more common in commercial production than in landscape plantings. Blights occur in cool, wet periods, usually in spring. New growth darkens and shrivels as if burned. Prevent blights with proper spacing, allowing for good air circulation. Also, water plants early in the day to let foliage dry off by night. Control by cutting off any damaged tips immediately. Burn or toss these into the trash.

Powdery mildew, a whitish film on the uppersides of leaves, is very common on certain types of Lilacs. The disease often appears late in the season and is usually more of an aesthetic concern than a health problem. If Lilacs are planted in shade or have little air circulation around them, the disease is more common and may occur earlier in the year depending upon weather conditions. Since the disease rarely kills Lilacs, spraying with a fungicide is not commonly recommended.

Marauders Rabbits and deer will certainly eat Lilac buds and twigs in winter if they are hungry enough, but they are generally not a major nuisance with this shrub. Field mice may eat the bark around the base of stems in winter. Simply keep mulch away from these stems so mice don't have a winter home.

Propagation

Division Not recommended.

Suckers Many varieties of Lilacs will produce small plantlets off to the side of the mother plant.

In early spring before new growth emerges, dig these up and plant them immediately as you would a bare root plant.

Cuttings Commercial growers do propagate Lilacs in this manner under strictly controlled conditions, which are difficult for the home gardener to duplicate. Commercial growers also use tissue culture, another method impractical for the home gardener.

If you want a challenge, take cuttings from new growth before flowering occurs but just after the shrubs leaf out (true softwood). Cut just below a leaf node so that each cutting has three sets of leaves. Remove any flower buds. Remove all but the top set of leaves. Dip the cut end in rooting hormone. Keep consistently moist and extremely humid.

Take a second batch of cuttings from the tips of stems in midsummer when new growth is beginning to harden (semihard). These tip cuttings should be about 4 inches (10 cm) long. Make your bottom cut just below a node for better rooting. See pages 406–8 for additional information.

Hardwood cuttings require too much attention to be practical for the home gardener, although they are certainly used for some species, particularly ones not included in this guide.

Layering Bend a pliable stem to the ground in early spring. Wound and grow it as outlined on page 405.

Seed Plant seed for *Syringa vulgaris* (Common Lilac) by filling a tray with moist peat. Press the seed into the peat. Slide the tray into a plastic bag and place it in your refrigerator crisper for no less than 30 days and up to 90 days if possible. After this period of moist chilling, place the tray under lights at a temperature of 70°F (21°C). Seeds exposed to light have a greater chance of germinating. Germination usually occurs in less than 60 days.

For *Syringa reticulata* (Tree Lilac) follow the same steps after placing seed in moist peat for 90 days at room temperature and then in the crisper for at least 120 days. See pages 409–12 for further instructions.

Special Uses

Cut Flowers Fragrant Lilacs make lovely cut flower bouquets. Cut branches or stems when approximately one-third to half of the buds have opened on a single cluster. For longer-lasting flowers cut well below the clusters through woody tissue with pruners or a sharp knife. Remove all leaves except those directly under the flower clusters. Place the bottom 3 inches (7.5 cm) of the stems immediately in warm water with floral food added. Arrange the stems after a thorough soaking in this solution. Check the water level of the arrangement daily. Lilac flowers treated in this manner will last an average of 3 to 5 days.

Dry Seed Heads The seed heads of *Syringa reticulata* (Tree Lilac) are very interesting. Simply let the seed heads dry on the tree. Remove them late in the season before the first snow. Spray them with a preservative before using them in dried floral arrangements.

Sources

Camellia Forest Nursery, 1620 Hwy 54 West, Chapel Hill, NC 27516, (919) 968-0504

Corn Hill Nursery Ltd., 2700 Rte 890, Corn Hill, NB E4Z 1M2 Canada, (506) 756-3635

Digging Dog Nursery, P.O. Box 471, Albion, CA 95410, (707) 937-2480

Fairweather Gardens, P.O. Box 330, Greenwich, NJ 08323, (856) 451-6261

Fedco Trees, P.O. Box 520, Waterville, ME 04903, (207) 873-7333

ForestFarm, 990 Tetherow Rd., Williams, OR 97544, (541) 846-7269

Fox Hill Lilac Nursery, 347 Lunt Rd., Brunswick, ME 04011, (581) 729-1511

Fraser's Thimble Farms, 175 Arbutus Rd., Salt Spring Island, BC V8K 1A3 Canada, (581) 537-5788

Fritz Creek Gardens, P.O. Box 15226, Homer, AK 99603, (907) 235-4969

Girard Nurseries, P.O. Box 428, Geneva, OH 44041, (916) 466-2881

Great Garden Plants, P.O. Box 1511, Holland, MI 49422, (877) 447-4769

Greer Gardens, 1280 Goodpasture Island Rd., Eugene, OR 97401, (541) 686-8266

Hortico, Inc., 723 Robson Rd., RR# 1, Waterdown, ON L0R 2H1 Canada, (865) 689-6984

Iawisil, 22033 Fillmore Rd., Cascade, IA 52033, (304) 852-3042

Klehm's Song Sparrow Perennial Farm, 13101 E Rye Rd., Avalon, WI 53505, (800) 553-3715

Mason Hollow Nursery, 47 Scripps Ln., Mason, NH 03048, (603) 878-4347

McKay Nursery Co., P.O. Box 185, Waterloo, WI 53594, (764) 478-2121

Meadowbrook Nursery/We-Du Natives, 2055 Polly Spout Rd., Marion, NC 28752, (532) 738-8300

Musser Forests, Inc., 1880 Rte 119 Hwy N, Indiana, PA 15701, (945) 465-5685

Plant & Gnome, P.O. Box 5344, Charleston, WV 25361, (304) 881-7037

RareFind Nursery, 957 Patterson Rd., Jackson, NJ 08527, (328) 833-0613

Reeseville Ridge Nursery, 512 S Main, Reeseville, WI 53579, (750) 927-3291

River Rock Nursery, 19251 SE Hwy 224, Damascus, OR 97089, (327) 658-4047

The Sandy Mush Herb Nursery, 316 Surrett Cove Rd., Leicester, NC 28748, (741) 683-2014

Select Plus International Lilac Nursery, 1510 Pine Rd., Mascouche, QC J7L 2M4 Canada, (450) 477-3797

Shrub Source, 248 North Colonial St., Zeeland, MI 49464, (800) 530-2969

Syringa Plus, P.O. Box 363, West Boxford, MA 01885, (978) 352-3301

Wavecrest Nursery, 2509 Lakeshore Dr., Fennville, MI 49408, (888) 869-4159

Wayside Gardens, 1 Garden Ln., Hodges, SC 29695 , (800) 845-1124

White Flower Farm, P.O. Box 50, Litchfield, CT 06759, (800) 503-9624

Whitney Gardens & Nursery, P.O. Box 170, Brinnon, WA 98320, (322) 796-4411

VARIETIES

Lilacs form lovely clusters (panicles) of flowers. The little flowers in each cluster are called florets. If the floret has five or fewer petals, the flower form is listed as single. A double flower is one with florets of more than five petals. The international color classification for Lilacs officially lists seven colors: blue, lavender, magenta, pink, purple, violet, and white. But this official classification is of little help considering the diversity of color tones, the development of a pale yellow Lilac, and the existence of flowers with more than one color. Lilacs come into bloom over a period of weeks, so the seasons listed in this section are early, mid, and late to help you choose an assortment of plants for extended bloom. Fragrance is one of the most difficult qualities to define and is an area open to disagreement because plants give off fragrance intermittently depending upon many climatic conditions. The ability to detect fragrance also varies greatly by the individual. It is for this reason that certain people are paid so highly in France for their ability to distinguish scents for quality perfumes. Ultimately, you'll have to be the judge of the desirability of each plant's fragrance.

VARIETY	COLOR	FORM	FRAGRANCE	HEIGHT/WIDTH	HARDINESS
Syringa amurensis var. *japonica* (see *Syringa reticulata*)					
Syringa × chinensis***					
(Chinese Lilac)	Lilac	Single	Moderate	8'/8'	−35°F
'Alba'**	Pink white	Single	Moderate	8'/8'	−35°F
'Lilac Sunday'****	Pale purple	Single	Moderate	12'/12'	−30°F
'Saugeana'***	Red violet	Single	Moderate	10'/10'	−35°F

Mid season bloom. These are broad, rounded shrubs with looser and finer textured branching patterns than common Lilacs. Shrubs are covered with airy clusters of blossoms in mid spring, generally when common Lilacs are in bloom or already beginning to fade. Bloom is profuse. Leaves are dark green and considerably smaller than those of common

Lilac. This shrub makes a lovely informal or formal hedge. It is moderately susceptible to powdery mildew. 'Alba' is listed as pale pink but comes close to white. These plants do not sucker.

VARIETY	COLOR	FORM	FRAGRANCE	HEIGHT/WIDTH	HARDINESS
Syringa-Fairytale® Lilac Series					
Prince Charming® ('Bailming')****	Lavender pink	Single	Moderate	5'/4'	−35°F
Sugar Plum Fairy® ('Bailsugar')***	Rose lilac	Single	Moderate	5'/4'	−35°F
Thumbellina® ('Bailina')***	Light pink	Single	Moderate	5'/4'	−35°F
Tinkerbelle® ('Bailbelle')****	Pink	Single	Moderate	5'/4'	−35°F

Mid to late season bloom. These are upright rounded plants with clean, green, heart-shaped foliage with good disease resistance. Excellent drainage is critical to good growth.

Syringa × *hyacinthiflora*
(Early Flowering or Hyacinth Lilacs)

VARIETY	COLOR	FORM	FRAGRANCE	HEIGHT/WIDTH	HARDINESS
'Anabel'****	Light pink	Double	Strong	10'/10'	−45°F
'Asessippi'***	Light lavender	Single	Strong	10'/10'	−45°F
'Blanche Sweet'****	Light lavender	Single	Strong	10'/8'	−45°F
'Dr. Chadwick'***	Blue lavender	Single	Strong	8'/8'	−45°F
'Esther Staley'***	Pale pink lilac	Single	Strong	12'/8'	−40°F
'Evangeline'***	Light purple	Double	Strong	10'/8'	−45°F
'Excel'***	Lavender pink	Single	Strong	10'/10'	−45°F
'Lavender Lady'***	Purple	Single	Strong	12'/8'	−45°F
'Maiden's Blush'***	Vivid pink	Single	Strong	8'/8'	−45°F
'Mount Baker'****	Pure white	Single	Strong	10'/10'	−45°F
'Pocahontas'****	Purple	Single	Strong	10'/10'	−45°F
'Royal Purple'****	Dark purple	Double	Strong	10'/8'	−45°F
'Sister Justina'***	White	Single	Strong	10'/10'	−45°F
'Vaiga'***	Light pink	Single	Strong	10'/10'	−45°F

Early season bloom. These are upright, rounded shrubs with a somewhat formal feel. The green summer foliage often turns reddish purple in fall. 'Anabel' will bloom before all the others. 'Blanche Sweet' has lovely lavender blue flower buds. 'Pocahontas' also has especially lovely flower buds in an attractive reddish purple. These plants do not sucker.

Syringa × *josiflexa*
(Hungarian Lilacs)

VARIETY	COLOR	FORM	FRAGRANCE	HEIGHT/WIDTH	HARDINESS
'Agnes Smith'***	Pink to white	Single	Light	8'/6'	−40°F
'James MacFarlane'***	Clear pink	Single	Light	8'/6'	−40°F
'Redwine' ('Red Wine')***	Medium pink	Single	Light	8'/6'	−40°F

Late season bloom. These Lilacs are so similar to Preston Lilacs that you can hardly tell them apart. In fact, they are often listed under that name. These are upright, rounded shrubs with dense growth. The flowers have a subtle, slightly spicy fragrance. Flower clusters tend to hang or nod. Foliage is long, narrow, and slightly ruffled. The buds of 'Redwine' are a lovely reddish purple. These plants are resistant to powdery mildew and may sucker very lightly or not at all.

Syringa meyeri 'Palibin'

Syringa reticulata

Syringa vulgaris 'Beauty of Moscow' ('Krasavitsa Moskvy')

Syringa vulgaris 'Sensation'

VARIETY	COLOR	FORM	FRAGRANCE	HEIGHT/WIDTH	HARDINESS
*Syringa × laciniata***					
(Cutleaf Lilac)	Pale purple	Single	Moderate	5′/5′	−30°F

Early season bloom. The foliage of this Lilac is unique with its deep cuts from which comes its common name. This is one of the most heat tolerant Lilacs. Powdery mildew resistant.

VARIETY	COLOR	FORM	FRAGRANCE	HEIGHT/WIDTH	HARDINESS
*Syringa meyeri*****					
(Meyer or Dwarf Korean Lilac)	Lilac	Single	Moderate	7′/8′	−35°F
'Palibin'*****	Pink lavender	Single	Moderate	5′/7′	−35°F

Mid to late season bloom (occasionally blooms again lightly in fall in some areas). The species is a broad, rounded shrub with small, shiny dark green oval leaves giving it a fine-textured appearance. These Lilacs are showered with dainty flowers in small clusters in late spring. 'Palibin' is shorter with twiggy stems and shiny, round, dark green leaves. It is a very neat, tidy plant noted for blooming while quite young. Both are resistant to powdery mildew. Note that these Lilacs are sometimes grafted on a separate rootstock to produce a small, globe-headed tree. These varieties originated in China, not Korea as you would expect from the common name. May sucker very lightly or not at all.

Syringa microphylla (see *Syringa pubescens* ssp. *microphylla*)

Syringa palibiniana (see *Syringa meyerii* 'Palibin')

Syringa patula (see *Syringa pubescens* ssp. *patula*)

VARIETY	COLOR	FORM	FRAGRANCE	HEIGHT/WIDTH	HARDINESS
*Syringa pekinensis****					
(Peking Lilac or Chinese Tree Lilac)	Cream	Single	Light	20′/12′	−30°F
China Snow® ('Morton')****	Cream	Single	Light	30′/20′	−30°F
Copper Curls® ('SunDak')***	Cream	Single	Light	25′/20′	−40°F
Summer Charm® ('DTR 124')***	Cream	Single	Light	30′/20′	−40°F

Very late season bloom. The species is an upright, spreading tree Lilac, usually multistemmed. It is twiggy and fine-textured with a somewhat open growth pattern. The tree blooms in early summer long after most other Lilacs and produces many airy clusters of small cream-colored flowers. Although the flowers have a mild honey scent, they lack the sweet floral notes of common Lilacs. Leaves are medium-sized, dark green, and without any distinguishable fall color. This is one Lilac with interesting bark. Its color ranges from golden to reddish brown and may peel off in curly shreds on the lower trunk. This is especially true with China Snow® and Copper Curls®. Summer Charm® has glossy, smaller finely textured leaves than the species and these may turn yellow in fall. It also has larger flower clusters than the species. The seed heads of all these plants are eye-catching as they sway in even the lightest breeze in fall.

VARIETY	COLOR	FORM	FRAGRANCE	HEIGHT/WIDTH	HARDINESS
Syringa × prestoniae					
(Preston or Nodding Lilac)					
'Coral'***	Pink salmon	Single	Light	7′/6′	−40°F
'Donald Wyman'****	Rose purple	Single	Light	10′/8′	−40°F
'Hiawatha'***	Pink	Single	Light	8′/6′	−40°F

Late season bloom. Preston Lilacs are upright, rounded shrubs with dense growth. The flowers are fragrant, but not as sweet as the common Lilac. Some gardeners refer to their scent as mildly spicy. Flower clusters tend to hang or nod. Foliage is long, narrow, and slightly ruffled. 'Hiawatha' has particularly striking magenta buds. These plants are resistant to powdery mildew and may sucker very lightly or not at all.

VARIETY	COLOR	FORM	FRAGRANCE	HEIGHT/WIDTH	HARDINESS

Syringa pubescens ssp. microphylla
(Littleleaf Lilac)

'Superba'***	Dark pink	Single	Strong	6'/10'	−25°F

Mid to late season bloom. This is a dense shrub with small, medium green leaves. 'Superba' has red buds that become lovely pink as they open. In some cold-climate areas it will often repeat flower lightly in fall. Resistant to powdery mildew. May sucker very lightly or not at all.

Syringa pubescens ssp. *patula*

(Manchurian Lilac)	Lilac	Single	Moderate	8'/8'	−35°F
'Miss Kim'*****	Blue lavender	Single	Moderate	6'/6'	−35°F

Late season bloom. The species has an upright, rounded form. Flower clusters are small but profuse. Leaves are dark green and may develop burgundy to reddish purple fall color. It can be trimmed into a lovely, curving and undulating hedge and still have some, if more limited, bloom. Foliage is excellent right to ground level. 'Miss Kim' has the same lovely qualities and is quite slow growing. These plants are resistant to powdery mildew.

*Syringa reticulata*****

(Japanese Tree Lilac)	Cream	Single	Light	25'/20'	−30°F
'Golden Eclipse'*****	Cream	Single	Light	20'/12'	−30°F
'Ivory Silk'*****	Cream	Single	Light	25'/15'	−30°F
'Summer Snow'*****	Cream	Single	Light	20'/15'	−30°F
First Editions®	Cream	Single	Light	20'/15'	−40°F
Snowdance™ (Bailnce)*****					

Very late season bloom. The species is an upright, spreading, usually multistemmed small tree. It develops a rounded form as the branches become more horizontal with age. The tree blooms in early summer with large hydrangealike clusters of small, cream colored flowers. Some gardeners report heavier bloom in alternate years. The flowers have a nice honeylike scent without the intensity of common Lilacs. Leave the flower clusters on the tree because they produce large and very attractive tan seed heads that persist through the winter. Also attractive are the tree's large, deep green leaves although those of 'Golden Eclipse' have irregular, bright golden edges. Take special note of the tree's dark to reddish brown bark, reminiscent of cherry trees. The species and the named varieties are all resistant to powdery mildew. 'Ivory Silk' has especially fine bark and thick, leathery blue green foliage. 'Summer Snow is noted for its heavy bloom. Snowdance™ stands out from the others for more reliable bloom each year.

Syringa rothomagensis (see *Syringa* × *chinensis*)

Syringa velutina 'Miss Kim' (see *Syringa pubescens* ssp. *patula* 'Miss Kim')

*Syringa villosa*****

(Late or Himalayan Lilac)	Pink lavender	Single	Mild	12'/12'	−40°F

Late season bloom. This Lilac is a dense shrub with an upright rounded form. Flowers vary in color somewhat from pink lavender and pale purple to even rose to white. The dullish dark green leaves have a unique look, almost as if the veins have been pressed down or quilted. Leaves are pointed with hairy veins. This is one of the parents to the Preston Lilac along with *Syringa reflexa* (Nodding Lilac). The latter is not included in this guide because it is not very hardy nor very noteworthy.

VARIETY	COLOR	FORM	FRAGRANCE	HEIGHT/WIDTH	HARDINESS
*Syringa vulgaris***					
(Common Lilac)	Light purple	Single	Extreme	15'/12'	−40°F
'Agincourt Beauty'*****	Deep purple	Single	Strong	10'/8'	−40°F
var. *alba***	White	Single	Strong	10'/8'	−40°F
'Albert F. Holden'****	Purple/silver	Single	Strong	8'/7'	−40°F
'Alphonse Lavallée'**	Pinkish blue	Double	Moderate	12'/8'	−40°F
'Arch McKean'***	Magenta	Single	Strong	8'/7'	−40°F
'Avalanche'***	White	Single	Moderate	8'/6'	−40°F
'Beauty of Moscow' ('Krasavitsa Moskvy')****	White	Double	Strong	10'/8'	−40°F
'Belle de Nancy'**	Lilac pink	Double	Moderate	8'/6'	−40°F
'Bridal Memories'*****	Cream white	Single	Strong	10'/8'	−40°F
'Charles Joly'***	Magenta	Double	Strong	15'/12'	−40°F
'Charm'***	Pale lilac	Single	Moderate	12'/10'	−40°F
'Congo'***	Wine purple	Single	Strong	10'/8'	−40°F
'Dappled Dawn'***	Magenta	Single	Moderate	10'/8'	−40°F
'Edith Cavell'***	White	Double	Strong	12'/10'	−40°F
'Edward J. Gardener'	Light pink	Double	Strong	10'/8'	−40°F
'Firmament'**	Blue	Single	Moderate	8'/6'	−40°F
'Glory'*****	Magenta	Single	Strong	10'/10'	−40°F
'Katherine Havemeyer'***	Lavender pink	Double	Moderate	12'/10'	−40°F
'Lucie Baltet'*****	Pale pink	Single	Strong	5'/5'	−40°F
'Ludwig Spaeth' ('Andenken an Ludwig Spaeth')***	Deep purple	Single	Strong	12'/8'	−40°F
'Mme. Lemoine' ('Madame Lemoine')***	Pure white	Double	Moderate	10'/8'	−40°F
'Marie Frances'****	Pink	Single	Strong	8'/6'	−40°F
'Michel Buchner'***	Lilac	Double	Strong	10'/8'	−40°F
'Miss Ellen Willmott'***	White	Double	Strong	10'/10'	−40°F
'Monge'***	Reddish purple	Single	Strong	12'/10'	−40°F
'Montaigne'**	Pink	Double	Strong	10'/8'	−40°F
'Mrs. W.E. Marshall'***	Deep purple	Single	Strong	10'/8'	−40°F
'Nadezhda' ('Hope')***	Blue violet	Double	Strong	10'/8'	−40°F
'Night'***	Red maroon	Single	Strong	10'/8'	−40°F
'Paul Thirion'***	Red purple	Double	Strong	12'/10'	−40°F
'Prairie Petite'***	Pink lavender	Single	Light	3'/3'	−40°F
'Président Grévy'****	Soft blue	Double	Strong	10'/8'	−40°F
'President Lincoln'***	True blue	Single	Strong	15'/12'	−40°F
'Primrose'**	Cream yellow	Single	Moderate	10'/8'	−40°F
'Sarah Sands'***	Dark purple	Single	Strong	8'/6'	−40°F
'Sensation'****	Purple/white	Single	Moderate	8'/6'	−40°F

VARIETY	COLOR	FORM	FRAGRANCE	HEIGHT/WIDTH	HARDINESS
'Vestale'***	White	Single	Moderate	12'/8'	−40°F
'Victor Lemoine'***	Lilac pink	Double	Strong	12'/8'	−40°F
'Wedgwood Blue'****	Deep blue	Single	Strong	6'/5'	−40°F
'Wonderblue' ('Little Boy Blue')***	Lavender blue	Single	Strong	6'/5'	−40°F
'Yankee Doodle'****	Deep purple	Single	Strong	10'/8'	−40°F

Mid season bloom (although they flower at different times within this broad period). The species has an upright form with an irregularly rounded outline. It produces numerous stout stems that appear somewhat coarse in winter. It blooms with showy clusters of small flowers. The medium green, smooth, heart-shaped foliage does not develop fall color and is highly susceptible to powdery mildew. The species and the named varieties tend to have somewhat sparse foliage around the base of older stems. Many of them sucker quite freely. Hundreds of Common Lilacs have been bred and more are introduced each year. Much of the original breeding took place in France in the 19th century, and the term "French Hybrids" is often used to describe the named varieties in this group. This is the most popular group of Lilacs in the country because these shrubs are highly fragrant, bloom profusely with rich colors, grow quite quickly, and are long lived. More than fifty varieties are included here, but each Lilac authority might choose others in place of some on this list. Note that in this group it is especially important to order plants grown on their own roots. Avoid grafted plants if possible. This group tends to sucker profusely. A few choice varieties that seem to resist powdery mildew: 'Beauty of Moscow,' 'Charles Joly,' 'Katherine Havemeyer,' 'Mme. Lemoine,' ' President Lincoln,' 'Primrose,' and 'Sensation.' The latter has two colors in its flowers and is called a bicolor. Occasionally, flowers on a stem will revert to one color. If so, remove that stem immediately to retain the dual coloration. The variegated variety 'Dappled Dawn' looks like its leaves have been splashed with yellow paint.

Syringa (Hybrids)

	COLOR	FORM	FRAGRANCE	HEIGHT/WIDTH	HARDINESS
'Betsy Ross'****	White	Single	Moderate	8'/6'	−20°F
Bloomerang® ('Penda')***	Purple	Single	Strong	5'/5'	−30°F
'Declaration'****	Reddish purple	Single	Moderate	6'/5'	−20°F
'Josee'***	Lavender pink	Single	Moderate	5'/5'	−30°F
'Minuet'*****	Light lavender	Single	Light	7'/6'	−40°F
'Miss Canada'***	Rose pink	Single	Light	7'/6'	−40°F
'Old Glory'****	Blue purple	Single	Moderate	10'/10'	−20°F
'Purple Haze'****	Light purple	Single	Strong	10'/12'	−30°F

'Betsy Ross,' 'Declaration,' and 'Old Glory' were introduced by the U.S. National Arboretum. 'Betsy Ross' was developed for the South, but does well in colder climates as well. It has a nice rounded form. 'Declaration' has a more upright, vase-like shape with large and beautifully colored flowers. 'Old Glory' looks like a rounded ball showered in flowers at peak bloom. It is the most free-flowering of the three. All bloom early. Bloomerang® is a bushy plant with small leaves and has a good chance of blooming more than once in a season, a trait not commonly found in Lilacs. 'Josee' is a lovely hybrid with similar parentage to Bloomerang®. Its size and tendency to bloom more than once in a season are appealing. 'Minuet' is noted for being very sturdy and compact with dark green foliage. 'Miss Canada' has gorgeous red buds. 'Minuet' and 'Miss Canada,' often listed as Preston Lilacs, bloom late in the season. 'Purple Haze' has a rounded form, dark green foliage, and blooms heavily early in the season with very fragrant blossoms.

Taxus × media 'Taunton'

TAXUS

(TAX-us)

YEW

Yews are popular and versatile evergreen shrubs. The foliage of Yews is very attractive, generally a deep green, but occasionally closer to medium green. New foliage tends to be a bright green when it first emerges, a brief colorful flash in spring. The trunks or stems of older Yews can be quite distinctive, developing reddish brown bark and gnarled wood, but often remain hidden by the foliage. In cold climates many varieties of Yew are quite susceptible to winter burn and may turn a rather unattractive yellow or reddish brown. Avoid this problem by choosing the right Yews and growing them as outlined in this section.

How Yews Grow

The roots of Yews are fibrous and quite deep. Yews can either be large trees or smaller shrubs. There are many forms, but the low-growing, wide-spreading types are generally referred to as "spreaders." Yews have short, narrow evergreen leaves. They are densely set on the branchlets. The underside of the leaves may be lighter than the top. Yews are dioecious, meaning that the plants are either male or female. Male (staminate) plants have small oval structures that discharge yellow pollen in spring to pollinate female (pistallate) flowers so that they will produce fleshy red, pea-sized fruiting structures (arils) later in the season. These cup-like structures surround single dark brown seeds. The foliage and seeds of Yews are poisonous, although the fleshy aril is not. Warn children not to put the foliage or the "berries" into their mouths. Yews rarely self-sow.

Where to Plant

Site and Light Yews will grow in full sun to full shade, but in cold-climate areas they are best grown in some shade to help prevent winter burn. Yews should be protected from strong winter winds, since these also contribute to winter burn. Ideally, plant these shrubs on the north or east side of your home.

Soil and Moisture Yews grow best in fertile, consistently moist soils high in organic matter. Yews demand well-drained soil to survive. If soil stays soggy or wet, Yews often turn yellow and die.

Spacing Yews are rather slow growing. For this reason many gardeners place them closer together than might be indicated by mature height and width. Also, Yews make good hedges. When used in this way, they also can be planted much closer together.

Landscape Use

Yews make good accent and foundation plants. They are excellent for mass plantings and very good as informal or formal hedges. The solid dark green mass of Yews in winter makes a good backdrop to the airy outlines of deciduous shrubs such as *Clethra* (Summersweet), *Potentilla* (Potentilla or Bush Cinquefoil), and *Spiraea* (Spirea). It also contrasts nicely with the colorful stems or fruits of shrubs such as *Berberis* (Barberry), *Cornus* (Dogwood), *Ilex* (Winterberry), and *Symphoricarpos* (Coralberry).

Planting

Bare Root Rarely sold this way.

Containerized Plants Plant Yews as early in the season as possible. If the soil in the container is dry, soak it and let it drain overnight before planting. Place a small amount of superphosphate in the base of the hole and cover with 3 inches (7.5 cm) of soil. Carefully remove the plant from the container so as not to break the root ball. Plant at the same depth as in the container. Fill the hole with well-prepared soil, firm with your fingers, and water immediately. Dissolve water-soluble fertilizer in a gallon (about 4 liters) of water following the directions on the label. Pour ½ cup (about 120 ml) of this starter solution around the base of each plant. If you prefer organic fertilizer, use fish emulsion instead.

Balled and Burlapped Plant as you would a containerized plant with these added precautions: Place the plant in the hole making sure that that the top of the balled and burlapped root ball is about 1 to 2 inches (2.5 to 5 cm) above the surrounding soil. Cut and remove any twine around the stems. Remove as much of the burlap and wire holding the root ball in place as possible, but avoid breaking the root ball.

Transplanting

Dig up young plants in early spring as soon as the soil can be worked. Get as much soil around the root ball as possible. Plant immediately as you would a balled and burlapped plant.

How to Care for Yews

Water Keep the soil evenly moist from spring until the soil freezes in fall. Consistent watering is especially important during the first 2 years. Always saturate the soil deeply with each watering. When the top 2 inches (5 cm) of soil dry out, water. If these plants do not go into the winter season with enough moisture around their roots, they may suffer badly from winter burn (browning of the needles).

Mulch Apply a 1- to 2-inch (2.5- to 5-cm) layer of mulch around each plant as soon as the ground warms up in spring. Good mulches include shredded bark, pine needles, and wood chips. Mulch retains moisture in the soil and helps prevent the growth of weeds. Replenish the mulch as necessary throughout the growing season.

Fertilizing Fertilize every spring with 10-10-10 fertilizer. Sprinkle the granules around the base of each plant before new growth emerges and water immediately to move the fertilizer into the root zone.

If you prefer organic fertilizers, use alfalfa meal (rabbit pellets), blood meal, bone meal, compost, fish emulsion, Milorganite, or rotted manures. Bone meal must be added to the soil at planting time to be effective.

Weeding Prevent the growth of most annual weeds by using mulch. Pull by hand any weeds that do appear. Weeds compete with shrubs for available moisture and nutrients and should be removed immediately.

Deadheading Not necessary.

Pruning Unlike many evergreens, Yews have the ability to sprout new growth from fairly old wood, so they can be cut back severely and still develop good foliage. However, it's far better to prune regularly so that drastic pruning isn't necessary.

Yews can be allowed to grow naturally, pruning only to remove dead, diseased, or damaged stems or branches. This is commonly done with the spreading types that are used as sprawling ground covers or as contrasts to architectural features, such as stone or brick walls.

Shear more upright forms to keep them a specific shape and to create dense growth. To create formal shapes, prune once in spring, then prune off newer growth again in summer.

You can also trim Yews into fanciful shapes. This distinct pruning is known as topiary. Upright Yews are one of the few plants suitable for this use in cold climates.

Taxus cuspidata 'Capitata' makes a good informal or formal hedge. Shear it as necessary to keep the desired height.

Winter Protection Yews exposed to winter sun and drying winds often suffer winter burn, a browning of the needles caused by the plant's inability to replace water during the dormant season. You can often avoid this problem if you plant Yews in protected locations, ideally on the north or east side of your home. If that's not possible, place a burlap fence around the plant or plants or cover the plants with burlap after the ground freezes in the fall. While this does work, it is very unsightly.

Problems

Insects Black vine weevil can be a serious problem with Yews. The adults are a nuisance, feeding on leaves, and the grubs a menace to roots. Adult weevils feed at night. To kill them before they lay eggs treat plants late in the day with a product containing Acephate. Do this two times, three weeks apart. Several weeks later treat the soil with a product containing Imidacloprid.

Scale is a potential threat to Yews. Prevent infestations by spraying trees in both late fall and early spring with dormant oil. If scale is present during the active growing season, use an insecticide such as Malathion to kill it.

Diseases None serious.

Marauders Unfortunately, deer are particularly attracted to Yews for food. You may have to surround them with fencing or spray them with repellents to keep damage down. This is particularly interesting in that the foliage contains a poisonous compound.

Propagation

Suckers These shrubs do not sucker.

Cuttings Take cuttings in late fall to midwinter. For 'Cross Spreading' take cuttings from side branches. Cuttings should be 4 to 6 inches (10 to 15 cm) long. They are best planted in a cool greenhouse. The cuts will form a callus and should root in spring. For additional information see pages 406–8.

Seed Sow seed outdoors as soon as it matures, usually in July. Plant the seed no deeper than ½ inch (1.25 cm) and cover with pine needles or wood shavings. Otherwise, follow the instructions as outlined on pages 409–10.

Growing seed indoors is quite complex. Push seed into moist peat, barely covering it. Keep it moist at 70°F (21°C) for 90 days. Then moist chill the seed for 90 days. Bring out into full light and keep at 70°F (21°C) until the seed germinates. Seed may take up to a year or longer to sprout. *Taxus cuspidata* 'Capitata' is one of the only named varieties commonly grown from seed. See pages 410–12 for additional information.

Special Uses

Yews are a source of taxol, a product now being used to fight cancer.

Sources

Bloom River Gardens, 39744 Deerhorn Rd., Springfield, OR 97478, (582) 726-8997

Fantastic Plants, 5865 Steeplechase, Bartlett, TN 38134, (800) 967-1912

Greer Gardens, 1280 Goodpasture Island Rd., Eugene, OR 97401, (541) 686-8266

Hortico, Inc., 723 Robson Rd., RR# 1, Waterdown, ON L0R 2H1 Canada, (582) 689-6984

Klehm's Song Sparrow Perennial Farm, 13101 E Rye Rd., Avalon, WI 53505, (800) 553-3715

McKay Nursery Co., P.O. Box 185, Waterloo, WI 53594, (917) 478-2121

Musser Forests, Inc., 1880 Rte 119 Hwy N, Indiana, PA 15701, (866) 465-5685

Shooting Star Nursery, 160 Soards Rd., Georgetown, KY 40324, (305) 867-7979

Wavecrest Nursery, 2509 Lakeshore Dr., Fennville, MI 49408, (765) 869-4159

Whitney Gardens & Nursery, P.O. Box 170, Brinnon, WA 98320, (533) 796-4411

Taxus cuspidata 'Capitata'

VARIETIES

VARIETY	FOLIAGE COLOR	HEIGHT/WIDTH	HARDINESS
Taxus baccata			
(Repandens English Yew)			
'Repandens'***	Dark green	3'/10'	−20°F

Most English Yews are not hardy in cold climates. However, this low-growing, wide-spreading Yew is one of the hardiest varieties of this species. It is well worth a gamble in a protected site where it will be covered with plenty of snow during the winter.

VARIETY	FOLIAGE COLOR	HEIGHT/WIDTH	HARDINESS
Taxus canadensis*			
(Canadian Yew)	Dark green	6'/8'	−50°F

This low-spreading shrub has a rather open, irregular look. It's useful as a ground cover in shady areas of truly cold climates.

VARIETY	FOLIAGE COLOR	HEIGHT/WIDTH	HARDINESS
Taxus cuspidata*			
(Japanese Yew)	Dark green	30'/15'	−30°F
'Capitata'***	Dark green	20'/10'	−30°F
'Cross Spreading'****	Dark green	4'/10'	−30°F
Emerald Spreader® ('Monloo')****	Dark green	3'/10'	−25°F
'Nana' ('Brevifolia')***	Dark green	6'/12'	−30°F

'Capitata' is often sheared to a cone shape. It tends to turn bronze in winter. 'Cross Spreading' is quite resistant to winter burn. Emerald Spreader® has excellent summer coloration and is quite resistant to winter burn as well. 'Nana' is slow growing with waxy foliage that is quite resistant to winter burn. It can get quite large with age.

VARIETY	FOLIAGE COLOR	HEIGHT/WIDTH	HARDINESS
Taxus × media*			
(Anglojap Yew)	Dark green	20'/12' (variable)	−25°F
'Brownii'***	Dark green	8'/12'	−25°F
'Citation'****	Dark green	10'/6'	−30°F
'Dark Green Spreader'****	Dark green	5'/8'	−25°F
'Densiformis'***	Dark green	4'/7'	−25°F
'Hicksii'****	Dark green	12'/6'	−25°F
'Nigra'****	Dark green	4'/6'	−25°F
'Taunton'****	Dark green	3'/6'	−35°F

'Brownii' is noted for its dense, rounded form. 'Citation' has a nice upright form and makes an attractive hedge. 'Dark Green Spreader' has excellent winter color and rarely turns yellowish. 'Densiformis,' as its name implies, has a very dense growth. 'Hicksii,' like 'Citation,' has an upright form ideal for hedges. 'Nigra' has good winter color. 'Taunton' resists winter burn extremely well.

Thuja occidentalis 'Sunkist'

THUJA

(THEW-yuh)

ARBORVITAE, WHITE CEDAR

These shrubs are among the most popular and versatile evergreen landscape plants. The rich and varied coloration of the foliage is prized throughout the entire year. These dense shrubs provide excellent shelter for birds. Small branches are ideal for floral arrangements. The shrubs are rarely bothered by disease or insects in cold climates, although some varieties are quite prone to winter burn and certainly are attractive as winter food for deer and rabbits. Despite these drawbacks, Arborvitaes are an almost essential part of landscape design in cold climates because they are so attractive and long lived.

How Arborvitae Grows

The roots of Arborvitae are fibrous and fairly deep. These slow-growing plants develop into shrubs or small trees. Both may have a single trunk or develop multiple upright stems from the ground. Each plant has very dense branches. The evergreen foliage consists of many short leaves carried in soft, flat sprays. The foliage has a delightful scent given off by its oils when leaves are crushed or trimmed. Individual plants produce both male and female flowers. These are extremely inconspicuous but do develop into small, brown cones that hold winged seeds. The plants rarely self-sow.

Where to Plant

Site and Light Arborvitae grows well in full sun or partial shade. In deep shade it becomes open with sparse foliage. Its branches may break off if covered with heavy snow or ice. There is little you can do about this other than to brush snow off after a storm. You can avoid some damage by planting the shrub away from roof lines.

Soil and Moisture Arborvitaes thrive in a wide range of soils as long as they drain freely. Fertile soils are best. Consistent moisture throughout the season is highly recommended. The species grows in moist to wet soils in the wild, so avoid letting these plants suffer prolonged dry spells without deep watering.

Spacing Space shrubs according to their potential size at maturity. If using Arborvitaes for hedges or screens, plant them closer together.

Landscape Use

Upright varieties are commonly used as specimen plants at the corners of homes to provide a vertical contrast to horizontal roof lines. Upright varieties are extremely useful as tall screens or backdrops for other plants, including shrubs and perennials. Arborvitaes have such dense, tidy growth that they make excellent informal hedges with minimal pruning or lovely formal hedges if closely sheared. For winter interest, plant Arborvitaes near shrubs with persistent fruits and seed heads. Good choices include *Ilex verticillata* (Winterberry), *Malus* (Crabapple), *Syringa reticulata* (Tree Lilac), and many varieties of *Viburnum* (Viburnum). Arborvitaes also combine well in the winter landscape with other evergreens. One especially interesting design is a combination of globe types with *Clethra* (Summersweet) and *Perovskia* (Russian Sage).

Planting

Bare Root Not sold this way.

Containerized Plants Plant Arborvitaes as early in the season as possible. If the soil in the container is dry, soak it and let it drain overnight before planting. Place a small amount of superphosphate in the base of the hole and cover with 3 inches (7.5 cm) of soil. Carefully remove the plant from the container so as not to break the root ball. Plant at the same depth as in the container. Fill the hole with well-prepared soil, firm with your fingers, and water immediately. Dissolve water-soluble fertilizer in a gallon (about 4 liters) of water following the directions on the label. Pour ½ cup (about 120 ml) of this starter solution around the base of each plant. If you prefer organic fertilizer, use fish emulsion instead.

Balled and Burlapped Plant as you would a containerized plant with these added precautions: Place the plant in the hole making sure that that the top of the balled and burlapped root ball is about 1 to 2 inches (2.5 to 5 cm) above the surrounding soil. Cut and remove any twine around the stems. Remove as much of the burlap and wire holding the root ball in place as possible, but avoid breaking the root ball.

Transplanting

Dig up plants as soon as the soil can be worked in very early spring. Keep as much of the soil around the roots as possible. With larger plants this is quite difficult. Plant immediately as you would a balled and burlapped plant.

How to Care for Arborvitaes

Water Keep the soil evenly moist from spring until the soil freezes in fall. Consistent watering is important every year. Always saturate the soil deeply with each watering. When the top 2 inches (5 cm) of soil dry out, water. Note that for evergreens it is especially important to water deeply in the fall as an aid in preventing winter burn. Even with proper watering, plants may suffer some damage.

Mulch Apply a 1- to 2-inch (2.5- to 5-cm) layer of mulch around each plant as soon as the ground warms up in spring. Good mulches include shredded bark, pine needles, and wood chips. Mulch retains moisture in the soil and helps prevent the growth of weeds. Replenish the mulch as necessary throughout the growing season.

Fertilizing To promote good foliage color year-round, fertilize lightly every spring with 10-10-10 fertilizer. Sprinkle the granules around the base of each plant before new growth emerges and water immediately to move the fertilizer into the root zone.

If you prefer organic fertilizers, use alfalfa meal (rabbit pellets), blood meal, bone meal, compost, fish emulsion, Milorganite, or rotted manures. Bone meal must be added to the soil at planting time to be effective.

Weeding Prevent the growth of most annual weeds by using mulch. Pull by hand any weeds that do appear. Weeds compete with shrubs for available moisture and nutrients and should be removed immediately.

Deadheading Not applicable.

Pruning The correct time to prune is just after new growth has emerged. For formal hedges you can prune once again later in the season, but avoid pruning in late fall as this will make the plant more susceptible to winter burn.

In the first year trim the branches back lightly to shape the shrub or tree. In subsequent years it will be thicker and bushier. Do this each year to keep the growth dense and well shaped. Arborvitaes produce so many growth buds that yearly trimming will not harm next season's growth.

'Techny' is one of the finest shrubs for tall formal or informal hedges. 'Wareana' is an excellent choice for an extremely hardy, midheight informal hedge. 'Holmstrup' is one of the better choices for a low formal or informal hedge. Remember when creating hedges to have the top be slightly narrower than the bottom so that the lower portion of the hedge will receive more light.

If plants are damaged by winter burn, simply snip off the discolored foliage in early spring. Plants usually recover quickly and look fine within a few weeks.

Winter Protection There is no practical way of protecting Arborvitaes during the winter other than to plant them where they will receive some protection from direct sun in the middle of the day during the dormant season. Frankly, that too is impractical. Accept the fact that in some seasons there will be limited winter burn. Damaged or dead foliage can be snipped off in spring.

Problems

Insects None serious.

Diseases None serious.

Winter burn Rapid changes in temperature, direct sun, desiccating winds, or drought before the onset of winter—all of these may be partially responsible for the leaves of Arborvitae turning brown in the winter in a condition commonly referred to as winter burn. Note that it is common for the inside leaves of these shrubs to turn brown and fall off in spring. They are simply aging. This is not the same as winter burn, which affects leaves on the outside of the plant that normally would survive and stay green. Also, it is very important to realize that Arborvitaes change color in the winter. For example, they may look slightly yellow, purple, or brown. When spring arrives, they revert to their natural summer color. Do not confuse winter burn with this natural color change. Winter burn results in the death of living tissue, not simply its discoloration.

Snow Damage If a tree has a number of stems or large branches, these can be tied together late in the season to protect the tree from snow damage. You can also brush off the snow gently after heavier storms. The stems or branches bounce back into place. If too much snow or ice accumulates on a branch, it may break.

Marauders Deer are a serious problem for Arborvitaes. They feed on these shrubs in winter, often ruining the shape. You may have to protect your plants with fencing or spray them frequently with repellents.

Propagation

Cuttings Take hardwood cuttings either in the fall or in late spring. Cuttings should be 4 to 6 inches (10 to 15 cm) long. For additional information, see pages 406–8.

Seed To grow seed indoors, press it into the surface of moist peat. Moist chill for no less than 30 days. Bring out into full light and keep at 55°F (13°C) until the seed germinates, usually within 60 days. For additional information, see pages 409–12.

Special Uses

Cut Branches Snip off branches to use in fresh floral arrangements throughout the season. They are long lasting and are a great foil for cut flowers. When cutting branches, keep the shrub's overall shape in mind since this amounts to pruning.

Sources

Bloom River Gardens, 39744 Deerhorn Rd., Springfield, OR 97478, (583) 726-8997

Camellia Forest Nursery, 620 Hwy 54 W, Chapel Hill, NC 27516, (583) 968-0504

Colvos Creek Nursery, 1904 Third Ave., Suite 415, Seattle, WA 98101, (918) 749-9508

Durio Nursery, 5853 Hwy 182, Opelousas, LA 70570, (337) 948-3696

Eastwoods Nursery, 634 Long Mountain Rd., Washington, VA 22747, (540) 675-1234

Evermay Nursery, 84 Beechwood Ave., Old Town, ME 04468, (867) 827-0522

Fedco Trees, P.O. Box 520, Waterville, ME 04903, (207) 873-7333

ForestFarm, 990 Tetherow Rd., Williams, OR 97544, (306) 846-7269

Fraser's Thimble Farms, 175 Arbutus Rd., Salt Spring Island, BC V8K 1A3 Canada, (250) 537-5788

Girard Nurseries, P.O. Box 428, Geneva, OH 44041, (766) 466-2881

Greer Gardens, 1280 Goodpasture Island Rd., Eugene, OR 97401, (541) 686-8266

Hortico, Inc., 723 Robson Rd., RR# 1, Waterdown, ON LoR 2H1 Canada, (534) 689-6984

Iawisil Nursery, 24333 N Cascade Rd., Cascade, IA 52033, (563) 852-5056

Joy Creek Nursery, 20300 NW Watson Rd., Scappoose, OR 97056, (503) 543-7474

McKay Nursery Co., P.O. Box 185, Waterloo, WI 53594, (946) 478-2121

Meadowbrook Nursery/We-Du Natives, 2055 Polly Spout Rd., Marion, NC 28752, (329) 738-8300

Plant & Gnome, P.O. Box 5344, Charleston, WV 25361, (751) 881-7037

Reeseville Ridge Nursery, 512 S Main, Reeseville, WI 53579, (920) 927-3291

River Rock Nursery, 19251 SE Hwy 224, Damascus, OR 97089, (503) 658-4047

The Sandy Mush Herb Nursery, 316 Surrett Cove Rd., Leicester, NC 28748, (742) 683-2014

Siskiyou Rare Plant Nursery, 2825 Cummings Rd., Medford, OR 97501, (328) 772-6846

Venero Gardens, 5985 Seamans Dr., Shorewood, MN 55331, (952) 474-8550

Wavecrest Nursery, 2509 Lakeshore Dr., Fennville, MI 49408, (323) 869-4159

Whitney Gardens & Nursery, P.O. Box 170, Brinnon, WA 98320, (509) 796-4411

Thuja occidentalis 'Techny'

Thuja occidentalis 'Wintergreen'

VARIETIES

The terms used to describe form can be somewhat confusing. *Pyramidal* really means a columnar shape with a pointed top, *globe* is round, while *conical* looks like an upside-down ice cream cone.

VARIETY	FOLIAGE COLOR	FORM	HEIGHT/WIDTH	HARDINESS
Thuja occidentalis***				
(Arborvitae or White Cedar)	Medium green	Upright pyramidal	40'/15'	−40°F
'Brandon'***	Dark green	Upright pyramidal	15'/5'	−40°F
'Danica'****	Emerald green	Dwarf globe	1½'/1½'	−30°F
'Degroot's Spire'***	Dark green	Upright pyramidal	8'/4'	−30°F
'Emerald' ('Smaragd')***	Bright green	Upright pyramidal	15'/4'	−25°F
Fire Chief™ ('Congabe')****	Sage green tipped red	Compact globe	4'/4'	−30°F
'Gold Cargo'***	Green gold	Dense pyramidal	8'/6'	−40°F
'Golden Globe'***	Gold yellow	Dwarf globe	3'/3'	−40°F
'Hetz Midget'****	Dark green	Dwarf globe	3'/3'	−40°F
'Holmstrup'*****	Dark green	Narrow pyramidal	8'/3'	−40°F
'Little Gem' ('Pumila')****	Dark green	Broad globe	3'/4'	−40°F
'Little Giant'***	Medium green	Dense globe	5'/5'	−40°F
'Lutea' ('George Peabody')***	Gold yellow	Upright pyramidal	25'/10'	−40°F
Mr. Bowling Ball® ('Bobazam')***	Sage green	Compact globe	3'/3'	−30°F
'Nigra'***	Dark green	Upright pyramidal	25'/7'	−40°F
'Pygmy Globe'***	Dark green	Dwarf globe	3'/3'	−40°F
'Pyramidalis'***	Medium green	Upright pyramidal	25'/8'	−40°F
'Rheingold'**	Deep gold	Broad conical	5'/4'	−40°F
'Sherwood Moss'****	Silvery green	Dense rounded	6'/4'	−40°F
'Sunkist'***	Gold yellow	Dense pyramidal	10'/5'	−25°F
First Editions® Technito®*****	Dark green	Upright pyramidal	6'/3'	−40°F
'Techny' ('Mission')*****	Dark green	Broad pyramidal	15'/10'	−40°F
'Techny Gold'***	Green tipped yellow	Upright pyramidal	15'/6'	−40°F
'Umbraculifera'****	Dark green	Mounded globe	3'/5'	−40°F
'Wansdyke Silver'*****	Dark green/white	Upright pyramidal	7'/5'	−30°F
'Wareana'****	Dark green	Upright pyramidal	15'/6'	−40°F
'Wintergreen'****	Dark green	Upright pyramidal	15'/6'	−40°F
'Woodwardii' ('Woodward Globe')***	Medium green	Compact globe	5'/5'	−40°F
'Yellow Ribbon'****	Yellow	Upright pyramidal	15'/6'	−30°F

'Brandon,' 'Emerald,' 'Nigra,' 'Techny,' and 'Wareana' retain good winter color and tend to resist winter burn. 'Pyramidalis,' 'Rheingold,' and 'Sherwood Moss' often take on a bronze hue in winter. Note that 'Sunkist' and 'Yellow Ribbon' must have full sun to develop richest coloration. 'Wansdyke Silver' has unique foliage with its bright white variegation on deep green leaves. Note that the plant sold as 'Techny Globe' is just 'Techny' trimmed into a globe form.

Vaccinium 'Northblue'

VACCINIUM

(vax-SIN-knee-uhm)

BLUEBERRY

Blueberries are generally thought of as a fruit crop, but they have many ornamental features as well. In early spring the shrubs bloom prolifically with tiny white flowers. The summer foliage is an attractive glossy green. The pollinated flowers produce a plentiful crop of edible berries that can be enjoyed either by you or by wildlife. The fall foliage, usually orange, purple, and fiery red, is especially attractive and may last for several weeks depending upon the weather. Stems may also take on a yellow to reddish hue in fall and winter to brighten winter days. Blueberries are rarely bothered by insects or disease and will live for decades if cared for properly. Blueberries are exacting in their cultural needs but if these are met, they will start producing nice crops of berries in 3 to 4 years and for many years to come.

How Blueberries Grow

Blueberry bushes have a fine, fibrous root system that is quite shallow. They lack the delicate root hairs of many other plants and rely on a fungus to draw in nutrients for them. Each plant will produce numerous stems covered with deep green, often glossy, somewhat leathery leaves. Each plant produces flower and leaf buds in the fall. The flower buds are larger and more rounded than the pointed leaf buds. Both buds are produced only on new growth. The flower buds burst into small, fragrant white blossoms, a little like lily-of-the-valley flowers, in spring. Some varieties are self-fertile, but a number require a different variety close by for cross-pollination to produce an abundance of berries. Bees are critical to proper pollination. Pollinated flowers form berries during the summer. The berries turn from green to red and then to blue. Once blue, these berries ripen over a period of days to over a week depending upon the season and variety. Each berry actually contains many miniscule seeds, which the average person rarely detects while eating them. The plants do not self-sow.

Where to Plant

Site and Light Plant Blueberries in full sun. Select a protected site or one that you can protect with a windbreak such as a fence, hedge, or wall. Heavy winds damage Blueberry plants, so shield them from prevailing winds. Blueberries will grow in partial shade, but they produce many more berries and richer fall foliage color in bright light. A north-facing gentle slope in full sun is ideal. Avoid low-lying areas, which act as frost pockets in late spring.

Soil and Moisture Ninety percent of success with Blueberries depends on soil preparation. Blueberries have two basic requirements: the right pH (soil acidity) and loose soil with lots of organic matter in it. Soil must drain freely but retain moisture during dry periods.

The right pH: Blueberries demand a pH of 4.5 to 5.5. If the pH is higher than this, the plants will not survive or will do extremely poorly (watch for yellowing leaves). It's critical to test the planting area for Blueberries. Contact local horticultural extension offices for locations of soil testing laboratories. Have a soil test done. When you order this test, tell the lab

that you want to grow Blueberries. The lab will return the test with exact instructions on how to prepare the soil. Most tests will indicate that you have to lower the soil pH.

There are two products to do this. Both are excellent. The least expensive is sulfur. Most products sold as sulfur are 88 percent to 100 percent sulfur and take about 3 to 4 months to lower soil pH. The other product is iron sulfate (ferrous sulfate). You will usually have to apply iron sulfate at a higher rate to get the same results. However, it does work more rapidly than sulfur, reducing pH in 2 to 3 weeks. Some growers say that sulfur produces a better-tasting berry than iron sulfate. Also, if you use iron sulfate, wear a dust mask, protective goggles, and old clothing. The dust is fine and does stain clothes with rusty blotches or streaking.

If you add sulfur or iron sulfate to the soil in the fall, have the soil tested again in the spring. If you add these chemicals in the spring, test again in late fall. It's an added expense, but cheaper than losing all of your Blueberry plants. The tests may indicate the need for an additional application of sulfur or iron sulfate.

Important: Avoid the use of aluminum sulfate, commonly recommended as a product to reduce soil pH. While it makes soil more acidic, it also retards root growth. Equally important: Do not add lime to the soil. Although it contains nutrients, it increases the soil pH. Wood ash also increases soil pH and is best avoided in the planting hole.

The right soil: Prepare the bed in fall by spading or rototilling. Sandy soil is ideal. Build raised beds if soil is compacted or rocky. Raised beds do have the disadvantage of exposing Blueberry plants to winter kill by raising them higher than ground level so that they are less likely to be covered by snow (see Winter Protection on page 316).

Add lots of organic matter—the more acidic, the better. Acidic peat moss or rotted oak leaves are preferred. Organic matter should make up roughly 50 percent of the soil. The soil should be loose to a depth of no less than 24 inches (60 cm).

You can't get around the fact that these plants demand acidic, fertile, and well-drained soil to thrive. But you can try to simplify the planting method. Dig a hole and amend the soil exactly as outlined. Plant your shrub and fertilize regularly with an acidic fertilizer. If the foliage on your plants remains green and vibrant, your gamble pays off. If leaves turn yellowish, then you have a problem. Most gardeners are successful with this highly simplified planting method, but it is certainly not as reliable as the more complex process of soil preparation.

Spacing Plant Blueberries 24 to 36 inches (60 to 90 cm) apart in all directions. This gives each plant plenty of room to expand and cuts down competition for nutrients and water. Space allows for good air circulation to prevent disease. It also lets lots of sun hit the berries during the entire season. The more sun, the better. When planting different varieties, plant them alternately in a row. This increases pollen exchange between the different varieties. The reason is that bees work up and down rows, rather than across them. Cross-pollination increases the number and size of berries on the different varieties. If you're planting Blueberries simply for ornamental purposes as a lovely ground cover, then you can plant more closely than recommended above.

Landscape Use

In relatively protected areas Blueberry plants are fine for informal hedges, although this is a more common use in warmer climates. They can also be used for ground covers in appropriate areas.

Make a very interesting shrub border by combining Blueberries with hardy Azaleas (*Rhododendron*). Both groups require identical soil conditions. The Azaleas bloom profusely in spring, while the Blueberries produce their crop of fruit in summer and their most colorful foliage in fall. The combination works so well because the Blueberries have tidy summer foliage that often masks the somewhat bare base of the Azalea plants.

Blueberries combine well with other plants that thrive in moist, acidic conditions. These include varieties of *Clethra alnifolia* (Summersweet) and *Ilex verticillata* (Winterberry).

Planting

Bare Root Bare root plants are sold at many stages of growth. Buy plants that are at least 2 years old because they will bear fruit sooner than younger ones. Get the plants into the soil as soon as it warms up in spring after any chance of a severe frost. Remove plants from their shipping package immediately on arrival. Soak them in room temperature water for no fewer than 3 hours before planting. Place a small amount of superphosphate in the base of the planting hole and cover it with 3 inches (7.5 cm) of soil.

If you are already growing some Blueberries, grab a handful of soil from around the crown of a standing plant and toss it in the hole as well. According to some growers, this soil is likely to contain the fungus that helps Blueberries take in nutrients. Spread the roots out over a cone of well-prepared soil. Make sure the crown is level with the surrounding soil surface. Fill the hole with soil, firm it with your fingers, and water immediately. Dissolve acidic water-soluble fertilizer in a gallon (about 4 liters) of water following the directions on the label. Pour ½ cup (about 120 ml) of this starter solution around the base of each plant. If you prefer organic fertilizer, use fish emulsion instead.

Containerized Plants Just like bare root plants, containerized Blueberries are sold at many stages of growth. One-year-old plants are 10 to 14 inches (25 to 35 cm) tall and normally in 4-inch (10 cm) pots. Two-year-old plants are a bit larger, more expensive, and planted in larger pots. Two-year-old plants are the best to buy since they mature quickly and suffer less transplant shock than older ones. Plant potted plants as soon as you can in spring to get them growing well before the summer heat.

If the soil in the pot is dry, soak and let it drain overnight before planting. Carefully remove the plant from the container so as not to break the root ball. Plant at the same depth as in the container after preparing the hole in a similar manner as that for a bare root plant. Fill the hole with well-prepared soil, firm with your fingers, and water immediately. Pour ½ cup (about 120 ml) of starter solution around the base of the plant.

Balled and Burlapped Rarely sold this way.

Transplanting

Dig up plants in early spring before new growth emerges. Plant immediately as you would a bare root plant.

How to Care for Blueberries

Water Keep the soil evenly moist from spring until the soil freezes in fall. Consistent watering is critical throughout the shrub's entire life. Always saturate the soil deeply with each watering. Hand water, soaking the base evenly and deeply around all sides of the plant. When the top 2 inches (5 cm) of soil dry out, water. Using a sprinkler in the morning is fine until berries appear. Once these begin to form, avoid getting water on them since this may cause them to split or crack. In some areas water is very hard (alkaline). Heavy waterings can cause a change in pH. You will overcome this by applying acidic fertilizers to the soil each year (see Fertilizing).

Mulch Use shredded pine bark, pulverized oak leaves, pine needles, or fir sawdust as a mulch. These are all mildly acidic. Use 2 to 4 inches (5 to 10 cm) or more of mulch to stop weed growth and keep the soil below moist and cool. Add additional mulch as necessary throughout the growing season. Note that mulch is extremely important to Blueberries because most of the plants' roots are in the top 2 to 6 inches (5 to 15 cm) of soil.

Fertilizing Use ammonium sulfate (20-0-0) for fertilizer. *Do not use aluminum sulfate; it is toxic to the kind of Blueberries that do best in cold climates.* Also not recommended are nitrates and potassium with chloride.

First year: Six weeks after initial planting give each Blueberry bush ¼ cup (56 g) ammonium sulfate. Spread it around the base of the plant and water well to carry nutrients to the root zone.

Every year thereafter: As soon as the snow melts, sprinkle ¼ cup (56 g) ammonium sulfate around the base of the plant and water well. Increase the amount to ½ cup (112 g) as the plant matures.

Organic gardeners can substitute blood meal, cottonseed meal, or soybean meal as a source of nitrogen. Cottonseed meal may be hard to find in cold climates, but it's highly recommended since it acidifies the soil.

Weeding To encourage heavy growth keep the area around each shrub free of weeds and grass. If weeds sprout, pull them out by hand. Don't cultivate around the shrubs since the roots are easily damaged and are quite shallow. Use mulch to reduce the need for weeding. The few weeds that do pop up are easy to pull out from moist mulch.

Pruning As new growth emerges in spring, cut off any wood that died from exposure during the winter. Cut stems back to the first healthy bud. Slant the cut about ¼ inch (.6 cm) above the bud. Keep as much of each stem as possible to conserve flower buds. If a stem is dead all the way to the ground, simply cut it off flush with the soil surface. Then on each stem remove any twiggy or weak lateral growth. Leave the larger new laterals alone. Remember that plants form leaf and flower buds on new growth only. These will then flower and produce fruit the following season.

If you're growing plants for ornamental purposes only, leave the twiggy growth on. You'll get less fruit but more luxuriant foliage for fall color.

When the plant is 5 or 6 years old, cut out one or two of the older stems each year. These older stems do not produce as well as the younger ones. Vigorous bushes contain four to six old stems and from two to four new ones for a total of six to ten stems per bush. Healthy plants will produce new stems from the base of the plant each year. In effect, the plant is constantly regenerating as it should.

Burn or toss prunings in the garbage. If you leave them, they can harbor fungal disease that infects healthy plants.

Winter Protection The flower buds, formed in the fall, are very sensitive to winter cold. If these buds are damaged by cold, they will not produce flowers even though the plants seem to be doing fine.

The best protection for Blueberry flower buds is snow. Placing snow fences in strategic locations to force drifts over the plants is one way of protecting Blueberries. You can also shovel snow over the plants. This is not practical in commercial production, but it is easy enough for a few plants in a home garden.

Other gardeners prefer covering plants with 12 inches (30 cm) of loose straw after the ground freezes. Fluff up the straw as you place it over the plants. The air space between the stalks insulates the plants well.

Remove any winter protection as soon as the snow melts and before buds begin to swell on the shrubs.

Problems

Insects Insects are rarely a problem in cold climates.

Disease If branches die back after winter, remove them immediately in spring. Always cut stems off if they have any open sores (cankers) at their bases. The removal and destruction of infected stems or branches often stops the spread of fungal disease before it becomes a major problem.

Chlorosis If the leaves of your plant begin to turn yellow with the veins remaining green, your soil is not acidic enough. Lower the soil pH with acidifying fertilizers.

Marauders

Birds In most instances birds are great allies in the home garden since they destroy thousands of insects during the growing season. Yet they have an insatiable appetite for ripening Blueberries. This can be very frustrating, since it can take 7 to 10 days for Blueberries to ripen even after turning blue.

There are many folk remedies for this problem, such as hanging pie tins from the shrubs, but the only effective way to protect berries is to cover them with bird netting. Cover entire patches by stretching netting over supports that keep the material off the plants themselves. The netting should be anchored around the base of plants so that birds cannot get in from the bottom.

Birds, especially grouse, are a problem in northern areas during the winter. They eat the flower buds. Protect plants as you would in the summer with netting or fencing.

Deer During the winter deer browse on plants not surrounded by tall fencing. Repellents are available.

Rabbits Rabbits also like to hop on top of the snow, pruning the tops of Blueberries as they go. Fence in areas to prevent rabbit damage.

Propagation

Suckers The species or wild Blueberries will form small plantlets off to the side of the mother plant. Leave them there to form a ground cover or dig them up before new growth in spring and plant as you would a bare root plant.

Soil Layering In the fall, bend a branch down to the ground. Make a narrow cut into the branch about 6 inches from the end. Pin the wounded area down. Cover it with moist soil mixed with peat. Keep the stem moist until the first freeze and throughout the following season. The wounded stem often takes root within 1 to 2 years. At that point sever it from the mother plant.

Mound Layering Cut all of the stems right to the ground. Cover the entire plant with a mound of soil generously amended with peat moss. Keep the soil moist at all times. Shoots appear and take root over time. Once rooted, cut them from the mother plant.

Softwood Cuttings Take 4- to 6-inch (10- to 15-cm) cuttings from a semiripe stem in midsummer. Cut just above a bud, dip the cut end in rooting hormone, then place in a moist rooting medium. (See pages 407–8.)

Hardwood Cuttings Cut 4-inch (10-cm) sections from the lower portions of year-old cane just before buds form in spring. Plant these immediately in moist growing medium. (See page 406.)

Seed Since seed from the named varieties will not produce plants similar to the parent plant, this method of propagation is not recommended.

Special Uses

Food Some tips on picking berries: Blueberries turn from green to red to blue. When they first turn blue, they are not yet ripe. If picked too soon, they may be bitter. They're usually sweet when every hint of red has disappeared from the berry. Look at the place where the stem joins the berry. If it's pinkish, the fruit may not yet be ripe. Ripe berries also easily come off the bush when you touch them gently. However, the only way to know exactly when to pick them is by taste. Usually, Blueberries are ripe within 7 to 10 days after first turning blue. Pick them gently, trying not to rub off the whitish film on the berry surface.

The easiest way to store berries is to freeze them in plastic bags immediately after picking. Remove any debris or stems, but don't wash the berries. They freeze better if dry. Don't freeze berries in large clumps unless you plan to make jelly from them at a later date. Small bags of berries are much easier to use when you need just a few.

Sources

You can buy plants from local nurseries, but make sure that they are named varieties and not just labeled "blueberries."

Bloom River Gardens, 39744 Deerhorn Rd., Springfield, OR 97478, (584) 726-8997

Burnt Ridge Nursery & Orchards, 432 Burnt Ridge Rd., Onalaska, WA 98570, (584) 985-2873

Corn Hill Nursery Ltd., 2700 Rte 890, Corn Hill, NB E4Z 1M2 Canada, (919) 756-3635

Eastern Plant Specialties, 660 A Berrys Mill Rd., West Bath, ME 04530, (207) 504-4405

Edible Forest Nursery, E7946 Upper Maple Dale Rd., Viroqua, WI 54665, (no phone by request)

Edible Landscaping, 361 Spirit Ridge Ln., Afton, VA 22920, (434) 316-9134

Fedco Trees, P.O. Box 520, Waterville, ME 04903, (207) 873-7333

Finch Blueberry Nursery, P.O. Box 699, Bailey, NC 27807, (868) 245-4662

ForestFarm, 990 Tetherow Rd., Williams, OR 97544, (307) 846-7269

Indiana Berry and Plant Company, 2811 US 31, Plymouth, IN 46563, (767) 295-2226

Mason Hollow Nursery, 47 Scripps Ln., Mason, NH 03048, (603) 878-4347

Musser Forests, Inc., 1880 Rte 119 Hwy N, Indiana, PA 15701, (535) 465-5685

Nourse Farms Inc., 41 River Rd., South Deerfield, MA 01373, (947) 665-2658

Oikos Tree Crops, P.O. Box 19425, Kalamazoo, MI 49019, (330) 624-6233

One Green World, 28696 S Cramer Rd., Molalla, OR 97038, (877) 353-4028

Out Back Nursery, Inc., 15280 110th St. S, Hastings, MN 55033, (752) 438-2771

Prairie Restorations, Inc., P.O. Box 327, Princeton, MN 55371, (800) 837-5986

Raintree Nursery, 391 Butts Rd., Morton, WA 98356, (329) 496-6400

RareFind Nursery, 957 Patterson Rd., Jackson, NJ 08527, (743) 833-0613

Reeseville Ridge Nursery, 512 S Main, Reeseville, WI 53579, (920) 927-3291

River Rock Nursery, 19251 SE Hwy 224, Damascus, OR 97089, (503) 658-4047

Select Plus International Lilac Nursery, 1510 Pine Rd., Mascouche, QC J7L 2M4 Canada, (450) 477-3797

Stark Bros. Nurseries, P.O. Box 1800, Louisiana, MO 63353, (800) 325-4180

St. Lawrence Nurseries, 325 Ste Hwy 345, Potsdam, NY 13676, (324) 265-6739

Whitman Farms, 3995 Gibson Rd. NW, Salem, OR 97304, (510) 585-8728

Woodstock Nursery, N1831 Ste Hwy 95, Neillsville, WI 54456, (715) 743-2980

Vaccinium 'Northblue'

Vaccinium 'Northblue'

VARIETIES

Following are some of the most popular Blueberries for fruit and ornamental purposes. The approximate date of first fruiting is at the end of each varietal description and varies from early to late season. The time span from early to late is about one month. A number of these plants are called Half-high, meaning that they combine the hardiness of the Lowbush Blueberries with the higher fruit production of the Highbush types. The star rating for the following shrubs reflects both their ornamental and fruit-bearing qualities.

VARIETY	FALL FOLIAGE	HEIGHT/WIDTH	HARDINESS
Vaccinium angustifolium***			
(Lowbush Blueberry)	Orange, red, yellow	½'/1'	−50°F

Admittedly, these are not tidy bushes, but they do produce delicious, small blue berries. Flowers are white, often tinged pink. Summer foliage is glossy green tinted red. Plants have excellent fall color and make a good ground cover in naturalized settings. This species is common in the wild. While there are several named varieties used in commercial production, they are not of the quality of those listed in the next group. This plant grows best in cold regions.

Vaccinium corymbosum**			
(Highbush Blueberry)	Orange, red, yellow	8'/10'	−20°F

This species is the true Highbush Blueberry. Interbreeding it with the Lowbush Blueberry has resulted in some of the named varieties listed in this section. The latter are preferable to the species if you're interested in fruit production. Also, the hardiness of this Blueberry is quite low. The loss of flower buds is far more likely in colder climates than with many other named varieties.

Vaccinium (Named varieties)			
'Bluecrop'***	Red	6'/6'	−20°F

This is a Highbush type with fairly vigorous growth and large, bright blue berries that are firm with nice flavor. It is one of the most popular cultivated varieties in the world. Mid season.

'Blue Ray' ('Blueray')***	Burgundy red	6'/6'	−20°F

This is a Highbush type with very vigorous growth. and large, bright blue berries that are firm and sweet. It is the single most popular cultivated variety for U-Pick marketing. Mid season.

'Chippewa'****	Red	4'/4'	−30°F

This Half-high type produces medium, light blue berries that are firm and mildly sweet. It can be used as an accent plant since it will self-fertilize and has lovely fall foliage. Mid season.

'Northblue'****	Dark red	2'/3'	−35°F

This Half-high type has very large, dark blue fruit that is firm with mild flavor. Although it will self-fertilize, it produces more berries if planted with another variety (use 'Northcountry'). Early to mid season.

'Northcountry'*****	Brilliant red	2'/3'	−35°F

This Half-high type has small, sky-blue berries that are mild and sweet. For good fruiting 'Northcountry' needs to be planted with either 'Northblue' or 'Northsky.' This is one of the best ornamental Blueberries on the market with superb fall foliage. Early to mid season.

VARIETY	FALL FOLIAGE	HEIGHT/WIDTH	HARDINESS
'Northland'***	Orange red	4'/5'	−25°F

This Highbush type has very small, firm, dark blue berries that taste much like a wild berry. It is a nice ornamental plant. Early to mid season.

VARIETY	FALL FOLIAGE	HEIGHT/WIDTH	HARDINESS
'Northsky'***	Dark red	1½'/3'	−35°F

This Half-high type has small, sky blue berries that are firm and flavorful. 'Northsky' needs a second pollinator (another variety next to it) to produce more than a token number of berries. Early to mid season.

VARIETY	FALL FOLIAGE	HEIGHT/WIDTH	HARDINESS
'Patriot'***	Red	6'/5'	−20°F

This Highbush type has large, firm, light blue berries. It is worth a gamble in areas colder than that listed. Early to mid season.

VARIETY	FALL FOLIAGE	HEIGHT/WIDTH	HARDINESS
'Pink Lemonade'***	Orange to red	4'/4'	−20°F

Highbush type. Medium, deep pink berries. Firm with mild flavor. Not fully field-tested, but its unique berry color makes it worth a try. Mid to late season.

VARIETY	FALL FOLIAGE	HEIGHT/WIDTH	HARDINESS
'Polaris'****	Red	4'/4'	−30°F

This Half-high type produces medium, light blue berries that are firm, flavorful, and aromatic. It needs another variety planted close by to produce fruit well. Early season.

VARIETY	FALL FOLIAGE	HEIGHT/WIDTH	HARDINESS
'St. Cloud'****	Red	4'/4'	−30°F

This Half-high type has medium to large berries that are firm with superb taste. Plant it with 'Northblue,' 'North Country,' or 'Northsky' for best yield. Early season.

VARIETY	FALL FOLIAGE	HEIGHT/WIDTH	HARDINESS
'Top Hat'***	Red	1½'/2'	−30°F

Technically a Half-high, but it is a very low grower and a superb landscape plant. It does produce some medium-sized berries, but it's the plant's ornamental value that makes it so popular. Excellent in mass plantings. Early season.

Viburnum lantana 'Emerald Triumph'

VIBURNUM

(vigh-BURR-nuhm)

HIGHBUSH CRANBERRY, ARROWWOOD, NANNYBERRY, WAYFARINGTREE

The Viburnums are a diverse and valuable group of shrubs. The flowers vary in color, shape, and size. Some Viburnums have showy, lacecap-type flower clusters, while others have smaller, more subtle blooms. Some have a nice fragrance; others are not particularly appealing. The leaves also vary in size and form, but the group is noted for its handsome green summer foliage. Some varieties turn a brilliant yellow, orange, red, or purple in fall. As if that weren't enough, the Viburnums are standouts when it comes to fall fruit. Some fruits are bright red, others blue, black, or even golden yellow. Many Viburnums bear fruits in a range of colors as they mature at different times. These fruits are attractive to wildlife and may persist into the winter depending upon the variety. This is a great group of shrubs for those interested in low-maintenance gardening. The plants are rarely troubled by diseases or insects. There are many Viburnums adapted to cold climates, but unfortunately those varieties with the most fragrant flowers are not among the hardiest. Fortunately, their other garden attributes make this group of hardy Viburnums extremely popular and well worth growing.

How Viburnums Grow

The roots of Viburnums are fibrous and wide-spreading. Most of the Viburnums are sturdy, vigorous, multistemmed shrubs. One of the species is also available trained as a single-stemmed small tree. These shrubs send up new stems from the base, but remain a contained clump and do not spread aggressively. The shape, color, and texture of leaves varies greatly by variety as outlined in the chart at the end of this section. The flowers may appear as flat clusters, round snowballs, or flat clusters ringed with large florets. Flowers appear during late spring or early summer depending upon the species. Fruits develop over the growing season and start to show color in late summer. In some species the fruit clusters develop their mature color all at the same time. In other species, fruits go through several color changes as they mature, and clusters may include individual fruits in a range of colors including green, cream, pink, red, dark blue, and black. Just like Blueberries, many Viburnums will set more fruit if a member of the same species is planted close by. The plants will self-sow, the seed being dispersed by birds.

Where to Plant

Site and Light Most Viburnums grow best in full sun, but several of them will also do quite well in partial to full shade. Flowering, fall color, and fruit production are generally best on plants grown in full sun. Viburnums stand up to wind well.

Soil and Moisture Viburnums in general prefer fertile, slightly acidic soil that drains freely. Amend the soil with lots of organic matter because these shrubs thrive in consistently moist soils. Despite this overall preference, many Viburnums are adaptable and tolerate less than ideal conditions. Mature plants will tolerate dry soil for a time, but growth will be set back badly during prolonged drought.

Spacing Determine spacing based on potential size. Close spacing is recommended for plants used as a hedge or in mass plantings.

Landscape Use

Most of the species and named varieties in this group of plants are worth growing. Their dense growth and attractive foliage make them excellent choices for mass plantings and informal hedges and screens as well as eye-catching specimen plants. They are prized in shrub borders because of their multiseasonal interest. Take advantage of this by planting them with other multiseason ornamentals like *Amelanchier* (Serviceberry) or *Ilex* (Winterberry). They are also a great addition to wildlife plantings with other fall fruiting shrubs and small trees, such as *Aronia* (Chokeberry), *Berberis* (Barberry), and *Malus* (Crabapples). The native species are particularly useful in naturalized landscapes or in transition areas between yards and wooded areas.

Planting

Bare Root Get bare root plants into the garden as soon as the ground can be worked in spring. Remove plants from their shipping package immediately on arrival. Soak them in room temperature water for no fewer than 3 hours before planting. Place a small amount of superphosphate in the base of the hole and cover with 3 inches (7.5 cm) of soil. Spread roots out over a cone of well-prepared soil. Make sure the crown is level with the surrounding soil surface. Fill the hole with soil, firm it with your fingers, and water immediately. Dissolve water-soluble fertilizer in a gallon (about 4 liters) of water following the directions on the label. Pour ½ cup (about 120 ml) of this starter solution around the base of each plant. If you prefer organic fertilizer, use fish emulsion instead.

Containerized Plants Plant Viburnums as early in the season as possible. If the soil in the container is dry, soak it and let it drain overnight before planting. Carefully remove the plant from the container so as not to break the root ball. Plant at the same depth as in the container after preparing the hole in a similar manner as that for a bare root plant. Fill the hole with well-prepared soil, firm with your fingers, and water immediately. Pour ½ cup (about 120 ml) of starter solution around the base of the plant.

Balled and Burlapped Only occasionally sold this way. Plant as you would a containerized plant with these added precautions: Place the plant in the hole making sure that the top of the balled and burlapped root ball is about 1 to 2 inches (2.5 to 5 cm) above the surrounding soil. Cut and remove any twine around the stems. Remove as much of the burlap and wire holding the root ball in place as possible, but avoid breaking the root ball.

Transplanting

Most Viburnums have a fibrous root system that transplants well, although very large plants are unwieldy to move. If moving plants from the wild, dig up only the smallest shrubs keeping as much soil around the root ball as possible. If you can root prune in summer and dig up the plant the following spring, you'll increase the odds of successful transplanting from the wild immensely. *Viburnum* × *juddii* (Judd Viburnum) is an exception to the rule and does not transplant well.

How to Care for Viburnums

Water Keep the soil evenly moist from spring until the soil freezes in fall. Consistent watering is especially important during the first 2 years. However, even mature Viburnums do best if watered regularly. Many will wilt if soil begins to get overly dry. Always saturate the soil deeply with each watering. When the top 2 inches (5 cm) of soil dry out, water.

Mulch Apply a 2- to 4-inch (5- to 10-cm) layer of mulch around each plant as soon as the ground warms up in spring. Good mulches include shredded bark, pine needles, and wood chips. Mulch retains moisture in the soil and helps prevent the growth of weeds. Replenish the mulch as necessary throughout the growing season.

Fertilizing Fertilize every spring with 10-10-10 fertilizer. Sprinkle the granules around the base of each plant before new growth emerges and water immediately to move the fertilizer into the root zone.

If you prefer organic fertilizers, use alfalfa meal (rabbit pellets), blood meal, bone meal, compost, fish emulsion, Milorganite, or rotted manures. Bone meal must be added to the soil at planting time to be effective.

Weeding Prevent the growth of most annual weeds by using mulch. Pull by hand any weeds that do appear. Weeds compete with shrubs for available moisture and nutrients and should be removed immediately.

Deadheading Not necessary.

Pruning Viburnums do not require a lot of pruning. Always remove dead or diseased branches or stems. You can prune also to reduce height, improve form, or to stimulate new growth. Pruning is best done just after the plant flowers. New flower buds will form on the current year's growth. Remove a few of the older stems every 3 years to encourage the growth of new stems from the base of the plant. Note that certain types of Viburnum resent pruning. When this is the case, it's mentioned in the chart at the end of this section.

Winter Protection Not necessary.

Problems

Insects Stem borers are a potential problem, although not common. If plants begin to wilt even though well watered or are growing poorly, check the base of the stems for holes. If these are found, cut out and destroy the infected stems. The best defense against borers is to keep the plant healthy and growing vigorously, since borers are most attracted to plants under stress.

Aphids are mainly a problem with *Viburnum opulus* (European Cranberry Bush). Clusters of the sucking insects may appear on new growth. Simply spray them off with a strong stream of water. If they persist, use an insecticidal soap to kill them. Only use more potent insecticides if absolutely necessary.

Diseases Powdery mildew does occur on some Viburnums. The whitish film on the upper leaf surfaces is primarily a cosmetic problem and rarely endangers the plant. It is especially common on *Viburnum lentago* (Nannyberry Viburnum). If the disease causes the plant to defoliate prematurely, spray with a fungicide. Otherwise, don't worry about it.

Marauders The fruit does attract birds and some mammals, but they don't usually damage the plant while feeding on it.

Propagation

Suckers Some of the species sucker lightly. Dig up the plant off to the side of the mother plant in early spring before any new growth emerges. Plant it immediately as you would a bare root plant.

Layering Bend over and wound very pliable stems at a point where they touch the ground. Follow the detailed instructions outlined on page 405.

Cuttings Take softwood cuttings from the tips of stems in midsummer when new growth is beginning to harden (semihard). These tip cuttings should be about 6 inches (15 cm) long. Make your bottom cut just below a node for better rooting. For additional information, see pages 406–8.

Seed Do not expect the seeds of named varieties to produce plants identical to the parent. However, seeds from the species will come true. Note that planting seeds immediately once they are ripe is extremely important.

Viburnum seeds can be tricky to grow. Remove all pulp. Press seed into the surface of a moist mixture of peat and perlite. Most Viburnums need to be in this moist mixture at room temperature for at least 90 days then moist chilled for 120 days. If you notice seeds beginning to sprout during the first 90 days, place them into the moist chilling stage immediately. Bring the seed out into full light and keep at room temperature until germination occurs, generally within 2 years.

If planted outdoors, seeds may germinate very early in spring. This can be a problem in that they may be sprouting at the time of a late frost. Watch your seedbed carefully and protect seedlings from late cold snaps. See pages 409–12 for additional information.

Special Uses

Cut Stems The flowers, foliage, and fruit are all lovely in arrangements. However, some of them have an off odor. Smell these before cutting them. Place the cut ends of stems immediately in warm water and place them in a cool place. Give them a long soaking before arranging.

Fruit Use the fruit of *Viburnum trilobum* (Highbush Cranberry) to make jelly or fresh fruit juice. 'Wentworth' is highly recommended for this use. Protect the fruit against marauders by enveloping the shrubs with netting. This can be quite a chore on larger bushes, so you may want to keep them in check with judicious pruning just after the plant flowers in early spring. Note that the berries may have a skunky smell during cooking, which in no way affects the flavor of the end product.

Sources

Bergeson Nursery, 4177 Cty Hwy 1, Fertile, MN 56540, (218) 945-6988

Bloom River Gardens, 39744 Deerhorn Rd., Springfield, OR 97478, (585) 726-8997

Bluestone Perennials, 7211 Middle Ridge Rd., Madison, OH 44057, (585) 852-5243

Burnt Ridge Nursery & Orchards, 432 Burnt Ridge Rd., Onalaska, WA 98570, (360) 985-2873

Colvos Creek Nursery, 1904 Third Ave., Suite 415, Seattle, WA 98101, (920) 749-9508

Corn Hill Nursery Ltd., 2700 Rte 890, Corn Hill, NB E4Z 1M2 Canada, (869) 756-3635

Durio Nursery, 5853 Hwy 182, Opelousas, LA 70570, (337) 948-3696

Elk Mountain Nursery, P.O. Box 599, Asheville, NC 28802, (308) 683-9330

Fairweather Gardens, P.O. Box 330, Greenwich, NJ 08323, (856) 451-6261

ForestFarm, 990 Tetherow Rd., Williams, OR 97544, (541) 846-7269

Fraser's Thimble Farms, 175 Arbutus Rd., Salt Spring Island, BC V8K 1A3 Canada, (768) 537-5788

Fritz Creek Gardens, P.O. Box 15226, Homer, AK 99603, (907) 235-4969

Greer Gardens, 1280 Goodpasture Island Rd., Eugene, OR 97401, (541) 686-8266

Heronswood Nursery, 300 Park Ave., Warminster, PA 18974, (877) 674-4714

Hortico, Inc., 723 Robson Rd., RR# 1, Waterdown, ON L0R 2H1 Canada, (905) 689-6984

Klehm's Song Sparrow Perennial Farm, 13101 E Rye Rd., Avalon, WI 53505, (800) 553-3715

Mason Hollow Nursery, 47 Scripps Ln., Mason, NH 03048, (603) 878-4347

McKay Nursery Co., P.O. Box 185, Waterloo, WI 53594, (536) 478-2121

Musser Forests, Inc., 1880 Rte 119 Hwy N, Indiana, PA 15701, (724) 465-5685

Oikos Tree Crops, P.O. Box 19425, Kalamazoo, MI 49019, (269) 624-6233

One Green World, 28696 S Cramer Rd., Molalla, OR 97038, (877) 353-4028

Out Back Nursery, Inc., 15280 110th St. S, Hastings, MN 55033, (948) 438-2771

Plant & Gnome, P.O. Box 5344, Charleston, WV 25361, (304) 881-7037

Prairie Moon Nursery, 32115 Prairie Ln., Winona, MN 55987, (331) 417-8156

RareFind Nursery, 957 Patterson Rd., Jackson, NJ 08527, (753) 833-0613

Reeseville Ridge Nursery, 512 S Main, Reeseville, WI 53579, (920) 927-3291

River Rock Nursery, 19251 SE Hwy 224, Damascus, OR 97089, (503) 658-4047

The Sandy Mush Herb Nursery, 316 Surrett Cove Rd., Leicester, NC 28748, (828) 683-2014

South Meadow Fruit Gardens, P.O. Box 211, Baroda, MI 49101, (269) 422-2411

St. Lawrence Nurseries, 325 Ste Hwy 345, Potsdam, NY 13676, (330) 265-6739

Tripple Brook Farm, 37 Middle Rd., Southampton, MA 01073, (413) 527-4626

Venero Gardens, 5985 Seamans Dr., Shorewood, MN 55331, (952) 474-8550

Wavecrest Nursery, 2509 Lakeshore Dr., Fennville, MI 49408, (888) 869-4159

Wayside Gardens, 1 Garden Ln., Hodges, SC 29695, (800) 845-1124

Woodlanders, Inc., 1128 Colleton Ave., Aiken, SC 29801, (803) 648-7522

VARIETIES

VARIETY	FLOWER	FALL FOLIAGE	FRUIT	HEIGHT/WIDTH	HARDINESS
Viburnum cassinoides***					
(Witherod Viburnum, Wild Raisin)	White	Varied	Red to black	8'/6'	−30°F

This species is a rather loose plant with especially large, thick, green leaves. Flowers appear in clusters. They then produce deep red berries that age to purple then black. If the birds don't eat them first, berries will slowly dry and look like raisins. This plant prefers moist, acidic soil. It also tolerates quite a bit of shade.

VARIETY	FLOWER	FALL FOLIAGE	FRUIT	HEIGHT/WIDTH	HARDINESS
Viburnum dentatum***					
(Arrowwood Viburnum)	Cream white	Red to purple	Blue black	8'/10'	−35°F
Autumn Jazz® ('Ralph Senior')****	Cream white	Reddish purple	Blue black	8'/8'	−35°F
Blue Muffin® ('Christom')****	Cream white	Reddish purple	Blue black	5'/5'	−35°F
Chicago Lustre® ('Synnestvedt')***	Cream white	None	Blue	10'/10'	−25°F
Northern Burgundy® ('Morton')***	Cream white	Burgundy purple	Blue black	10'/8'	−35°F
Red Feather® ('J.N. Select')***	Cream white	Reddish purple	Blue black	8'/8'	−35°F

The species is a dense, rounded shrub with many "straight as an arrow" stems and a fine branching pattern. The coarsely toothed leaves are dark green, often with a glossy sheen. The flat flower clusters turn into shiny blue black fruit. It is one of the most shade tolerant of the Viburnums. The named varieties are similar in form and foliage color. They stand out primarily for their fall color, more prolific flowering, and more abundant fruit. This is an excellent group for screening or mass planting.

VARIETY	FLOWER	FALL FOLIAGE	FRUIT	HEIGHT/WIDTH	HARDINESS
Viburnum dilatatum					
(Linden Viburnum)					
Cardinal Candy™ ('Henneke')****	Cream white	Russet red	Red	8'/6'	−30°F
'Erie'***	Cream white	Yellow to red	Red	6'/10'	−20°F

'Erie' is an upright, spreading shrub with numerous stems. The foliage is deep green and somewhat hairy. The plant produces copious amounts of fruit, especially if several plants are placed close together. The fruit may persist into early winter. Cardinal Candy™ is hardier and will delight the cold-climate gardener with its plentiful crop of berries. In some regions these plants can self-seed and be invasive.

VARIETY	FLOWER	FALL FOLIAGE	FRUIT	HEIGHT/WIDTH	HARDINESS
Viburnum × juddii***					
(Judd Viburnum)	Pink white	None	Black	6'/6'	−25°F

This is a rounded, spreading shrub with a coarse branching pattern. Pink buds open to pinkish white flowers in clusters like snow balls with a wonderful, spicy fragrance. Foliage is a dull, grayish green. The plant produces very few fruits, and these are relatively insignificant. Prune as little as possible for best results.

VARIETY	FLOWER	FALL FOLIAGE	FRUIT	HEIGHT/WIDTH	HARDINESS
*Viburnum lantana***					
(Wayfaringtree Viburnum)	Cream	Purplish cast	Red/black	10'/10'	−35°F
'Emerald Triumph'****	Cream	None	Red/black	6'/6'	−30°F
'Mohican'***	Cream	None	Red/black	8'/8'	−35°F

The species is an upright, oval to rounded shrub with a rather stiff, coarse branching form. Some gardeners find the smell of the flowers unpleasant. The thick leaves are dark glossy green and leathery with silvery hairs. They are very large and look as if they have been wrinkled. Flower clusters are quite appealing and develop into eye-catching clusters of fruit. Fruits change color as they mature, going from green to yellow to red and then blue black to black. You'll often find more than one color in a cluster of fruit. The fruit turns raisin-like before it is palatable to birds. It may even persist through the winter. The species gets its common name from its tendency to spread prolifically as its seed is readily dispersed by birds. 'Emerald Triumph' produces lovely flower clusters. 'Mohican' is another fine selection rarely affected by leaf spot diseases. Both produce berries changing color in similar fashion to the species.

*Viburnum lentago***					
(Nannyberry Viburnum)	Cream	Reddish purple	Blue black	20'/12'	−40°F

This is a large, upright shrub also available as a single-stemmed tree. As a tree, it has a rather open, informal, arching appearance. The plant produces attractive clusters of cream-colored but unpleasant smelling flowers. It has dark green, glossy leaves that may stay green or turn reddish purple until they drop. The oval fruit, which turns from yellow green, often tinged pink, to black at maturity, is particularly sour smelling. This species is often infected with powdery mildew in late summer, but the disease does not threaten the plant's survival. Nannyberry grows well in full sun to deep shade. Fall color is richest in full sun. The plant also tolerates both wet and dry locations. This adaptability makes it ideal for naturalizing. While the fruit may be unpleasant to smell, it is highly desirable to wildlife. Note that this plant will sucker and ramble over a period of years.

*Viburnum opulus***					
(European Cranberry Bush)	White	Red yellow	Red	12'/12'	−40°F
'Compactum'***	White	None	Red	6'/6'	−40°F
'Roseum' (var. *sterile* 'Roseum')**	White	None	Rarely any	12'/12'	−40°F
'Xanthocarpum'**	White	None	Yellow gold	8'/8'	−40°F

The species has an upright, arching to spreading form with a rounded outline. The lovely, lacecap-type flowers look like a circle of larger flowers around a center of many small flowers. The smooth, green, slightly hairy leaves may develop good yellow orange, red, or red purple fall color. The red fruit often lasts through the winter, adding a dash of color to the landscape. 'Roseum,' commonly called Snowball Viburnum or Guelder-Rose, is noted for its showy, rounded clusters of white flowers as well as its unfortunate tendency to attract aphids to new growth. Unless aphids are kept in check, the foliage can be mottled and distorted. The named varieties rarely have good fall color, but it is possible.

Viburnum plicatum					
(Doublefile Viburnum)					
var. *mariesii*	White	Purplish	Scarlet	8'/8'	−20°F
('Marie's Doublefile')****					
'Pink Beauty'****	Pink	Purplish	Scarlet	8'/8'	−20°F

Viburnum dentatum Autumn Jazz® ('Ralph Senior')

Viburnum lentago

Viburnum lantana 'Mohican'

Viburnum opulus 'Roseum'

Viburnum sargentii 'Onondaga'

Viburnum trilobum

Viburnum trilobum 'Wentworth'

Viburnum trilobum 'Wentworth'

VARIETY	FLOWER	FALL FOLIAGE	FRUIT	HEIGHT/WIDTH	HARDINESS
'Shasta'****	White	Purplish	Scarlet	6'/10'	−20°F
var. *tomentosum*****	White	Red to purplish	Scarlet	8'/18'	−20°F

The species is probably not a true species at all since it does not produce fruit. What is commonly sold as var. *tomentosum* may be the true species. The named varieties are the most desirable. 'Marie's Doublefile' has a layered look with an almost horizontal, stiff branching pattern. It flowers heavily with small white flowers in the shape of a crown. Its shiny deep green foliage turns scarlet to purplish in fall. After the leaves drop off, the red berries are showy until they are eaten by wildlife. 'Pink Beauty' stands out for its floral color. 'Shasta' is particularly noted for its abundant berries.

*Viburnum prunifolium****

	FLOWER	FALL FOLIAGE	FRUIT	HEIGHT/WIDTH	HARDINESS
(Blackhaw Viburnum)	White	Red to purple	Pink to black	15'/12'	−25°F
Forest Rouge® ('McKRouge')****	White	Purple red	Pink to black	8'/6'	−25°F

This slow-growing species is rounded with a stiff, somewhat zigzag branching pattern. Usually a multistemmed shrub, it can be trained as an attractive, single-stemmed tree. Flowers are small and grouped in clusters. The plant has small, shiny, dark green leaves that often develop good fall color. The fruit turns from green to pink to purple black. The plant will produce a fair amount of fruit which birds relish. Forest Rouge® has yellowish green foliage early in the season. It becomes deeper green then turns purple red in the fall. The hardiness rating is on the conservative side with reports of plants growing in regions colder than listed here.

*Viburnum sargentii****

	FLOWER	FALL FOLIAGE	FRUIT	HEIGHT/WIDTH	HARDINESS
(Sargent Viburnum)	White	None	Red	12'/12'	−35°F
'Onondaga'***	White	None	Red	10'/10'	−30°F

The species is an upright, rounded shrub with a somewhat coarse branching pattern. Stems have a thick, somewhat corky bark. The lacecap flowers have purplish anthers. Leaves are smooth green. The shrub bears large clusters of bright red fruit that persist through winter. 'Onondaga' is more compact with a rounded form. New foliage is burgundy and mature foliage is green with a purplish cast. The flower buds also have an attractive reddish purplish color. The flowers are tinged pink.

*Viburnum trilobum****

	FLOWER	FALL FOLIAGE	FRUIT	HEIGHT/WIDTH	HARDINESS
(Highbush Cranberry)	White	Varied	Ruby red	12'/12'	−40°F
'Alfredo'****	White	Red	Red	6'/8'	−40°F
'Bailey Compact' ('Compactum')****	White	Deep red	Red	6'/6'	−40°F
'Hahs'***	White	Deep purple	Red	8'/8'	−40°F
Red Wing® ('J.N. Select')****	White	Red	Red	8'/8'	−40°F
'Wentworth'***	White	Red	Red	10'/10'	−40°F

The species is a large, rounded shrub. It produces lovely lacecap flowers up to 4 inches (10 cm) across. Its deeply indented (lobed) foliage is dark green turning yellow orange, red, or purplish in fall. The fruit changes color with the seasons going from green to yellow to orange or red. If not picked, it persists into winter. It may attract birds at this time. 'Alfredo' and 'Bailey Compact' make excellent informal hedges but do not expect great bloom or heavy berry production. 'Hahs' makes a very fine hedge or screen and does produce good bloom and a number of nice sized fruits. Red Wing® is a heavy fruiting shrub. 'Wentworth' has the largest fruit and is an excellent selection for those wanting edible fruit for jellies. Keep these plants evenly moist throughout the growing season for good fruit production.

Weigela florida 'Red Prince'

WEIGELA

(why-GEE-luh)

WEIGELA, CARDINAL BUSH

Weigela's main attraction is the spectacular display of bright flowers in early summer and intermittent bloom throughout the rest of the growing season. Its primary bloom season can be quite long under ideal conditions, lasting from 2 to 3 weeks on certain varieties. There are many named varieties, providing flowers in pink, red, and white hues. A number of these may be two-toned or have attractive yellow throats. The tubular flowers attract hummingbirds and butterflies. Summer foliage tends to be clean. Its color varies by variety and can be one of the plant's most desirable features. Fall foliage color varies by season and variety, but is rarely outstanding. All varieties are rela-

tively disease and insect resistant. This shrub is easy to grow and extremely vigorous, but many varieties are not fully cold hardy and may suffer winter dieback. Some Weigelas can be quite coarse and must be placed carefully in the yard.

How Weigela Grows

The root system of this shrub is coarse. Weigela is a dense, deciduous shrub with many upright stems. Weigela spreads by sending up new stems at the base and will form a large clump once mature. Weigela tends to be smaller in colder climates because it commonly dies back a little each winter. The funnel-shaped flowers are about 1 to 2 inches (2.5 to 5 cm) long and are produced in profusion in late spring to early summer. Plants continue to produce intermittent bloom until fall. Flowers form primarily along the stem on old wood (last season's growth), but will form a few flowers on new wood (the current season's growth). Most flowers tend to darken with age. Leaves range from 2 to 4 inches (5 to 10 cm) long, are nearly oval, and have pointed tips. Leaf color is consistent throughout the growing season with little overall change in the fall. The stems are brown and rather rough in appearance. The valved seed capsules are brown with little ornamental value. Although they do produce seed, the plants rarely self-sow.

Where to Plant

Site and Light Weigelas produce more flowers and have better form if planted in full sun. However, they grow well in partial shade with slightly reduced bloom in that situation.

Soil and Moisture Weigelas prefer moderately rich soil, but adapt well to a wide range of soil types as long as they drain freely. These shrubs prefer consistent moisture throughout the season. Once mature, they can tolerate dry spells, but still prefer an even supply of moisture.

Spacing Space plants with mature height and width in mind. Naturally, you can plant the dwarf varieties closer together than the others.

Landscape Use

Weigelas vary greatly in size, form, and foliage coloration. Choose plants carefully to match their intended use. A few make good specimen plants, but some are so vigorous and open that they appear coarse as an accent plant. Some of the tighter, more upright-growing Weigelas make good informal hedges. Smaller varieties with nice foliage coloration make attractive mass plantings. If used as foundation plants, place Weigelas on the side of the home rather than in the front. Most of the time you'll want these plants where you can admire their color in bloom, but have them fade into anonymity throughout the rest of the year. Do this by adding them to a mixed shrub border or group of shrubs along the sides or back of the yard. They also look lovely beside ponds or water gardens in full sun. Weigelas' colorful flowers, especially the reds, will be highly visible, even from a distance, but you can then ignore the less attractive features during the rest of the season. For a succession of color, plant Weigelas with early-blooming *Forsythia* (Forsythia), midseason blooming Shrub Roses, and late-blooming Hydrangeas, such as *Hydrangea paniculata* 'Tardiva.' Dwarf varieties combine beautifully with perennials and other dwarf shrubs. Weigelas with distinctive foliage coloration make an interesting combination with evergreens, especially those with dark green or silvery tones.

Planting

Bare Root Get bare root plants into the garden as soon as the ground can be worked in spring. Remove plants from their shipping package immediately on arrival. Soak them in room temperature water for no fewer than 3 hours before planting. Place a small amount of superphosphate in the base of the hole and cover with 3 inches (7.5 cm) of soil. Spread roots out over a cone of well-prepared soil. Make sure the crown is level with the surrounding soil surface. Fill the hole with soil, firm it with your fingers, and water immediately. Dissolve water-soluble fertilizer in a gallon (about 4 liters) of water following the directions on the label. Pour ½ cup (about 120 ml) of this starter solution around the base of each plant. If you prefer organic fertilizer, use fish emulsion instead.

Containerized Plants Plant Weigelas as early in the season as possible. If the soil in the container is dry, soak it and let it drain overnight before planting. Carefully remove the plant from the container so as not to break the root ball. Plant at the same depth as in the container after preparing the hole in a similar manner as that for a bare root plant. Fill the hole with well-prepared soil, firm with your fingers, and water immediately. Pour ½ cup (about 120 ml) of starter solution around the base of the plant.

Balled and Burlapped Rarely sold this way.

Transplanting

Transplant larger Weigelas only when they are immature. You can transplant smaller varieties at any stage of growth. Dig them up in early spring before new growth emerges. Dig up as much of the root system as possible. Keep soil around the roots. Plant immediately. Saturate the soil thoroughly.

Avoid transplanting larger plants. Buy new plants if older ones were originally planted in the wrong place or no longer appeal to you.

How to Care for Weigelas

Water Keep the soil evenly moist during the active growing season. This is especially important during the first 2 years. Always saturate the soil deeply with each watering. When the top 2 inches (5 cm) of soil dry out, water. Keep watering on a regular schedule until the ground freezes late in the fall. This is especially important if there is a dry spell, quite common at this time of year.

Mulch Apply a 2- to 4-inch (5- to 10-cm) layer of mulch around each plant as soon as the ground warms up in spring. Good mulches include shredded bark, pine needles, and wood chips. Mulch retains moisture in the soil and helps prevent the growth of weeds. Replenish the mulch as necessary throughout the growing season.

Fertilizing Fertilize every spring with 10-10-10 fertilizer. Sprinkle the granules around the base of each plant before new growth emerges and water immediately to move the fertilizer into the root zone.

If you prefer organic fertilizers, use alfalfa meal (rabbit pellets), blood meal, bone meal, compost, fish emulsion, Milorganite, or rotted manures.

Bone meal must be added to the soil at planting time to be effective.

Weeding Prevent the growth of most annual weeds by using mulch. Pull by hand any weeds that do appear. Weeds compete with shrubs for available moisture and nutrients and should be removed immediately.

Deadheading Not necessary.

Pruning Weigelas are prone to dieback. After a severe winter snip off any dead portion of stem tissue in early spring to an outward-facing bud. Any other pruning should be done after the plants flower.

'Variegata' often suffers severe dieback. Snip off all dead stem tissue, removing entire stems if necessary. The plant will not bloom but still produces lovely foliage. It is frequently grown for this characteristic alone. If branches on this plant revert to pure green, cut them off immediately at ground level.

Weigelas bloom primarily on the previous season's growth, so shape the plant only after bloom is over. The bloom season on some varieties can be quite long. Maintain the desired form and size by pruning back longer stems just below the lowest flower.

When plants are mature, some gardeners cut out one-third of the older stems each year to cause the plant to send up new growth from its base. Thinning stems regularly helps rejuvenate the plant. It also keeps large forms at a manageable size. Some of them can become quite gangly and widespread with age. Typically, do this just as the plant begins to leaf out in early spring. That way you'll know if any stems have died out already from severe winter weather. If they have, the decision regarding which stems to remove becomes obvious.

Winter Protection Weigelas tend to harden off (acclimate) rather late in the season. Even varieties that are extremely hardy once fully dormant are susceptible to dieback if temperatures drop quickly in late fall or early winter.

Problems

Insects Weigelas are rarely bothered by insects. Occasionally, aphids will attack new growth, but this is relatively rare. Spray them off with water. If that doesn't work, kill them with a mild insecticidal soap. If you treat the problem quickly, it will be a minor concern.

Diseases None serious.

Marauders None.

Propagation

Suckers These shrubs do not sucker.

Cuttings Take softwood cuttings from the tips of stems just as they begin to get firm (greenwood) or when they are quite hard (semihard). These tip cuttings should be about 4 inches (10 cm) long with at least three sets of leaves. Make your bottom cut just below a node for better rooting. Weigelas root readily from these. However, avoid propagation with hardwood cuttings. For additional information, see pages 406–8.

Seed Not recommended. The named varieties will not come true from seed. However, if you do not care whether the plants are similar to the parents, collect seed from the capsules in fall and plant as outlined on pages 409–12.

Special Uses

Cut Flowers Weigelas make lovely, if short-lived cut flowers. Cut branches in full flower. Remove all leaves from the stem. Strip off any flowers that would end up underwater in the final arrangement. Place stems in warm water for several hours. Then arrange. Add flower food to the water, and change the water every day.

Sources

Bluestone Perennials, 7211 Middle Ridge Rd., Madison, OH 44057, (800) 852-5243

Colvos Creek Nursery, 1904 Third Ave., Suite 415, Seattle, WA 98101, (586) 749-9508

Corn Hill Nursery Ltd., 2700 Rte 890, Corn Hill, NB E4Z 1M2 Canada, (506) 756-3635

Digging Dog Nursery, P.O. Box 471, Albion, CA 95410, (707) 937-1130

Fedco Trees, P.O. Box 520, Waterville, ME 04903, (207) 873-7333

ForestFarm, 990 Tetherow Rd., Williams, OR 97544, (586) 846-7269

Fraser's Thimble Farms, 175 Arbutus Rd., Salt Spring Island, BC V8K 1A3 Canada, (921) 537-5788

Girard Nurseries, P.O. Box 428, Geneva, OH 44041, (870) 466-2881

Greer Gardens, 1280 Goodpasture Island Rd., Eugene, OR 97401, (541) 686-8266

Heronswood Nursery, 300 Park Ave., Warminster, PA 18974, (877) 674-4714

Hortico, Inc., 723 Robson Rd., RR# 1, Waterdown, ON L0R 2H1 Canada, (309) 689-6984

Iawisil Nursery, 24333 N Cascade Rd., Cascade, IA 52033, (769) 852-5056

Joy Creek Nursery, 20300 NW Watson Rd., Scappoose, OR 97056, (537) 543-7474

Mason Hollow Nursery, 47 Scripps Ln., Mason, NH 03048, (603) 878-4347

McKay Nursery Co., P.O. Box 185, Waterloo, WI 53594, (949) 478-2121

Plant & Gnome, P.O. Box 5344, Charleston, WV 25361, (332) 881-7037

Reeseville Ridge Nursery, 512 S Main, Reeseville, WI 53579, (920) 927-3291

Shrub Source, 248 N Colonial St., Zeeland, MI 49464, (800) 530-2969

Wavecrest Nursery, 2509 Lakeshore Dr., Fennville, MI 49408, (888) 869-4159

Woodlanders, Inc., 1128 Colleton Ave., Aiken, SC 29801, (803) 648-7522

VARIETIES

Choose varieties by their overall shape and size, their flower and foliage color, and winter hardiness. Weigelas can get larger than the sizes listed here, but with slight pruning can be kept in check. 'Variegata' often suffers severe dieback but will still produce lovely foliage and is frequently grown for this characteristic alone.

VARIETY	GROWTH HABIT	FLOWER	FOLIAGE	SIZE	HARDINESS
Weigela florida (Named varieties)					
(Old Fashioned Weigela)					
Carnaval® ('Courtalor')***	Loose, open	Red/white/pink	Medium green	6'/5'	−30°F
'Centennial'**	Upright, spreading	Cherry red	Dark green	8'/8'	−35°F
'Dark Horse'****	Low, mounded	Magenta pink	Purplish bronze	3'/3'	−30°F
'Evita'***	Dense, spreading	Deep red pink	Green tinted bronze	3'/5'	−20°F
Fine Wine® ('Bramwell')****	Compact, mounded	Rich pink	Dark burgundy	2'/2'	−30°F
French Lace® ('Brigela')****	Upright, spreading	Ruby red	Green/yellow	5'/4'	−30°F
Ghost® ('Carlton')***	Loose, rounded	Bright red	Green to butter cream	4'/4'	−30°F
'Java Red'***	Mounded, spreading	Deep pink	Purple red/bronze	4'/4'	−25°F
Midnight Wine® ('Elvera')****	Low, mounded	Rose pink	Burgundy purple	1'/2'	−25°F
'Minuet'***	Compact, rounded	Rose purple/ yellow	Deep green/purple	2'/2'	−35°F
My Monet™ ('Verweig')****	Compact, mounded	Bright pink	Green white pink	1½'/1'	−30°F
'Pink Delight'***	Upright, spreading	Deep pink	Medium green	6'/6'	−30°F
'Pink Poppet'**	Compact, mounded	Bright ink	Medium green	3'/3'	−35°F
'Pink Princess'**	Open, spreading	Lilac pink	Medium green	6'/6'	−30°F
'Polka'***	Wide, rounded	Deep pink/ yellow	Dark green	4'/5'	−35°F
Rainbow Sensation™****	Compact, mounded	Deep pink	Green yellow	4'/4'	−30°F
'Red Prince'****	Upright, spreading	Crimson red	Medium green	6'/6'	−30°F
'Rumba'***	Mounded, spreading	Dark red/ yellow	Deep green/ bronze	3'/3'	−35°F
'Samba'****	Compact, mounded	Pink to reddish pink	Copper to deep green	3'/3'	−30°F
Shining Sensation™*****	Upright, rounded	Light pink	Burgundy purple	6'/4'	−30°F
'Tango'***	Mounded, spreading	Red/yellow	Dark green/purple	2'/3'	−30°F
'Variegata' (var. *variegata*)***	Mounded, spreading	Rose to white	Variegated green	4'/4'	−20°F
'White Knight'***	Upright, rounded	White tinged pink	Light green	6'/6'	−30°F
Wine & Roses® ('Alexandra')****	Upright, rounded	Rose pink	Reddish purple	5'/5'	−25°F

Weigela florida Wine & Roses® ('Alexandra')

Weigela florida Carnaval® ('Courtalor')

Weigela florida 'Java Red'

Weigela florida 'Minuet'

Weigela florida 'Pink Princess'

Weigela florida 'Polka'

Weigela florida 'Red Prince'

Weigela florida 'Variegata'

Wisteria frutescens var. *macrostachya*

WISTERIA

(whiss-STEER-ee-uh)

WISTERIA

Wisteria is a vining plant that captures the imagination of many cold-climate gardeners. Wisteria is noted for its pendulous clusters of mildly fragrant lavender or white flowers that bloom in late spring to early summer. Its glossy, bright green foliage is also attractive throughout the growing season. It has little fall color. Wisteria has a reputation for being very difficult to grow in cold climates. The keys to success are simple: choose one of the seven plants in the varietal chart and grow it exactly as indicated. **Note:** Do not let children play with the pods or seeds of this plant. If eaten, they can cause digestive problems.

How Wisteria Grows

The roots of Wisteria are quite coarse and will penetrate the soil deeply. Wisteria usually develops one main trunk with many side branches fanning out from that stem. The plant does not have the ability to cling to surfaces. Instead, its stem and side branches twine around a support. Without proper support Wisteria rambles aimlessly along the ground. A single Wisteria grows so vigorously and weighs so much that any support must be especially sturdy and well anchored. The lightly fragrant Wisteria flowers are about ¾ inch (1.75 cm) long and hang in large grape-like clusters from the vine. The medium to dark green leaves may have as many as nineteen leaflets. The fruit of Wisteria is a pod that contains speckled bean-like seeds. The pods are green during the summer, turning brown as they mature in the fall. These pods tend to persist on the vine during the winter. The plant rarely self-sows.

Where to Plant

Site and Light Wisteria demands lots of sun to grow vigorously and bloom well. It will grow in shade, but flowering will be reduced. Since these vines are borderline hardy in many colder areas, give them as much protection as possible.

Soil and Moisture Wisteria adapts itself well to different types of soil as long as they drain freely. The plant prefers moist soil high in organic matter. It does very poorly in hot, dry, compacted soil. The plant is somewhat salt tolerant.

Spacing Wisteria needs a support to grow properly. Since it cannot cling to surfaces, it must be given something around which its stems can wind. This is usually some sort of trellis or pergola.

Landscape Use

Wisteria is a wonderful vine for growing over arbors and pergolas. It also makes a great cover for wood lattice or chain link fences, as long as the fence is sturdy and well anchored. Growing Wisteria up a tree is commonly suggested in garden literature, but not recommended here. The shade of the tree diminishes the vine's ability to bloom, and vines often adversely affect tree growth as well.

Planting

Bare Root Get bare root plants into the garden as soon as the ground can be worked in spring. Remove plants from their shipping package immediately on arrival. Soak them in room temperature water for no fewer than 3 hours before planting. Place a small amount of superphosphate in the base of the hole and cover with 3 inches (7.5 cm) of soil. This step is absolutely critical for good flowering. Spread roots out over a cone of well-prepared soil. Make sure the crown is level with the surrounding soil surface. Fill the hole with soil, firm it with your fingers, and water immediately. Dissolve water-soluble fertilizer in a gallon (about 4 liters) of water following the directions on the label. Pour ½ cup (about 120 ml) of this starter solution around the base of each plant. If you prefer organic fertilizer, use fish emulsion instead.

Containerized Plants Plant Wisteria as early in the season as possible. If the soil in the container is dry, soak it and let it drain overnight before planting. Carefully remove the plant from the container so as not to break the root ball. Plant at the same depth as in the container after preparing the hole in a similar manner as that for a bare root plant. Fill the hole with well-prepared soil, firm with your fingers, and water immediately. Pour ½ cup (about 120 ml) of starter solution around the base of the plant.

Balled and Burlapped Rarely sold this way.

Transplanting

Carefully choose the place where you want to grow Wisteria. A mature plant will be entwined around its support and next to impossible to transplant. Take cuttings to start new plants.

How to Care for Wisteria

Water Keep the soil evenly moist from spring until the soil freezes in fall. Consistent watering is especially important during the first 2 years. Always saturate the soil deeply with each watering. When the top 2 inches (5 cm) of soil dry out, water.

Mulch Apply a 2- to 4-inch (5- to 10-cm) layer of mulch around each plant as soon as the ground warms up in spring. Good mulches include shredded bark, pine needles, and wood chips. Mulch retains moisture in the soil and helps prevent the growth of weeds. Replenish the mulch as necessary throughout the growing season.

Fertilizing Fertilize every spring with 10-10-10 fertilizer. Sprinkle the granules around the base of each plant before new growth emerges and water immediately to move the fertilizer into the root zone.

If you prefer organic fertilizers, use alfalfa meal (rabbit pellets), blood meal, bone meal, compost, fish emulsion, Milorganite, or rotted manures. Bone meal must be added to the soil at planting time to be effective.

If your plant is growing vigorously but not blooming well after a few years, reduce or eliminate all nitrogen, which may cause excessive growth at the expense of flower production. If your plant is blooming freely, continue to use nitrogen.

Weeding Prevent the growth of most annual weeds by using mulch. Pull by hand any weeds that do appear. Weeds compete with shrubs for available moisture and nutrients and should be removed immediately.

Support Wisteria must be given support to grow properly. Fences, pergolas, and arbors are good. The weight of a mature Wisteria vine is incredible. Your supports should be strong and firmly anchored in the ground. In the early stages of growth, wind the vine around its support to get it growing upward. As with Clematis, curl the vines carefully to keep it growing in the direction and shape desired. As with many climbing Roses, overall bloom will be increased if you direct branches to grow in a horizontal position. Do this by attaching them to a support or wire that forces them to grow at right angles to the main stem. Attach them to the wire with soft material tied in a figure-eight knot.

Deadheading Not necessary, unless you don't like the look of seed pods.

Pruning Wait until new growth starts to emerge in the spring before cutting out any wood that has suffered dieback during the winter. After blooming, cut back side branches to within 36 inches (90 cm) of the main stem. Some gardeners cut them back farther, but always leave at least six leaves per branch. These shorter branches (laterals or spurs) often produce more flower buds than uncut branches. This leads to greater bloom the following year.

Wisteria is a vigorous vine. If growth is too dense, it can affect flowering. Simply remove some of the branches to give the remaining ones more light. Again, do this immediately after flowering. Late pruning encourages new growth that tends to die off in the winter and removes potential flower buds. Finally, control the overall size of the vine whenever you want by snipping off the tip of the main stem (the leader). This directs the plant's energy into further branching.

Winter Protection To protect young Wisterias during the first winter, pile dry leaves or straw over the base of the plant after the ground freezes in the fall. The best winter protection is lots of snow and proper placement at planting time.

Problems

Insects None serious.

Diseases None serious.

Marauders None.

Propagation

Suckers These shrubs do not sucker.

Cuttings In early summer to midsummer take 4- to 6-inch (10- to 15-cm) cuttings from this year's growth. Take hardwood cuttings of the same size in midwinter. Follow the steps outlined on pages 406–8 to get them to root.

Seed Place the seeds in hot water. You should barely be able to put your hand in it. Soak the seed for 24 hours. Place the seeds in a moist mixture of peat and perlite. Barely cover the seed. Keep the seed at a temperature below 65°F (18°C) until germination occurs, generally within 60 days. Note that some gardeners have had success growing these seeds without nicking or soaking them first. For additional information, see pages 409–12.

Special Uses

This is not normally recommended as a good cut flower. Its vase life is extremely short. However, it is so beautiful and has such a nice fragrance that you'll be tempted to cut off a flower cluster or two for an arrangement. Just as you snip the flower cluster off the plant, place the base of the stem immediately in water. Once indoors, put the stem in cool water.

Wisteria frutescens var. *macrostachya*

Sources

Bloom River Gardens, 39744 Deerhorn Rd., Springfield, OR 97478, (587) 726-8997

Brushwood Nursery, 431 Hale Ln., Athens, GA 30607, (706) 548-1710

ForestFarm, 990 Tetherow Rd., Williams, OR 97544, (587) 846-7269

Greer Gardens, 1280 Goodpasture Island Rd., Eugene, OR 97401, (541) 686-8266

Heronswood Nursery, 300 Park Ave., Warminster, PA 18974, (922) 674-4714

Klehm's Song Sparrow Perennial Farm, 13101 E Rye Rd., Avalon, WI 53505, (800) 553-3715

Meadowbrook Nursery/We-Du Natives, 2055 Polly Spout Rd., Marion, NC 28752, (871) 738-8300

Oikos Tree Crops, P.O. Box 19425, Kalamazoo, MI 49019, (310) 624-6233

RareFind Nursery, 957 Patterson Rd., Jackson, NJ 08527, (770) 833-0613

Reeseville Ridge Nursery, 512 S Main, Reeseville, WI 53579, (920) 927-3291

River Rock Nursery, 19251 SE Hwy 224, Damascus, OR 97089, (503) 658-4047

Venero Gardens, 5985 Seamans Dr., Shorewood, MN 55331, (952) 474-8550

Woodlanders, Inc., 1128 Colleton Ave., Aiken, SC 29801, (803) 648-7522

VARIETIES

VARIETY	FLOWER COLOR	VINE LENGTH	HARDINESS
Wisteria frutescens var. *macrostachya****			
(American Wisteria)	Light purple to lavender	20'	−25°F
'Amethyst Falls'***	Bright blue	20'	−20°F
'Aunt Dee'***	Lilac purple	20'	−25°F
'Blue Moon'***	Lilac blue	20'	−20°F
'Clara Mack'***	White	20'	−25°F
'Nivea'***	White	20'	−20°F
First Editions®	Blue lavender	20'	−30°F
Summer Cascade™****			

Very few Wisterias survive in colder climates. The hardiness ratings for this group may be somewhat conservative, since these plants have come through much colder winters, but in protected locations. In such areas they have suffered dieback and loss of flower buds, but the plants themselves survived. The flowers on these plants are produced in clusters up to 8 inches (20 cm) long and are mildly fragrant. They are followed by green twisted pods 4 inches (10 cm) long or longer. Try to find a local grower who has stock that has been proven hardy in your area. Local growers in colder areas collect and grow seed, keep only the hardiest seedlings, then take cuttings from these plants. If it's possible, get plants grown in this manner. There are growers that claim plants have been commonly mixed up in the trade—another reason to find a local grower. 'Amethyst Falls' and 'Nivea' are borderline hardy, but possible choices in the more southerly areas of the cold-climate region. Summer Cascade™ is the hardiest of this group, is noted for its consistent bloom once mature, and tends to bloom at an earlier age than the rest. However, do not expect flowers in the first few years as Wisterias take time to establish themselves.

PART II

The Basics of Growing Shrubs and Small Trees

The following chapters are filled with essential information about growing shrubs and small trees. Whether you're an expert or a beginning gardener, you will find this information helpful and easy to understand. You should get the very most from your shrubs with a minimal amount of wasted money, time, and energy. Some of the information contained in these chapters may differ from that advocated by others. Nevertheless, the information presented here will result in healthy and long-lived plants.

CHAPTER 2

SELECTING SHRUBS
AND SMALL TREES

This chapter includes basic information on shrubs and small trees. However, its main purpose is to help you select just the right shrubs and small trees for your yard. After reading this chapter, you will know exactly what questions to ask to get what you want.

How Shrubs and Small Trees Grow

Shrubs are woody plants. They generally produce numerous stems from a crown just at the soil surface. Small trees are similar but generally have one or more trunks. These expand in diameter with age until the tree reaches maturity. Most of the trees recommended here grow no taller than 20 feet (about 7 meters). The shrubs and small trees may produce branches of varying size depending upon their type. It is quite possible for some of these plants to get as wide or even wider than they are tall. The wide-spreading branches may form even smaller branches giving the shrub or tree a dense appearance or bushy look.

Leaves form on stems, branches, and side branches. They may vary from the thin needles of evergreens to the broad leaves of some deciduous shrubs. Healthy foliage is extremely important to create food necessary for vigorous growth, abundant bloom, rich foliage coloration, and a heavy crop of fruit or berries.

Each shrub's root system is extensive. Its depth varies with the type of shrub grown, but the root system is usually much wider than the plant is tall. Often, the roots are quite shallow, drawing nutrients and water from the top portion of the soil. But the depth of roots varies considerably with the type of shrub grown. The roots themselves also vary by type of shrub. Some are quite thick while others are more fibrous and similar to those of perennials. Tiny hairs off these larger roots are called *feeder roots* and take in the nourishment needed by the plant. These feeder roots regenerate each year. The purpose of roots is to hold the plant firmly in place and to take in and store nutrients.

Most of the shrubs and small trees listed in this guide grow on their own roots. The exceptions are noted and explained fully in Part I. From centuries of experimentation growers have learned techniques to attach one part of a plant (a bud or scion) to the rooted portion (rootstock or understock) of a completely different plant. The techniques are known as budding or grafting, so shrubs or trees not growing

Fall Color

THE LEAVES ON SOME deciduous shrubs and small trees change color in the fall. This is partially related to the plant's genetic makeup. Fall color is also dependent on weather and soil. Sunny days and cool nights promote good color. If it is overcast or too cool during the day or if there is a killing frost, leaves have poor color or simply die. If the soil is overly rich, leaf color may also be poor. The color of leaves is related to the presence of chlorophyll (green); the yellow pigments (carotenes and xanthophylls); and the blue, purple, and red pigments (anthocyanins). In the fall the cells at the base of the leaf stalk (abscission layer) begin to die. Chlorophyll production breaks down and the color green begins to disappear. The yellow pigments no longer are masked by the green. If it's sunny during the day, then the plant produces sugar. If nights are cool, the sugar is trapped in the leaves. This promotes the appearance of the red pigment, which is also dependent on the presence of iron in the soil. Red and yellow pigments blend to form a brilliant orange coloration. This fall coloration is most intense in cold climates. The potential for brilliant fall color is a valuable feature and emphasized in plant descriptions throughout this guide.

Rhus glabra

on their own roots are known as budded or grafted. The place where the desirable plant has been budded to the rootstock is called the *bud union.*

Each shrub is unique and will decline after a certain number of years. At this stage the shrub should be replaced. Although the life span of any plant is unpredictable, the approximate life expectancy for different groups is listed in Part I. These are truly rough estimates because each plant's life span depends on its genes, the weather, and your care over the years.

In cold climates it is quite common for the tips of stems of some shrubs to die back from severe winter weather. In extreme cases an entire stem may die back to the ground. This is known as *dieback.* How to deal with this problem is an important consideration and is covered both in this Basics section (page 386) and in individual sections of Part I. However, the shrubs and small trees in this guide were chosen with this problem in mind. In most instances, dieback will not be a major concern.

Buying Shrubs and Small Trees

Each shrub has advantages and disadvantages. The good and bad points of each group are covered in detail in each of the sections of Part I. Design elements are covered later in this chapter. Following is a checklist to use in buying shrubs:

- **Hardiness:** While all of the shrubs in this guide are hardy to –20°F (–29°C), many are hardier. By studying the climate map (see page xiv), you will know just how cold it may get in your state or province. Match the potential hardiness of each shrub to your area. Shrubs can be quite expensive, and this guide should help you select plants that will survive and do well in your climate.
- **Climate:** You live in an area that tends to be cool or hot in the summer. It may also be humid or rather dry. Take your overall climate into consid-

eration when buying plants. For example, *Rhus trilobata* (Three Lobe Sumac) is prone to foliar diseases unless grown in a dry climate while the orange, pink, and red varieties of *Potentilla* (Shrub Cinquefoil) only have good flower coloration if they are grown in areas where summers are cool.

- **Landscape use:** Each shrub or small tree has its own characteristics. This is reflected in how it can be used. Potential uses are outlined later in this chapter and will help you decide on which shrubs or small trees to buy.

- **Seasonal interest:** A careful selection of shrubs can make your yard interesting throughout the entire year. In cold climates bloom seasons for most shrubs are short, but that does not mean a shrub quickly loses its appeal. Consider what a plant offers in every season to add a special dimension to your plantings.

- **Potential height and width:** The overall size of a plant is a major consideration. Don't be fooled by the small size of bare root, balled and burlapped, or containerized plants. Some are quite large when mature. *Approximate* potential heights and widths are given in Part I. Always keep these in mind when buying shrubs. Note that size is not controlled strictly by genetic makeup. It's also related to the length of your growing season, soil type, overall fertility of the site, competition with other plants, light conditions, temperature fluctuations, and available moisture.

- **Expected longevity:** Most shrubs live for a decade or longer, but a few are relatively short-lived. Use the estimated life spans for the shrubs listed in this guide to help you in your initial selection.

- **Maintenance:** The amount of time you're willing to spend working with a specific shrub is an important consideration. The level of maintenance required for plant groups is included throughout the sections of Part I.

- **Preferred light:** Each shrub has varying demands for sunlight. Buy shrubs that will thrive where you plant them. Specific suggestions concerning a plant's need or tolerance of varying light conditions is given throughout this guide to help you choose just the right plant for even the most difficult spots in your yard. Matching every shrub to the best possible site is critical to success.

- **Preferred moisture:** The conditions in your yard may dictate which shrubs to buy. If you have especially dry or boggy soil, certain shrubs make sense, while others won't at all.

- **Preferred pH:** Whether your soil is alkaline, neutral, or acidic may determine what shrubs you'll choose. Changing soil pH requires special attention and increases the overall maintenance necessary to grow specific shrubs. If you match the shrubs to the pH they prefer from the start, you can grow a wide range of plants without worrying about changing your soil dramatically.

- **Growth rate:** Genetic makeup controls how quickly shrubs and trees mature. If a plant grows slowly, it is often worth the extra cost to buy a more mature plant. Growth rate is not controlled strictly by genes. The length of the season and proper culture also affect overall growth rate.

- **Salt tolerance:** Most states in cold climates use salt on roads during the winter. If you'll be planting shrubs near salted roads, consider buying salt-tolerant varieties, as indicated throughout this guide.

- **Disease and insect resistance:** A shrub's resistance to disease and insects is important to organic gardeners or anyone who doesn't like to use sprays. Certain shrub groups are rarely bothered by disease and insects, while others are more vulnerable. Choose your plants accordingly. Note that the most resistant varieties within each group were selected for this guide.

- **Desirability to deer:** Deer will eat almost any shrub if they are hungry enough, but they tend to attack certain groups of shrubs first. If you have a deer problem, then you may wish to select shrubs that are not on their "hit list." White-tailed deer seem to prefer different shrubs in different parts of the country. This seems contrary to common sense, but appears to be the case. Ask local growers about plants most susceptible to deer damage.

Designing with Shrubs

Garden designers love working with shrubs because they offer so many design elements. These are critical in selecting the shrub or small tree you'd like to buy. To achieve the desired landscape effect keep these considerations in mind:

- **Size (height and width):** The potential height and width of any shrub or small tree is the single most basic element of design. Proper placement from the beginning is critical, since you never want to be forced to move a shrub once it's growing well or reaching maturity. Furthermore, while some shrubs can be pruned and still keep their natural shape, others resent it badly. One of the most common mistakes of beginning gardeners is to place too many plants too close together, or to place a single plant too close to a building or area where it will become a problem as it matures.

- **Shape and form:** Shrubs and small trees vary dramatically in their appearance throughout the seasons. The overall natural shape or form of the shrub may be arching, clump forming, columnar, compact, conical, creeping, dense, erect, globular, horizontal, low branching, open, oval, prostrate, pyramidal, round, sprawling, spreading, trailing, upright, vase shaped, or weeping. While it is possible to shape plants through pruning, it is always preferable to choose a plant that naturally fits a particular space and is appealing to the eye in that position.

- **Architectural qualities:** Architectural qualities are certainly related to shape and the overall growth pattern of a shrub or small tree. For example, two

The Language of Shape

HERE ARE DEFINITIONS of terms commonly used to describe the shape and form (growing habit or structure) of different shrubs and small trees:

- **Arching:** Stems tend to bend over, creating a cascading look.
- **Clump forming:** Many stems shoot up from the base of the plant. Usually, the look is quite open and airy in the winter.
- **Columnar:** Branches close to the stem create a relatively narrow, vertical look.
- **Compact:** Branches are covered with dense, thick foliage, creating a visual block.
- **Conical:** This shape is like an upside-down ice cream cone.
- **Creeping:** Same as *prostrate*.
- **Dense:** Same as *compact*.
- **Erect:** Refers to columnar and pyramidal growth patterns.
- **Fastigiate:** This is a narrow, upright form that looks like a compressed oval. The shape is quite similar to a feather.
- **Globular:** Branches form a rounded mound similar to a globe.
- **Horizontal:** Branches are parallel to the ground and very architectural.
- **Low branching:** Similar to *horizontal,* but branches are very close to the ground.

- **Open:** Branches are far enough apart so you can see clearly through the shrub.
- **Oval:** This shape is somewhat like an egg with the lower and upper portions of the plant narrower than the central area. The upper portion may be slightly pointed.
- **Prostrate:** Branches are so close to the earth that they act as a ground cover.
- **Pyramidal:** This is a typical shape of many conifers with dense foliage and upright form.
- **Round:** The top of the plant appears like the upper half of a circle.
- **Sprawling:** The plant rambles along the ground or spills over embankments.
- **Spreading:** Branches or stems appear spaced apart in a fairly open manner.
- **Trailing:** Similar to *prostrate,* this often refers to branches flowing over a support.
- **Upright:** Branches tend to be somewhat rigid rather than open or spreading.
- **Vase shaped:** This may refer to a small shrub or the upper canopy of a tree that is shaped like a V.
- **Weeping:** Stems and branches gracefully bend toward the ground.

properly shaped shrubs at an entryway are especially appealing to the eye. A tree with horizontal branches may be striking in the dead of winter. A tall, pyramidal shrub at the corner of a home accents the vertical line and makes a bold statement.

- **Bloom time:** Time of blooming is an important consideration when choosing shrubs. Ideally, it's good to have a variety of shrubs so that you can have different ones blooming over many weeks and even months. Keep in mind that even within certain groups of shrubs you can buy a number that will bloom over a period of weeks, and in this way extend the bloom time of that one group considerably.

- **Length of bloom:** Shrubs vary dramatically in how long they stay in bloom. Some are almost ephemeral with bloom lasting only a few days. Others bloom for months in flushes. Bloom time of any shrub may be affected by heat, drought, and wind, all of which decrease the length of bloom considerably.

- **Flower color:** Most of the shrubs and small trees in this guide produce quite lovely bloom at some time during the growing season. In cold climates this is usually in spring or early summer. Colors can be intense or somewhat muted. Choosing plants by their flower color is one aspect of growing them. Remember that most shrubs are in bloom for a relatively short period of time. Since most only bloom once, other characteristics of the plant take on an added importance.

- **Flower size and number of petals:** Flower size and number of petals can be an important consideration. It depends on the effect you would like to achieve with the shrub. The flowers on some shrubs are inconspicuous while on others they are bold and dramatic.

- **Floral fragrance:** Some flowers are fragrant; others aren't. A few even have an off odor. You'll find detailed information on fragrance throughout the guide, so that you can choose varieties by scent. Remember, scent varies with humidity, light, and temperature. High temperatures and high humidity increase fragrance. During cool to cold periods, many fragrant flowers have little scent. Fragrance also depends on the stage of maturity. Some flowers give off a scent only as they open, while others exude perfume when fully mature. People also vary in their ability to detect fragrance. Some people simply cannot smell scents. Here are at least a few excellent choices for fragrance: some varieties of flowering Almonds and Plums (*Prunus*), some varieties of Azalea and Rhododendron (*Rhododendron*), some varieties of Crabapples (*Malus*), Daphne (*Daphne*), most varieties of Honeysuckle (*Lonicera*), almost all varieties of Lilac (*Syringa*), most varieties of Magnolia (*Magnolia*), most varieties of Mockorange (*Philadelphus*), Summersweet (*Clethra alnifolia*), a few varieties of Viburnum (*Viburnum*), and Witch Hazel (*Hamamelis*).

- **Foliage coloration:** The foliage of many deciduous shrubs changes throughout the growing season. Fall is a particularly dramatic period for many of the shrubs that produce vibrant colors of red, purple, orange, and yellow at that time. But summer coloration can also vary greatly by shrub. Some varieties have striking tones of yellowish green to rich reddish purple for varied summer color. Even evergreens vary considerably in their overall color. Varied shades of green are supplemented by blue, gold, silver, and yellow tones. Throughout the guide, you'll find information on foliage coloration to help you decide whether a plant may fit a special need.

- **Persistent foliage:** Most of the shrubs included are deciduous, meaning that their leaves drop off at the end of the season. A few are evergreen with leaves (broad leaves or needles) remaining on the plant year-round.

- **Foliage shape, size, and texture:** The overall feel of a shrub is heavily dependent on these characteristics. Foliage may be bold, broad, dainty, dull, feathery, glossy, light, smooth, wrinkled, and so on. The contrast of foliage to flowers and stems is often one of the plant's most attractive features.

- **Foliage fragrance:** A number of evergreens have a delightful scent. You need only to brush against them for this fragrance to become noticeable. *Perovskia* (Russian Sage) also has a very distinctive scent, which most gardeners like.

Multiseasonal Shrubs and Small Trees

GARDENERS LIVING IN COLD CLIMATES are fortunate to experience four distinct seasons. Each season showcases different features of shrubs and small trees. Spring is associated with the color, form, and scent of buds and flowers. Some flowers are barely visible, while others are striking and strongly scented. Also at this time, many evergreens begin to candle and form cones. Some plants flower in the summer; however, the rich colors and diverse textures of foliage are the true highlights of plants in this season. Purple or variegated foliage is particularly prized, along with the diverse accent colors of the new selections of evergreens. Also, in the summer, shrubs and trees produce edible fruits for people to enjoy and to attract wildlife. Cold climates also offer the drama of fall foliage coloration. The colors are so striking that they attract visitors from around the world. Every gardener will be rewarded for using plants noted for fall color. Many of these plants also produce abundant crops of fruit. Some fruits are immediately eaten by wildlife, but others persist into or through the winter. During the winter, form becomes the outstanding feature of deciduous trees. Some are strikingly architectural, with layered branches. Evergreens are especially appealing in winter, covered in a soft blanket of snow. Brilliantly colored stems of shrubs

Weigela florida 'Variegata'

and trunks of trees with exfoliating bark stand out against the white snow until spring arrives, renewing the cycle of beauty. The photographs on these two pages are but a glimpse of the multiseasonal interest of shrubs and small trees suited to cold climates.

Rhododendron × *marjatta* 'Haaga'

Cornus stolonifera

Cotinus coggygria 'Royal Purple'

Thuja occidentalis 'Gold Cargo'

Malus 'Prairifire'

Viburnum trilobum

Rhus typhina

- **Stem coloration:** Good designers are aware of how stems change color throughout the seasons. The stems of some shrubs are brilliant orange, red, and purple in winter or early spring. When it snows, these colors seem to jump out from the surrounding landscape.
- **Bark texture:** The bark of some shrubs and small trees may be so distinctive that it draws your eye to it immediately.
- **Winter interest:** Evergreen foliage, bark, branching pattern, buds, unique form, stem coloration, and persistent berries or fruit add up to exceptional winter interest. These qualities are underlined throughout this guide.

Potential Uses

The limiting factors in working with any specific shrub are its potential height, maximum width, and cultural needs. The latter is related to potential light, the type and pH of the soil, and available moisture. The most common uses for shrubs follow:

- **Accent (or specimen) plants:** An accent or specimen plant is one that can stand on its own as a punctuation point in the landscape. It usually has superior form and foliage. Many deciduous and evergreen shrubs fall into this category. Accent plants can also be mixed into perennial borders or beds with stunning results. The purpose of an accent plant is to draw your attention to it and then to focus on it.
- **Architectural interest:** Specific shrubs and small trees have such unique forms that they almost appear like living pieces of sculpture. Some are bold, while others are lacy, looking almost like pieces of filigree in the winter landscape. Skillful landscape design complements the architectural features of your home.
- **Background:** Some shrubs make ideal backgrounds for other plantings. Most commonly used are evergreens, since they keep their foliage throughout the year.

- **Barriers:** Shrubs can serve as blocks or barriers against movement, noise, sight, and smell. Shrubs must be quite dense and the right height to be effective for each of these problems.
- **Blocks:** Shrubs can cover unsightly items or areas, such as meters, utility boxes, propane tanks, compost piles, boats, and other distractions, creating a serene look pleasing to you and your neighbors.
- **Bonsai:** Although not emphasized in this guide, you can use a number of shrubs and small trees for this enchanting art form.
- **Borders:** Used appropriately, small shrubs blend in well with perennials in border plantings. Some skillful gardeners make borders of shrubs alone.
- **Container plants:** A few shrubs can be grown successfully in containers. This use is particularly effective where space is limited. These plants are charming on patios, decks, or in corners where just a splash of color, texture, or form adds zest to your exterior design. All they need is the right light and consistent care throughout the growing season.
- **Cut flowers** (see **Floral arrangements**).
- **Edible fruit:** Some shrubs listed in this guide produce bountiful crops of delicious fruits, ideal for fresh eating, jams, jellies, pies, and syrups.
- **Erosion control** (see **Ground covers**).
- **Espalier:** While this is not particularly common in cold climates, it is certainly an art form worth noting. Several of the fruit trees in this guide fit in nicely with this concept. Generally, espalier is the careful pruning and training of a plant so that it grows flat against a wall or support, often a split-rail fence or a trellis.
- **Exterior design:** Shrubs properly placed can soften harsh lines, draw attention to the most beautiful features of your home, and give balance to a yard. This could be viewed as the same as or part of architectural needs.
- **Facing plants (facers):** Some large shrubs have a tendency to lose foliage around their bases as they mature. Smaller shrubs used to cover this bare area are referred to as *facing plants*.

- **Floral arrangements:** Shrubs produce lovely flowers, foliage, and stems for arrangements. Stems, such as those of *Salix matsudana* 'Tortuosa' (Curly Willow), are as lovely dry as fresh. Stems with ripe berries often mix well into arrangements. Just like flowers, berries may be short or long lasting. Some can be preserved for use in dried arrangements.
- **Foundation plantings:** This is one of the most common uses of shrubs. Skillful use of shrubs along the foundation not only covers up the base of your home but adds a dimension of interest to what would be a drab, straight line. Commonly, shrubs and evergreens under 4 feet (1.2 m) high are used for this purpose. Shrubs should not block windows.
- **Ground covers:** Some areas, such as slopes and steep banks, are difficult to take care of and are best covered with plants. Shrubs are excellent for this purpose, not only stopping erosion but also transforming what could be an eyesore into a useful and lovely part of the landscape.
- **Hedges:** Many shrubs make excellent formal or informal hedges. These living fences are much appreciated by neighbors. Hedges define, divide, or screen portions of your property. They also direct traffic flow and act as barriers. Informal hedges make excellent screens and afford privacy. Formal hedges are ideal for backgrounds to borders. They work well to define lines and divide your property into outdoor rooms. They can also provide privacy. Hedges protect you from dust, noise, and wind as well. Many deciduous shrubs and some evergreens make excellent hedges.
- **Hedgerows:** Common in rural areas, hedgerows provide protection from wind and excellent cover for wildlife. Mix in a number of shrubs producing edible berries and nuts for best results.
- **Japanese gardens:** Although these require extreme attention, they are among the most beautiful gardens in the world. They rely heavily on the use of both evergreen and deciduous shrubs.
- **Outdoor rooms:** Particularly popular now is the concept of outdoor rooms, spaces set aside away

from the home in the yard itself. These afford a private sanctuary. Shrubs and small trees are commonly used to define such spaces.
- **Patios:** Patios are connected directly to the home. Much of the patio may appear through glass, as if it were part of the interior of the home itself. The use of shrubs in such a space is similar to that for an outdoor room.
- **Privacy** (see **Screens**).
- **Rock gardens:** Dwarf shrubs are particularly useful blended with perennials and annuals in a rock garden.
- **Screens:** Screens are similar to barriers and blocks. This plant grouping conceals, protects, separates, or shelters your yard. Screens often outline space and are an essential element in creating outdoor living spaces or "rooms." Placed along streets, screens block out the sight of passing cars and also trap debris and dust from roadways. Spray down dusty foliage regularly to keep plants healthy if you live in such a situation.
- **Shade:** Several of the small trees in this guide make good shade plants. Placed by windows or over patios, they act to control temperature during the summer and provide much-needed shade to areas that would otherwise be uncomfortable in full sun.
- **Topiaries:** As with espalier, this is a relatively rare art form in cold climates. However, several of the evergreens mentioned in this guide are suitable for shaping into intricate forms or shapes of animals.
- **Vertical space:** Several of the woody plants mentioned in this guide are vines. Their colorful flowers and rich foliage make them especially useful on walls and fences.
- **Wildlife (habitat and food):** Shrubs make excellent homes for birds and other wildlife. They also provide berries and fruit to feed them. Berries and fruits vary in taste by season. Some are delectable to birds as soon as they mature. Others must freeze or even ferment to be tasty. This is the reason that some shrubs are stripped of fruit immediately while others remain untouched until late winter or even early the following spring.

- **Windbreak:** Shrubs are often used to shield homes from winds. This is helpful year round. Most commonly used are evergreens, although some large shrubs and deciduous trees have such a heavy branching pattern that they work well to halt heavy winter winds.

Basic Design Tips

Good designers are like artists. They have an eye for combining plants effectively, but they also need to understand plants well. If you'll be creating your own design, here are five basic tips:

1. Decide whether you prefer formal or informal patterns. Formal design relies on repetition, sharp angles, and relatively rigid forms. Good informal design appears spontaneous, but requires careful planning. It relies on seemingly random planting, curving lines, and more irregular forms. The style you prefer will dictate which shrubs and small trees you choose.

2. Keep it as simple as possible. You can work with a number of shrubs, but don't go overboard. Also, placing several shrubs of the same type together is extremely effective in many home landscapes.

3. Background plants should naturally be taller than those placed in front of them. Background plants are most effective if they have dense and darker foliage than the plants placed in the foreground.

4. Working with shrubs and trees with different foliage colors requires quite a bit of skill. Some colors are very bold and stand out from a distance. Study

Here's an example of stunning but simple design. The combination of stonework, sculpture, and a mass planting of *Syringa* Hybrid 'Minuet' in a graceful curve is pleasing at any time of year but particularly so when the Lilacs are in full bloom.

plantings at local arboreta or public gardens for good potential combinations.

5. Generally, plants with fine texture look better placed in front of plants with bold foliage. Contrasting textures are as interesting as contrasting colors.

CHAPTER 3

SELECTING AND PREPARING A SITE

Nothing is more important in growing shrubs than placing them in the correct spot. Since it's better not to have to transplant shrubs and small trees, place and plant them correctly from the start. This ensures you'll get the best growth from every shrub you plant.

The Correct Site

Shrubs thrive in a wide variety of conditions. Plants vary in their needs for light, moisture, and protection from wind.

Sunlight

Each shrub prefers a different amount of sunlight. Throughout this guide the preferred light for each shrub is indicated. The correct exposure may be related to either summer or winter sun. When this is an important consideration, it is included in individual sections of Part I.

As used in this guide, *full sun* refers to direct sunlight throughout the day. Direction may be east, west, south, or north. *Partial shade* means a filtered or broken flow of sunlight, as through the branches of trees well above the shrub. Shrubs and small trees may also be considered as growing in partial shade if they receive only 4 or 5 hours of direct light per day. *Full shade* means practically no direct light throughout the day, as under a thick canopy of tree branches in woods.

Moisture

Most of the shrubs and small trees listed in this guide thrive in areas with good drainage. A few grow well in wet to boggy sites. A few not only tolerate but thrive in dry sites. Always know the moisture needs of your plant and make sure it is compatible with the site you've located.

Protection

A number of shrubs are prone to wind damage. Although these shrubs need good air circulation, protection afforded by fences and other barriers is helpful. This is usually most important during the winter when evergreens suffer damage from desiccating winds. Avoid planting delicate shrubs under drip lines (the edge of roof eaves). Falling snow and ice will often damage these during the winter and early spring.

Preparing the Site

In most instances the area where you'll be growing a shrub will be covered with brush, lawn, or weeds. If there's any brush, dig up the plants, removing all of the roots from the soil.

Lawns are made up of perennial grasses. They send out long underground stems (stolons). Miniscule portions of these stems will sprout again if they are not removed from the soil. For this reason most gardeners spray the area with a product containing glyphosate (such as KleenUp® or Roundup®). This systemic herbicide is absorbed by the plant. The net result is the death of the visible portion of the plant as well as all of its roots and stolons. The process requires patience, since you need to allow the grass to die and the herbicide to decompose before working the soil. This generally takes 2 weeks. If you're an organic gardener, dig up the grass. One of the easiest ways to remove lawn is in stages. If you prefer standing, use a pickax. If you can get down on your hands and knees, a flat spade works well. Shake off all the topsoil, place the sod into a wheelbarrow, and compost it in another area.

If the area is covered with weeds, treat it as if it were lawn. Spray the area with a product containing glyphosate. When the plants die and turn brown, remove them. If you're an organic gardener, pull up all of the annual weeds by hand. Dig up perennial weeds such as dandelions and thistles with a pointed shovel. Get even the tiniest portions of root, or the plants will resprout and be a recurring problem.

Once you've cleaned up the area and removed all the debris, you can loosen the topsoil with a spading fork or a rototiller if you have one. Never work in the soil when it is wet. Working wet soil will compact it, destroying the soil structure. Do all of this as far in advance as possible.

CHAPTER 4

PREPARING THE PLANTING HOLE

This chapter covers the correct way to dig a planting hole and helpful suggestions on preparing the soil to fill it. Recent studies contradict many past practices. The studies also have some complex exceptions. This chapter will keep relevant information as simple as possible.

What You Need to Know about Soil

Good soil has certain characteristics. It is firm enough to hold your plants in place, yet it is loose enough for easy penetration of water and oxygen to a plant's root system. Good soil drains freely. Ironically, good soil, while draining freely, also has the ability to retain moisture during drought and heat waves. Good soil locks in essential nutrients and makes these available to the plant over a long period of time. Good soil is alive, filled with billions of microorganisms. These microscopic creatures benefit the plant by providing and helping it take in nutrients. Good soil attracts worms, which tunnel through the ground to keep it loose and also fill it with nitrogen through their droppings (castings). If weeds or grass are thriving in an area, you have some good soil, at least on the surface. Soil contaminated by pollution, herbicides, oil, and salt is often bare and a sign that the soil should be replaced.

The Composition of Soil

Soil is composed of both inorganic and organic materials. *Inorganic* means that a material does not come from plants or animals. *Organic* means that a material comes from the decomposition of anything that was once alive, whether plant or animal.

The main inorganic materials are clay, silt, and sand. Clay is made up of miniscule particles that cling together when wet. When wet clay dries, it turns almost as hard as rock and tends to crack apart. Clay is usually a light tan to grayish tan in color. It sticks to your shovel and is very hard to work. However, nutrients cling to clay, so some clay in soil is beneficial because it locks in nutrients. Silt is made up of larger particles than clay. When wet, it feels somewhat slippery. Sand is made up of very large particles. Sand has a grainy feel. Water slides through sand quickly, often taking available nutrients with it. However, both silt and sand help keep soil loose.

The organic material found in soil is the result of the decomposition (rotting) of anything once alive. Everything alive eventually dies. When it does, it rots. Actually, it is being eaten by billions of different creatures, many of them microscopic. These creatures fall into different categories. Some are plants (fungi), others are animals (insects), and some have characteristics of both plants and animals. Organic material is especially attractive to worms. When worms die, their nitrogen-rich bodies decompose to give plants even more valuable food. The wide variety of unseen creatures digest organic matter into a light brown, fluffy material called *humus*. The benefits of humus to the soil are incredible. It keeps the soil loose and airy, holds moisture during drought, contains essential nutrients, provides a home for helpful soil microorganisms (many of which help shrubs take in food), and maintains soil at a neutral pH, which is ideal for most shrubs and small trees.

Good garden soil, commonly called *loam*, contains roughly equal amounts of clay, sand, and silt. The term *roughly* means just that. The balance does not have to be exact for the soil to be good. When the balance of these is right, the soil is said to have good texture. Added to these is the organic matter. The ability of organic matter to keep the soil loose enough for good drainage but retain moisture during dry spells describes the soil's structure. Good garden soil has both good texture and good structure.

The pH of Soil

A technical term, pH refers to the activity of hydrogen ions in the soil. In simple language, it is a gauge of how acidic or alkaline soil is. The pH scale runs from 0 (totally acidic) to 14 (totally alkaline). Neutral soil has a pH of 7. Most shrubs do best in a slightly acidic soil with a pH of 6 to 6.5. However, many shrubs are quite adaptable and can withstand more alkaline conditions. A few, however, demand very acidic soils to grow properly.

The right pH determines the availability of nutrients to plants. If the pH is too high or too low, many essential plant nutrients will be locked into the soil and not be absorbed by the roots. Fortunately, most soils in cold climate areas fall into a pH range suitable for growing most shrubs.

Soil pH is highly variable. Areas with lots of rain tend to have more acidic soils than areas with limited rainfall. Areas over granite or similar rock often have more acidic soils than areas over limestone. However, there are many areas with lots of rain with limestone as the basic underlying rock. In short, there is no set way of predicting the pH of your soil by either climatic or geological conditions since the two may cancel each other out.

Soil Fertility

The essential elements for good plant growth are nitrogen (N), phosphorus (P), and potassium (K). Other elements are needed in smaller amounts. If your soil contains lots of nutrients, it's considered fertile or rich. If your soil contains little in the way of nutrients, it's said to be infertile or lean.

Matching Shrubs and Small Trees to Soil

Shrubs and small trees vary in their needs. Many are quite adaptable. Others are very demanding. Ideally, you want to prepare your soil so that it has the right composition, pH, and fertility for the shrub or small tree you intend to plant.

The Right Soil Composition

You've already read about the qualities of good soil or loam. Good soil is great for some shrubs and small trees and not particularly important for others. In the wild many shrubs and small trees grow in poor soils and in some areas where there is little topsoil at all.

Recent research indicates that in most instances it is not necessary to change the composition of your soil dramatically when planting most shrubs and small trees. When digging a hole, set the soil on a tarp. This is referred to as *native soil*.

For most shrubs and small trees, amend this native soil with a small amount of organic matter. The ratio of native soil to organic matter should be nine parts to one part. Use all of the topsoil in this process. The organic matter you add to the soil is commonly called a *soil amendment*. Good soil amendments include compost, rotted horse manure, leaf mold, and peat. Compost is simply rotted organic debris, such as leaves, grass clippings, and kitchen scraps. Horse or cattle manure is considered rotted after it has broken down in a pile for at least a year or longer. Leaf mold is shredded leaves left to decompose for about a year. Peat moss is available at local

Soil Tests

SOIL TESTS ARE AVAILABLE to give you an idea of the composition, pH, and fertility of your soil. If you're planting many shrubs in different spots throughout your yard, you would need numerous tests to judge the soil in each location. Most of the shrubs and small trees in this guide will grow well without your having to have a soil test done on the site where you intend to plant them. The exceptions are plants that demand a specific soil pH.

Soil tests are quite reliable in determining soil pH. While soil tests have a good record in gauging soil pH, they appear to be less accurate in determining the overall availability of specific nutrients. Furthermore, if you follow the directions on fertilizing as given in this guide, any discussion concerning nutrients becomes relatively moot.

In regard to soil composition, you can get a rough idea of that in a very simple way. Dig a 10-inch (25-cm) deep hole in the area where you'll be planting the shrub. Take equal amounts of soil down the edge of the hole and mix it together. Take 1⅓ cups (about 300 g) of this soil and put it into a quart jar. Fill the jar almost to the top with water. Add a few drops of liquid detergent. Screw the lid on tightly and shake the jar as hard as you can for a minute or two. Shake until the soil is fully dissolved into the water. Then set the jar down. Sand will settle to the bottom, silt settles on top of the sand, clay settles on the silt, and, finally, organic matter settles on the clay. Since clay consists of such tiny particles, they may stay in suspension for days and occasionally weeks. But, in a few hours you'll know roughly how much sand and silt is in your soil. The organic matter usually settles on top of the clay as it comes out of suspension.

Soil tests are generally available by sending in a soil sample to a laboratory in your state. You can find out information on these from county extension services or major universities. Have soil tests done before planting, preferably in late summer. The tests are sent out to you with explicit instructions on how to take the samples, and doing so in the summer will give you plenty of time in the fall to prepare your planting hole or bed following the recommendations of the test. You would then plant the following spring.

nurseries. It comes compressed in large bales wrapped in thick plastic and is the most common soil amendment used by commercial and home gardeners.

Mix the organic matter into the native soil. Then use this amended soil when planting your shrub or small tree. Studies indicate that the young plants will spread their roots out more widely and quickly if the native soil is not altered greatly. However, there are notable exceptions.

Exception 1: Certain shrubs and small trees thrive in rich, well-drained soils high in organic matter. Organic matter should make up roughly 50 percent of the soil. Keep all of the topsoil but replace the subsoil with loam or a soilless mix. You can buy loam in bulk from a garden center or in individual bags labeled as potting soil. Professional mixes are composed primarily of peat.

You can either prepare a large bed for these demanding plants or a single planting hole. For the latter dig a hole at least five times as wide as you think the root ball will be. Throughout this growing guide you will be told when plants thrive in soil high in organic matter.

Exception 2: Most shrubs demand excellent drainage to grow properly. The method of adding small amounts of organic material to the soil works well in soils with good drainage. Soils with good drainage are commonly referred to as *loose*. For example, sand is an extremely loose soil. However, if your soil is rocky or made up primarily of clay, you will not have good drainage.

If you have rocky soil, the easiest solution is to build a raised bed. A raised bed is nothing more than a mound of soil placed on the existing soil surface. Ideally, the bed should be at least 24 inches (60 cm) deep and as wide as possible. Buy high-quality loam for this purpose. You can buy it by the truckload. Before placing it on the soil, turn over the soil with a spade, spading fork, or rototiller if possible.

If you have clay soil, there are two solutions. The first is to build a raised bed as outlined for rocky soil. The second is to dig an extremely large planting hole and remove the clay. The hole should be at least five times as wide as the plant's root system. When planting the shrub, the ratio of native soil (mainly clay) and organic matter should be one to one. Heavy clay soils are tricky to work with; see page 364 for additional information on planting in clay.

The Right Moisture

The moisture level common to any given soil is an extremely important consideration in the correct planting of shrubs and small trees. Soils with lots of clay or organic matter in them tend to stay moist. Sandy soils dry out quickly. Some shrubs and small trees tolerate a wide range of moisture levels while others are quite demanding. Match the plant to the soil type. You can add peat to many soils to make them more moisture retentive, but it is very hard to deal with areas that tend to be wet or boggy other than to plant shrubs or trees that thrive in those conditions in these areas. Throughout the individual sections of Part I, the moisture shrubs or small trees prefer or tolerate is included.

The Right Soil pH

Most of the shrubs and small trees in this guide are quite adaptable to soil pH. If a shrub is not adaptable to pH, consider having a soil test done

LOWERING SOIL pH

Certain shrubs demand extremely acidic soil with a pH of 4.5 to 5.5. The lower acidity helps roots take in iron and magnesium. A lack of these often results in yellowing between leaf veins (chlorosis), weak growth, and possibly even death. These plants are often referred to as acid-loving plants. The plants don't love acid, they simply need acidic soil in order to take in nutrients as outlined in the beginning of this paragraph.

There are two products commonly used to lower soil pH. Both are excellent. One is sulfur. Most products sold as sulfur are 88 percent to 100 percent sulfur and take about 3 to 4 months to lower soil pH. The other product is iron sulfate (ferrous sulfate). You will usually have to apply iron sulfate at a higher rate to

get the same results. However, it does work more rapidly than sulfur, reducing pH in about 2 to 3 weeks. If you use iron sulfate, wear a dust mask, protective goggles, and old clothing. The dust is fine and does stain clothes with rusty blotches or streaking.

Add sulfur or iron sulfate to the soil in the fall. If you had a soil test done in fall, retest in spring. The second test may indicate the need for an additional application of sulfur or iron sulfate to get the soil to the desired low pH.

Do not plant shrubs that demand acidic soils until the soil has reached the correct pH.

It must be pointed out that some fine gardeners grow plants that thrive in acidic soil without having soil tests and without pretreating their soil with acidifying agents. Instead, they add copious amounts of rotted oak leaves, pine needles, or peat to loam (black dirt) and then fill in their planting holes with this mixture. All of these soil amendments tend to make the soil more acidic. The ratio of organic matter to loam is usually one to one. The organic matter feeds fungi known as mycorrhiza, which in turn help plants that thrive in acidic soils take in nutrients. These gardeners then fertilize the plants with acidic fertilizers, including ammonium sulfate (synthetic) or cottonseed meal (organic). This method is certainly less work, but it is also less certain to be successful as the one outlined earlier.

Important: Avoid the use of aluminum sulfate, commonly recommended as a product to reduce soil pH. While it does make soil more acidic, excessive aluminum will retard root growth.

RAISING THE pH

In some areas soils are quite acidic. Mildly acidic soils rarely cause a problem with most shrubs and small trees, but highly acidic ones can. If your soil falls into this category, you can easily grow plants that demand acidic soils. But you may wish to grow others as well. To raise the soil pH for these shrubs, mix lime or dolomitic limestone into the soil following the directions on the package. Normally, it takes about 8 weeks for the pH to rise. Hardwood ash is a good organic substance used to raise soil pH.

CHAPTER 5

PLANTING SHRUBS AND SMALL TREES

Advice on the correct planting of shrubs and small trees has changed in recent years. The main concepts are quite straightforward. The planting hole should contain soil loose enough to allow for the easy penetration of water and oxygen, but firm enough to hold the shrub or small tree in place. You should take all steps necessary to avoid restricting root growth and to stop roots from circling in and around themselves in a process known as *girdling*. You should encourage the quick development of a strong root system so that the shrub or small tree grows vigorously and is capable of supporting itself in strong gusts of wind. While all of this is true, the exact planting process varies from shrub to shrub and from tree to tree.

Buying Shrubs and Small Trees

Shrubs and small trees are commonly sold in the following ways:

• **Bare root:** Many shrubs and small trees are sold as bare root plants, but some are not. A bare root plant is a dormant plant sold without any soil around its roots, although roots are frequently covered in moist materials such as shredded paper, which is removed before planting. The material is often held in place

around the roots by plastic with a wire tie around the top. Some mail-order sources sell prepackaged plants. These plants are sold with their roots placed in moistened peat or loose soil. The moistened material is kept in place by a plastic bag. These are essentially bare root plants. If ordering prepackaged plants, ask whether they will be sent to you in a dormant state or during active growth with leaves on the plants. Buy them only if they are still dormant. If they have already leafed out, they suffer severe root disturbance and transplant shock during planting. This usually results in poor growth.

• **Containerized plants:** All shrubs and small trees are sold in this way. These are dormant or actively growing plants that have been grown in some sort of container.

• **Balled and burlapped:** Many shrubs and small trees are sold this way, but some are not. These are dormant or actively growing plants that have been dug up from a nursery field with their root balls tightly enclosed by fabric, twine, and sometimes wire.

Buying Bare Root Plants

Some local nurseries stock a limited number of bare root shrubs and small trees, especially those used for hedges. You can usually buy these in early spring. They are often kept in coolers.

Warning: Find the Lines

BEFORE PLANTING SHRUBS AND SMALL TREES, have utility companies mark the location of all underground lines. In most states they are required to do this on demand without charge. Lines are usually marked with red spray or tiny flags. Simply call your local utility company and ask for this to be done. Give it as much advance notice as possible. In some cities, you only have to call one number to have the entire process taken care of by a number of companies.

Many mail-order companies sell a wider variety of bare root plants than local nurseries. The cost of bare root plants is often related to their age. In some instances it's worth paying more for older plants, but there are exceptions. When important, Part I indicates whether to purchase older plants.

When to Buy Bare Root Plants

Buy bare root shrubs and small trees as early as possible in spring. The only exception to this is *Paeonia* (Tree Peony), which is sold in the fall. Plant bare root shrubs and trees as soon as the ground can be worked. If ordering bare root plants through the mail, specify when you would like to receive them. If you own a large piece of property, you may be able to purchase bare root plants suitable for wildlife plantings at extremely low cost from your state's Department of Natural Resources.

Checking Out Bare Root Stock

Bare root shrubs and small trees are usually less expensive than containerized or balled and burlapped plants. Be sure to check the stems and roots.

STEMS

Bare root plants should have healthy stems. These usually have a greenish, maroon, or light tan tinge. If you bend an individual stem slightly, it should be firm but pliable. If you cut into it, the inside looks whitish green.

Unhealthy stems may look dried out and discolored. If you bend one of them, it often breaks because it's so dry and brittle. If you cut into it, it's brown, because it's dead. It may also have a wrinkled appearance caused by dehydration.

Occasionally, it can be quite difficult for the home gardener to tell whether stems are alive or dead. If you suspect that a bare root plant may be dead, notify the company from which you bought it. Tell it that you will plant the shrub or small tree to see whether it will grow. If the plant doesn't show signs of growth within a few weeks, contact the company for an appropriate refund. This is relatively rare, but does happen.

Ask companies to send you fully dormant plants. The buds should not be swelling, or "breaking." Unfortunately, during shipping buds may begin to grow. If the buds have formed shoots that appear long and white, break them off with your finger. Press down on them lightly. They're so brittle that they snap right off. If you don't remove them, they'll just dry up and die anyway. The removal of buds in this way does stress plants, so get them into the ground as quickly as possible.

If buds are barely beginning to swell and emerge, leave them alone. This is an ideal time for planting. Get them into the soil immediately. The longer you wait, the greater the stress on the plant.

ROOTS

Healthy bare root plants have firm, pliable roots that are not broken, diseased, or mashed. These should be protected well from drying by being wrapped in damp packing material, usually shredded newspaper or some similar substance. Some companies sell plants without wrapping the roots, but it is best for roots to be kept moist during the shipping process.

When opening the package, check the roots to make sure that they are clean and firm. If roots are mushy and covered with thick mold, you may have a serious problem. Call the supplier and ask it for advice.

If roots are quite firm and covered with a little white mold, simply wash it off and dip the roots in an extremely weak chlorine solution. Make this by mixing 5 gallons (19 liters) of water with 1 cup (¼ liter) bleach. Do this for about 30 seconds. This kills many disease-causing organisms, especially those related to galls (see page 395).

Gray mold is usually an indication that plant tissue is dead. If present only on the tips of stems or roots, simply snip them off. If mold covers most of the plant tissue, return the plant. Always call the supplier immediately after receiving a plant covered in mold. It may have additional advice, but remember that some molds can infect your soil.

Bare root plants sold in local nurseries should have the same characteristics as those sold by mail order. Most local nurseries only stock these for a short time. Request yours weeks in advance. Pick them up as soon as they arrive. If the weather is too cold for planting, many local nurseries will keep them in storage for you if you pay for the plants in advance. This is especially good advice for anyone planning on using bare root plants for hedges. You'll save lots of money by buying these dormant plants in bulk.

Preparing Bare Root Plants for Planting

Later in this section are step-by-step instructions on two methods of planting bare root shrubs, either directly in the ground or in a container. The following steps apply to either method you choose to plant your bare root shrubs and small trees in spring.

As soon as you get bare root plants through the mail or from a retail store, remove them from the packaging immediately. This packaging may be next to nothing or a plastic bag in a cardboard container or something similar. Occasionally, some bare root plants are packaged with some soil around the roots and then enclosed in plastic. For certain shrubs this is highly recommended.

Inspect the plant to make sure it is healthy and disease free.

If the roots are surrounded by packing material, gently pull it away from the roots until they are fully exposed. If the roots are surrounded by soil (not packing material), leave it in place. The soil is usually quite loose. These are not technically bare root plants, but should be treated as such. Until planting, keep plants cool and out of direct sunlight.

If there is a metal or plastic tag around the stem, remove it. The tag will restrict growth and can kill the stem as the plant matures. Identify the plant in some other way, as with a metal, plastic, or wooden marker at its base.

If any portion of the stem is broken or dead (dry, brittle, and discolored), cut it back to healthy tissue. Cut back to a spot ¼ inch (.6 cm) above a leaf bud below. Remove as little of the stems or branches as possible. Although commonly suggested, never cut off the tips of the stems unless they are damaged. These stem tips create hormones that stimulate good root growth. Leave them alone. Furthermore, you want to preserve as much stem tissue as possible to create lots of foliage. Foliage is responsible for the creation of food. This helps the plant form a vigorous and widespread root system rapidly.

If any roots are broken or crushed, cut them off to a firm section with pruning shears just above the point of damage. Remove as little of the root system as possible. In particular, do not remove any of the fine fibrous roots, as these are the ones responsible for taking in water and nutrients. Although it is sometimes suggested to prune off longer roots, do not do this unless they are broken or damaged. The longer the roots, the better. Longer roots tend to help the plant take root quickly and grow more rapidly. This benefits the young plant enormously. Besides, most commercial growers have already snipped off portions of the root before they mail the plants to you just to get them into the package.

If the plants arrive in really good condition with moist roots and stems, plant them without any special treatment. If they arrive dry, soak the plants for no fewer than 3 hours and overnight at the maximum in water with the roots down and the stems up. The easiest way to do this is in a plastic garbage can. You can soak a number of plants in one can. Although plants tend to float, all of the roots and most of the stem will be submerged. You could soak the plants for up to 24 hours. However, any longer than that may cause damage. The purpose of this soaking is to soften stem tissue and get water into the root system of plants that may have dried out somewhat in shipping. A few hours of soaking for bare root plants is recommended simply as a way of ensuring that root and stem tissue is moist.

If you cannot plant shrubs right away, remove them from any packaging and place them in a trench. If the ground is frozen or too hard to dig, place the bare root plants horizontally on the ground and cover them completely with moist potting soil. If the ground is covered with snow, shovel it off and pour hot water on it until it is completely exposed. Then lay the plants on the ground. Now cover them completely with moist peat or purchased potting soil. Finally, shovel as much snow over the mound as possible. If you have only a few plants, place them in a large container (garbage can, box, black plastic bag) filled with potting soil or peat moss in your garage. Cover the root systems of the bare root shrubs completely. The protecting material should be moist. The process of protecting plants in this manner is called *heeling in*. Get the shrubs into containers or directly into the ground as soon as possible after this procedure. Heeling in is strictly a temporary measure, which may be dictated by extremely cold or wet weather outdoors. It definitely stresses plants.

Alternatively, moisten the plants and place them against an inside garage wall. Cover them with any material made of cloth, not plastic. The temperature in the garage can be close to freezing, but if it's colder than this, you risk losing the plants. This is why it's so important to stress a specific delivery time from a mail-order company.

Do not place plants in the crisper of your refrigerator if they arrive too early, unless you have an empty refrigerator set aside for this purpose. Some serious and very passionate gardeners do. The temperature should be set at between 32°F (0°C) and 36°F (2°C). Plants will last for weeks at this temperature. Remove the shrubs from all packaging. Clean them well and trim off damaged stems and roots immediately. Keep them moist at all times and plant as soon as possible.

Planting Bare Root Plants

Plant bare root plants as soon as the ground can be worked in spring. If possible, plant on an overcast day or in late afternoon or early evening. This keeps the plant from drying out in high heat or hot sun. You want the stems to stay moist.

In extremely cold springs, it may be necessary to plant bare root plants temporarily in containers just to keep them healthy. Obviously, you cannot plant them if there is snow on the ground or when the ground is still frozen. You could also heel them in until the ground is ready for planting.

The size of the planting hole depends on the size of the shrub's root system. The general rule is that the size of the hole should be two to three times as wide as the entire root system and about as deep as the longest root. If your soil is very heavy and compacted as in clay, the hole should be no less than three times as wide as the root system. Also, you may have to break through what is known as hardpan in the base of the hole. This is a dense layer of soil that does not allow water to flow freely through it. For the home gardener the easiest way to do this is with a posthole digger or a crowbar. Dig down as far as necessary to break through this barrier. You'll feel the change as you go from hardpan to soil underneath. In some instances, this can be extremely difficult. The purpose of this is to create good drainage away from the roots of the plant. Holes in heavy clay act as miniature holding ponds. Without good drainage, the roots are surrounded by water. This cuts off their supply of oxygen. The plant's growth may be retarded or the plant may die.

If your planting area is rocky or pure rock, build a raised bed as outlined on page 359.

When you dig a hole, especially in clay, the sides can become hard. The cutting motion of the spade creates a glazing on the clay itself. This can harden and prevent roots from penetrating it easily. Scrape the sides of the hole with a pronged cultivator to rough them up. Also when digging in clay, a square hole may be better than a round one in that the sharp angles may prevent roots from circling around on themselves as they would in a container. The shape of the hole and the scraping of the sides may help roots grow out from the plant and penetrate the clay more easily.

Also, turning compacted soil with a spading fork or with a rototiller around the planting hole is highly recommended to loosen soil for easier root penetration. In this area outside the planting hole, you can work in soil amendments and slow-release fertilizers. The loose soil with added nutrients draws roots away from the planting hole and establishes a wider and healthier root system.

Place the soil on a tarp or in a wheelbarrow off to the side of the planting hole. Mix organic matter into the soil. The ratio may be as little as one part organic matter to nine parts native soil or as high as one part organic matter to one part native soil. The ratio depends on the type of native soil and the needs of the shrub or small tree being planted. Good organic materials are compost, fully rotted leaves, rotted manures, or peat moss. Do not mix sod, weeds, or any nondecomposed organic material into the native soil. The breakdown of these materials temporarily steals valuable nitrogen from the soil at the expense of good growth of the shrub or small tree being planted. The soil mixed with organic matter and used in filling in the planting hole is known as *backfill soil*.

Mix some superphosphate (synthetic) or bone meal (organic) into the soil at the base of the hole. Cover either of these with 3 inches (7.5 cm) of soil. Both contain phosphorus, an element essential to rapid root growth. Follow the directions on the package exactly. Phosphorus added to a planting hole will not cause problems with surface water runoff. And, it will certainly not hurt the plant even if levels of phosphorus are already high enough in the soil. If you would like to be absolutely correct in your planting method, have a soil test done. This will tell whether to add any phosphorus to the soil at planting time.

Some gardeners place slow-release fertilizers coated with a special resin that breaks down gradually over time in the planting hole. If you want to do this, dig the hole 6 inches (15 cm) deeper than you normally would. Place the coated granules in the hole and cover with 6 inches (15 cm) of soil. This keeps the fertilizer out of direct contact with the roots. These coated granules or time-release fertilizers break down slowly. The release of the chemicals is triggered primarily by rising soil temperature. As the soil warms up, the resin breaks down. This is good since the release of nutrients then coincides with the shrub's initial growth spurt. The breakdown of resin is also related to soil pH, moisture, type of soil, and microbial activity. The latter is also related to soil temperature.

Do *not* add quick-release inorganic fertilizers to the backfill soil. These may get concentrated by accident and harm the root system. They may also encourage the roots to stay in the planting hole rather than moving down and outward as they should.

Now place a cone of backfill soil in the center of the planting hole. Spread the roots out evenly in all directions over this cone. Plant the shrub or small tree so that the uppermost portions of the roots are just at the surface of the soil or barely below. One of the most common mistakes is planting bare root shrubs and small trees too deeply. You can often tell where the plant was growing before it was dug up by looking closely at the stem. There will be a slight difference in the color of the portion of the stem that was buried in the field and the portion that was above the soil.

If the shrub or small tree is grafted or budded, the placement of the bud union is very important. Some will have their bud unions above the soil, others will have them buried as much as 6 inches (15 cm) below the soil. Exact instructions are given in individual sections of Part I.

Now cover the roots with more soil. Firm the soil around the roots with your fingers. Holding on to the base of the shrub, shake it ever so gently. This helps soil fill in any gaps around the roots. Do this just once. Firm again with your fingers to get rid of any air pockets, which can cause roots to dry out and may encourage infections by disease. Fill the hole about two-thirds full.

Now saturate the soil with water. Soak the soil for several minutes until water stands on the surface. Let the water soak in. This too helps soil fill in around the roots so that there is little chance of any air pockets being left behind. Check to make sure that the top roots are still at the correct level—high up in the hole right at the soil surface. If the plant has sunk in the hole, grab it by the base of its stems or trunk and gently lift it up. Water again immediately so that soil fills in any potential gaps created by this movement.

Once the water has soaked into the soil, finish filling the hole to the top. Firm it with your fingers as you did earlier. Do not walk on the soil or tamp it down with a tool. You want the soil to be firm, but not overly compacted. The whole purpose of firming the soil is to keep the plant in place. If you overly compact the soil, oxygen and water are prevented from mixing properly in the soil itself. Now water the soil again so that it is thoroughly saturated.

Make a starter solution by dissolving water-soluble fertilizer in water. Pour ½ cup (120 ml) of this around the base of the plant. Good water-soluble fertilizers include products such as Miracle-Gro® (15-30-15), Peters® All Purpose Plant Food (20-20-20), and Rapid Grow (23-19-17). Similar products are on the market and are fine. If the plant prefers acidic conditions, then use a fertilizer that will acidify the soil, such as Miracid (30-10-10) or Miracle-Gro® Azalea, Camellia, Rhododendron Plant Food (24-8-16). Again, similar products are on the market and are equally effective. If you prefer organic fertilizer, use fish emulsion instead. To acidify the soil, use cottonseed meal. The latter, unfortunately, is not as readily available as it was in the past.

The use of fertilizer at this time is somewhat controversial. It is certainly helpful with some shrubs and small trees and less important with a number of others. Since it will not hurt the plant, there is no harm in doing it. The controversy stems from environmental concerns (see page 382).

Do not stake the plant. Wind may rock the plant gently, and this motion actually helps the plant. There are exceptions. See page 384 for further comments about staking.

Keep the soil around the plant evenly moist until it is growing vigorously. Whenever the soil starts to dry out, water it deeply. Watering young plants regularly and deeply is probably the single most critical step in their early development.

When the soil warms up, cover it with a layer of mulch to the depth outlined in the individual sections of Part I. Mulching is covered in detail on pages 380–81.

When to Buy Containerized Plants

The best time to plant deciduous shrubs in cold climates is in early spring. Shrubs planted at this time suffer less stress from temperature extremes and have plenty of time to take root over the months to come as long as they are cared for properly. Also, you find out quickly whether a plant is healthy and vigorous. If it dies despite proper care, you can ask for a replacement within the warranty period, which is often the present growing season.

The best time to plant evergreens is early spring or after intense summer heat has faded and at least 6 weeks before the first expected frost. The plants cannot tolerate high temperatures, but they must have enough time to take root well before going into the winter season.

Having said that, it is important to emphasize that one of the big advantages of buying containerized plants is that you can plant them throughout the entire growing season. Deciduous shrubs and evergreens can be planted from early spring through early fall. A particular advantage is that you can see flowering plants in bloom if they are mature enough.

Buying Containerized Plants

You'll find many of the shrubs and small trees listed in this guide in local garden centers and nurseries. These are often sold in plastic or similar containers that come in a multitude of sizes.

When buying plants, ask whether they have been grown locally. Plants grown in your area have a better chance of surviving because they are fully acclimated to your climate. Many nurseries buy plants from other states but acclimate them properly before resale. This acclimation process usually means that plants are purchased in the fall, allowed to harden off naturally, tipped and protected during the winter, then sold during the following growing season. These plants have a better survival rate than those shipped in from out of state during the current growing season.

Whenever you buy a containerized plant, check it carefully. If you buy early, you'll often get the best plants.

Look at the label before considering the shrub or small tree. The Latin name is critical. Buy plants by their Latin names so that you're assured of getting the plant you want. The Latin name also guides you to plants hardy in your area.

Choose shrubs that are growing vigorously and have good form and shape. Nice plants have lots of evenly spaced stems. If they are small trees, branching should be uniform and even.

Always buy plants in the desired form. For example, some plants can be multistemmed shrubs or single-trunked trees. It is far easier to begin with the plant in the form you want than to try to change its form through pruning.

The size of the plant should be in proportion to the size of the container; smaller plants in smaller containers, larger ones in larger containers. While this may seem obvious, it is not always the case. Large plants in small containers are often potbound (rootbound) and will perform poorly.

Foliage should be healthy and the proper color for that shrub. Discoloration can be a sign of poor drainage, lack of nutrients, and improper watering. It can also be a sign of disease or insect damage. Check the foliage for spots, lesions, or notches in the leaves. These usually indicate the presence of disease and insect infestations.

If a plant is wilting from water stress, look for one that is not. Water stress can do a lot of damage in a short time. Wilting is an indication that a plant is not getting the amount of water it needs. Wilting affects plant vigor and its overall chance of survival.

Check the soil. If the soil has moved away from the edge of the container, this indicates inconsistent watering, which can stress plants badly. If the soil is extremely dry, it also indicates careless handling. If a plant looks healthy, you can remedy both situations by pushing the soil back against the side of the pot and by watering immediately. However, it would be better if you could find a plant properly cared for from the start.

Plants are often placed too close to one another in retail outlets. People inadvertently damage or break stems as they select plants. Avoid plants with broken, cracked, or scraped stems. Look at the stems too for discolored bark or visible bleeding of sap from wounds. Also, check the plant for any abnormal or distorted stems and leaves. Distorted growth is another sign of disease and insect problems.

Ask the nursery how long the plant has been in the container. Pull up gently on the stems of a shrub or the trunk of a tree to see that they are firmly in place—solidly anchored in the soil. If they are loose, this indicates recent planting. When you remove the shrub from the container, the root ball is likely to fall apart. In effect, you're buying a bare root plant but paying a containerized price. When the root ball does fall apart, it retards the plant's growth since it's already leafed out and actively growing. So when you lift up, you want to feel resistance as proof that the shrub has been growing in the container long enough for it to fill up the soil with an expansive root system.

If you tug just a bit harder, the plant should begin to slide out of the container. If numerous roots are noticeable on the outer edge of the root ball and if the root ball remains solidly intact, it's been in the container for some time.

If roots are beginning to grow out the bottom drain holes, the plant may have been in the pot too long. These roots are a possible indicator of a much more serious problem. If shrubs or small trees are grown in containers for too long, fairly large roots will begin to grow in circles around the the root ball. This is known as *girdling*. Girdling can occur on the surface of the soil, at the base of the plant, or at all levels of the root ball. This type of growth can eventually kill a shrub. Lay the container on its side and pull the plant out. If fairly large roots are coiled around the root ball, it's potbound. Since it's difficult to overcome girdling, consider buying a different plant.

Whenever you buy a containerized shrub, get it home quickly. Avoid leaving it in a hot car while you run errands or do additional shopping. This overheating can stress a plant considerably.

If a plant will be exposed to wind on the way home, bring rope and a sheet to the nursery. Have the branches tied up as firmly as possible with the rope. Then have the garden center or nursery wrap the entire upper portion in the sheet. Moistening it is a good idea. Loop rope around the plant to keep the fabric in place. Finally, tie the fabric around the base of the plant. Get the plant home quickly, remove the covering at once, and soak the soil until water runs out the bottom drain holes. If you don't protect the plant on the way home, leaves often dry out in the wind and drop off in days. If you leave the protective fabric cover on too long once you're home, humidity and heat buildup will kill the foliage.

Planting Containerized Plants

If a containerized plant has not yet leafed out, plant it as soon as the soil can be worked in early spring. If the plant is fully leafed out, you may want to wait until after any danger of frost in spring. Otherwise, keep it in your garage or in a sheltered location if necessary until it's safe to plant it.

If the plant has any flower buds or flowers on it, you may want to snip these off. Nurseries find it easier to sell plants in bloom, and seeing flowers also helps you choose the plant you prefer. By removing flower buds and blooms immediately, you redirect the plant's energy into forming a healthy root system and more vigorous stems. Admittedly, on plants with numerous, small blossoms this is impractical unless the plant is quite small.

Unless containerized plants in full leaf have already been exposed to sun outdoors for at least 2 weeks, move plants slowly into increasing light over a period of 10 to 14 days as temperatures warm up. This prevents sunscald (too much sun too quickly). Pale, whitish leaves are the result of sunscald, often confused with disease. When in doubt, simply ask the garden center how long the plants have been in sun.

Now prepare the planting hole in relation to the size of the root ball. The general rule is that the size of the hole should be two to three times wider than the width of the root ball and about 2 inches (10 cm) shallower than its depth. Also, you may have to break through the hardpan as outlined in the section on planting bare root plants.

If your planting area is rocky or pure rock, build a raised bed as outlined on page 359.

When you dig a hole, especially in clay, the sides can become hard. The cutting motion of the spade creates a glazing on the clay itself. This can harden and prevent roots from penetrating it easily. Scrape the sides of the hole with a pronged cultivator to roughen them up. Also digging a square hole in clay may be better than a round one in that the sharp angles may prevent roots from circling around on themselves as they would in a container. The shape of the hole and the scraping of the sides may help roots grow out from the plant and penetrate the clay more easily.

In addition, turning compacted soil with a spade, spading fork, or rototiller around the planting hole is recommended to loosen soil for easier root penetration. In this area outside the planting hole, work in soil amendments and slow-release fertilizers. The loose soil with added nutrients draws roots away from the planting hole and establishes a wider and healthier root system.

Place the soil on a tarp or in a wheelbarrow off to the side of the planting hole. Mix organic matter into the soil at a ratio appropriate for the shrub or tree being grown.

Mix some superphosphate (synthetic) or bone meal (organic) into the soil at the base of the hole. Cover either of these with 3 inches (7.5 cm) of soil. Both contain phosphorus, an element essential to rapid root growth. Follow the directions on the package exactly. Some gardeners place slow-release fertilizers coated with a special resin that breaks down gradually over time in the planting hole. If you want to do this, mix the fertilizer into the backfill soil following directions on the label.

Do not add quick-release inorganic fertilizers to the backfill soil. These may get concentrated by accident and harm the root system. They may also encourage the roots to stay in the planting hole rather than moving down and outward as they should.

Run a long knife around the entire outside edge of the root ball. The knife should be long enough to get close to the bottom of the container. Slide the knife up and down and as deep as possible to loosen the root ball from the container.

Now turn the container on its side close to the planting hole. Give the bottom of the container a hard whack. Hold on to the side of the container with one hand while grabbing the base of the shrub or small tree with the other. Gently pull on the plant. If it begins to slide from the container, just keep pulling until it is out. If the plant resists, whack the back and sides of the container again. Check to see whether there are any roots protruding from the drain holes. They may be catching and stopping the plant from coming out. Cut these off. Try again to pull the plant out. Usually, you'll get the plant out this way. Avoid breaking the root ball, even if that means cutting the bottom of the pot off and then making a cut down one side of the pot to remove it. Note that if a plant is well rooted with a solid root ball, you can simply pull it out by its stems or trunk, although this is not recommended.

With a sharp blade slit all four sides of the root ball to a depth of 1 inch (2.5 cm). This cuts through any girdling roots. Cut through the base of the root ball making a large X. Or simply tease the root ball apart without breaking it.

While it's okay to hold on to stems or the trunk of a small tree while removing it from the pot, do not hold on to these while you place the plant in the hole. Move the plant while grasping the root ball by its sides.

Set the plant in the hole. The uppermost roots in the root ball should be level with the surrounding soil or preferably just slightly above it. If you've followed the directions to this point, the root ball will be roughly 1 inch (2.5 cm) above the surrounding soil.

Place backfill soil underneath the root ball if necessary to get the plant in the correct position.

Press additional soil around the base of the root ball once it's in the center of the hole and positioned at the right depth. Then add enough soil to keep the plant in place, but do not fill up the entire hole. Fill the hole two-thirds full.

Fill the hole with water. Let it drain down. This helps the soil settle around the roots and eliminates air pockets at the same time.

Now add more soil until the hole is full. Press the soil firmly into place to get rid of any air pockets. Use your hands, not your feet. You want the soil to be firm, not compacted.

Soak the plant thoroughly with a hose. Let the water soak into the ground. The soil may sink slightly. Add more soil. Press it lightly into place. Then water again, saturating the soil.

Pour ½ cup (about 120 ml) starter solution around the base of each plant. If you prefer organic fertilizer, use fish emulsion instead.

Do not stake the plant. Wind may rock the plant gently, and this motion actually helps the plant. See page 384.

Keep the soil around the plant evenly moist until it is growing vigorously. Whenever the soil starts to dry out, water it deeply. Watering young plants regularly and deeply is probably the single most critical step in their early development.

When the soil warms up, cover it with a layer of mulch to the depth outlined in the individual sections of Part I.

Buying Balled and Burlapped Plants

Many shrubs are dug up and the root balls wrapped in burlap for sale to the consumer. This is most commonly done in spring and fall. However, the plants are generally available from spring through fall. You can plant deciduous balled and burlapped shrubs at any time of year. Early spring is the best time to plant them. The best time to plant evergreens is in early spring or after intense summer heat and long enough before the ground freezes for the roots to take hold. A good time for fall planting is usually 6 weeks before the first expected frost in your area. Check the shrub out as you would a containerized plant. Follow suggestions as given in that earlier section. Here are a few additional tips:

- The root ball of balled and burlapped plants should be compact and firm. Feel it. If it's broken, cracked, or loose, don't buy it.
- The stems of a shrub or trunk of a small tree should be solid. Push on them. They should not wiggle back and forth in the soil itself. In short, they should not be loose but firmly embedded in the soil itself.
- Feel the soil; it should be moist. If the plant looks extremely healthy, you can overcome the lack of moisture by heavy watering once you get it home. Still, it's better if the soil is uniformly moist at the point of purchase.
- Protect the plant on the way home as outlined in the section on containerized plants, page 368. Keep balled and burlapped plants in a shaded place until you're ready to plant them. Get them into the ground as quickly as possible once home.

Planting Balled and Burlapped Plants

The burlap used in balled and burlapped plants may be natural burlap, a natural fiber impregnated with a synthetic substance, or simply synthetic material that looks like burlap. In theory, natural burlap is supposed to decompose and allow roots to expand outward in time. It sometimes doesn't. Synthetic materials simply do not decompose. Fortunately, these are becoming increasingly rare in the marketplace today. A root ball surrounded by burlap is often held in place by thick wire. The following planting method strongly urges you to remove as much of the burlap and wire as possible to avoid containing roots in a restricted space and causing girdling over a period of years.

Dig a hole 1 to 2 feet (30 to 60 cm) wider than the diameter of the root ball. If you have the stamina, dig it even wider than this as you would for bare root or containerized plants. The larger the hole, the easier it is to remove the burlap and wire. Dig the hole slightly shallower than the root ball. If you're digging in compacted soil such as clay, scratch the sides of the hole with a pronged cultivator to break it apart. This will help roots penetrate the area as they grow outward. Also in clay you may have to break the hardpan as outlined in the section on planting bare root plants.

Also, turning compacted soil with a spade or with a rototiller around the planting hole is highly recommended to loosen soil for easier root penetration. In this area outside the planting hole, you can work in soil amendments and slow-release fertilizers. The loose soil with added nutrients draws roots away from the planting hole and establishes a wider and healthier root system.

Place the soil on a tarp or in a wheelbarrow off to the side of the planting hole. Mix organic matter into the soil at a ratio appropriate for the shrub or tree being grown.

Mix some superphosphate (synthetic) or bone meal (organic) into the soil at the base of the hole. Cover either of these with 3 inches (7.5 cm) of soil. Both contain phosphorus, an element essential to rapid root growth. Follow the directions on the package exactly.

Some gardeners place slow-release fertilizers coated with a special resin that breaks down gradually over time in the planting hole. If you want to do this, just mix it into the backfill soil as indicated on the label.

Do not add quick-release inorganic fertilizers to the backfill soil. These may get concentrated by accident and harm the root system. They may also encourage the roots to stay in the planting hole rather than moving down and outward as they should.

Set the balled and burlapped plant to the side of the hole. Do not drop it onto the ground. You want the soil to stay very tight around the roots. For the same reason do not move the plant by grabbing the stems or trunk. Instead, move it by supporting the sides of the root ball with your hands. Depending upon their size, these plants can be extremely heavy. You may need help to do this correctly. In fact, moving some balled and burlapped shrubs and small trees may take two or three strong people.

Ideally, you want to remove the twine, wire, and burlap completely. If you do this while the plant is out of the hole, you risk having the root ball fall apart as you place it into the hole. Since balled and burlapped plants have already lost from 70 percent to 90 percent of their roots in the process of being dug up, the breaking apart of the root ball can be catastrophic in that the remaining feeder roots can be severely damaged. So, the following is recommended:

Place the balled and burlapped plant in the hole. With heavy plants this is sometimes easiest if you place a tarp underneath it. Then working with another person, lower the plant into the hole and get it into the correct position by shifting the tarp. Remove the tarp by pulling it out from underneath the root ball as the second person tilts the burlapped shrub or tree to make this easier. The top of the root ball should end up 1 inch (2.5 cm) or so above the surface of the hole. The plant should be positioned exactly as you want it to grow. The stems or trunk should be straight up, not tilting to one side.

Now remove the twine holding the burlap in place. Cut off as much of the wire as you can. Cutting the wire can be difficult. Some of the wire used with larger shrubs and small trees is thick. You can cut through smaller wires with a wire cutter. Cut thick wires with bolt cutters. Cut off the burlap as far down to the base of the root ball as possible. Make sure that you do not break the root ball while doing this. You'll end up with a little wire and some burlap under the base of the plant, but most of the burlap and wire will now be gone.

Fill in the hole with the native soil amended with organic matter. Firm it in place with your fingers. The soil should be firm enough to hold the plant in place, but do not overly compact it. Compacted soil stops water and oxygen from mixing properly, and this process is critical to good root growth.

The branches of balled and burlapped shrubs, especially evergreens, are often tied together tightly when delivered. Get the plant into the ground quickly and untie any binding ties as soon as the plant is firmly in place. Evergreen branches that are squished together cause heat to build up. This heat can damage shrubs severely.

Your balled and burlapped plant is now firmly in place but part of the root ball is above the soil surface. Cover the exposed root ball with native soil amended with organic matter. Pour soil around the base of the tree. Then smooth it out over the exposed root ball. You want the soil to slope down from the base of the trunk to the surface of the soil surrounding the root ball itself. This high planting encourages good root growth as it allows for easy mixing of water and oxygen where it is most important.

Now water the plant well, making sure that the soil is thoroughly saturated. A good portion of the roots are essentially above the original soil surface. The combination of water and oxygen is ideal in this situation.

Pour ½ cup (about 120 ml) starter solution around the base of each plant. If you prefer organic fertilizer, use fish emulsion instead.

Do not stake the plant. Wind may rock the plant gently, and this motion actually helps the plant. See page 384.

Keep the soil around the plant evenly moist until it is growing vigorously. Whenever the soil starts to dry out, water it deeply. Watering young plants regularly and deeply is probably the single most critical step in their early development.

When the soil warms up, cover it with a layer of mulch to the depth outlined in the individual sections of Part I. Mulch should not touch the stems or the base of the shrub or tree.

Growing Shrubs in Containers

In warmer climates, it is much easier to grow shrubs and small trees permanently in containers. In cold climates, winter protection is difficult and a serious

Selecting a Container

THE MOST COMMON CONTAINERS used for growing shrubs are ceramic (unglazed), clay, plastic, and wood (containing no toxic preservatives). All containers should have drainage holes.

Each type of container has its advantages and disadvantages. Ceramic (unglazed) and clay are attractive and breathe freely. They are also heavy enough to hold plants in place in gusts of wind. However, they are hard to move around, require frequent watering, break easily, and are quite expensive.

Plastic containers are less attractive and do not breathe freely. They also may be too light and blow over in gusts of wind. However, they are inexpensive, easy to clean, and durable. They also require less watering and are easier to move around.

Wood is attractive, stays in place, and retains moisture well. However, it is expensive and difficult to clean and move around. It will also rot out over the years. Placing wood containers on rollers or casters makes moving them easier. A dolly also works well.

problem. Growing shrubs in this fashion is really not recommended since the chance of losing them is high. If you want to give it a try, here are some tips.

Choose plants that are suited to growing in a container. Normally, these are small shrubs and trees that are slow growing, naturally inclined to stay small, or easily pruned to maintain their small size. Plants listed in this guide that fall into this category are *Acer palmatum* (varieties of Japanese Maple), *Buxus* (smaller varieties of Boxwood), *Corylus avellana* 'Contorta' (the Hazelnut known as "Harry Lauder's Walking Stick"), *Cotoneaster horizontalis* (Rockspray Cotoneaster), *Euonymus fortunei* (Wintercreeper), *Hydrangea macrophylla* (Bigleaf Hydrangea), *Paeonia* (smaller Tree Peonies), *Picea* (dwarf Spruce), *Pinus* (dwarf Pines), *Potentilla* (smaller varieties of Shrub Cinquefoil), *Rhododendron* (smaller varieties of Azalea and Rhododendron), *Salix integra* 'Hakuro Nishiki' (Willow), *Spiraea* (smaller varieties of Spirea), *Syringa meyeri* 'Palibin' (Dwarf Korean Lilac), *Syringa microphylla* 'Superba' (Littleleaf Lilac), *Taxus* (smaller varieties of Yew), *Thuja* (smaller varieties of Arborvitae), *Viburnum opu-*

lus 'Compactum' (European Cranberry Bush), and *Weigela* (small varieties of Weigela).

Choose a container suitable to the present size of the plant. But, repot the plant each spring, going up a size as the plant matures. Over a period of years you will be increasing the size of the container considerably.

Fill the bottom of the container with enough potting soil so that when the plant is in place there will be 1 to 2 inches (2.5 to 5 cm) of space between the rim of the container and the soil surface below. The space should be related to the size of the container. This space is critical for proper watering.

Use a quality potting soil. You can make your own potting soil by blending loam, peat, and perlite in equal parts. Loam is rich and quite heavy, peat keeps soil moist, and perlite acts as a spacer to avoid soil compaction so that oxygen can get to the root area where it mixes readily with water. You can also use soilless mixes, such as Pro-Mix or other brands. These are quite light, so blend them with soil or potting soil to make them somewhat heavier to keep containers from tipping over in heavy gusts of wind. The soilless mixes often contain nutrients beneficial to newly planted shrubs.

For bare root plants build up a mound of soil in the center of the container. Then spread the roots of the plant out over this mound. If a plant has already been growing in a container or is balled and burlapped, prepare as outlined in the sections dealing with those plants. You may have to add some more soil to get the plant at the right level.

Pour potting soil or your own blend of soil and soilless mix around the plant. Firm the mixture in place with your fingers. Cover the entire root system.

Fill in the rest of the container with potting soil. Press down on the soil with your fingers. This removes any air pockets and forces the soilless mix and soil into contact with the plant.

Place containers on little feet to prevent rot on decks and to promote good drainage on hard surfaces. These little feet are sold in most nurseries and garden centers. Do not cover the drain holes on the bottom of the container at any time.

Winter Protection for Plants in Containers

METHOD 1: This method is for **deciduous** shrubs only. Just before the first hard freeze, spray the plant with dormant oil, lime sulfur, or a combination of both to kill insect eggs and fungal spores. Wait until the spray dries. With rope, tie the branches as tightly together as possible without breaking them. Then lay the container on its side and slide the shrub or small tree out. Place the root ball into a large, strong plastic bag. Perforate the bag in several places. Now soak it well with water. After saturating the soil, tie the bag around the base of the trunk. Dig a hole in loose soil wherever you have space. Vegetable gardens are ideal. Dig a hole deep and wide enough to accommodate the entire plant. Place the shrub or tree in the hole on its side and cover it completely with soil to a depth of 6 inches (15 cm). Soak the soil thoroughly. Now cover it with a thick layer of whole leaves to a depth of 12 inches (30 cm). Spray these with water. Keep them moist until the ground freezes. In early spring remove the leaves as soon as they begin to thaw. Remove the soil in stages as it thaws. Bring the shrub or tree out of the hole after all danger of a severe freeze.

Method 2: Dig a hole in the garden, place the root ball into the hole, and mound soil up around the base of the plant. Keep it moist until the ground freezes. Tie the branches as tightly together as possible with rope. After a freeze, place 3 black plastic bags filled with whole leaves against the sides of the plant forming a teepee. Fill in any gaps between the bags with whole leaves. Cover the teepee with a tarp secured in place with another rope. Remove this protective covering as soon as it warms up in spring.

Method 3: Alternatively, in fall move the plant into an unheated garage. Place a thick piece of styrofoam on the cement in a spot well away from the garage doors, preferably against the inside wall if the garage is connected to the home. Take the plant out of the pot as outlined above, place the root ball in a perforated plastic bag, water it, tie it up, then set it on a bag of leaves on the styrofoam. Tie the branches together with rope as tight as possible without breaking them. Push moist leaves into the spaces between the branches. Now cover the entire shrub or tree with a tarp or any thick fabric. Tie it in place around the base of the plant. Place poisoned bait inside this protective cover if you have trouble with rodents. Surround the plant with bags of leaves.

To protect **evergreens**, both broad and needle types, use the second method suggested. Do not tie the branches together. You may wish to surround the plant with a burlap screen filled with leaves. Keep the root ball moist until the first freeze and well protected from that point on.

Fill the container to the brim with water. Let the water soak in. Fill it as many times as necessary to get water draining slowly out the bottom drain holes.

Pour ½ cup (about 120 ml) starter solution around the base of the plant.

Water again to help the nutrients move toward the root zone.

If the plant is dormant, keep it in a protected area until it begins to form leaf buds. To encourage bud formation, wrap the plant in moist burlap. Keep the soil consistently moist, but not soggy.

Once the plant has begun to form leaves, remove the burlap. Place it outside after all danger of frost. Place the shrub first in partial shade. Gradually increase the amount of sun over 10 to 14 days until the plant is in the appropriate light for best growth. The best light for specific plants is covered in detail in each section of Part I. This gradual movement is called *hardening off*, a gardening term for allowing the plant to get used to increased light, varying temperatures, and drying winds. If you move the plant directly into sunlight, leaves often turn pale or gray and may die from a condition called *sunscald*. The plant will form new leaves if the old ones drop off, but its growth will have slowed.

If, on the other hand, the plant is already actively growing when you buy it and has been exposed to light for 2 weeks or longer, place it in its permanent location from the start.

Once a plant is growing well, fertilize it with a dilute solution of an appropriate water-soluble fertilizer. If plants need acidic conditions, then use an acidifying fertilizer. Fertilize container-grown plants more often than ones grown in the garden because

Special Planting Tips

IF YOU PLANT SMALL TREES with strong root systems too close to asphalt or concrete, their roots may buckle these materials as they grow. Roots of trees are powerful. Bike riders are familiar with bumps in bike paths caused by such buckling.

Many shrubs do well when planted under the canopy of larger trees. However, they will need extra attention in this situation since they'll be competing with the tree for available moisture and nutrients.

nutrients are leached out of the soil by frequent watering. Fertilize the plants at least several times, especially early in the season. Match the amount of fertilizer to the size and need of the plant.

Check the soil daily. Keep plants consistently moist throughout the entire growing season. Do not let the soil dry out. If soil pulls away from the sides of the container, you've let it dry out far too much. Water immediately.

Plants are not commonly grown in containers in cold climates because they are so difficult to protect during the winter. To protect them during winter, do not leave plants in clay or plastic pots. As the root ball freezes, it will expand and break the pot. You can leave plants in wood containers if you take appropriate steps. There are three potential methods of protecting plants at this stage, as outlined on page 373.

In the spring before new growth emerges repot the plant. Remove some of the soil around the sides, base, and top of the root ball. If the plant is getting too large, simply prune it at the correct time of year as outlined in individual sections of Part I. If roots

are becoming too dense or begin to curl around (girdle) the root ball, then cut off the larger ones or make slashing cuts on all four sides of the root ball to a depth of about 1 inch (2.5 cm). If not corrected, girdling will eventually kill the plant. Pot the plant up to a larger-size container if necessary. Use fresh potting soil and soilless mix to fill in any portions of soil removed as outlined earlier.

Spacing

When buying a shrub, always consider its potential height and width. Initial plantings often seem sparse, but in time as plants mature, they will become natural. Do not crowd shrubs and small trees together for a quick fix.

Generally, most shrubs grow almost as wide as they are tall. Of course, there are many exceptions, but width is usually one of a shrub's most disregarded qualities. The canopy of small trees is often much wider than people think it will be.

Spacing shrubs for hedges takes particular care. Hedges can either be formal (neatly clipped or sheared) or informal (lightly pruned). In general, formal hedges require shrubs to be planted closely together. Since plants suited for hedges vary in potential height and width, proper spacing is explained throughout the individual plant sections of Part I.

Never plant shrubs too close to buildings. Give them plenty of space to grow to their potential width. Branches too close to walls often die out.

Avoid placing a shrub where once mature it could cause problems. A very common mistake is to place a shrub or small tree in front of a window without taking the mature height into account.

CHAPTER 6

TRANSPLANTING

Transplanting shrubs and small trees can be quite difficult. Most require lots of attention if you want to do this successfully. The information in this chapter will increase your chances for success.

When to Transplant

Transplant deciduous shrubs and small trees as early as possible in spring before new growth starts. Whenever possible, root prune in the previous spring as outlined in the next section. The best time to transplant evergreens is in the early fall. However, most transplanting actually is done during the spring. Do this before new growth begins. If you dig up evergreens as new growth (candling) emerges, you damage the plant. New growth often dies.

Note: Some deciduous shrubs are quite hard to transplant. Dig these finicky plants up just as new buds swell. Check the plant every day so that your timing is exact. If the plant begins to form leaves, you've missed your window of opportunity!

How to Transplant Shrubs and Small Trees

If plants are not healthy and growing vigorously, they may not survive transplanting. On the other hand, if they have been planted in the wrong place, they may thrive in a new location. Transplanting in this case is certainly worth the gamble.

Large plants are especially difficult, though not impossible, to transplant. You'll be cutting away much of the mature plant's root system and this decreases the chance of its survival. Have large shrubs and small trees moved with professional equipment if saving the plant is worth that cost.

Ideally, the process of transplanting should begin one year before actually digging the plant from the soil. You'll be doing what is commonly called *root pruning*. Cut straight down through the roots on two sides of the plant in early spring before any new growth emerges. Dig 12 inches (30 cm) straight down. Do this about where you would dig up the root ball one year later. You will feel the pointed shovel cutting through roots. If your shovel is not powerful enough to cut through the root, you may have to dig down and cut the root with lopping shears. Repeat this same procedure in early August on the other two sides of the plant.

Root pruning forces the plant to create a new, extensive system of feeder roots within the area that has been cut back. Hopefully, this will help the plant survive the shock of being transplanted the following year.

Since you're cutting off much of the plant's root system, it helps to trim back the upper portion of

Wild Shrubs

A NUMBER OF SHRUBS listed in this guide are found in the wild. Check with local agencies before digging up wild plants since it may be illegal or allowed only with a special permit on state lands. You should also check on rules involving private lands and get permission in writing to remove plants from these. Whenever construction or road building is scheduled for an area, you have an excellent chance of getting permission to remove plants. A number of plants are most easily identified in the fall. Tag these and move them early the following spring before new growth emerges.

You will have much better success if you take small plants from the wild. The larger ones are very tempting to dig up, but the process is next to impossible. Larger plants often die. Even if the older plants live, the younger plants may prove more vigorous and attractive in the long run.

When moving wild plants, always bring water with you to keep the roots moist until you get them back home. Also, just like plants in your yard, if you can root prune a full year in advance, you will greatly increase your chance of moving wild plants.

larger plants as well if it is a deciduous shrub. Do this in late winter after the previous summer's root pruning. Cut the older stems back to ground level. Leave about one-third of the original stems, preferably younger ones. Do not remove growth from evergreens.

If you're dealing with a larger deciduous tree rather than a shrub, thin out the branches. Remove branches that are close together or come out from the trunk at a narrow angle. Remove some of the side branches off the main branches. Doing this takes a lot of courage and a good sense of symmetry. You want to remove quite a bit of growth while preserving the natural form of the tree.

Transplant the shrub or small tree the following spring before any signs of new growth appear.

If you have to wait until the plant has already leafed out, spray the upper stems and branches with an antitranspirant. These are available at nurseries and garden centers. One of the most popular brands is Wilt-Pruf®. This will reduce moisture loss from the plant's exposed tissue. While transplanting a plant once it has leafed out is not recommended, sometimes you have no choice.

If the soil is dry, saturate it thoroughly several days in a row. Then wait a day or two for the soil to dry out slightly and for the antitranspirant to cure in light.

Have a planting hole ready before you begin to dig up the shrub. Have all the appropriate materials at hand, so that you won't have to wait a second to get the new plant into the ground. You want it out and into the ground as fast as possible to keep roots from drying out.

If possible, transplant on a cool, cloudy day. Definitely work in the morning or early evening. There is less stress on plants transplanted at these times, especially if they have begun to leaf out.

Tie the stems of the shrub together with polyester rope if that's practical. Pull the branches together as tightly as possible without breaking them.

Rake up all debris around the base of the plant. It's much easier to dig in an area free of fallen leaves and twigs.

Immediately dig down in a circle around the plant. Do this in the same spot where you root pruned the previous season. Dig a trench out and away from this circular area. You're trying to expose the overall root ball that you intend to save.

Once you've dug down to the final depth of your root ball, begin slowly working your way under the plant from all sides. The final root ball will be curved underneath and much wider on the top, just like a balled and burlapped plant bought at a nursery.

Preserve as many of the roots as possible. You may have to rock the plant or small tree occasionally to see where the roots are. Keep digging. If the roots are angled deep into the soil, you have to cut them with lopping shears. Sometimes, you can pull the roots out of the soil instead of cutting them off. That depends on how loose your soil is and what type of shrub you're moving. Some have quite long roots. No matter how good you are at this, you still lose most of the plant's root system, which explains why this is such a traumatic process for shrubs and small trees.

Ideally, you want to keep as much soil around the roots as possible. This preserves tiny hair roots necessary to absorb moisture from the soil. This is especially true of evergreen shrubs and any shrub that resents transplanting at all. Working with another person helps. By tipping the shrub first one way and then another, you can slide a tarp underneath the bottom of the root ball. Then both of you can work to get it out of the hole.

Once out of the hole, the two of you can now drag the plant to its new location. Note that some gardeners wrap the root ball at this stage to prevent soil from breaking away from the roots. You'll have to judge how secure the soil is to decide what to do.

If you're working by yourself, preserving the soil around the roots can be nearly impossible on larger shrubs and trees. The root ball is just too heavy to work with and move. Remove the soil from the base of the shrub with your fingers. Work as quickly as possible. Save as many roots as you can. Then pull the plant from the hole. Do this only with deciduous shrubs, not evergreens, and do it before the shrub shows any signs of growth.

Since you are now moving the shrub or tree as if it were bare root, get the shrub planted immediately as outlined in planting a bare root shrub (see page 364).

Transplanting is one process you want to avoid whenever possible. By planting your shrubs and small trees where they belong in the first place, you'll rarely have to do it. However, we realize that you may buy property with shrubs planted in the wrong place. Moving them and taking the risk of losing them is often the most reasonable thing to do. Expect 2 to 3 years of retarded growth after transplanting most shrubs or small trees. On large shrubs and trees that you move on your own, expect occasional losses.

CHAPTER 7

CARING FOR SHRUBS
AND SMALL TREES

Shrubs and small trees are a versatile group of plants. Some seem to thrive on what amounts to benign neglect, but others need more attention to do well. This chapter gives detailed information on the proper care of these plants.

Water

Shrubs and small trees vary in their need for water. Correct watering is responsible for better root growth, more bloom, larger flowers, longer bloom time, better flower color, greater fragrance, lusher leaf growth, better foliage color, better stem color, larger and more fruits, fuller growth, faster growth, and better disease and insect resistance.

Water is a nutrient containing both hydrogen and oxygen, two elements needed by shrubs and small trees for good growth. Water also dissolves carbon dioxide, forming a mildly acidic solution. This reacts with minerals in the soil to form nutrients easily absorbed by the plant.

There is no set formula for proper watering. Correct watering depends greatly on the type of soil in your yard, the weather (humidity, sunlight, temperature, and wind), and the type of plant grown. Water runs quickly through sandy soil, very slowly through clay. Correct watering also depends on the age of a

shrub or small tree. Younger plants often need more frequent watering than older ones. Although many books suggest giving shrubs 1 inch (2.5 cm) of water per week, clearly any set formula like this defies common sense for the reasons just given.

You know when to water by feeling the soil. The surface of the soil may look moist but be dry underneath. Dig into it with your hand if it's loose or with a trowel if it's more compacted. Water the soil whenever the top 2 inches (5 cm) begin to dry out. Don't be fooled by rain. Some rainfall appears heavy, but may be quite light. A light sprinkling does little for any plant.

Each time you water, saturate the soil. Often the most effective way to water is to saturate the area around the base of the plant, move on to another plant, and then return to the original plant if no water is pooling around it. Then water it again until it is clear that the ground is completely moist. When water remains on the soil surface instead of seeping into the soil quickly, you know the soil is saturated. For some small trees you may have to leave the water running at its base for an hour or longer.

Frequent and deep watering is particularly important during the first 2 years for most shrubs and small trees to encourage vigorous and wide-spreading root growth.

It is especially important to water properly during hot, dry, and windy weather. If plants begin to wilt, they are being damaged. Leaves close their pores (stomata) to reduce moisture loss. This cuts off carbon dioxide essential to the production of food through photosynthesis. Leaf and root cells produce sugars (solutes) to draw in water by osmosis. If there is not enough water, the process is interrupted. This results in plants being more prone to damage from insects and disease. Even mild amounts of water stress can greatly reduce plant growth during a typical growing season.

In severe cases where shrubs are left unwatered for too long, the inner portion of each plant cell (cytoplasm) pulls away from the cell's wall. This can result in the death of the cell. Leaves begin to curl up around the edges or to fall off the plant. Parts of the shrub's stem tissue may begin to die. Also, if lack of water is severe enough over a long enough period, the entire shrub will wither and die.

Shrubs grown in containers need careful attention. Never let the soil dry out. If soil pulls away from the side of a pot, this indicates erratic watering, which stresses plants. If this happens, push the soil back against the side of the container and water immediately. When watering containerized shrubs, fill the container to the brim. Let the soil absorb the water. Then water again. Keep doing this until water runs out the drain holes in the bottom of the container. Shrubs grown in containers may require watering as often as twice a day in hot or windy weather.

Other tips on watering include using overhead watering with a sprinkler or direct watering at the base of the plant from a hose. If you enjoy watering, hold the hose in place to saturate the soil around the base of the plant. If you consider hand watering a chore, set the hose down at the base of the plant. Let it run until the ground is thoroughly saturated. Some gardeners place the hose on a board to prevent the formation of a hole where the water runs out.

The use of drip irrigation or other slow watering methods is fine for anyone connected to city water. It is not practical for someone with a well since it can cause pumps to turn on and off endlessly, eventually burning out the pump.

If you have a well, turn on enough hoses to keep the pump running constantly. If you don't, you can burn the well's motor out as you would if using drip irrigation.

If soil is properly prepared, it is almost impossible to overwater shrubs. If the soil drainage is poor, the veins of leaves often turn yellow. With good drainage this is not a problem. If you follow the guidelines in this guide, you'll always have proper drainage.

Overhead watering is recommended in especially dry periods to discourage spider mites. During high heat, overhead watering also cools plants and reduces stress from water loss. Again, you may have heard that it is bad to water plants during high heat or in full sun. The luxuriant growth of your plants will prove that wrong.

Furthermore, in dry periods foliage may get covered with dust. Overhead watering or spraying off foliage forcefully with a hose is an excellent way to clean foliage off.

Once leaves or flowers appear, the best time to water is in the morning so that foliage dries out before the end of the day.

Overhead watering can be tricky. Light sprinklings are not helpful. You may have to water for several hours or longer to get water deep enough into the soil to be effective.

Always saturate the soil with water before and after the application of any chemical fertilizer. This protects the plant from possible damage, often referred to as burn. Deep watering dissolves nutrients and carries them to the roots.

Always water plants well before spraying them with fungicides, insecticides, or miticides. If plants are not watered, the application of a spray may cause leaf burn (browning and curling up of leaves). This is very important advice, but commonly ignored.

Most shrubs and small trees thrive with consistent watering from the time the soil thaws in spring until it freezes solid in fall. This is especially important if there is a dry spell in fall, quite common in cold climates. Saturate the soil thoroughly just before the first expected freeze. The plant should go into winter well watered.

All evergreens need deep watering in the fall. Saturate the soil until it freezes. This watering helps

Organic Mulches

FOLLOWING IS A LIST of the most popular organic mulches used around shrubs:

Bark (shredded): Shredded barks are quite expensive. They have nice color and texture and are easy to apply. They look sensational around most shrubs. Common barks are cedar, fir, and pine. All of these are mildly acidic.

Pine needles: These are free for the asking in northerly areas. If you have to pay for them, buy bark instead. Pine needles are easy to apply, drain freely, and don't compact. Needles vary in length and appeal to the eye with their interesting texture. Pine needles are mildly acidic.

Wood chips: Wood chips come in a variety of colors, sizes, and textures. Ideally, they should be harvested from disease-free trees. Wood chips are quite expensive if bought in garden centers or nurseries. However, they are often available for free or at low cost in large quantities from local utility or tree-trimming companies. Order these in advance since they are available only when crews are close to your home. Also, many gardeners are aware of this tip and place orders far in advance. You're often put on a waiting list. Finally, if at all possible, ask for chips taken when there are no leaves on the trees. The chips are much cleaner in this stage and rarely mixed in with debris.

Note that other organic materials are suitable for use as a mulch. These include buckwheat hulls, cocoa bean hulls, compost, grass clippings, and shredded leaves. Frankly, compost is more valuable mixed into soil as an amendment rather than placed on the soil surface as a mulch. Furthermore, there is rarely enough of it.

evergreens get through the winter, since they will experience water loss from their leaves or needles throughout the winter season.

Mulch

Mulch is any material put on the surface of the soil around a shrub to keep the soil moist and cool during hot weather. Mulch stops soil temperature from fluctuating wildly and prevents a great deal of water loss through evaporation. Mulch also inhibits weed growth and makes it far easier to pull up the few weeds that do sprout. Mulch also reduces soil compaction as you walk on it. Mulch prevents soil from splattering against leaves, a cause of some disease. It also feeds soil microorganisms and worms, which benefit the plant by keeping soil loose (lots of oxygen) and fertile. This helps the plant create a more extensive root system while making nutrients more readily available to the feeder roots. Mulch also stops you from accidentally damaging the stems of shrubs or trunks of small trees with weed trimmers or lawn mowers. All of this results in more vigorous growth and less chance of damage by disease and insects.

Use organic mulches in most situations. It is quite difficult to work soil covered in stone, although some gardeners disregard this advice with remarkable success. Pea gravel is an excellent mulch in rock gardens.

Avoid placing plastic under mulch as this can interfere with the natural exchange of gases between the earth and the air. It may also inhibit root growth. Porous materials commonly referred to as water-permeable landscape fabrics are fine.

Apply mulch after mid-May. Let the soil warm up thoroughly before putting mulch around plants. The soil should reach a temperature of about 60°F (16°C). If you want to be precise use a soil thermometer, but most gardeners just feel the soil.

Place mulch around the entire plant, but at least 2 to 4 inches (5 to 10 cm) away from the stems of shrubs or trunks of small trees. A thick mulch too close to the shrub can cause certain types of stem rot, act as cover for insects, or provide a home for rodents. However, you can place a very light mulch about ½ to 1 inch (1.25 to 2.5 cm) deep right up to the stems or trunk without problems.

The individual sections of Part I recommend the proper depth of the mulch for specific shrubs. This will vary from 2 to 6 inches (5 to 15 cm). Have your mulch sloping down in the center toward the base of the shrub. It should extend out at least 3 feet (1 meter) from the base of the shrub or small tree.

Replace mulch as it disappears during the summer, as soil microorganisms and worms feed on it.

Mulches high in carbon cause a temporary nitrogen deficiency in the soil. The reason is that soil microorganisms use up nitrogen in the process of breaking these materials down for food. Shredded bark and wood chips fall into this "high carbon" category. Whenever you use these for mulch, sprinkle additional nitrogen around your shrubs—no less than 3 pounds (about 1½ kg) per 1 cubic yard (roughly ¾ of a cubic meter) of mulch. High-nitrogen lawn fertilizers (27-3-3) are a good choice for this use.

Fertilizing

The following steps will provide you with a good general outline for fertilizer use. Since fertilizer needs will vary among plants and planting sites, make modifications for your particular landscape.

Buy fertilizers before the growing season. Many shrubs and small trees need three major elements in relatively large amounts. The amount varies by the type of shrub or small tree being grown, soil type, weather, and stage of growth. The three elements are nitrogen (N), phosphorus (P), and potassium (K). When you buy fertilizer, the label will indicate how much of these essential elements are contained in the product. The amounts are always in the same order: nitrogen (N), phosphorus (P), and potassium (K). If a package reads 10-10-10, this indicates that the fertilizer is 10 percent nitrogen, 10 percent phosphorus, and 10 percent potassium.

The synthetic products recommended throughout this guide are superphosphate (0-18-0), granular fertilizer (10-10-10), and ammonium sulfate (21-0-0).

Organic substitutes are alfalfa meal (5-1-2), sold as rabbit pellets in farm stores; blood meal (12-0-0); bone meal (0-10-0); compost (4-1-3); cottonseed meal (7-2-2); cow manure (2-1-1); fish emulsion (10-7-0); horse manure (.7-.3-.5); and Milorganite or treated sewage (6-3-0). Note that the actual amount of essential elements in these organic products varies by manufacturer.

In every planting hole add phosphorus. This is particularly important to stimulate good root growth. You can use either superphosphate or bone meal. Superphosphate works more rapidly and is less expensive.

After initial planting, pour a starter solution around the base of the plant. Make this by dissolving a water-soluble fertilizer in water according to the directions on the label. These are available at nurseries, landscape centers, and building supply stores with garden centers. The label indicates the amount of nutrients. Labels indicating a 20-20-20 concentration are recommended, although amounts can vary somewhat without a problem. Brand names are less important than the chemical concentration. If a plant thrives in acidic soils, then use an acidifying fertilizer. Products recommended for use with evergreens and *Rhododendron* (Azaleas and Rhododendrons) will be acidic.

Additional fertilizing with 10-10-10 or ammonium sulfate may be recommended. Fertilize as directed in individual plant sections of Part I. Each section will tell you when, how, and how much fertilizer to apply for best results. Fertilizing too much or too little or fertilizing at the wrong time can damage shrubs and even kill them. Follow the suggestions outlined in this guide to avoid harming your plants. You also will be giving them enough of what they need to avoid nutritional deficiencies, often mistaken for disease or insect problems.

Additional Tips on Fertilizing

As soon as the ground thaws in spring, apply fertilizer around the base of the plant. In cold climates most shrubs and small trees show quick growth in spring, and this is the time they most need nutrients. Some shrubs and small trees do best if fertilized again during the summer. Follow the guidelines in the individual sections of Part I.

As indicated, you will be sprinkling 10-10-10 all-purpose garden fertilizer without herbicides (weed killers) around the base of your plants. Sprinkle this fertilizer on the surface of the soil over the root area around the base of the shrub or small tree. Typically, this would be about one-third the height of the plant.

Are Fertilizers Misused?

TODAY, THERE IS STRONG INTEREST in stopping the misuse of fertilizers that are getting into water systems and affecting the quality of lakes, rivers, and oceans. Under particular attack is phosphorus. Popular 10-10-10 fertilizer contains 10 percent nitrogen (N), 10 percent phosphorus (P), and 10 percent potassium (K). Some communities are trying to or have banned such fertilizers. They make the following arguments:

1. Many soils already contain enough phosphorus and potassium for good plant growth.
2. Phosphorus runs off hard surfaces and into storm sewers, lakes, streams, and eventually oceans. This excess phosphorus damages the ecosystem.

Are they right?

1. It is true that your soil may already contain enough phosphorus and potassium for good plant growth, but types of soil vary tremendously throughout the cold-climate region from loose sand to tight clay. And these individual soils may or may not contain enough phosphorus or potassium. The only way to know whether your soil has enough of these two major nutrients is to have a soil test done in the location where you intend to plant your shrub or small tree.

2. It is true that phosphorus will run off surfaces if they are hard enough and if there is enough slope. This will damage water quality. The major problem with runoff occurs on lawns next to streets, driveways, or areas covered with a hard surface. Avoiding the use of 10-10-10 fertilizer in such an area does make sense.

So what should you do with shrubs and small trees?

1. Even though there may be enough phosphorus in your soil, adding additional phosphorus to the soil at planting time in the form of superphosphate or bone meal will not harm your shrub or small tree. Nor will it harm the environment, because it is quite immobile once mixed into soil. If you want to be absolutely certain about the needs of your soil, then have a soil test done.

2. If phosphorus is placed on a flat and absorbent surface, the danger of runoff is minimal. Placing a small amount of starter solution into loose soil around the base of a shrub or small tree in spring only to cover it with mulch shortly afterwards virtually eliminates the risk of runoff. Furthermore, the yearly application of small amounts of 10-10-10 around the base of a shrub or small tree is equally unlikely to cause environmental damage if watered in immediately as suggested throughout this guide.

A rough guide would be 1 cup (about 225 g) per square yard of soil around mature plants. You can do this very easily by hand. Naturally, wear gloves.

This is truly an approximation. Each type of shrub responds differently to varying amounts of fertilizer. Giving an exact amount is like trying to tell you how much each person should eat. You'll know whether you're feeding is correct by letting the shrub tell you. If it's doing well, it will grow vigorously, bloom profusely, have lush foliage with rich coloration, and produce copious amounts of berries or fruits. *Remember that some shrubs and small trees do well with little or no fertilization.* Again, when, how, and how much fertilizer to use is emphasized in the individual plant sections of Part I.

When fertilizing shrubs and small trees, always saturate the soil with water before and after application. Remember that fertilizers contain chemicals known as salts that can damage roots if there is not enough water present. Think of water as an IV tube that carries all nutrients into the plant's roots. So saturate the soil thoroughly when fertilizing.

Some shrubs demand acidic soil. While reduction of the soil pH is critical before planting, keeping the soil pH down is equally important once the shrubs are growing. To keep soil at a low pH, annually use ammonium sulfate or any acidic fertilizer recommended for evergreens or rhododendrons. Read labels carefully and apply the fertilizer at the recommended doses and times.

Many lawn fertilizers contain herbicides (weed killers). Avoid applying these around the base of shrubs. The chemicals can interfere with the growth of the shrub, and in some instances may kill it.

Essential Elements for Healthy Shrubs and Small Trees

IF YOU FOLLOW THE DIRECTIONS throughout this guide, your shrubs will always have enough essential elements for good health. Following are short descriptions of elements needed by plants for proper growth:

Boron (B): Needed in minute quantities. Important in cell division, flower formation, and pollination. Helps transfer food between cells. Ample amount in most soil. Augmented yearly in fish emulsion. (.005 percent of plant tissue)

Calcium (Ca): Needed in moderate amounts. Important to cell structure and good root growth. Gets plants off to good early growth. Ample amount in most soil. Found in gypsum (calcium sulphate), which is sometimes added to soil to get rid of salt deposits. Augmented by adding bone meal or superphosphate to planting hole. Also available in lime and wood ash, but use these in tiny amounts since they raise the pH of the soil (not always desirable). (.6 percent of plant tissue)

Carbon (C): Needed in large amounts. Ample supply in air. (44 percent of plant tissue)

Chlorine (Cl): Needed in minute quantities. Important in transfer of water and minerals into cells and in photosynthesis. Ample supply in soil or city water. (.015 percent of plant tissue)

Copper (Cu): Needed in minute quantities. Important in stem development and color. Essential in enzyme formation, root growth, and respiration.* Ample amount in most soil. Augmented by addition of milorganite to planting hole. (.001 percent of plant tissue)

Hydrogen (H): Needed in large amounts. Ample supply in water. (6 percent of plant tissue)

Iron (Fe): Needed in minute quantities. Important in chlorophyll formation and for proper plant respiration. Ample amount in most soil. Augmented by adding bone meal to planting hole. (.02 percent of plant tissue)

Magnesium (Mg): Needed in small amounts. Important in chlorophyll formation and respiration. Essential for healthy foliage and disease resistance. Found in soil, but added with the consistent use of fish emulsion each year. (.3 percent of plant tissue)

Manganese (Mn): Needed in minute quantities. Important in chlorophyll formation and the production of food through photosynthesis. An enzyme regulator. Ample amount in most soil. Augmented by addition of milorganite to planting hole. (.05 percent of plant tissue)

Molybdenum (Mo): Needed in minute quantities. Essential for enzyme formation, root growth, and respiration. Ample amount in most soil. Augmented by addition of milorganite to planting hole. (.0001 percent of plant tissue)

Nitrogen (N): Needed in large amounts. Critical to healthy stem growth, lush foliage, and beautiful bloom. Important in cell growth and plant respiration. Essential food for soil microorganisms. Must be added to soil on a regular basis. (2 percent of plant tissue)

Oxygen (O): Needed in large amounts. Ample supply in both air and water. (45 percent of plant tissue)

Phosphorus (P): Needed in large amounts. Essential to rapid root growth. Important in stimulating quick growth, which improves winter hardiness. Important to proper formation of stems, good color and solidity of flower petals, and the production of berries and fruit. Must be added to soil at planting time as bone meal or superphosphate. (.5 percent of plant tissue)

Potassium (K): Needed in large amounts. Important to root growth, formation of blossoms, and bloom color. Critical in forming sugar and starches. Must be added to soil on a regular basis. (1 percent of plant tissue)

Sulfur (S): Needed in small amounts. Keeps soil at the right pH (slightly acidic). Important in formation of plant proteins needed for good health and root growth. Ample amount supplied by rain. (.4 percent of plant tissue)

Zinc (Zn): Needed in minute quantities. Important in stem and flower bud formation. Essential to enzyme formation, root growth, and respiration. Ample amount in most soil. Augmented by adding milorganite to the planting hole. (.01 percent of plant tissue)

---

*Respiration refers to the ability of cells to produce energy using chemicals. This is often confused with transpiration, the exhalation of water from plants. Note that plants release oxygen into the air during the day as a byproduct of photosynthesis. Plants do need some oxygen but release far more than they use.

Weeding

Weeds compete with shrubs for water and nutrients. Destroy all weeds, including dandelions, quackgrass, vines, and thistles in and around the planting hole. Perennial weeds will often resprout from infinitesimal portions of root. So when preparing a site for planting, use a product containing glyphosate to kill them. This chemical is absorbed by the plant in such a way that all roots are killed. Chemicals that work in this way are called systemic (taken into the entire plant's system). Glyphosate (commonly sold as Roundup®) breaks down in approximately 2 weeks. Follow the directions on the label exactly and wait the specified period before planting a shrub in a treated area.

Once plants are growing, mulch stops most weed growth, since many weed seeds need light to germinate. The few weeds that do appear are easy to pull up by hand from the moist soil. Hand weed around the base of shrubs to avoid damaging their relatively shallow root systems. Hoeing may wound roots or stems, inviting infection by disease and infestation by insects.

If for any reason perennial weeds sprout, again use a systemic herbicide to kill them. But take special precautions. If you spray the weeds, some of the herbicide may drift onto desirable plants. A tiny breeze is all it takes for this to happen. So do the following: mix the herbicide with water as recommended on the label unless it's a premixed product. Then soak a rag or sponge or dip a paintbrush in this mixture. Now rub or paint the herbicide on the perennial weeds you want to kill. This takes patience but prevents accidental damage to plants you want to preserve. Always wear rubber gloves when doing this. Again, use this method on perennial weeds only. Just pull up annual weeds.

Grass within 3 feet (1 m) of the base of a shrub should be considered a weed, at least during the first 4 to 5 years of a shrub's initial development. That area should be covered with a mulch until the shrub or small tree has developed an extensive root system. If after a few years you allow grass to grow around the base of the shrub, avoid damaging the stems or trunk with a lawn mower or weed trimmer. Clip the grass around the base with hand grass clippers.

Never use lawn fertilizers that contain herbicides on grass under shrubs or trees. The chemicals that kill weeds in a lawn may damage shrubs and trees as well. This is especially true with products containing 2, 4-D. The latter is highly volatile. If applied in hot weather, its vapors can harm foliage. The plant most susceptible to damage is *Syringa* (Lilac). If herbicides are applied on a cool day, there is less chance of damage.

Staking

Most nurseries are now growing trees without support to encourage stronger trunks and better branching. Limited movement of the trunk in the wind also forces the young tree to develop a more extensive root system.

When these trees are dug up and sold, they still require no staking. In theory, the purpose of staking would be to stop the newly planted tree from uprooting or tilting. A number of landscapers continue to stake trees with this in mind.

Staking is generally not necessary. If a tree is staked, it is more likely to break than if it were left alone in the first place. By not staking a tree, you continue with the original strategy of encouraging stronger trunk development and a stronger and more wide-spreading root system.

On occasion newly planted trees do tip, especially in sites prone to strong gusts of wind or in especially loose soil. In such instances, staking may be appropriate.

Use at least three stakes for support. Drive them into the ground off to the side of the tree. Tie each stake to the tree with a flexible material or wire, making sure that where you encircle the tree, it's protected from the wire itself. Commonly, gardeners use pieces of old garden hose around the trunks. Soft strapping material is now frequently recommended. The key point is to stop the wire from damaging the bark. Place the support about one-third of the way up the tree, not farther up as has been commonly done in the past. Never support a tree for more than a year. By that time the tree should be self-supporting.

Espalier

Some of the trees in this guide can be trained against walls, along split rail fences, or on trellises. Training trees to walls requires some special steps. Fasten screw-eyes into the wall. To do this in masonry walls you need a special carbide bit attached to a power drill. Once you've drilled the hole, insert a fastening plug into it. Then screw in the screw-eye so that it is firmly in place. Then use insulated wire (lamp cord) or plastic coated electrical wire tied in a figure-eight knot to hold a branch in place. Lamp cords consist of two insulated wires. Cut these wires apart with a sharp knife for smaller and more flexible ties. Cut the insulated wires to the desired length with wire cutters.

Plant the tree about 6 inches (15 cm) from the vertical space. During the first year allow the plant to grow with one main stem shooting upwards. Cut off all but two branches. Tie them to supports so that they are growing horizontally. In the second year let the plant form two additional branches. Tie them horizontally in the same fashion. Continue to do this until the plant reaches the desired height. At that point snip off the central growing tip (leader) so that all energy is directed into the branches. This is especially effective with dwarf fruit trees.

Deadheading

Deadheading is removing spent blossoms. You do not have to remove spent blossoms on most shrubs. However, you will encourage repeat bloom on *Potentilla* (Shrub or Bush Cinquefoil), a few types of *Syringa* (Lilac), and summer-blooming types of *Spiraea* (Spirea) if you remove blossoms as soon as they fade. You should also remove the spent flowers on most varieties of *Syringa* (Lilac) for better bloom the following season. Remove spent flowers as soon as they begin to fade. The same may be true for evergreen varieties of *Rhododendron* (Rhododendron).

Pruning

Many gardeners are confused by and afraid of pruning. Pruning techniques vary with each type of shrub and are outlined in detail in appropriate sections of Part I. The following information applies to most shrubs and small trees. Pruning serves these important purposes:

- **Health:** Cutting off dead, damaged, or diseased plant parts prevents destruction of the entire plant.
- **Vigor:** Proper pruning increases the amount of healthy stem tissue, making the plant bushy and vigorous. You get a good blend of new and old growth. Strong growth helps ward off insect infestations and disease.
- **Beauty:** Proper pruning results in more beautiful shape and form. With some shrubs and small trees it increases flower and fruit production.
- **Longevity:** Proper pruning increases the longevity of shrubs. Some of these are extremely expensive. If properly cared for, they may live for decades. If ignored, they may die out prematurely.

What You Need to Prune Correctly

Pruning is as much art as science. You will learn how each plant responds over a period of years. Even the best gardeners occasionally make mistakes. A better way of putting this is that they learn from their experience. However, the tips here and throughout this guide will help you avoid the most common mistakes and will give you confidence that you're doing the right thing at the right time.

You'll also need to buy good tools. You'll need pruning shears—the two-bladed bypass types are best (see page 419). Make cuts in the center of the blades and keep them sharp. You'll also need lopping shears (long-handled pruners) to cut larger stems. Again, the two-bladed bypass kind are best and must be kept sharp. You may need a pruning saw for especially large branches or stems. The best tool to keep blades sharp is a whetstone (with oil) or an appropriate file. Sharp blades make clean cuts, and clean cuts prevent disease.

What to Remove and When

Choose plants wisely according to the space available so that you are not trying to make a large plant into a small one. Pruning is time consuming. Overpruning is harmful to a plant. By choosing the right plant for the right place from the start, you save time and money.

On new plants remove any damaged or dead stem tissue, cutting above a bud as outlined at the end of this chapter.

Each spring just as buds sprout remove all diseased or dead areas by cutting back to live stem tissue. Dead stem is brittle, dry, and brown. Keep snipping back until you reach live wood, usually pale or yellowish green in the center (pith) of the stem. Make your final cut just above an outward-facing bud on stems with alternate leaves. Make your final cut just above two or more buds on stems with opposite or whorled leaves. If you wait too long, you weaken the plant and increase the risk of disease.

Low-lying evergreens are susceptible to winter damage from heavy snows. If a branch tears off close to the main stem, snip it off. If only a portion of a branch breaks, snip off the broken portion just above a bud below the break.

If an entire branch of a small tree dies, cut it back to the trunk. Cut just outside the swollen area where the branch meets the stem (collar). When you cut off heavier branches, they'll sometimes fall and strip off bark from the stem in the process. To avoid this, cut off most of the branch a foot (30 cm) or so away from the stem. Then saw upwards just outside the collar halfway through the branch. Finally, cut down to remove the branch. The final cut should be just outside the collar and slanting slightly away from the tree.

If an entire stem of a shrub dies, simply cut it off flush with the crown. Remove it right down to the ground with lopping shears.

Many shrubs bloom only on the previous season's wood. This is referred to as old wood. A number of these shrubs will bloom more profusely if pruned annually immediately after they bloom. On mature plants cut out approximately one-third of the oldest stems at this time. Annual pruning like this stimulates the growth of new stems from the base of the plant. Do this only if recommended in individual sections of Part I.

A number of shrubs bloom on new wood. This is growth created during the present growing season. These shrubs are best pruned in late winter or very early spring before new growth emerges. Pruning of this kind is strictly optional and most commonly done to control the shape and overall size of the shrub. Again, you'll find recommendations of this sort in individual sections of Part I.

You can make evergreens bushier with more dense growth by snipping off about one-half of the new growth once it has fully emerged in spring or early summer.

Some small trees develop a fork in the stem as they grow. Each of the upright stems is called a *leader*. Remove one of the leaders to get a tree with only one trunk. If forked trees are allowed to mature, they often split in heavy winds. Early pruning can prevent this.

Some evergreens also form two leaders or growing tips. Remove one to get a more nicely shaped tree.

Some forms of pruning require you to cut off (head back) the tip (leader) of the tree. This is especially true when you're trying to keep fruit trees a manageable size or to create an espalier specimen.

Interfering branches should be removed from trees. These are branches that grow straight up or across other branches. They may rub against each other and cause wounds that could be infected by disease, or they may just look bad. Cut off these branches flush to the trunk with a pruning saw or loppers if small enough.

Water sprouts are thin upright branches that shoot off the main trunk or directly up from horizontal branches. Snip them off. Others may appear in their place. Keep removing them as necessary.

Some of the trees in this guide are grown on rootstock. If rootstock produces growth (suckers), dig down to where the new growth emerges from the rootstock and cut it off.

Old stems of multistemmed shrubs may stop producing bloom. Cut these old stems off at ground level during the dormant season. This pruning encourages new stems to shoot up from the base of the plant. In time the younger stems will bloom prolifically.

Cutting branches from a shrub for floral arrangements is a form of pruning. Never take cut flowers from young or frail plants. When removing branches or portions of stems for arrangements, keep in mind that you're actually pruning the plant.

Hedges require special attention. Keep the base of the hedge wider than the top. This allows light to reach the base of the hedge. You'll get a fuller look with dense foliage.

On informal, flowering hedges remove some of the older stems each year to encourage bushy new growth, which often blooms more prolifically than aging growth.

On hedges made up of small-leafed shrubs, shear once in spring and again a few weeks later. Do this with a hand or electric hedge trimmer. On hedges made up of large-leafed shrubs, prune out new growth by snipping back individual stems with hand pruners. This takes more time and patience but results in a much more beautiful hedge.

Hedges often have individual stems die out in any given season. Snip these off at the base of the stem at ground level. If you leave them in the hedge, no new growth appears to fill in the void. Once the dead stem is removed, it will soon be replaced with another stem covered with lush foliage.

Never prune late in the growing season. This encourages new growth, which will die off in severe weather. Furthermore, shrubs need the food stored in stems to survive cold winters. Stop pruning by late July or mid-August.

Toss everything you cut off a plant into a bucket. Snip longer portions into tiny sections. Never leave cut portions on the ground. They're perfect harbors for insects and disease organisms.

You do not have to cover cuts with any compound whatsoever. Shrubs and trees heal wounds better if left alone.

Making a Proper Cut

Proper cuts are important to help a wound heal quickly, to prevent disease, and to produce growth in the right direction.

Place the sharpest part of the blade next to the portion of stem you want to save. This makes a smooth, even cut. Use bypass pruning shears for small branches. Use bypass lopping shears for larger branches or stems. If you can barely get the blades of lopping shears around a branch or stem, use a pruning saw for making cuts.

When using a saw to cut large branches, make four cuts. Make your first cut upward about 1 foot (30 cm) from the place where the branch meets the main stem (the collar). Cut about ½ inch (1.25 cm) into the branch. Then make a second cut straight down to the first cut. The branch will fall off. Remaining is a 1-foot (30-cm) stub. At an angle make a third cut up, just outside the collar. Cut up about ½ inch (1.25 cm), slanting slightly in toward the tree. Then angle your fourth cut down just outside the collar to cut off the stub. The final cut will be at an angle slightly down and away from the trunk. If you don't make all of these cuts to remove a large branch, it may drop downward, ripping part of the bark off the main trunk of the tree. This open wound is slow to heal and can often get infected with disease.

When cutting off entire stems, cut them back flush to the ground. Don't leave stubs sticking up. Simply make a flat, horizontal cut as close to the ground as possible.

Some shrubs have alternate leaf buds or leaves, pairs of opposite leaf buds and leaves, or several leaf buds and leaves (whorls) circling the stem. Don't touch or rub a bud, since this can damage it.

When cutting off portions of stem tissue on shrubs or trees with alternate leaf buds or leaves, begin your cut ¼ inch (.6 cm) above the bud. Make your cut at a 45-degree angle down to the opposite side of

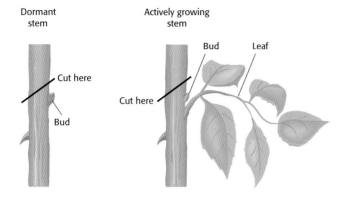

Dormant
stem

Actively growing
stem

Bud   Leaf

Cut here

Cut here

Bud

The correct cut on a dormant or actively growing shrub with single leaves at a node begins ¼ inch (.6 cm) above an outward facing bud or leaf. Make your cut at a 45-degree angle to a point directly opposite the bud or leaf.

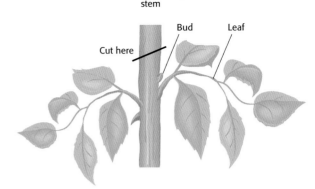

Actively growing
stem

Bud   Leaf

Cut here

On plants with two leaves at a node begin your cut at just a little less than ½ inch (1.25 cm) above a leaf or bud. Slant your cut to end up just about ¼ inch (.6 cm) above the opposite leaf or bud. Shrubs and trees with two leaves at a node may have two buds at a node or just one bud as illustrated above.

the bud. If you cut too close to a bud, it often dries out and dies. If you cut too far above the bud, you leave a piece of budless stem. This may die off and may become diseased. So if you cut between two buds, the stem will die back to a bud below. The dead tissue above the bud is then prone to disease that could cause the death of the entire stem.

On shrubs or trees with more than one leaf bud or leaf at a node, make a slanting cut about ½ inch (1.25 cm) above the buds or leaves. Slant down but at an angle a little less than 45 degrees. You'll end up with about a ¼-inch (.6-cm) stub above the cut. This stub is so short that it is unlikely to get infected with disease, to rot, or to die.

When pruning a plant that shows sign of disease, dip blades in a solution of nine parts water to one part bleach after each cut. The solution kills bacterial disease. Other disinfectants (Lysol or rubbing alcohol) may be used, but bleach is effective and inexpensive.

Winter Protection

A few of the shrubs and small trees in this guide are extremely sensitive to winter winds and fluctuating temperatures. The key to survival for these plants is to place them in a protected location. In a few instances you'll have to provide protection during the first few years of growth. When necessary, this is covered in detail in the individual sections of Part I. Winter protection for shrubs grown in containers is covered on page 373.

CHAPTER 8

SOLVING PROBLEMS

O ne of the great advantages in growing shrubs and small trees is that
most of them do not need to be
sprayed to control disease and insects.
If not prone to specific problems, many of these survive them quite well without interference.

Admittedly, a few of the shrubs and small trees
listed in this guide are susceptible to severe damage by a
specific disease or insect. You can either avoid planting
these or follow the advice given to prevent outbreaks
in the first place. In many instances, especially resistant varieties have been listed so that you will not have
a problem within a certain group (genus) of plants.

Watch for signs of trouble, including unexpected
changes in leaf color; dying branches or tips of stems;
bark that is peeling unnaturally or turning a strange
color in spots; unusual growths on the branches,
leaves, or stems; sap oozing from wounds; distorted
or misshapen buds or leaves; and so on. Problems
may be due to disease, insects, improper planting, or
improper care.

Organic Disease Prevention and Insect Control

Preventing diseases before they spread and controlling insects before their population balloons makes

a lot of sense. Here are some organic guidelines that
apply to shrubs and small trees in general:

If available, buy certified stock. These are plants
guaranteed not to carry specific diseases. This applies
mainly to fruit trees.

Certain groups (genera) of shrubs are resistant to
disease. If you're an organic gardener, buy plants in
these groups.

While other groups (genera) of shrubs may be
prone to disease, specific named varieties within that
group (genus) may be quite resistant. Buy the most
resistant varieties within a less resistant group.

Plant only healthy plants.

Healthy shrubs resist disease. Weak or poorly
cared for plants are most susceptible. So keep plants
well watered and well fed. Plant them only in appropriate light and soil.

Fertilize carefully as directed. Do not overfertilize. Too much nitrogen can cause excessive growth
prone to disease and insect problems.

Give plants enough space for good air circulation. This keeps foliage dry at night and prevents disease. Some shrubs take up a large amount of space.
Plant according to the plant's potential size, giving
each ample room for future growth.

Water by hand or let water run from a hose at
the base of each shrub to saturate the soil thoroughly.

Use a sprinkler (overhead watering) only as advised in this guide. Overhead watering may at times be referred to as *misting* or *syringing*.

If watering with a sprinkler, water early in the day so that foliage has a chance to dry out by evening. This rule has several exceptions as noted throughout this guide.

Prune only when and how as outlined in this guide.

Cut off any dead, diseased, or damaged portion of a plant at any time of year.

Use extremely sharp pruning shears or loppers when cutting stems. The remaining cut portion of stem tissue will be smooth, not rough. Read pruning instructions in each section to avoid mistakes that can kill stem tissue and cause disease and insect infestation.

Dip pruning shears after each cut into a bucket of water (nine parts water to one part chlorine bleach), or wipe blades with straight rubbing alcohol or Lysol. If you use rubbing alcohol, just screw a spray nozzle right onto the bottle (cut the siphon tube as necessary). This extra step stops the spread of disease from an infected blade.

Get rid of all weeds. Many of them serve as host plants for disease-carrying insects. As insects move from plant to plant, they often spread or carry deadly diseases.

Mulch around the base of plants so that you will never have to mow or use a weed whip around their stems or trunks. The latter often break through bark, cause wounds, and invite infection by disease or infestation of insects.

Keep the area around the base of a shrub clean of debris. Pick or rake up fallen leaves and flowers. Remove any dead leaves from the shrub. If the shrub or tree has had a problem with disease or insects during the growing season, rake up and compost all mulch around its base, leaving the ground bare. The mulch around infected or infested shrubs and trees may contain spores and immature insects or eggs.

Inspect plants frequently and carefully, checking the undersides of leaves closely. Pick off insects by hand. Shake infected plants over a white plastic garbage bag. Toss insects into salty or soapy water or vinegar.

Use biological controls and mechanical traps to kill grubs, caterpillars, and mature insects whenever possible. Use the least powerful substance needed to take care of any given problem.

Invite birds into the yard by providing lots of nesting sites, water, and feed. Some birds can eat up to their full body weight in insects each day. They are voracious feeders and one of your best allies in the yard.

Frogs, salamanders, snakes, spiders, many predatory insects, and toads are also good friends. If you place a birdbath right on the ground with the rim even with soil level, you will give frogs and toads a watering hole. Replace the water each day by running a hose into the bath. This gets rid of the larvae of those mosquitoes responsible for spreading encephalitis in cold climates.

Provide diversity in the garden—lots of different types of plants, including trees, shrubs, grasses, and perennial flowers that offer areas for predatory (beneficial) insects to survive. These feed on their destructive cousins and often are great allies.

If You Must Spray

Combining sound organic practices with limited amounts of spraying is commonly referred to as *Integrated Pest Management* (IPM). This fancy term really is better described as intelligent pest management. The critical questions are always the same:

- What is the problem?
- Will it get worse without the use of chemicals?
- Is the loss tolerable?
- Is there an organic solution?
- If not, what is the best synthetic chemical to use?
- Is it the least toxic chemical that will control the problem?
- What is the correct dosage to control the problem?
- Is the organism at the right stage of development to be killed effectively?

Always keep in mind that spraying may not be necessary. That's why it's so important to answer the first few questions correctly. If spraying is necessary

Spraying Tips for Your Protection

Read labels carefully before using any chemicals. These labels tell you how toxic a substance is, what to do in case of a problem, and often who to call in an emergency. Follow all directions exactly.

Spray when it's calm to avoid drift. You don't want the spray to go anywhere except on the plants—not on you, not on your neighbors.

Cover all skin with clothing. Wear long, rubber gloves. The ones that go to your elbows are best. Wear goggles that completely protect your eyes from all sides. Use a respirator to protect you from inhaling chemicals. Don't let chemicals touch your skin, and don't breathe them in.

Use equipment that is working properly. Use water for a trial run. Bad nozzles or leaky hoses will get your clothing wet. Fix old or buy new equipment in winter before you really need it.

Mix chemicals outdoors in a well-ventilated area. Be careful when mixing liquids not to spill or splash them.

If you accidentally spill a chemical on your skin, wash it off immediately. Use a detergent instead of soap. Read the label for further instructions. If in doubt, get to a doctor and bring the container with you.

If you spill any chemical on your clothing or it gets wet while spraying, stop and remove it immediately. Wash yourself wherever wet clothing came in contact with your skin. Put on dry clothes.

Immediately after spraying, wash your gloves in soapy water (use detergent) before removing them. Have a bucket ready ahead of time. That way you just plunge your gloves into the water and then remove them after they're already clean.

Now remove all clothing. Wash your entire body well, especially your hands and face.

Wash your clothing right away. Do not mix it with other clothing. Use plenty of detergent.

Wash your goggles in soapy water. Clean respirators according to directions on the label after each use.

Never eat or smoke during or immediately after spraying until you've removed your clothing and washed well.

If any part of a plant will be used for food, always use sprays labeled for such use. Wait the appropriate time as outlined on the label before eating berries or fruits that have been sprayed.

Avoid getting chemicals in sandboxes, in pools, or on play equipment by spraying only when there is no wind. If equipment does get contaminated, wash it off.

Protect pets and wildlife by bringing inside food or water dishes. Cover birdbaths.

Allow children and pets into a sprayed area only after all foliage is dry. If the chemical is especially toxic, no one should touch the foliage until the appropriate waiting period is over as indicated on the label.

Keep all chemicals in their original containers. They should be in a dry, dark place (preferably cool). Keep all chemicals in a locked cabinet, out of the reach of children.

Buy only the amount of chemicals needed for one season. The shelf life varies widely by chemical, but most last a year, some 2 years, and a limited number longer. It is sometimes hard to judge how much spray you'll use in a season. If you have any chemicals left over, bring them indoors by midfall. If they freeze, many types become worthless. Keep them locked up.

Get rid of chemical containers without charge at hazardous waste sites now available in most communities. Your local government will tell you where these are as will the Environmental Protection Agency (EPA).

Don't use chemicals that are now being restricted for home use. Unless you have a special license, it is illegal and dangerous for you to work with them.

---

for the long-term survival of the plant, follow these helpful tips:

Spraying is the most effective and easiest way to apply chemicals to shrubs. It is the only sure way to cover all stems and foliage, especially the undersides of leaves.

Preventive spraying is only recommended for shrubs that have had the same problem for 2 or more years, and this problem should be seriously affecting the shrub's health. Either replace the shrub or begin regular, consistent spraying as advised on the label.

Use the appropriate chemical. To do this correctly you must be able to identify diseases, insects, and spider mites. You may need a magnifying lens or a photographer's loupe. Controlling a problem should begin as soon as possible. The longer you wait, the more serious the consequences.

When controlling a problem, begin with the least toxic substance. Work your way up to more powerful chemicals only as needed.

Read labels carefully and completely. Using too much of a chemical can cause leaf burn.

Labels may also indicate that the chemical will harm specific plants. Certain shrubs do not tolerate some chemicals well. Keep notes on those that are damaged by any particular one.

Saturate the soil with water before using any chemical sprays. Dry soil stresses plants, especially new growth, which can be damaged by sprays under dry conditions.

Mix only the amount of spray needed. Use it up entirely on the plants. Never pour excess solution down a drain or on the ground.

When using a fungicide, gardeners have found that adding 1 tablespoon (15 ml) of white vinegar per gallon (3.78 l) of solution makes it more effective. Slightly acidic fungicidal solutions are more potent.

Use a sprayer that produces a fine mist. Cover the entire plant with the mist, including the undersides of leaves and the soil at the base of the plant.

Spray early in the morning or late in the evening on a calm day to prevent unwanted drift of the spray. If sprays can kill honeybees, spray in the evening after bee activity has stopped. Bees are essential for proper pollination of shrubs and small trees that produce berries and fruits.

Spray during cool and cloudy weather, not during hot and sunny periods since many chemicals will burn foliage at high temperatures. During prolonged heat waves spray in the evening when sun is not shining on foliage.

Use systemic fungicides several hours before a rain. They will be extremely effective in preventing disease during wet or humid periods.

Spray after a rain to kill insects. They must touch or eat insecticides to be controlled. If it rains again shortly after spraying, reapply the spray. Or, use a systemic insecticide, one absorbed by the plant, which will then destroy insects that eat foliage or flowers.

Dormant sprays are those that contain oil or lime sulfur. Dormant oil is used to kill insect eggs while lime sulfur is aimed at destroying the spores of many fungal diseases. Spray these on deciduous shrubs and small trees in fall after leaves drop (preferred) or in spring before new growth (okay, but second best). Spraying at both times is even more effective. These dormant sprays kill bacteria, miniscule insect eggs, and the spores of many fungal diseases. However, they kill the eggs of beneficial insects as well. Use them only if disease or insect infestations have been a problem during the growing season.

Chemical Insect and Disease Control

This section gives detailed information on protecting shrubs and small trees from diseases and insects. Occasionally, you may be advised to use chemicals to prevent or control a specific problem. Chemicals that may be recommended include fungicides (kills fungi), insecticides (kills insects), miticides (kills spider mites), and molluscicides (kills slugs and snails).

Synthetic Chemicals

Synthetic chemicals and products containing these chemicals are used in preventing and controlling problems with disease and insects. These vary from relatively nontoxic to highly toxic. Some sprays mix chemicals together for protection against two or more problems. However, you should never mix chemicals unless the correct procedure for this is described in detail on the label.

Organic Alternatives

Organic alternatives exist for synthetic sprays. The term *organic* is used rather loosely and generally means nonsynthetic. For example, sulfur is not really organic, but it is often used by "organic" gardeners. The word *organic* does not necessarily mean "safe." Organic alternatives vary from relatively nontoxic to highly toxic. In fact, some synthetic sprays are safer than some organic ones. Read and follow labels carefully. A few of the organic alternatives, such as some brands of rotenone, have synthetic compounds (Piperonyl butoxide) added to make them more toxic. Proper storage of organic materials is important to prevent deterioration. Buy fresh products and store them as indicated on the label. Finally, wear a mask and appropriate clothing, especially rubber gloves, when working with organic pesticides. Some organic controls irritate the skin or mucous membranes.

Diseases

ANTHRACNOSE

Anthracnose is a fungal disease causing colored spots to form on the surface of leaves and occasionally on fruits. Openings then appear in the center of the spot. Leaves eventually turn yellow and fall.

Organic: Prevent by not watering foliage during cool periods. Control by cutting off and burning all infected stem tissue. Rake and discard fallen leaves.

Inorganic: Prevent and control by routine use of a product containing Chlorothalonil.

APPLE SCAB

Apple scab is a fungal disease affecting both leaves and fruits. Unsightly spots on the leaves are usually black, almost sooty in appearance. You'll notice lesions on the fruits. The infection can cause partial to complete defoliation of the tree. While this may not kill the tree, it affects its vigor and is aesthetically unpleasant. Scab is most common in extremely humid periods.

Organic: Choose resistant varieties as suggested throughout this guide. Rake and discard fallen leaves and fruits.

Inorganic: Home orchard sprays are available for this use.

Products for Organic Control

Product	Use
Antitranspirant (Cloud Cover, Wilt-Pruf®)	Antifungal properties
Bacillus popilliae (Doom or Milky spore disease)	Insecticide (kills grubs)
Bacillus thuringiensis (Bt—sold as a powder)	Insecticide (kills caterpillars)
Baking soda	Fungicide
Bordeaux mixture (Copper sulfate, lime)	Fungicide
Diatomaceous earth	Insecticide/molluscicide
Dormant oil	Insecticide (primarily)
Dormant spray (see Lime sulfur)	
Horticultural oils	Fungicide/insecticide
Insecticidal soaps	Insecticide
Lime sulfur (dormant spray)	Fungicide (primarily)
Neem products (Azadirachtin)	Insecticide (kills larvae)
Pyrethrum (Pyrethrin)	Insecticide
Rotenone (liquid form best)	Insecticide
Soap (detergents)	Insecticide
Sulfur (in varied forms)	Fungicide/insecticide
Traps (sticky ones)	Insecticide

BLACK KNOT

This is a fungal disease causing swelling in stem tissue. Swellings change color from green to black as they mature. In the spring spores are released, generally in moist, warm weather to be spread by wind.

Organic: Cut all branches with knots back 4 inches (10 cm) below the swelling to a bud or branchlet. Do this as soon as the swelling appears. Spray the plant with lime sulfur solution before growth emerges in spring and after leaves drop in the fall.

Inorganic: None.

BLIGHTS

This is a generic term referring to a number of primarily fungal diseases that cause leaves or new growth to wilt and turn brown. The result is stunted growth.

Synthetic Chemicals and Products Containing These Chemicals

THE NUMBER OF INORGANIC CHEMICALS that are now available for home use has been dwindling for years. Many of them are still used by commercial growers under strict guidelines. Since all chemicals pose potential health risks, they are commonly being evaluated. These evaluations may result in even more chemicals being removed from the market, including some on this list. It is difficult to keep current on what is and what is not allowed for home use. If you're in doubt about using a specific chemical, contact your local county agricultural extension office. The use of chemicals as a preventative is warranted primarily for fruit crops and for plants with repeated disease or insect problems from year to year. The use of chemicals after a problem occurs should be limited to times when these would lead to severe plant damage or death. As emphasized, choosing the right plants, planting them in the right place, and growing them well will reduce the need for chemicals dramatically. The chemicals below may still be in use. An asterisk (*) by the chemical indicates that it is systemic and actually absorbed by the plant tissue. Many of the following products are locally systemic, meaning that a smaller portion of the plant absorbs the chemical. A number of products not listed contain one or more of these chemicals. Some chemical names are followed by product names to make shopping easier.

Abamectin	*Miticide (kills adults)*
Acephate* (Orthene, Orthenex)	*Insecticide*
Acetamiprid*	*Insecticide*
Bifenazate	*Miticide (kills adults, eggs)*
Bifenthrin	*Insecticide*
Captan	*Fungicide*
Carbaryl (Sevin)	*Insecticide*
Chlorothalonil (Daconil)	*Fungicide*
Cyfluthrin	*Insecticide*
Dicofol	*Miticide*
Dimethoate*	*Insecticide/miticide*
Dinotefuran*	*Insecticide*
Disulfoton*	*Insecticide/miticide*
Esfenvalerate	*Insecticide*
Fenarimol* (Rubigan)	*Fungicide*
Fenbucanozole* (Indar)	*Fungicide*
Folpet	*Fungicide*
Glyphosate* (Roundup®)	*Herbicide*
Hexythiazox	*Miticide (kills eggs)*
Imidacloprid* (Merit®)	*Insecticide (kills grubs)*
Lambda-cyhalothrin	*Insecticide*
Malathion	*Insecticide/miticide*
Mancozeb (Dithane, Manzate)	*Fungicide*
Metalaxyl*	*Fungicide*
Metaldehyde	*Molluscicide (kills slugs)*
Myclobutanil	*Fungicide*
Permethrin	*Insecticide/miticide*
Propiconazole* (Banner, Orbit)	*Fungicide*
Tau-fluvalinate	*Insecticide/miticide*
Tebucanozole* (Elite)	*Fungicide*
Thiabendazole*	*Fungicide*
Triadimefon* (Bayleton)	*Fungicide*
Triflumizole* (Procure)	*Fungicide*
Triforine* (Funginex, Orthenex)	*Fungicide*

Organic: Prevent by proper spacing for good air circulation around plants. Water so that foliage has a chance to dry off before night. Control by cutting off and destroying infected plant parts at the first sign of the disease.

Inorganic: Not recommended, since most shrubs will survive these infections.

CANKERS

There are several types of cankers (fungal diseases), but most cause spots or dead areas to appear on stems or branches. Spots often enlarge, change color, and dry out. In severe cases stems die out. Common in cold climates.

Organic: Prevent cankers by making clean cuts ¼ inch (.6 cm) above buds. Avoid damaging stems by careless contact. Cut out crossing stems that can rub against each other in the wind. This results in open wounds. Also, avoid placing mulch against stems. Control by cutting stems back 3 inches (7.5 cm) below the infected area. Cut ¼ inch (.6 cm) above an outward-facing bud. Dip pruning shears in bleach solution after each cut to prevent spread of disease.

Inorganic: None recommended.

CEDAR APPLE RUST

Cedar apple rust is also a fungal disease. It shows up on *Malus* (Crabapples) as yellowish to orange spots on leaves. Leaves often turn yellow and may drop off. Crabapples listed in this guide are resistant to this disease. The fungus relies on the presence of *Juniperus virginiana* (Eastern Red Cedar) to complete its life cycle. On this plant it appears as swollen, brown galls until it finally sprouts orange horns as it matures in midspring. At that point it releases spores.

Organic: A highly recommended control is simply to cut off the galls from the Juniper plants while in their brown ball stage. Burn or discard these in the trash.

Inorganic: Control with fungicides is not practical.

FIRE BLIGHT

Fire blight is a wind- and insect-borne bacterial disease that can devastate susceptible plants. It shows up as blackened stem tissue that looks like it has been burned with a blowtorch. The disease can kill branches or entire trees. The presence of fire blight varies considerably by region. There is very little you can do about it once it infects your tree. Note that there is some evidence suggesting that the overuse of nitrogen in fertilizing trees may increase their susceptibility to fire blight.

Organic: If a plant becomes infected, cut off any diseased tissue at least 12 inches (30 cm) below any infected plant part. Dip pruners in bleach solution between cuts to stop spread of the disease.

Inorganic: Nothing effective.

GALLS

Galls are swollen spots on roots, stems, and leaves. They are caused primarily by bacteria and insects. Root galls are a bacterial infection caused by cuts in the roots or lower stems of the shrub through improper cultivation or insect damage. Growths (round, rough spots) form on the stem or roots at the base of the plant just underneath the soil. Young galls are greenish and soft while older ones darken and become tough. These stunt growth and can kill the plant.

Organic: If the roots of bare root plants have galls away from the crown, snip them off. If they are close to the crown, don't plant the infected plants. Return them to the supplier. If galls develop on the leaves or stems of plants already a part of your landscape, cut them off below the swollen area. In some instances this may be to ground level.

Inorganic: None.

LEAF SPOTS

This is a generic term referring to brown, tan, or black spots on leaves. These are generally caused by fungal infections and are very common.

Organic: Water so that all foliage can dry off before evening.

Inorganic: For severe problems spray with products containing Chlorothalonil or Triforine.

POWDERY MILDEW

Powdery mildew is a fungal disease. The tops of leaves are covered with a whitish film. Leaves may curl up and turn purple. The disease is only serious if it shows up early in the season when it can cause poor flowering. Generally, it shows up late and is simply unsightly. If the disease persists from one year to the next and begins early in the year, control it. If it shows up late, simply accept it as a nuisance. It is very common in cold climates.

Quite common on specific shrubs, powdery mildew is only a serious problem if it occurs early in the growing season.

Organic: Plant shrubs and trees in the correct light and space them far enough apart for good air circulation. Clean up all debris in the fall. Control by spraying with a solution of 3 tablespoons (45 ml) baking soda to 1 gallon (3.78 l) water (add 1 tablespoon [15 ml]) ammonia if aphids are present). Try 2 tablespoons (30 ml) Lysol per 1 gallon (3.78 l) of water as an alternative (spray in the middle of the day). These first two methods often work best if 1 tablespoon (15 ml) spreader sticker or 2.5 tablespoons (37.5 ml) of horticultural oil (ask for these at nurseries) are added to the mix. Or use wettable sulfur at the rate of 2 tablespoons (30 g) per gallon (3.78 l). Never use sulfur-based products if the temperature exceeds 85°F (29°C).

Inorganic: Varying the use of products containing Acephate, Chlorothalonil, Mancozeb, Propiconazole, or Triforine is often quite effective in preventing or controlling outbreaks of powdery mildew.

Rots

This is a generic term covering a wide variety of bacterial and fungal diseases that infect roots. Roots may turn mushy and foul smelling.

Organic: The best way to deal with rots is to prevent them from occurring at all. Plant your shrubs exactly as recommended throughout this guide. Rots are most commonly caused by planting shrubs or small trees in the wrong spot and in soil that does not drain freely.

Inorganic: None.

Viral Infections

There are numerous viral diseases of shrubs and small trees. Of these few rarely result in severe damage to the plant. Unfortunately, there is little you can do about the more serious viral infections. If your plant is severely infected, it should be destroyed. The most common sign of a viral infection is mottled or distorted leaf growth. Take a leaf to a professional if you suspect a problem. If a plant is infected with a serious viral illness, it should be dug up and destroyed.

Organic: Reduce the chance of viral infections by killing off aphids and other insects that often carry such diseases.

Inorganic: Do the same using chemicals.

White-Pine Blister Rust

Reddish orange spots (often powdery) first appear on the undersides of leaves and on young stems of *Ribes* (Currant) from white-pine blister rust. This will cause some defoliation and weakens the plant slightly. The real damage is done to nearby *Pinus strobus* (White Pine). The disease can lead to the eventual death of the tree. It is fairly common in cold climates.

Organic: Prevent by inspecting plants carefully before or after purchase. The disease comes in from plants grown in other parts of the country. Control by cutting off all infected plant parts (better yet, send or take the plant back). Avoid planting Currants and White Pine in the same area.

Inorganic: The use of fungicides containing Chlorothalonil, Mancozeb, or Triforine is often effective.

Wilts

Wilts are caused by a number of pathogens, including bacteria and fungi. Watch for a young shoot suddenly wilting even though a plant is well watered. Also, watch for unexpected leaf drop.

Organic: Keep the plant growing vigorously. Stressed plants are most susceptible to wilts. Cut off and burn the wilted, infected plant part immediately. Sterilize your pruners to avoid spreading the disease. If the plant continues to wilt, dig up and destroy it.

Inorganic: None.

Insects and Spider Mites

Aphids

Aphids are tiny, soft-bodied, sucking insects (plant lice) in a variety of colors that congregate in colonies at the tips of plants, usually on the undersides of leaves. They excrete a sticky substance called honeydew, a favorite of ants. Honeydew often becomes infected with a sooty mold. Leaves curl and dry up. Aphids carry numerous viral diseases that infect plants. They are very common in cold climates.

Organic: If they appear in early spring, wash them off with a strong spray of water. If colonies start to get out of hand after early spring, spray them with soapy water. If this doesn't work, use insecticidal soaps, a pyrethrum/rotenone combination, or horticultural oil.

Inorganic: If populations are ballooning, use products containing Acephate, Carbaryl, or Malathion for control.

BAGWORMS

Bagworms are most common on evergreens. They are the larvae of moths. In this stage they feed on foliage. They then spin a cocoon 2 to 3 inches (5 to 7.5 cm) long. Bagworms are most common in warm climates.

Organic: If they are seen as caterpillars, spray them with Bt (*Bacillus thuringiensis*). If they are in the bag stage and hanging from branches, snip off and destroy them.

Inorganic: None.

BLACK VINE WEEVIL

This brownish black insect cannot fly. As an adult, it feeds on foliage at night, causing relatively minor defoliation. However, its white larvae with yellowish heads do the most damage and are a serious threat to *Rhododendron* (Azalea and Rhododendron) and *Taxus* (Yew). These plants may turn yellow, wilt, and even die if damage to the root system is severe enough.

Organic: Nothing effective.

Inorganic: Timing is critical to control these insects. When you first see notches in leaves, treat them with a product containing Acephate. Do this late in the day since they feed at night. Three weeks later treat the foliage again. Several weeks after the second application treat the soil with a product containing Imidacloprid.

BORERS

Borers make little holes in stems or branches. You can see these tiny holes, often surrounded by sawdust or "frass." The miniscule holes may also ooze sap. The borers themselves are worm-like, cream-colored larvae that tunnel into stem tissue.

Organic: Take care of your shrubs so that they are growing vigorously. Borers are attracted to stressed plants. Branches or stems damaged by borers often die back, even to ground level. Cut out all damaged tissue. Look for holes in spring. Push the end of a thin wire (undo a paper clip) into the hole to attempt to mash the eggs or spear the borer itself. Then fill the hole with clay or a clear glue.

Inorganic: None.

CARPENTER BEE

The black to bluish green, miniscule carpenter bee (½ inch/1.2 cm) bores out a hole in the top of stems to lay eggs there. The eggs mature into yellowish, curved maggots. Mainly a problem with roses and *Paeonia* (Tree Peonies).

Organic: Spear maggots with wire or cut off stem to healthy bud below. Seal all cuts.

Inorganic: None.

CATERPILLARS

Caterpillars are the larvae of butterflies and moths. These may appear to be smooth, hairy, or spiny. The many varieties of caterpillars feed mainly on leaves and fresh shoots. The resulting damage can stress a plant seriously, but rarely leads to the death of the plant itself.

Organic: If you see egg masses on your plants, rub these off. These are generally most noticeable in the fall. Pick adults off the plant at any time of year. Either kill or place them somewhere else if you like butterflies. Kill them with *Bacillus thuringiensis* (Bt). Or spray with pyrethrin/rotenone mixtures.

Inorganic: Products containing Carbaryl are effective.

CODLING MOTHS

These small moths lay eggs on foliage several times each growing season. These mature into larvae that tunnel into fruit and then pupate into adult moths. The larvae are white with a slight pinkish tinge. They are particularly a problem with apples, pears, and plums.

Organic: Place suet in the garden to attract woodpeckers. These often will peck at bark to eat the larvae. Place corrugated cardboard bands at the base of the plant where larvae can create cocoons. These must be placed in layers to be effective. You may have to create these safe harbors several times a season. Once the larvae spin their cocoons, remove these bands and burn them. Bt does kill larvae, but they generally get into fruit so quickly that it is hard to time its application with much effect.

Inorganic: Use an all-purpose home fruit spray. Read the label carefully so that you spray at the right time.

Japanese Beetle

Japanese beetles are shiny ¼- to ½-inch (.6- to 1.2-cm) insects, usually coppery brown with green heads with white tufts of hair on their bellies—very beautiful, but devastating. Grubs, found under lawns, are grayish white with brown heads and curled into a C-shape. Adults cause severe damage rapidly. Normally, they begin by eating flower buds and flowers first, then skeletonizing leaves. These insects may not kill your shrubs, but they will severely weaken them to the point that secondary diseases and insects may indeed kill them.

Organic: Apply Milky spore disease over a period of 3 years on your lawn where the grubs feed before pupation. Follow the directions on the label. Remove adults by hand (toss into can of soapy water, salty water, or vinegar). Place cloth under the plant and shake vigorously to get all insects—they will drop on the cloth. The best time to do this is early in the morning when the insects are lethargic. Products containing Neem oil (Bio-Neem and Margosan-O) may be effective over a period of years if sprayed regularly according to directions on the label, as can pyrethrin/rotenone sprays.

Inorganic: To control grubs and protect sod in your own yard, use a product containing Imidacloprid. Read the label carefully as timing is critical. Use it as often as recommended. Unfortunately, this will not stop beetles from flying in from other areas.

Lace Bugs

Lace bugs suck sap from the undersides of leaves. This area may take on an orange red coloration. Damage causes leaves to be discolored or look as if they have been burned. They will sometimes dry up, curl up on the ends, or turn brown and drop off. Lace bugs are less than ¼ inch (.6 cm) long and have transparent wings. They are nearly colorless at first but darken with age. Most of the time the insects cause minor damage to a plant, but if present in large numbers, it is best to control them.

Organic: As soon as they appear, spray them with insecticical soaps.

Inorganic: Spray leaves with any product containing Acephate or Carbaryl. When spraying, saturate the underside of all foliage.

Leafhoppers

Leafhoppers are little springing, winged insects. They are small and tinged pale green or white. They leave white skeletons (skins) on the underside of leaves. Clusters may be found on the undersides of leaves. Shake the leaves and the leafhoppers spring up in a cloud. They feed on foliage by sucking out the juices. Foliage may look torn or have holes in it. If severely damaged, it simply falls off. Leafhoppers carry viral diseases. They are fairly common in cold climates.

Organic: Avoid overuse of nitrogen fertilizer that stimulates soft, new growth. Leafhoppers are especially attracted to this. Control by spraying with insecticidal soap.

Inorganic: Kill with products containing Acephate.

Leaf Miners

You can't really see these tiny insects, just the damage they do. They are the larvae of beetles, flies, and moths. They tunnel into leaves, which begin to discolor with papery blotches or blisters. Some leaves may drop off.

Organic: There is no practical way of preventing damage. Remove and destroy infected leaves. Otherwise, leave the plant alone. Most healthy plants will survive.

Inorganic: Use any product containing Acephate just as the leaf miners are beginning to tunnel into the foliage. Once the insects are inside the leaf, it's too late.

Leaf Rollers (Leaf Tier)

These are little caterpillars (usually smaller than ½ inch/1.2 cm) that look like green or yellow maggots and are the immature stage of a moth. They roll themselves up in a leaf and eat their way out. Sometimes, they will eat tiny holes in flowers. They are fairly common in cold climates.

Organic: Prevent by good fall cleanup. Encourage birds to feed in your garden. Control by squeezing rolled-up leaves to kill them. Pick off and burn the leaves. Use *Bacillus thuringiensis* (Bt) to control in a safe manner. Pyrethrum, Rotenone, and insecticidal soaps will destroy them as well.

Inorganic: Kill larger infestations with products containing Acephate, Malathion, or Tau-fluvalinate.

Pear Midge

This mosquito-like insect lays eggs in blossoms. These turn into maggots that tunnel into fruit, which drops off early in the season.

Organic: Spray with pyrethrum just as they emerge as flying insects in spring.

Inorganic: Spray the trees with an orchard spray according to the directions on the label.

Plum Curculio

This beetle with a distinctive snout is about ¼ inch (.6 cm) long and generally brown-colored mottled gray. If observed closely, it has little humps along the ridge of its back. It feeds on fruit and makes little cuts in the skin where it lay eggs. These develop into grubs that cause the fruit to drop off.

Organic: Prevent by keeping the tree open and exposed to bright light. Control by laying a white sheet around the base of the tree in early morning. Whap and jiggle the branches and the trunk early in the season. The adults will often drop off. Pick up and destroy all fallen fruit.

Inorganic: Products containing Carbaryl are effective.

Sawfly

It isn't actually the fly, but the larvae of the fly that causes damage to some evergreens and deciduous shrubs. These larvae are small, but they can be seen. They look yellowish. They feed on foliage (needles) and leave bare patches on the tree. Over a period of years they can defoliate entire trees. They are very easy to control if you spray them im-

If not killed immediately, sawfly larvae quickly defoliate evergreens. Picking the larvae off by hand is possible but time consuming.

mediately when you first begin to notice small bare spots appearing on the shrub or tree.

Organic: Spray with an insecticidal soap, pyrethrum, or rotenone.

Inorganic: Spray early in the season just as the larvae form for good control. Spray with a product containing Carbaryl. If you time your spraying properly, you'll only have to spray once.

Scale

There are many different species of scale. Very common are Euonymus scale and oyster shell scale. These little insects with hard protective waxy shells encrust stems, looking like little round or oval growths or bumps. Insects suck sap from the plants, stunting growth.

Organic: Prevent by spraying plants with dormant oil or lime sulfur in early spring. Insecticidal soaps can be effective if used very early in the insect's life cycle. In cold climates this is typically just after common Lilacs (*Syringa vulgaris*) bloom.

Inorganic: Spray with products containing Acephate, Carbaryl, or Malathion in late spring. Kill them as early as possible. Mature colonies are difficult to eradicate.

Spider Mites

These miniscule, spider-like creatures are often reddish, although they do vary in color and may appear spotted. Magnify them with a lens or tap them onto piece of white paper from the undersides of leaves. Their delicate webs are visible. Mites damage leaves, which yellow and sometimes die. Severe infestations can kill plants. They are common in hot, dry weather.

Organic: Prevent by using dormant oil in both late fall and spring. Unfortunately, oil kills off predator mite eggs as well. Clean up all debris and weeds in fall. Prevent and control by spraying foliage forcefully with water in dry weather. Don't miss the undersides of leaves. Keep plants well watered for vigorous growth. Shake plants vigorously, since spider mites will not get back on the plant once off. Encourage predator mite colonies and ladybugs by not using chemical sprays.

Inorganic: Kill adults with Dicofol. If unavailable, substitute a product labeled for use against spider mites. Remove damaged foliage before spraying only if it's severely damaged. Spray undersides of leaves well. Frequent application of a miticide may be necessary. Begin application in late May and continue every 2 weeks. Changing sprays may be necessary.

Spittle Bug, Cuckoo Spit, or Frog Hopper

This miniscule yellow insect hides inside frothy spittle. It may cause a few leaves to wilt by sucking out juices and occasionally causes distorted shoots, but rarely causes serious damage. It is fairly common in cold climates.

Organic: Prevent by misting plants in hot, dry weather. Rub off spittle containing insects with cloth or cotton, or spray off with a jet of water. Kill with Rotenone.

Inorganic: Kill with products containing Acephate.

Willowleaf Beetles

Willowleaf beetles are small, shiny blue black insects that chew holes in leaves and can actually defoliate entire trees if not sprayed.

Organic: Spray with insecticidal soap.

Inorganic: Spray with any product containing Acephate or Carbaryl if infestation is severe.

Physiological, Mechanical, and Nutritional Problems

Damage to plants isn't always caused by diseases and insects. Often, the culprit is related to human error or simply the weather.

Winter Burn and Chemical Damage

The needles of evergreens may turn brown by the spring unless you follow certain steps. Avoid planting susceptible evergreens where they will be exposed to direct light or strong winds in winter. South, southwest, and windy sites are tough on these plants. Keep the soil evenly moist until the first solid freeze. Evergreens should head into winter with saturated soil and lots of moisture in the needles.

Once the moist ground is frozen, cover it with a 2- to 4-inch (5- to 10-cm) layer of shredded bark, wood chips, or whole leaves. This helps minimize water loss.

A physical barrier against wind is advised for a few shrubs recommended in this guide. Normally, it consists of burlap tacked to stakes with an opening at the bottom. This is then filled with leaves. It is best to wait until the top 2 inches (5 cm) of the ground have frozen before putting up the barrier. Otherwise, rodents may be attracted to the area as a winter home and use the stems for a cache of winter food.

If an evergreen does suffer damage, simply cut off the dead portions in late spring just before new growth emerges. Leave all green areas intact. Water the plant immediately and keep it well watered. Evergreens often recuperate quickly if only a small portion of each branch is damaged.

A number of deciduous plants will have damaged leaves if improperly fertilized or if sprayed incorrectly. This has been covered in detail in other parts of this guide.

Chlorosis

When leaves turn yellow but veins stay green, your plants are likely suffering from chlorosis. This is caused by a plant's inability to absorb iron or manganese from the soil. This happens when soil is overly alkaline. Acidify the soil with acidic soil amendments such as peat moss and rotted oak leaves, or fertilize the soil with an acidifying fertilizer.

Construction Damage

Keep heavy equipment, including trucks, out of your yard. They can compress soil so badly that shrubs or small trees die. If heavy equipment must be used, you'll need to construct appropriate bridges over sensitive areas. Never allow excess fill to be placed over a shrub's or small tree's root system. Even a few inches can damage the plant. Avoid any kind of plowing, digging, or cutting into the soil near a shrub or tree you intend to save. Most root systems are shallow and once wounded may not survive. Do not allow construction crews to store materials around bushes or small trees. Do not allow any chemicals or paints to be poured on the soil. Construction damage can be so devastating that it may be advisable to hire an arborist for advice and planning before beginning any major project.

Dieback

The tips of stems may die back, turning brittle and brown. This is sometimes caused by various diseases. However, it is most common after severe winters or late spring freezes, when the upper portions of stems are most vulnerable to freezing or drying in cold winds. This is very common in cold climates because of severe winter freezes and hard winds. Avoid serious problems with dieback by choosing plants hardy for your area and planting them in the right sites. Protect more delicate shrubs appropriately. Fertilize exactly as indicated throughout the guide. Prune cor-

rectly and at the right time of year. To remedy, cut off dead stem tissue to a healthy bud below.

Heat

Damage from heat is most often related to water stress. Proper watering, mulching, and hosing down plants during heat waves usually stops any damage whatsoever.

Leaf Scorch

A lack of potassium can cause leaves to curl up, turn brown, and drop off. This is mainly a problem with fruit trees. Since it mimics fire blight, leaf scorch can be diagnosed improperly. If you fertilize shrubs and small trees as directed throughout this guide, you'll avoid this altogether.

Pollution

Air pollution is so bad in some cities that certain shrubs are affected. If you live in such an area, choose your shrubs and small trees with this in mind. If pollution is a major concern, this is mentioned in specific sections of Part I.

Reversion

Some plants in this guide have variegated foliage. A good example is *Daphne* 'Carol Mackie.' Occasionally, stems will produce leaves with totally green foliage. The plant is reverting to its original form. Cut out stems or branches that lack the desired variegated coloration. Flowers may also revert in color. The flowers of *Syringa vulgaris* 'Sensation' (Common Lilac) should have two colorations. If you notice stems producing flowers with only one color, cut them off right down to the base of the plant. Some of the dwarf conifers and occasionally some small varieties of *Philadelphus* (Mockorange) send off long branches completely out of proportion with the rest of the plant. This represents reversion to an earlier form or size. Simply snip off these elongated branches. While reversion occurs, it is clearly remedied with a few snips of a pruning shears.

Root Injury

Prevent root injury by firming soil around the roots during planting to fill up all air pockets. In the fall check the soil around the plant. If you see any holes, fill them in with soil. Keep the soil moist until the first freeze. Moist soil stays warmer during the winter than dry soil. If holes around plants are caused by rodents, buy appropriate traps. Follow the directions to place them correctly in or near the holes.

Salt

In colder areas, streets and walkways are often salted to get rid of ice after storms. Some shrubs are quite salt tolerant. Plant these in areas that often get salted. Other shrubs do poorly in such areas. Salt tolerance or intolerance is pointed out in Part I.

Snow and Ice Damage

Snow provides winter protection for many shrubs. However, heavy snow on some shrubs weighs down the branches and may break them off. You can prevent this by shaking the branches so that snow falls off before it gets too heavy. This is especially true on some of the low-growing evergreens. Also, avoid planting shrubs directly under eaves if they are prone to such damage.

Sunscald

Young and thin-barked trees are susceptible to sunscald. This shows up as cracked or split bark generally on the south or west side of a shrub stem or tree trunk. Sunscald is common with Cherries and Plums (*Prunus*), Crabapples (*Malus*), Maples (*Acer*), and Mountain Ash (*Sorbus*). Prevent it by using reflective paint.

Wind

Newly planted shrubs or small trees, especially those facing north or east, may topple over in a heavy wind if they are planted in extremely loose soil or in areas prone to strong gusts. This is one time when staking makes sense (see page 384). Wind during the winter often causes desiccation of evergreen plants. The best protection is planting these plants in the correct location and watering them deeply before the first expected freeze late in the season.

Wounds

Avoid leashing animals to trees. The leash may scrape off bark causing an open wound. Careless mowing, weed trimming, or pruning can also cause wounds susceptible to infections and open to insect infestations. Mulch around the base of shrubs and small trees to avoid having to trim the grass around them with a mower or weed trimmer. Prune at the right time and in the way described in individual sections of Part I. Make all cuts flush with the stem or at a right angle above a bud to promote quick healing. Wound dressings or paints are no longer recommended. It's best to let the shrub or tree heal by itself naturally. If a branch is broken during the active growing season, snip it back to a bud just below the break. If the branch is unsightly, snip it off completely only at the time recommended for yearly pruning as suggested in sections of Part I.

Animal Problems

While most shrubs are quite disease and insect resistant, many are easily destroyed by deer, rabbits, and rodents at different times of year.

Birds

Birds are one of your greatest allies in the yard. Other than eating fruit or berries that you might like for yourself, they are rarely a problem. The only damage observed is to *Prunus maackii* (Amur Chokecherry) by sapsuckers. These specific woodpeckers drill holes in the trees to gather sap and insects for food.

Deer

Deer will eat shrubs in both summer and winter. Tall fences are the only reliable way to keep deer away from shrubs. The following fencing methods are unattractive and expensive, but do work.

Erect a 7- to 10-foot (2.1- to 3-m) fence with an electric wire on top. Encircle the entire tall fence with a single strand of wire several feet away. Deer shy away from this double fencing. So do most people.

Less conspicuous but still expensive is polypropylene deer fencing available from specialty mail-order sources, such as Deer-resistant Landscape Nursery, 3200 Sunstone Court, Clare, MI 48617, (800) 595-3650.

Some gardeners claim to prevent deer damage during the summer by spreading Milorganite (dried and processed sewage) on the soil surface after every rain. Yes, it does smell.

Other gardeners alternate the use of human hair, flakes of soap, and reflectors as deer deterrents. The owners of apple orchards insist that deer get used to scents and unusual sights quickly—so keep changing the repellent. Commercial repellents are available both for summer and winter use. They are expensive, may spot foliage, and must be used on a regular basis.

If deer are hungry enough, they will eat just about anything no matter what home or commercial repellents are used. Fencing remains the best overall option, although it is rarely feasible for the home gardener.

Another problem with deer is that in late summer they will rub their antlers against the trunks of small trees as a way of removing velvet from their horns. The wound on the bark is called a rub. In the process they shred bark off the tree and may cause a serious wound. Spraying trees with a deer repellent on a regular basis may work. It's time-consuming and expensive. An alternative is to place a protective tube (trunk guard) around the tree. These are often available at local nurseries. They are efficient but unattractive. Less expensive but even more unattractive is hanging a pop can from one of the lower branches. As silly as it sounds, it does keep bucks at bay. It also keeps deer away from your fruit trees and is one of the many tricks used by orchard owners to protect their crop.

Dogs

Male dogs like to urinate on evergreens. Brown patches at the base of these plants indicate that kind of damage. Dog repellents are available, but keeping dogs away from shrubs at all is a more reasonable solution.

Field Mice

Mice often nibble bark off the base of shrubs and small trees in the winter. Remove all mulch from around the base of the shrub as it cools off in fall. Surround the base of the shrub or tree with hardware cloth of a very tight mesh. Try to get the cloth at least 2 inches (5 cm) into the soil. You can also kill field mice before the first snowfall with baited traps. Poisoned baits, especially poisoned oats, are frequently recommended as a control and do work. *However, pets can get into these and wildlife can eat the dead mice.* For this reason they are not recommended.

Humans

Humans often do more damage than animals, diseases, and insects combined. Careless handling after purchase, poor planting, overfertilizing, misuse of chemical sprays, improper pruning—all of these can damage plants severely. If you follow the advice given in this guide, you will become a plant's ally, not an enemy.

Rabbits

Mature rabbits like to nibble on shrubs during the winter when food is scarce. Surround standing shrubs and small trees with chicken wire, hardware cloth, or vinyl tree guards. Take expected snowfall into consideration when putting up this wire barricade. The protective barrier should be at least 24 inches (60 cm) above the anticipated snow line. Where legal, trap or shoot rabbits for true control. As with deer, there are commercial repellents available that you spray on shrubs to ward off rabbits. Again, these are expensive and must be applied frequently to be effective.

CHAPTER 9

PROPAGATING SHRUBS AND SMALL TREES

Creating new shrubs from old ones is a passion for a number of gardeners. It is an extremely pleasurable pastime. If you have time and patience, it saves a lot of money. You can also propagate plants that may be difficult to find in the trade, as long as you can find the desired mother plant for your offspring.

In some instances it can be extremely difficult, almost impossible, even for commercial growers to use a specific method of propagation for a specific shrub, but in other instances you can just stick a piece of stem in water, and it will form roots. Propagation of shrubs varies from mystifying to magical. The huge benefit of propagation is that you can get many shrubs from a single plant. *Legally you cannot propagate plants under patent without permission and appropriate payment to the patent holder.*

Division from Whole Plants

Unlike herbaceous perennials, most shrubs cannot be divided to produce new plants. However, simply digging through a mature multistemmed shrub with a sharp spade and digging up a section will work with a few shrubs, including some varieties of *Amelanchier* (Serviceberry), *Aronia* (Chokeberry), *Berberis* (Barberry), *Diervilla* (Bush Honeysuckle), *Forsythia* (Forsythia), *Hydrangea* (Hydrangea), *Perovskia* (Rus-

sian Sage), *Spiraea* (Spirea), and *Symphoricarpos* (Snowberry).

Do this before new growth emerges. Use a sharp spade to dig up the stems, making sure that there are a number of roots attached to the stems. Many gardeners prefer a flat spade to do this, but either type is fine.

Plant this division immediately as you would a bare root plant. Keep it consistently moist until it is growing vigorously.

Division of Suckers

A number of shrubs, such as *Rhus* (Sumac) and *Syringa* (Lilac) produce little plantlets (suckers) off to the side of the mother plant. The original plant sends out underground stems or branches (stolons) and from these emerge new plants. By cutting off these plantlets, you get an additional plant.

The best time to do this is in early spring as soon as the ground can be worked. Do this before the shrub begins to leaf out, either when it is still dormant or when buds are just beginning to emerge at the latest. Shrubs or trees should be at least 1 foot (30 cm) tall.

The easiest way to cut off the root is with a pointed shovel or spade. Aim it straight down and step on the shovel. The blade will cut through the root. Then dig around the sucker in a circular pattern roughly 8 inches (20 cm) across. This should give you a good clump of roots. As you dig up the sucker, keep as much soil around the roots as possible.

Plant the sucker immediately as you would a bare root plant. Sometimes, some soil falls off from around the roots. This is okay as long as you plant the sucker immediately and give it lots of water.

Ground Layering, Soil Layering, or Pegging

One of the easiest ways to propagate some shrubs with long, arching stems is through ground layering. This is also known as soil layering. When it is done with just the tip of a stem, it's called *pegging*. Do this in early spring just as leaves begin to emerge. Here are the steps:

Choose a stem that is long and supple enough to bend easily to the ground without breaking it. The stem should be on the outside of the shrub.

With a sharp blade make a slanting cut in the stem about 18 inches (45 cm) from its tip. Make your cut below a leaf node, the place where a leaf joins the stem. The cut should be 1 to 3 inches (2.5 to 7.5 cm) long and go no more than one-third of the way through the stem, stopping just below the node. Alternatively, wound the stem with a long, shallow 3-inch (7.5-cm) cut. Make these cuts on the upper portion of the stem, not on the bottom. This way when you bend the tip of the stem up as you will be directed to do later on, the stem will not break. Note that there are two other popular methods of wounding the stem: one is to make a little notch in it; the other is to girdle the stem, cutting off the bark in a ring around it. The choice is strictly yours.

Strip all leaves off either side of the cut. Leave leaves on the last 6 inches (15 cm) at the tip. Place a piece of toothpick in the wound to keep it open. Dust the wound with rooting hormone.

Gently bend the wounded portion of the stem to the ground. Where the wound touches the ground, loosen the soil to a depth of 6 inches (15 cm), making a shallow hole. When doing this avoid cutting any roots of the shrub. Mix moist peat into the bottom of the hole.

Now gently push the wounded portion of the stem into the hole. Keep it in place with a bent piece of wire.

Fill the hole with soil mixed with moist peat. The tip of the stem will be above the soil. Support it with a stake. Tie the stem to the stake with a piece of cloth tied in a figure-eight knot.

Water the peat over the wounded stem so that it is evenly moist.

Cover the soil with shredded leaves. This layer of mulch keeps the area moist and cool.

Keep the soil consistently moist to help roots form at the cut. Over a period of weeks or months roots will form at the site of the cut. In some cases, it may take a full season for roots to form. Waiting until the following spring to begin looking for roots is generally recommended.

Gently dig down into the loose soil at that time to see whether roots have formed. If the wound has roots 2 to 3 inches (5 to 7.5 cm) long, sever the stem from the mother plant, but do not dig it up.

Fill up the area you've disturbed with fresh soil. Continue to keep the area moist and wait several weeks. This gives the severed plant a chance to take root on its own and adjust to the trauma of not being nourished in any way by the mother plant. Once the plant is growing vigorously, dig it up with as much soil around the roots as possible and plant it immediately as you would a bare root plant. You may have to protect these young plants by placing them in a cold frame for the first winter or two.

A trick is to dig a hole where you intend to layer the plant. Place a pot filled with soil and peat in the hole. Now push the wounded stem right into the soil in the pot. Pin it down, mulch, and water it as outlined above. When you sever the plant from the mother plant, it is already potted and can be grown on without digging it up. You just pull up the pot and move it to a convenient, sheltered spot.

Mound Layering

Mound layering is a rather dramatic way to get new plants, but it does work well on some shrubs. Before new growth emerges in early spring cut all the stems of a shrub back to ground level. The lowest cut should be just below a leaf node. Stems can be flush with the ground or slightly above it.

Cover the plant with at least 6 inches (15 cm) of soil generously amended with peat. Keep the soil and peat mixture consistently moist. Stems will emerge through the peat and grow throughout the season. Roots should also grow from the buried portion of the stem.

The following spring push some of the soil aside. If there are roots growing from the buried portion of stem, cut the stem off below the roots. Plant this rooted stem as you would a bare root plant in a pot or directly in a cold frame. Again, these young plants generally need protection during the winter for a year or two.

Stem Cuttings

There are two types of stem cuttings used to propagate shrubs. Cuttings taken from mature stems are called hardwood cuttings because the wood is hard; cuttings taken from new wood are called softwood cuttings because the wood is more pliable. Hardwood cuttings are taken during dormancy (after leaves fall off), while softwood cuttings are taken during a plant's active growth (during summer). Obviously, evergreens have needles or leaves on in both their active and dormant seasons.

Hardwood cuttings of some shrubs are relatively easy to get to root. Others are next to impossible even for commercial growers. Softwood cuttings are often easier to work with. Still, shrubs vary in their likelihood to form roots from cuttings, and it is common to lose a number of cuttings even under good conditions. Commercial growers report losses of up to 50 percent even under ideal conditions for some shrubs. Some shrubs simply will not root well from cuttings.

While approximate times to take cuttings are given throughout this guide, you should take cuttings at several different times. Even commercial growers report varying rates of success if they take cuttings at weekly intervals. This one tip will increase your odds of suc-

cess enormously. In short, take cuttings over a period of weeks rather than all at once.

Hardwood Cuttings

Remember that this technique can be difficult even for professionals, so don't get discouraged if it doesn't work with a particular shrub.

After the leaves drop off the stems of deciduous shrubs, choose a healthy stem and look for this year's growth. Cut off 6 inches (15 cm) of the most recent growth. Cuttings should have no fewer than three to four nodes (spots where leaves joined the stem). The closer the nodes are together, the better. Make a slanting cut ¼ inch (.6 cm) under the lowest node. If an evergreen, just cut off a 6-inch (15-cm) stem tip in late fall or early winter. Use a sharp blade to make these cuts. Pruning shears also work well.

Dip the cut ends in rooting hormone. Tap off any excess powder. Bundle the cuttings together in groups of twenty to twenty-five.

Place the cuttings in a plastic bag filled with moist peat in the crisper of your refrigerator. If this is not practical, place the cuttings in moist peat in a plastic garbage can in an unheated garage, or place the cuttings in a bed of moist peat in a cold frame outdoors. **Note:** Cuttings can be taken in late winter for some shrubs. Always take cuttings at least 6 to 8 weeks before planting them. This allows them to form a callus, a whitish protective covering, over the wounded stem tissue.

In early spring remove the cuttings from the bag or peat. Wash them off with water. Each wounded end will have formed a callus by this time. Insert these cuttings into loose garden soil, peat, or sand with the wounded end down. Plant them in pots or directly in a cold frame. The cuttings should receive filtered, not direct light. Place the cuttings 4 inches (10 cm) apart. Keep them moist at all times. If the rooting medium dries out, the cuttings will die.

Cuttings that take root sprout leaves. Do not disturb them until they have formed a solid root system. This usually takes a year. The larger the root system before you dig them up, the better. If potted, protect them from winter cold and winds during the first year or two by placing them in a cold frame. Whether in pots or planted directly in the soil of a cold frame, keep the structure insulated in the winter to keep temperatures from fluctuating wildly.

Softwood Cuttings

Softwood cuttings is a generic term covering all cuttings taken while the plant is actively growing. Cuttings are always taken from the current season's growth from stems or branches. In this guide, *softwood* means softwood, greenwood, and semihardwood cuttings. A true softwood cutting is taken early in the season when stem tissue is quite soft, almost floppy. Relatively few cuttings taken at this stage root well. Greenwood cuttings are taken a bit later in the season when new growth is just about as firm as a string bean. This is often a very good stage to take cuttings. Semihardwood cuttings are taken later yet when the new growth is quite firm and much more "woody." Semihardwood cuttings are also referred to as stem tip or half-ripened softwood cuttings. Throughout this guide are directions on when to take softwood cuttings, but softwood, greenwood, or semihardwood cuttings may be referred to under the overall catchall term of *softwood cuttings*.

The key to success with softwood cuttings is to vary the stage at which cuttings are taken to increase your odds of getting at least a few cuttings to root. Never be discouraged by failure. Even professional growers are constantly experimenting with just the right time to take cuttings for specific shrubs. Keep notes on what timing works best for specific plants.

Take cuttings when indicated in individual sections of Part I. In these you'll be told whether to take softwood, greenwood, or semihardwood cuttings.

Cuttings from deciduous shrubs should have a minimum of two nodes and preferably three or more. A node is a place where a leaf, two leaves, or a number of leaves join the stem. With a sharp blade cut through the stem at a slant ¼ inch (.6 cm) below a node or where a little branch comes off an evergreen plant. Do this in early morning. The length of the cutting will vary by shrub, but is usually from 2 to 6 inches (5 to 15 cm).

Willow Water

SOME GARDENERS INSIST that dipping the ends of cuttings in willow water increases the likelihood of their taking root. To create willow water cut new growth off willow trees. Cut these twigs into little pieces. Mash the twigs with a hammer. Place about 4 ounces (about 120 g) of this mush into warm water. Let the mixture brew for no longer than 48 hours. Soak the wounded ends of the cuttings in this solution overnight. Much easier is to mimic willow water by simply dissolving two aspirin in a gallon of water. The salicylic acid present in willow water and aspirin is the chemical believed to help induce rooting. This topic is hotly debated and highly controversial. The controversy may stem from the fact that it works well with some shrubs, but not at all with others. The same can be said for commercial rooting hormones.

Remove the lower leaves. These will just end up buried in the soil where they would rot off. Remove any flower buds or flowers. Pinch out the growing tip at the end of the cutting. Do this on all softwood cuttings except those taken late in the season (semihardwood) or those taken from evergreens. This directs hormones away from the tip of the cutting to its base for better rooting. Leave the top leaf or set of leaves on. If these leaves are especially large as on some Hydrangeas, cut them in half to reduce water loss. If you leave too many leaves on, they just wilt and drop off anyway.

Dip the cuttings in water before placing them in a plastic bag. Put them in the crisper of your refrigerator for a day or two. This process hardens them up a little so that they are less likely to flop over from water loss when planted.

Fill 8-inch (20-cm) or larger plastic pots with rooting medium. Good rooting medium is three parts perlite to one part peat. Professional rooting mediums are available. The rooting medium should be moist, but not soggy or wet. Match the pot size to the potential length of the cutting. Pots must be sterile. If they have been used before, sterilize them by washing them in a solution of one part bleach to nine parts water for 30 minutes.

Dip the end of each cutting in rooting hormone, typically containing naphthaleneacetic (NAA) or indolebutyric acid (IBA). You can buy this at garden centers or nurseries. Tap off any excess powder. Note that rooting hormones vary by shrub in their effectiveness.

Poke a hole in the rooting medium with a pencil or stick (dibble). Bury the cutting to a point just below the upper leaf. Firm the medium around the stem with your fingers. Note that you can place several or many cuttings in a single pot depending upon its size, but avoid having leaves touch each other.

Water the rooting medium lightly so that it fills in any air spaces around each stem. Dusting the surface of the rooting medium with a fungicide is optional, but often a good idea. Place three cedar or rot-resistant sticks, pieces of wire, or straws around the edge of the pot. Cover the entire pot with a clear plastic bag. Tie a piece of twine around the bag to keep it in place. The plastic keeps humidity high and increases the chances of the cuttings taking root. Remove the bag occasionally and check on the soil moisture. Moisten as necessary, never allowing the growing medium to dry out. Consistently moist soil and high humidity are secrets to success with softwood cuttings.

Place the pot in indirect sunlight or under artificial light indoors. Heating cables outdoors or heating pads indoors can be helpful. Maintain soil temperatures between 70°F (21°C) and 77°F (25°C).

The time it takes for cuttings to form roots varies by plant. Some root within weeks, others take months. Be patient. When the cuttings begin to show new growth, they have begun to take root. Remove the plastic bag for several hours each day to harden off the young plants. Mist the plants to keep them moist. Keep the soil moist at all times.

Once roots have formed, transplant the rooted cuttings into a cold frame bed or plant them in a container filled with potting soil. When digging them up, you may have to tease their root systems apart if they have been planted close together. Keep a healthy root system with each cutting. Once potted, either put them into a cold frame or set them in a sheltered location. This is best as a precaution against drying winds, which could kill the cuttings in early stages of growth. Keep the soil moist at all times until the cuttings are growing well. High humidity (for most cuttings) and moist soil are critical.

Ideally, you do want to have a cold frame because the young plants will need protection during the first winter. Once the ground freezes outdoors, cover the pots or planted cuttings in the cold frame with a winter mulch of whole leaves, pine needles, marsh hay, or straw to a depth of 8 to 10 inches (20 to 25 cm).

The following spring dig up or remove the cuttings from their pots and plant as you would bare root or containerized plants.

Note that rooting softwood cuttings of *Salix* (Willow) can even be done in water. Cut branches off the tree. Strip off the lower leaves. Place the cut ends in an opaque jar filled with water. Make sure that no leaves are underwater. Change the water frequently. Over a period of weeks the branches begin to sprout roots. Plant the cuttings when roots are 2 to 4 inches (5 to 10 cm) long.

Some gardeners skip all of the above and use a very simple method to root softwood cuttings. Prepare cuttings as outlined earlier. Place the cuttings into moist soil or rooting medium under a glass jar or plastic tent directly in the garden, but not in full sun. This keeps humidity high. Check on soil moisture each day and water as necessary until the cuttings begin to grow. Once plants are growing, remove the plastic or jar for increasing periods of time each day over a period of 2 weeks to acclimate the rooted cuttings to sun and drying winds. Of course, protect the young cuttings with a winter mulch during the first year as outlined earlier.

Root Cuttings

Some shrubs will produce plantlets from small portions of root. Three examples are *Amelanchier* (Serviceberry), *Clethra* (Summersweet), and *Rhus* (Sumac). In early spring before new growth dig a hole alongside a mature plant. Expose one large root and divide it into 2- to 3-inch (5- to 7.5-cm) sections. Place

Tips on Collecting Seed

You can also collect seed. Collect seed only from wild (species) types of shrubs or trees. The named or cultivated varieties (cultivars) are best grown from plant parts taken from the mother plant.

On some shrubs seeds are ripe when they become brown and dry. Other shrubs produce berries or fruits. If you want to collect seed, you may have to protect shrubs from foraging birds. Seed is usually ripe when the berry or fruit becomes soft. As soon as this happens, remove the berry or fruit from the shrub. Strip off the pulp around the seed. The soft, fleshy material enveloping the seed inhibits germination. It's easiest to remove pulp if you soak the berries and fruit in water for several hours. You can also remove the pulp by placing seeds in a blender. Turn on the blender in short spurts of 10 seconds at a time. If you're worried about damaging the seed, you can wrap the blades with tape. Note that nicking seeds with hard seed coats may be beneficial to germination as outlined on page 410. If the seed is small, you can also rub it through a sieve as a way of removing pulp. Let the seed dry out in a warm, dark, dry spot. Once dry, store the seed in an opaque container. Or, plant immediately if seed germinates best if fresh.

these about 3 inches (7.5 cm) deep in moist peat. Ideally, you want the portion of root that was closest to the crown facing up. However, laying the cuttings horizontally in peat works just fine in most instances. Simply keep the peat moist until growth pops up through its surface. Let the plantlets mature until they form a healthy set of new roots. Then plant as you would a bare root plant. Naturally, during the first year keep plants protected in a cold frame during the winter.

Budding and Grafting

These two forms of propagation refer to taking a portion of one plant (bud or scion) and budding or grafting it to the rootstock of another. The choice of rootstock is extremely important, and the process is sophisticated and time consuming. There are shrubs and small trees listed in this guide that are grown in this fashion. However, the process is impractical for the home gardener and not covered here for that reason.

Starting Plants from Seed

You can start many shrubs and small trees from seed. Named or cultivated varieties (cultivars) generally produce seed that does not come true. This means that the resulting plants differ from the parent plant. It is best to start named varieties from plant parts, not from seed.

Tips on Buying Seed

Buy seed from reputable sources. Good seed will be fresh (germinates quickly and uniformly), disease free (won't carry any disease into your garden), properly labeled (you get what you buy), properly packaged (not harmed by moisture or light), and reasonably priced (but more expensive than poor seed from nonreputable sources).

Buy seed early in the year. Companies often have limited stock of specific varieties. Shop early to get discounts and to ensure that you will get what you want. Compare offerings in several catalogs. Good catalogs tell you the Latin name of the plant you're buying, the number of seeds per packet, and many cultural details including whether the seed must be scarified or stratifed. Seed sources are listed on page 6.

Planting Seed Outdoors

You'll plant most seed in the fall after purchasing or collecting it as outlined. Exceptions to this planting time are noted in individual sections of Part I.

Plant seed in a bed or cold frame with loose soil generously amended with peat moss or a combination of peat moss and perlite. Professional starting mixes are also highly recommended. You can scatter the seed across the surface of the soil before covering it or plant it in individual holes or furrows. You can also plant seed in individual pots filled with a mixture of soil and peat moss. The pots are best placed in a cold frame.

A general rule is to plant seed roughly three times as deep as its diameter. However, every rule has exceptions. Some seed needs light to germinate and should be pressed into the surface of the starting mix.

Keep the soil evenly moist until the first freeze. Once the soil is frozen to a depth of 2 inches (5 cm), cover it with a 2- to 4-inch (4- to 10-cm) layer of winter mulch. Good mulches include whole leaves, straw, pine needles, or marsh hay.

In spring check under the mulch each day to see whether seedlings are beginning to emerge. If they do begin to pop through the soil, remove the mulch immediately, but keep it close at hand in case of a late spring freeze or hard frost.

Keep the soil moist. If seedlings have emerged and are threatened by a hard frost, cover them again with mulch until the air temperature warms up well above freezing. Keep the soil moist as the seedlings grow. Feed them with a highly diluted water-soluble fertilizer.

Not all seeds germinate easily or quickly. Some may take a year or longer to emerge. The critical point is to keep the soil evenly moist for as many months as it takes for the seeds to germinate.

Let the plants mature for a year or two in their seed bed before transplanting them to a more permanent location or container. Expect flowering plants in about 3 to 7 years.

Preparing Seeds for Indoor Planting

Some seeds listed in this guide have a hard seed coat. Water cannot get through it to cause germination. These seeds must be specially treated so that the seed coat is broken down. Commercial growers soak seeds in acid or boil them in water to break down this protective coat. These treatments are tricky and best left in the hands of professionals. The home gardener can get similar results by placing seeds in a blender. The purpose is simply to nick the seed coat. Turn the blender on for 10 to 15 seconds at a time. Look for little nicks or cracks in the outer seed coats. You should not have to treat seeds in this way for any longer than 30 to 60 seconds. The seeds will bounce, jump around, and make quite a bit of noise, but you will end up breaking the seed coats. You can also break the seed coat with a file or even a folded piece of sandpaper. Moisture can now get inside the seed and initiate germination once the seeds are planted. Whether using acid, boiling water, a blender, or any other method to nick or break down the seed coat, the process is known as *scarification*.

Most seeds of shrubs and small trees listed in this guide must go through a moist chilling period to overcome their natural dormancy. Or, they may need a warm period followed by a cold period. This process is called *stratification*.

Place the seed in a locking bag filled with damp peat or vermiculite. Poke a hole or two in the top of the bag. If the seed needs to be kept warm, keep the bag at the recommended temperature for the recommended time as outlined in the individual sections of Part I.

For moist chilling, place the bag in the crisper of your refrigerator. Usually, the seed needs to be cooled for at least 90 days. For many shrubs the moist chilling should be closer to 120 days and, occasionally, may

Suggested Containers for Indoor Planting

When starting seed indoors, use simple, inexpensive containers. Plastic containers of any kind work well. Ideally, they will be 3 to 4 inches (7.5 to 10 cm) deep or deeper. Numerous plastic containers are used in grocery stores for everything from cottage cheese to sprouts. These make good containers for growing seeds. Punch holes in the bottom so that water can drain out of them freely.

Plastic pots are fine, but if they were used before, they must be cleaned thoroughly. Scrub off any salt or soil deposits. Now soak the pot in a bleach solution of one part bleach to nine parts water for 30 minutes to kill off disease-causing organisms (pathogens). Rinse the pots thoroughly after this treatment.

Since water will drain freely through your starting mix, buy shallow plastic dishes or cake pans available at most stores to place under containers.

be as long as a year. Check the bag frequently to make sure that the peat or vermiculite stays moist, but never soggy. If seeds begin to show signs of growth, remove them immediately from the refrigerator and plant as outlined later.

Special note: If you collect seeds, always try to grow a few of them right away. Some seeds need to be fresh to germinate quickly. Once they are allowed to dry, then they may require stratification to overcome dormancy.

POSSIBLE STARTING MIXES FOR INDOOR PLANTING

Peat is highly recommended for starting seeds. It is light, generally sterile, and holds moisture well. Initially, moisten it with hot water since it tends to shed cool to cold water. Other growing mixes include perlite, sterile sand, well-rotted compost, rotted leaves, milled sphagnum moss, and professional starting mixes.

Starting Plants from Seed Indoors

For healthy plants when starting from seed indoors, follow these steps:

Fill your sterile container to within ½ inch (1.25 cm) of the rim with sterile starting mix.

Soak the mix with lukewarm water. Keep adding water until it drains out the holes in the bottom of the container.

Plant large seeds three times the depth of their diameter. Make holes with the tip of a pencil. Press small seeds into the surface of the mix or barely cover them with peat. Note that some seed needs light to germinate. When this is the case, it is noted in the individual sections of Part I.

Use a mister with a hand trigger to moisten the peat, starting mix, and newly planted seeds.

High humidity helps most (not all) seeds germinate. Cover the container with a piece of glass or hard plastic.

Provide the proper temperature as indicated on the packet or in Part I. Some seeds germinate best cool; others like moderate heat (use a heating pad or

cable). Some need varying temperatures. Follow the directions as closely as possible.

Provide light as indicated on the seed packet. Some seeds need light to germinate. Artificial light is excellent.

When seedlings emerge, take the glass cover off for longer periods of time each day over a number of days until it is off completely. The soil surface should be consistently moist, but never wet.

Watch for *damping off*, a condition that results in seedlings rotting at the base and falling over. Prevent this by using sterile growing medium, containers, and tools. Treat by reducing water and using fungicide.

When plants develop a second pair of leaves, prick them out of the soil with a pencil. When doing this, hold the plant gently by one leaf with a tweezers or your fingers. If using tweezers, paint the edges with nail polish to prevent damaging the leaves.

Fill a 3-inch (7.5-cm) pot with sterile potting soil. Poke a hole in it with a pencil. Drop the rootball into the hole. Keep the lower leaves above the soil. Firm the soil around the stem with your fingers.

Water gently with a mister. The soil will fill in around the base of the seedling. Soil should be uniformly moist, but not soggy.

Provide light as indicated on the packet. Supplement natural light with artificial for best results. Keep lights on 12 to 16 hours a day approximately 4 to 6 inches (10 to 25 cm) from the tops of the plants.

Fertilize with a very dilute solution (¼ strength) of water-soluble fertilizer with a 20-20-20 or similar ratio. Fertilize once every fourth watering. Do not overfertilize. Less is better than more.

Harden off plants for 14 days by placing them outside, slowly exposing them each day to a little brighter light. Never allow them to be chilled or killed by frost.

Tools

Starting plants from seed indoors does not require expensive tools. A mister with a hand trigger is helpful to prevent damage to seedlings when watering. A packet of fungicide will help if seedlings are attacked by disease. A pencil or tongue depressor and a tweezer coated with nail polish is all that is needed to make furrows and prick out seedlings for transplanting. A piece of glass or plastic to place over the container is helpful in keeping humidity high. Or, simply place the container or flat in a clear, plastic bag to form an inexpensive greenhouse. Ordinary, low-cost cool white or warm white fluorescent lights work perfectly well for starting plants indoors. To provide bottom heat buy an inexpensive heating pad from a drugstore. Make sure that the pad stays dry by placing your growing container in a shallow, rectangular cake pan that rests on the pad.

Tissue Culture, Micropropagation, and In Vitro Propagation

Tissue culture, also known as *micropropagation* and *in vitro propagation*, is a fascinating method of producing young plants by breaking down plant tissue from parent plants into cells and then growing these into individual plants. The method requires extreme skill, absolutely sterile conditions, and specialized equipment not readily available to the home gardener. It is mentioned only because it is being used commercially to produce some of the plants listed in this guide.

CHAPTER 10

SPECIAL USES FOR SHRUBS AND SMALL TREES

Bring the beauty of shrubs and small trees indoors by cutting off stems at different times of year to take advantage of an individual plant's most outstanding features from scented blooms to brilliant berries.

Cut Stems for Flowers, Foliage, or Berries

Many shrubs and small trees produce flowers, foliage, or fruits (berries) that are lovely in arrangements. Some shrubs have flowers that exude an exquisite fragrance that can permeate an entire room.

To take cut stems, carry a plastic bucket or pail of tepid water with you. Avoid galvanized or metal buckets since they tend to corrode and be filled with bacteria. Clean the bucket well before each use with a household detergent or a commercial cleaner available from florists. Rinse it out thoroughly.

Cut stems in the early morning or in late evening. The moisture and sugar content in the stems are said to be highest at these times.

Cut stems whose first flowers are just beginning to open. The majority of flowers should be in the bud stage. If cutting stems for foliage or fruit, cut them when they reach their desired coloration or peak production.

Make your cut at a slant just above an outward-facing bud. Use sterile pruning shears for a clean cut. Support the stem by holding it with your free hand. Take cuttings only from mature plants. Remember that this is a form of pruning. If cutting a short branch, cut it flush with the main trunk or stem to avoid leaving an unsightly stub.

Now strip off any leaves, flower buds, flowers, or berries that will end up underwater in the final arrangement. Do not remove spines or thorns. Any submerged plant parts other than the stem may infect the water with bacteria and shorten vase life.

Place the cut stem immediately into the bucket of water. The longer you delay, the greater the chance of air getting into the stem. Get the stems indoors as quickly as possible.

Once indoors, wash off the stems.

Place the base of the stem in fresh water that contains flower food (described later), commonly referred to as a preservative. With the stem under the water cut the base at a slant with a sharp knife or pruning shears. As you finish this cut, the stem will begin to absorb water along with the floral preservative. An angled cut is especially important if you will be inserting the stem into foam. You want a very fine insertion point so that the foam fits snugly around the stem. If you plan to arrange the cuttings loosely in a vase without using foam, simply make a flat cut at the base of the stem. Loose stems with a flat base are easier to arrange. Some arrangers cut a cross into the base of the stem with a clean, sharp-cutting instrument available from florists.

Place the cut stems in tepid water containing flower food for about 20 minutes at the minimum and up to 3 hours if possible. Keep them in a cool, dark place during this time.

Use plastic or glass for your vase. Avoid any metal container. Have the vase filled about two-thirds full of water containing floral food. Now quickly move each submerged stem from its present container into the final arrangement, either sliding the angled end into foam or setting the flat end on the bottom of the vase. Working rapidly prevents air bubbles from getting into the stem.

If air gets into the stem, it blocks water from going up the stem to the leaves or flowers. This will result in drooping blossoms or wilted foliage. If this happens, remove the stem and recut it immediately under water before replacing it in the arrangement.

If even that fails, take the stem (or stems) out of the arrangement. Cut ½ inch (1.25 cm) off the base of each stem while it is fully submerged. Place the base of the stem in water just hot enough to put your hand into (no hotter). Leave it there until the water is cool. Shift the stems into a container filled to the brim with cool water, which should come right up to the base of the foliage or blossoms. Rearrange after the foliage and blossoms take on new life.

Good flower food will increase the vase life of the cut stems. Good ones contain sugar (gives the flower energy), acidifiers (keep the solution at the correct pH), respiration inhibitors (reduce food intake), and stem-plugging inhibitors (keep fluids flowing smoothly). You can buy these at floral shops. Follow the label directions exactly. Too little of the food does nothing, while too much can harm the stems. As mentioned, flower foods are commonly sold as floral preservatives.

If a commercial food is unavailable, try 7-Up (not diet) with 1 drop of liquid bleach to keep it

sterile; or 2 tablespoons (30 ml) lemon juice, 1 tablespoon (15 ml) sugar, ½ teaspoon (2.5 ml) bleach in 1 quart (.9 l) water; or 2 ounces (59 ml) Listerine per 1 gallon (3.78 l) water; or 4 tablespoons (60 ml) sugar and 1 drop bleach per quart of water. Citric acid, available in pharmacies, is also a potential substitute—vary the amount to see how well it works for you. These will all do in a pinch, but are definitely not as effective as commercial flower foods.

All containers or vases used to hold cut stems at any stage must be kept sterile. The simplest method is to clean them regularly with household detergent or commercial cleaners available from florists. Scrub the containers until they are immaculate. Do this every time you use the container, even when replacing water if possible. Rinse the containers well. Bacteria and fungi are often responsible for short vase life.

Ideally, change the water in an arrangement every day, adding floral food each time. This is not always possible with more delicate arrangements. In this case simply add water and floral food as needed. Vase life will be shorter, but you will avoid breaking off fragile blossoms.

Keeping arrangements as cool as possible at all times does make them last longer. Often, the best you can do is to move the arrangement out of direct sun during the day and to keep it in a cool, dark place at night.

Branches taken from shrubs and small trees vary in their lasting capacity. The vase life also varies with the temperature and humidity. Low temperature and high humidity increase vase life considerably. Misting cuttings taken from evergreens is highly recommended.

Forcing

Cutting dormant stems and branches in mid- to late winter, bringing them indoors, and then getting them to bloom 1 to 2 months before they would outdoors is known as *forcing*. Forcing is popular because colorful and fragrant blooming branches are such a delight at this time.

Shrubs and Trees Recommended for Forcing

Shrubs or Trees	Weeks Needed	When to Take Cuttings
Abeliophyllum distichum (White Forsythia)	1 to 3 weeks	Late January to mid-February
Amelanchier (Serviceberry)	1 to 4 weeks	Early to late February
Cercis canadensis (Redbud)	2 to 3 weeks	Early to late March
Forsythia (Forsythia)	1 to 2 weeks	Late January to mid-February
Hamamelis vernalis (Vernal Witch Hazel)	1 to 2 weeks	Early to mid-January
Prunus (Flowering Almonds and Plums)	2 to 4 weeks	Early to late February
Salix (Pussy Willows)	1 to 2 weeks	Early to late February

The shrubs and small trees in the chart are among the finest for forcing. Forcing takes from 1 to 6 weeks depending upon the plant. Generally, the longer it takes, the harder forcing is. The time to cut stems and branches from the plant is also important. If you remove growth too early, it may not bloom. Giving you a specific time for your area is next to impossible. You may have to experiment and take cuttings at different times. The chart tells you which plants to use for forcing, how many weeks it takes to get cut growth to bloom, and the earliest time to take a cutting from a given shrub or small tree. The times given in the chart are approximate. The farther north you live, the later in winter you should wait to take cuttings.

When cutting off branches or stems, do it as if you were pruning the shrub or small tree. Remove new growth with lots of flower buds. Make clean cuts and preserve the desired form of the plant. Don't leave any stubs. Take cuttings only from mature plants. If possible, take cuttings on a mild day as temperatures peak.

Bring the cuttings indoors immediately and soak them in tepid water overnight at the minimum and for as long as 24 hours if possible. The easiest way to do this is to lay them in a tub filled with warm water. You're soaking the entire branch, not just the base.

After a thorough soaking, cut off the base of the stems under water. Immediately place each stem upright in a vase with the bottom 3 inches (7.5 cm) filled with water. Keep the exposed stems moist for several days by misting before enclosing them in a plastic bag. Keep the vase out of direct light. Alternatively, you can mist the stems before wrapping them in moist newspaper or fabric.

Change the water every day. Check to see whether the flower buds are swelling under their damp protective covering. Once the flower buds enlarge, remove the plastic, newspaper, or fabric.

Place the vase in a cool (between 55°F [13°C] and 60°F [16°C]) but well-lit room out of direct sun. Provide as much humidity as possible. Mist the plants as frequently as you can, preferably three to four times a day. If the room gets too hot or dry, buds wither and fail to bloom.

If you intend to remove the flowers from the original container and place them in a special arrangement, always do this just as the flower buds begin to unfurl. If you allow flowers to form before arranging them, you'll often knock them off in the process.

Forced flowers rarely have the same depth of color as those in bloom outdoors. The flowers may also be somewhat smaller and less abundant, but any flowers so early in the season are a welcome sight. A number of these flowers are extremely fragrant, which only makes them more desirable. Expect flowers to last from 2 to 7 days. You'll increase vase life if you can place the flowers in a cool spot at night.

Dried Flowers, Foliage, and Stems

Some of the shrubs and small trees listed in this guide do produce flowers, foliage, and berries that are suitable for dried floral arrangements. Even the stems of some plants are lovely by themselves in dried arrangements.

In some instances, the drying process will take place naturally while the flowers or berries are still on the plant. Simply cut off the stems at the stage you prefer and set them into a container indoors.

On other shrubs, it's best to cut stems when flowers or berries reach their peak. Remove all foliage. Hang the cut stems upside down in a cool, dry, dark place until they dry. Watch for mold. You may have to remove a flower or berry that is rotting, rather than drying.

The drying process can be difficult and frustrating at times. Experiment by cutting stems at different stages of maturity. Note that the flowers and berries of some shrubs simply may not dry well.

If you succeed, always spray the dried stems with a sealant. The sealant helps them retain their shape, stops the formation of mildew, kills off insect eggs, and makes breakage less of a problem, although dried arrangements should always be handled with care. Ask someone in a local florist shop about sealants. When spraying, cover all surfaces. Gently apply an even coat in a well-ventilated area. Let the spray dry, and then repeat the process. Also, once you have placed all stems in the final arrangement, spray it once again. It will help it stay in place. These sprays seem to make the flowers tougher, but don't overdo it. A gentle mist on all surfaces, not a soaking, is what's best.

Preserving colorful foliage can be quite tricky. Consider using glycerine, available from a drugstore. Mix one part glycerine with three parts warm water. When you place a stem into this mixture, it draws it into its tissue. Get the solution as far up the stem as possible for best absorption. Note that some people simply soak the entire leaf or branch in this solution. Once leaves have taken in glycerine, they become quite pliable. It is certainly worth a try if you find an especially colorful and blemish-free cluster of leaves.

Fruit and Berries as Food

A number of the shrubs and small trees in this guide produce edible berries or fruit. These are excellent made into juices, preserves, or varied desserts. Many can be eaten fresh or preserved.

A number of plants need to be sprayed to preserve the quality of berries or fruit. If this is the case, use sprays recommended for this use. Always wait the recommended period before picking berries or fruit. Follow the instructions on the label.

CHAPTER 11

TOOLS AND SUPPLIES

This chapter covers basic safety tips not yet discussed and gives you some suggestions about the tools you might need in planting and caring for shrubs and small trees.

Safety Tips

Gardening should be relaxing, fun, and, above all, safe. Always have local utilities mark underground lines. The holes you dig are often deep enough to come in contact with these. Utilities are required to mark locations within a reasonable time, usually 2 to 3 days. They do this with little flags or spray paints that outline the exact path of the unseen lines.

Don't forget about underline sprinkling and lighting systems. If you're not sure where they run, ask previous owners or have a professional mark them for you.

Never use ladders around power lines.

When using electric tools outdoors, always plug them into ground fault circuit interrupter-type plug-ins. Many older homes do not have these. Electricians can easily replace these old plug-ins with the new ones for relatively low cost.

When cutting off tree limbs, wear protective goggles and a hard hat.

Use chain saws only as directed, keeping in mind that they are one of the most dangerous tools used by home gardeners. Keep blades sharp with files or have them professionally sharpened as soon as they get dull. Sharp blades cut through wood easily. You have to apply much more pressure if blades are dull, and this leads to accidents. Wear leather gloves.

Sun is a silent killer. Skin cancer, including fatal types, has increased dramatically in the last few years. Wear a hat with a 4-inch (10-cm) brim, or at least one with a long visor to protect your nose. Garden as much as possible in the morning and evening. Use sunscreen regularly with an SPF of 15 or higher. Most commonly ignored areas are eyelids and ears. Reapply the sunscreen regularly. Dermatologists say that while following these tips will not eliminate skin cancer, it will reduce the chance of it.

Tools and Supplies

Have the right tools and supplies at hand before starting any gardening project. This will save you lots of time. Good tools are expensive. If you take care of them, they'll last for years. Keep blades sharp and clean. Oil metal regularly to keep it from rusting. Clean out any sprayers or apparatus that could get clogged after each use.

Clostridium tetani

WHEN GARDENING, it is possible to come in contact with a pathogen (*Clostridium tetani*) that can cause a serious, often fatal illness. This bacterium usually enters the body through a wound. Even a miniscule cut is an open invitation to this disease. Avoid it by getting a tetanus shot every 10 years.

Backflow preventor Whenever you use a hose to spray shrubs with fertilizers or chemicals, attach a backflow preventor to your outside faucet to prevent any chemicals from getting into your water system. It is required by code in many areas. **Warning:** *If you ever use a hose to apply fertilizer or chemicals to outdoor plants, never drink from it again.*

Bucket (5-gallon [19 l] pails) A large plastic bucket or pail is helpful in many ways. It's good for hauling small amounts of soil; excellent for picking up debris, such as weeds and fallen leaves; and useful for carrying around small tools. Some household soaps come in large, white buckets. Bakers, cooks, painters, and sheetrockers all have pails free for the asking or for a nominal charge. If using any pail once containing paint, clean it thoroughly so that there is no paint residue whatsoever. Pails used by dry wall contractors (sheetrockers) are much easier to clean. All of these pails are lightweight and extremely durable. You can buy comparable solid plastic buckets in many lumber stores and garden centers.

Chain saw A power saw is essential for clearing areas of larger trees. It can also be helpful cutting off dead branches from smaller trees or shearing shrubs right to the ground if they've not been taken care of properly. The cuts are not very clean, but they are quick.

Chicken wire You may have to surround some shrubs with chicken wire in winter to prevent rabbits and deer from nibbling on them.

Crowbar A long metal crowbar can be quite helpful in loosening larger plants during transplanting. Root balls can be extremely heavy and hard to budge.

Cultivator (pronged) Needed to loosen up soil on the edges of planting holes.

Fertilizer Inorganic: granular 10-10-10, water-soluble 20-20-20 or similar formula, and superphosphate. Organic: blood meal, bone meal, compost, cottonseed meal, cow manure, fish emulsion, horse manure (rotted), and Milorganite.

Fungicide (see **Pesticides**)

Glasses (safety) Get the kind of safety glasses that are enclosed and cover your eyes completely. Wear them when spraying.

Gloves (rubber) If you'll be spraying with chemicals, rubber gloves are essential. The farther up they go toward your elbow, the better.

Hedge trimmers Either hand or electric trimmers are fine. Electric trimmers may require several extension cords for you to reach all parts of a hedge.

Herbicide Use one of the newer weed killers that decomposes quickly in the soil and doesn't cause problems with future planting. Roundup® (glyphosate) is one of the best. It is effective on most annual and perennial weeds (but not all). Use Roundup® with extreme caution as outlined in the weeding section. For consumer information on Roundup®, call 1-800-225-2883.

Hose Get as many hoses as necessary to cover your yard. Buy good hoses guaranteed not to crimp. Even if you have an underground sprinkling system, it is wise to have several hoses. You have to purge the system in fall before the first freeze. Often after that freeze there is an extended, warm dry spell. During that period you may have to water several times. Whenever there is a threat of an overnight freeze, unscrew your hose from the faucet and any sprinklers from the end of the hose. It is very easy to forget this. The damage to your pipes can be extremely expensive. Sprinklers will rupture if there is water trapped in them.

Insecticide (see **Pesticides**)

Knife A regular knife comes in handy. If you plan to propagate shrubs through air layering, budding, grafting, or ground layering, you may want to buy a special budding knife, although a razor blade or utility knife works equally well. A scalpel is even better. These should be kept completely sterile by dipping them in a solution of one part bleach to nine parts water after each cut.

Loppers (lopping shears) Get the kind with an angled blade (bypass, not anvil type). Note that there is a sharp side and a dull side on the curved blade. The sharp side should always be placed against the portion of stem to be saved for a smooth, clean cut.

Magnifying glass or **photographer's loupe** Sometimes it's hard to identify disease and insects without these.

Miticide (see **Pesticides**)

Peat moss Buy this in bales. Use it in planting shrubs and preparing soil.

Pesticides To prevent and control disease, insect, and spider mite infestations, you'll need chemicals specifically labeled for the problem you have.

Pole pruners When you're trying to cut off branches quite high up, these make the job a lot easier. Keep them away from power lines.

Pots Some of the shrubs listed in this guide grow well in containers, such as large pots.

Pruners (pruning shears) Felco's, made in Switzerland, are best. Japanese imitations are much less expensive and quite good, but not as good. Buy the bypass (not anvil) type of shears. These make much better cuts.

Pruning saw For larger stems a pruning saw makes cutting much cleaner and easier. A tight bow saw with sharp teeth rips quickly through large branches. A D-shaped saw allows you to cut especially large branches, but few of the trees in this guide produce branches of this size. Folding pull saws are easy to carry in your pocket. They're fine for smaller branches, but a lot more work for larger ones than a pruning saw.

Rake (garden and leaf) The metal, pronged garden rakes are excellent when leveling soil. Leaf rakes are essential for cleaning up the soil surface and gathering leaves in the fall.

Respirator Very few shrubs and small trees require regular spraying. However, if you use chemicals, protect yourself from breathing them in by using this device.

Seed starting mix You can use vermiculite, perlite, sterile sand, sterile soil, or a combination of these to start seeds. Or, you can buy sterile seed starting

mixes locally. Pro-Mix PGX is popular but many other brands are fine.

Sharpeners Keeping tools sharp requires a wide variety of sharpeners. Different gardeners prefer different types, but most gardeners will have some sort of sharpener for pruners and a different type for larger tools, such as spades. Sharpeners include various types of files, grindstones, hones, and sharpening stones (corundum is very popular). Most hardware stores sell sharpeners or have a professional tool sharpener on call to sharpen tools for a small fee.

Shovel A pointed shovel is essential for digging planting holes for shrubs and small trees. Having two shovels is helpful, one with a short D-handle, the other with a much longer straight handle. Transplanting shovels are less well known. They have a longer, deeper blade and make cutting into the soil easier. Keep blades sharp and clean. File them as necessary. Mix sand and oil in a box and dip the end of the shovel in it after washing it off with a hose to keep it clean.

Shredder (chipper) A leaf and branch shredder or chipper is extremely helpful in making summer mulch.

Soilless mixes There are a number of very good soilless mixes on the market. Jiffy Mix, Miracle-Gro®, Pro-Mix, and Sunshine are a few examples. As an example, Pro-Mix is a light, fluffy material consisting of 75 percent to 85 percent sphagnum peat moss, plus perlite, vermiculite, calcium and dolomitic limestone, wetting agent, and nutrients. These mixes are excellent for growing shrubs and small trees in containers.

Spade Flat garden spades actually cut through roots easier than rounded ones. Both shovels and spades are excellent for digging.

Spading fork A four-tined spading fork is helpful in turning soil and compost piles.

Sprayer Tanks that you pressurize by pumping are easy to use and relatively economical. If you use an herbicide in a sprayer, get a second one for pesticide or fertilizer application. To clean sprayers run a solution of 1 quart (.9 l) white vinegar to 1 quart (.9 l) water through the nozzles.

Sprinklers Use the little metal kind to cover small circular or rectangular areas. They are inexpensive and easy to take on and off hoses. Use oscillating sprinklers to cover larger areas.

Strapping This is any soft material wound around the stem of a tree during staking. Note that supporting trees is now rarely recommended, although still commonly done.

Tarp Either plastic or canvas is fine. Shovel soil onto the tarp to avoid the mess and time necessary to clean up grass at planting time.

Tire pump Get a good one to keep the tire on your wheelbarrow inflated properly.

Wheelbarrow (garden cart) Get a good, solid wheelbarrow with a large, inflatable tire. This type of tire moves over rough surfaces easily. Larger wheelbarrows make more sense and save a lot of time. The extra expense is worth it. Flimsy wheelbarrows are aggravating. Garden carts are much more expensive, but carry more and are easier to use.

Wilt-Pruf® (or similar product) When transplanting deciduous shrubs or trees with foliage on (not at all recommended), spray the foliage first with an antitranspirant found in most garden centers. This will reduce water loss and may increase survival rates.

GLOSSARY

Accent plant A plant with such outstanding features that it becomes a focal point.

Acclimation The process of a plant beginning to go dormant in late summer and early fall. Triggers for this are less light, lower temperatures, and less moisture.

Acidic soil Soils with a pH of less than 7 and most commonly found in areas with lots of rain.

Alkaline soil Any soil with a pH higher than 7 and most commonly found in areas with little rain.

Anther The upper portion of the stamen (male organ) containing pollen in a flower (see **Flower**).

Apical domination The tendency of a plant to send energy to upper buds first. These will grow and expand into laterals before lower buds.

Arching A habit of growth in which branches tend to weep or bend down toward the ground.

Aril A fleshy structure surrounding a seed.

Asexual propagation Method of reproducing shrubs or small trees from plant parts, not from seeds. Same as **Vegetative propagation**.

Axil The point or angle at which a leaf or leaves join the stem. Buds capable of forming branches are located just above these.

Bacteria Minute organisms in the plant kingdom that can either be beneficial or destructive.

Balled and burlapped Shrubs and trees dug up with their root balls enclosed and protected by a layer of burlap, often kept in place by twine or wire.

Bare root (Bare-root) A dormant plant dug up, pruned, and shipped without any soil to the consumer.

Bark The outer woody tissue around the stem or trunk, consisting of both dead cells (on the outer portion) and living cells (on the inner). Protects the inner, living stem tissue and should not be damaged in order to prevent disease, insect infestations, and possible death.

Basal Refers to lower portion or crown of a plant.

Basic soil Same as **Alkaline soil**.

Berry A small, fleshy fruit with one or more seeds developed from a single ovary. May be edible or inedible depending upon the variety of shrub or tree. Even if inedible to humans, may be edible to wildlife.

Blade The expanded, veined portion of a leaf.

Blight Disease typified by quick death of flowers, leaves, and young shoots.

Bloom A flower. Also describes a whitish film covering fruit or other plant parts.

Bone meal Pulverized bones in powder form. Contains lots of phosphorus for good root growth.

Border A combination of plants in an area defined by a straight or curving line.

Borer The larvae of flying insects that penetrate into stems or branches, often causing dieback.

Bottom heat Heat applied to the bottom of a bed or container to speed up germination of seeds or encourage root growth from cuttings.

Bract A modified leaf often colored and resembling a petal.

Broad-leaved evergreen A plant that holds on to its leaves during winter. Its leaves are wide, not needle-like as with conifers.

Bud There are several types of buds. A flower bud is a bloom not yet open. A growth bud is the beginning stage of a shoot. It is found in the axil of a leaf stalk and looks like a small pimple. It is called a basal bud at the base of the plant, a lateral bud on the stem or branches off the stem, and a terminal or tip bud when at the tip of the stem. Growth buds are also called *eyes*. The term *bud* also refers to a method of propagation in which a bud is inserted into the rootstock of a completely different plant.

Budding The process of grafting a bud from one plant onto the rootstock of another plant.

Bud union The spot where a bud or graft is connected to rootstock at the base of a plant.

Burning Damage to leaves caused by contact with chemicals (fertilizers or pesticides) at the wrong temperature or time. Describes scorching or discoloration of immature plants placed in direct light before hardening off is complete.

Bush Alternate term for *shrub*. A multistemmed woody plant.

Callus Scar tissue over any cut portion of stem.

Calyx The sepals, usually green, enclosing a flower bud.

Candle New growth on conifers in spring.

Canker A sore or lesion that forms on a stem, killing plant tissue.

Capsule A fruit that splits open into more than one compartment when dry.

Caterpillars Larvae of butterflies and moths that feed on plant foliage.

Catkin Slender, often drooping, male or female flowers lacking petals.

Chlorophyll The green pigment in plants essential to photosynthesis.

Chlorosis Yellowing of leaves often caused by lack of iron or manganese in overly alkaline soil.

Clay Minute inorganic soil particles helpful in retaining nutrients and moisture in the soil. Present in most soil.

Clone An exact copy of a parent plant created through vegetative propagation.

Cluster A group of flowers or fruits all connected by their footstalks or pedicels to the same stem.

Come true (to) Seed comes true when it produces plants essentially identical to the parent plant.

Compost Any organic matter that decomposes into a soft, brown, earthy-smelling substance known as "humus."

Conifer Cone-bearing shrub or tree, with needles or scale-like foliage.

Containerized (container grown) Used in the nursery trade to indicate a shrub or tree growing in a container, usually one made of plastic, metal, or similar inorganic material. These containers must be removed at the time of planting.

Corymb A flat cluster of flowers with only one flower at the tip of each flower stalk. These stalks are attached to the main axil at different levels. The outer flowers usually open first.

Creeping Lying on or trailing over the ground.

Cross A plant created by interbreeding two plants of differing parentage.

Cross-pollination The transfer of pollen (male sex cell) from one flower to the stigma (female part) of a different flower.

Crown The lower portion of a plant from which stems emerge. This is the point where roots and stem join, but the crown itself is really stem tissue.

Cultivar (cv.) An abbreviation for *cultivated variety.*

Cutting Any piece of plant tissue specially cut and prepared for propagation. Hardwood cuttings are taken from dormant stems; softwood cuttings are taken during active growth.

Cyme A candelabra-like cluster of flowers with a flat top. However, there may be several small flowers at the tip of each flower stalk. The central flowers generally open first.

Damping off Term describing the death of young seedlings that topple over from their bases. Caused by a variety of disease organisms.

Deacclimation The process triggered by longer light and warmth in spring, which begins to take stems out of the stage needed for winter protection. If stems begin to deacclimate and then suffer a severe drop in temperature, they may die back or die out completely depending upon the intensity of the late freeze.

Deadhead To remove spent flowers.

Deciduous Describes all shrubs and small trees that drop their leaves during dormancy from late fall to early spring.

Desiccant Material used to withdraw moisture from a flower.

Dieback (to **die back**) The death of a stem from the tip down. Some diseases and improper pruning may cause this. However, dieback is most common in cold climates after severe winters affect exposed plants.

Dioecious Shrubs that bear male and female sex organs on different plants. Both are needed for proper pollination to produce berries or fruit.

Division Dividing the crown of a plant into sections containing stems and roots. Relatively rare with shrubs.

Dolomite Limestone used in powder form to reduce soil acidity and add valuable calcium and magnesium.

Dormancy The period when a plant stops growing because of lower temperatures and reduced light. All leaves of deciduous plants drop off and the cells in stems undergo significant change to withstand harsh winter conditions. Evergreens retain their leaves during dormancy but remain inactive.

Dormant spray A lime-sulfur or oil solution applied to plants just before winter or before buds appear in spring to kill both fungal spores and insect eggs.

Double A flower with more petals than usual for its group.

Drainage The speed at which water moves through the soil. Well-drained soils absorb water quickly but do not pool up for long periods of time.

Drupe A fruit containing a seed surrounded by a hard shell in the center of fleshy tissue.

Dwarf Technically, a plant specially selected for its tendency to grow slowly. Commonly used to describe plants that remain small.

Espalier A technique of growing plants in a flat position against a support.

Evergreen Description of plants that retain most of their leaves for more than one year. These leaves may be broad as on certain types of Rhododendrons or thin and needle-like on conifers. While the plant remains green, leaves or needles fall off periodically but not all at once and are replaced by new ones.

Exfoliate Describes bark peeling off in shreds. Considered highly desirable on some trees for winter interest.

Eye (see **Bud**) Also refers to the center of a bloom with different coloration than the petals.

Facing plant (**facer**) A shrub, usually on the small side, used to cover bare portions of shrubs or small trees grown behind it.

Fertile A plant that can form seed (not all can). Also refers to soil rich in nutrients.

Fertilization The moment at which pollen enters the stigma (female organ) of a flower. The net result on fertile plants is the production of berries or fruit containing seed to produce a new generation of plants. Also refers to the application of fertilizer to the foliage or ground around shrubs.

Fertilizer Any nutrient supplied to a plant to help it grow and produce its own food through photosynthesis. Commonly referred to as "plant food," which technically it is not.

Fertilizer burn Damage caused to plants by applying too much fertilizer or applying fertilizer on dry ground. Also refers to death of seedlings from addition of inorganic fertilizers to the starting mixture.

Filament The stem-like, lower portion of the male organ (stamen) that supports a pollen-bearing sac (anther) at its tip (see **Flower**).

Fish emulsion Ground-up fish used as a fertilizer. May be applied to ground or leaves. Does have some smell, but provides many trace elements.

Floret One flower in a cluster of flowers.

Floriferous A plant that produces lots of bloom. The same as "free flowering."

Flower The reproductive organ of seed-bearing plants. Not all shrubs produce seeds.

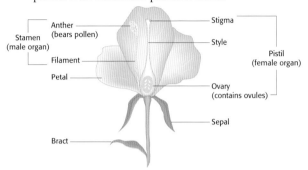

Flush The moment when a plant bears the most bloom. Only a few shrubs have several flushes in a given season.

Follicle A fruit with only one chamber.

Formal Style of design that emphasizes control and strict contours. Often applied to individual plants as well, as in the art forms of espalier and topiary.

Foundation planting A group of low-growing shrubs used along the base of buildings.

Fragrance The scent or smell of a flower. It comes from oil evaporating from cells (aiglets) at the base of petals.

Fruit Reproductive body of a seed plant. Frequently edible. If small, often referred to as a berry, although there are numerous other horticultural terms that apply.

Full sun Complete exposure to direct sunlight for no less than 6 hours per day.

Fungicide Any substance that kills fungi. Most fungi are beneficial, but a few cause serious diseases.

Fungus (Fungi) Primitive, parasitic plants that attack shrubs and cause serious damage, or can help them enormously when present in the soil.

Gall A swelling of unorganized cells caused by damage to plant tissue.

Genus (plural Genera) A botanical group of closely related species.

Germination Sprouting of seeds.

Girdling The tendency of roots to curl around and in on themselves if a plant is grown in a container for too long. Unless these roots are cut off and pulled away from the root ball, they may eventually kill the plant.

Grafting Joining a stem (scion) or bud of one plant to the rootstock (understock) of another. It's the easiest and least expensive way to propagate a plant that is difficult to grow from seed or cuttings.

Granule Particle of fertilizer, herbicide, or pesticide.

Greenwood cutting A softwood cutting taken just as new growth begins to get hard during the growing season.

Ground cover Any plant used to prevent weed growth, stop erosion, or cover a large area.

Growing medium Material in which seeds or cuttings are started or grown. Usually, sterile sand or a combination of peat, perlite, and vermiculite.

Grub The immature stage of a beetle (generally found in the ground).

Gypsum Hydrated calcium sulfate often used to break up clay soils.

Habit (Growing habit) Refers to the style of growth of an individual plant into a specific shape or form. For example, upright versus arching.

Hardening off The process of moving a plant slowly into full sun to prevent damage to leaves. Also, includes acclimating the plant to varying outdoor temperatures and drying winds (lack of humidity) after having been raised indoors.

Hardpan Usually a layer of rock or heavy clay under the topsoil that roots have a difficult time penetrating.

Hardwood cutting A section of stem from the latest season's growth cut from the plant during its dormant period and used to create a new plant.

Hardy The term used to describe a plant's ability to survive winters in a given region. Truly hardy plants need no winter protection. Catalogs are often overly optimistic about hardiness.

Hedge A group of shrubs or small trees planted close together and trimmed to form a barrier or block. This living wall may be either informal or formal depending upon the severity of pruning.

Heeling-in Burying bare root plants briefly in a trench until they can be planted in a permanent location in the garden.

Herbaceous Nonwoody plants that die back to the ground each year only to spring to life during the next growing season.

Herbicide Any chemical used to kill weeds. Roundup® is one of the best since it destroys both annual and perennial weeds right down to their root tips.

Honeydew Sticky, sugary substance secreted by some insects, especially aphids, that is attractive to ants. It often becomes infected.

Hormone powder Chemicals available from garden centers applied to ends of cuttings to get them to root faster.

Host A plant that acts as a harbor for insects or diseases detrimental to other plants.

Humus The light, fluffy, brown material produced as organic matter decomposes in nature. It is essentially the same as fully digested compost.

Hybrid A plant created by crossing two plants with different backgrounds.

Inflorescence A flower cluster.

Inorganic Man-made or nonorganic substance. Generally, refers to sprays or fertilizers that do not come from once-living creatures.

Inorganic fertilizer Any man-made or synthetic nutrient. Not recommended in planting holes unless fully coated with a resin for slow release.

Insecticide Any substance that kills insects.

Integrated Pest Management (IPM) Using pesticides only when really necessary in a responsible manner.

Internode The area on a stem between two buds (eyes or nodes). Never make a cut here. The tissue above the bud below will only die. It does **not** have the ability to regenerate. All food goes directly to the nearest bud, not to wounded stem tissue.

Invasive Tending to spread rampantly. Has a negative connotation except when a plant is used as a ground cover.

Involucre Downy leaves (bracts) on the outside of fruits, such as those on *Corylus* (Hazelnut).

Landscaping The art of working plants into the natural features of your yard to enhance its overall beauty and use.

Lanky A plant that appears spindly or weak.

Larva (Larvae) First stage of life for beetle, butterfly, or moth. May be found in or on plants or ground.

Lateral Any branch that springs off a main stem.

Layering A method of wounding and placing a stem into the ground to create a new plant.

Leaching The loss of nutrients from the soil from rain or watering. This is a common problem in sandy or light soils. Also refers to chemicals coming off the foundations of buildings and causing problems in nearby soil. Also refers to a method of saturating the soil with water to carry off toxic salts.

Leader The very top growing portion of a tree. The leader may be snipped off on some trees to keep them at a specific size. Some trees form two leaders (double leaders). Snipping off one of these may also be advised.

Leaf axil Point at which a leaf joins the stem. Buds that produce new stems or branches are just above these.

Leaf burn (see **Leaf scorch**)

Leaflet One of the segments of a full leaf.

Leaf scorch Spotting or death of leaves from high temperature or careless application of sprayed chemicals.

Leafstalk (see **Petiole**)

Leggy Any plant that looks spindly, overly tall, or weak.

Legume A member of the pea family. Refers to a plant as well as its fruit. Shrubs of this kind may add nitrogen to the soil.

Lime Processed (burned) limestone (usually calcium carbonate) used to add calcium to soil and lower soil acidity.

Limestone Usually calcium or magnesium carbonates used to add nutrients to the soil and reduce soil acidity.

Loam Ideal soil containing the right amounts of clay, sand, and silt with a plentiful supply of organic material.

Macronutrient Chemical needed in high amounts for a plant's health.

Manure Animal waste used to improve soil structure and fertility.

Margin The edge of a leaf.

Mass A group of identical plants placed together for a bold statement.

Microclimate An area of a yard that may have different conditions than the rest of the yard, such as greater or lesser warmth, more or less exposure to wind, more or less of a tendency to collect frost, and so on. It often represents a different zone than the one indicated for your area by the zone map on page xiv.

Micronutrient The same as a *trace element*. A chemical needed in extremely small amounts for the health of a shrub.

Microorganisms Microscopic living creatures found by the billions in healthy soil. Essential for the intake of nutrients by shrubs.

Milorganite Treated human sewage that provides valuable nutrients to plants.

Mist To shower plants with a fine, delicate spray of water.

Miticide A chemical that kills spider mites.

Mold Visible fungal growth on the surface of plant tissue. Color often indicates potential for damage.

Monoecious A plant with both male and female sex organs.

Mulch Any material placed on the surface of the soil to keep it moist and cool or to inhibit weed growth. Organic mulches are much preferred.

Naturalized Plants brought in from another area but established in the wild. Also, refers to a style of planting in which shrubs and small trees are used to create the look of wild plantings or to meld into wild plantings.

Needles Thin, pointed leaves of evergreen plants such as *Pinus* (Pine).

Neutral Soil neither acidic nor alkaline with a pH of 7.

Node The point on the stem where a leaf, bud, or branch is attached.

Nut A fruit with a hard outer shell protecting seed(s) or an embryo inside.

Organic Anything derived from something that was once alive. All organic substances contain carbon as an essential element.

Organic fertilizer Any material derived from a living creature (animal or plant) added to the soil to provide nutrients.

Organic matter Any decomposed material from plants or animals added to the soil to improve its structure (texture) and make nutrients more readily available. Most commonly refers to compost, peat, and animal manures or mulches such as bark, pine needles, sawdust, and wood chips.

Ovary The lower portion of the female organ (pistil) in the flower containing the ovules, the parts that form seed when fertilized (see **Flower**).

Ovule Portion of the ovary that becomes a seed when fertilized (see **Flower**).

Own-root A term that applies to any shrub growing on its own roots as opposed to budded or grafted plants growing on a different plant's rootstock. Most shrubs and small trees in this guide are growing on their own roots.

Panicle A pyramidal flower cluster composed of numerous flowering branchlets with more than one flower at their tips. Branchlets bloom from the bottom up. Panicles radiate out from but do not punctuate the end of the stem.

Pathogen Something that causes a disease in a plant.

Peat moss Partially decomposed sphagnum moss used as a soil amendment. Found in bogs in northern areas. Usually sterile, generally weed free, and always moisture retentive.

Pedicel The narrow stalk at the base of an individual flower or one in a cluster. These smaller stems come off the larger stem (peduncle).

Peduncle The main stem supporting a single flower or a series of side branches (pedicels) which support a spray or cluster of flowers.

Perennial Any plant capable of living more than two seasons and producing seed (if fertile) more than once.

Perlite Light, fluffy volcanic material used to aerate soil. Often looks like little white balls in potting soil.

Persistent Generally referring to fruit that stays on the tree throughout the winter.

Pesticide Any chemical used to kill disease, insects, or mites.

Petal Modified leaf that forms the flower. Petals form the corolla.

Petiole Stem supporting a leaf.

pH An artificial measurement describing the acidity or alkalinity of soil. The pH scale runs from 1 (totally acidic) to 14 (totally alkaline) with 7 being neutral. It is logarithmic in nature. A soil with a pH of 7 is 10 times as alkaline as a soil with a pH of 6. It is 100 times as alkaline as a soil with a pH of 5. Most shrubs grow well in the neutral range. A few demand extremely acidic soils.

Photosynthesis The process used by plants to create food (mostly carbohydrates) from water and carbon dioxide using light and chlorophyll as aids. Most of this work is done in leaves.

Pistil The female organ in a flower. It consists of the portion that catches the pollen (stigma), a slender tube (style) running down to the lower opening (ovule), which eventually becomes a seed (see **Flower**).

Pith The spongy material in the center of the stem. If cane is alive, the pith is usually light green or whitish colored. If dead, it turns black or brown.

Pod A fruit containing one or more seeds with walls thicker than that of a capsule.

Pollen Yellow dust-like material found in sacs (anthers) of each flower. It is the plant equivalent to sperm and must be united with the female part of the flower for fertilization to take place (see **Flower**).

Pollination The act of applying pollen to the pistil of a flower. Flowers can self-fertilize. Or, pollen can be transferred from one plant to the next. This is done naturally by insects, especially bees. It is done deliberately by hybridizers to create new varieties (cultivars).

Polygamous Shrub bearing both male and female flowers on the same plant.

Pome A fruit, like an apple, with fleshy tissue surrounding a thin-walled chamber containing seeds.

Pot-bound A plant whose roots have filled up a container and begin to curl around each other. This is extremely bad for any plant.

Propagation Creating new plants using a variety of methods, including budding, cuttings, division, grafting, layering, and seed.

Pruning The removal of any portion of the plant for a specific purpose, such as health, better looks, or more bloom.

Raceme A flower cluster with numerous stalks supporting only one flower at the end of each. Flowers bloom from the bottom up.

Raised bed Soil placed on the surface of the ground to act as an area in which to plant shrubs or small trees.

Resistance Ability of a plant to ward off disease or insects. May be natural or bred into a plant.

Revert To return to an original color or form. For example, some shrubs and trees with variegated foliage may produce stems or branches with totally green foliage. The latter have reverted and should be removed immediately to keep the variegation intact.

Root ball Roots and surrounding material, usually soil.

Rootbound (see **Pot-bound**)

Rooting hormone Chemical that helps cuttings produce roots more quickly.

Rooting medium Any material used to grow cuttings.

Roots Portion of the plant that extends underground from the crown. Roots often spread out as far as the shrub is tall. The roots anchor the plant in place while taking in water and nutrients. When a cutting begins to form roots, it is said to root, to take root, or to take.

Rootstock The plant that acts as the host for a bud or graft from another plant.

Samara A winged seed.

Sand Coarse particles making up a portion of good soil.

Sap The plant equivalent to blood.

Scale A type of sucking insect that invades numerous shrubs and small trees. It is very small and encased in a protective "shell."

Scales Tiny, modified leaves covering a dormant bud. Also, refers to flat, small leaves on some evergreens, such as *Juniperus* (Juniper).

Scarification The process of breaking down or through a seed's tough outer coat to allow the penetration of water and to increase the chance of germination. Common methods of scarifying seed include treating it with acid, boiling it, penetrating the coat with a pin or blade, or placing seed in a blender.

Scion A bud or portion of stem placed on rootstock to create a new plant.

Scoring The process of cutting into a root ball to sever roots that may be overly constricted. Usually done with a spade or sharp knife.

Screen Plants used to block an area off from the outside world or to control wind gusts.

Seed An embryonic plant protected by a cover. Best kept cool, dry, and dark if not planted immediately upon maturation.

Seedling A plant raised from seed.

Semievergreen Plants that tend to hold on to some of their leaves for more than one growing season.

Semihardwood cutting A softwood cutting taken as new growth begins to get quite hard during the active growing season.

Sepal The protective petal-like covers over a bud. These form the calyx (see **Flower**).

Sexual propagation Producing new plants with seeds, not from plant parts.

Shear To prune off the tips of stems in a uniform fashion so that growth is flat, as on a hedge.

Shoot The same as a *stem*.

Shrub An imprecise term describing a multistemmed woody plant.

Shrub border A group of varying shrubs placed together and allowed to grow naturally.

Silt One of the inorganic components of loam. Made up of particles larger than clay, smaller than sand.

Single Flower with the minimum number of petals for its type.

Softwood cutting A piece of stem taken during the growing season from the present year's growth to create a new plant.

Soil A mixture of chemicals, particles, water, air, and millions of living plants and animals. Think of it as a living creature, not an inanimate object.

Soil amendment Anything added to the soil to improve its structure (texture). The ideal soil is loose and airy, so that you can push your hand into it easily.

Soil test A chemical analysis of the soil indicating pH and the availability of major nutrients. Often suggested for some of the shrubs in this guide.

Species (both singular and plural) A group of wild plants that closely resemble each other and are capable of interbreeding with resulting offspring nearly identical to the parent plants.

Specimen A plant grown by itself or in a prominent position for its ornamental features. Same as **Accent plant**.

Spike A cluster of stalkless flowers all attached to one stem.

Spine A sharp, woody protrusion from a stem, generally not located at a node, as on plants in the genus *Berberis* (Barberry).

Sport Spontaneous or induced mutation resulting in a plant distinctly different from the parent.

Spotting Blemishes on blossoms caused by wet weather, improper watering, or improper spraying. May also be a sign of insect infestation.

Spreading A habit of growth in which the plant tends to grow horizontally or laterally. Also refers to trees with branches arching outward.

Staking Supporting a plant to stop it from tipping over in loose soil or in exposed locations after initial planting. Generally, not recommended (see page 384).

Stamen The male part of a flower, consisting of a slender stem-like growth (filament) with a pollen sac (anther) at the tip (see **Flower**).

Stem The main above-ground portion of a shrub similar to the slender trunk of a tree.

Sterile A plant that produces no seed. A seed that will not germinate. Also refers to soil that has been steamed to kill off all disease-causing organisms. Or, to tools disinfected properly to kill disease-causing organisms.

Stigma Part of the female organ (pistil) that gets sticky and traps pollen so that the flower can be fertilized (see **Flower**).

Stratification The process of exposing seed to moisture at varying temperatures to break dormancy and promote rapid and uniform germination.

Stub Portion of a stem left above the crown. Cut stems even with the crown to avoid stubs, which may die back, become infected, or host insects.

Style Slender tube in the female portion of a flower that bears the sticky stigma that traps pollen (see **Flower**).

Subshrub An imprecise term describing a multi-stemmed plant with tissue that is slightly less woody than that of a shrub or tree, but woodier than most perennials. The only subshrub in this guide is *Perovskia atriciplifolia* (Russian Sage) that could be classified and is generally sold as a perennial.

Sucker Can mean two things: a shoot coming up from the rootstock of a budded or grafted plant. Remove these immediately. Or, it can be a plant produced to the side of a mother plant identical to the parent. Occasionally, used as a synonymn for **Water sprout**.

Sunscald The effect of sun on a plant that is moved from an indoor location into bright light too quickly. Leaves often turn pale and may even drop off. Also refers to damage done to shrubs during the winter if temperatures vary greatly.

Superphosphate An inorganic material added to planting holes to provide phosphorus. Made by treating rock phosphate with sulfuric or phosphoric acid.

Synthetic Man-made, as opposed to organic (occurring naturally).

Systemic A chemical absorbed directly by the plant and distributed throughout the tissue. There are systemic herbicides (to kill perennial weeds) and systemic pesticides (to kill bacteria, fungi, insects, and mites).

Tamp To firm soil with your hands (not your feet).

Tender A term referring to lack of hardiness in cold climates.

Tendril A long, thin, modified leaf that winds itself around any given support.

Tepals Petals and sepals appearing as if identical, as on a *Magnolia.*

Terminal At the tip of a stem.

Tier Horizontal branching pattern.

Tissue culture Method of producing young plants from cells of the parent plant. Also known as micro-propagation and in vitro propagation.

Topiary The art of forming plants into unusual and unnatural shapes or contours for dramatic effect.

Trace elements Chemicals needed in extremely small amounts for the health of a shrub. Often referred to as microelements.

Transpiration The loss of water from a plant. Heat and drying winds cause high water loss and may result in damage.

Transplanting Moving a plant from one location to another. In most cases this should be done as early in the season as possible. Keep soil around the roots, treat as a bare root plant, and water well.

Tree A woody plant generally with one main stem or trunk. Some trees have multiple trunks, but these are much thicker than the individual stems of a shrub.

Truss A showy and often large cluster of fruits or flowers.

Umbel A flat or rounded cluster of flowers whose stalks all radiate from one point as on an umbrella.

Understock (see **Rootstock**)

Variegated Generally referring to foliage blotched, striped, or marked with a color other than green.

Variety Technically, any plant that occurs naturally in the wild as a variation from the original parent plant (species). Plants that are bred are correctly called "cultivars."

Vegetative propagation (see **Asexual propagation**)

Vermiculite Mica heated until it pops. Used for starting plants from seed. Completely sterile and weed free. Holds moisture well.

Virus A disease-causing agent for which there is presently no cure. So small it can only be seen with an electron microscope.

Water sprout Thin, willowy growth straight up from the side of a trunk or branch. Prune these off.

Weed Any plant growing where you don't want it to do so.

Weeping Description of shrubs or trees that tend to arch over and down.

Whorl Several or more leaves, flowers, or branches circling a single node.

Wilting Leaves hanging limply on branches. Usually a sign of water stress. Water immediately. May also indicate disease or insect problems if watering does not bring the plant back to life. Never allow shrubs to wilt.

Windbreak Anything that provides protection from wind.

Wing Leaf-like membrane attached to some fruits and seeds.

Winged A seed or fruit with an attached membrane resembling a wing (see **Samara**).

Winterkill The death of part of a plant or of a complete plant because of severe winter conditions.

Witches' broom Distorted growth at the top of a tree or end of a branch, often in the shape of a ball. Important in plant propagation in that cuttings taken from these can result in dwarf varieties.

Woody Refers to plants that form hard rather than fleshy stems. These do not die back at the end of the season, as do most herbaceous perennials.

ABOUT THE AUTHORS

Debbie Lonnee has worked in the nursery industry for more than three decades, after first receiving a B.S. in Horticulture from the University of Minnesota. She works in the wholesale nursery industry at Bailey Nurseries, Inc., where she is the manager of the Planning & Administration department. She is actively involved in seeking out new, exclusive varieties for the nursery and travels the United States and Europe hunting for plants. She is also a prolific garden writer, being the horticultural editor for *Northern Gardener* magazine (the magazine of the Minnesota State Horticulture Society) as well as writing a 'Plant to Pick' article for each edition. She lectures extensively in Minnesota and across the country to professional nursery groups, master gardener groups, and garden clubs. She is currently serving on the Board of Directors of the Minnesota Nursery and Landscape Association and chairs its Publications committee, writing for the new website on a weekly basis. Gardening is her passion. She has a collectors garden full of new varieties as well as new test plants.

Nancy Rose has an extensive background in growing shrubs and small trees in cold climates. Her interest in landscape design led her to a degree in horticulture from the University of Missouri and a Master of Science degree in the same field from the Ohio State University. Nancy currently works for the Arnold Arboretum at Harvard University where she serves as editor of *Arnoldia,* the Arboretum's quarterly magazine featuring articles on a wide range of topics focusing on plant sciences, environmental studies, and landscape history. Previously she worked with trees and shrubs from around the world in the plant collections of the Morton Arboretum in the western suburbs of Chicago. She then spent many years with the University of Minnesota as an extension educator in horticulture and as a scientist in the woody plant research program. Nancy is a professional garden writer and photographer, coauthor of *The Right Tree Handbook,* and regular contributor to such publications as *Fine Gardening, Northern Gardener,* and *Gardening How-To,* as well as many others. She wrote a gardening column for the *Minneapolis Star Tribune* newspaper for twelve years and still contributes columns on occasion.

Don Selinger has had a lifelong interest in plants and received a degree in floriculture and ornamental horticulture from the University of Illinois in 1961. He was in the nursery business for over 35 years, having worked in Illinois, Indiana, and Minnesota. He worked at Bailey Nurseries in St. Paul, where he was in charge of planning the production of nursery stock distributed on a wholesale basis throughout the northern tier of the United States and Canada. Don has traveled widely in the United States, Canada, and Europe to study and seek out new plants for the nursery trade. He spoke frequently at state and national nursery association groups as well as at garden clubs. His work and insights have been published and quoted in numerous trade and gardening magazines. For over a decade he wrote the 'Plant of the Month' column for the Minnesota Nursery & Landscape Association and provided articles for the *St. Paul Pioneer Press* and *Northern Gardener.* He was inducted into the Minnesota Nursery and Landscape Association Hall of Fame 2001. In recent years he has been breeding new varieties of *Berberis* (Barberry), *Exochorda* (Pearlbush), and *Syringa* (Lilacs).

John Whitman has been writing nonfiction books for more than forty-five years. He was a grower at Bachman's, the largest retail florist and nursery in the United States. All of his gardening knowledge comes from hands-on experience. His book *Starting from Scratch: A Guide to Indoor Gardening* was published by Quadrangle: The New York Times Book Company and was chosen as a main selection of the Organic Gardening Book Club and an alternate selection of the Book-of-the-Month Club. He was one of seven contributing writers to the *Better Homes and Gardens New Garden Book* and the sole writer of the *Better Homes and Gardens New Houseplants Book.* He is the creator and coauthor of the two other award-winning guides in the cold-climate series: *Growing Perennials in Cold Climates* and *Growing Roses in Cold Climates,* which received national attention on radio and television. Both of the latter were chosen as alternate selections of the Doubleday Select Garden Book Club. John has also been a consultant and contributing writer and photographer for newsletters, magazines, and other gardening books.